Guns in American Society

Guns in American Society

AN ENCYCLOPEDIA OF HISTORY, POLITICS, CULTURE, AND THE LAW

Second Edition

Volume I: A–F

Gregg Lee Carter, Editor

ABC-CLIO

Santa Barbara, California • Denver, Colorado • Oxford, England

1657795

NOV 28 2012

Copyright 2012 by ABC-CLIO, LLC

Library of Congress Cataloging-in-Publication Data

Guns in American society : an encyclopedia of history, politics, culture, and the law / Gregg Lee Carter, editor. — 2nd ed.
   p. cm.
Includes bibliographical references and index.
ISBN 978–0–313–38670–1 (hard copy : alk. paper) — ISBN 978–0–313–38671–8 (ebook)
1. Gun control—United States—Encyclopedias. 2. Firearms—Law and legislation—United States—Encyclopedias. 3. Firearms—Social aspects—United States—Encyclopedias.
4. Violent crimes—United States—Encyclopedias. 5. Social movements—United States—Encyclopedias. I. Carter, Gregg Lee, 1951–
HV7436.G8783   2012
363.330973—dc23   2011043435

ISBN: 978–0–313–38670–1
EISBN: 978–0–313–38671–8

16 15 14 13 12   1 2 3 4 5

This book is also available on the World Wide Web as an eBook.
Visit www.abc-clio.com for details.

ABC-CLIO, LLC
130 Cremona Drive, P.O. Box 1911
Santa Barbara, California 93116-1911

This book is printed on acid-free paper ∞

Manufactured in the United States of America

Contents

Preface

Public debate and discussion about guns in American society are rarely guided by research, at least not in the academic sense of looking at the distribution of findings accumulated across a large number of scholarly studies. Based on positive or negative personal experiences—for example, having had a father who took you hunting as a youth, or having felt revulsion after seeing the aftermath of a shooting spree on the web or on television—individuals, with the help of those nearest to them, talk themselves into either a pro- or antigun position. There is good reason why most people do not rely on the relevant research: it is massive and contradictory; it uses arcane statistical methodologies and esoteric legal language and theories that are far beyond the ken of the average academic and the average public-policy maker, let alone the average citizen.

Enter the present three-volume *Guns in American Society: An Encyclopedia of History, Politics, Culture, and the Law*. Its goal is help the reader navigate the research and become educated enough on any particular aspect of the gun issue to make an informed decision—for example, whether to support stricter or more lenient gun control; whether to become a gun owner; whether to support a particular political party or candidate; or whether to develop or to refine a particular

philosophy, simple or complex, regarding guns. The encyclopedia, the most comprehensive single source on the gun issue published to date, draws on a vast array of research in criminology, history, law, medicine, politics, and social science. It covers all aspects of the issue: gun violence, gun control, gun rights, government regulations; legislation, court decisions, gun organizations (both gun control and gun rights), gun owners, gun subcultures (for example, hunters and collectors), and attitudes toward guns. Many of the more than 450 entries place the topics in historical and cross-cultural perspective.

Guns in American Society proposes no easy solutions to the problem of gun violence, and it is not "pro" or "anti" gun control or gun rights. Entries have been carefully cross-referenced and are appended with suggested readings, representing the best of current scholarship. In short, there is more than enough information—for anyone who cares to do the perusing—for each reader to make up his or her own mind on the benefits or harms that the strict control of firearms may incur, as well as the obstacles facing those who would like to strengthen or weaken the current level of control.

The members of the Editorial Board for *Guns in American Society* are first-rate scholars, and each one made a significant contribution to all three volumes. I am grateful for their diligence, writing, and manifold editorial efforts. They are James A. Beckman of the University of Central Florida, Walter F. Carroll of Bridgewater State University in Massachusetts, David B. Kopel of the Independence Institute and Denver University in Colorado, Robert J. Spitzer of the State University of New York at Cortland, and Harry L. Wilson of Roanoke College in Virginia. Readers with even a modest background on the gun debate will recognize that this group represents a diverse range of perspectives on the gun debate—diverse in their scholarly approaches, diverse in their more personal and editorial-page pronouncements. They will also recognize David Kopel and Robert Spitzer as luminaries in the field.

My editing work benefited greatly from the library staff at Bryant University. Reference librarians Laura Kohl and Colleen Anderson were particularly helpful. The secretarial staff at Bryant is always ready to lend a hand. Joanne Socci and Sue Wandyes performed many valued services, as did my student research assistant Kyle Baldwin. The Bryant administration was also very cooperative and supportive, and I especially thank David Lux, dean of the College of Arts and Sciences. My editors, David Paige, Sandy Towers, and John Wagner, were encouraging and enthusiastic from the moment each of them joined the project. On a personal note, I finally want to thank Lisa H. Carter for her constant and loving encouragement and support, and my children—Travis, Kurtis, Alexis, and Davis— for their love and forbearance.

Guns in American Society has been written for researchers, teachers, students, public officials, law-enforcement personnel, journalists, and members of the general public having an interest in this critical area of American life. I hope that it will stimulate and clarify every reader's thinking on the key issues surrounding guns in the contemporary United States, especially on the debate over gun control.

Gregg Lee Carter
North Smithfield, Rhode Island

Introduction

There is hardly a more contentious issue in American politics than the ownership of guns and various proposals for gun control.

> —National Research Council, *Firearms and Violence* (2005, 1)

[G]un control advocates assume that if they win the argument about the public health consequences of gun violence, they will win the broader debate about how to regulate firearms. This line of thinking fails to account for our opponents' claims about the importance of guns to our cultural and political values. Gun control advocates have spent the past three decades trying to persuade the public that guns are dangerous, while gun rights groups have been arguing that guns are essential to our freedom.

> —Joshua Horwitz and Casey Anderson, *Guns, Democracy, and the Insurrectionist Idea* (2009, 226)

Politics is inherently controversial because human beings are passionately attached to their opinions by interests that have nothing to do with the truth.

> —Harry V. Jaffa, Distinguished Fellow, Claremont Institute (2011, BR16)

Ultimately, the debate over guns in American society boils down to a philosophical argument about the role of government in modern society, and more particularly in American society. To scholars, policy makers, politicians, and thoughtful citizens who believe in strong gun control, the problem is the massive destruction to human life created by the presence of guns in the United States—mainly from homicide and suicide, much less so—but no less important—from accident (in total, 30,000 to 32,000 lives per year lost to homicides, suicides, and accidents; plus tens of thousands of serious injuries). They view this state of affairs as a "public health" problem, akin to the classic public health problems of infectious diseases or uncontrolled dangerous products and substances (e.g., lead-based paint). The public health approach does not ignore the importance of individual choices, attitudes, and behaviors; but the emphasis tends toward the more sociological, the more structural, the more regulatory. That is, set up the situation so that when bad individual choices are made, the cumulative negative effects are minimized. The conquest of infectious disease via vaccination, sewage control, and quarantine is the archetype of this approach.

More closely related to the public health problem of gun violence is the much-heralded achievement of the public health approach in reducing the fatalities, injuries, and economic-social-personal costs of motor vehicle accidents. In the early 1950s, such accidents and their resultant deaths and injuries were considered a major problem of public health. The focus of the times was on bad drivers and their bad driving behaviors: They did not get enough training; they did not follow traffic laws very well; they did not sleep enough before driving; they drank alcohol or took drugs and then drove. Focusing on drivers and bad driving habits yielded some returns, but not nearly the returns achieved when the focus turned to the situations of accidents—and then to alter these situations so that bad driving yielded the minimum of harm. Thus, for example, roads were widened, shoulders were added, street lighting was improved; guardrails were redesigned and their use increased; at the vehicle level, collapsible steering wheel columns were developed, shatterproof glass replaced the hard-glass windshields that formerly sliced and shredded the heads and necks of accident victims; shoulder straps were added to seat belts and their use made easier; bumpers were redesigned to absorb more shock; air bags were developed; headlights were made brighter—and the list goes on. Changing the focus from who caused the accident to what caused the death or injury resulted in huge gains: Deaths from car accidents today are fewer than they were in the early 1950s (for example, 38,310 deaths in 1953 versus 33,808 deaths in 2009), despite the huge increases in the number of drivers and the number of vehicles on the road (24.3 deaths per 100,000 population in 1953, versus 11.0 per 100,000 population in 2009).

Many in the public health community, as well as some in the general public itself, see the parallels and possibilities for reducing gun violence: To be sure, let individuals know that they must be trained to use their firearms, that they must be licensed to carry concealed weapons (save for the few states where such a license is not required), and that they will be dealt with severely by the criminal justice system if they commit crimes with their weapons. But, beyond this focus on the individual, there are many more situational, more sociological, more regulatory actions that can reduce gun violence and its manifold costs to society (economically speaking, $100 billion a year, according to one sophisticated estimate). Here are a small handful of examples: (1) trigger pressure can be increased—reducing the chances of a small children firing it; (2) as is common knowledge, it is an "unloaded gun" that is often involved in accidents (the shooter is playing around, incorrectly thinking the gun is empty—which often seems believable for semiautomatic handguns when the ammunition magazine has been removed—but in fact there can still be a round in the chamber), and thus simple "loaded chamber" indicators can reduce the likelihood of these kinds of accidental shootings; (3) although purchases from retailers require a background check of the buyer, there is no federal law requiring that purchases in the private market involve a background check (even though some states do require such checks—note that the need for standardized laws across all 50 states is a paramount goal of those in the gun control camp, as a little driving can often overcome the strict law of state A versus the absence or more lenient version of the law in state B); (4) technologies exist—and which can be further refined—that imprint unique markings/numbers on shell casings and bullets that allow spent ammunition to be traced to a particular gun and a particular retail dealer (rogue dealers, willing to cut corners and even break the law to sell more guns, are a central focus of the gun control movement)—though only California has developed regulations in this area; relatedly, more traditional bullet identification systems could be used much more widely— e.g., two states require "ballistic fingerprinting" in which handguns have spent bullets and cartridge casings scanned and saved digitally in a database; when a spent bullet or casing is found at a crime scene, it can then be checked against the database to identify the gun and its last owner—but much better would be a federal requirement that all new guns be test-fired at the manufactory and the digital images of spent casings and bullets be added to the existing National Integrated Ballistic Information Network (which currently keeps only images of cartridge cases and bullets found at crime scenes); (5) critical to the success made in reducing the human and economic costs of motor vehicle accidents was the development of a sophisticated, *comprehensive* system of data reporting, so that the manifold details about the conditions of accidents could be used to make situational changes to reduce death, injuries, and damages (the Fatality Analysis Reporting System operated by the National Highway Traffic Safety Administration); such a system for violent deaths (most of which occur from firearms via homicide and suicide) has the same potential, yet federal funding on such a project has been sporadic and incomplete, with currently only 18 states using such a system (the National Violent Death Reporting System).

Overall, any one policy, any one regulation, any one program, would be expected to have only small effects at the margins; that is, produce only a small reduction in the total number of deaths or injuries related to firearms. However, these effects are often cumulative, and thus a multitude of such policies/regulations/programs can combine to produce significant reductions of death and injuries. Indeed, one of the better-known public health organizations advocating strong gun control laws, the Firearm and Injury Center at Penn (2009, 4), states in no uncertain terms that "firearm injury and its subsequent repercussions are preventable. Research on firearm injury provides evidence that specific changes can be made that will reduce the deaths, disability, and costs to society."

As a final point, for many of those in the gun control camp, who are joined in this sentiment by a good many gun owners, the gun issue is not simply about the deaths and injuries associated with firearms, but also about the insecurity they feel when guns are in their presence. They shudder at the thought of being in a tavern or restaurant or sporting arena—or any public gathering—where there are individuals strapping firearms (legal or not, concealed weapons permits be damned).

To scholars, policy makers, politicians, and thoughtful citizens who believe in strong gun rights, the problem of the significant destruction to human life created by the presence of guns in American society is regrettable, but is also one that can and should be mitigated by vigorous government enforcement of existing laws against gun misusers—as well as by lawful armed self-defense. Some in the gun rights camp acknowledge the power of the public health approach in solving human misery—and even those who believe in the absolute minimum of government regulation often recognize the validly of public-health-research-based government regulations that require, say, lead be removed from paint or that private septic systems be maintained to prevent the pollution of groundwater. This said, those in the gun rights camp believe that guns and paint, guns and many of the products that are regulated to increase the safety of consumers, of the public, are very different entities with very different purposes. Although guns and paint can increase the happiness of the individual (from feeling the satisfaction of accurately sighting and then shattering a flying clay target, to feeling the pleasure of looking at a freshly painted room, or house, or portrait), the ultimate aim of guns in the hands of the average nonviolent and mentally stable citizen is to ensure that the individual, that the home, that the neighborhood, that the community, that the commonwealth, that property connected with any and all of these, is protected (via the efforts of law enforcement agencies and state-organized militias, yes, but also, as is sometimes required, via individual wherewithal). Protected from marauders and villains when public law enforcement is not up to the task; protected from the government when those in power pervert it to serve their needs and not those of the people—and are willing to use violence to ensure this. The venerated right to keep and bear arms guaranteed in the Second Amendment is not primarily about protecting the joy of hunting or target shooting; it is about protecting the people—individually and collectively, as affirmed by the 2008 (*Heller*) and 2010 (*McDonald*) landmark decisions of the U.S. Supreme Court. In short, to those in the gun rights camp, the difference between all other consumer products and guns is fundamental, and they thus believe the public health approach misses the point. Guns are not germs; rather, they are critical tools in the quest for greater individual and public safety.

As for the discomfort many might feel being in public places where some citizens are carrying concealed firearms, this is a function of culture—"shall-issue" concealed-carry laws are relatively new, and most Americans,

even those who grew up in areas where guns are common, are not accustomed to the idea of armed citizens in their midst. However, gun rights advocates hold that people must become used to the civil right of lawful concealed carry and, moreover, that the recent history of American society reveals multiple examples of significant cultural shifts in how we view the world, of what we think is proper, of how we act. To wit, the dramatic changes in gender roles and race relations since the early 1970s; the transformation of smoking thought to be somewhat cool to becoming a near stigma since the 1980s; the increasing acceptance of openly gay and lesbian individuals, couples, and families since the 1990s—and the list goes on.

Given this fundamentally different worldview of those strongly for gun control versus those strongly for gun rights, the data really do not matter. This may sound startling to the average lay reader. But even partial immersion in the writings of gun control versus gun rights organizations, and even scholars, makes this conclusion easier to see. For the past several decades, gun control advocates have been quick to promulgate cross-national studies that show firearms availability and gun violence are positively correlated: The more guns that circulate in society, the greater the gun violence and—because a gunshot generally magnifies the wound trauma that would have been inflicted by a fist, foot, club, or knife— the greater the overall homicide rate, the greater the serious-injury rate, and, for selected subpopulations (e.g., adolescents), the greater the suicide rate. At the same time, those in the gun rights camp promulgate the "more guns, less crime" thesis, with both cross-national and cross-U.S.-state tour-de-force statistical analyses; they also point to empirical studies extolling the reality and salience of defensive gun use (by ordinary, armed citizens against criminal attacks). But the data each camp promotes do not sway the other side. To wit, as avid and well-known gun control advocate Dennis Henigan (2009, 6) sees it: "critics of gun regulation . . . dress up their arguments in the arcane language of academia and in mountains of statistics, but their basic claims [can] be boiled down to . . . the bumper sticker arguments of the National Rifle Association and its allies" (e.g., "Guns don't kill people—people kill people"; "When guns are outlawed, only outlaws will have guns"; and "An armed society is a polite society"). And owning up to how the gun rights camp sees much of the data and statistical analyses emanating from the public health research community, high-profile gun control advocates Josh Horwitz and Casey Anderson (2009, 226) concede that the arguments for more control are "based on *contested* factual claims" (emphasis added).

Given this fundamentally different worldview, there is a strong tendency in the gun rights camp not to compromise. Such compromise, they fear—and some scholarship indicates that their fear is justified—will result in a slippery slope ending in guns being viewed no differently than lead-based paint. This little-to-no-compromise approach frustrates, enormously, those in the gun control camp. This frustration stems from one of the major tenets of the public health approach— the approach whose research dominates the home pages of gun control organization: That from each single gun control regulation, policy, or program, we can only expect modest marginal returns. Thus, if one regulation is opposed by the gun rights side, okay, we don't have to go that way (at least not right now)— but can't we agree to work together to bring about this other regulation? (Tit for tat; *quid pro quo*; can't we negotiate a deal that gives

each side a little satisfaction?) Going with the other regulation might well still produce some positive benefits. But "no" is the reply from the gun rights side: The stakes are too high, and the risk of the slippery slope too great. The debate is sometimes muddied because many from the gun rights side believe, more generally, in minimal government regulation of the ordinary affairs of the citizenry, while many in the gun control camp take a more communitarian approach— that the free market, that individual choice, cannot solve many of our most vexing social and economic problems (at least not as many as those with a more libertarian bent believe). But, as already stated, the real point is that no matter how the core of one's more general political philosophy is constituted, those with the strongest gun rights orientation hold that guns are unique: They need to be readily accessible; they need to be reasonably commercially available; they need to be regulated no more than is truly necessary for public safety; and no matter what, the government must not keep a registry of who owns them (lest these individuals be more easily disarmed should the government make war on its own citizens, as so often been the case in human history—right up to the present day). Since there can be no compromise on any of these tenets, why even bother to talk with the other side? In the words of NRA executive Wayne LaPierre, "Why should I or the NRA go sit down with a group of people that have spent a lifetime trying to destroy the Second Amendment in the United States?" (as quoted in Calmes 2011, A24).

References

Calmes, Jackie. "N.R.A. Declines to Meet with Obama on Gun Policy," *New York Times*, March 15, 2011. http://www .nytimes.com/2011/03/15/us/politics/15guns .html (accessed July 18, 2011).

Firearm Injury in the U.S. Philadelphia: Firearm and Injury Center at Penn, 2009. http://www.uphs.upenn.edu/ficap/resource book/pdf/monograph.pdf (accessed July 18, 2011).

Henigan, Dennis A. *Lethal Logic: Exploding the Myths that Paralyze American Gun Policy.* Dulles, VA: Potomac Books, 2009.

Horwitz, Joshua, and Casey Anderson. *Guns, Democracy, and the Insurrectionist Idea.* Ann Arbor: University of Michigan Press, 2009.

Jaffa, Harry V. "Aristotle and the Higher Good," *New York Times*, July 3, 2011. http://www.nytimes.com/2011/07/03/ books/review/book-review-aristotles-nico machean-ethics.html?scp=1&sq=Harry %20V.%20Jaffa&st=cse (accessed July 18, 2011).

Lindgren, James, and Franklin E. Zimring. "Regulation of Guns." In *Encyclopedia of Crime and Justice*, edited by Sanford H. Kadish, 836–41. New York: Free Press, 1983.

National Research Council. *Firearms and Violence: A Critical Review.* Washington, DC: National Academy Press, 2005. http:// www.nap.edu/openbook.php?isbn=030909 1241 (accessed July 18, 2011).

Chronology

The following chronology presents the long and broad range of watershed events that have shaped the contemporary gun debate in American society.

1787–1791   The place of militias in the new nation is one of a myriad of issues during the U.S. Constitutional Convention's deliberations in 1787. States' rights advocates emphasize that citizens in new republics should fear standing armies at all costs. This zeal of some such advocates is tempered by the ineffective governance existing under the Articles of Confederation (1778–1789), which have kept the federal government weak and the governments of the states strong. Many are concerned about the need for a strong central government to suppress uprisings such as the recent Shays' Rebellion in Massachusetts.

Federalists are also fearful of standing armies, but see the survival of the United States depending upon a strong national government—a government that, among many other things, has its own army and navy (that does not depend upon grants from the individual states to support). One of the compromises between proponents and opponents of federalism is reflected in Article I, Section 8, of the Constitution and the Second Amendment of the Bill of Rights. In Article I, Section 8, Congress is granted the power to raise and support an army (8.12); provide and maintain a navy (8.13); call forth the militia to execute the laws of the Union, suppress insurrections, and repel invasions (8.15); provide for organizing, arming, and disciplining the militia, and for governing such part of them as may be employed in the service of the United States (8.16).

Concessions to satisfy the Anti-Federalists include the right of the states to appoint officers to the militia and to train militiamen (according to standards set by Congress). State militias are seen as counteracting forces to the potential might of a standing federal army, as well as reducing the need for a large standing army in the first place. Fears of a standing army are further assuaged by giving the civilian Congress control over the military's purse strings, and by limiting military appropriations to no more than two years.

1787–1791
(cont.)

Nagging doubts over the power of the states to maintain and control militias are addressed in the First Congress and eventually alleviated with the passage of the Second Amendment. States' rights advocates want certainty that federal power will not be used to annul state sovereignty. As ratified in 1791, the Second Amendment declares: "A well regulated Militia, being necessary to the security of a free State, the right of the people to keep and bear Arms, shall not be infringed."

These 27 words eventuate in a furor of controversy in the last decades of the twentieth century and the first decade of the twenty-first century—controversy over their original meaning, and controversy on their applicability to contemporary American society. Federal appeals courts, with the backing of many historians and legal scholars, interpret the amendment as a *collective* right granted to the states to maintain the capacity for arming their own militias—this is also the interpretation emphasized by most gun control activists. Selected scholars and many from the gun rights camp agree with this interpretation, but see it as only a partial understanding of the amendment—which they see as also guaranteeing the right of *individuals* to keep and bear arms for personal self-defense. Finally, a few scholars hold that neither the collective-right interpretation (which focuses on the first clause of the amendment) nor the individual-right interpretation (focusing on the second clause) truly hits the mark. Rather, the amendment was intended to outline a civic duty, that is, individuals were indeed granted the right to keep and bear arms, but only to meet their duty to serve in a *well-regulated* militia, as to ensure the common defense. Not surprisingly, those in the gun control camp are much more likely to accept the civic-duty interpretation than their counterparts in the gun rights camp.

1792–1990

On May 1 and 8, 1792, President George Washington signs the First and Second Militia Acts of 1792, which set a minimum standard for the federal militia. The acts require free, able-bodied, 18- to 45-year-old white men to enroll in the militia (men employed as postmen, stagecoach drivers, and ferrymen are exempted). Each militiaman is required to supply his own gun, powder, ammunition, shot-pouch, powder horn, and knapsack and to "appear so armed, accoutered, and provided, when called out to exercise or into service" (*Annals of Congress* 1792, 1392).

Washington uses the act to muster the militia and put down the "Whiskey Rebellion" of August 1794. The act is amended in 1795. It is revised in 1862 to allow all African Americans to serve. In the Militia Act of 1903, the "organized militia" is revamped into the "National Guard" and separated from the "unorganized militia" (able-bodied male citizens—or immigrants on the path to citizenship—between the ages of 17 and 45).

In 1916, Congress passes the National Defense Act, increasing federal support for the Guards, and also further subsumes them under national military rules, organization, and authority. Starting in 1933, they operate under a dual enlistment system, whereby a guard member is simultaneously part of the relevant *state* Guard and the *National* Guard; and Congress asserts that its authority over the National Guard is based on Congress's army power, not its militia power.

Federal authority over the state Guards is recognized by the Supreme Court in 1990 in *Perpich v. Department of Defense*, where it rules that state governors have control over their state Guards for state purposes, but that the governors cannot prevent the U.S. government from using the state Guards as it sees fit, such as sending them to Central America. As the Supreme Court observes in its 1965 *Maryland v. United States* decision, "The National Guard is the modern Militia reserved to the States by Art. I . . . of the Constitution."

1800–1900   Even though stories of frontier violence are popular, the level of violence—especially gun violence—in nonfrontier America is actually but a fraction of that actually occurring on the frontier, which itself is considerably less than that depicted in the Wild West shows and dime novels of the latter part of the era. As soon as a frontier area is secured and towns established, violence quickly recedes—especially personal violence—and so does gun carrying. In established metropolitan areas, violence tends to be at the *group* level, coming in periodic waves in the form of riots. Such frays pit older immigrant groups against more recent arrivals: Protestants against Catholics, Yankees against Irishmen, blacks and their white abolitionist friends against Irishmen and other whites, Chinese against whites, Mexicans against "Anglos." The issues are usually economic and involve disputes over jobs, turf, and the public largess. Even though some killing occurs, most egregiously during the 1863 New York City draft riots where Irish immigrants ran amuck and murdered dozens of African Americans, the fighting in New York and elsewhere rarely involves guns and is often limited to fisticuffs. When fists are not the order of the day, bats, rocks, swords, and fire are the weapons of choice.

In response to the group violence, cities start organizing police forces in the 1840s. By the middle of the 1870s, all major cities have professional police forces, and by the century's end, so do most smaller communities. In the last quarter of the nineteenth century, urban police forces are buttressed by state National Guard units, which are formed to help deal with the labor violence that is becoming common in northern and midwestern cities.

Frontier peoples' readiness to cooperate for their mutual protection belies the myth of frontier individualism and of the lone pioneer—as extolled in dime novels—conquering the West with rifle and six-shooter. The gun violence associated with famous range wars (as in Johnson County, Wyoming, in 1891), gun fighters (like Billy the Kid, Bat Masterson, and Wild Bill

1800–1900
(cont.)

Hickok), cattle towns (such as Dodge City and Abilene, Kansas), mining towns (à la Deadwood, South Dakota; Tombstone, Arizona; Virginia City, Nevada), and stagecoach robberies (as of the Butterfield line and of Wells Fargo) are, for the most part, the vivid exaggerations and often outright creations of pulp fiction writers.

As frontier settlements become "civilized," local officials are quick to put controls on guns. Thousands of municipal, county, and state gun control laws are passed to protect the public and maintain law and order. A typical gun law is the Indiana statute that "every person, not being a traveller, who shall wear or carry any dirk, pistol, sword in a sword-cane, or other danger-ous weapon concealed, shall upon conviction thereof, be fined in any sum not exceeding one hundred dollars" (*Laws of Indiana, 1831*; as quoted in Cramer 1994, 72). Prohibitions against concealed weapons are increasingly common by the mid-1800s, as are laws against the discharging of a weapon within city limits. By the late 1800s, many communities have laws dictating that firearms cannot be carried publicly unless a person is hunting, taking the weapon for repair, or going to or from a military muster.

With few exceptions, challenges of such laws in the courts fail. Most of the legal arguments are based on right-to-bear-arms provisions of state constitu-tions, and occasionally on the Second Amendment. However, the courts rou-tinely rule along the lines of an 1840 judgment by the Alabama Supreme Court: "A Statute, which, under pretence of *regulating* the manner of bearing arms, amounts to a destruction of the right, or which requires arms to be so borne as to render them wholly useless for the purpose of defence, would be clearly unconstitutional. But a law which is intended merely to promote personal security, and to put down lawless aggression and violence, and to that end inhibits the wearing of certain weapons in such a manner as is calculated to exert an unhappy influence upon the moral feelings of the wearer, by making him less regardfull of the personal security of others, does not come in collision with the constitution" (*State v. Reid*, 1 Ala. 612 [1840]). In other words, Alabama could ban concealed carry of handguns, since open carry is allowed. A few decisions from the South, after white supremacists regain control of state governments following Reconstruction, are more restrictive—upholding laws designed to make any carrying diffi-cult and inconvenient (e.g., mandating that the handgun be actually carried in the hand).

1865–1866

In the post–Civil War South, *Black Codes* are enacted in Alabama, Arkansas, Florida, Georgia, Louisiana, Mississippi, North Carolina, South Carolina, Tennessee, and Texas. These statutes deprive African Americans of many basic rights, including the right to own and carry firearms. For example, a Mississippi law dictates that "no freedman, free Negro, or mulatto not in the military service of the United States government, and not licensed so to do by the board of police of his or her county, shall keep or carry firearms of any kind, or ammunition, dirk, or Bowie knife" (as quoted in Cramer 1994, 72). Such laws contribute to keeping African Americans servile.

1871–1977   The National Rifle Association (NRA) is founded in 1871. In its early years, it is a small shooting association sponsoring rifle matches and sharpshooter classes. Prestigious retired army officers, such as former President Ulysses Grant and 1880 Democratic presidential nominee Winfield Scott Hancock, serve as early president, supporting the NRA's purpose of helping to keep the general population militia-ready. As part of this task, the NRA is commissioned to train members of the New York National Guard to shoot well, as well as to create a marksmanship training model to be adopted by other state militias. However, its state funding is cut off in 1879, and by 1892, the organization has fallen into disarray.

Revived a few years later, the NRA receives a substantial boost in 1903, when Congress creates the National Board for the Promotion of Rifle Practice (NBPRP) to promote civilian rifle practice (another attempt by the military to ensure that civilians are militia-ready). An appendage of the War Department, the civilian-run NBPRP includes all eight NRA trustees on its executive board, pursuant to congressional command. This is a critical turning point for the organization, as these trustees work with Congress to achieve passage in 1905 of Public Law 149, authorizing the sale of surplus military weapons, at cost, to rifle clubs meeting NBPRP standards. As implemented, one of these standards is that the club must be affiliated with the NRA, and Congress formally makes this a requirement in 1924. The NRA is also chosen to run the National Matches, the rifle championships created by the 1903 law.

In 1910, Congress authorizes the giving away of surplus weaponry to NRA-sponsored clubs, and in 1912, Congress begins funding NRA rifle championships. The association benefits greatly, and membership climbs from several hundred to several thousand by 1917. The end of World War I greatly increases the number of surplus weapons made available to the NRA, and membership rises steadily as prospective members are motivated by the allure of a free new rifle and a place to shoot it. Closely focusing on supporting the National Guard during the early twentieth century, the NRA in the 1920s broadens itself into a more general organization for participants in the shooting sports; at the same time, its political agenda broadens beyond the promotion of rifle and handgun marksmanship, and it is generally successful in defeating proposals for handgun control (Gilmore 1974). By the mid-1930s, the organization's membership grows to 35,000.

Compared to the organization it will become in the 1970s, the NRA of the 1930s is moderate and restrained in its attempts to influence public policy. In response to the proposed National Firearms Act of 1934, the NRA rejects

1871–1977
(cont.)

provisions for federal registration and a $200 tax for owning a handgun, but has no objection to the same restrictions applied to automatic firearms. Handguns are for virtuous citizens, and machine guns are not, in the NRA's view at the time. The NRA likewise blocks attempts to impose federal gun registration in 1937–1938, and 1957–1958. This philosophy is refined over the years until the late 1970s, when it is solidified to its present status, which is that virtually all new gun control regulations should be resisted, existing ones being more than sufficient, if enforced. (Note: the NRA supports the National Instant Check System, which goes into effect in 1998, and supports state versions of the system starting in 1989. The NRA also supports the NICS Improvement Act of 2008, which is aimed at improving the record keeping necessary to perform adequate background checks of potential firearms purchasers; however, the organization does so only because it claims that the improved instant check system does not represent any new form of "gun control"—that is, there are no new restrictions placed on those who are legally qualified to buy firearms.

The decision to oppose the gun-registration portion of the 1934 bill is accompanied by the development of a set of tactics that remains with the NRA to the present day. It circulates editorials, press releases, and open letters throughout the sporting and gun-owning communities. It urges its members and potential sympathizers to telegram or write congressional representatives. The NRA is rewarded with a huge influx of anti-registration mail, resulting in the eventual deletion of the reference to handguns in the final version of the National Firearms Act of 1934.

The NRA's growing involvement in public policy results in an invitation to work with the Justice Department and Congress in the developing the Federal Firearms Act of 1938. As with the earlier legislation, the NRA accepts minimal regulation but makes sure strong restrictions, such as a system of national registration, are kept out of the law.

Although the NRA is not especially large or well-funded in the 1930s, it finds its interests more or less readily accepted, because there is no gun control movement and no organization dedicated to gun control (like the modern-day Brady Campaign to Prevent Gun Violence).

After World War II, nine million demobilized veterans reenter civilian life with a new interest in firearms. Tens of thousands of ex-GIs join the NRA, giving it a much greater potential to wield power over public policy. However, the vast majority of these new members have little interest in gun control issues per se and great interest in recreational shooting. The NRA's programs and publications begin to reflect this transformation in membership. The NRA changes from an organization motivated by the nation's need for military preparedness to one reflecting the interests of hunters, target shooters, and other recreational gun enthusiasts.

Through the 1960s, the NRA continues on a moderate course. For example, some in the NRA of the late 1960s and early 1970s endorse the banning of Saturday night specials (cheaply made handguns). In 1968, the NRA editorializes: "Shoddily manufactured by a few foreign makers, hundreds of thousands of these have been peddled in recent years by a handful of U.S. dealers. Prices as low as $8 or $10 have placed concealable handguns within reach of multitudes who never before could afford them. Most figure in 'crimes of passion' or amateurish holdups, which form the bulk of the increase in violence. The Administration . . . possesses sufficient authority to bar by Executive direction these miserably-made, potentially defective arms that contribute so much to rising violence" (National Rifle Association 1968a, 16; as quoted in Sugarmann 1992a).

The NRA reaffirms its stance against Saturday night specials by observing that it does "not necessarily approve of everything that goes 'Bang!' " (National Rifle Association 1968b, 16; as quoted in Sugarmann 1992a). In what sounds astounding by the position of the NRA today, Executive Vice President Franklin L. Orth testifies before Congress that "the National Rifle Association concurs in principle with the desirability of removing from the market crudely made and unsafe handguns . . . [because] they have no sporting purpose, they are frequently poorly made . . . On the Saturday Night Special, we are for [banning] it 100 percent. We would like to get rid of these guns" (as quoted in Sugarmann 1992b, 42). As for the place of the Second Amendment in debate over gun control, the official *NRA Fact Book on Firearms Control* in the 1970s notes that the amendment is of "limited practical utility" in arguing against gun control (as quoted in Sugarmann 1992b, 48).

The voices of moderation and compromise within the NRA recede in 1977, when Second Amendment hard-liners oust those leaders wanting to withdraw the NRA from politics and move the headquarters to Colorado Springs (see "Revolt at Cincinnati" below).

1876   In *United States v. Cruikshank*, the U.S. Supreme Court renders its first major decision on the Second Amendment. The court rules that the Second Amendment is a guarantee against federal infringement of a preexisting right that "is found wherever civilization exists." However, the Second Amendment right is not one of the "privileges or immunities of citizens of the United States," which the Fourteenth Amendment empowered Congress to defend against state violations. Rather, "privileges or immunities" refers only to rights that are created by the U.S. Constitution (e.g., the right to travel the waterways of the United States), not preexisting rights that are simply protected by the Constitution. The case arises out of the infamous "Colfax massacre" on Easter Sunday 1873; after a disputed election, a gang of whites attacked a courthouse that was being guarded by blacks and their white Republican allies. The gang slaughters the blacks and, among other

1876 *(cont.)*	things, takes away their guns. Some of the gang leaders, including William Cruikshank, are convicted of conspiring to deprive the blacks of the First Amendment right to assemble, and their Second Amendment right to keep and bear arms—in violation of a federal statute (enacted under Congress's Fourteenth Amendment powers) against violations of civil rights on account of color. The court rules that the Second Amendment applies only to the federal government, not to state governments. The states do not have to honor it. Despite this decision supporting their contention that the Second Amendment should pose no barrier to the enactment of strict gun control laws, at least at the state level, many advocates of the gun control movement are not particularly eager to tout *United States v. Cruikshank*. The racist ruling prevents Congress from acting against racist gangs, which, unrestrained by state or local governments, can keep former slaves unarmed and in a position of vassalage in the South, thereby partly counteracting the effect of the Emancipation Proclamation. This fact is not lost either on many African American and Jewish jurists or on interest groups opposing gun control such as the National Rifle Association. Even though African Americans and Jews generally tend to support strict gun control, some contend that regulations on gun possession are a means for suppressing a society's minorities and for allowing unjust rulers to hold sway because they control most weaponry.
1886	The U.S. Supreme Court addresses the Second Amendment for a second time in *Presser v. Illinois*. Herman Presser, the leader of a German-American labor group called the *Lehr und Wehr Verein* (the "Learning and Defense Club"), is arrested for parading the group through downtown Chicago while carrying a sword, and while club members were carrying unloaded rifles. He is accused of conducting an "armed military drill," which could legally be done only with a license, under Illinois statutes in force at the time. Presser appeals, invoking the Second Amendment in his defense. The Supreme Court rules against him, citing the *United States v. Cruikshank* decision discussed above. Again, the court contends that the Second Amendment does not directly apply to the individual states, and is not made applicable to them by the privileges or immunities clause of the Fourteenth Amendment. And, as was the case with *Cruikshank*, the Supreme Court's decision smacks of bigotry—in this instance, through the repression of exploited immigrant laborers trying to improve their collective lot via unionization.
1903–1990	Congress passes the Militia Act of 1903, also known as the Dick Act (named after the Ohio congressman who sponsors the legislation, Rep. Charles Dick, himself a National Guard officer). The act separates the organized militia, to be known as the "National Guard" of the state, from the "unorganized

militia" (which, in actuality, has not existed for decades). It provides federal support for state governments to arm, train, and drill the Guards.

In 1916, Congress passes the National Defense Act, increasing federal support for the Guards, and also further subsumes them under national military rules, organization, and authority. They operate under a dual enlistment system, whereby a guard member is simultaneously part of the relevant *state* National Guard and the *U.S.* National Guard.

Federal authority over the state Guards is recognized by the Supreme Court in 1990 in *Perpich v. Department of Defense*, where it rules that state governors have control over their state Guards for state purposes, but that the governors cannot prevent the U.S. government from using the state Guards as it sees fit—and more particularly to deploy them outside of the country without gubernatorial consent. As the Supreme Court observes in its 1965 *Maryland v. United States* decision, "The National Guard is the modern Militia reserved to the States by Art. I . . . of the Constitution."

1911	New York State passes the Sullivan Law, requiring a license for both the purchase and carry of handguns. Such licenses are rarely issued for carrying. However, gun rights advocates point out that it has little effect on violent crime and is motivated, at heart, by xenophobic fears within the mainstream leadership of New York, who want to keep firearms out of the hands of Italian and other recent immigrants. It is estimated that 7 of 10 of those arrested during the first three years of the law are of Italian descent. While the Sullivan Law applies to the entire state, it is actually aimed at New York City, where the large foreign population is thought overly turbulent and prone to criminal activity (Beckman 2002). Due to the xenophobic nature of the Sullivan Law, some critics point to it as an example of using "gun control" to quash minority interests.
1927	Congress passes the Mailing of Firearms Act of 1927, also known as the Miller Act, prohibiting sending concealable firearms through the U.S. Post Office. As originally proposed, the act would ban the interstate shipping of all handguns except service revolvers. However, strong opposition from legislators in gun manufacturing states combined with similarly strong opposition from legislators in the southern and western states, many of whom believe it violates the Second Amendment's right to keep and bear arms, almost completely neutralize the act by restricting its provisions to the U.S. Post Office. The law is easy to skirt until passage of the Gun Control Act of 1968, because mailers can legally send guns via private mail delivery companies such as UPS (United Parcel Service).
1929	The Saint Valentine's Day Massacre in Chicago shocks the nation. Four members of Al Capone's gang, two dressed as police officers, ruthlessly mow down seven members of a rival Chicago gang using Thompson

1929 *(cont.)*	submachine guns. The murders prompt several gun control proposals in Congress, two of which eventually pass (the National Firearms Act of 1934 and the Federal Firearms Act of 1938).
1934	The first major federal gun control legislation is passed as the National Firearms Act of 1934. It mandates all persons engaged in the business of selling gangster-type weapons—machine guns, sawed-off shotguns, and silencers—and all owners of these to register with the collector of internal revenue and pay applicable taxes for the firearm transfer. Because criminals are unlikely to register their weapons, the effect is to give law enforcement authorities a new reason to arrest gangsters (possession of an unregistered weapon). Lawful trade in these weapons is also dramatically reduced due to the hefty taxes.
1938	The second major federal gun control legislation is passed as the Federal Firearms Act of 1938. It imposes the first federal limitations on the sale of ordinary firearms. It requires manufacturers, dealers, and importers of guns and handgun ammunition to obtain a federal firearms license. Dealers must maintain records of the names and addresses of persons to whom firearms are sold. Gun sales to persons convicted of violent felonies are prohibited.
1939–1942	In *United States v. Miller* (1939), the U.S. Supreme Court makes its third major ruling bearing on the Second Amendment. The court rules that the federal government has the right, which it exercised in the National Firearms Act of 1934, to control the transfer of (and in effect, to require the registration of) certain firearms. In this particular case, the sawed-off shotgun, a favorite weapon of gangsters, is deemed unprotected by the Second Amendment. The ruling reads, in part: "In the absence of any evidence tending to show that possession or use of 'shotgun having a barrel of less than eighteen inches in length' at this time has some reasonable relationship to the preservation or efficiency of a well regulated militia, we cannot say that the second amendment guarantees the right to keep and bear such an instrument." Lower-court decisions involving the National Firearms Act and the kindred Federal Firearms Act use even more direct language. In upholding the National Firearms Act, a Florida district court declares in *United States v. Adams* (1935) that the Second Amendment "refers to the Militia, a protective force of government; to the collective body and not individual rights." A later Third Circuit Court of Appeals decision, *United States v. Tot* (1942), cites this ruling in upholding the Federal Firearms Act. These court decisions make clear that no personal right to own arms exists under the federal Constitution.
	On the other hand, gun rights advocates point out that in its *Miller* ruling, the Supreme Court noted that the writers of the Constitution clearly intended that the states had both the right and the duty to maintain militias and that a "militia comprised all males physically capable of acting in concert for

the common defense. . . . And, further, that ordinarily when called for service, these men were expected to appear bearing arms supplied by themselves and of the kind in common use at the time. . . . This implied the general obligation of all adult male inhabitants to possess arms, and with certain exceptions, to cooperate in the work of defense. The possession of arms also implied the possession of ammunition, and authorities paid quite as much attention to the latter as to the former." Thus, the full text of the Supreme Court decision mitigates the impact of its decision on sawed-off shotguns. Such weapons have no place in a militia and thus are not protected, but the general principle of ordinary citizens owning arms and ammunition is clearly preserved.

1961   An amendment to the Federal Aviation Act of 1958—by Public Law 87-197 of 1961—bars individuals from bringing on board a passenger aircraft any concealed firearm (except in the form of check-in luggage).

1963   Using a false name, Lee Harvey Oswald buys an imported Italian military rifle for less than $20 from a mail-order dealer in Chicago. He uses it to assassinate President John F. Kennedy. The ease with which he has obtained the weapon stuns many Americans, and soon there are numerous bills brought before Congress to regulate the gun market. These bills are combined and reformulated many times until they result in the Omnibus Crime Control and Safe Streets Act of 1968 and its sister legislation, the Gun Control Act of 1968.

1965   The Texas Tower shooting shocks the nation. On August 1, former Marine sharpshooter Charles Whitman climbs the clock tower on the University of Texas campus in Austin with seven firearms. He methodically kills 15 people and wounds 31 others. Whitman's victims include the unborn child of an 18-year-old pregnant student, whom he shot through the abdomen. The shooting spree ends when two Austin police officers and a civilian subdue and kill the sniper. An autopsy reveals a golf-ball sized tumor in Whitman's brain.

The Texas Tower massacre and its immediate aftermath are played out many times over the next five decades: A mass-murder shooting shocks the nation and sparks local, state, and national legislative proposals to control guns; within a few months, however, emotions die down and almost all of the proposals fail enactment.

1968   The assassinations of Reverend Martin Luther King and Senator Robert F. Kennedy, as do the urban riots exploding in hundreds of urban areas since 1965, increase national attention on gun violence and, according to many observers, the need for stronger gun control. Congress is finally motivated to pass twin bills containing serious gun control measures—the Omnibus Crime Control and Safe Streets Act of 1968 and the Gun Control Act of

1968
(cont.)

1968 (GCA). More recent federal gun laws, including the 1993 Brady Law and the 1994 federal Assault Weapons Ban, are enacted as amendments to the GCA statutes (or, less often, to the 1934 National Firearms Act).

The GCA places severe restrictions on the importation of firearms and on the sale of guns and ammunition across state lines. Interstate pistol sales are banned. Interstate long gun sales are also banned, except when contiguous states enact laws to authorize such sales. Mail-order and package delivery service (e.g., UPS) gun sales are prohibited. Interstate ammunition sales are prohibited. The GCA also creates a "prohibited persons" list of those barred from possessing guns. The list is originally comprised of convicted felons, alcoholics, drug users, "mental defectives," fugitives, persons dishonorably discharged from the military, and persons who renounced their citizenship. In 1994, the list is expanded to include those convicted of domestic violence or subject to a domestic violence restraining order (for a concise, comprehensive, and current list of the criteria prohibiting a person from possessing a firearm, see U.S. Department of Justice 2011, 12).

The GCA leads to the creation of the Bureau of Alcohol, Tobacco, and Firearms (ATF)—upgraded from its previous status as a division—within the Department of the Treasury (and moved to the Deparment of Justice in 2003). The ATF is the key federal agency assigned to effectuate gun control, but its advocates complain that it is hampered by lack of funding and by restrictions placed on it by the gun-rights-leaning Congresses of the 1986 and of the post-1994 era.

1972

The Consumer Product Safety Commission is created to "protect against unreasonable risks of injuries associated with consumer products." However, firearms are excluded from the commission's oversight. Congress further clarifies its intent with a follow-up piece of legislation, the Firearms Safety and Consumer Protection Act of 1976, which excludes ammunition from regulations by the Consumer Product Safety Commission. Gun control advocates rue these exclusions. Toward the end of the century, these advocates begin pointing to Massachusetts as an example of the potential of consumer product laws to promote the cause of gun control: In 1996, Massachusetts attorney general Scott Harshbarger uses the state's Consumer Protection Act to create strict regulations over handguns—declaring them as inherently unsafe consumer products unless they meet a number of stringent criteria, e.g., having a "loaded chamber indicator" (letting a user know that a round is in the chamber, even if the ammunition magazine has been removed from the gun). In 1998, the state legislature codifies the Harshbarger requirements into state law.

1973–1978

From October 1973 through April 1974, the Zebra Killings in the San Francisco area captivate the public's attention and eventually strengthen the gun control movement both locally and nationally. The label given the killings is attributed to the fact that the killers are black and the victims white. Fourteen people are murdered and seven wounded during the five-month killing spree.

Eight members of a Black Muslim cult called the "Death Angels" are eventually arrested; their motive is to incite a race war. Four are released for a lack of evidence, but the other four are convicted in 1976 and sentenced to life in prison.

The Zebra Killings, as well as the 1978 handgun murders of Mayor George Moscone and Supervisor Harvey Milk, are instrumental in strengthening political and public support for stricter gun control measures within the San Francisco Bay Area. The City and County of San Francisco approve a handgun ban in 1982, though it is subsequently overturned in state court.

The Zebra killing of college student Nick Shields leads his father, Pete Shields, to become a gun control activist. Shields leaves an executive position with DuPont to become executive director of a fledging advocacy group, Handgun Control, Inc. He plays a critical role in developing it into the premier organizational advocate for strengthening gun controls in the United States (it is renamed the Brady Campaign to Prevent Gun Violence in 2001).

1974–2011   The modern gun control movement begins in 1974 when Mark Borinsky founds the National Council to Control Handguns in Washington, D.C. In the late 1970s, it is renamed Handgun Control, Inc., and in 2001, the Brady Campaign to Prevent Gun Violence.

Borinsky had been robbed at gunpoint as a graduate student. The traumatic experience stays with him, and upon graduation, he decides to join a national group promoting gun control. Alas, none exists. He fills the void by starting his own.

The new organization finds sympathy for its cause abounding within the federal government. Many members of Congress are eager to work with an organization devoted to gun control. Indeed, many of them were part of the 78th Congress that had passed the Omnibus Crime Control and Safe Streets Act of 1968 and the kindred Gun Control Act of 1968. Though the acts ban the sale and possession of guns to felons, drug addicts, illegal aliens, and the mentally incompetent, they include no serious enforcement mechanisms to block such sales, as opposed to simply prosecuting such persons who are caught possessing guns. Many members of Congress feel that rectifying this shortcoming is critical to realizing effective gun control.

The Treasury Department's Bureau of Alcohol, Tobacco, and Firearms (ATF) welcomes an organization that will help in its fight to regulate and monitor firearms. ATF's efforts to fulfill the promise of the federal gun control legislation of 1968 are stymied every step of the way by gun rights legislators (prodded, in part, by the NRA), and it is looking for allies. Perhaps

1974–2011
(cont.)

most notably, the ATF's proposal to begin a computerized system to record the serial numbers of all new weapons and every firearms transaction of the nation's 160,000 federally licensed firearms dealers provokes the U.S. House in 1978 to vote down the idea 314–80; and because the ATF says it can implement the $5 million registration system from its existing budget, ATF's budget is cut by that amount.

Other divisions of the Department of Justice also welcome an organization devoted to gun control. For example, the department's recently formed Bureau of Justice Statistics has many staffers who are shocked by the gun-violence statistics they are amassing and are subsequently eager to provide these statistics in editorialized format ("guns are bad, just look at these data!") to an organization like Borinsky's.

In the 1990s, the organization finds an ally in the federal government's Centers for Disease Control (CDC), whose staffers are emotionally affected by the gun-violence data they are analyzing in much the same way as the emotions of their counterparts in the Bureau of Justice Statistics. In the early 1990s, through its National Center for Injury Prevention and Control division, the CDC produces several studies that frame gun violence as a serious *public health* problem and that include recommendations for the control of firearms that inflame many in the gun rights community, including the strong gun-rights members of Congress. Congress responds by demanding that the CDC not publish papers that "may be used to advocate or promote gun control." Since 1996, funding and motivation for gun-violence research has been severely constrained.

The 1990s and early 2000s also sees Handgun Control, Inc., now the Brady Campaign, greatly develop—through its tax-exempt educational arm, the Center to Prevent Handgun Violence—its Legal Action Project, which uses lawsuits to push firearms manufacturers and dealers to develop products and practices aimed at reducing gun violence. After a mostly unsuccessful string of suits involving private plaintiffs, starting in 1998, the Legal Action Project assists more than two dozen city governments, as well as the state of New York, to file suits to recover the costs of gun violence to the general public—including those associated with the police and courts, as well as with emergency medical care. The governments claim that gun manufacturers fail to take advantage of safe-gun technologies, and that their distribution system encourages straw purchases and the flow of firearms into the black market. (A "straw purchaser" is an individual who can pass a federal background check, but who buys a gun for someone who cannot pass such a check; the black market consists largely of stolen guns and those acquired through straw purchases.) Although many in the gun control community see promise for the strategy (cases are not won in court, but sometimes result in out-of-court settlements), it is rejected by most courts, hamstrung by laws enacted by 32 states to block such suits, and finally brought to a near halt with the 2005 passage of the federal Protection of Lawful Commerce in Arms Act—which shields gun and ammunition dealers and manufacturers from civil liability suits based on the criminal misuse of their products. Subsequent court challenges to the act fail.

1977   The "Revolt at Cincinnati" occurs at the annual meeting of the National Rifle Association. It is a watershed event that will change the organization from one largely dedicated to promoting the sporting uses of firearms to one largely dedicated to fighting any and all forms of gun control.

Although some of the NRA's membership and leadership in the 1960s and early 1970s are radically opposed to any form of gun regulation, they are in the minority. In 1972, however, this minority begins an all-out—and eventually successful—effort to redefine the meaning and the primary mission of the NRA.

Executive committee member Harlon B. Carter leads this redefinition effort. In a July 1972 address to the NRA executive committee, Carter argues that the NRA philosophy on gun control—that some was necessary and good for society—is wrongheaded and needs to be replaced by a new philosophy, one of absolute resistance to any and all forms of gun regulation: "Any position we took [on gun control] back at that time is no good, it is not valid, and it is simply not relevant to the problem that we face today. The latest news release from NRA embraces a disastrous concept . . . that evil is imputed to the sale and delivery, the possession of a certain kind of firearm, entirely apart from the good or evil intent of the man who uses it and/or . . . that the legitimate use of a handgun is limited to sporting use" (as quoted in Sugarmann 1992b, chap. 2).

Carter further argues that every gun has a legitimate purpose and that every law-abiding person should have the right to choose his or her own weapon according to what he or she thinks best.

Largely through Carter's efforts, the minority view begins appearing more and more in the NRA's public statements. The moderate editorials that had occasionally appeared in the NRA's leading publication, the *American Rifleman*, vanish as its editor is replaced, partly through pressure applied by Carter, by a new editor who promotes the idea that there can be nothing good about any kind of gun control aimed at law-abiding citizens, and there are no bad guns, only bad gun owners.

During the mid-1970s, only 25 percent of the organization—according to the NRA's own estimate—consists of "nonshooting constitutionalists" (people who do not own firearms but who join the NRA to support its political agenda). But this does not prevent the complete takeover of NRA leadership positions by the hardest of the hard-liners against gun control at the NRA's

1977
(cont.)

1977 annual meeting. The coup is led by Neal Knox (at the time, editor of the gun magazines *Rifle* and *Handloader*), Robert Kukla (the new head of the NRA's lobbying wing, the Institute for Legislative Action), and Joseph Tartaro (then and now the editor of *Gun Week*).

Knox, Kukla, and Tartaro lay the foundation for their revolt by using their access to gun publications to condemn the moderate direction the NRA is taking (on being a hunting and conservation organization). At the convention itself, they use their knowledge of parliamentary procedure to methodically replace top leaders with hardcore gun-rights advocates such as themselves. The "New NRA," as Carter called it, would become almost synonymous with the "gun lobby."

1980

On the evening of December 8, Mark David Chapman uses a Charter Arms .38-caliber revolver to gun down John Lennon in New York City. Lennon's murder stokes national interest in gun control and the still-fledgling Handgun Control, Inc. (renamed the Brady Campaign to Prevent Gun Violence in 2001) rockets from 5,000 to 80,000 contributing members in a matter of weeks.

In *Lewis v. United States*, the Supreme Court upholds a provision of the Gun Control Act of 1968; in a footnote, it states that "restrictions on the use of firearms are neither based upon constitutionally suspect criteria, nor do they trench upon any constitutionally protected liberties," and cites the 1939 *United States v. Miller* case for support.

In *Lewis*, the court addresses the case of an individual convicted of a burglary in Florida in 1961, whose conviction for the offense is never overturned, even though it is ruled unconstitutional under the Sixth and Fourteenth Amendments (the individual had not been provided with counsel to assist in his defense). The court holds, however, that the constitutionality of the petitioner's conviction has no bearing on his liability under the Gun Control Act of 1968. The court maintains that any felony conviction, even an invalid one, is a sufficient to prohibit possession of a firearm.

1981

John Hinckley uses a cheap handgun in March to wound President Ronald Reagan and his press secretary, James Brady, as well as Secret Service agent Timothy McCarthy and local police officer Thomas Delahanty. The assassination attempt results in a boon for Handgun Control, Inc., and the gun control movement. The event generates huge media focus on handguns—where the emphases are on their easy acquisition, and their strong connections to crimes of violence (especially, homicide). The event motivates Sarah Brady, James Brady's wife, to dedicate herself to the gun control movement; she joins HCI, takes on leadership roles, and eventually becomes its president.

The assassination attempt also moves Congress to renew its discussions on gun control, and encourages its support of legislation that eventually becomes the 1988 Undetectable Firearms Act (banning the manufacture, importation, possession, receipt, and transfer of "plastic guns"—those with less than 3.7 ounces of metal, which could potentially defeat metal detectors; a symbolic victory for the gun control movement, as commercially manufactured guns have always met this standard) and the 1993 Brady Handgun Violence Prevention Act (requiring a five-day waiting period and a criminal background check before an individual can purchase a handgun). Relatedly, the assassination attempt is in the mind of Congress when, at the urging of Handgun Control, Inc., it retains the 1968 Gun Control Act's ban on the interstate sale of pistols when enacting the 1986 Firearms Owners' Protection Act. The act also bars the future possession and sale of machine guns, but is otherwise seen as gun rights legislation because of its relaxing of several provisions of the 1968 Gun Control Act and of its improving due-process protections for gun owners and licensed firearms dealers.

1982   In *Quilici v. Village of Morton Grove*, the Seventh Circuit of the U.S. Court of Appeals upholds a ban on the possession of handguns by ordinary persons in Morton Grove, Illinois. The court declares that the Second Amendment preserves the *collective* right of a state's citizens to form a militia, and not the absolute right of an *individual* to keep and bear firearms.

The 1981 Morton Grove law exempts those needing a handgun for occupational purposes—such as police officers, prison officials, members of the armed forces, and security guards. It also exempts licensed gun collectors. A resident owning a handgun before the ban is enacted can keep it, as long as the gun is stored at a local gun club (although nonworking, antique firearms may be kept at home).

Soon after enactment, gun rights advocates file a lawsuit claiming that the Morton Grove law is in violation of both the U.S. and Illinois State Constitutions. A lower federal court rules in favor of Morton Grove, as does the appeals court. The appeals court declares that "construing the [Second Amendment] according to its plain meaning, it seems clear that the right to bear arms is inextricably connected to the preservation of a militia." The plaintiffs ask the U.S. Supreme Court to hear the case, but the court declines.

The ruling in *Quilici* is consistent with other federal court decisions finding a militia-based meaning of the Second Amendment—though in 2001, a federal appeal court rules in *United States. v. Emerson* that the amendment guarantees an individual right to possess and bear firearms (see below).

Quilici v. Village of Morton Grove receives enormous publicity and fuels the increasingly hot fires of the national debate over gun control. The village's law banning handguns, as well as the lower and appeals court decisions in favor of it, are huge symbolic victories for those favoring stricter gun control.

1982
(cont.)

Ironically, the *Morton Grove* case turns out well for the NRA in other states. The Morton Grove ban (plus a similar 1983 ban in Chicago) and other bans in Chicago suburbs enacted in the next several years, are the perfect examples for the NRA to use to convince many state legislatures to enact "preemption laws"—a statute forbidding local governments to enact gun control laws.

In addition, gun rights advocates work with public officials in the small town of Kennesaw, Georgia, to pass a local ordinance *requiring* that all heads of households own a firearm and ammunition. The law is entirely symbolic, as there is no provision for enforcement; moreover, the law itself includes several clauses "excusing" those not wanting to own a gun for moral or religious reasons, or because they are a convicted felon or mentally or physically disabled.

1984–1989

On July 18, 1984, James Huberty leaves his home announcing to his wife that he is "going to hunt humans." He enters a McDonald's restaurant in San Ysidro, California and uses three high-powered weapons to methodically slaughter 20 patrons and employees, wounding another 19. The carnage stops when he is mortally wounded by a police sniper Because one of his weapons is an Uzi semiautomatic rifle, gun control advocates press state legislators for restricions on assault weapons, but it will take another California massacre, four and a half years later in Stockton, before action is finally taken. Soon after Patrick Purdy uses an semiautomatic assault rifle to kill five children in a Stockton schoolyard (wounding 29 others), the state legislature passes the Roberti-Roos Assault Weapons Control Act of 1989.

The Armed Career Criminal Act of 1984 increases the penalties for firearm possession by convicted felons as specified in the Gun Control Act of 1968. The 1984 act is amended in 1986 and 1988, and its guidelines receive several updates over the years. These amendments and updates represent an effort to meet the true spirit of the legislation, which is aimed at incapacitating hardened criminals—those with three or more previous violent felony or serious drug offense convictions—by putting them in prison for a minimum of 15 years if they are found in possession of a firearm (Levine 2009).

1986

The Firearms Owners' Protection Act (FOPA)—known also as the McClure-Volkmer Act—is passed against the protests of gun control advocates. FOPA curtails many of the more stringent provisions of the Gun Control Act of 1968. Most notably, it (1) allows federally licensed firearms dealers to sell guns not only at their principal place of business, but also at gun shows as long as the sales comply with all relevant laws; (2) limits the Bureau of Alcohol, Tobacco, and Firearms' (ATF) compliance inspections of a gun dealer to once per year, while allowing unlimited inspection as part of a "bona fide" criminal investigation; (3) prohibits the ATF from creating a national gun registry; (4) removes federal restrictions on interstate ammunition sales; and (5) re-legalizes interstate long gun sales (if the seller is a federally licensed firearms dealer, and the sale is legal in both states).

The Law Enforcement Officers Protection Act bans so-called "cop killer" handgun bullets—or more accurately, bullets with very dense cores made from certain metals—that are capable of piercing some bullet-resistant vests and other body armor. Amended in 1994, the statute defines "armor piercing ammunition" as a handgun bullet "constructed entirely" from "tungsten alloys, steel, iron, brass, bronze, beryllium copper, or depleted uranium," or with a jacket having a weight greater than one-quarter of the projectile's total weight (18 U.S.C. § 922(a)(7) and 18 U.S.C. § 921(a)(17)(B). Because rifles are more effective in defeating police body armor than any handgun, cop-killer bullets represent a symbolic, rather than substantive, issue in the debate over gun control (Vizzard 2000)—an issue won by gun control advocates, an issue they use to rail at the NRA in public discourse ("How could any organization not support legislation aimed at removing 'cop-killer bullets' from the market?").

1989   On January 17, Patrick Purdy enters a Stockton, California, schoolyard and fires 105 rounds from a semiautomatic assault rifle, killing 5 children and wounding 29 others. The slaughter mobilizes public and political support for gun control throughout the nation. California responds quickly and enacts the Roberti-Roos Assault Weapons Control Act of 1989. Over the next few years, six other states follow with legislation restricting the sale of assault weapons (Connecticut, Hawaii, Maryland, Massachusetts, New Jersey, and New York). At the federal level, President George H. W. Bush, even though a member of the NRA and a gun rights proponent during his election campaign, responds in March by placing a temporary ban on the importation of assault rifles and selected similar weapons. Several bills are introduced in Congress to outlaw or restrict assault pistols, rifles, and shotguns. President Bill Clinton eventually pushes one of these through Congress as part of the Violent Crime Control and Enforcement Act of 1994.

1990   Enacted as Public Law 101-647, the Crime Control Act of 1990 bans the importing of certain semiautomatic firearms designated as "assault weapons," as well as manufacturing them domestically with some foreign parts. The act also creates gun-free school zones, making it a federal crime to carry a firearm with 1,000 feet of a school; however, this provision is overturned in a circuit court ruling in 1993, which is subsequently upheld by the Supreme Court in *United States v. Lopez* (1995). Congress, however, soon reenacts the ban with small changes.

1991–2002 The Killeen, Texas, massacre unfolds on the afternoon of October 16, 1991, when George Hennard Jr. plows his truck into Luby's Cafeteria. Repeatedly firing and then reloading two handguns, he slaughters 23 people and wounds 21 others.

1991–2002
(cont.)

Two of Hennard's victims are the parents of Suzanna Gratia. Gratia normally travels with a handgun for self-protection, but keeps it in her car to be in compliance with Texas law, which in 1991 does not allow ordinary citizens to carry concealed weapons. She testifies ruefully at a public hearing that she might have been able to save her parents if she had had her gun in her purse: "I had a perfect shot at him. It would have been clear. I had a place to prop my hand. The guy was not even aware of what we were doing. I'm not saying that I could have saved anybody in there, but I would have had a chance" (as quoted in Kopel 2002, 335).

Gratia's testimony becomes instrumental in changing the political climate in Texas and many other states regarding right-to-carry laws. And in the mid-1990s, 11 states, including Texas, adopt a right-to-carry law. (Note that as of 2011, 34 states are classified as "shall-issue"—allowing an ordinary citizen to obtain a concealed-carry permit with a background check [usually based on fingerprints] and, in most cases, after having passed a safety course; another four states—Alaska, Arizona, Vermont, and Wyoming—do not require any license for law-abiding citizens to carry concealed weapons; two states, Alabama and Connecticut, have statutes that are nominally discretionary, but in practice, most applicants who would qualify in a shall-issue state are granted permits. Illinois allows only licensed security, hunters in the field, and a few other special categories [such as some elected officials] to carry guns in public, while in the remaining eight states [California, Delaware, Hawaii, Maryland, Massachusetts, New Jersey, New York, and Rhode Island], local and state authorities have considerable discretionary power—with permits often being denied; see Appendix II, "State Gun Laws"; also see Galloway 2011 and National Rifle Association 2010.)

Along with the wave of state laws allowing concealed carry, the 1990s see "preemption laws" passed or judicially clarified in dozens of states. Such laws preempt local ordinances that would be more restrictive than state gun laws. By 2011, all states but Hawaii have at least limited preemption, while the majority have complete preemption of all local firearm laws. Massachusetts, a limited-preemption state, allows more restrictive local ordinances if approved by the state legislature. In 2002, the California Supreme Court rules that the state's limited preemption law, which prohibits local licensing or registration of gun sales, does not preempt a county's ban on gun shows on county-owned property. In Ohio, in *Cleveland v. State* (2010), the Ohio Supreme Court upholds the state's preemption law on a 5–2 vote and thus ends a Cleveland ban on assault weapons, as well as the gun laws of many other Ohio municipalities.

1993–2001

On July 1, 1993, Gian Luigi Ferri, a disgruntled former client, enters the law office of Pettit and Martin at 101 California Street in San Francisco. Armed with three handguns, two of them TEC-DC9 assault pistols, he kills eight people and wounds another six in the law office and in neighboring offices. The police quickly arrive and corner him in a stairwell, where he commits suicide. Although California had banned the sale of assault weapons after the Stockton schoolyard massacre of 1989, Ferri easily obtains his at a gun show and pawn shop in Nevada.

The 101 California Street massacre sparks outcries for strong gun controls and contributes to the passage of the 1994 federal Assault Weapons Ban. The massacre also spawns the historic lawsuit *Merrill v. Navegar*, resulting in the first appeals court decision to rule that under certain circumstances, a gun manufacturer can be held negligent when its weapons are used in the commission of crime.

Navegar, under the business name Intratec Firearms Inc., is manufacturing high-capacity assault pistols under the names KG-9 and TEC-9 during the 1980s. The weapons are popular with criminals and street gang members. When the District of Columbia and other jurisdictions enact laws restricting the TEC-9 (and other assault weapons by model name), Navegar responds by making a minor alteration to the pistol and renaming it the "TEC-DC9" to evade the laws (according to some former employees, the "DC" is inserted to mock the Washington "DC" *Assault Weapons Control Act of 1990*; see DeBell 2002). The features appealing most to criminals remain unchanged—a high-capacity magazine and a threaded barrel to screw on a silencer. The company touts the TEC-DC9's "firepower" and "excellent resistance to finger-prints" (see Henigan 2002).

The *Merrill v. Navegar* lawsuit is filed in May 1994. California (101) Street victims and their families argue that Navegar's negligent actions contributed to the massacre. The company's advertising is said to appeals to criminals. Indeed, Navegar executives testify that they are well aware of their product's stature as the preeminent assault weapon used in crimes, and that they welcome the publicity stemming from its use in notorious acts of violence because of the resulting spike in sales.

A California Superior Court judge dismisses the suit before trial, ruling that Navegar's guns are legally manufactured and sold, and that the company cannot be held liable for what others do with their guns. In a landmark ruling in September 1999, the California Court of Appeals disagrees. The court holds that Navegar owes the plaintiffs and the general public a duty to exercise reasonable care and not to create risks above and beyond those inherent in the presence of firearms in society.

On August 6, 2001, the California Supreme Court votes 5–1 to reverse the court of appeals ruling on other grounds, finding that a California statute, passed in 1983, bars imposing any liability on Navegar.

1993–2001
(cont.)

On November 30, 1993, President Clinton signs the Brady Handgun Violence Prevention Act, requiring a five-government-business-day waiting period for the purchase of a handgun. The waiting period allows time for at least a minimal background check of the prospective buyer; it also allows for a "cooling-off" period to minimize impulse purchases that might lead to suicide or criminal violence. Five years after enactment, the five-day waiting period sunsets by its own terms and is replaced by the National Instant Criminal Background Check System (NICS), which allows background checking for both handgun and long gun sales (rifles and shotguns). The check must be completed within three days; firearms dealers sometimes get a response in a matter of seconds, while in some states the check can take several hours, due to backlogs. When the dealer is told to "delay" the transaction (because of inadequate information to determine whether there is a true match with the "prohibited persons" list on file, e.g., a criminal conviction is not noted whether it is a felony or misdemeanor), a decision can often be completed within several hours. However, over 90 percent of the calls involve buyers not on any computer list that would delay or deny their purchases, and in these cases the background check is completed in well under a minute (U.S. Department of Justice 2011).

Several county sheriffs, with the assistance of the National Rifle Association, challenge the Brady Act as a violation of states' rights under the Tenth Amendment. In 1997, the U.S. Supreme Court strikes down the provision requiring local police to conduct background checks in *Printz v. United States*. Despite the ruling, handgun background checks continue on a voluntary basis in most areas until the NICS is operational in late 1998 (Kopel 1999).

Gun control advocates bemoan that background checks only apply to licensed retail dealers. Private, informal sales by unlicensed individuals—including at flea markets and many gun show venues—are legal in most states.

On December 7, 1993, Colin Ferguson shoots 25 people, killing six of them, on a Long Island commuter train in Garden City, New York. Carolyn McCarthy's husband is killed and her son seriously injured in the attack. She successfully runs for Congress in 1996 after her representative, Dan Frisa, votes to repeal the federal Assault Weapons Ban. McCarthy's campaign focuses heavily on one issue, gun control.

1994–2004

The Gun Free Schools Act of 1994 requires that any state receiving federal education funds "shall have in effect a State law requiring local educational agencies to expel from school for a period of not less than one year a student who is determined to have brought a weapon to a school."

Enacted under Title XI as part of the Violent Crime Control and Law Enforcement Act of 1994, the federal "Assault Weapons Ban" prohibits for 10 years the future manufacture and transfer of 19 named assault weapons, and approximately 200 firearms covered by the law's generic definition of an "assault weapon." It also bans large-capacity ammunition feeding devices ("magazines")—those that can hold more than 10 rounds. The ban does not apply to assault weapons or magazines already in circulation.

Although gun rights advocates complain that it is impossible to give a generic, operational definition of an "assault weapon," Congress agrees with gun control groups that there are certain characteristics differentiating military-style from sporting arms. Among these characteristics are a pistol grip or thumbhole stock, a folding or telescoping grip, a threaded barrel for adding a silencer or flash suppressor, and the ability to receive a detachable ammunition magazine.

Gun rights members of Congress organize to repeal the Assault Weapons Ban but lose support in the wake of the April 19, 1995, terrorist attack of Timothy McVeigh and Terry Nichols on the Alfred P. Murrah federal building in Oklahoma City. Antiterrorism legislation in 1996 originally contains gun control language, which is removed before final passage of the Anti-Terrorism and Effective Death Penalty Act.

Both the gun control and the gun rights camps are in strong agreement that the swift and effective enforcement of existing firearms laws is critical to solving the problem of gun violence. Two promising strategies are developed during the 1990s: gun courts and gun-focused, place-oriented community policing.

The first modern gun court is created in Providence, Rhode Island, in September 1994 (note that Chicago had created one in the 1930s to handle an onslaught of gun crime in that era). Before its existence, the average time for the disposition of a gun case—via a plea bargain or the start of a trial—is 518 days, with a conviction rate of 67 percent. After the court is created, the maximum time for the disposition of a gun case falls to 126 days, while the conviction rate rises to 87 percent (U.S. Department of Justice 2000, Profile No. 37). These impressive results encourage the creation of gun courts in other cities, with a handful of high-profile courts appearing in Birmingham, Boston, Cambridge (Massachusetts), New York City, Philadelphia, and Wilmington.

The U.S. Department of Justice, working in conjunction with state and local authorities, and coordinating key law enforcement groups (the ATF, FBI, and Drug Enforcement Administration [DEA]), develops Project Triggerlock in 1991. Over the years, Triggerlock is expanded and reformulated—to accommodate the unique circumstances of various metropolitan areas—under

1994–2004
(*cont.*)

dozens of guises in hundreds of local and regional jurisdictions (program titles include Project Exile, Operation Ceasefire, Project Felon, Project Safe Neighborhoods, Triggerlock II, and many others). Funding for most of these comes through Project Safe Neighborhoods, the centerpiece of the federal government's efforts to control gun violence during President George W. Bush's two terms in office. Other funding is channeled through the Community Oriented Policing Services (created as part of the Violent Crime Control and Law Enforcement Act of 1994), and the Safe Streets Violent Crime Initiative. These programs use federal firearm statutes—for example, those barring the possession of firearms by high-risk individuals, including convicted felons, drug dealers, and domestic abusers—to prosecute gun-carrying offenders in *federal* ("U.S. District") courts, where conviction rates are typically much higher and penalties much stiffer than in state and local courts. For example, during this period, approximately 86 percent of those arrested on a federal weapons charge are convicted, and 92 percent of them serve prison time, averaging 107 months. In contrast, only about 16 percent of those arrested on a state or local weapons charge are convicted, while 67 percent of them end up in prison, averaging only 45 months (see Southwick 2002, Table 1; cf. Scalia 2000 and Bureau of Justice Statistics 2004). The programs often contain media campaigns to increase public awareness of gun crime and its ramifications, including the death and maiming of innocent victims, the financial losses suffered by the community, and the stern penalties gun-carrying criminals will face when turned over to the federal judicial system. Sometimes the programs incorporate a "carrot" approach—for example, increasing funding for school and community development agencies, especially those that seek to take teens and young adults off the streets through recreational, educational, and job-placement programs.

Triggerlock-type programs suffer two setbacks during their first decade. First, in December 1995, the U.S. Supreme Court rules in *Bailey v. United States* (516 U.S. 137, 116 S.Ct. 501) that persons in possession of a gun when arrested for a violent or drug-trafficking crime must have actually used it (e.g., firing or brandishing) if they are to be charged with the separate offense of having used a gun in the crime. This immediately reduces the number of weapons charges filed in federal district courts (see Scalia 2000). Before *Bailey*, for example, if a college student selling drugs has a unloaded rifle in an upstairs closet, while selling marijuana in his downstairs living room, federal prosecutors charge the individual not only with drug dealing, but also with using a weapon in the commission of a crime; the additional weapons charge adds significant prison time if the individual is convicted on the drug charge. However, if the drug dealer is already a convicted felon, then an illegal firearm possession charge can of course still be made.

A second setback comes at the end of 2004, when Congress cut $45 million that is directly earmarked to fund gun prosecutions from the proposed budget for Project Safe Neighborhoods. Another $106 million is cut from the budget that would have funded an ATF program meant to track and intercept illegal purchases of guns by youths.

However, both setbacks are temporary. In the case of *Bailey v. United States*, federal prosecutors begin channeling many of the weapons-possession cases for first-time drug and violent-crime offenders to state court systems (where many are prosecuted for violations of particular state-level firearms laws). More importantly, there are an increasing number of gun-focused, place-oriented, community-policing efforts. Thus, even though the two years immediately following the *Bailey* decision (1996–1997) see consecutive decreases in the number of federal firearms cases brought to U.S. district courts (bottoming out at 3,162), by 1998, the number climbs back to pre-*Bailey* levels and rises every year until 2005, peaking at 9,617. As national crime rates fall, so do firearms arrests, but the 2010 figure of 8,327 is still well above 1980s and 1990s numbers—when gun crimes are at their peak levels (see Maguire and Pastore 2004, Table 5.10: 405, as well as the *Sourcebook of Criminal Justice Statistics Online* 2011a–e). The larger figures after 1998 also reflect the impact of 1998 federal legislation commonly referred to as the "Bailey Fix," which dictates that the mere possession of a firearm during a crime of violence or drug-trafficking crime allows for an additional charge and for enhanced sentencing (18 U.S.C. § 924[c]).

1996   The Lautenberg Amendment to the Gun Control Act of 1968, also called the Domestic Violence Offender Gun Ban, expands prohibition of gun purchase, ownership, or possession to include persons convicted of domestic violence misdemeanor offenses (18 U.S.C. § 922[g][9]). The amendment strengthens the existing regulation that prevents gun possession by a person under a court order that restrains him or her "from harassing, stalking, or threatening an intimate partner or child of such intimate partner" (18 U.S.C. § 922[g][8]; per the "Wellstone Amendment" in the Violent Crime Control and Law Enforcement Act of 1994).

1997   On June 4, Massachusetts attorney general Scott Harshbarger sets forth the state's new *Consumer Protection Regulations on Handgun Safety*. Harshbarger bases the sweeping new gun controls on a state statute against "unfair or deceptive trade practice." He claims it is unfair or deceptive to sell handguns that: (1) do not have tamper-resistant serial numbers; (2) do not meet high standards for accidentally discharging when dropped on a hard surface; (3) do not have trigger locks; (4) do not have strong trigger pulls (that can prevent the average five-year-old child from firing it); and (5) have a barrel less than three inches long.

1997
(cont.)

In protest, gun industry represenatives file a lawsuit claiming that Harsh-barger has overstepped his authority. Harshbarger loses, but the Massachusetts Supreme Court overturns the decision in June 1999. To prevent further suits, the Massachusetts legislature enacts a law giving the attorney general the necessary authority to create the new handgun regulations. The Brady Campaign to Prevent Gun Violence and other gun control organizations extol Harshbarger's efforts as a model for emulation by other states.

1998–2005

A wave of schoolyard shootings stun the nation and spark dozens of state and federal legislative proposals to tighten up gun laws, almost none of which are enacted. The most shocking shootings occur in 1998, in Littleton, Colorado, and in 2005, in Red Lake, Minnesota. In Littleton, two Columbine High School students kill 12 fellow students, one teacher, and then themselves; while in Red Lake, a 16-year-old shoots to death his grandfather and his companion in their home, and then 7 others on his high school campus—the murdering halted when he shoots himself to death. In this same late 1990s-early 2000s era, many other shooting sprees by teenage boys gain national attention, including those in Santee, California; Springfield, Oregon; Pearl, Mississippi; West Paducah, Kentucky; Jonesboro, Arkansas; Edinboro, Pennsylvania; Richmond, Virginia; and Conyers, Georgia. Typical of the reaction following each of these shootings is the introduction of a bill in the U.S. Congress following the Columbine tragedy that would have required background checks on *all* gun purchasers, not just those buying their weapons from federally licensed dealers. Much of the general public and many members of Congress are motivated to support this particular legislation when it is learned that three of the weapons used at Columbine were acquired through straw purchases from private vendors at a gun show (a friend of one of the killers made the "straw purchases"—that is, she bought the guns not for herself, but to give them to the boys). Legislation is proposed in both houses of Congress aimed at closing the "gun show loophole," but none survives.

2000–2010

President Clinton announces the Smith & Wesson Settlement Agreement on March 17, 2000. The agreement involves the gun manufacturer and industry giant Smith & Wesson, the federal government, the states of New York and Connecticut, and several cities and counties. In return for the dismissal of lawsuits that the governmental bodies had filed (seeking compensation for the gun-related violence they had incurred), Smith & Wesson agrees to implement major changes in the design and distribution of its guns. More specifically, the company promises to begin incorporating the following safety features: internal locking systems; "authorized user technology" (making the gun functional only for an authorized user, normally the owner); "chamber loaded" indicators; child safeties; and hidden serial numbers to prevent obliteration. Moreover, Smith & Wesson agrees to distribute their guns only to dealers willing to: make no sales at gun shows unless there are background checks on all purchasers at the show; make sales only to individuals passing a certified firearms safety course or exam; pass a comprehensive exam on recognizing suspect buyers (e.g., "straw purchasers"); and implement security procedures to prevent gun thefts. Finally, Smith & Wesson agrees that all of its future practices will be overseen by a monitoring board.

The landmark agreement represents the first time that any gun manufacturer has been willing to alter its sales and distribution practices to prevent criminals, juveniles, and other high-risk individuals from obtaining guns. However, fierce opposition to the agreement quickly arises from other gun manufacturers, gun retailers, gun rights organizations, and many gun owners. The opposition is successful. Indeed, the agreement never goes into effect. Smith & Wesson's sales plummet. Its United Kingdom corporate owners (who had ordered Smith & Wesson to make the deal) sell the company to Saf-T-Hammer, which renames the manufacturer the Smith & Wesson Holding Corporation. Even though Saf-T-Hammer produces safety devices that prevent unauthorized gun use and unintentional firearm accidents, it wants to reverse Smith & Wesson's plummeting sales and introduces a .50-caliber revolver in 2003. Its introduction receives huge criticism from gun control advocates. However, gun rights organizations applaud Smith & Wesson's return to the fold. For example, in the NRA publication the *American Rifleman*, there is the acclamation that "Smith & Wesson has re-established itself as an American handgun icon—a status it lost in the backlash of its now infamous agreement with the Clinton administration" (Mayer 2003, 55).

Many seasoned political observers credit the power of the NRA and the gun rights movement for George W. Bush's victory over Al Gore in the 2000 presidential election (e.g., see Feldman 2008, 274–75; Carville and Begala 2006, 49–50; Wilson 2007, 162–63). More particularly, Gore loses in his home state of Tennessee, Bill Clinton's home state of Arkansas, and the normally strongly Democratic state of West Virginia. A win in any of one of these would have given the presidency to Gore. The NRA had strongly targeted these states, railing against Gore for his generally strong support of gun control legislation, both existing (e.g., the Brady Act; the Assault Weapons Ban) and proposed (e.g., handgun licensing, closing the "gun show loophole," and opposing protections for gun dealers and manufacturers against civil liability suits). Although this interpretation for Gore's loss is disputed by some (e.g., see Henigan 2009, 2; Spitzer 2004, 98), because NRA-backed candidates lose other and just-as-crucial races (to wit, Pennsylvania, Michigan, and Wisconsin), it is given more credibility when, in the 2004 election, John Kerry loses the hotly contested state of Ohio. Had he triumphed, he would have won the Electoral College. Gun rights observers contend that Kerry's association with the gun control movement cost him

2000–2010
(*cont.*)

several hundred thousand Ohio votes—and he loses by 120,000 (see Feldman 2008, 277–78). In the 2004 congressional races, NRA-backed candidates win 14 of 18 Senate seats and 241 of 251 House races (see Gottlieb and Tartaro 2004). However, the Brady Campaign (2004) quickly withholds any credit to the NRA and explains the victories as the result of most of the seats belonging to incumbents—who have a strong edge in most elections.

The various interpretations of the 2000 and 2004 elections reveal how difficult it is for the average citizen, even if well educated, to uncover the truth. Nevertheless, it seems clear that elections increasingly favor the gun rights camp. The 2006 and 2008 elections demonstrate, however, that the curve of change is jagged, as NRA-backed candidates do not fare well in either the 2006 midterm congressional races (Violence Policy Center 2006) or in the 2008 presidential and congressional elections (*New York Times* 2008). But the trend favoring gun rights candidates rebounds in 2010 with a vengeance—as 19 of 25 NRA-endorsed Senate candidates and 227 of 272 NRA-endorsed House candidates are victorious in the midterm elections (Horwitz and Grimaldi 2010). Indeed, some observers, including former NRA insider Richard Feldman, contend that the 2006 midterm elections, the worst faring of the NRA in nearly 15 years, is a blessing in disguise: It allows the organization to whip up fear in its members resulting in increased donations and increased campaign efforts on behalf of the organization's favorite candidates ("the National Rifle Association ha[s] *enemies* again . . . [it] 'could not have bought itself better results' " [Feldman 2008, 282, in part, quoting one of his friends—a high-profile executive in the firearms industry]; compare the similar assessment of Cummins 2007).

By the early 2000s, many, if not most, politicians favoring gun control (mainly Democrats) begin to mute their cries for more regulation—in part, because they fear public challenges from the NRA (if not its outright wherewithal to make them lose in the next election), and, in part, because they see efforts in this area as wasted. For example, gun control advocate and representative Jan Schakowsky (D-IL) complains that the lack of any real national movement for stronger regulations on the sale and possession of firearms is because the "NRA has pretty much set the agenda for the Congress" regarding guns (as quoted in Cummings 2007). Similarly, gun control advocate and representative Alcee L. Hastings (D-FL) observes that that the majority of congressional representatives are in one way or another "captives . . . of the NRA" (as quoted in Cummings 2007). Brady Campaign president Paul Helmke complains that attempts to increase gun regulations represent an uphill fight and that "if anything, we've gone backwards" (as quoted in Cummings 2007). Helmke's colleague—and founder of the Brady Center's Legal Action Project—Dennis Henigan concurs that the gun lobby is winning, in part, because of the "fear of the gun issue . . . within the Democratic Party . . . [indeed] the perception continues to persist that crossing the NRA is risky business" (Henigan 2009, 4). At the end of 2010, the *Washington Post* publishes a lengthy, analytical article on how and why "The NRA-led gun lobby wields powerful influence over [the] ATF [and] U.S. politics" (Horwitz and Grimaldi 2010).

2001–2011   In *United States v. Emerson*, the New Orleans–based Fifth Circuit Court of Appeals becomes the first federal appeals court to decide a case based on the determination that the Second Amendment guarantees ordinary individuals— as opposed to members of groups such as the National Guard—the right to own guns. The court concludes "that the history of the second amendment reinforces the plain meaning of its text, namely that it protects individual Americans in their right to keep and bear arms whether or not they are a member of a select militia." The *Emerson* ruling is a striking departure from many previous federal court decisions, which emphasize that the Second Amendment is meant to grant a collective right to the citizens of a state to maintain a militia. Gun control advocates criticize the court's interpretation but take heart that the court also makes clear that the federal government has the right to regulate arms. More specifically, the court notes that the individual-rights interpretation of the Second Amendment "does not mean that those rights may never be made subject to any . . . restrictions." In this particular instance, the court upholds the indictment of Dr. Timothy Joe Emerson, who has challenged his criminal prosecution for possessing a gun after being served with a domestic-violence-related restraining order (Dr. Emerson was challenging 18 U.S.C. § 922(g)(8)(C)(ii), as it amended the 1968 Gun Control Act and which allowed for the prosecution).

On September 11, 2001, the United States suffers the worst terrorist attack in its history, with nearly 3,000 people dying on a single day. Over the next decade, attempts are made to strengthen gun control via legislation aimed at antiterrorism, but all fail. Most contentious is that being on the FBI's Terrorist Screening Center's watch list does not prevent an individual (if otherwise qualified, e.g., not being a convicted felon) from legally buying a firearm (Government Accounting Office 2010: also see Lilllis 2011a, 2011b, 2011c; Riggs 2011). If anything, the 9/11 attack enhances public attitudes toward self-defense and gun rights legislation—including of the Arming Pilots against Terrorism Act of 2002, allowing airline pilots to carry firearms on passenger flights (if they so desire, and after having gone through a TSA training program; see Elias 2003). Also signed into law is the 2004 Law Enforcement Officers Safety Act (LEOSA), allowing current and retired, qualified law enforcement offices to carry concealed firearms throughout the country without a concealed-carry permit, with a few restrictions (e.g., they may not carry into state government buildings in contravention of state law; they cannot carry their firearms into federal courtrooms, buildings, and lands where firearms are banned). The LEOSA is amended in 2010, refining the definition of "qualified," and is extended to include Amtrak police and

2001–2011
(*cont.*)

selected other federal agents. The operational definition of "qualified" is straightforward and fits common-sense notions regarding its meaning, e.g., the officer, whether currently employed or retired, is in good standing with his or her agency; the officer has (or had) authorization from his agency to carry a firearm; the officer's firearms training is current. Between the original 2004 and the amended 2010 versions of the law, LEOSA is tested in court. Manuel Rodriguez is a Pennsylvania state constable. The state gives its constables the authority to cross state lines to serve warrants. While doing so in New York City, he is arrested for criminal weapons possession. In *People v. Rodriguez* (2006), he uses as his main defense LEOSA; the judge agrees and dismisses the case.

In 2007, gun rights advocates in Florida push for legislation barring physicians from asking routine questions about firearms ownership and storage, as well as recording any such information they might receive in interviews with patients. The advocacy effort comes to fruition on June 2, 2011, when Florida governor Rick Scott signs HB-155 into law. HB-155 "Provides that [a] licensed practitioner or facility may not record firearm ownership information in [a] patient's medical record . . . unless [the] information is relevant to [the] patient's medical care or safety or safety of others," [furthermore] "inquiries regarding firearm ownership or possession should not be made"; [and it . . .] "prohibits harassment of [a] patient regarding firearm ownership during examination; prohibits denial of insurance coverage, increased premiums, or other discrimination by insurance companies issuing policies on [the] basis of [an] insured's or applicant's ownership, possession, or storage of firearms or ammunition" (Florida House of Representatives 2011). Within days, three Florida physicians and the Florida chapters of the American Academy of Pediatrics, the American Academy of Family Physicians, and the American College of Physicians file suit in federal district court requesting that it declare the law unconstitutional and enjoin its enforcement (*Wollschlaeger et al.v. Scott et al.* [2011]). More broadly, the legislation represents the long-held distrust of scholars and activists associated with the gun rights camp of public health research showing harmful outcomes of gun ownership, gun carrying, and having guns in the home (e.g., see the conclusion of Kates, Lattimer, and Boen [1997, 123] that "medical and public health discussion of firearms issues have consistently exemplified . . . inventing, selecting, or misinterpreting data to validate preordained conclusions"; compare Faria's [2001] similar assessment).

2002

John Allen Muhammad and John Lee Malvo use a Bushmaster assault rifle in October to murder 10 people and injure 3 others in the Washington, D.C., area. The shooting spree prompts gun control advocates to call for the creation of a national ballistic fingerprinting database, in which all firearms would have digital images of their shell casing and (in the case of rifles and handguns) bullet markings on file. They contend that such a database would have led law enforcement authorities to identify the snipers much sooner. These advocates also contend that the shooting spree is strong evidence for strengthening and extending the federal ban on assault weapons.

The U.S. Customs Service and the Bureau of Alcohol, Tobacco, Firearms and Explosives (ATF) announce that they will begin enforcement of the Nonimmigrant Aliens Firearms and Ammunition Amendments to the Gun Control Act of 1968 (as enacted by Congress in 1998 as Public Law 105-277). These amendments require nonimmigrant aliens wanting to bring firearms or ammunition into the United States for hunting or sporting purposes to obtain an import permit from ATF prior to entering the country.

2004   Tucked away in an omnibus spending package approved by both houses of Congress in January are provisions reducing the length of time the Department of Justice can maintain background-check records on firearm sales: from 90 days to 24 hours. Records are kept on file to ensure that if an individual prohibited from buying guns (e.g., a convicted felon) is inadvertently allowed to make such a purchase, the mistake can be corrected. Gun control advocates complain that requiring these records to be destroyed within 24 hours makes it nearly impossible for the Justice Department to correct errors, and the end result will be the arming of more criminals. This contention has empirical support: In a 2002 study, the federal government's General Accounting Office asserts that if background records are destroyed within 24 hours "the FBI would lose certain abilities to initiate firearm-retrieval actions when new information reveals that individuals who were approved to purchase firearms should not have been. Specifically, during the first 6 months of the current 90-day retention policy, the FBI used retained records to initiate 235 firearm-retrieval actions, of which 228 (97 percent) could not have been initiated under the proposed next-day destruction policy" (General Accounting Office 2002, 4).

On the other hand, supporters of the legislation point out that the congressional statute creating the National Instant Check System already requires the government, after approving a sale, to "destroy all records of the system with respect to the call (other than the identifying number and the date the number was assigned) and all records of the system relating to the person or the transfer." They also point out that existing federal law forbids the creation of any national registry of guns or gun owners, and that keeping records for all retail firearms sales in the United States approved by NICS in the previous 90 days amounts to an illegal registry.

Also passed in 2004 is the so-called "Tiahrt amendment" (named for one of its sponsors, Rep. Todd Tiahrt, R-KS), which removes from public access a government database of traces of guns. Guns may be traced because they were recovered at crime scenes, or because they were stolen and then recovered, or for various other reasons. Gun control advocate Chuck Wexler,

2004
(cont.)

director of the Police Executive Research Forum, calls the amendment "the most offensive thing you can think of . . . the tracing data, which is now secret, helped us see the big picture of where guns are coming from" (as quoted in Grimaldi and Horwitz 2010). Gun control advocates point to a study of ATF tracing data by criminologists Glenn Pierce, LeBaron Briggs, and David Carlson (1995) showing that a very small fraction of dealers are the original sellers of more than half the guns found at crime scenes. Gun rights advocates retort that the Tiahrt Amendment protects gun dealers from lawsuits that would unfairly hold the dealers liable for the crimes committed with the guns they have sold. Moreover, some scholars and many gun rights activists question the legitimacy of ATF trace-data studies, contending the findings are more reflective of the political agenda of gun control advocates than of any social scientific depiction of reality (e.g., see Blackman 1999; Kopel 1998). For example, NRA Institute for Legislative Action representative Paul H. Blackman (1999, 58–59) observes that "Criminological research based on firearm tracing data conducted by the Federal Bureau of Alcohol, Tobacco, and Firearms (ATF) is suspect because ATF is asked to conduct traces on a small minority of firearms used in crimes, including homicide . . . It is not representative of all firearms recovered by police. . . . Because of these data deficiencies, while ATF trace data may be useful for law enforcement purposes, it is not useful for research purposes."

Gun rights advocates also dispute the claim that a relatively high number of traces proves that a particular firearms store is a rogue operation. Rather, stores that sell the most guns will usually have the most traces, since some customers' guns will eventually be stolen. More broadly, the advocates point that out ATF itself has unlimited access to its own trace data, and can use that data for whatever law enforcement purposes it sees best, including investigating a particular store. The trace information should not be made available to any and all comers, including antigun politicians who might use it to persecute local gun owners.

Finally, gun rights advocates point out that if the trace reports are available to local politicians, they are also, under the federal Freedom of Information Act, available to anyone else. So sophisticated criminals could obtain trace reports to get a list of the gun owners in an area, the better to burglarize their homes while the gun owner is at work, and put more guns into the black market.

Despite the protests of gun control advocates, the 1994 federal Assault Weapons Ban, originally enacted to last for 10 years, is allowed to expire in September. U.S. manufacturers had been generally successful in evading the ban by making cosmetic changes to their assault weapons. The most infamous example is the Bushmaster assault rifle that John Allen

Muhammad and John Lee Malvo use in their October 2002 Washington, D.C., killing spree.

A Department of Justice study reveals that the use of assault weapons in crime dropped significantly in the years following the ban, and that this drop was not explainable by the overall drop in gun crime during the late 1990s. Assault weapons specifically named in the 1994 ban declined from about 5 percent of all crime guns, according the ATF National Tracing Center data, to about 1 percent between 1993 (the year before it took effect) and 2001 (see Koper 2004; Roth and Koper 1999; note that some scholars and gun rights advocates challenge the study because it is based on gun-tracing data—see the Blackman quote above for criticisms of these data).

In December, the U.S. attorney general's office publishes a lengthy memorandum concluding that "the Second Amendment secures a personal right of individuals, not a collective right that may only be invoked by a State[,] or a quasi-collective right restricted to those persons who serve in organized militia units" (U.S. Department of Justice 2004). Gun rights activists applaud the opinion, even though its interpretation of the Second Amendment is disputed by some constitutional historians and all organizations advocating for strong gun control.

2005   In June, a landmark gun control bill is introduced in the California state legislature requiring that semiautomatic pistols be equipped with technology that can imprint microscopic identifying information on the shell casing fired from a particular gun. Subsequent research reveals flaws in the technology, including that imprinted marking are often illegible and the firing pin marker is easily degraded (e.g., see Howitt et al. 2006; Krivosta 2005). Despite this research, which others challenge (see Page 2008), microstamping legislation is passed in California in 2007 (as of 2011, however, the legislation has yet to be implemented because of patent disputes; see National Shooting Sports Foundation 2011).

Congress passes the Protection of Lawful Commerce in Arms Act of 2005. The act prohibits civil liability actions against manufacturers, distributors, dealers, and importers of firearms or ammunition products, and their trade associations, for any harm caused by the criminal or unlawful misuse of firearms or ammunition. The act does not exempt those in the gun industry breaking the law or selling defective weapons or ammunition. However, gun control advocates see this legislation as a major setback. Although civil lawsuits are not won in the courtroom, they have the potential for yielding out-of-court settlements that promote reform in the gun industry. For example, a $2.5 million settlement against gun retailer Bulls Eye and gun manufacturer Bushmaster is reached in 2004 for their responsibility in the 2002 Washington, D.C., sniper shootings. Both the retailer and the manufacturer revise their inventory-control procedures to reduce the probability of the

2005
(*cont.*)

theft of their guns and to let law enforcement know immediately if a theft actually occurs.

Hurricane Katrina devastates the Gulf Coast states of Mississippi and Louisiana on August 29, 2005. Severe flooding in New Orleans breaks down the public safety system, and government responses, at all levels (federal, state, local), are inadequate. In reaction to looting and criminal assaults, some area residents arm themselves—but on September 8, city officials announce a ban on possession of firearms and instruct law enforcement to confiscate all guns they come across. Local and state police join in the effort, as does the National Guard (Berenson and Broder 2005). Gun rights advocates, and many in the gun control camp, are outraged, and numerous lawsuits and modifications to state laws ensue over the next year (Price 2005; Walsh 2005). In 2006, the Robert T. Stafford Disaster Relief and Emergency Assistance Act is signed into federal law, banning the disaster-related confiscation of guns. Many states, including Louisiana, enact similar legislation.

2007

On the morning of April 16, 2007, Virginia Tech student Seung-hui Cho uses two semiautomatic pistols to slay a total of 32 students and faculty. Before authorities can stop the carnage, he turns one of his guns on himself—ending the worst case of mass murder in U.S. history.

The shock of the Virginia Tech massacre is magnified when it is discovered that despite Cho's lifelong history of mental illness, he had obtained his firearms *legally* in the preceding months. Gun control proponents use the tragedy to bemoan the inadequacy of current U.S. gun regulations, while gun rights proponents note that had Cho's adjudicated mental illness been properly registered with the federal government, he would have failed a background check and never been sold the guns he used in the massacre.

In a rare display of cooperation (albeit motivated for different reasons), the major gun control organization in the nation, the Brady Campaign, and the major gun rights organization, the NRA, work with congressional representatives to fashion the NICS Improvement Act—intended to improve the quality and quantity of criminal, mental health, and related data used by the National Instant Criminal Background Check System (NICS)—with which federally licensed firearms retailers check the backgrounds of prospective gun buyers. More hard-line groups on both sides of the gun issue (e.g., the Gun Owners of America, and the Coalition to Stop Gun Violence) are disappointed by the final legislation. But many on both sides of the gun debate extol the act's carrot-and-stick approach to getting the states to improve and then to submit their relevant computerized data to the NICS system in a timely manner, while enhancing the ability of prospective gun buyers previously judged as ineligible because of having been placed under a court order related to mental illness to seek relief. On December 17, 2007, the NICS Improvement Act is passed with strong bipartisan support, and signed into law (PL 110-180) by President George W. Bush on January 8, 2008. (As of 2011, the act has seen mixed success: Gun rights groups are pleased to see mental health–related provisions of the act regarding restoration of gun rights being increasing adopted by more and more states. One such provision ends gun bans on people who have never been adjudicated mentally ill, but have simply sought counseling at some point—e.g., military veterans who received Veterans Administration counseling for post-traumatic stress disorder. Likewise, a provision making it easier for those having lost their gun rights due to mental disabilities to have them restored (e.g., a person who was temporarily committed to an institution for a few days several decades ago during a personal crisis) is being increasingly adopted by the states. However, many states are still lax in reporting their records on arrests, domestic-violence orders, and court-ordered treatments for mental illness to the NICS system—and indeed, Alaska, Delaware, Idaho, New Mexico, Pennsylvania, and Rhode Island have submitted no records mental health records at all (see Luo 2011; *New York Times* 2011a).

Another upshot of the Virginia Tech massacre is the invigoration of the gun rights movement to allow college students and employees who have government permits to carry licensed concealed handguns everywhere else in the state to bring their weapons to campus, and to carry them concealed in accordance with state law. Founded on the evening of the massacre, Students for Concealed Carry on Campus grows to more than 43,000 members by early 2011—at which time they observe that "the eleven U.S. colleges/universities that currently allow concealed carry on campus (and have done so for a combined total of more than eighty semesters) have not seen any resulting incidents of gun violence, gun accidents, or gun thefts" (Students for Concealed Carry on Campus 2011; also see Kopel [2009] for an extended discussion on state legislative initiatives to allow students, faculty, and staff—who would otherwise be legally allowed to possess a firearm—to carry and store a gun while on campus; Kopel further argues that the passage of such initiatives would, on balance, make for safer campuses). In 2011, Wisconsin joins Utah in allowing adults with carry licenses to carry at all state colleges and universities.

Other survivors of the Virginia Tech massacre and members of the public have a completely opposite reaction from those founding and joining Students for Concealed Carry. For example, survivor Colin Goddard—shot four times and one of the 17 who survived their gunshot wounds on April 16—examines the gun control literature and finds a few themes very prominent, one being the "gun show loophole." He tests the contention that just about anyone can buy a gun at selected gun shows by attending several in Ohio and Texas. Indeed, without any background checking, he has little problem purchasing an AK-47-style rifle, 9 mm semiautomatic handguns, and other weapons. Though not touted in the gun control literature, he finds that some

2007
(cont.)

of those selling him guns without a background check consider it a "service" and thus charge him slightly higher prices than dealers doing background checks. He eventually takes a high-profile job with the Brady Campaign and tells his story in the much-heralded documentary film *Living for 32*, which includes hidden-camera scenes of some of his gun show purchases. (The "32" is a double entendre, representing the 32 victims of the Virginia Tech massacre and the average of 32 gun murders each day in the contemporary United States; see Goddard [2011]. Many press accounts about Goddard and his life story can be found online, e.g., see Molloy [2010]; Stone [2010]; and Todd [2011])]).

2008–2011
(and beyond)

In June 2008, in a landmark 5–4 decision in *District of Columbia v. Heller*, the U.S. Supreme Court holds that the District's ban on handgun possession in the home and its prohibition against rendering any lawful firearm in the home operable for the purposes of immediate self-defense violates the Second Amendment. The court holds that the Second Amendment protects an individual right to possess a firearm unconnected with service in a militia and to use that firearm for traditionally lawful purposes, such as self-defense within the home.

The majority rules the Constitution guarantees that "the right of the people, to keep and bear arms, shall not be infringed," and this mandate is independent of the "well regulated militia." Preserving the militia is the foremost reason that led the Founders to protect the right to keep and bear arms, but the right they guaranteed is not just for service in the militia.

In a follow-up 5–4 vote in June 2010, the sharply divided court extends its ruling to include the 50 U.S. states and their municipalities in *McDonald v. City of Chicago*. The majority—Justices Alito, Roberts, Scalia, and Kennedy basing their decision on the due process clause of the Fourteenth Amendment, and Justice Thomas on the basis of the amendment's privileges or immunities clause —holds that the Fourteenth Amendment makes the Second Amendment applicable to state and local governments, as it does most of the rest of the Bill of Rights. Both decisions are watershed victories for the gun rights movement, though gun control activists note that the Supreme Court acknowledges in both cases that the individual-right interpretation does not mean the right is unlimited. To quote from the *Heller* decision, "Like most rights, the Second Amendment right is not unlimited. It is not a right to keep and carry any weapon whatsoever in any manner whatsoever and for whatever purpose: For example, concealed weapons prohibitions have been upheld under the Amendment or state analogues. The Court's opinion should not be taken to cast doubt on longstanding prohibitions on the possession of firearms by felons and the mentally ill, or laws forbidding the carrying of firearms in sensitive places such as schools and government buildings, or laws imposing conditions and qualifications on

the commercial sale of arms [nor on . . .] the historical tradition of prohibiting the carrying of dangerous and unusual weapons" (such as sawed-off
shotguns or submachine guns). And in the *McDonald* case, the majority
opinion included the statement that their ruling would allow for "[s]tate . . .
and local experimentation with reasonable firearms regulations [to be]
continue[d] under the Second Amendment."

Gun control advocates also take solace in Justice Breyer's dissenting obser-
vation that: "Since *Heller*, historians, scholars, and judges have continued to
express the view that the Court's historical account was flawed" (Breyer's
dissent is joined by Justices Ginsburg and Sotomayor). The separate dissent
of Justice Stevens, his last opinion as a Supreme Court justice, is a paragon
of the thinking of gun control activists and scholars regarding the limitations
of the Second Amendment to contemporary American society. Among
Stevens's observations these activists and scholars extol are: "The practical
impact of various gun-control measures may be highly controversial, but this
basic insight should not be. The idea that deadly weapons pose a distinctive
threat to the social order—and that reasonable restrictions on their usage
therefore impose an acceptable burden on one's personal liberty—is as old
as the Republic. . . . The idea that States may place substantial restrictions
on the right to keep and bear arms short of complete disarmament is, in fact,
far more entrenched than the notion that the Federal Constitution protects
any such right. Federalism is a far 'older and more deeply rooted tradition
than is a right to carry,' or to own, 'any particular kind of weapon.' "

Thus, the strong dissent of Justices Breyer, Ginsburg, Sotomayor, and
Stevens in the *McDonald* case leaves open the possibility that a change in
the court's composition might eventuate in a reversal of the *Heller* and
McDonald decisions. Before any such reversal, however, both sides of the
gun debate expect many lower-court cases in which the constitutionality of
particular gun control laws is challenged. The Supreme Court cases do not
include a detailed standard against which to judge the reasonability of
restrictions on the right to keep and bear firearms, thus opening up an
onslaught of especially difficult litigation in the lower courts. Some legal
scholars expect new and existing gun control law must hold up to "inter-
mediate scrutiny," meaning the law in question should be substantially
related to an important government interest (see Rosenthal and Malcolm
[2010] for the variety of possible standards that can be invoked and which
of these might become dominant).

Gun control advocates are especially prone to emphasize the importance of
these post-*McDonald* court cases, as national legislative efforts seem
doomed with a Republican-controlled House of Representatives and the
president of the United States declaring that the "Second Amendment guarantees an individual right to bear arms" (Obama 2011). Moreover, his aides

2008–2011 (and beyond) (*cont.*) report to the *New York Times* that the president "has no plans to take the lead in proposing further gun control legislation" (Calmes 2011).

These comments are especially disturbing to gun control advocates because they come on the heels of the horrific January 8, 2011, shooting spree in Tucson, Arizona, where a mentally ill gunman, uses a legally purchased semiautomatic handgun, a Glock 19, to severely wound U.S. congresswoman Gabrielle Giffords and kill six others—including federal district court judge John Roll and nine-year old Christina Taylor-Green. Traditionally, gun control legislation is motivated by terrible acts of violence, and some in the gun-control advocacy community have thoughts, if not hopes, that the Tucson massacre will motivate federal movement in the areas of stronger background checking and restrictions on high-capacity (greater than 10 rounds) ammunition holders (magazines) for semiautomatic weapons. The shooter passes a computerized background check when he purchases the handgun in late 2010; however, it is unlikely that he would have passed a traditional background check (involving law enforcement officials interviewing acquaintances, neighbors, coworkers). The shooter empties a 31-round magazine, which magnifies the destruction wrought; indeed, it is while he is trying to switch to a fresh magazine that bystanders tackle and disarm him (thus a "regular" 10-shot magazine would have reduced the damage). The *Washington Post* (2011) soon publishes an article detailing that many of the nation's worst shooting sprees/mass murders having involved high-capacity (11+ round) magazines—including Patrick Purdy's killing of six schoolchildren in Stockton, California (1989); George Hennard's murdering of 23 customers in Luby's Cafeteria in Killeen, Texas (1991); Gian Luig Ferri's slaughter of eight workers in a San Francisco office building (1993); Eric Harris and Dylan Klebold's killing of 12 students and a teacher at Columbine High School in Littleton, Colorado (1999); Seung-hui Cho's murdering of 32 at Virginia Tech (2007); Nidal Hasan's killing of 13 at Fort Hood in Texas (2009); and Mar Thornton's slaughter of eight former coworkers in Manchester, Connecticut (2010). Only a handful of states have retained the (now expired) 1994 federal Assault Weapons Ban legislation limiting semiautomatic firearms' magazines to 10 rounds or fewer (the District of Columbia, Hawaii, Massachusetts, New Jersey, and New York ban both sale and possession of magazines greater than 10 rounds, while California and Maryland ban their sale but allow possession).

Adding fuel to the disappointment of gun control advocates in Obama's performance as president is his signing of pro–gun rights legislation between the landmark 2008 *Heller* and 2010 *McDonald* Supreme Court decisions. In May 2009, he signs a credit-card reform bill that has tucked away in it a provision to allow the legal carry of firearms in the national park system (*New York Times* 2009). And in December 2009, he signs an appropriations bill that includes a reversal of a post-9/11 ban on the transporting of firearms in locked luggage on Amtrak trains (Urbina 2010). Notably, these changes in federal law are enacted when Democrats hold large majorities in both the House and the Senate.

Finally, gun control advocates are crestfallen when Obama's attorney general, Eric Holder, appears to be reined in and silenced by the administration soon after announcing his desire to act on candidate Obama's multiple campaign speeches in which he had declared the need for the federal government to make the ban on assault weapons permanent, to shut down unscrupulous gun dealers, and to close the "gun show loophole." Because so many assault-style weapons are allegedly being bought at U.S. retailers near the Mexican border and have contributed to the magnitude of the violence of the Mexican drug cartel wars, Holder is especially interested in renewing the 10-year federal ban on assault weapons, which had gone into effect in 1994 but failed congressional renewal in September 2004. Upon hearing the announcement, famed NRA executive Wayne LaPierre fires back: "I think there are a lot of Democrats on Capitol Hill cringing at Eric Holder's comments right now . . . A semi-automatic is a quintessential self-defense firearm owned by American citizens in this country . . . it is clearly covered under *Heller* and it's clearly, I think, protected by the Constitution" (Ryan 2009).

In the spring of 2011, a secret ATF operation, "Fast and Furious," is exposed for having gone wrong and is heavily criticized in the media. The program allows selected "straw buyers"—those believed to be supplying Mexican drug cartels with weapons—to purchase assault-style and other firearms at U.S. retailers along the border; the intent is to follow the buyers and to document their handing-over of the weapons to drug cartel members. However, many of the weapons are lost track of, smuggled into Mexico, and two are eventually recovered at the scene of a shootout where a U.S. Border Patrol agent is killed. When Holder is asked about details of the operation, he claims ignorance of many of them—and almost immediately, the NRA starts a national petition to have him fired (National Rifle Association 2011a). Other fallout includes the call for ATF acting director Kenneth Melson's resignation, as well as calls for the dissolving of the bureau itself (Gerstein 2011; Stolberg 2011)—long a target of the gun rights movement and continually hamstrung, at least in the eyes of gun control advocates, from enforcing federal gun control laws (in the words of a *New York Times* editorial, the ATF is "perennially hogtied by the gun lobby's power over Congress"; *New York Times* 2011c).

Public attitudes in support of strong gun control laws are at nearly all-time lows, e.g., the National Opinion Research Center's national probability sample of U.S. adults, the General Social Survey, tracks public opinion toward gun control with the question: "Would you favor or oppose a law which

2008–2011
(and beyond)
(*cont.*)

would require a person to obtain a police permit before he or she could buy a gun?" The percentage "in favor" of police permits peaks in 1998 at 83.7 percent, but falls steadily ever since—and as of 2010, it stands at 74.3 percent (National Opinion Research Center 2011). More dramatically, the Gallup Poll tracking of gun control with the question "In general, do you feel that the laws covering the sale of firearms should be made more strict, less strict, or kept as they are now?" reveals that those favoring more strict laws has declined from 78 percent in 1990 to 44 percent in 2010. And the Gallup item "Do you think there should or should not be law that would ban the possession of handguns, except by the police and other authorized persons?" reveals a drop from 43 percent in 1990 to 29 percent in 2010 (Newport and Saad 2011).

The combination of declining public support and fear of the NRA prompts more liberal—generally Democratic—candidates for congressional Senate and House seats to avoid the topic of gun control. As a *Washington Post* column entitled "Aiming to Win" concludes at the end of 2010, "lawmakers have come to fear the [NRA's] 4 million members" (Keating et al. 2010).

In short, as of 2011, at the national level (and gun control proponents posit, correctly so, that this is the level at which the most important policies, programs, and legislation must occur), current and recent court decisions, legislative measures, executive actions, and public opinion polls reveal that there is little pointing to success for the gun control movement in the coming years, but much for the gun rights movement. That said, the strongest gun control advocates see the current situation as a long string of setbacks, but little more. They have lost many key battles, yes, but in no way do they see the war as lost. Brady Center vice president Dennis Henigan, who has been a central figure in the gun debate for nearly two decades, maintains that "it is absurd to pronounce the political death of gun control" (Henigan 2009, 5). Likewise, the former president of the Brady Campaign, Paul Helmke, declares: "It isn't easy going up against a well-funded gun lobby with the resources to scare congressional members into keeping gun laws weak. But Jim and Sarah Brady continue to inspire me to stay in the fight. . . . I've learned that every step towards gun safety, no matter how seemingly small, can potentially save a life" (Helmke 2011). Finally, Josh Horwitz, executive director of the gun control advocacy group the Campaign to Stop Gun Violence, declares that we must and should "abide by the American political tradition that the people without guns can tell people with guns what to do" (Horwitz and Anderson 2009, 214).

Evidence that the hopes and goals of these high-profile leaders of the gun control movement are not in vain is slim but not absent. For example, in July 2011, the Obama administration sidesteps Congress and instructs the Department of Justice to decree that the 8,000 firearms dealers along the

U.S.-Mexican border must report multiple sales of semiautomatic rifles larger than .22 caliber and having detachable magazines. (Handguns are already under such a system; note that the application of multiple sales reporting for long guns is complicated by a federal law forbidding the ATF to require licensed dealers to provide it with any reports beyond what is "expressly" authorized by statute). The goal, according to deputy attorney general James Cole, is to help the ATF "detect and disrupt the illegal weapons trafficking networks responsible for diverting firearms from lawful commerce to criminals" and in particular to "help confront the problem of illegal gun trafficking into Mexico" (Savage 2011; note the magnitude of this problem is highly contested; for example, the *New York Times* [2011b] reports that "at least 70 percent of the weapons recovered in Mexico's bloody drug war originate in the United States, where shady gun buyers operate freely thanks to loopholes in American law," but a U.S. Department of Justice study of the relevant trace data concludes that "most seized guns are not traced" and thus claims such as that of the *New York Times* are unsubstantiated; see U.S. Department of Justice 2010, 75). Immediate court and legislative challenges from gun rights groups, including the NRA, follow—and the fires of the gun debate remain hot.

Lost in the many battles in recent years over local and state laws, federal legislation, and federal agencies like the ATF and CDC is the growing concern of many in the gun rights camp over international law, policy, and programs. More particularly, the long-term efforts of the United Nations to move forward on its Arms Trade Treaty (ATT) raises serious concerns in the gun rights community. The aspects of the ATT most bothersome to this community involve the record keeping, registration, micro-stamping, and other means for the accounting of civilian-owned, traded, and manufactured arms; many UN member states see these as potentially effective methods for reducing the international market in illegal firearms. In the words of NRA executive Wayne LaPierre, if approved, and if acceded to by the United States, these aspects of the ATT would pose an "infringement on the constitutional freedom of American gun owners" (National Rifle Association 2011b; also see Second Amendment Foundation 2011).

In sum, as of 2011, both sides of the gun debate believe there is much to be accomplished in the coming days, months, and years. In the words of the public face and voice of the NRA, Wayne LaPierre, gun owners and gun rights advocates must "stay ready . . . we know that the first chance Obama gets, he will pounce on us" (as quoted in Urbina 2010, A1).

References

Note: In addition to the materials cited below, this chronology draws selectively from the following sources: Chapters 1–3 in Gregg Lee Carter, *Gun Control in the United States: A Reference*

Handbook (Santa Barbara, CA: ABC-CLIO, 2006); Chapters 1–5 in Gregg Lee Carter, *The Gun Control Movement* (New York: Twayne Publishers, 1997); and selected entries in the current three volumes and their predecessor (Gregg Lee Carter, ed., *Guns in American Society: An Encyclopedia of History, Politics, Culture, and the Law*, vols. 1 and 2 [Santa Barbara, CA: ABC-CLIO, 2002]).

Annals of Congress. 2nd Cong., 1st sess. (1791–92). http://memory.loc.gov/cgi-bin/ampage ?collId=llac&fileName=003/llac003.db&recNum=68 (accessed June 20, 2011).

Beckman, James A. "Sullivan Law." In *Guns in American Society: An Encyclopedia of History, Politics, Culture, and the Law*, edited by Gregg Lee Carter, vol. 2, 568. Santa Barbara, CA: ABC-CLIO, 2002.

Berenson, Alex, and John M. Broder. "Police Begin Seizing Guns of Civilians." *New York Times*, September 9, 2005. http://www.nytimes.com/2005/09/09/national/nationalspecial/09storm .html (accessed June 30, 2011).

Blackman, Paul. "The Limitations of BATF Firearm Tracing Data for Policymaking and Homicide Research." In *National Institute of Justice Research Forum: Proceedings of the Homicide Research Working Group Meetings, 1997 and 1998*, 58–59. Washington, D.C.: U.S. Department of Justice, Office Justice Programs, May 1999 (NCJ-175708). https://www.ncjrs.gov/ pdffiles1/nij/175709.pdf (accessed July 13, 2011).

Brady Campaign to Prevent Gun Violence. "No Mandate for Gun Extremism." http://www.brady campaign.org/media/press/view/607 (accessed July 6, 2011).

Bureau of Justice Statistics. *State Court Sentencing of Convicted Felons, 2002: Statistical Tables.* Washington, DC: Office of Justice Programs, U.S. Department of Justice, 2004.

"Bursts of Gunfire." *Washington Post*, January 12, 2011. http://www.washingtonpost.com/ wp-dyn/content/graphic/2011/01/23/GR2011012300266.html?sid=ST2010121406431 (accessed July 13, 2011).

Calmes, Jackie. "N.R.A. Declines to Meet with Obama on Gun Policy." *New York Times*, March 14, 2011. http://www.nytimes.com/2011/03/15/us/politics/15guns.html (accessed July 8, 2011).

Carville, James, and Paul Begala. *Take It Back: Our Party, Our Country, Our Future.* New York: Simon and Schuster, 2006.

Cleveland v. State (128 Ohio St.3d 135, 2010-Ohio-6318). Decided December 29, 2010. http:// www.supremecourt.ohio.gov/rod/docs/pdf/0/2010/2010-Ohio-6318.pdf (accessed July 7, 2011).

Cook, Philip J., and Jens Ludwig. *Gun Violence: The Real Costs.* New York: Oxford University Press, 2000.

Cramer, Clayton E. *For the Defense of Themselves and the State: The Original Intent and Judicial Interpretation of the Right to Keep and Bear Arms.* Westport, CT: Praeger, 1994.

Cummings, Jeanne. "Why the Gun Lobby Usually Wins." Politico, April 17, 2007. http://www .politico.com/news/stories/0407/3563.html (accessed July 7, 2011).

DeBell, Matthew. "TEC-DC9 Pistol." In *Guns in American Society: An Encyclopedia of History, Politics, Culture, and the Law*, edited by Gregg Lee Carter, vol. 2, 575–76. Santa Barbara, CA: ABC-CLIO, 2002.

Editorial: "Dangerous Omissions." *New York Times*, July 10, 2011a. http://www.nytimes.com/ 2011/07/11/opinion/11mon2.html (accessed July 13, 2011).

Editorial: "The Gun Lobby's Loss." *New York Times*, December 12, 2008. http://www.nytimes .com/2008/12/02/opinion/02tue3.html?_r=1 (accessed July 7, 2011).

Editorial: "Gun Mayhem along the Border." *New York Times*, July 13, 2011b. http://www.nytimes .com/2011/07/14/opinion/14thurs3.html?ref=politics (accessed July 27, 2011).

Editorial: "Guns in Parks: Safe, Scary or a Sideshow?" *New York Times*, May 22, 2009. http:// roomfordebate.blogs.nytimes.com/2009/05/22/guns-in-parks-safe-scary-or-a-sideshow/?ref =politics (accessed July 7, 2011).

Editorial: "No Excusing the A.T.F., or Congress." *New York Times*, July 28, 2011c. http://www .nytimes.com/2011/07/29/opinion/no-excusing-the-atf-or-congress.html?_r=2&emc=tnt &tntemail0=y (accessed July 29, 2011).

Elias, Bartholomew. *Report to Congress: Arming Pilots Against Terrorism: Implementation Issues for the Federal Flight Deck Officer Program*. Washington, DC: Congressional Research Service, Library of Congress, 2003. http://www.policyarchive.org/handle/10207/bitstreams/ 1575.pdf (accessed June 28, 2011).

Faria, Miguel A. "Doctors to Ask Patients About Gun Ownership." *Medical Sentinel* 6 (2001): 115–17. http://www.haciendapub.com/medicalsentinel/doctors-ask-patients-about-gun -ownership (accessed December 28, 2011).

Feldman, Richard. *Ricochet: Confessions of a Gun Lobbyist*. Hoboken, NJ: Wiley, 2008.

Galloway, Pam. "Concealed Carry Signed into Law." Wisconsin State Senate, July 8, 2011. http:// legis.wisconsin.gov/senate/galloway/PressReleases/Pages/Concealed-Carry-Signed-Into-Law .aspx (accessed July 18, 2011)

General Accounting Office. *Potential Effects of Next-Day Destruction of NICS Background Check Records* (Report No.: GAO-02-653). http://www.gao.gov/new.items/d02653.pdf (accessed June 28, 2011).

General Accounting Office. *Terrorist Watchlist Screening: FBI Has Enhanced Its Use of Information from Firearm and Explosives Background Checks to Support Counterterrorism Efforts*. (Highlights of Report No.: GAO-10-703T). http://www.gao.gov/new.items/d10703t.pdf (accessed June 28, 2011).

Gerstein, Josh. "Could Controversy Kill the ATF?" Politico, July 8, 2011. http://www.politico .com/news/stories/0711/58532.html (accessed July 10, 2011).

Gilmore, Russell S. "Crackshots and Patriots: The National Rifle Association and America's Military-Sporting Tradition, 1871–1929." PhD diss., University of Wisconsin, 1974.

Goddard, Colin. *Living for 32*. 2011. http://livingfor32.org/home.html (accessed July 8, 2011).

Gottlieb, Alan M., and Joseph Tartaro. "Election 2004." *The Gottlieb-Tartaro Report* 119 (2004). http://www.saf.org/gt/gt119.pdf (accessed July 6, 2011).

Grimaldi, Josh, and Sari Horwitz. "Industry Pressure Hides Gun Traces, Protects Dealers from Public Scrutiny." *Washington Post*, October 24, 2010. http://www.washingtonpost.com/ wp-dyn/content/article/2010/10/23/AR2010102302996.html (accessed July 13, 2011).

Helmke, Paul. "Leaving Brady, But Not the Fight to Prevent Gun Violence." Washington, DC: Brady Campaign to Prevent Gun Violence, July 8, 2011. http://blog.bradycampaign.org/ ?p=3435 (accessed July 13, 2011).

Henigan, Dennis A. "California Street (101) Massacre." In *Guns in American Society: An Encyclopedia of History, Politics, Culture, and the Law*, edited by Gregg Lee Carter, vol. 1, 95–96. Santa Barbara, CA: ABC-CLIO, 2002.

Henigan, Dennis A. *Lethal Logic: Exploding the Myths that Paralyze American Gun Policy*. Washington, DC: Potomac Books, 2009.

Horwitz, Joshua, and Casey Anderson. *Guns, Democracy, and the Insurrectionist Idea*. Ann Arbor: University of Michigan Press, 2009.

Horwitz, Sari, and James V. Grimaldi. "NRA-Led Gun Lobby Wields Powerful Influence over ATF, U.S. Politics." *Washington Post*, December 15, 2010. http://www.washingtonpost.com/wp-dyn/content/article/2010/12/14/AR2010121406045.html?sid=ST2010121406431 (accessed July 7, 2011).

Kates, Don B., Jr., John K. Lattimer, and James Boen. "Sagecraft: Bias and Mendacity in the Public Health Literature on Gun Usage." In *The Great American Gun Debate: Essays on Firearms and Violence*, edited by Don B. Kates, Jr. and Gary Kleck, 123–35. San Francisco: Pacific Research Institute for Public Policy, 1997.

Keating, Dan, et al. "Aiming to Win." *Washington Post*, December 15, 2010. http://www.washingtonpost.com/wp-dyn/content/graphic/2010/12/14/GR2010121408340.html?sid=ST2010121406431 (accessed July 7, 2011).

Kennett, Lee, and James LaVerne Anderson. *The Gun in America: The Origins of a National Dilemma*. Westport, CT: Greenwood Press, 1975.

Kopel, David B. "The Brady Bill Comes Due: The *Printz* Case and State Autonomy." *George Mason University Civil Rights Law Journal* 9 (1999): 189–205.

Kopel, David B. "Clueless: The Misuse of BATF Firearms Tracing Data." *Law Review of Michigan State University* 1999 (1999): 171–84.

Kopel, David B. "Killeen Texas, Massacre." In *Guns in American Society: An Encyclopedia of History, Politics, Culture, and the Law*, edited by Gregg Lee Carter, vol. 1, 333–36. Santa Barbara, CA: ABC-CLIO, 2002.

Kopel, David B. "Pretend 'Gun-Free' School Zones: A Deadly Legal Fiction." *Connecticut Law Review* 42 (2009): 515–84. http://www.connecticutlawreview.org/documents/Kopel.pdf (accessed July 4, 2011).

Koper, Christopher S. *Updated Assessment of the Federal Assault Weapons Ban: Impacts on Gun Markets and Gun Violence, 1994–2003*. Philadelphia, PA: Jerry Lee Center of Criminology, University of Pennsylvania, 2004. http://www.sas.upenn.edu/jerrylee/research/aw_final2004.pdf (accessed July 6, 2011).

Krivosta, George G. "NanoTag™ Markings from Another Perspective." *AFTE Journal* 39 (2005): 41–47.

Levine, James G. "The Armed Career Criminal Act and the U.S. Sentencing Guidelines: Moving toward Consistency." *Harvard Journal on Legislation* 46 (2009): 537–67. http://www.harvardjol.com/wp-content/uploads/2009/09/537-568.pdf (accessed July 10, 2011).

Lillis, Mike. "Gun Lobby Questions Accuracy of Terrorist Watch List." *Washington Independent*, June 22, 2009. http://washingtonindependent.com/48240/terrorist-watchlist-is-no-barrier-to-gun-purchasesterrorist-watch-list (accessed June 28, 2011).

Lillis, Mike. "Terrorist Watch List is No Hurdle to Gun Purchases." *Washington Independent*, June 23, 2009. http://washingtonindependent.com/48316/gun-lobby-questions-accuracy-of-terrorist-watch-list (accessed June 28, 2011).

Lillis, Mike. "247 on Terror Watch List Bought Guns." *The Hill*, April 28, 2011. http://thehill.com/homenews/news/158235-suspected-terorists-unhampered-in-buying-guns (accessed June 28, 2011).

Luo, Michael. "Some with Histories of Mental Illness Petition to Get Their Gun Rights Back." *New York Times*, July 2, 2011. http://www.nytimes.com/2011/07/03/us/03guns.html (accessed July 3, 2011).

Maguire, Kathleen, and Ann L. Pastore, eds. *Sourcebook of Criminal Justice Statistics 2002*. Washington, DC: U.S. Department of Justice, 2004.

Mayer, Scott. " 'Do You Feel Lucky . . . ' .500 S&W Magnum." *American Rifleman* 151 (2003): 54–57, 93.

McDowall, David, Allan J. Lizotte, and Brian Wiersema. "General Deterrence through Civilian Gun Ownership: An Evaluation of the Quasi-Experimental Evidence." *Criminology* 29 (1991): 541–59.

Molloy, Joanna. "Colin Goddard, Survivor of Tragic Virginia Tech Shooting, Has Message with Film 'Living for 32.' " *NYDailyNews.com*, November 17, 2010. http://www.nydailynews .com/ny_local/2010/11/17/2010-11-17_32_big_reasons__to_watch_chilling_documentary_on _guns_by_va_tech_massacre_surviv.html (accessed July 8, 2011).

National Opinion Research Center. General Social Survey. "Would you favor or oppose a law which would require a person to obtain a police permit before he or she could buy a gun?" http://www.norc.uchicago.edu/GSS+Website/ (accessed July 7, 2011).

National Rifle Association. "Are We Really So Violent?" *American Rifleman*, 1968a.

National Rifle Association. "Firearms Preemption Laws." 2006. http://www.nraila.org/Issues/ FactSheets/Read.aspx?id=48 (accessed July 5, 2011).

National Rifle Association. "Restraint on TV, Cheap Handguns Wins Favor." *American Rifleman*, 1968b.

National Rifle Association. "National Campaign to Fire Attorney General Eric Holder." July 2011a. https://www.nra.org/fireholder/ (accessed July 13, 2011).

National Rifle Association. "NRA Delivers Remarks at United Nations Concerning Proposed Arms Trade Treaty," July 14, 2011b. http://www.nraila.org/Legislation/Read.aspx?ID=6993 (accessed July 15, 2011).

National Rifle Association. "Right-to-Carry 2010." http://www.nraila.org/Issues/FactSheets/ Read.aspx?ID=18 (accessed July 18, 2011).

National Shooting Sports Foundation. "California Microstamping Law Not In Effect." 2011. http://www.nssf.org/GovRel/news/california-microstamping-law-not-in-effect.cfm (accessed July 27, 2011).

Newport, Frank, and Lydia Saad. "Gallup Review: Public Opinion Context of Tucson Shootings: Less Support for Gun Control in Recent Years, Evidence of Increased Polarization." *Gallup*, January 10, 2011. http://www.gallup.com/poll/145526/gallup-review-public-opinion-context -tucson-shootings.aspx (accessed July 7, 2011).

Obama, Barack. "We Must Seek Agreement on Gun Reforms." *Arizona Daily Star*, March 13, 2011. http://azstarnet.com/news/opinion/mailbag/article_011e7118-8951-5206-a878 -39bfbc9dc89d.html (accessed July 8, 2011).

Page, Douglas. "Microstamping Calls the Shots: A Revolutionary Identification Technology Finds Favor and Foes." *Law Enforcement Technology* 35 (2008): 54, 56–59. http://www.officer.com/ article/10249197/microstamping-calls-the-shots (accessed July 6, 2011).

Pierce, Glenn L., LeBaron Briggs, and David A. Carlson. *The Identification of Patterns in Firearms Trafficking: Implications for Focused Enforcement Strategies: A Report to the United*

States Dep't of Treasury, Bureau of Alcohol, Tobacco and Firearms Office of Enforcement. Boston: Northeastern University, December 13, 1995.

People v. Rodriguez. "Indictment Number 2917/06, Decision & Order." http://www.handgunlaw. us/documents/agopinions/NYCtLEOSARulingPeoplevsRodriguez.PDF (accessed July 8, 2011). (Note: Because this case was dismissed, it was not published on any court-related websites maintained by the state of New York.)

Price, Joyce Howard. "Groups Call Arms Seizures 'Arbitrary.' " *Washington Times*, September 23, 2005, A14. http://www.infowars.com/articles/2nd_amendment/no_gun_seizures_groups_call _arbitrary.htm (accessed July 7, 2011).

Riggs, Mike. "House Democrat Tries, Fails, to Use Patriot Act to Pass New Federal Gun Control Law." Reason.com, May 13, 2011. http://reason.com/blog/2011/05/13/house-democrat-tries -fails-to (accessed June 28, 2011).

Rosenthal, Lawrence, and Joyce Lee Malcolm. "*McDonald v. Chicago*: Which Standard of Scrutiny Should Apply to Gun-Control Laws?" *Northwestern University Law Review* 105 (2010): 85–114. http://www.law.northwestern.edu/lawreview/colloquy/2010/24/LRColl2010n24 Rosenthal&Malcom.pdf (accessed July 6, 2011).

Roth, Jeffrey A., and Christopher S. Koper. *Impacts of the 1994 Assault Weapons Ban: 1994–96.* Washington, DC: National Institute of Justice, U.S. Department of Justice, 1999 (NCJ 173405). http://www.ncjrs.org/pdffiles1/173405.pdf (accessed July 6, 2011).

Ryan, Jason. "Obama to Seek New Assault Weapons Ban." ABCNews.com, February 25, 2009. http://abcnews.go.com/Politics/story?id=6960824&page=1 (accessed July 13, 2011).

Savage, Charlie. "New Reporting Rules on Multiple Sales of Guns Near Border." *New York Times*, July 11, 2011. http://www.nytimes.com/2011/07/12/us/politics/12guns.html?_r=2 (accessed July 13, 2011).

Scalia, John. *Federal Firearm Offenders, 1992–1998.* Washington, DC: U.S. Department of Justice (NCJ-180795), June 2000.

Second Amendment Foundation. "News Release: Report from the U.N. by Julianne Versnel Second Amendment Foundation Director of Operations." July 14, 2011. http://www.saf.org/ viewpr-new.asp?id=368 (accessed July 15, 2011).

Sourcebook of Criminal Justice Statistics Online. "Criminal Defendants Disposed of in U.S. District Courts, 2006." 2011a. http://www.albany.edu/sourcebook/pdf/t5242006.pdf (accessed July 13, 2011).

Sourcebook of Criminal Justice Statistics Online. "Criminal Defendants Disposed of in U.S. District Courts, 2007." 2011b. http://www.albany.edu/sourcebook/pdf/t5242007.pdf (accessed July 13, 2011).

Sourcebook of Criminal Justice Statistics Online. "Criminal Defendants Disposed of in U.S. District Courts, 2008." 2011c. http://www.albany.edu/sourcebook/pdf/t5242008.pdf (accessed July 13, 2011).

Sourcebook of Criminal Justice Statistics Online. "Criminal Defendants Disposed of in U.S. District Courts, 2009." 2011d. http://www.albany.edu/sourcebook/pdf/t5242009.pdf (accessed July 13, 2011).

Sourcebook of Criminal Justice Statistics Online. "Criminal Defendants Disposed of in U.S. District Courts, 2010." 2011e. http://www.albany.edu/sourcebook/pdf/t5242010.pdf (accessed July 13, 2011).

Southwick, Lawrence, Jr. "Enforcement of Gun Control Laws." In *Guns in American Society: An Encyclopedia of History, Politics, Culture, and the Law*, edited by Gregg Lee Carter, vol. 1, 86–90. Santa Barbara, CA: ABC-CLIO, 2002.

Spitzer, Robert J. *The Politics of Gun Control*. 3rd ed. Washington, DC: CQ Press, 2004.

Stolberg, Sheryl Gay. "Firearms Bureau Finds Itself in a Rough Patch." *New York Times*, July 4, 2011. http://www.nytimes.com/2011/07/05/us/politics/05guns.html (accessed July 6, 2011).

Stone, Andrea. "Virginia Tech Survivor Is 'Living for 32' in War to Tighten Gun Laws." AOLNews.com, December 31, 2010. http://www.aolnews.com/2010/12/31/colin-goddard -virginia-tech-shooting-survivor-fights-to-tighte/ (accessed July 8, 2011).

Sugarmann, Josh. *National Rifle Association: Money, Firepower, Fear*. Washington, DC: National Press Books, 1992b.

Sugarmann, Josh. *National Rifle Association: Money, Firepower, Fear* (online ed.). http://www .vpc.org/nrainfo/chapter1.html#32 (accessed July 7, 2011).

Students for Concealed Carry on Campus. "About Us." 2011. http://concealedcampus.org/ aboutus.php (accessed July 4, 2011).

Supreme Court of the United States. *District of Columbia, et al., Petitioners v. Dick Anthony Heller*. No. 07-290. 554 U.S. 570; 128 S. Ct. 2783; 171 L. Ed. 2d 637; 2008 U.S. LEXIS 5268; 76 U.S.L.W. 4631; 21 Fla. L. Weekly Fed. S 497. March 18, 2008, Argued. June 26, 2008, Decided. http://www.supremecourt.gov/opinions/07pdf/07-290.pdf (accessed July 5, 2011).

Supreme Court of the United States. *Otis Mcdonald, et al., Petitioners v. City of Chicago, Illinois, et al*. No. 08-1521. 130 S. Ct. 3020; 177 L. Ed. 2d 894; 2010 U.S. LEXIS 5523; 22 Fla. L. Weekly Fed. S 619. March 2, 2010, Argued. June 28, 2010, Decided. http://www.supreme court.gov/opinions/09pdf/08-1521.pdf (accessed July 5, 2011).

Todd, Chuck. "Outgunned." *Hardball with Chris Matthews*, March 31, 2011. http://www.msnbc .msn.com/id/3036697/vp/42348115%2342348115#42348115 (accessed July 8, 2011).

Urbina, Ian. "Fearing Obama Agenda, States Push to Loosen Gun Laws." *New York Times*, February 24, 2010. http://www.nytimes.com/2010/02/24/us/24guns.html (accessed July 19, 2011).

U.S. Department of Justice. *National Instant Criminal Background Check System (NICS) Operations 2010*. 2011. http://www.fbi.gov/about-us/cjis/nics/reports/2010-operations-report/2010 -operations-report-pdf (accessed July 16, 2011).

U.S. Department of Justice. *Promising Strategies to Reduce Gun Violence*. Washington, DC: U.S. Department of Justice, NCJ 173950, 2000. http://www.ojjdp.gov/pubs/gun_violence/contents .html (accessed July 13, 2011).

U.S. Department of Justice. *Review of ATF's Project Gunrunner*. Washington, DC: Evaluation and Inspections Division, Office of the Inspector General, U.S. Department of Justice (I-2011-001), November 2010. http://www.justice.gov/oig/reports/ATF/e1101.pdf (accessed July 27, 2011).

U.S. Department of Justice. "Whether the Second Amendment Secures an Individual Right: Memorandum Opinion for the Attorney General." August 24, 2004. http://www.justice.gov/ olc/secondamendment2.pdf (accessed June 28, 2011).

Violence Policy Center. "National Rifle Association Suffers Self-Proclaimed 'Biggest Election Disaster in Nearly 15 Years.' " Washington, DC: Violence Policy Center, 2006. http://www .vpc.org/press/0611elect.htm (accessed July 7, 2011).

Vizzard, William J. *Shots in the Dark: The Policy, Politics and Symbolism of Gun Control*. Lanham, MD: Rowman & Littlefield, 2000.

Walsh, Bill. "Police Ordered to Stop Disarming Residents." *New Orleans Times Picayune*, September 23, 2005, A3. http://www.nola.com/katrina/pages/092405/0924PAGEA03.pdf (accessed June 30, 2011).

Wilson, Harry L. *Guns, Gun Control, and Elections: The Politics and Policy of Firearms*. Lanham, MD: Rowman & Littlefield, 2007.

A

Aborn, Richard (1952–)

Richard Aborn served as president of Handgun Control, Inc. (HCI), and of the Center to Prevent Handgun Violence from 1992 to 1996 (these organizations were renamed the Brady Campaign to Prevent Gun Violence and the Brady Center to Prevent Gun Violence, respectively, in June 2001). During his presidency, he lobbied and testified before Congress and a number of state legislatures and made numerous media appearances across the country. He helped mobilize support for the passage of the Brady Bill (Brady Handgun Violence Prevention Act), the ban on the import of assault weapons (Assault Weapons Ban of 1994), and the ban on large-capacity clips. He is among the most visible advocates of gun control and has been active in a variety of ways in many different arenas.

Aborn first became involved with gun control issues when he served from 1979 to 1984 in the Manhattan District Attorney's Office. In that capacity he investigated and prosecuted cases of gun violence and distribution and increasingly came to believe in the importance of restrictions on guns. After Aborn left the District Attorney's Office, he began work as a volunteer at HCI. His visible and effective advocacy led to his election to the Board of Trustees in 1988 and to the presidency of the organization in 1992.

While he was president of HCI, Aborn established a broad agenda. He lobbied the federal and state governments for laws mandating licenses to buy handguns, for mandatory fingerprint checks and safety training for those who apply for licenses, a mandatory seven-day cooling-off period, and the registration of handgun transfers. He sought to ban possession of guns by those convicted of violent misdemeanors and to ban semiautomatic weapons and certain types of ammunition.

He served a concurrent term as president of the Center to Prevent Handgun Violence, which focuses on public education and community involvement. During his term he worked to develop and implement the STAR (Straight Talk About Risks) program, a curriculum for prekindergarten through 12th grade that seeks to educate students about the risks of gun injuries. Aborn was instrumental in winning adoption for the program by the New York City public schools.

Aborn also served on a task force in New York State that focused on violent crime as a public health issue; he contributed to its published report, "New York State Strategy to Reduce Gun Violence." He was a visiting fellow at Columbia University, where he lectured on gun control, and has served as a consultant to the Ford Foundation project on violence, youth, and schools. In 2001, Aborn was senior counsel and director of policy at the Kamber Group, a media consulting group. He also serves on the board of New Yorkers Against Gun Violence and Harlem Mothers SAVE. In his various roles, he is often interviewed and quoted in new stories and makes regular media guest appearances, such as on the Fox News Network.

Currently, Aborn is a managing partner at the firm law Constantine Cannon, which focuses on antitrust litigation and counseling but offers services in other legal domains as well. He is also president of Constantine & Aborn Advisory Services, which provides consulting, project management, technology solutions in e-discovery, compliance monitoring, investigative services and public policy areas to private- and public-sector clients. Aborn also advises U.S. and European police and criminal justice agencies on a range of issues, from police integrity to building effective interagency relationships. His clients include the Los Angeles Police Department, Hartford Police Department, Transport for London, the MET Police, British Transport Police, and the Crown Prosecution Service. Managing several roles, Aborn is also president of Citizens Crime Commission, a New York–based non-profit organization that researches and educates on the issues of illegal gun crime, juvenile crime, counterterrorism, and crime prevention.

In 2009, Aborn ran against Cyrus Vance Jr., son of the secretary of state under Jimmy Carter, and Leslie Crocker Snyder, a former judge, in the Democratic primary for the office of district attorney of New York County (Manhattan), a position that had been occupied by only two individuals since 1941. The office was most recently held by Robert Morris Morgenthau for 35 years. Vance won the race with 44 percent of the vote, while Snyder garnered 30 percent and Aborn, 26 percent. Since there was no Republican candidate running, the Democratic primary, which received heightened coverage, was decisive. Aborn ran primarily on his gun-control record and was endorsed by the Brady Campaign, Million Mom March, and New Yorkers Against Gun Violence; some critics claim that Aborn's loss was a repudiation of the gun-control agenda he advocated.

Clyde Wilcox and Christine Kim

See also: Assault Weapons Ban of 1994; Brady Campaign to Prevent Gun Violence; Brady Center to Prevent Gun Violence; Brady Handgun Violence Prevention Act (Brady Bill)

Further Reading

Brady Campaign to Prevent Gun Violence. "Additional Biographies." http://www.bradycampaign.org/about/bio/additional (accessed May 16, 2011).

Cannon, Constantine. "Richard M. Aborn, Esq." http://www.constantinecannon.com/attorneys/raborn.php (accessed May 16, 2011).

Citizens Crime Commission of New York City. "Citizens Crime Commission of New York City." http://www.nycrimecommission.org/ (accessed May 16, 2011).

Constantine & Aborn Advisory Services. http://www.caasny.com/index2.html (accessed May 16, 2011).

Accidents, Gun

Unintentional firearm deaths, often called gun accidents in the popular press, are only a small fraction of gun suicides or gun homicides, but they still represent a substantial public health problem. According to Vital Statistics data, between 1965 and 2007, over 66,000 Americans died from accidental firearm shootings, more Americans than were killed in all the wars during that period. From 2003 to 2007, over 680 Americans per year were killed unintentionally with firearms.

Data from the National Violent Death Reporting System (which has more comprehensive data on each shooting but is currently operating in only 17 states) show that two-thirds of these shooting deaths occur in someone's home, about half the victims are under age 15, and half the deaths are other-inflicted—the victims are typically shot accidently by a friend or family member, often an older brother. Children aged 5–14 in the United States are *11* times more likely to be the victim of a fatal gun accident than similarly aged children in the rest of the developed world.

Not surprisingly, where there are more guns, there are more accidental gun deaths. One study found that for every age group—men and women, blacks and whites—those living in states with more guns were far more likely to die of gun accidents. The differences were enormous. A study published in 2001 found that the typical resident from one of the four states with the most guns (Louisiana, Alabama, Mississippi, and Arkansas) was *eight* times more likely to die in a gun accident than someone from one of the four states with the fewest guns (Hawaii, Massachusetts, Rhode Island, and New Jersey). Although there were virtually the same number of children in both groups of states, between 1979 and 1997, 104 children between birth and age 4 died from accidental gunshot wounds in the high-gun states, compared to only 6 in the low-gun states. Among 5- to 14-year-olds, 565 children died from accidental gunshot wounds in the high-gun states, compared to only 42 in the low-gun states.

The fatal injury problem is, of course, only the tip of the iceberg. In the 2000s, for every unintentional firearm fatality, there were more than 10 individuals injured seriously enough to be treated in hospital emergency rooms. In other words, from 2003 to 2007, almost 20 Americans each day were shot unintentionally but did not die. This number does not include any of the more than 45 people each day who were treated in emergency rooms for BB/pellet gun

wounds or the many others injured unintentionally by firearms in other ways (e.g., powder burns, struck with a firearm, injured by the recoil of a firearm).

One study of nonfatal accidental firearm injuries found that over one-third required hospitalization, most involved handguns, and many occurred during fairly routine gun handling—cleaning a gun, loading and unloading, hunting, or target shooting.

Like death rates from most other types of unintentional injury, the U.S. unintentional firearm fatality rate has been falling over the past four decades, as has the unintentional firearm fatality rate in other developed nations. The reduction is probably due to a rising standard of living (injury rates are lower among higher-income populations), improvements in emergency medicine (e.g., helicopter transport, pre-hospital advanced life support), and increased suburbanization (accidental gun fatality rates are higher in rural than in non-rural areas). The percentage of households with an adult hunter has fallen over time.

Many policies can further reduce the number of accidental gun injuries. Currently, there are no federal safety standards for domestically manufactured firearms. New regulations might require that firearms do not go off when dropped and that guns have minimum trigger-pull standards to help prevent very young children from being able to pull a gun's trigger. One study found that three safety devices —a loaded chamber indicator, magazine safeties (that prevent a gun from firing once the ammunition magazine has been removed), and personalization devices—could have prevented over 40 percent of unintentional gun deaths in Maryland and Milwaukee.

Prevention advocates argue that we have more safety standards for toy guns than we currently have for real guns. They find it difficult to justify why we do not child-proof guns when we know that child-resistant packaging of aspirin and prescription drugs has prevented hundreds of deaths among children. Since even the most basic camera indicates whether it is loaded, why can't the same determination be made by users of firearms?

Unfortunately, unintentional firearm injuries remain a serious public health problem in the United States. In the early 2000s, when 34 injury prevention experts were asked to prioritize home injury hazards for young children, based on frequency, severity, and preventability of the injury, the experts rated access to firearms in the home as the most significant hazard.

David Hemenway

See also: Gun Violence as a Public Health Problem; Guns in the Home; Loaded-Chamber Indicator; Victimization from Gun Violence; Violence Prevention Research Program

Further Reading

Hemenway, David. *Private Guns, Public Health*. Ann Arbor: University of Michigan Press, 2006.

Hemenway, David, Catherine Barber, and Matthew Miller. "Unintentional Firearm Deaths: A Comparison of Other-Inflicted and Self-Inflicted Shootings." *Accident Analysis and Prevention* 42 (2010): 1184–88.

Katcher, Murray L., et al. "Use of the Modified Delphi Technique to Identify and Rate Home Injury Hazard Risks and Prevention Methods for Young Children." *Injury Prevention* 12 (2006): 189–94.

Miller, Matthew, Deborah Azrael, and David Hemenway. "Firearm Availability and Unintentional Firearm Deaths." *Accident Analysis and Prevention* 33 (2001): 477–84.

Richardson, Erin G., and David Hemenway. "Homicide, Suicide and Unintentional Firearm Fatality: Comparing the United States with Other High-Income Countries, 2003." *Journal of Trauma* 70 (2011): 238–43.

Sinauer, Nancy, Joseph L. Annest, and James A. Mercy. "Unintentional, Nonfatal Firearm-Related Injuries." *Journal of the American Medical Association* 275 (1996): 1740–43.

Vernick, Jon S., et al. "Unintentional and Undetermined Firearm-Related Deaths: A Preventable Death Analysis for Three Safety Devices." *Injury Prevention* 9 (2003): 309–11.

Acquisition of Guns

Patterns of acquisition of guns have changed over the years. In the eighteenth century, civilian firearms were custom-made by gunsmiths and obtained directly from them. With the expansion of mass production in the nineteenth century, firearms were commonly ordered direct from the manufacturer. By the twentieth century, manufacturers had established marketing systems whereby the manufacturer sold to a wholesaler, or "jobber," who in turn sold to local dealers. An exception to this pattern was the mail-order house, which sold arms (mostly military surplus) and shipped them direct to its customers; mail-order houses vanished after the Gun Control Act of 1968, which generally prohibited interstate sales to nondealers.

A lively trade in used firearms, either person-to-person or through a dealer, exists in addition to these commercial outlets. Gun shows are especially popular, as many federal firearm regulations—e.g., background checks—are often sidestepped.

The total number of firearms acquired and owned by Americans can only be roughly approximated. In 2008, the National

Opinion Research Center reported that 36 percent of American households reported owning a firearm, a figure that has fallen steadily over the past four decades (e.g., in 1973, it was 49.1 percent). Although Smith (2001) documents several reasons for the decline in gun ownership (e.g., there has been a steady decline in the popularity of hunting), studies of underreporting errors suggest the real figure may be higher. Most households claiming to possess firearms report that they own several guns. The total number of firearms owned by Americans has been estimated at 235 million. All these figures may be greatly affected by the increase in firearm purchases that began in 2009. These are reflected in federal excise taxes on new firearms and ammunition, whose returns increased 38 percent over the previous year.

The acquisition of firearms by criminal elements has been the subject of a U.S. Bureau of Justice Statistics survey (2000, 10), which tallied responses from over 12,000 inmates who had used firearms while committing the criminal offense for which they were imprisoned. The inmates reported the following sources of the firearms they used: a friend or relative (35 percent), their drug dealer (15 percent), a licensed gun dealer (15 percent), and a gun show or flea market (1.7 percent). Those groups suspicious of strong gun control efforts are especially quick to highlight these data, as they show that a large portion of the criminal population is able to sidestep regulations meant to keep guns out of their hands, while rarely resorting to gun shows.

David T. Hardy

See also: Black Market for Firearms; Felons and Gun Control; Firearm Dealers; Gun Control Act of 1968; Gun Shows; Mail-Order Guns

Further Reading

Bureau of Justice Statistics. *Federal Firearms Offenders 1992–98*. Washington, DC: U.S. Department of Justice, 2000.

National Opinion Research Center. General Social Survey, 2008 ("Do you happen to have in your home [or garage] any guns or revolvers?" If yes, "Is it a pistol, shotgun, rifle, or what?"). http://www.norc.org/GSS +Website/ (accessed February 14, 2011).

National Shooting Sports Foundation, "Quarterly Firearm and Ammunition Taxes Up 29 Percent." http://www.nssf.org/newsroom/releases/show.cfm?PR=020110.cfm&path =2010 (accessed February 14, 2011).

Smith, Tom W. *2001 National Gun Policy Survey of the National Opinion Research Center: Research Findings*. Chicago: National Opinion Research Center, 2001.

Adames, et al. v. Beretta U.S.A. Corp. (2009)

In *Adames, et al. v. Beretta U.S.A. Corp.* (2009), the Illinois Supreme Court granted summary judgment for both a county sheriff and a gun manufacturer regarding the accidental death of a teenager. Thirteen-year-old William (Billy) Swan accidentally killed his friend Joshua (Josh) Adames in May 2001 while playing with his father's service gun. Billy's father, David Swan, was a correctional officer employed by the Cook County Sheriff's Department. According to Billy, while home alone, he removed an unlocked and loaded Beretta 92FS handgun from his father's closet and shot his friend Josh in the stomach, killing him. Billy believed the gun was unloaded because he had removed the magazine. As a lieutenant for the Cook County sheriff, David Swan had previously carried a gun as part of his duties, but no longer did. He disputed that the lockbox in which Billy found three handguns was unlocked and claimed that the ammunition was stored separately. However, it was presumed that the lockbox was unlocked for purposes of summary judgment.

Billy was found delinquent for the shooting and placed on probation after a finding that he committed involuntary manslaughter and recklessly discharged a firearm. David was found not guilty of the improper storage of a firearm in a premise in which a minor under 14 is likely to have access to the firearm.

The co-special administrators of Adames's estate filed claims against the Cook County sheriff (Michael F. Sheahan) and Beretta USA Corporation. The trial court entered summary judgment for Sheahan on plaintiff's wrongful-death and survival claims and for Beretta "on plaintiff's claims for product liability design defect, negligent design, failure to warn, and breach of the implied warranty of merchantability." The appellate court affirmed in part and reversed in part. The Illinois Supreme Court affirmed in part and reversed in part the appellate court, affirming the judgment of the circuit court. The court held the following:

Sheahan's Appeal: The court held that Sheahan was entitled to summary judgment; he was not liable for the tort of his employee because the torts were not committed within the scope of employment. At the outset, the Illinois Supreme Court found that the issue of respondent superior was properly before the court. The court found that the case was factually distinguishable from *Gaffney v. City of Chicago* (302 Ill. App. 3d 41 (1998)) and concluded that none of the three criteria under the Second Restatement of Agency were met: "David's negligent storage of his guns was not the kind of conduct David was employed to perform, nor was it incidental to his employment"; "David's negligent storage of the gun was

not within the authorized time and space limits of his employment"; and "there is no evidence that David was motivated, at least in part, by a desire to serve his employer when he negligently stored his gun."

Beretta's Appeal: The court then held that the Protection of Lawful Commerce in Arms Act (PLCAA) "requires dismissal of plaintiffs' failure to warn claim against Beretta." The court found that the lawsuit qualified as a civil liability action under the PLCAA because the "use" of the gun "constituted a criminal or unlawful misuse of the Beretta for purposes of the PLCAA." The court then analyzed whether the conduct fell under an exception to a qualified civil liability action under 7903(5)(A)(v). The court found that the conduct did not meet the exception because "the discharge of the Beretta in this case was caused by a volitional act that constituted a criminal offense, which the PLCAA provides 'shall be considered the sole proximate cause of any resulting death, personal injuries or property damage.' " Thus, the plaintiff's failure to warn claims did not fall under section 7903(5)(A)(v) and were barred by the PLCAA. Furthermore, the court found that "[t]he PLCAA does not require a finding that the volitional act that constituted a criminal offense be the sole proximate cause of any resulting death." The court also rejected the plaintiff's claim that the PLCAA was unconstitutional as violating the Tenth Amendment to the U.S. Constitution. The court found that "the PLCAA is a valid exercise of the federal power to regulate interstate commerce, Congress has not intruded upon an area of authority traditionally reserved to the states and does not impermissibly commandeer the states or their officials in violation of the tenth amendment."

Plaintiff's Cross-Appeal: Using the same reasoning, the court found that, like the failure to warn claims, the plaintiff's design defect claims were barred by the PLCAA.

In December 2009, the U.S. Supreme Court denied certiorari (refusing to hear the case).

Travis H. Carter

See also: Lawsuits against Gun Manufacturers; Protection of Lawful Commerce in Arms Act of 2005

Further Reading

Adames, et al. v. Beretta U.S.A. Corp. Supreme Court of Illinois. 2009. http://www .scotusblog.com/wp-content/uploads/2009/ 08/Illinnois-SCt-Adames-ruling.pdf (accessed January 27, 2011).

Christensen, Anna. "Wednesday Round-up." SCOTUSblog. http://www.scotusblog.com/ 2009/12/wednesday-round-up-13/(accessed January 18, 2011).

Garcia, John. "High Court Rejects Challenge to Gun Law." WLS-AM 890 Local News .http://abclocal.go.com/wls/story?section =news/local&id=7171294 (accessed January 18, 2011).

Adames v. Sheahan. *See* Protection of Lawful Commerce in Arms Act of 2005

African Americans and Gun Violence

Gun violence has disproportionately affected the African American community. For much of American history, firearms were used as a means to subjugate African Americans and deny them full economic and political rights. While overall crime rates, including gun-related crime, have declined among the general population during the past decade, gun violence has increased among African Americans. African American youths, especially young males, have been particularly affected by gun violence. In addition to higher rates of violent crime, suicide rates among the African American community have also increased. This has led community leaders to decry the self-destruction of younger generations and call for increased gun control measures.

In 1619, the first African Americans were brought as slaves to the region that would become the United States. Within the first few decades after the establishment of the initial colonies, laws were passed that denied African Americans, both slaves and freemen, access to firearms. In 1640, Virginia became the first colony to enact legislation that prohibited African Americans from carrying weapons in public. This was followed by legislation throughout the colonies that prohibited African Americans from even possessing firearms. The fear of a slave revolt was the main rationale for these laws. However, they also served to further disenfranchise and alienate African Americans from full participation in the socioeconomic mainstream.

Following the American Revolution, laws were passed at the national level to deny African Americans access to firearms. In 1792, Congress enacted the Uniform Militia Act. This legislation called upon every "able-bodied white citizen" to be a member of his respective state militia and possess a rifle, bayonet, and ammunition if called up for service. This effectively banned African Americans from service in the militias.

Even as northern states outlawed slavery, many continued bans or added new bans on gun ownership among the African American community. Concurrently, southern states continued to restrict gun ownership. A law passed in 1825 even allowed the Florida militia and law enforcement to arbitrarily search African American homes for guns. As new slave states joined the Union, they

A suspect being searched by two armed police during the Watts race riots in Los Angeles, California, June, 1965. (Harry Benson/Getty Images)

also enacted bans on gun ownership by slaves. Texas passed such laws in 1840. When challenges to these laws were brought in state courts by free African Americans, they were uniformly rejected on the basis that African Americans, whether slave or free, were not considered to be citizens of the United States. Examples of these cases included the North Carolina case *State v. Newsom* in 1840 and Georgia's *Cooper v. Savannah* in 1848. In the infamous Supreme Court case *Dred Scott v. Sandford* in 1857, the nation's highest court held that African Americans who were slaves or the descendants of slaves were not entitled to the rights of citizenship, including the right to carry or possess firearms.

Until the Civil War, guns were the primary tools used to keep African Americans in bondage. The inequity of power that resulted from the white monopoly on gun ownership meant that African Americans could not effectively resist slavery. The most significant slave revolt in American history, Nat Turner's Revolt in Virginia in 1831, demonstrated the inability of African Americans to overcome the well-armed state militia. Turner and his band of about 60 followers killed 55 white men, women, and children. However, within a week, the revolt was put down by the militia. Turner and the majority of his supporters were either hanged or summarily executed. Whites throughout the state undertook reprisals against suspected sympathizers of Turner, killing dozens of innocent African Americans.

When the Civil War ended, various measures were passed to try to integrate African Americans into the broader society. However, in the immediate aftermath of the conflict, southern states such as Mississippi, Louisiana, and Alabama again passed laws that forbade African Americans from owning or possessing weapons. Such laws were part of the "Black Codes," which were designed to restrict the newly won freedoms of African Americans. Congress attempted to overturn the Black Codes through the Civil Rights Act of 1866, which specifically stated that laws prohibiting African Americans from "having firearms" were illegal. The Civil Rights Act was bolstered by the ratification in 1868 of the Fourteenth Amendment. This amendment made African Americans full citizens of the United States and guaranteed all Americans equal protection of the law.

The passage of the Fourteenth Amendment led white supremacists to seek other means to prevent African Americans from having access to guns. From the end of the Civil War onward, African Americans faced terror and harassment from such groups as the Ku Klux Klan (KKK). These groups sought to intimidate African Americans into leaving the South or to keep them subservient by maintaining the prewar social order. If African Americans had been able to defend themselves, such intimidation would not have been successful. Therefore, state legislatures throughout the nation enacted legislation to deny access to weapons based on economic constraints. In 1870, Tennessee banned the sale of all handguns, except the expensive models (which most whites already owned as a result of their service in the Civil War). Other states, including Arkansas, Alabama, and Texas, passed similar laws. It is important to note that these laws affected new sales of weapons, so that the white population was able to retain the firearms it already possessed. African Americans suffered a further setback in their efforts to acquire firearms to protect

themselves when the Supreme Court ruled in *United States v. Cruikshank* (1875) that the national government did not have the power to stop the KKK from disarming African Americans. Instead, African Americans had to rely on state and local law enforcement to protect them. These institutions were often dominated by white supremacists or were unwilling to act for fear of alienating themselves from the white population.

Throughout the early period of the twentieth century, guns continued to be concentrated in the hands of white citizens, and African Americans continued to face terror and oppression. The revival of the KKK in 1915 led to a renewed wave of lynchings and racially motivated killings in the South and Midwest. Such violence continued through the modern civil rights movement of the 1950s and 1960s. Efforts to empower African Americans in the South were met with resistance, often armed resistance, and those working to expand civil rights were frequently targeted for violence. The 1964 slaying of three civil rights workers in Mississippi exemplified this trend.

Frustration over continued discrimination and economic disparities sparked a series of race riots in the mid-1960s. For instance, the 1965 Watts riot in Los Angeles left 34 dead while riots in Newark, New Jersey, in 1967 killed 26, and similar riots in Detroit killed at least 40. These dramatic periods of violence occurred simultaneously with a general rise in violent crime rates. From the end of World War II onward, the availability of inexpensive handguns, often called Saturday night specials, was partially responsible for this upswing in violence. Public reaction to the growth in crime rates and the 1968 assassinations of both Martin Luther King Jr. and Robert F. Kennedy prompted Congress to pass the Gun Control Act of

1968. This was followed by a number of state Saturday night special laws that banned certain types of inexpensive handguns.

Violent gun crime in the United States peaked in the 1970s. However, while overall crime rates have declined since then, gun violence continued to increase in the African American community. The dramatic increase in violent crime as a result of the proliferation of certain illicit drugs, including crack cocaine, has been worsened by a new wave of inexpensive handguns. Since 1993, half of all new firearms have been handguns, and since 1973, more than 40 million new handguns have become available in the United States.

From 1985 through 1992, homicide rates and arrest rates for homicide among African American males doubled. Concurrently, homicide rates among the general population decreased by 27 percent. African Americans are three times as likely to be victims of handgun violence as are whites. In addition, rates of gun violence among African American youth increased by 300 percent, and African American youth are four times as likely as their white counterparts to be victims of gun violence. These factors have partially contributed to a four-fold increase in the nation's prison population since 1980 (to a total of 1.3 million in 2001). By the 1990s, almost one-quarter of African American males between the ages of 18 and 30 were either in prison or had served time in prison. Although African Americans comprise about 12 percent of the population, almost 50 percent of homicide victims are African American. Significantly, the majority of gun violence that is now directed toward African Americans is perpetuated by African Americans. By 2000, almost 90 percent of gun violence suffered by African Americans was committed by other African Americans.

Meanwhile, African Americans reported far lower rates of gun ownership than other groups. For instance, while 44 percent of white households reported owing a firearm in 2010, only 27 percent of African American homes owned a gun (*Sourcebook of Criminal Justice Statistics* 2011a). There were also differences in attitudes toward gun control. While 42 percent of whites agree with the notion that controlling gun ownership is more important than protecting gun rights, 66 percent of African Americans agree (*Sourcebook of Criminal Justice Statistics* 2011b).

Through the early 2000s, African Americans continued to be disproportionately impacted by gun violence, even as violent crimes declined across the nation. Between 2002 and 2007, homicide rates among African Americans increased by more than 30 percent, while homicide rates by firearms rose by more than 50 percent. By 2008, the murder rate for African Americans was 18 per 100,000, while the national average was approximately 5 per 100,000, and the average among whites was 3 per 100,000. The majority of the victims were male, more than 85 percent, and the average age was 30. Handguns continued to the most common weapons used in homicides in the African American community. On average, handguns were used in approximately 75 percent of homicides each year. Higher gun crime rates among African Americans were concentrated in 17 states and in specific urban areas in those states, including cities such as St. Louis, Missouri; Philadelphia, Pennsylvania; Detroit, Michigan; and Memphis, Tennessee. Studies indicated that urban areas with significant gang activity had higher rates of gun crime. California, New York and Texas were the states with the highest total incidents of gun crimes among

African Americans (Violence Policy Center 2011).

Tom Lansford

See also: Black Codes; Black Panthers; Crime and Gun Use; *Dred Scott v. Sandford*; Ku Klux Klan; Militia Act of 1792; NAACP and Gun Control; Poverty and Gun Violence; *United States v. Cruikshank*; Vigilantism; Youth and Guns

Further Reading

Alexander, Rudolph, Jr., ed. *Race and Justice*. Huntington, NY: Nova Science Publishers, 2000.

Carter, Gregg Lee. *The Gun Control Movement*. New York: Twayne, 1997.

Griffin, Sean Patrick. *Black Brothers, Inc.: The Violent Rise and Fall of Philadelphia's Black Mafia*. New York: Milo, 2005.

Kedia, P. Ray, ed. *Black on Black Crime: Facing Facts, Challenging Fictions*. Bristol, IN: Wyndham Hall Press, 1994.

Ogletree, Charles, Jr. *Beyond the Rodney King Story: An Investigation of Police Conduct in Minority Communities*. Boston: Northeastern University Press, 1995.

Sourcebook of Criminal Justice Statistics. "Table 2.60.2010: Respondents Reporting Having a Gun in their Home or on Property. By Demographic Characteristics, United States, 2010." 2011a. http://www.albany.edu/sourcebook/tost_2.html#2_ak (accessed June 25, 2011).

Sourcebook of Criminal Justice Statistics. "Table 2.0040.2010: Respondents Reporting Whether They Think Gun Control or the Right to Own a Gun is More Important— by Demographic Characteristics, United States, 2010 (Question: 'What do you think is more important–to protect the right of Americans to own guns, or to control gun ownership?')." 2011b. http://www.albany.edu/sourcebook/tost_2.html#2_ak (Accessed June 25, 2011).

Sulton, Anne T., ed. *African-American Perspectives on Crime Causation, Criminal Justice Administration, and Crime Prevention*. Englewood, CO: Sulton Books, 1994.

Tolnay, Stewart E., and E. M. Beck. *A Festival of Violence: An Analysis of Southern Lynchings, 1882–1930*. Urbana: University of Illinois Press, 1995.

Violence Policy Center. *Black Homicide Victimization in the United States: An Analysis of 2008 Homicide Data*. Washington, DC: Violence Policy Center, January 2011. http://www.vpc.org/studies/ (accessed June 25, 2011).

AK-47

The AK-47 was one of the first assault rifles ever built and is the most numerous and widely used assault rifle in the world. Millions of this model and its close cousins (such as the AKM, a modernized version of the AK-47 first produced in 1959, and the Norinco Type 56, a Chinese copy) were used as standard infantry weapons in the Soviet Union, the former Warsaw Pact countries, China, and many other countries, starting in the late 1940s. In later decades, it continued to see wide use in military, revolutionary, insurgent, and terrorist forces around the world, including Afghanistan, Colombia, Iraq, and other locations. The Israeli Galil and Finnish Valmet assault rifles use the same basic action. The AK-47 was replaced in Soviet service with the very similar AKM, which was subsequently replaced with the similar but smaller-caliber AK-74. The name AK-47 is short for "Automatic Kalashnikov model 1947."

The AK-47 is a selective-fire (capable of semiautomatic or automatic fire at the flip of a switch), gas-operated assault rifle that feeds 7.62 × 39 mm ammunition from a detachable 30-round magazine and has an effective range of about 300 meters. It weighs nearly 10 pounds and is about 34

An ATF officer holds an AK-47. (AP Photo/Lynne Sladky)

inches long. It is generally regarded as robust, reliable, and easy to manufacture.

AK-47s, like all automatic weapons, are subject to rigorous control in the United States. This has been the case since the passage of the National Firearms Act of 1934. Very few AK-47s are in civilian hands. However, thousands of semiautomatic derivatives of the AK-47 have been sold in the United States, including the Chinese Norinco Type 56S. Although the semiautomatic versions meet the definition of an "assault *weapon*" under U.S. and state statutes, they are not "assault *rifles*" per se— since an assault rifle is a selective-fire automatic rifle (Defense Intelligence Agency 1988), a semiautomatic rifle cannot be an assault rifle. Conversely, an AK-47 assault rifle is not an "assault weapon" as the term has been defined in the *United States Code* because an "assault weapon" is semiautomatic while an AK-47 is automatic.

Although semiautomatic derivatives of the AK-47 have a reputation for being particularly dangerous or lethal, this reputation is not entirely accurate. Semiautomatic versions of the AK-47 have a shorter range and less penetration and wound-causing potential than many ordinary center-fire hunting rifles. (The AK-47's intermediate-power 7.62 mm cartridge produces wounds less serious than common deer-hunting cartridges such as the .308 Winchester or .30-06, especially when military-type full metal jacket bullets are used.) Their rate of fire is similar to that of other semiautomatic rifles, and their rate of accurate, aimed fire is not dramatically higher than that of bolt-action rifles (Kopel 1994).

In 1989, Patrick Purdy used a Norinco Type 56S, which looks like an AK-47 but is semiautomatic, in his infamous attack on an elementary school playground in Stockton, California. He killed 5 people and wounded 30. As is not unusual in notorious mass shooting cases, the Stockton murders galvanized gun control efforts. California responded by passing the Roberti-Roos Assault Weapon Control Act of 1989, and President George H. W. Bush banned the importation of several kinds of semiautomatic weapons that same year, including the Norinco Type 56S.

Matthew DeBell

See also: Assault Weapons; Assault Weapons Ban of 1994; National Firearms Act of 1934; Stockton, California, Massacre

Further Reading

Defense Intelligence Agency. *Small Arms Identification and Operation Guide— Eurasian and Communist Countries.* Washington, DC: Government Printing Office, 1988.

Ezell, Edward. *The AK-47 Story.* Harrisburg, PA: Stackpole Books, 1986.

Kopel, David B. "Rational Basis Analysis of 'Assault Weapon' Prohibition." *Journal of Contemporary Law* 20 (1994): 381–417.

Alcohol and Gun Violence

Alcohol and gun violence have little to do with each other per se. Fewer than 4 percent of violent crimes involving alcohol also involve firearms (Bureau of Justice Statistics 1998). But alcohol, drugs, and firearms are designated "criminogenic commodities" because they are each so frequently involved in crime, especially violent crime (Moore 1983).

Since the failure of Prohibition, its proponents' identities and concerns have been obscured by decades of uncomprehending ridicule. Its proponents were truly the best and the brightest of three generations of humane and progressive Americans: William Lloyd Garrison, Horace Mann, Frederick Douglass, Susan B. Anthony, the Beechers (Harriet, Lyman, and Henry), Horace Greeley, Jane Addams, and William Jennings Bryan. Far from being narrowly religious, they were motivated by the involvement of alcohol in a vast amount of violent criminal behavior, including sex crimes and all varieties of homicide, particularly domestic homicide. "The Bottle," a late nineteenth-century cartoon by D. W. Moody, typifies their attitudes: It shows a husband being dragged off by the police in front of his children, who also witnessed the father beating their mother to death with the liquor bottle that now lies broken next to her head. The caption reads, "The husband in a state of furious drunkenness, kills his wife with the instrument of all their misery."

Indeed, the arguments for Prohibition closely parallel modern arguments for banning handguns. Comparatively, 28.7 percent of violent crimes involve firearms (primarily handguns), while roughly 35–40 percent of violent crimes are committed by offenders who were drinking. Handguns are the weapons used in 50–55 percent of murders, while nationally, at least 37–44 percent of murderers were drinking (Bureau of Justice Statistics 1998). Local and regional studies show that anywhere from 19 up to 86 percent of offenders have been drinking when the murder was committed (Kates 1989, 143–44). Additionally, 35–72 percent of robbers were drinking, as were 33–50 percent of rapists and child molesters (Bureau of Justice Statistics 1998; Kates 1989). Roughly 25 percent of robbers use firearms (mostly handguns), as do 4 percent of rapists (Kleck 1997, 217). More generally, a 2009 study by epidemiologists at the University of Pennsylvania found that risk of being a victim of gun violence increases with higher alcohol consumption and proximity to places that sell alcohol to go (Branas et al. 2009).

Beyond the toll of intentional crime is that from liquor-induced accidents. Drunk drivers kill over 13,400 people annually. There are roughly 850 accidental gun deaths each year; though there are no figures on how many of these are alcohol-related, the kinds of people who cause such accidents tend to have records of alcohol and drug abuse. Adding in alcohol-related illnesses, alcohol is involved in perhaps 10 percent of all American deaths annually, while handguns are involved in 1 percent or fewer.

At the same time, it should be emphasized that these problems are not associated with either drinking or gun ownership by ordinary people. If the incidence of alcohol-related criminal violence seems very large viewed on its own, it is minuscule compared to the vast number of Americans (roughly half of all adults) who drink without causing any harm. Alcohol-related crimes and accidents are usually linked to heavy drinkers. Even so, the great majority of heavy drinkers do not harm anyone.

By the same token, the incidence of gun violence (27.8 percent of all serious violent crime) is infinitesimal if viewed in the context of 250 million firearms contained in 41 percent of American households. Serious violent crime is not "caused" by the possession of alcohol or guns by normal people. Rather, violent crimes are committed by abnormal individuals as part of a pathology of highly aberrant behavior that includes regularly inebriating themselves (with alcohol or narcotics, or both) and inflicting harm on others with firearms or other weapons.

Another area in which firearms may be compared to alcohol is the ease with which restrictions, or total prohibition, of each are enforceable. Prohibiting or severely restricting guns among the general populace raises more or less the same enforceability problems as did alcohol prohibition—only more

so. The single most important difference is that guns are not consumed by their use. Temperance advocates recognized that many drinkers might defy Prohibition, but nevertheless counted on the fact that continued drinking would expose drinkers to the risks of detection as they made repeated purchases of alcohol. But for the owners of the nation's 250 million guns, defying a ban would require merely doing nothing, i.e., the low-visibility, low-risk failure to turn in their guns. (Of course, for the gun to continue to be useful for either criminal activity or for self-defense, the owner would need to procure fresh ammunition at least once every 20–40 years.)

Motivations for gun owners to violate a ban in many ways parallel the motivations that impelled even otherwise law-abiding drinkers to violate Prohibition. One motivation for violation in each case is the feeling by responsible drinkers/gun owners that they are being blamed, and their liberty circumscribed, for the misbehavior of a tiny minority of highly aberrant drinkers/gun owners whom the responsible majority despises and sharply differentiates from themselves. The outrage and anger this generates among the responsible majority inclines them to regard the ban as egregiously unjust. In the case of gun owners, anger and outrage are fueled by the deep belief (whether it is correct or not is irrelevant) that the ban is unconstitutional because the right to bear arms is guaranteed in the Bill of Rights. This argument was not available to drinkers because Prohibition was unquestionably legally valid, having been enacted by constitutional amendment.

Also crucially important is the immediate impetus for defying the law. Obviously, alcoholics during Prohibition experienced severe pressure to continue drinking, regardless of the law. But for the great majority of drinkers, i.e., social drinkers, the pressure to continue drinking was far less. In contrast, those who believe a gun is a vital tool for defending themselves and their families clearly have a greater impetus for violating a gun ban.

None of this should be misunderstood as meaning that defiance of a firearms-confiscation measure would be universal. After all, despite the mythology that grew up after its repeal, many Americans did stop drinking in response to Prohibition. Unfortunately, in gun prohibition as in alcohol prohibition, the result is likely to be less than desirable: The people most likely to comply are the responsible law-abiding people whose drinking or gun ownership represents no problem, while those most likely to resist are the people whom it is most desirable to affect.

Don B. Kates Jr.

See also: Availability of Guns, Effects on Crime; Average-Joe Thesis

Further Reading

Branas, Charles C., et al. "Alcohol Consumption, Alcohol Outlets, and the Risk of Being Assaulted with a Gun." *Alcoholism: Clinical and Experimental Research* (2009): 906–15.

Bureau of Justice Statistics. *Alcohol and Crime: An Analysis of National Data on the Prevalence of Alcohol Involvement in Crime.* Washington, DC: U.S. Department of Justice, 1998. http://bjs.ojp.usdoj.gov/content/pub/pdf/ac.pdf (accessed December 28, 2011).

Kates, Don B. "Handgun Banning in Light of the Prohibition Experience," *Firearms and Violence: Issues of Public Policy*, edited by Don B. Kates, 139–65. Cambridge, MA: Ballinger, 1989.

Kleck, Gary. *Targeting Guns: Firearms and Their Control.* Hawthorne, NY: Aldine de Gruyer, 1997.

Moore, Mark H. "Controlling Criminogenic Commodities: Drugs, Guns and Alcohol." In *Crime and Public Policy*, edited by James Q. Wilson, 125–44. San Francisco: Institute for Contemporary Studies, 1983.

Amateur Trapshooting Association. *See* Skeet, Sporting Clays, and Trap Shooting

American Academy of Pediatrics (AAP)

The American Academy of Pediatrics (AAP) is a nationwide medical association dedicated to the health of all children. The AAP takes one of the strongest firearm policy positions in the medical community, calling for the banning of handguns, assault weapons, and deadly air guns. The AAP's activities include supporting model gun control legislation, educating pediatricians and lay people about the dangers of firearms for children, and providing resources related to firearm injuries and violence. On its Healthy Children website, the AAP succinctly states its position on gun safety, updated in 2010.

Founded in 1930 by 35 pediatricians, the AAP today has 60,000 members, including over 34,000 board-certified Fellows. The mission of the AAP is "to attain optimal physical, mental, and social health and well-being for all infants, children, adolescents, and young adults." AAP programs in relation to firearms reflect that commitment and its position that gun violence is a public health issue. Through its "Periodic Survey of Fellows," the AAP gets feedback from members. The latest survey on guns and children indicates widespread agreement with AAP positions on gun control and on the importance of pediatricians educating parents about firearm safety.

In an updated policy statement in 2000, since reaffirmed in 2004, the AAP examined data on firearm-related deaths and injuries over the past decade. Although acknowledging slight decreases in gun violence in recent years, the AAP noted that 4,223 firearm-related deaths of children and adolescents occurred in 1997; 85 percent of all homicides and 63 percent of all suicides for adolescents aged 15–19 were committed with a firearm; 306 adolescents died from unintentional gun-related injuries in 1997; and the rates of firearm-related deaths for the United States are the highest among industrialized countries. In fact, the overall rate of firearm-related deaths for U.S. children under 15 is nearly 12 times greater than that for 25 other industrialized countries, and the rate of firearm-related homicide is nearly 16 times higher than that in all the other countries combined.

Reaffirming its long-standing position that children are safest when there are no guns in their environment, the AAP policy statement renewed its support for banning handguns, semiautomatic assault weapons, and dangerous air guns. The policy states, "Because firearm-related injury to children is associated with death and severe morbidity and is a significant public health problem, child health care professionals can and should provide effective leadership in efforts to stem this epidemic." In supporting such bans, the AAP had suggested that the Second Amendment does not grant individuals the right to bear arms.

Recommendations for firearm safety to parents stress that the safest thing is not to have a gun in the home, especially a handgun. The Healthy Children initiative includes concise advice to parents on "Gun Safety: Keeping Children Safe." For homes in which there are guns, the AAP emphasizes the importance of securely locking guns and ammunition in separate, secure places. The AAP also recommends ensuring that children do not have access to keys to the locations of guns and ammunition, asking police for advice on safe storage and gun locks, and talking with children about the risk of gun injury outside of the home. The AAP also strongly urges parents to work at making their homes safe, nonviolent places, discouraging overt displays of hostility between parents and among siblings.

The AAP has also expressed concern with the level of violence depicted in mass media, especially television. Reflecting this concern, the AAP made 11 recommendations for pediatricians in regard to media violence. These include recommending that pediatricians urge the entertainment industry to be more sensitive to media violence issues, contact local stations regarding violent programming, urge parents to monitor and limit their children's television viewing, and become better educated about media violence. In regard to parents, the AAP recommends limiting children's television watching to one to two hours a day, talking to children about television violence, and discussing with children nonviolent ways of resolving disagreements and solving problems.

In its Violence Intervention and Prevention Program Database, the AAP provides additional resources on firearms, some developed by other groups or organization. These include a Speaker's Kit on "Preventing Firearm Injury: Protecting Our Children"; the brochure "Keep Your Family Safe from Firearm Injury" for distribution by pediatricians; the "Firearm Injury Prevention Resource Guide," a directory of groups working to prevent firearm injuries; and the "Steps to Prevent (STOP) Firearm Injury Kit," developed jointly with the Center to Prevent Handgun Violence and available to health care professionals. Many of these resources are available on the AAP website, and the website provides information on where other such resources are located.

The AAP has supported various pieces of legislation aimed at preventing or reducing firearm injuries to children. These include the Children's Gun Violence Prevention Act of 1998, the Children Firearm Access Prevention Act, and a model bill, the Protection of Children from Handguns Act. The AAP has also supported legislation to close the gun show loophole and also supported the Student Pledge against Gun Violence and First Monday 2001, which focused on gun issues. A special article that appeared in *Pediatrics* in 2006 discussed and disapproved legislation introduced that year in the Virginia and West Virginia state legislatures that would prohibit pediatricians from asking parents if they owned firearms if they did so to counsel the parents. Both bills were defeated at that time. The AAP is a member of the Coalition to Stop Gun Violence (CSGV).

Walter F. Carroll

See also: Accidents, Gun; Assault Weapons Ban of 1994; Brady Handgun Violence Prevention Act (Brady Bill); Child Access Prevention (CAP) Laws; Coalition to Stop Gun Violence (CSGV); Media Violence; Million Mom March; Suicide, Guns and; Trigger Locks; Youth and Guns; Youth Gun Control Legislation: The Juvenile Justice Bill of 1999

Further Reading

American Academy of Pediatrics. http://www.aap.org (accessed February 28, 2011).

Committee on Injury and Poison Prevention, American Academy of Pediatrics. "Firearm-Related Injuries Affecting the Pediatric Population." *Pediatrics* 105 (2000): 888–95. Revised October 1, 2004: http://aappolicy.aappublications.org/cgi/content/full/pedia

trics;105/4/888 (accessed February 28, 2011).

Committee on Psychosocial Aspects of Child and Family Health, American Academy of Pediatrics. "The New Morbidity Revisited: A Renewed Commitment to the Psychosocial Aspects of Pediatric Care." *Pediatrics* 108 (2001): 1227–30.

Healthy Children. http://healthychildren.org (accessed February 28, 2011).

Vernick, Jon S., Stephen P. Teret, Gary A. Smith, and Daniel W. Webster. "Counseling about Firearms: Legislation is a Threat to Physicians and Their Patients." *Pediatrics*.118 (2006): 2168–72. http://www.ncbi.nlm.nih.gov/pubmed/17079591 (accessed February 28, 2011).

American Bar Association (ABA)

The American Bar Association (ABA), the national professional association for lawyers, consistently advocates the enactment of stronger gun control measures. The ABA's policymaking group, the House of Delegates, has drafted a number of positions in support of restricting the use and sale of guns. In addition to taking policy positions on gun control, the ABA has also been active in presenting its strong gun control stances to congressional committees considering firearm regulation bills. These actions have been controversial among some members of Congress. Some conservative lawmakers have expressed concern that the ABA has no special expertise in the issue of gun control and that it thus should not advocate positions on an issue divided along ideological lines. However, the ABA has remained committed to reducing gun violence in society through careful regulation of firearms. In fact, the ABA House of Delegates has deemed gun control to be one of its critical legislative priority issues.

After the assassination of President John F. Kennedy in 1963, the ABA responded by forming a task force to examine the regulation of firearms. As a result, the House of Delegates, in 1965, advocated requiring the licensing of firearm dealers; prohibiting sales to felons, mental incompetents, and minors; and controlling importation of firearms. In subsequent years, the House of Delegates continued to support a number of bills and proposals aimed at reducing gun violence in society by regulating the use and sale of guns.

In 1973, the House of Delegates supported legislation limiting the sale and possession of inexpensive imported handguns. In 1975, the ABA supported amending the Gun Control Act of 1968 to tighten up the licensing requirements of firearm dealers and to require background checks and waiting periods prior to firearm purchases. In 1983, the group opposed efforts to repeal parts of the Gun Control Act of 1968. In 1993, ABA policy supported legislation to regulate assault weapons. In 1994, the ABA endorsed providing the federal government authority to regulate firearms as consumer products, adopting required safety features such as gun locks and load indicators, and requiring gun owners to obtain and maintain a current handgun license. In 1996, the ABA supported amending the Gun Control Act of 1968 to include a private cause of action for persons suffering injury or damage as a result of a violation of gun control laws. And, in 1998, they backed a program to address gun violence by youths at schools that included peer mediation programs, firearm education programs, and enforcement and enactment of gun laws emphasizing prevention, adult responsibility, and safety.

The ABA believes gun control provisions are consistent with a proper legal interpretation of the Second Amendment.

In 1998, the chairperson of the ABA's Coordinating Committee on Gun Violence submitted to the Senate Subcommittee on the Constitution, Federalism, and Property Rights a statement of the ABA's views on issues arising under the Second Amendment. In it, the group wrote that federal and state court decisions have been consistent in the view that the Second Amendment gives all levels of government broad authority to limit private access to firearms. The statement closed by urging Congress to enact appropriate gun control measures to reduce tragic gun-related deaths and injuries in the United States, and emphasizing that the Second Amendment is not a valid reason for failing to adopt appropriate gun control measures. In 2008, the ABA filed an *amicus curiae* brief in support of gun control in *District of Columbia v. Heller*.

However, the ABA's focus on reducing violent crime in society reaches beyond the advocacy gun control positions in Congress. For example, in 1994, the group committed to a joint effort with colleagues in the public health, law enforcement, and religious communities to reduce gun violence. The ABA held a "Summit on Crime and Violence" where leading members of the bar, representatives of other organizations, and government officials planned strategies on the war against crime and violence.

Keith Rollin Eakins, with updates by Andrea Boggio

See also: Gun Control Act of 1968; Gun Violence as a Public Health Problem; Interest Groups and Gun Legislation; Second Amendment; United States Congress and Gun Legislation

Further Reading

American Bar Association. "American Bar Association Special Committee on Gun

Violence." ABA Network, 2010. http://www.abanet.org/dch/committee.cfm?com=CC108570 (accessed January 26, 2011).

American Bar Association. "Legislative and Governmental Advocacy: Letters and Testimony." ABA Network, 2010. http://www.abanet.org/poladv/letters (accessed January 26, 2011).

American Bar Association. "Letter Commenting on Proposed Changes in Federal Gun Law and Regulation (Committee on the Judiciary)." ABA Governmental Office Affairs, May 16, 2006. http://www.abanet.org/poladv/letters/crimlaw/060516letter_clmay.pdf (accessed January 26, 2011).

Brief of *Amicus Curiae*, American Bar Association, *District of Columbia v. Heller*, 554 U.S. 290 (2008) (No. 07-290).

Cottrol, Robert J., ed. *Gun Control and the Constitution: Sources and Explanations on the Second Amendment*. New York: Garland, 1994

McMillion, Rhonda. "Targeting Gun Control Again." *ABA Journal* 86 (2000): 104.

O'Connor, Karen, and Graham Barron. "Madison's Mistake? Judicial Construction of the Second Amendment." In *The Changing Politics of Gun Control*, edited by John M. Bruce and Clyde Wilcox, 74–87. Lanham, MD: Rowman & Littlefield, 1998.

Patterson, Samuel C., and Keith R. Eakins. "Congress and Gun Control" in *The Changing Politics of Gun Control*, edited by John M. Bruce and Clyde Wilcox, 45–73. Lanham, MD: Rowman & Littlefield, 1998.

Podgers, James. "Tackling Crime in the Streets." *ABA Journal* 80 (1994): 104.

Spitzer, Robert J. *The Politics of Gun Control*. 5th ed. Boulder, CO: Paradigm Publishers, 2012.

American Civil Liberties Union (ACLU)

Founded in 1920, the American Civil Liberties Union (ACLU) describes itself as "our nation's guardian of liberty," devoted to defending and preserving the "individual rights and liberties" guaranteed by the U.S. Constitution and laws (ACLU 2011a). The ACLU supports a collective interpretation of the Second Amendment. In a statement on *Gun Control*, the organization disagreed with the U.S. Supreme Court decision for *District of Columbia v. Heller*—in which the court supported the individual-right interpretation. Some of the organization's efforts are lauded by gun control advocates, while, ironically, some of its other efforts are supported by those in the opposing gun rights camp. These varying efforts reflect the organization not having an official position on gun control; no position is taken because the ACLU does not see the possession or regulation of guns as a civil liberties issue (ACLU 2011b).

The ACLU was formed during a period when fundamental personal freedoms were under serious government attack. For example, in its first year, it joined battle with U.S. attorney general A. Mitchell Palmer over the rights of union and antiwar activists to organize, hold meetings, and distribute materials. In 1925, it arranged the services of renowned attorney Clarence Darrow to defend biology teacher John T. Scopes, charged for teaching evolution, in the famous criminal trial in Tennessee. The ACLU also was instrumental in overturning a U.S. Customs Service ban on importing James Joyce's novel *Ulysses*, fought the unconstitutional 1942 internment of Japanese Americans, supported the civil rights movement, opposes attempts to criminalize flag-burning, and litigates against racism, sexism, homophobia, religious intolerance, and censorship of unpopular speech.

A national board of directors in New York sets ACLU policy. The policy is implemented through a network of autonomous affiliate offices in the 50 states. The organization has over 500,000 members, about 200 staff attorneys, and thousands of volunteer attorneys. ACLU lawyers take on about 6,000 cases each year. The organization receives no government funding.

Some ACLU statements on gun control present a sore point with gun rights activists. It holds, for example, that "the individual's right to bear arms applies only to the preservation of efficiency of a well-regulated militia. Except for lawful police and military purposes, the possession of weapons by individuals is not constitutionally protected. Therefore, there is no constitutional impediment to the regulation of firearms," according to ACLU Policy #47 ('Lectric Law Library, 2011). To the ACLU, the question is not whether to restrict gun ownership, but how much to restrict, a question it concludes is for Congress to decide.

Some local affiliates of the ACLU have been involved in opposing restrictions on firearm ownership when collateral civil liberties issues are implicated. For example, local affiliates opposed as excessive and ineffective the imposition of enhanced additional prison terms for use of guns in crimes in California, as well as legislation in Connecticut authorizing law enforcement officials to confiscate the firearms of anyone found to be an immediate danger to himself and others.

At the national level, the ACLU joined forces in the 1990s with the Gun Owners of America (GOA), a group that relentlessly criticizes the National Rifle Association for being too soft. Headed by Larry Pratt, often credited with being one of the founders of the "militia" movement, the GOA forged a coalition with the ACLU and other civil libertarian groups to fight legislation perceived as infringing on other civil rights. Thus, for example, although the GOA and the ACLU opposed different parts of an omnibus antiterrorism bill, they joined forces and were thus able to lobby effectively both conservative and liberal members of Congress, whom one or the other would have had difficulty otherwise engaging.

Thomas Diaz, with updates by
Walter F. Carroll

See also: *District of Columbia v. Heller*; Gun Owners of America (GOA); National Rifle Association (NRA); Pratt, Larry

Further Reading

ACLU (American Civil Liberties Union). "About the ACLU." 2011a. http://www.aclu.org/about-aclu-0 (accessed April 12, 2011).

ACLU (American Civil Liberties Union). "FAQ: What Is the ACLU's Position on the Second Amendment?" 2011b. http://www.aclu.org/faqs#3_5 (accessed April 12, 2011).

ACLU (American Civil Liberties Union). "Heller Decision and the Second Amendment."

ACLU (American Civil Liberties Union). "Organization News and Highlights: Second Amendment: March 4, 2002, Gun Control." Updated July 8, 2008. http://www.aclu.org/organization-news-and-highlights/second-amendment (accessed April 12, 2011).

ACLU Blog of Rights, July 1, 2008. http://www.aclu.org/2008/07/01/heller-decision-and-the-second-amendment (accessed April 12, 2011).

Diaz, Tom. *Making a Killing: The Business of Guns in America.* New York: New Press, 1999.

'Lectric Law Library, The. "ACLU Policy #47: Gun Control." (2011). http://www.lectlaw.com/files/con11.htm (accessed April 12, 2011).

Mehren, Elizabeth, "Knocking Guns from the Hands of Potential Killers." *Los Angeles Times*, October 2, 1999, A1.

American Firearms Industry Magazine

The *American Firearms Industry* magazine is a trade publication for federally licensed firearms dealers (FFLs) and over 800 gun industry–related manufacturers. It is the official monthly publication of the Professional Gun Retailers Association (PGRA) and the National Association of Federally Licensed Firearms Dealers (NAFLFD). According to the AFI website, the NAFLFD was incorporated in Illinois in 1972 and is the oldest association serving firearms dealers in the United States. Andrew Molchan, president of PGRA and NAFLFD, started the magazine in 1972, and published the first issue in January 1973.

The August 2010 issue of the magazine includes the final part of a three-part series on "The Celebration of Handguns," and the cover features pictures of three weapons. In addition to the series, this issue includes columns on Industry News and Industry Insights. As would be expected, the magazine features numerous advertisements by gun manufacturers that are aimed at gun dealers. The magazine also includes ads for various types of shooting products and a table providing numbers of National Instant Criminal Background Checks. The website for the magazine has a section of statistics that might potentially be useful, especial those on firearms production. The crime statistics section is not useful because of a lack of context for the statistics, lack of sources for some of them, and odd juxtapositions such as "Murder vs. Marital Fertility." The statistics are not providing objective evidence but are there to make certain points.

The Industry Insights column provides Molchan's analysis of the 2012 presidential election. Many Facebook postings and articles in the magazine focus heavily on politics and economics from an idiosyncratic right-wing perspective. Sometimes these are linked to gun issues, but they seem to be more broadly political and economic and feature name-calling and invective. For example, in "How to Survive the 21st Century," the 57th article in his "How to Survive Series," he examines "Crackpot Economics, Liberalism, and Demagoguery. . . . A Recipe for Disaster." He refers to Treasury Secretary Ben Bernanke, Fed chairman Timothy Geithner, and President Barack Obama as the "three stooges." Similarly, he castigates Senator Charles Schumer (D-NY) for focusing on the role of guns sold in Midwestern states in New York City crime. He suggests that Schumer and his "fellow Communist crackpots" avoid the real reasons for that crime. In this article, he does not explain what the real reasons are, but his use of the term "diversity" and "diversities" in quotes several times suggest that race and ethnicity might have something to do with it, although Molchan insists that he is not "anti-Black." Molchan does not just criticize Democrats. For example, he refers to George W. Bush as "insane."

Walter F. Carroll

See also: Firearm Dealers; National Instant Criminal Background Check System

Further Reading
American Firearms Industry. http://www .amfire.com/ (accessed May 16, 2011).

American Handgunner. *See* Gun Magazines

American Hunter. *See* Gun Magazines

American Jewish Congress (AJC)

The American Jewish Congress (AJC) is a lobbying, legal, and cultural organization. In recent years, the AJC has become a strong proponent of restrictive gun laws.

World War I had a profound effect on Jewish life in the United States. The war was accompanied by a marked awakening of Jewish consciousness among those who had earlier stood aloof from their Jewish heritage. As the United States prepared to enter the war, a group of American Jews believed that a united American Jewish voice could best protect their convictions, desires, and dreams. This resulted in a preliminary conference held in Philadelphia in 1916. The first American Jewish Congress was convened in Philadelphia's Metropolitan Opera House in December 1918. In 1920, Rabbi Stephen Wise was charged with the task of transforming the succession of haphazardly planned Jewish gatherings into a permanent organization intended to safeguard Jews everywhere—in the United States, overseas, and especially in what was then the British colony of Palestine. After the threat of Nazi Germany had passed with the end of World War II, the AJC broadened its scope of activism to include extensive work on civil rights for blacks and many other issues.

The AJC has a membership of approximately 50,000 and is headquartered in New York City. It also maintains an Israeli office in Jerusalem. The group holds a convention every two years, at which time it sets the organization's agenda and elects a president who serves a two-year term. Policy is formulated in the interim by the AJC's Governing Council and the Executive Committee. The American Jewish Congress is sometimes confused with a separate group, the American Jewish Committee, which shares the same acronym.

The centerpiece of the AJC's gun control work is a petition campaign called "Stop the Guns: Protect Our Kids!" The petitions demand that the U.S. Congress enact legislation to require that (1) all gun buyers pass a government test to receive a license; (2) all guns be registered with the government; (3) prospective gun buyers provide fingerprints and a photograph to receive a license; (4) firearm manufacturers be "required to install safety devices to prevent accidental and inadvertent firing"; and (5) licensing and registration rules that currently apply to retail firearm dealers be applied to all firearm transfers. The petition campaign is supported by a variety of gun prohibition and gun control organizations, and the AJC coordinates its work with other antigun lobbies and works in support of a wide variety of other proposed gun laws.

The AJC was party to an *amicus curiae* brief in the U.S. Supreme Court case *District of Columbia v. Heller* (2008), supporting the District's de facto ban on firearms as a means of self-defense. The brief stated that "the Second Amendment was designed to protect state authority," and did not protect an individual right to keep and bear arms.

Opinion polls typically show that Jews are strongly supportive of gun control, though some American Jews do not share the AJC's views on firearm ownership. For example, Jews for the Preservation of Firearms Ownership (JPFO) calls gun control "victim disarmament" and charges that the AJC's gun control activism undermines traditional Jewish values. The JPFO believes that "Jews, like everyone else, have a duty to protect and defend themselves and their families against violence."

Paul Gallant and Joanne Eisen

See also: *District of Columbia v. Heller*; Gun Control; Jews for the Preservation of Firearms Ownership (JPFO)

Further Reading

American Jewish Congress. http://www.aj congress.org/site/PageServer (accessed June 12, 2011).

American Jewish Congress. "Stop the Guns: Protect Our Kids." http://www.ajcongress .org/site/PageServer?pagename=gcimage6_2 (accessed June 12, 2011).

Jews for the Preservation of Firearms Ownership. http://www.jpfo.org/ (accessed June 12, 2011).

American Medical Association (AMA)

The American Medical Association (AMA) is an organization of physicians whose goal is "to promote the art and science of medicine and the betterment of public health." The AMA believes that private firearm ownership is a public health menace and has consistently advocated strong gun control provisions to reduce citizen access to firearms.

The AMA was founded in 1847 by Nathan Davis at the Academy of Natural Sciences in Philadelphia. In 2010, approximately 15 percent of practicing physicians in the United States belonged to the organization, and it had a combined membership of approximately 216,000 medical students and physicians (significantly smaller than it was a decade earlier, when this total was closer to 300,000; see AMA 2011, 27; see Peck 2010 for a discussion of the decline).

According to the AMA, the ownership and use of firearms, especially handguns, pose serious threats to public health. The AMA believes that handguns are one of the main causes of intentional and unintentional injuries and death in the United States.

In 1992, the AMA's Council on Scientific Affairs promulgated a report and position paper on assault weapons (guns with a military appearance), and declared them to be a public health hazard in the United States. It recommended legislation to restrict the sale and private ownership of such firearms.

Among the critics of the AMA report was Dr. Edgar A. Suter. In 1994, Suter said, "The AMA Council on Scientific Affairs did not conduct a rigorous scientific evaluation before supporting a ban on assault weapons. The Council appears to have unquestioningly accepted common misperceptions and even partisan misrepresentations regarding the nature and uses of assault weapons. . . . While an assault weapon ban may have appeared to the Council to be a simple solution to America's exaggerated 'epidemic' of violence, a scholarly review of the literature finds no reliable data to support such a ban. Unfortunately the Council's faulty call for prohibition may distract legislators and the public from addressing effective methods of controlling violence" (1994b).

The AMA encourages its members to use regular checkups as an opportunity to inquire from patients whether firearms are present in their household, to educate patients about the dangers of firearms, to advise patients to educate their children and neighbors about the dangers of firearms, and to remind patients to obtain firearm safety locks, lock up all firearms, and store ammunition separately.

The AMA supports numerous legislative initiatives dealing with firearms. These include: waiting periods and background checks for all handgun purchases; the requirement that manufacturers incorporate a variety of features in all firearms, including visible loaded-gun indicators, trigger locks, and an increased minimum force needed to activate a trigger; increased licensing fees for firearm dealers; increased federal and state surtaxes on manufacturers, dealers, and purchasers of handguns and semiautomatic firearms, as well as on the ammunition such firearms use, with the revenue allocated for health and law enforcement activities related to the prevention and control of violence in the United States; mandatory destruction of any firearms obtained in gun-surrender programs; a ban on certain types of bullets; and a ban on the possession and use of firearms and ammunition by unsupervised youths under the age of 18.

In his inauguration address delivered at its annual meeting on June 20, 2001, incoming president Richard F. Corlin renewed the AMA's push for more restrictive firearm laws. In a speech devoted entirely to the issue of firearm-related violence, Corlin declared that "gun violence—both self-inflicted and against others—is now a serious public health crisis," one that is "a uniquely American epidemic." According to Corlin, "The very language of the Second Amendment refutes any argument that it was intended to guarantee every citizen an unfettered right to any kind of weapon. . . . [W]e don't regulate guns in America. We do regulate other dangerous products like cars and prescription drugs and tobacco and alcohol. . . . In fact, no other consumer industry in the United States—not even the tobacco industry—has been allowed to so totally evade accountability for the harm their products cause to human beings. Just the gun industry."

Corlin called for re-funding of firearm research by the Centers for Disease Control and Prevention (CDC) and its National Center for Injury Prevention and Control, including the establishment of a National Violent Death Reporting System for both fatal and nonfatal gun injuries. (CDC funding for firearm research was terminated by Congress in 1996. While Corlin blamed the loss of funding on "heavy lobbying by the antigun control groups," critics had charged that the CDC's research on firearms was biased, promoted an antigun agenda, and failed to address any of the benefits accruing to private firearm ownership, such as self-defense. The outcome of the congressional action was a prohibition on public funding by the CDC "to advocate or promote gun control.")

A few physician groups have been highly critical of the AMA and its position on private firearm ownership. For example, Doctors for Responsible Gun Ownership (DRGO) believes that social activists in the medical and public health fields (including the AMA) have used their authority to misrepresent gun ownership as a "disease." According to DRGO, organized medical groups like the AMA use discredited advocacy research and poor medical scholarship to justify their political stand against firearms and gun owners. Furthermore, they ignore legitimate criminological research because it generally proves that good citizens use guns wisely.

DRGO has criticized the AMA's practice of encouraging doctors to use their professional authority and patient trust as a means of advancing a political agenda for gun control. A doctor's responsibility is to place the patient's needs above all else. However, a physician reverses this priority when, because of passionate political beliefs, he tries to influence a patient about guns and firearm ownership. In doing so, that doctor crosses the line from healer to political activist. DRGO maintains that this approach places such intervention in the area of unethical physician conduct called "boundary violations" (see Claremont Institute 2011).

The AMA's best-known publication is the *Journal of the American Medical*

Association (*JAMA*), published weekly. While *JAMA* explicitly states that its editorials do not reflect the views of the AMA, they nevertheless often mirror its philosophy. Each year, *JAMA* publishes a number of "theme" issues. One of these is usually on the subject of violence. The editorials accompanying these issues articulate the empathy, anguish, and frustration physicians face in the aftermath of violence, and their desire to prevent and eliminate violence. However, while many of *JAMA*'s violence "theme" issues have contained articles dealing with guns and firearm-related violence, none of them have addressed the positive elements of firearm ownership (e.g., self-defense) that may prevent violence.

Although the vast majority of *JAMA* articles on firearms have supported gun control, a notable exception was an article in 2000 by Jens Ludwig and Philip Cook, which found that the Brady Bill had no significant effect on homicide rates or on overall suicide rates. A *JAMA* editorial that accompanied the study by Ludwig and Cook argued that the flaw in the Brady Bill was that its provisions applied only to sales by licensed gun dealers, and not to informal transactions among family, friends, or other acquaintances.

For a full policy statement on firearms and a discussion of the AMA's fundamental contention that "uncontrolled ownership and use of firearms, especially handguns, is a serious threat to the public's health," see the organization's *National Advisory Council on Violence and Abuse, Policy Compendium April* (2008, 30–33).

Paul Gallant and Joanne Eisen

See also: Brady Handgun Violence Prevention Act (Brady Bill); Child Access Prevention (CAP) Laws; Doctors for Responsible Gun Ownership (DRGO); Gun Buyback Programs; Gun Violence as a Public Health Problem; National Violent Death Reporting System; Trigger Locks

Further Reading

American Medical Association. http://www.ama-assn.org/ (accessed June 12, 2011).

American Medical Association. *National Advisory Council on Violence and Abuse, Policy Compendium*. April 2008. http://www.ama-assn.org/ama1/pub/upload/mm/386/vio_policy_comp.pdf (accessed June 14, 2011)

American Medical Association. *2010 AMA Annual Report: Moving Medicine Forward.* April 2010. http://www.ama-assn.org/resources/doc/about-ama/2010-annual-report.pdf (accessed June 14, 2011).

Claremont Institute for the Study of Statesmanship and Political Philosophy. "Doctors for Responsible Gun Ownership." http://www.claremont.org/projects/projectid.39/project_detail.asp (accessed June 12, 2011).

Cook, Philip J., Bruce A. Lawrence, and Jens Ludwig. "The Medical Costs of Gunshot Injuries in the United States." *Journal of the American Medical Association* 282 (1999): 447–54.

Council on Scientific Affairs. "Assault Weapons as a Public Health Hazard in the United States." *Journal of the American Medical Association* 267 (1992): 3067–70.

Faria, Miguel A., Jr. "Public Health and Gun Control—A Review." *Medical Sentinel* 6 (2001): 11–18. http://www.haciendapub.com/gunpage4.html (accessed June 12, 2011).

Ludwig, Jens, and Philip J. Cook. "Homicide and Suicide Rates Associated with Implementation of the Brady Handgun Violence Prevention Act." *Journal of the American Medical Association* 284 (2000): 585–91.

McAfee, Robert E. "Physicians and Domestic Violence: Can We Make a Difference?"

Journal of the American Medical Association 273 (1995): 1790–91.

Peck, Peggy. "AMA: Little to Cheer About as AMA Meetings Open." *MedPage Today*, June 13, 2010. http://www.medpagetoday.com/PublicHealthPolicy/GeneralProfessionalIssues/20640 (accessed June 14, 2011).

Rosenfeld, Richard. "Tracing the Brady Act's Connection with Homicide and Suicide Trends." *Journal of the American Medical Association* 284 (2000): 616–18.

Suter, Edgar A. " 'Assault Weapons' Revisited —An Analysis of the AMA Report." *Journal of the Medical Association of Georgia* 83 (1994a): 281–89.

Suter, Edgar A. "Guns in the Medical Literature—A Failure of Peer Review." *Journal of the Medical Association of Georgia* 83 (1994b): 133–48.

Wheeler, Timothy. "Boundary Violations: Gun Politics in the Doctor's Office." *Medical Sentinel* 4 (1999): 60–61.

American Revolution

Personal firearms were vitally important for the success of the American Revolution. The brunt of the initial fighting during the war was borne by state militias, composed of citizen-soldiers who carried their own hunting rifles and personal weapons into combat. However, ultimate victory over the British rested on the ability of the Continental army to acquire heavy military weapons, including artillery. Nonetheless, the importance of a well-armed citizenry in the struggle for independence would continue to impact American politics as debate over the role and necessity of firearms in society continues into the twenty-first century.

In many ways, the American Revolution was an anomaly. Compared to people in Europe and other areas of the world, the white citizens of the British colonies of

A line of Minute Men are fired upon by British troops at the Battle of Lexington, April 19, 1775. (Library of Congress)

North America had greater political freedom and higher standards of living. Since their initial establishment, the various colonies had been granted considerable political latitude by the British Crown. In fact, the colonies were left essentially to run themselves, with the exception of trade and foreign policy. However, this tradition of "benign neglect" came to an end following the French and Indian War (1756–1763). The colonial militias had not been able to defend the 13 colonies, and London had been forced to send troops to North America and spend considerable sums on the defense of the colonies. Following the war, London attempted to recoup its expenditures, but the British met considerable resistance from the colonies. Because the colonists had no direct representation in the British Parliament, many felt that it was unfair for them to be subject to "taxation without representation." The colonists undertook sporadic acts of civil disobedience against the new tax measures, including the famous Boston Tea Party. Colonists also opposed the issuance of writs and general warrants that allowed the British to search homes and seize property without specific search warrants. Finally, the quartering of British troops in personal homes, without the consent of the owners, was a source of resentment toward the Crown.

In response to British actions, the colonists established a Continental Congress in 1774 to organize their resistance efforts and coordinate their policies toward the Crown. The colonies had several significant advantages in their conflict with the British. The most obvious was the great distance between Great Britain and the colonies. In addition, since their formation, the defense of the colonies had rested on the white male population, rather than the regular British army. During instances of conflict with

Native American tribes or when there were bandit gangs or pirates in operation or during episodes of civil disturbance, it usually fell to each colony's individual militia units to take action. All able-bodied white males over the age of 18 were liable for service in the militia. In addition, many colonies also mandated militia service by free African Americans and slaves under specific conditions. Each individual was expected to provide his own firearm, and mounted units required the militiaman to provide his own horse and equipment. Each colony maintained a variety of military equipment and supplies for use by the militia. Such equipment included cannon and artillery equipment, firearms, and such miscellaneous military supplies as tents, carriages, and entrenching equipment. The colonies also maintained supplies of ammunition.

As tensions grew between the colonies and London, the various militia units were reorganized. The main purpose behind the reforms was to ensure that the militia units would be loyal to the individual colonies and not to the Crown. The militias were also given expanded training to ready them for potential military action against regular British forces. There were alarm systems in place to alert the citizen-soldiers to hostile action so they could be called up and deployed quickly. Each individual militiaman was supposed to be ready to muster at a moment's notice. Because of this, the militia troops began to be popularly known as "minutemen."

The first shots of the American Revolution came during an attempt by the British to seize the ammunition and heavy weapons of the New England colonies' militias. In April 1775, British troops moved to confiscate the militia stores of the Massachusetts colony at the depot in Concord. On April 19, the first shot of the revolution was fired at

Lexington, and eight minutemen were killed and nine wounded during the ensuing skirmish with British regulars. The militia retreated and the British marched to Concord where they captured some minor equipment (the militia had hidden most of the supplies). After a second brief skirmish, the British marched back to Boston. However, during the British retreat, the minutemen used the unconventional guerrilla tactics that they employed against Native Americans and sniped at the British troops. The militia inflicted 273 casualties on the regulars while suffering 90 dead and wounded. In many ways, the battles at Lexington and Concord foreshadowed much of the combat of the coming war. The American forces were able to inflict significant casualties on the British, but had difficulty beating the regular British forces in pitched battles.

On July 4, 1776, the Continental Congress approved the Declaration of Independence from Great Britain. Following the Declaration, the Continental Congress dispatched envoys to Europe to seek support against the British. The Americans specifically sought foreign aid to help offset British naval superiority and to acquire military weapons, especially heavy artillery. The American forces also needed standard firearms, since the militia forces brought their own guns, which often used different ammunition. In addition, the American forces needed military training.

The minutemen had several distinct advantages over the British. They were more mobile than the British forces and could exist without the large supply infrastructure required by the Crown's forces. More significantly, many of the American forces had superior firearms. At the start of the war, the most common weapon was the smoothbore Brown Bess musket. The highly disciplined British troops could fire three times

as fast as their American counterparts, but the massed volley fire of the British was fairly inaccurate. Americans tended to have slower rates of fire, but they were more accurate. However, the accuracy range of the Brown Bess was only about 60 yards. As the revolution progressed, more and more Americans began using the Pennsylvania or Kentucky rifle. This firearm was rifled with twisting groves through the barrel, which made the bullet spin. It also has a longer barrel than the Brown Bess. These factors greatly increased the accuracy and range of the weapon. In the right hands, the rifled firearms of the minutemen were accurate at 200 yards and had an extreme range of 400 yards. These guns made American soldiers highly effective as snipers and irregular troops.

Throughout the American Revolution, the majority of American soldiers served in their respective state militia units. Usually, the troops preferred militia service because it kept them closer to their homes and they were only called to service for short periods of time. After the Battle of Bunker Hill, Gen. George Washington realized that to defeat the British, the Americans would need to establish a regular standing military force with the kind of training and discipline that was the hallmark of the British army. The result was the Continental army. During the winter of 1777–1778, Washington camped his army in Valley Forge. With the aid of foreign soldiers who had been attracted to the American cause, Washington transformed the collection of militia units and volunteers into an effective fighting force.

The American victory at Saratoga in 1778 was a major turning point in the revolution since it demonstrated to the major European powers the capability of the Continental army. After the victory, France and Spain began

murder rate in the United States greatly exceeds those of other industrialized democracies. It argues that only effective firearm-related legislation can reduce high levels of firearm-related murders and injuries.

Walter F. Carroll

See also: Assault Weapons Ban of 1994; Background Checks; Brady Handgun Violence Prevention Act (Brady Bill); Child Access Prevention (CAP) Laws; Coalition to Stop Gun Violence (CSGV); Democratic Party and Gun Control; Ideologies—Conservative and Liberal; Interest Groups and Gun Legislation; Lautenberg, Frank R.

Further Reading

Americans for Democratic Action. "*Handgun Control* No. 251." http://www.adaction.org/pages/issues/all-policy-resolutions/politics-amp-government/251-handgun-control.php (accessed February 28, 2011).

Americans for Democratic Action. http://www.adaction.org/ (accessed February 28, 2011).

Brock, Clifton. *Americans for Democratic Action: Its Role in National Politics*. Westport, CT: Greenwood Press, 1985.

Gillon, Steven M. *Politics and Vision: The ADA and American Liberalism, 1947–1985*. New York: Oxford University Press, 1987.

Americans for Gun Safety.
See Third Way

America's First Freedom

America's First Freedom is a magazine published monthly by the National Rifle Association (NRA) that focuses on guns and politics. Complementing the NRA's two other main publications, *American Rifleman* and *American Hunter*, *America's First Freedom* is sold as an alternative to what the NRA views as the mainstream media's bias against guns. *America's First Freedom* was first published in 1997 as *The American Guardian*, but was changed to its current title in June 2000.

NRA leaders introduced *America's First Freedom* a little over a year after the Columbine High School tragedy and shortly before the 2000 elections. The name change signaled a redoubling of the organization's efforts to oppose candidates who supported gun control and as a way to mobilize its surging membership. The new magazine's first task was to warn of the loss of gun rights if Democratic presidential candidate Al Gore was elected. As vice president, he and President Bill Clinton sought several gun control measures, highlighted by their support for what became the Brady Handgun Violence Prevention Act (1993) and the Assault Weapons Ban of 1994. Gore expressed support for additional forms of gun control during his presidential campaign, including child safety locks and background checks on all purchases at gun shows. The first cover of *America's First Freedom* featured a morphing of facial features of Clinton and Gore, along with the caption, "He's Clinton to the Gore: The Face of Gun Hatred in America" (Melzer 2009). The premiere issue of *America's First Freedom* captured what would be the magazine's and the NRA's core arguments throughout the next decade: the Democratic Party and its leaders pose the greatest threat to gun rights, threats to gun rights are greater today than at any moment in the NRA's history, and defending gun rights is essential if other individual rights and freedoms are to be preserved for future generations.

America's First Freedom identifies various groups and individuals it views as threats to gun rights, including the United Nations, political parties around the world, individual politicians (typically Democrats, with an occasional Republican), gun control groups, organizations that have supported gun control measures (such as the American Medical Association), media organizations and journalists, and celebrities such as Michael Moore. Magazine content revolves around firearms as they relate to federal and state legislation and laws, court cases, media coverage, and crime, and is accompanied by slick artwork as well as a bevy of advertisements mostly associated with guns and gear.

Each month, *America's First Freedom* includes columns written by the NRA executive vice president, the current NRA president, and the magazine's editor, along with a report from the NRA's Institute for Legislative Action. "The Armed Citizen" is a collection of news stories featuring people who have lawfully used guns in self-defense, fending off burglars, robbers, and other offenders. It first appeared in the *American Rifleman* many decades ago as a way to highlight the NRA's argument that guns can reduce crime, and is a regular feature in *America's First Freedom*. Other regular pieces reflecting the magazine's tenor have included a "Freedom Index" (and later a meter), which the NRA offered as a barometer of the status of gun rights based on current events such as gun legislation and election results, and a monthly "BAN-DE-MODIUM" award given to someone whom the NRA deemed a threat to gun rights. The magazine also dedicates a small fraction of its coverage to non-political issues such as new guns and shooting products. *America's First Freedom*'s primary purpose remains informing NRA members about threats to gun rights, whether legislative, judicial, or social.

Scott Melzer

See also: *American Rifleman*; Assault Weapons Ban of 1994; Brady Handgun Violence Prevention Act (Brady Bill); Clinton, William J.; Columbine High School Tragedy; Democratic Party and Gun Control; National Rifle Association (NRA)

Further Reading

Melzer, Scott. *Gun Crusaders: The NRA's Culture War*. New York: New York University Press, 2009.

National Rifle Association. *America's First Freedom*. http://www.nrapublications.org/index.php/first-freedom/ (accessed June 4, 2011).

Ammunition, Large Capacity Magazines. *See* Assault Weapons Ban of 1994; Boxer, Barbara

Ammunition, Regulations of

Federal Law

The Gun Control Act of 1968 requires a federal license to make (except for personal use) or deal in ammunition. Dealers may not sell long-gun ammunition to a person under 18, or handgun ammunition to a person under 21. The sale of ammunition to any person who is prohibited by federal law from possessing a firearm is forbidden. Likewise, a person forbidden to possess a firearm may not possess ammunition, either. As with firearms, any participation in the sale or transport of ammunition that is known to be stolen is illegal. When ammunition is shipped in interstate or foreign commerce, it must be labeled, and the carrier must obtain a written acknowledgement of receipt.

Congress is sometimes careful to ensure that general laws are not implemented by administrators so as to ban ammunition. For example, the 1972 Consumer Product Safety Act specifically forbade its use as an administrative vehicle to restrict firearms.

But in response to requests from gun control advocates, the Consumer Product Safety Commission declared that although it had no jurisdiction over firearms, it had jurisdiction to consider outlawing handgun ammunition. So Congress enacted the Firearms Safety and Consumer Protection Act of 1976, to make it clear that the commission had no authority over ammunition, either.

Similarly, the Toxic Substances Control Act (TSCA) gives the Environmental Protection Agency broad powers to ban almost anything that EPA determines to "present an unreasonable risk of injury to health or the environment." But the statute specifically forbids TSCA from being used to regulate firearms or ammunition (15 U.S.C. § 2602(B)). A petition for EPA to regulate the lead component of ammunition was rejected by the agency in 2010, as forbidden by the statute.

In 1991, the U.S. Fish and Wildlife Service prohibited use or possession of lead shot during the hunting of waterfowl. The ban was accomplished by an administrative regulation, based on powers granted by the Endangered Species Act. Critics objected that the protection of endangered avian predators did not require an all-out ban in every waterfowl-hunting area in every state. Twenty-three states impose some type of additional, but limited, restrictions on the use of lead shot in the hunting of some upland game-bird species.

Like firearms, ammunition is subject to an 11 percent federal excise tax, pursuant to the 1937 Pittman-Robertson Act (16 U.S.C. § 669). The revenues are used for a matching grant program to the states to foster wildlife conservation, game management, hunter safety education, and the construction of shooting ranges. Since the tax is moderate and the revenues are used to foster Second Amendment activities, the tax appears constitutionally valid.

In contrast, there have sometimes been proposals to impose punitive taxes on handgun ammunition. For example, in 1993, Senator Daniel Patrick Moynihan (D-NY) proposed a 50 percent tax on all center-fire handgun ammunition (essentially, anything but .22-caliber ammunition), and a 10,000 percent tax on Winchester's "Black Talon" brand of defensive ammunition. Taxes intended to discourage the exercise of a constitutional right are generally considered unconstitutional. For example, when Louisiana governor Huey Long and the state legislature retaliated against press criticism of them by imposing a 2 percent gross revenue tax on large-circulation newspapers, the Supreme Court ruled it unconstitutional (*Grosjean v. American Press Co.*, 297 U. S. 233 (1936)). Likewise, when Minnesota, apparently without malign intent, imposed a special tax on paper and ink, the court ruled it unconstitutional (*Minneapolis Star & Tribune Co. v. Minnesota Commissioner of Revenue*, 460 U.S. 575 (1983)).

Armor-Piercing Ammunition

A 1986 federal law (amended in 1994) prohibits armor-piercing ammunition for handguns. The statute specifies that "armor piercing ammunition" is a handgun bullet "constructed entirely" from "tungsten alloys, steel, iron, brass, bronze, beryllium copper, or depleted uranium," or with a jacket whose weight comprise more than 25 percent of the projectile's total weight (18 U.S.C. § 922(a)(17)(B)).

Some persons—such as the producers of the film *Lethal Weapon 3*—imagine that a Teflon coating gives a bullet special penetrating powers; this is not correct, and the federal definition has nothing to do with Teflon. Teflon reduces the lead abrasion caused by the bullet's movement down the barrel of the gun. Thus, the barrel is kept cleaner and is protected from excessive wear. Also, reduced abrasion means that fewer tiny lead air particles are produced, so the air is cleaner—an especially important consideration at indoor shooting ranges.

In addition, a Teflon coating on a bullet also makes the bullet safer to use in a self-defense context. The Teflon helps the bullet "grab" a hard surface such as glass or metal, and thus significantly reduces the risk of a dangerous ricochet. Similarly, canes or walking sticks are often coated with Teflon, so that they will not slip on hard, smooth surfaces.

The federal definition is a content standard, based on the bullet's composition. From time to time, gun control advocates, such as President Clinton and Senator Edward Kennedy, have attempted to replace the content standard with a "penetration standard": any ammunition that could penetrate a standard police vest would be outlawed. Because police vests are designed to block handgun ammunition but not rifle ammunition (which is more powerful, in part because of higher velocity), most rifle ammunition would become illegal. Neither before 1986 nor thereafter has there ever been a case of an American police officer killed because a bullet penetrated his vest, or killed with "armor-piercing ammunition."

The federal ban prohibits the manufacture or import of certain ammunition, but does not apply to (1) the manufacture or importation of such ammunition for the use of the United States or any of its departments or agencies, or for the use of any state or any of its departments, agencies, or political subdivisions; (2) the manufacture of such ammunition for the purpose of exportation; and (3) the manufacture or importation for the purposes of testing or experiment authorized by the secretary of the treasury. Federal law also prohibits any manufacturer or importer to sell or deliver armor-piercing ammunition, with the same use and purpose exceptions as for the manufacture or import of such ammunition.

In addition, federal law requires that licensed importers and licensed manufacturers mark all armor-piercing projectiles and packages containing such projectiles for distribution in the manner prescribed by the secretary of the treasury by regulation. The secretary must furnish information to each licensed dealer defining which projectiles are considered to be armor-piercing.

Before the 1986 law, many persons possessed such ammunition, typically acquired from military surplus. Federal law does not criminalize the continuing possession or private transfer of these now-old, pre-1986 supplies. However, if a federally licensed firearms dealer sells some of the old ammunition, he must keep records of the residence and identity of the purchaser, similar to the records that must be kept for the sale of firearms. Except for armor-piercing ammunition, licensed dealers do not have to keep records of ammunition sales.

Federal law mandates an extra prison term of not less than five years for committing a federal crime of violence or a drug-trafficking crime by using or while carrying a firearm and at the same time possessing armor-piercing ammunition that can be fired in that firearm.

State and Local Laws

Most states have parallel provisions to the federal laws. A few states go further. For example, Massachusetts and Illinois require a firearm identification card to purchase and possess any ammunition. A number of states have complex regulations on armor-piercing ammunition—California and New Jersey, for example—as well as on incendiary ammunition—California, for example.

New Jersey bans hollow-point ammunition, with some exceptions. New York City bans the possession of ordinary rifle and shotgun ammunition, except for persons who hold a New York City rifle-shotgun license; when a consumer purchases such ammunition, she must display her license to the dealer. There is a variety of other state and local laws on ammunition, although the spread of statewide preemption laws in the last three decades has considerably reduced special local laws. Even so, prudence dictates that a person become familiar with the laws of a particular state and locality on the subject before attempting to possess, acquire, or transfer ammunition.

Case Law

In the 1939 case *United States v. Miller*, the Supreme Court stated that historically, the militiaman's "possession of arms also implied the possession of ammunition, and the authorities paid quite as much attention to the latter as to the former." The court also noted the seventeenth-century Massachusetts laws that provided that two-thirds of every militia company should be musketeers and that each of them should have not only a musket, but also other equipment, including ammunition comprising "one pound of powder, twenty bullets, and two fathoms of match."

As the court explained, mandatory ammunition ownership by militiamen (comprising most of the able-bodied adult male population) continued after independence. For example, a 1784 Massachusetts law directed that the militia comprise all able-bodied men under 60 years of age and required that every noncommissioned officer and private soldier of the militia "shall equip himself [with ammunition], and be constantly provided with a good fire arm" (180). A 1786 New York law required that all militiamen—that is, all able-bodied male citizens of the

state between 16 and 45 years of age residing within New York—had to provide themselves with a "good Musket or Firelock" as well as, among other things, "Twenty-four Cartridges . . . each Cartridge containing a proper Quantity of Powder and Ball" (181). And a 1785 Virginia militia statute required that every noncommissioned officer and private should appear at the appropriate muster field "armed, equipped, and accoutered . . . with a good, clean musket carrying an ounce of ball . . . a cartridge box properly made, to contain and secure twenty cartridges fitted to his musket . . . and . . . one pound of good powder, and four pounds of lead, including twenty blind cartridges" (181–82).

Thus, to the court, arms and ammunition were inextricably interwoven. Second Amendment arms possession necessarily implied the possession of suitable ammunition. The Supreme Court's modern cases on the Second Amendment agree.

McDonald v. City of Chicago (2010) explained that the Fourteenth Amendment was enacted in part to prohibit states from violating Second Amendment rights. Among such violations was a post–Civil War in Mississippi law, which said that no freedman "shall keep or carry fire-arms of any kind, or any ammunition."

Dissenting in *District of Columbia v. Heller* (2008), Justice Breyer argued that the D.C. handgun ban was permissible because "The law concerns one class of weapons, handguns, leaving residents free to possess shotguns and rifles, along with ammunition." As Justice Breyer recognized, the right to arms, whatever its scope, implies a parallel right to suitable ammunition.

The majority opinions in both *Heller* and *McDonald* both cited an 1871 Tennessee case, *Andrews v. State* (50 Tenn. 165) as correctly construing the Second Amendment. In *Andrews*, the Tennessee Supreme Court ruled that, pursuant to the Tennessee Constitution, all Tennessee citizens had a right to keep and bear arms and that the "right to keep arms necessarily involves the right . . . to purchase and provide ammunition suitable for such arms" (178).

David B. Kopel and David I. Caplan

See also: Ammunition, Types of; Armor-Piercing Ammunition; Ballistic Identification System; Black Talon; Cartridges; *District of Columbia v. Heller*; Gun Control Act of 1968; *McDonald v. City of Chicago*; Preemption Laws; *United States v. Miller*

Further Reading

Halbrook, Stephen P. *Firearms Law Deskbook: 2010–2011 Edition*. Eagan, MN: Thomson Reuters, 2010.

Ammunition, Types of

Ammunition types can be classified roughly by rim design, ignition system, and projectile type. For four centuries, humankind has struggled to "marry" projectile, powder, and ignition system into a conveniently loaded unit. In the seventeenth century, musketeers carried bandoliers of wooden capsules filled with powder and ball; since the musketeer also carried a burning match, these proved extremely dangerous to the user. In the eighteenth and nineteenth centuries, tubular paper cartridges, secured in a leather cartridge box, were employed; the user removed the cartridge, tore the paper open with his teeth, and emptied the contents down the barrel. As repeating firearms evolved in the nineteenth century, the modern "fixed" cartridge came into use, with powder contained in a brass case with the projectile held by friction at one end and the ignition system mounted at the other. Brass was used due to its springy nature; a brass cartridge would expand when the powder ignited, sealing the breech of the barrel, but spring back to nearly its original diameter to allow the fired cartridge to be easily removed from the gun. Mild steel has sometimes been used as a cartridge case material, but is much less satisfactory. Untreated steel cases will rust, and varnished ones can cause jamming as the varnish rubs off inside the chamber.

Fixed cartridges can be classified by their rim type, their ignition system, or their projectile. A repeating firearm must be able to mechanically extract and remove the empty cartridge after firing, a task accomplished by a metal hook-like device known as an extractor. The cartridge in turn must have a feature that the extractor can grasp. In a rimmed cartridge, the base of the cartridge extends outward in a disk, the rim, which the extractor can grasp. In a rimless cartridge, there is no protruding rim, but a groove is cut around the base of the cartridge, and the extractor grasps the groove. Variations include the semirimmed cartridge, which has a groove and a rim that protrudes only slightly; and the belted cartridge, in which the base of the cartridge case expands outward into a strengthening belt with a cut groove.

Cartridges can also be classed by their ignition system, the principal ones being rimfire and center-fire. Rimfire cartridges are rimmed, but the rim is hollow. An explosive primer compound is placed inside the rim, and when the firing pin strikes and crushes the rim, the compound explodes and ignites the powder. Since the metal of the rim must be quite thin to be crushable, rimfire ignition is restricted to cartridges of very low power. Today, only low-power .22-caliber cartridges are made in rimfire form. In the center-fire cartridge, the priming compound is placed in a metal capsule, the primer. The primer is mounted in the center of the cartridge's base; a cartridge

A pile of 5.56mm-caliber rifle cartridges. (Eldad Carin)

of center-fire form can withstand considerably higher pressures than a rimfire.

In addition to these main types, there are some rare forms of ignition. A few modern rifles use electronic ignition, in which an electric current passes through the primer to detonate it. Early cartridges (c. 1850) sometimes used a pin fire, in which the hammer struck a pointed pin extending sideways through the cartridge. The Prussian "needle gun" of the 1850s had a paper cartridge with primer located at the base of the bullet; a very long firing pin penetrated the cartridge and struck the primer.

Cartridges may further be classified by the nature of the projectile mounted in them. The earliest projectiles were simply solid lead or lead alloy. These materials were, however, too soft to take the higher velocities that arms designers reached in the late nineteenth century. At that point, jacketed bullets, with a lead core encased in a harder metal jacket, came into use; the harder jacket could take the higher velocities without smearing the inside of the barrel with lead. A copper-nickel alloy was first used for the jacket; it was found that this tended to leave hard-to-remove metal deposits inside the barrel, so "gilding metal," a copper alloy, then became standard jacket material. Mild steel has also been employed as a jacket material.

Jacketed bullets took several forms. In the full-metal-jacketed projectile, required for warfare by sundry international conventions, the copper alloy jacket covers the bullet's nose, inhibiting its expansion after impact. In the soft-point projectile, the jacket does not cover the nose; the exposed soft lead nose crushes upon impact and causes the projectile to expand. (The soft point originated as the military "Dum-Dum," whose use was subsequently outlawed in warfare.) In the hollow-point projectile, a hollow cavity of varying size is located in the nose, likewise promoting bullet expansion. Bullet designers have also evolved variations on these forms, in which the bullet's point is composed of a plastic or bronze tip, enabling it to keep a sharp point but still expand.

Military cartridges take an even greater variety of projectiles. The full-metal-jacketed bullet, described above, is the traditional form. Armor-piercing projectiles contain a large, pointed, steel core; currently many forms of full-metal-jacketed ammunition also contain a small steel penetrator under the nose. Incendiary projectiles contain compounds that produce an incendiary flash when the bullet nose is crushed by impact. Tracer projectiles contain a manner of flare compound that burns during the bullet's flight, making its path visible so that a machine gunner can correct his aim. Additionally, there have been experiments with small-caliber explosive projectiles. Different features are sometimes combined, the ultimate combination being the armor-piercing incendiary tracer (APIT) projectile.

These essentially comprise the forms of ammunition used in rifles and handguns; shotgun ammunition takes different forms. The most commonly produced form has a plastic cartridge case on which a brass base and rim are mounted, strengthening it at the most critical areas. After powder, a plastic wad, and the shot are loaded, the forward end of the cartridge is sealed by folding it inward. On occasion, shotgun cartridges have also taken an all-brass or all-plastic form, and prior to the evolution of plastic cartridges, rolled paper shells were standard. Common loading material are birdshot (small pellets used for birds and small game), buckshot (larger pellets used for deer and large game), and a slug (a single large projectile, also used for large game). Specialty loads are also available—flares for signaling, firecrackers to drive birds away from crops, tear gas, tracer pellets, plastic pellets for riot control, incendiaries, tiny

steel darts, and virtually anything else that can fit into a shotgun barrel.

Ammunition has generated fewer legislative controversies compared to firearms. In the 1970s, when efficient handgun soft-point and hollow-point ammunition became available, there were proposals to ban them on the ground that they were too deadly. In the 1990s, issues arose regarding armor-piercing handgun ammunition, whose projectile had a solid bronze core that increased its ability to penetrate. Critics charged that these projectiles would also pierce body armor and labeled them "cop-killer bullets." Congress ultimately outlawed civilian production of handgun ammunition with solid cores made of certain hard metals. A later controversy involved the "Black Talon" hollow-point produced by Winchester and aggressively marketed as an expanding projectile that inflicted greater injuries. After some of these rounds were used in the "101 California Street" murders, the marketing approach backfired on Winchester. The controversy ended after Winchester retitled the bullet the "Ranger Talon" and restricted sales to law enforcement personnel.

David T. Hardy

See also: Black Talon; California Street (101) Massacre; Cartridges; Dum-Dum Bullet; Gunpowder; Hollow Point Bullet

Further Reading

Hogg, Ian. *Jane's Directory of Military Small Arms Ammunition*. New York: Jane's Publishing, 1985.

Logan, Herschel C. *Cartridges: A Pictorial Digest of Small Arms Ammunition*. Harrisburg, PA: Stackpole, 1959.

Amnesty Programs

Gun amnesty programs, often run in conjunction with gun buyback programs, have been used by law enforcement agencies to remove firearms from circulation. In such programs, weapons that are turned in (often for cash or some other material inducement) are accepted with "no questions asked." Also, those turning in illegal guns are not prosecuted for illegal possession of a firearm. Typically, no background checks or criminal investigations of participants are conducted.

Not all gun buyback programs include amnesty provisions. Individuals who turned in guns through local programs funded by the U.S. Department of Housing and Urban Development (1999–2001) were required to show identification. The guns were then checked to determine whether they were stolen or used in a crime.

While amnesty and buyback programs have been politically popular (Callahan, Rivara, and Koepsell 1994, 472), there is no empirical evidence that they actually succeed in reducing gun violence. Many of the guns that are turned into these programs are obsolete and therefore not likely to be used in criminal activity. In 2009, a World War II–era mortar launcher was turned into the Syracuse, New York, police (Baker 2009). Also, those who turn in guns tend to be older people, who are less likely to be engaged in criminal activity. A study of the gun amnesty program in Sacramento, California, found that 40 percent of the program participants were 55 years of age or older, and none were under the age of 25 (Romero, Wintemute, and Vernick 1998).

There has also been some concern about amnesty programs in which guns are not checked. A gun, used in a crime, might be turned in anonymously. The gun is then destroyed, depriving the authorities of evidence and allowing a criminal to escape prosecution.

Even gun control advocates have recognized the limitation of such programs. In a 1998 interview, Robin Terry, a spokesperson for Handgun Control, Inc. (now called the Brady Campaign to Prevent Gun Violence), said that "any effort to get guns off the street is worthwhile. But I think they are more effective when they are used in connection with gun violence programs" (*Newark Star-Ledger* 1998, 4).

In recent years, advocates of these programs have tended to emphasize the safety aspects of the programs rather than crime control. Representative of this point of view was Newark, New Jersey, mayor Cory Booker, who, when announcing the 2009 amnesty program, said that "Many residents of Newark and surrounding communities may have unwanted firearms in their homes, inherited from family members, left behind by a building's previous occupants, or weapons discarded by fleeing criminals. These weapons could fall into the hands of dangerous criminals or persons unskilled in their use, and lead to tragedy. If you have an unwanted gun in your home, turn it in. You may save the life of yourself or a loved one" (Newark Press Information Office 2009).

Jeffrey Kraus

See also: Crime and Gun Use; Gun Buyback Programs; Guns in the Home

Further Reading

Baker, Robert A. "Artillery Piece Received during Gun Amnesty Program." Syracuse .com, February 11, 2009. http://www.syra cuse.com/news/index.ssf/2009/02/syracusans _turn_in_more_illega.html (accessed June 16, 2011).

Callahan, Charles M., Frederick P. Rivara, and Thomas D. Koepsell. "Money for Guns: Evaluation of the Seattle Gun Buy-Back Program." *Public Health Reports* 109 (1994): 470–77. http://www.ncbi.nlm.nih .gov/pmc/articles/PMC1403522/pdf/pubheal threp00059-0010.pdf (accessed June 16, 2011).

Newark Press Information Office. "Newark Gun Amnesty Buyback Program Resumes." http://www.thejerseytomatopress.com/stories/NEWARK-GUN-AMNESTY-BUY BACK-PROGRAM-RESUMES,2714? print=1 (accessed June 16, 2011).

"Newark Resurrects Gun Swap Program." *Newark Star-Ledger*, February 10, 1998.

Plotkin, Martha, ed. *Under Fire: Gun Buy-Backs, Exchanges and Amnesty Programs.* Washington, DC: Police Executive Research Forum, 1996.

Romero, Michael, Garren Wintemute, and Jon Vernick. *Reduction in Prevalence of Risk Factors for Firearm Violence among Participants in a Gun Amnesty Program.* Monterey, CA: Program on Security and Development, Monterey Institute of International Studies, 1998. http://blogs.miis.edu/sand/files/2011/02/sacgbb.pdf (accessed June 16, 2011).

Van Horn, Dwight. "What's Wrong with Gun Amnesty Programs." *Law Enforcement Alliance of America Newsletter* (1992): 2.

Antiterrorist Legislation

As Americans have had to deal with the specter of armed terrorist activities and bombings on American soil in recent years, Congress has responded with antiterrorist legislation intended to more effectively deter and punish terrorists and strengthen the ability of federal law enforcement to investigate these acts of violence. Legislative attempts to control the threat of terrorism are not new and date as far back as the passage of the Alien and Sedition Acts in 1798. However, events of more modern origin, such as the first attempted terrorist attack on the World Trade Center complex in 1993, the Oklahoma City bombing in 1995, and the terrorist attack on the United States on September 11, 2001, have raised a host of new concerns and legislation about how best to deter, investigate, prosecute, adjudicate, and punish terrorist acts that occur within the United States.

Modern attempts at antiterrorist legislation have included provisions for the stricter control of guns, though such provisions have been deleted from any laws finally enacted. While the main focus of antiterrorism legislation after September 11, 2001, has been generally in the enhancement of law enforcement powers in investigations and broadening criminal offenses relating to such offenses as the use of weapons of mass destruction, the post-9/11 legislation has been remarkably devoid of stricter laws pertaining to firearms in general. This is particularly intriguing in light of the specter of "lone wolf" terrorists such as John Allen Muhammad (the so called "D.C. Sniper" who utilized a Bushmaster XM-15 semiautomatic .223-caliber rifle in 11 of his 14 shootings in August–October 2002). In May 2010, the General Accounting Office released a report indicating the ease by which those on the terrorist watch list might be able to lawfully purchase firearms in the United States. Specifically, the report commented that "from February 2004 through February 2010, FBI data show[ed] that individuals on the terrorist watchlist were involved in firearm or explosives background checks 1,228 times; 1,119 (about 91 percent) of these transactions were allowed to proceed because no prohibiting information was found—such as felony convictions, illegal immigrant status, or other disqualifying factors—and 109 of the transactions were denied" (General Accounting Office 2010, 1).

Generally, it is possible to trace antiterrorism legislation in the United States back to the dawn of the European colonial presence

President George W. Bush signs the Patriot Act on October 26, 2001. (Harry Hamburg/ NY Daily News Archive via Getty Images)

in the New World. In fact, one author (Bruce Maxwell) has written in a 2004 book on the history of "homeland security" legislation in the United States that the first terrorist or "homeland security incident" occurred in 1607, only months after the establishment of the Jamestown colony, when one of the colony leaders (James Kendall) was tried and executed for a crime threatening the colony. Maxwell wrote that while the charges against Kendall "may have been mutiny, spying for Spain, or 'sowing discord' among the settlers," he was ultimately "executed because the jury believed that he threatened the security of the precarious 'homeland' established at Jamestown" (Maxwell 2004).

The first major law passed by Congress after the United States' independence that dealt with what could be called homeland security and/or antiterrorism legislation was the Alien and Sedition Acts in 1798. These laws undermined any notion of the First Amendment and free speech being absolute. The laws were originally justified as a means to combating domestic upheaval caused by newly arrived immigrants—by criminalizing seditious speech against the government and by authorizing the president to remove any alien deemed "dangerous" to the peace and security of the United States. However, the laws were also clearly politically motivated, as most immigrants associated with the opposition party (Thomas Jefferson's Democratic-Republicans) and the law was very politically implemented and enforced, as most prosecuted and/or deported under the acts were opposed to the Federalist Party. The law's focus on newly arrived immigrants is arguably comparable to the Sullivan Act/Law (New York's controversial gun law said by some to be originally directed at Italian immigrants to New York). Another early example of antiterrorism/homeland security legislation came in 1917 and 1918 with the passage of the Espionage and Sedition Acts. Part of the Espionage Act dealt with the exposure and transmission of sensitive information about the military. However, the law also outlawed all intentional attempts at causing insubordination, disloyalty, mutiny, or the refusal to serve, among members of the U.S. Army. While the Espionage and Sedition Acts were passed during a time of war, individuals continued to be prosecuted under like federal laws, or similar state laws, from the 1920s through the 1950s (laws like the Smith Act of 1940).

Additionally, during the turbulent years of the 1960s and 1970s, with contentious domestic issues involving civil rights and the Vietnam War, the FBI and CIA conducted investigations on Americans. A series of abuses committed by the FBI and the CIA were documented in such well-known U.S. Senate investigations as the Rockefeller Commission Report on CIA Activities (June 6, 1975) and the Senate Select Committee to Study Governmental Operations with Respect to Intelligence Agencies (known more commonly as the Church Committee Report on Rights Violations by Intelligence Agencies, April 26, 1976). The Church Committee Report noted numerous abuses and commented that "U.S. intelligence agencies had routinely and wantonly violated the civil liberties of Americans during domestic intelligence investigations. The FBI was one of the main culprits" (Maxwell 2004). As a result of these reports of abuses, among other things, Congress in 1978 passed the Foreign Intelligence Surveillance Act (FISA), the "exclusive means by which electronic surveillance" could be collected. The FISA legislation created a secret court comprised of a handful of federal district court justices (appointed by the chief justice of the U.S. Supreme Court), which was charged with overseeing requests from intelligence and law enforcement agencies to conduct electronic surveillance (which originally meant phone taps, but which was expanded to allow for e-mail and physical searches as well). FISA has been amended at several points thereafter, most recently in 2008.

While Americans have always been wary of terrorist acts, especially after attacks upon Americans at the Beirut compound in 1983 (killing 241 American service members) and the 1988 bombing of Pan Am Flight 103 over Lockerbie, Scotland (killing 270 people, including 189 Americans), there was a sense that these attacks occurred elsewhere and not on U.S. soil. This mind-set began to slowly change for many Americans in the 1990s, primarily after the attack on the World Trade Center masterminded by Ramzi Yousef in 1993, and the bombing of the federal Alfred P. Murrah Building in Oklahoma City, Oklahoma, on April 19, 1995, which resulted in the deaths of 168 individuals. The notion of giving law enforcement more tools to prevent such future attacks was the motivation in first proposing the legislation that would become the Anti-Terrorism and Effective Death Penalty Act (AEDPA) of 1996. Like the Patriot Act, which would be enacted a few short years later, a large portion of the AEDPA provides new tools to enable law enforcement and administrative agencies to more effectively combat terrorism both at home and abroad. Indeed, gun owners and their advocates largely believe that vesting law enforcement with more robust and "strong investigative tools to track down terrorists before they strike" is more appropriate than more onerous gun laws (Kouri 2011).

Consistent with this belief, the 1996 law put into effect new rules attempting to thwart the operation of terrorist organizations—something also continued with the Patriot Act in 2001. First, the secretary of state was empowered to designate groups as "terrorist organizations" if the group's activities threatened the peace and security of U.S. citizens, or the United States itself. Second, the law prohibited the financing of these organizations by individuals.

The third major aspect of the 1996 act dealt with the revision of immigration measures. Specifically, the law empowered the then Immigration and Naturalization Service (INS) to refuse asylum or citizenship requests from any member of a terrorist organization. The law allowed INS to deny asylum/citizenship on account of an individual's association with a particular group—even though the individual may not have ever acted in furtherance of the group's goals. The act also created a special federal court that could utilize "secret evidence" in making deportation decisions. Further, the law allowed for any single judge in these removal cases to consider evidence and testimony provided in camera or in an ex parte fashion in reaching a removal decision. This provision allows the government to utilize what has been described as "secret evidence" in deportation proceedings if the person is believed to be a member of a terrorist organization.

The attack on the United States on September 11 traumatized as it arguably has not been since Japan's surprise attack on the United States at Pearl Harbor in 1941. Within one week of the attacks, Attorney General John Ashcroft submitted a large antiterrorism proposal (a proposed legislative bill in excess of 300 pages) that would grant the federal government expansive powers in combating terrorism. President Bush called on Congress to pass the legislation within three days. While Congress took a little longer to pass the legislation (approximately 45 days), most agree that the legislation was subject to very little debate and scrutiny, and some senators and congressmen admitted to not even reading all of the provisions contained in the proposed legislation before voting.

The Patriot Act amended a variety of different laws on a great array of law enforcement tactics and tools in gathering intelligence during the course of an investigation. While the provisions are beyond the scope of this entry (as none of the provisions provided for in the Patriot Act provide new restrictions applicable to firearms), the act is quite notable as an expansion of law enforcement powers and generally allows law enforcement to gather private information and/or monitor individuals in ways not previously permitted, and subject to lesser amounts of judicial oversight (if any). The act, which amends over a dozen major preexisting federal statutes, broadens and redefines a number of different federal criminal offenses (e.g., making the criminal offense of conspiracies based upon terrorism subject to the provisions of the Racketeer Influenced and Corrupt Organization statute, broadening the definition of domestic terrorism, etc.). Finally, like the 1996 legislation, the law amends immigration law to strengthen the hand of federal law enforcement in deporting certain individuals. Namely, the act amends immigration laws to prohibit aliens from soliciting funds or members for a terrorist organization, or from providing material support to terrorist organizations. The act provides that that an alien can be refused entry into the United States for these activities, and more importantly, the act allows for the removal of those already legally in the country (i.e., under a temporary student visa or work visa) for committing these activities. This immigration change brought about by the Patriot Act has become a powerful tactic by the Department of Justice, especially in cases where the evidence may not support a conviction beyond a reasonable doubt in the federal court system for terrorism-related offenses. For instance, rather than having to prove by high standards of proof the violation of certain laws, the Department of Justice may institute deportation proceedings against any alien the attorney general has "reasonable grounds to believe" was a threat to national security. The level of proof/evidence is quite low, only such proof/evidence that reasonably supports the view of the attorney general's office. So, in cases with difficult evidentiary issues, the Department of Justice can simply institute deportation proceedings, and have the unwanted individuals expelled from the United States.

In June 2011, Adam Gadahn re-sparked a debate about whether gun control laws should be more rigorous in the United States. Gadahn, known as Azzam the American, is an al-Qaeda member who has released a series of al-Qaeda-related videos in recent years. As a result, he was indicted for treason by a grand jury in the U.S. District Court for the Central District of California (and the first American charged with treason since the 1950s). In a video released on June 4, 2011, and entitled "Do Not Rely on Others, Take the Task upon Yourself," Gadahn tells Muslim immigrants to obtain easily obtainable weapons and carry out random acts of violence in the United States. At one part in the video, Gadahn states that "America is absolutely awash with easily obtainable firearms." Gadahn went on to state that "you can go down to a gun show at the local convention center and come away with a fully automatic assault rifle

without a background check and, most likely, without having to show an identification card. So what are you waiting for?" (Kouri 2011).

It appears that the plethora of antiterrorism legislation promulgated in the last decade since 9/11 is here to stay. While legislation like the AEDPA and Patriot Act are the latest in the long list of legislation in the United States dealing with terrorism, they will likely not be the last. In future years, there will continue to be calls to make gun control and strict gun laws more a part of the country's antiterrorism strategy. In a June 20, 2011, article by Jim Kouri entitled "Senators See Gun Control as Anti-Terrorism Strategy," a number of Democratic senators are listed as being in support of stricter gun control laws as an aspect of a broader antiterrorism strategy. As described by Kouri in the above article, "Senator Frank Lautenberg (D-NJ) advised lawmakers to include the threat of armed terrorists acquiring more weapons and ammunition in the United States due to the nation's lax gun regulations in any legislation to control firearms. He reminded his colleagues of an al-Qaida video that urged jihadists to utilize the lack of gun restrictions to arm themselves and their comrades." Gun advocates in the Congress have generally responded that what is needed is not enacting more gun laws, but vesting law enforcement with more investigatory tools to ferret out potential terrorist threats. Furthermore, Congressman Lamar Smith, a Republican from Texas and the chairman of the House Judiciary Committee, has said the tightening of gun laws in response to the possible threat of terrorism would be like the unilateral surrender of beloved constitutional rights to the terrorists. Regardless of where one falls out on the debate, the history of antiterrorist legislation in the United

States makes clear that often the United States revises its laws or passes new more restrictive laws only after concrete threats or events (e.g., the adoption of the AEDPA after the 1996 Oklahoma City bombing, the adoption of the Patriot Act after the attacks on September 11, 2001, the adoption of the Gun Control Act of 1968 after the Kennedy assassinations of the 1960s). As such, adding more stringent gun control measures to antiterrorism legislation may come about only if the threat advocated by Gadahn becomes more palpable, or if such an event unfortunately comes to fruition.

James A. Beckman

See also: Bureau of Alcohol, Tobacco, Firearms and Explosives (ATF); Department of Justice, U.S.; Federal Bureau of Investigation (FBI); Gun Control Act of 1968; McVeigh, Timothy; Ruby Ridge; Sullivan Law; Terrorism; Waco, Texas, Raid; Washington, D.C., Sniper Attacks

Further Reading

Beckman, James. *Comparative Legal Approaches to Homeland Security and Anti-Terrorism.* London: Ashgate Publishing, 2007.

Daily Mail Reporter. " 'What Are You Waiting For': U.S. Born Al-Qaeda Spokesman Calls on Americans to 'Buy Guns and Start Shooting People.' " *UK Mail Online,* June 4, 2011. http://www.dailymail.co.uk/news/article-1394113/Al-Qaeda-spokesman-Adam-Gadahn-calls-Americans-buy-guns-shoot-people.html?ito=feeds-newsxml (accessed July 5, 2011).

Federal Bureau of Investigation. "Terrorist Screening Center." http://www.fbi.gov/about-us/nsb/tsc (accessed June 8, 2011).

Kopel, David, and Joseph Olson. "Preventing a Reign of Terror: Civil Liberties Implications of Terrorism Legislation." *Oklahoma City University Law Review* 21 (1996): 247–347.

Kouri, Jim. "Senators See Gun Control as Anti-Terrorism Strategy," Enter Stage Right, June 20, 2011. http://www.enterstageright.com/archive/articles/0611/0611guncontrolterror.htm (accessed July 5, 2011).

Maxwell, Bruce. *Homeland Security: A Documentary History.* Washington, DC: CQ Press, 2004.

President's Statement on Signing the Antiterrorism and Effective Death Penalty Act of 1996, 32 Weekly Comp. Pres. Doc. 719, 721 (April 29, 1996).

Smith, Roberta. "Note: America Tries to Come to Terms with Terrorism: The United States Anti-Terrorism and Effective Death Penalty Act of 1996 v. British Anti-Terrorism Law and International Response." *Cardozo Journal of International and Comparative Law* 5 (1997): 249–90.

U.S. Government Accountability Office. *Terrorist Watchlist Screening: FBI Has Enhanced Its Use of Information from Firearm and Explosives Background Checks to Support Counterterrorism Efforts* (Highlights of Report No.: GAO-10-703T). May 5, 2010. http://www.gao.gov/new.items/d10703t.pdf (accessed July 6, 2011).

Arming America **Controversy**

Arming America: The Origins of a National Gun Culture, published in 2000, quickly became that year's most celebrated and high-stakes book. Two years later, it was thoroughly discredited and its author, Emory University history professor Michael Bellesiles, had resigned from his tenured post. The history of the book's fall from grace was entwined from the first with its potential impact on whether the Second Amendment protected an individual's right to keep and bear arms. Bellesiles's insistence that there were few privately owned guns in early America and that these were subject to state control won his book enthusiastic praise from gun control advocates. When scholars discovered Bellesiles had seriously misrepresented his sources, he accused them of being either gun nuts involved in a political vendetta, or postmodernists for whom, as he put it, the next step was Holocaust denial. Bellesiles still claims, as does his current publisher, that he was the victim of a National Rifle Association plot. That notion apparently convinced the American Library Association to include *Arming America* on their list of Banned and Challenged Books—the odd nonfiction work among many celebrated literary volumes, all unfairly censored.

Five months before the publication of *Arming America*, the *New York Times* rushed to announce that Bellesiles's exhaustive search of some 11,170 eighteenth- and nineteenth-century probates found very few guns, let alone a so-called gun culture, in the United States prior to the Civil War. Bellesiles was blunt about the implications. The notion that guns were important in early America, he wrote, would have appeared "harebrained" to most Americans before the Civil War. It was all a myth. In the media blitz that followed publication, *Arming America* was heralded as a *tour de force* that "changed everything" and was warmly praised by distinguished scholars, many of whom favored gun control. Nor was its author reticent about his book's importance for debunking the claim that Americans had an individual right to be armed. In an interview with *Playboy* magazine, Bellesiles challenged the National Rifle Association to prove he was wrong, demanding facts and not folktales. Three months later, despite growing doubts about Bellesiles's own facts, *Arming America* was awarded Columbia University's prestigious Bancroft Prize for the best work of history published in 2000.

While Bellesiles dismissed his critics as political operatives, it was scholars from the many fields that his thesis affected who began to examine his evidence. If Americans were poorly armed, for example, then guns must have been rare and ineffective; hunting with guns unusual; militiamen not expected to own firearms; and famed shooting skills illusionary. Bellesiles's argument claims all these were the case. Bellesiles also equates firearms with higher homicide rates; therefore, if guns were rare, homicide rates must have been low.

The argument begins with his account of European gun use, especially English. He reports that only the wealthy could afford the expensive and dangerous new weapons, but in any case, the English government outlawed the use of firearms by commoners. The militia was required to be armed, but their guns were locked in storehouses. With few privately owned firearms, there was little violence. None of his sources support these contentions, and other evidence refutes them. Since the English militia were required to equip themselves with guns and kept these at home, large numbers of commoners necessarily owned and practiced using firearms. Pistols were the ordinary equipment of the numerous highway robbers. The English Bill of Rights of 1689 affirmed the right of Protestants—some 90 percent of the population—to have arms for their defense, which subsequent court cases interpreted broadly.

As for the United States, Bellesiles argues that before the mid-nineteenth century, guns were rare, expensive, highly regulated, inefficient, unwanted, and nearly useless for military purposes or hunting. He writes that colonists often perceived the ax as the equal of a gun and "completely failed" to care for guns or to learn their proper use. All guns were subject to storage in central arsenals. No gun belonged unqualifiedly to an individual. The United States, like England, had a broad-based militia. While it is generally agreed to have been unreliable, Bellesiles dubs it little more than a political gesture. As for hunting, he reports that his research into 80 travel journals and other documents finds hunting with guns the pastime of the idle rich or of those he labels the poorest fringes of civilization if not outright savagery.

The core evidence upon which Bellesiles relies to document the scarcity of guns is his data from 11,170 estate inventories from 40 counties between 1765 and 1859. He insists that each probate provided a complete listing of everything in the deceased's household, even items given away in his lifetime. The statistics for guns owned by adult white men in different counties and eras are presented in a series of graphs and tables in the appendix. Bellesiles calculates only 14.7 percent of men in the colonial era owned guns, of which 53 percent were described as old or broken. On the frontier, where firearms would seem especially essential, he finds even fewer. Not until Samuel Colt began advertising in 1849–1859 did Bellesiles's numbers increase.

Although *Arming America* had all the usual scholarly trappings, once the sources were checked, the volume's credibility began to dissolve. Travel accounts, even the journals Bellesiles cites, referred to widespread hunting with guns. The Englishman Charles Augustus Murray, for example, found few gentlemen hunters in the 1830s, but observed that nearly every man had a rifle and spent part of his time in the chase. Bellesiles omits the most famous traveler of the period, Alexis de Tocqueville, who described a typical "peasant's cabin" in Kentucky or Tennessee as containing a fairly clean bed, some chairs, and a good gun.

Were early guns useful weapons? Bellesiles claims it took three minutes to reload a musket, but experts point out that three to five shots could be fired off in one minute. Were guns kept in storehouses? Colonial legislatures insisted householders have and keep firearms at the ready. Bellesiles writes that the Militia Act of 1792, which enrolled all free white men between the ages of 18 and 45, required Congress to provide guns. In fact, that law explicitly states that every citizen so enrolled provide himself with a good musket and other supplies. Clayton Cramer, an independent scholar, was one of the first to report numerous errors in Bellesiles's work and received what became Bellesiles's typical rebuke about needing an introductory history lesson. As noted above, the claim on which Bellesiles bases his findings of gun scarcity is his search of 11,170 probates. It was inquiries about that evidence that led to discovery of wholesale fraud.

To begin with, Bellesiles is virtually alone in insisting probates list everything in a household. Some deal exclusively with real estate. In the southern and middle colonies, in 1774, 70 percent of estate inventories did not include cash, and 23 percent of those in a leading colonial database include no clothes. Many estates were never probated. The table and graphs drawn from his research fail to list the number of records Bellesiles examined for any of his 40 counties or for any of the time periods charted. When questioned, he flatly refused to explain how he weighted the sample from the various counties to arrive at his percentages. Experts have since demonstrated that his key percentages were mathematically impossible.

Then there is the database itself. When Professor James Lindgren of Northwestern

University asked to see Bellesiles's database, he was told he had none to share. Bellesiles said he had relied upon pencil checks on legal pads, and these were ruined in a flood at his office. He did name the archive where he worked, but archivists there reported that they never had the relevant probate records. Bellesiles then switched his story and said he had traveled the country for 10 years visiting country archives. He could not remember which ones. One of the 40 counties from which he drew data was San Francisco, where he did remember examining 1850s probates at the Superior Court. When a reporter inquired at the Superior Court, she learned that all its nineteenth-century documents had been destroyed in the great earthquake and fire of 1906. There was one set of probates Bellesiles specifically cited that were available, 186 inventories from early Providence, Rhode Island. Bellesiles writes that these probates were unusual because fully 48 percent mentioned guns, although he warns that if these 186 men comprised a militia company, half would have been unarmed while a third of the guns mentioned were described as old or broken. Lindgren found virtually everything Bellesiles had said about these records was false. Some were probates for women; 62 percent, not 48 percent, mentioned guns, of which only 9 percent, not 33 percent, were described as old. When Lindgren checked probates from one of Bellesiles's frontier counties, he found more guns than knives, more guns than books, and more guns than Bibles.

In May and June 2001, as criticism grew, Bellesiles claimed he had received death threats and retreated to an undisclosed e-mail address. In response, the governing councils of the American Historical Association, the Omohundro Institute of Early American History and Culture, and other organizations passed resolutions condemning harassment.

At this point, Emory University was sufficiently concerned to demand that Bellesiles offer a reasoned, measured, detailed, point-by-point response to his critics. The result was a symposium published in the *William and Mary Quarterly* two months later, in which three of the four scholars asked to examine *Arming America*, Gloria Main, Ira Gruber, and Randolph Roth, cited gross error and misuse of sources. Main found incredible Bellesiles's claim that probate inventories were complete and pointed to the astonishing difference between Bellesiles's low figure for gun ownership in Maryland and her far-higher figures. Gruber concluded Bellesiles methodically minimized the importance of guns, militia, and war in early America by a consistently biased reading of sources and careless use of evidence. Roth found Bellesiles's homicide information misleading or wrong in every instance. A month later, Emory launched an internal review followed by appointment of an external panel to examine Bellesiles's work. By this time, nearly all the early boosters of *Arming America* had gone silent.

In June 2002, when the soundness of Bellesiles's scholarship had become highly suspect, the National Endowment for the Humanities stripped its support for his Newberry Library fellowship. His response was to warn that the ghosts of McCarthyism had been reawakened. On July 10, the three distinguished historians asked by Emory to investigate Bellesiles's use of probate records and militia counts—Stanley Katz of Princeton University, Hanna Gray of the University of Chicago, and Laurel Thatcher Ulrich of Harvard University—issued their report. Their charge was surprisingly narrow, given serious doubts about other areas of Bellesiles's research. The committee found that every aspect of his work in the probate records were deeply flawed, that his work on militia records were consistently biased, that his scholarship fell short on every count, and that his scholarly integrity was seriously in question. Yet, they did not find that his use of Vermont and Providence probates involved intentional fabrication or falsification. While they were seriously troubled by his scholarly conduct and sloppy scholarship, they felt it did not prove a deliberate attempt to mislead, however misleading the result. Only in the case of his key probate table did they conclude there was deliberate falsification.

Bellesiles resigned his position at Emory, but minimized the significance of the report. He brushed off his mathematically impossible statistics as the result of his never having been good at math, but he insisted his thesis remained unchallenged. He had written a book with 1,347 footnotes, he pointed out, and the panel found problems with only five of them. However, other scholars have found many more inaccuracies scattered through those 1,347 footnotes.

Michael Bellesiles claims he was a victim who had innocently written on a controversial subject. Yet *Arming America*'s presumed impact on the gun rights debate gave it instant acclaim and the uncritical praise of reviewers who should have been more cautious. It allowed its author to dismiss critics as politically motivated. Had it not been for the dedicated work of scholars and reporters from across the political spectrum, *Arming America* would not have had its gross inaccuracies exposed.

Joyce Lee Malcolm

See also: Militia Act of 1792; United Kingdom—History of Gun Laws through 1900

Further Reading

Bellesiles, Michael A. *Arming America: The Origins of a National Gun Culture*. New York: Alfred A. Knopf, 2000.

Cramer, Clayton. *Armed America: The Remarkable Story of How and Why Guns Became as American as Apple Pie*. Nashville, TN: Nelson Current, 2006.

"Forum: Historians and Guns." *William and Mary Quarterly* 58 (2002): 203–68.

Katz, Stanley N., Gray, Hanna H., and Laurel Thatcher Ulrich. "Report of the Investigative Committee in the Matter of Professor Michael Bellesiles." http://www.emory.edu/news/Releases/Final_Report.pdf (accessed June 2, 2011).

Lindgren, James T. "Fall from Grace: *Arming America* and the Bellesiles Scandal." *Northwestern University School of Law: Public Law and Legal Theory Papers* 3 (2005).

Lindgren, James T., and Justin Lee Heather. "Counting Guns in Early America." *Northwestern University School of Law: Law and Economics Papers* 42 (2001).

Malcolm, Joyce Lee. "Review: *Arming America*." *Texas Law Review* 79 (2001): 1657–76.

Arming Women Against Rape and Endangerment (AWARE)

Arming Women Against Rape and Endangerment (AWARE) is a nonprofit organization formed in 1990 to provide training, information, and support for women and men seeking to resist violence against them. The organization was founded by Nancy Biddle, whose personal experience with violence encouraged her to study women's self-defense options. AWARE says that it works to prevent violence against women through education and training, but it also seeks to empower women by offering information and training in a variety of self-defense techniques, from pepper spray to handguns and shotguns. AWARE retains instructors made available to interested persons and organizations. The organization is based in Bedford, Massachusetts.

Robert J. Spitzer

See also: Second Amendment Sisters (SAS); Self-Defense, Reasons for Gun Use; Women and Guns

Further Reading

AWARE. http://www.aware.org/ (accessed January 31, 2011).

Homsher, Deborah. *Women and Guns.* Armonk, NY: M. E. Sharpe, 2001.

Armor-Piercing Ammunition

The penetration of any projectile or bullet depends upon its velocity, mass, and composition. The military has long classified some small-arms ammunition as armor piercing, although no uniform standard for penetration exists. This ammunition, commonly used in machine guns, has greater penetration against targets such as vehicles because of the bullet design and composition but is not capable of penetrating armor plate on tanks and other armored vehicles. Penetration of this armor plate requires projectiles from larger, crew-served weapons. The concept has had little application to the civilian ammunition market.

Beginning in the mid-1970s, bullet-resistant vests became standard equipment for most of the uniformed police in the United States. The vests became practical with the development of Kevlar, a synthetic fabric that, when layered, could resist penetration by bullets. The rising violent crime rate of the period ensured demand. None of

the vests would stop the penetration of rifle bullets, which routinely travel at over 2,000 feet per second, without the addition of heavy metal or ceramic plates that made the vests too cumbersome for routine police wear. Vests adequate to protect against most handgun and shotgun projectiles could be worn under the officer's uniform shirt on a regular basis.

Armor-piercing handgun rounds had existed for many years but failed to gain any popularity with police or civilian purchasers. Dealers seldom stocked the ammunition, and few buyers showed any interest in ordering it. Interest in pistol ammunition had primarily focused on development of more effective soft-point handgun ammunition that increased trauma by expanding when it struck a target. Armor-piercing ammunition had a sharp pointed bullet that reduced rather than increased trauma in the target. Since the bullet resistance of soft body armor resulted from the number of layers of fabric and the penetration characteristics of various cartridges varies, one can not rationally define an absolute point at which a cartridge becomes armor piercing. The issue of armor-piercing bullets and body armor reflects the historically shifting balance between offensive weapons that dates to castle walls and catapults. However, when a small ammunition company marketed Teflon-coated pistol bullets, capable of penetrating soft body armor, the symbolism generated widespread attention, particularly among the police (Davidson 1993).

In 1981, Representative Mario Biaggi (D-NY), a former New York police officer, became the visible advocate of federal legislation to outlaw these "cop-killer bullets." A dispute exists over the actual originator of the strategy to use armor-piercing ammunition as a wedge issue, but Handgun Control Incorporated (now the Brady Campaign) clearly assumed the lead role in advancing it (Vizzard 2000). The strategy called for pursuing a ban on the ammunition with police support, forcing the National Rifle Association (NRA) to either give tacit support to a gun control measure, or oppose it and alienate law enforcement and the public. The NRA responded by attempting to invoke a new paradigm, technology. Cop-killer bullets clearly constituted a symbolic, rather than substantive, policy issue (Vizzard 2000). Unfortunately for the NRA, their effort to invoke a rational technological paradigm in relation to this symbolic conflict proved unsuccessful. The issue defined them as unwilling to accept reasonable compromise on even the smallest issue. The resulting legislation banned the manufacture or importation of pistol ammunition with specific armor piercing components, except for military and law enforcement use (18 U.S.C. § 922(a)(7) and 18 U.S.C. § 921(a)(17)(B)).

Since the 1980s, the issue has essentially faded from the gun control debate with two short exceptions. President Clinton and some members of Congress again addressed the issue in 1995, proposing a broader definition of armor piercing to include any pistol ammunition capable of penetrating body armor. This initiative never gained traction, and the issue quickly faded. In 2005, the issue again arose when the Department of Homeland Security issued a bulletin regarding the capability of the FN Herstal 5.7 mm pistol to penetrate soft body armor, once again faded from the public agenda (Brady Campaign 2005). The proliferation of compact, semiautomatic, military-style rifles, commonly referred to as "assault weapons," proved to be far more effective in defeating police body armor than any pistol or revolver. In March 2010, two Oakland, California, SWAT officers wearing protective vests were killed by a barricaded subject using an AK-47-style rifle. Two weeks later, three Pittsburgh, Pennsylvania, officers were killed while responding to a domestic disturbance by a similar weapon, followed in May by the killing of two officers, and wounding of two more in West Memphis, Arkansas, by suspects armed with similar weapons.

William J. Vizzard

See also: Ammunition, Types of; Armor-Piercing Ammunition; Body Armor

Further Reading

Brady Campaign to Prevent Gun Violence, "Congress Must Act on Cop Killer Gun." http://www.bradycampaign.org/media/press/view/629 (accessed May 27, 2011).

Bruce, John M., and Clyde Wilcox, eds. *The Changing Politics of Gun Control*. Lanham, MD: Rowman & Littlefield, 1998.

Davidson, Osha Grey. *Under Fire: The NRA and the Battle for Gun Control*. Washington, DC: National Press Books, 1982.

National Rifle Association. "History of Federal Ammunition Law." http://www.nraila.org/Issues/FactSheets/Read.aspx?id=55&issue=005 (accessed May 27, 2011).

Vizzard, William J. *Shots in the Dark: The Policy, Politics and Symbolism of Gun Control*. Lanham, MD: Rowman & Littlefield, 2000.

Articles of Confederation and Gun Control

As the first written constitution of the United States, the Articles of Confederation neither contained any expressed provisions guaranteeing the alleged individual right to keep and bear arms nor gave to the new centralized government any means by which it could regulate guns or firearm possession or use. As the Articles of Confederation created only a league of 13 sovereign independent states and a nominal centralized government, any constitutional protection for gun ownership was derived, if at all, from each of the 13 state governments and constitutions. Similarly, any gun regulations or laws were instituted, if at all, on the state level as well. Under the Articles of Confederation, the centralized government lacked the basic authority to regulate interstate commerce and lacked a taxing power—two of the chief ways in which federal gun controls such as the National Firearms Act of 1934 and the Gun Control Act of 1968 have been enacted by the federal government in modern times. The centralized government also lacked the ability to enforce laws it could enact; there was no provision allowing for a chief executive or federal court system, and all "law enforcement" was left to the individual states. The centralized Congress, which was a unicameral body composed of delegates from each state, could not exert any of its limited powers over individuals. Lastly, in the only section of the Articles of Confederation to mention "arms," Article VI required that "every state shall always keep up a well regulated and disciplined militia, sufficiently armed and accoutred, and shall provide and constantly have ready for use, in public stores, a due number of field pieces and tents, and a proper quantity of arms, ammunition and camp equipage." This provision, which laid the foundation for the Second Amendment to the U.S. Constitution that followed later, illustrates the importance of the "militia" and the "collective right" theory to bear arms within the underpinnings of the Second Amendment.

Ratified in 1781 and remaining in effect until 1788, the Articles of Confederation established a loose confederation or league of states, rather than a strong centralized

federal government as was eventually created by the U.S. Constitution in 1787. The Articles of Confederation were literally born from the conflict with Great Britain. From the onset of the American Revolution, influential state leaders stressed the need for a stronger government sufficiently powerful to defeat Great Britain and, presumably, defend against future aggressions. However, most Americans remained overly suspicious of a new powerful centralized state. Thus, each state retained its "sovereignty, freedom and independence." Article III of the Articles of Confederation illustrates this concept of a limited union best by describing the confederation of American states as "a firm league of friendship" of states "for their common defense, the security of their liberties, and their mutual and general welfare." While the new centralized government was given some limited enumerated powers, these powers largely dealt with the handling of foreign affairs issues (e.g., power to declare war, power to raise and support an army and navy, and power to make treaties). Thus, regarding most domestic issues, the government created by the Articles of Confederation was largely a loose confederation or agency that enabled the actions of the individual states in their respective sovereign spheres.

James A. Beckman

See also: Federalism and Gun Control; Gun Control Act of 1968; Militias; National Firearms Act of 1934; Second Amendment

Further Reading

Articles of Confederation (ratified March 1, 1781). http://www.usconstitution.net/articles.html (accessed June 12, 2011).

Bowen, Catherine. *Miracle at Philadelphia*. Boston: Little, Brown and Company, 1966.

Jensen, Merrill. *The Articles of Confederation: An Interpretation of the Social Constitutional*

History of the American Revolution, 1774–1781. Madison: University of Wisconsin Press, 1940.

Assault Weapons

Assault weapons, first developed for military use, were designed as light machine guns, capable of firing in semiautomatic or fully automatic modes; they were subject to some federal regulation in the 1990s. Manufactured in rifle, pistol, and shotgun forms, these weapons began to come into civilian hands in large numbers with the sale of surplus M1 carbines in the 1960s, Chinese-made semiautomatic rifles (modeled after the Russian AK-47) in the 1980s, semiautomatic pistols like the MAC-10 in the 1980s, and the semiautomatic TEC-9 in the 1990s. A semiautomatic weapon fires one bullet with each pull of the trigger without manual rechambering; a fully automatic weapon fires bullets continuously and in rapid succession while the trigger is depressed until the bullet clip or magazine is empty.

American law dating to the 1930s has made possession of fully automatic weapons (usually called machine guns) difficult. Traditional machine guns were heavy, and it required more than one individual to properly operate them. The first significant departure from the crew-operated machine gun was the Tommy gun, developed at the end of World War I for use by a single soldier and popularized by gangster use in the 1920s. While modern fully automatic assault weapons are relatively lightweight, they were already regulated if they fired in a fully automatic fashion. The spread of semiautomatic assault weapons in recent decades, and their increasing use in sensational crimes, such as the Stockton, California, schoolyard massacre in 1989, prompted calls for stricter regulation. Despite such incidents, civilian sales of semiautomatic assault weapons increased dramatically in the late 1980s and 1990s. They were popularized not only by manufacturers' intensive advertising, but also through movies and television programs. They also proved popular among right-wing survivalist and self-created militia movements. In some instances, legally obtainable semiautomatic weapons could be easily altered to fire in full automatic mode.

Critics of proposed new regulations of assault weapons argued that it was difficult to produce an acceptable definition of what constitutes an assault weapon. They also noted that the firing process for many hunting rifles was the same as that of military-style assault weapons, rendering the distinction between legitimate semiautomatic hunting rifles and allegedly illegitimate semiautomatic assault weapons merely cosmetic.

Some assault weapons were finally subjected to national regulation when Congress passed the Assault Weapons Ban of 1994. This law resolved the definition problem by defining an assault weapon, configured specifically for military use, as having such characteristics as a more compact design, a barrel less than 20 inches in length, extensive use of stampings and plastics in its construction, lighter in weight (6–10 pounds), a pistol grip or thumbhole stock, a folding or telescoping stock, a grenade launcher, a bayonet fitting, a barrel shroud, a threaded barrel for adding a silencer or flash suppressor, and the ability to receive a large clip that holds 20–30 bullets. Gun control supporters argued that these guns' lighter weight and smaller size made them more appealing for criminal use—especially in the case of semiautomatic pistols—because their design facilitated concealability and spray fire, a firing technique incompatible with typical hunting or sporting purposes. The Assault Weapons Ban of 1994, passed as part of the

Violent Crime Control and Law Enforcement Act, banned 19 named types of assault weapons and several dozen copycat weapons. It also specifically exempted 661 sporting rifles. Existing assault-style weapons were also exempted from the ban. The Assault Weapons Ban lapsed in 2004 when Congress failed to reenact it.

In 1998, President Bill Clinton directed the Bureau of Alcohol, Tobacco and Firearms (ATF) to ban the import of 58 models of semiautomatic firearms. Several studies of guns used in crimes supported the concern that assault weapons were appealing to criminals. While assault weapons accounted for only about 2–3 percent of all firearms owned in the United States, they accounted for 6–8 percent of gun crimes in the 1990s. Seven states have also enacted assault weapons bans (California, Connecticut, Hawaii, Maryland, Massachusetts, New Jersey, and New York) as have several cities.

Robert J. Spitzer

See also: Assault Weapons Ban of 1994; Automatic Weapons Laws; Bureau of Alcohol, Tobacco, Firearms and Explosives (ATF); Semiautomatic Weapons; Sporting Purposes Test

Further Reading

Avery, Derek. *Firearms*. Ware, UK: Wordsworth, 1995.

Diaz, Tom. *Making a Killing*. New York: New Press, 1999.

Spitzer, Robert J. *The Politics of Gun Control*. 5th ed. Boulder, CO: Paradigm Publishers, 2012.

Vizzard, William J. *Shots in the Dark: The Policy, Politics, and Symbolism of Gun Control*. Lanham, MD: Rowman & Littlefield, 2000.

Assault Weapons Ban of 1994

Enacted under Title XI as part of the Violent Crime Control and Law Enforcement Act of 1994 (PL 103-322; 108 Stat. 1796), this provision banned for 10 years the future manufacture and transfer of 19 named assault weapons and approximately 200 firearms covered by the law's generic definition of "assault weapon." Under the terms of the law, semiautomatic assault weapons were defined under three categories: rifles, pistols, and shotguns. Semiautomatic rifles and pistols fell under the law if they had the ability to accept a detachable magazine and possessed at least two other characteristics of such weapons; shotguns were considered assault weapons if they possessed at least two of the assault weapon features. The law also specifically exempted 661 named weapons. In addition, it banned large-capacity ammunition-feeding devices (those that could hold more than 10 rounds). The ban did not apply to assault weapons already in circulation. Guns neither banned nor protected by the law were exempted from its regulations.

In the 1980s, several factors converged to build support for some kind of legal restriction on assault weapons (firearms designed for military use), including spiraling crime rates, the increasing availability of such weapons, and the belief that such weapons served no legitimate hunting or sporting purpose. The key event spurring control supporters was a senseless 1989 schoolyard massacre in Stockton, California, when five children were killed and 29 others were wounded in a shooting spree by drifter Patrick Purdy, who used a Chinese AK-47 assault rifle. Within weeks, 30 states and many localities were considering bans on these weapons. Two years later, an even more violent shooting occurred in Killeen, Texas, when George J. Hennard killed 22 people and himself, and wounded 23 others, in a cafeteria. Concern that criminals found assault weapons particularly appealing

President Bill Clinton holds a Colt AR-15 rifle during a ceremony at the White House in the spring of 1994. Dayton, Ohio Police Lt. Randy Bean, whose fellow officer Steve Whalen was gunned down with an AR-15 in 1991, looks on at left. (AP Photo/Dennis Cook)

was supported through studies of guns used in crimes. Assault weapons accounted for 6–8 percent of gun crimes in the United States during the 1990s, despite such weapons comprising only about 2–3 percent of all firearms owned in the United States.

Aside from the fierce political opposition to the ban from the National Rifle Association (NRA), regulation of such weapons posed a practical problem, since the definition of a semiautomatic weapon is one that fires a round with each pull of the trigger, which would include wooden-stocked hunting rifles. Assault-style semiautomatic weapons are distinguished from others in that they have large clips holding 20–30 bullets, are more compact in design, have barrels under 20 inches in length, take intermediate-sized

cartridges, include extensive use of stampings and plastics, are lighter in weight (about 6–10 pounds), and were designed for military use. In addition, they often have folding or telescoping stocks, heat-dispersing shrouds, pistol grips, grenade launchers, flash suppressors, and bayonet fittings.

President George H. W. Bush responded by passing an executive order in March 1989 placing a temporary ban on the import of certain assault rifles. The temporary ban became permanent and was later expanded to include a larger number of weapons, earning Bush the ire of the NRA. President Bill Clinton expanded the scope of the import ban in 1993, also by executive order, to include assault-style handguns, like the Uzi. Clinton expanded the order again in 1998.

In Congress, several bills aimed at curbing or banning assault weapons were introduced and debated in 1989, 1990, and 1991. In November 1993, the Senate passed a ban on the manufacture of 19 assault weapons, but also included a provision allowing gun dealers to sell guns that had already been produced. The measure, added to a crime bill, also exempted over 650 types of hunting weapons. In the spring of 1994, the House took up the Assault Weapons Ban. From the start, ban supporters shared little optimism that the House would approve the measure. While the majority of Democrats in Congress were more sympathetic to the measure, some of their leaders, such as Speaker Tom Foley (D-WA), were not. In April, Clinton weighed in strongly for the ban, enlisting the help of several Cabinet secretaries, most notably treasury secretary and gun owner Lloyd Bentsen. Ban supporters received unexpected help from Rep. Henry Hyde (R-IL), a staunch conservative who had opposed gun measures in the past. Thanks in part to Hyde's support, the measure was approved by the Judiciary Committee on April 28, despite the opposition of committee chair Jack Brooks (D-TX).

Even though a final preliminary tally showed that the measure lacked the necessary votes for passage, the Assault Weapons Ban managed to pass in the House in a stunning finale by a two-vote margin, 216–214, on May 5. The drama was heightened when Rep. Andrew Jacobs Jr. (D-IN), at the urging of several colleagues, switched his vote to support the ban in the final seconds of the roll-call vote. As with other gun control legislation, the political pressures were intense. A staff person for one freshman Republican representative who supported the bill commented, "You don't know the threats we received."

Because the Assault Weapons Ban was part of a larger crime bill that had passed in different versions in the two houses, a conference committee was called to iron out those differences. Typically, a bill that survives the legislative gauntlet up to the point of conference committee is all but assured final passage. Such was not the case for the Assault Weapons Ban. Bill supporters initially predicted that the conference committee would complete its work by the end of May. Yet it did not report a bill back to the House and Senate until the end of July, during which time Representative Brooks, a member of the House-Senate conference, attempted repeatedly to kill the Assault Weapons Ban. Brooks's efforts failed, but he did succeed in inserting provisions that exempted pawnbrokers from the Brady Bill and that barred all antihunting protests from taking place on federal lands. Meanwhile, Republican leaders launched a full-scale assault on the $33 billion crime bill, calling it a wasteful piece of legislation laden with pork-barrel spending. Anxious to

win final approval, and with an eye toward the fall elections, Clinton and his congressional allies pushed for an early vote in the House. This proved to be a serious tactical blunder, however, because they had not lined up the necessary support. In a dramatic reversal on a procedural vote to adopt a rule for the bill, the House rejected the crime bill on August 11 by a vote of 225–210.

Under normal circumstances, a defeat on a rules vote would spell the end of the legislation. Yet Clinton would not accept the bill's defeat. He launched an intense public campaign, enlisting the assistance of police organizations and several members of his Cabinet. Congressional leaders vowed to bring the bill back, and in another departure from normal procedure, they negotiated a new version of the bill, this time cutting the bill's spending by about 10 percent.

On August 21, after three days and two nights of intense negotiation, the revised bill was again brought before the House in a highly unusual Sunday session. This time, with the help of moderate Republicans and four members of the black caucus who were persuaded to vote with the president, the bill passed by a vote of 235–195. The bill then went to the Senate, where after considerable partisan wrangling, the bill was passed. Clinton signed the bill, HR 3355, on September 13. After the Republicans won control of Congress in the 1994 elections, party leaders promised to repeal the ban. In 1996, a measure to repeal passed in the House, but no Senate vote was taken, ending the effort to repeal.

Despite public support for renewal of the Assault Weapons Ban, the law lapsed in 2004, as Republican congressional leaders opposed its renewal, and President George W. Bush did nothing to boost its reenactment.

Robert J. Spitzer

See also: Assault Weapons; Clinton, William J.; Congressional Voting Patterns on Gun Control; Interest Groups and Gun Legislation; Killeen, Texas, Massacre; National Rifle Association (NRA); Semiautomatic Weapons; Sporting Purposes Test; Stockton, California, Massacre

Further Reading

Spitzer, Robert J. *The Politics of Gun Control.* 5th ed. Boulder, CO: Paradigm Publishers, 2012.

Vizzard, William J. *Shots in the Dark: The Policy, Politics, and Symbolism of Gun Control.* Lanham, MD: Rowman & Littlefield, 2000.

Windlesham, Lord. *Politics, Punishment, and Populism.* New York: Oxford University Press, 1998.

Assize of Arms. *See United States v. Tot*

Association of Firearm and Tool Mark Examiners (AFTE)

The Association of Firearm and Tool Mark Examiners (AFTE) was formed in 1969 to professionalize the identification of firearms and tool marks. The main issue was, and is, to render professional opinions in both in investigations and in court on matching and identification of firearms and tool marks. As of 2000, it had more than 600 members. Members are expected to abide by a Code of Ethics that requires that they testify only to what their analyses can conclude with a high degree of certainty. The *AFTE Journal* is "dedicated to the sharing of information, techniques, and procedures." AFTE also provides scholarships for research.

A tool mark (or toolmark) is a mark made on some piece of evidence that has been made by a tool. This may be as simple as a chisel or a hammer and the item cut or the surface hit. The idea is that tools such as these may have slight but identifiable differences resulting from the manufacturing processes or to the later usages to which it has been put. Frequently, these differences may be identifiable only microscopically. The receiving surface may record these marks if it is an appropriate surface.

The next steps in a criminal case are to connect the tool to the person charged and the mark to the victim. This will establish the chain of connection between the person charged and the victim. These latter two connections are generally done by others than the professionals who make the connection from the tool to the mark.

A major part of this work at present is the connection of a firearm to a bullet fired. Most handguns and rifles have rifling, which is a spiral groove inside the barrel that imparts a spin to the bullet. This spin makes the bullet more accurate. Shotguns typically do not have this rifling. The "twist rate" is the distance the bullet has to travel down the barrel to revolve once. Some guns have twist rates that increase as the bullet travels down the barrel; as the bullet increases in speed traveling down the barrel, the speed of rotation will increase. This may result as incidental to the gunsmith's desire to ensure that there not be a reduction in twist that would decrease accuracy and range. The result of all this is small differences in the marks made on the bullet by the gun.

Given the varying characteristics of different firearms as well as the differences across firearms of a given type/manufacturer, it may be possible to make the connection using the marks on the bullet and comparing them with the marks on another bullet fired by the tester from the gun under consideration. The particular similarities and differences need to be analyzed and be presented as part of the chain of evidence in court.

In making the connection between the tool and the mark, it is important that the witness cannot be impeached in court; otherwise, the testimony is essentially worthless. Thus, having professional certification (as with CPA, MD, etc.) is valuable to the person doing the testimony. The AFTE has a program that provides certification in three areas: Firearms, Toolmarks, and Gun Shot Residue/Distance. As of 2011, there were just 81 persons certified in Firearms, 57 certified in Toolmarks, and 31 certified in GSR/Distance. The written examinations are given at AFTE's annual Training Seminar, while the practical examinations are offered at the Bureau of Alcohol, Tobacco, Firearms and Explosives Laboratory in Annandale, Maryland.

For any expert witness, not only may certification be useful, but so is a reputation for integrity and thoroughness. Ideally, the presentation to the court should be the same and the conclusions the same whether the expert is working for the defense or for the prosecution (this is true for any expert). By creating methodology and databases that help standardize the work, the AFTE is working to help in that outcome.

Lawrence Southwick Jr.

See also: Bureau of Alcohol, Tobacco, Firearms and Explosives (ATF)

Further Reading

Hamby, James E., and James W. Thorpe. "The History of Firearm and Toolmark Identification." *Association of Firearm and Tool Mark Examiners Journal* 31 (1999): 266–84.

Science Daily. "Using Telltale Toolmarks to Fight Crime." http://www.sciencedaily .com/releases/2004/04/040414004703.htm (accessed May 31, 2011).

Attitudes toward Gun Control.

See Gun Control, Attitudes toward

Automatic Weapons Laws

Federal government regulation of automatic weapons—those capable of firing bullets in rapid succession by depressing and holding down the gun trigger—dates to 1934. The use of submachine guns, such as the infamous Tommy gun, by gangsters in the 1920s and 1930s sparked public outrage and calls for government regulation.

Created for military use at the end of World War I, the Tommy gun was developed by U.S. Army colonel John M. Thompson for use in trench warfare. Referred to by Thompson as a "trench broom," it was designed so that a single soldier could deliver numerous shots in a brief space of time, comparable to the heavier and more cumbersome machine guns used so devastatingly in the war. After the war, Thompson tried to market his gun, but had little success until Chicago gangsters began using the gun in 1925. Soon, other gangsters followed suit. Because automatic weapons could fire hundreds of rounds in a minute and produced recoil that made aim and control difficult to impossible, they had no legitimate hunting or sporting use and posed a considerable danger to anyone in the vicinity of such a weapon.

In response, several states passed anti–machine gun laws, but the federal government failed to act until 1934. In a bill backed by President Franklin D. Roosevelt and referred to as the "Anti-Machine Gun Bill," Congress considered a measure that would have required national registration and taxation of several types of firearms that were considered appealing to criminals, including handguns, sawed-off shotguns, cane guns, and automatic weapons. The original proposal also called for fingerprinting individuals who purchased such weapons. This proposal drew opposition from the National Rifle Association and other gun interests. Responding to these pressures, the bill that was reported out of committee omitted pistols. As enacted, the National Firearms Act of 1934 (48 Stat. 1236) requires automatic weapons to be registered with the U.S. Treasury Department. The owner must be fingerprinted, undergo a background check, and pay a fee.

There were no major changes in the law until the Firearms Owners' Protection Act of 1986, which barred future possession or transfer of automatic weapons. However, pre-1986 weapons can be sold by federally licensed Class III firearm dealers if the buyer passes the necessary background check and pays the federal tax. About a quarter-million fully automatic weapons are registered in the United States. Half are owned by private individuals, and the other half by various law enforcement and other government agencies. Law enforcement officials have noted that automatic weapons hold special appeal for criminals, especially those involved in drug trafficking, but crime statistics do not support the idea that such weapons are widely used by criminals, probably owing to the government's early and strict regulation of such weapons.

Robert J. Spitzer

See also: Assault Weapons; Firearms Owners' Protection Act of 1986; Gun Control; National Firearms Act of 1934; Tommy Gun

Further Reading

Kennett, Lee, and James LaVerne Anderson. *The Gun in America.* Westport, CT: Greenwood Press, 1975.

Leff, Carol Skalnik, and Mark H. Leff. "The Politics of Ineffectiveness: Federal Firearms Legislation, 1919–38." *Annals of the American Academy of Political and Social Science* 455 (1981): 48–62.

Yenne, Bill. *Tommy Gun: How General Thompson's Submachine Gun Wrote History.* New York: St. Martin's Press, 2009.

Availability of Guns, Effects on Crime

Multiple theories have been offered as to the effect of gun availability on crime, including the following:

1. *Guns Facilitate Crime by Those Inclined to It:* Besides being almost self-evident, this is amply supported by empirical evidence. Gun robberies net far more than do robberies in which other weapons are used, because without a gun, a robber is basically limited to attacking individuals. Also, guns allow robbers to attack such lucrative targets as banks and stores, whose proprietors might be armed (Kleck 1997, 239).

   By the same token, American and foreign data both show victims are less likely to suffer injury from robbers using guns. This is because victims are much more likely to comply if confronted with a gun; and robbers armed with lesser weapons may feel the need to start out by gratuitously hurting the victim to preempt resistance. Of course, if a gun robber actually shoots a victim, death is likelier than from injury with some lesser weapon (Cook 1987, 361; Kleck 1997, 238). Also, guns enable the weak to prey on the strong, though, in fact, criminals are mostly younger and stronger than victims.

2. *Guns Allow Victims to Resist Attack:* Neither martial-art skills nor chemical sprays provide a real option for victims faced by attackers who are stronger or armed. Indeed, sprays like Mace are

ineffective against attackers who are high on alcohol or drugs, or are intensely angry or excited—i.e., just the people who are most likely to attack and be the most dangerous (Jacobs 1989).

It bears emphasis that those who deprecate self-defense with guns do *not* recommend using any other kind of weapon instead. Their advice to victims threatened with robbery or rape is "the best defense against injury is to put up no defense—give them what they want or run" (Handgun Control Staff 1976; Shields 1981; Zimring and Zuehl 1986).

That advice is only partly supported by the evidence. Victims resisting with a lesser weapon than a gun are about twice as likely to suffer injury as victims who submit. But victims who pull guns find criminals generally flee. As a result, analysis of decades of national data shows victims who resist with a gun are only half as likely to suffer injury as those who submit—and of course, are much less likely to be robbed or raped (Kates 1991; Kleck 1997).

There is intense controversy as to just how often victims armed with guns actually do confront attacking felons. While the Federal Bureau of Investigation (FBI) compiles and publishes annual data on crimes, there is no protocol for self-defense incidents; so, even when they are reported, police agencies do not record them as such. In surveys of prison inmates sponsored by the National Institute of Justice, "Seventy percent of the respondents reported having been 'scared off,' shot at, wounded, or captured by a [gun-]armed crime victim" (Sheley and Wright 1995, 63; Wright and Rossi 1986, 154). From

responses to more than 15 national and state surveys in which the general populace was asked about defensive gun use, Gary Kleck (1995, 1997) estimated that 2 million to 2.5 million victims annually use handguns to repel criminal attackers. Handguns are used by citizens to defend against crime about three times as often annually as by criminals to commit crimes. (Many of these incidents do not involve victims confronting criminals with guns, however. Less than 30 percent of all violent crime involves guns [Bureau of Justice Statistics 1998, table 3-116]; for instance, guns are involved in only 25 percent of robberies and 4 percent of rapes [Kleck 1997].)

Kleck's estimate has been vindicated by subsequent research (Southwick 1997) and proved persuasive even to a criminologist who was deeply antipathetic to firearms (Wolfgang 1995). Many others have felt Kleck's estimate to be highly exaggerated. But the principal critics' own national survey yielded the even-higher figure of 3 million defensive uses annually. At that point, they decided that surveys cannot provide a reliable index to defensive firearm use (Cook and Ludwig 1998). They and other scholars opposed to defensive firearm ownership point to a different survey vehicle (the National Crime Victimization Survey) that suggests—but without directly posing the question—the incidence of defensive gun use is less than 100,000 annually (Cook and Ludwig 2000; McDowall and Wiersema 1994; however, contrast Kleck and Kates 2001).

3. *Guns Deter Criminal Attack:* The National Institute of Justice prison surveys found "36% of the respondents [imprisoned felons] in our study

Dezhbakhsa, Hashem, and Paul Rubin. "Lives Saved or Lives Lost: The Effects of Concealed Handgun Laws on Crime." *American Economic Review Papers and Proceedings* 88 (1998): 468–74.

Handgun Control Staff (Matthew G. Yeager, Joseph D. Alviani, and Nancy Loving). *How Well Does the Handgun Protect You and Your Family? Handgun Control Staff Technical Report 2.* Washington, DC: United States Conference of Mayors, 1976.

Jacobs, James B. "The Regulation of Personal Chemical Weapons: Some Anomalies in American Weapons Law." *University of Dayton Law Review* 15 (1989): 141–59.

Kates, Don B. "The Value of Civilian Arms Possession as Deterrent to Crime or Defense against Crime." *American Journal of Criminal Law* 18 (1991): 113–67. http://homepage.usask.ca/~sta575/cdn-firearms/Kates/crime-deterrent.html (accessed February 23, 2011).

Kates, Don B., and Daniel D. Polsby. "Long Term Non-Relationship of Firearm Availability to Homicide." *Homicide Studies* 4 (2000): 185–201.

Kleck, Gary. "Guns and Violence: An Interpretive Review of the Field." *Social Pathology* 1 (1995): 12–47.

Kleck, Gary. *Targeting Guns: Firearms and Their Control.* Hawthorne, NY: Aldine de Gruyter, 1997.

Kleck, Gary, and Don B. Kates. *Armed: New Perspectives on Gun Control.* Amherst, NY: Prometheus Books, 2001.

Lott, John R., Jr. *More Guns, Less Crime: Understanding Crime and Gun Control Laws.* 2nd ed. Chicago: University of Chicago Press, 2000.

McDowall, David, and Brian Wiersema. "The Incidence of Defensive Firearm Use by U.S. Crime Victims, 1987 through 1990." *American Journal of Public Health* 84 (1994): 1982–84. http://ajph.aphapublications.org/cgi/reprint/84/12/1982.pdf (accessed February 23, 2011).

Pridemore, William A. "Using Newly Available Homicide Data to Debunk Two Myths about Violence in an International Context: A Research Note." *Homicide Studies* 5 (2001): 267–75.

Sheley, Joseph, and James D. Wright. *In the Line of Fire: Youth, Guns, and Violence in Urban America.* Hawthorne, NY: Aldine de Gruyter, 1995.

Shields, Pete. *Guns Don't Die—People Do.* New York: Arbor House, 1981.

Shugart, William F. "More Guns, Less Crime: Understanding Crime and Gun Control Laws." *Southern Economic Journal* 65 (1991): 978–81.

Southwick, Lawrence. "Do Guns Cause Crime? Does Crime Cause Guns? A Granger Test." *Atlantic Economic Journal* 25 (1997): 256–73.

Wolfgang, Marvin E. "A Tribute to a View I Have Long Opposed." *Journal of Criminal Law and Criminology* 86 (1995): 188–92.

Wright, James D., and Peter H. Rossi. *Armed and Considered Dangerous: A Survey of Felons and Their Firearms.* Hawthorne, NY: Aldine de Gruyter, 1986.

Zimring, Franklin E., and Gordon Hawkins. *The Citizen's Guide to Gun Control.* New York: Macmillan, 1987.

Zimring, Franklin E., and James Zuehl. "Victim Injury Death in Urban Robbery: A Chicago Study." *Journal of Legal Studies* 15 (1986): 1–40.

Average-Joe Thesis

The central conundrum of gun control is that those for whom it is most urgent to disarm are at the same time least subject to being disarmed, while those likely to comply are the law abiding—for whom it is least important to disarm. This conundrum is dismissed by those who assert that murderers are mostly otherwise law-abiding people ("average

Joes") who would comply with a law banning firearms and who killed only because a gun was available in a moment of ungovernable anger (Christoffel 1991, 300; National Coalition to Ban Handguns n.d.).

If that were true, banning guns would be a cheap and effective way of reducing murder. However, murders are rarely, if ever, committed by ordinary, law-abiding persons. For as long as homicide studies have been done, they have shown murderers to be people who are unlikely to comply with either gun laws or laws against violence in general. In almost every instance, murderers' lives are characterized by violence (often irrational) and other crime, substance abuse, psychopathology, and automobile, firearm, and other dangerous accidents (Braga, Piehl, and Kennedy 1999; Bureau of Justice Statistics, 1993; Dowd, Knapp, and Fitzmaurice 1994, 872; Kennedy and Braga, 1998; Kennedy, Piehl, and Braga 1997; Langford, Isaac, and Adams 2000; Mulvihill, Tumin, and Curtis 1969, 532; Robin 1991, 46–48; Rojek 2000; Straus, 1986; U.S. Federal Bureau of Investigation 1972, 38, and 1976, 42ff). Indeed, even those responsible for fatal gun accidents have a similar profile (Cook 1982; Kleck 1997, 29–30). These are people who have remarkably little concern for laws or lives, even their own lives.

Federal Bureau of Investigation (FBI) national data show homicide arrestees averaging a prior adult criminal career of at least six years, including four major felony arrests (U.S. Federal Bureau of Investigation 1976, 42ff). Though only 15 percent of Americans have any kind of criminal record, national, state, and local studies consistently show criminal records for upward of 70–80 percent of arrested murderers. For instance, the Bureau of Justice Statistics study of "murder defendants [under indictment] in the nation's 75 largest counties" found

76.7 percent "had a criminal history" (Bureau of Justice Statistics 1993). Moreover, murderers' criminal records tend to be robust. Without even considering other offenses they may have committed, 80 percent of Atlanta murder arrestees in 1997 had at least one prior drug offense; fully 70 percent had three or more prior drug offenses (Rojek 2000).

Nor would it be correct to assume that if 70–80 percent of murderers have prior adult records, the other 20–30 percent must be the kind of ordinarily law-abiding people who would comply with a gun-confiscation order. In the first place, 10–15 percent of murderers are juveniles who, by definition, cannot have adult criminal records. But, insofar as their juvenile records are available, they show the same pattern as for adult murders. Researchers who have obtained access to criminal records for juvenile murderers in Minneapolis, Boston, Baltimore, and Kansas City describe them as "a relatively small number of very scary kids" (Kennedy, Piehl, and Braga 1997; cf. Dowd, Knapp, and Fitzmaurice 1994; Kennedy and Braga 1998). So extensive are their records that the combined priors of the 125 minors who killed other minors in Boston in the years 1990–1994 totaled 3 previous murder charges; 160 armed violent crimes; 151 unarmed violent crimes; 71 firearms offenses and 8 involving other weapons; and hundreds of property offenses, drug offenses, and other crimes (Kennedy, Piehl, and Braga, 1997).

Assuming adult murderers have juvenile crime records similar to these Boston juvenile murderers, their combined juvenile-cum-adult records would average 10–14 priors per murderer. Another reason 20–30 percent of murderers have no official record of prior crime is that much or all of their violence has been directed against their family members. Such victims are less likely to press charges, and the police are loath to interfere in a family matter. A study of police responding to domestic disturbance calls in Kansas City, Missouri, found that 90 percent of all family homicides were preceded by previous disturbances at the same address, with a median of five calls per address. Thus homicide—of a stranger or someone known to the offender—is "usually part of a pattern of violence, engaged in by people who are known . . . as violence prone" (Robin 1991, 47–48).

Perpetrator studies that delve beyond crime records find that, whether murderers also have such records of deviance, virtually all have life histories studded with violence and other crimes that may not have led to arrest. So, while a Massachusetts domestic murder study found at least 74.7 percent of perpetrators had priors, it also found 23.6 percent "were under an active restraining order at the time of the homicide. Forty percent of perpetrators had a history of having been under a restraining order at some time prior to the homicide, taken out by the victim or some other person" (Langford, Isaac, and Adams 2000). Another form of aberrant behavior sharply distinguishing murderers from ordinary people is that often during childhood or adolescence, the former tortured and/or killed animals.

To some extent, the myth that murderers are just "average Joes" stems from a misunderstanding of the often-used description "domestic and acquaintance murder." That does not mean murderers are ordinary, law-abiding people. National data show that the largest proportion of gun murders occurring in homes involve people who became acquainted through prior illicit drug dealings. Among New Orleans murder victims, 85 percent of those autopsied in 1992–1993 tested positive for metabolites of cocaine.

In Los Angeles, 71 percent of minors injured in drive-by shootings "were documented members of violent street gangs." In Washington, D.C., 80 percent of all murders are estimated to be drug-related. Of Philadelphia murder victims in 1990–1996, between 84 and 93 percent tested positive for illegal drug use or had criminal histories (Cook and Ludwig 2000, 23; Kleck 1997, 236; Hutson, Anglin, and Pratts 1994, 235).

For several years, a colloquium on juvenile murder in Boston has been conducted by a group consisting of academics, police, probation officers, and youth workers. Initially, "the practitioners felt strongly that the youth homicide problem was almost entirely a gang problem." But on closer examination, it was realized that a distinction had to be made. Yes, virtually all youth murders are committed by gang members. Yet many of these murders are unrelated to a gang, e.g., a gang member beating his girlfriend to death or shooting a drug dealer in the course of ripping him off (Braga, Piehl, and Kennedy 1999, 283–84).

In sum, while "domestic and/or acquaintance murder" literally describes many homicides, it does not refer to murders by "average Joes" in ordinary neighborhoods and families. Typical domestic and/or acquaintance murders involve gang members; drug dealers, their competitors, and/or customers; and men who kill women they have brutalized on prior occasions. While it is only sensible to prohibit firearm possession by such people, the fact that our laws already do so attests to the difficulty of disarming those who are inclined toward violence and determined to possess arms for that purpose.

Don B. Kates Jr.

See also: Crime and Gun Use; Homicides, Gun; Women and Guns

Further Reading

Bureau of Justice Statistics. *Murder Cases in 33 Large Urban Counties in the United States, 1988.* Washington, DC: U.S. Department of Justice, 1993.

Braga, Anthony, Anne M. Piehl, and David M. Kennedy. "Youth Homicide in Boston: An Assessment of the Supplementary Homicide Report Data." *Homicide Studies* 3 (1999): 277–99.

Christoffel, Katherine Kaufer. "Toward Reducing Pediatric Injuries from Firearms: Charting a Legislative and Regulatory Course." *Pediatrics* 88 (1991): 294–305.

Cook, Philip J. "Guns and Violence: An Interpretive Review of the Field." *Social Pathology* 1 (1995):12–47.

Cook, Philip J. "The Role of Firearms in Violent Crime." In *Criminal Violence*, edited by Marvin E. Wolfgang and Neil Alan Weiner, 236–91. Beverly Hills, CA: Sage, 1982.

Cook, Philip J., and Jens Ludwig. *Gun Violence: The Real Costs.* New York: Oxford University Press, 2000.

Dowd, M. Denise, Jane F. Knapp, and Laura S. Fitzmaurice. "Pediatric Firearm Injuries, Kansas City, 1992: A Population-Based Study." *Pediatrics* 94 (1994): 867–76.

Hutson, H. Range, Deirdre Anglin, and Michael J. Pratts. "Adolescents and Children Injured or Killed in Drive-By Shootings in Los Angeles." *New England Journal of Medicine* 333 (1994): 324–27.

Kates, Don B., and Clayton Cramer. "Second Amendment Limitations and Criminological Considerations." *Hastings Law Journal* 60 (2009): 1339–70. https://www.uchastings .edu/hlj/archive/vol60/Kates-Cramer_60 -HLJ-1339.pdf (accessed July 23, 2011).

Kennedy, David, and Anthony Braga. "Homicide in Minneapolis: Research for Problem Solving." *Homicide Studies* 2 (1998): 263–90.

Kennedy, David, Anne M. Piehl, and Anthony Braga. "Youth Violence in Boston: Gun Markets, Serious Youth Offenders, and a Use Reduction Strategy." *Law and Contemporary Problems* 59 (1997): 147–96.

Kleck, Gary. *Targeting Guns.* Hawthorne, NY: Aldine de Gruyter, 1997.

Langford, Linda, Nancy Isaac, and Sandra Adams. "Criminal and Restraining Order Histories of Intimate Partner-Related Homicide Offenders in Massachusetts, 1991–95." In *The Varieties of Homicide and Its Research*, edited by Paul H. Blackman et al. Quantico, VA: U.S. Federal Bureau of Investigation, 2000.

Mulvihill, Donald J., Melvin M. Tumin, and Lynne A. Curtis. *Crimes of Violence.* Washington, DC: U.S. Government. Printing Office, 1969.

National Coalition to Ban Handguns. *A Shooting Gallery Called America.* Washington, DC: n.d.

Robin, Gerald D. *Violent Crime and Gun Control.* Cincinnati, OH: Anderson Publishing, 1991.

Rojek, Dean G. "The Homicide and Drug Connection." In *The Varieties of Homicide and Its Research*, edited by Paul H. Blackman, et al. Quantico, VA: U.S. Federal Bureau of Investigation, 2000.

Straus, Murray A. "Domestic Violence and Homicide Antecedents." *Bulletin of the New York Academy of Medicine* 62 (1986): 446–61.

U.S. Federal Bureau of Investigation. *Crime in the United States 1971.* Washington, DC: U.S. Government Printing Office, 1972.

U.S. Federal Bureau of Investigation. *Crime in the United States 1975.* Washington, DC: U.S. Government Printing Office, 1976.

Aymette v. State. *See United States v. Tot*

Ayoob, Massad. *See Miniguns*

B

Background Checks

A background check entails an examination of the background of prospective gun buyers, conducted to determine whether the buyer has a criminal record, a history of mental illness, or other circumstances that should bar the individual from completing the gun purchase. The idea of conducting background checks of prospective gun buyers dates back at least to the 1930s, when a 48-hour waiting period was applied in the District of Columbia; the drafting of that rule was assisted by the National Rifle Association (NRA), which continued to support the idea until the 1970s, when it reversed its position.

A concerted effort to enact a national waiting period for the purchase of a handgun to conduct background checks began in 1986. Those efforts succeeded in 1993 with the passage of the Brady Handgun Violence Prevention Act, which imposed a five-business-day waiting period for handgun purchases, during which time local law enforcement authorities were to conduct the necessary background checks. According to the law, handgun purchases are to be rejected if the applicant has been convicted of a crime that carries a sentence of at least a year (not including misdemeanors); if there is a violence-based restraining order against the applicant; or if the person has been convicted of domestic abuse, has been arrested for using or selling drugs, is a fugitive from justice, is certified as mentally unstable or is in a mental institution, or is

an illegal alien or has renounced U.S. citizenship. Opponents of the law, including the NRA, filed suit against the Brady Bill, challenging its constitutionality—not as a violation of the Second Amendment's right to bear arms, but as a violation of states' rights under the Tenth Amendment. In 1997, the U.S. Supreme Court struck down the law's provision requiring local police to conduct background checks in the case of *Printz v. United States* (521 U.S. 898). The ruling did not challenge the propriety of restricting handgun sales. Despite the ruling, handgun background checks generally continued.

In 1998, the five-day waiting period lapsed, as per the terms of the law, and was replaced by the Federal Bureau of Investigation's (FBI) National Instant Criminal Background Check System (NICS). This system is designed to allow an immediate background check to occur. The check must be completed within three days, but 95 percent of the background checks are completed within two hours, according to a U.S. Justice Department report. From 1994 to 2008, about 1.8 million handgun purchases have been blocked as the result of background checks. This represented a rejection rate of about 2 percent of all handgun purchases. In 2009, the government passed its 100 millionth background check. Most states conduct their own background checks; the rest relied on FBI data. State checks result in a slightly higher rejection rate, probably owing to better and more complete state data. Even though waiting periods are no longer required by the national government, 11 states have their own, ranging from a few days to several months. Control proponents have argued for a restoration of a national three-day waiting period, in part because of the perceived value of a cooling-off period before handgun purchases. Since 2004, federal law has required the destruction of background check data within 24 hours (known as the Tiahrt Amendment, named after Rep. Todd Tiahrt (R-KS), who sponsored the measure), making it unavailable for law enforcement examination.

One area of gun sales continues to be omitted from nationally mandated background checks. In most places, "secondary-market" gun sales by unlicensed individuals can occur without background checks. Referred to generally as the "gun-show loophole," these sales at gun shows, flea markets, and other unregulated venues account for as much as 40 percent of gun sales. As of 2008, 17 states required background checks for all handgun purchases, even those from unlicensed sellers.

Robert J. Spitzer

See also: Black Market for Firearms; Brady Handgun Violence Prevention Act (Brady Bill); Coalition to Stop Gun Violence (CSGV); Gun Shows; National Rifle Association (NRA); *Printz v. United States*; Safety Courses; Waiting Periods

Further Reading

Hemenway, David. *Private Guns, Public Health*. Ann Arbor: University of Michigan Press, 2004.

Spitzer, Robert J. *The Politics of Gun Control*. 5th ed. Boulder, CO: Paradigm Publishers, 2012.

Bailey v. United States (1996)

In *Bailey v. United States* (516 U.S. 137 (1996)), the U.S. Supreme Court held that the government must show "an active employment" or active use of a firearm by a defendant for the defendant to be held criminally liable under a statute (i.e., the pre-amendment version of 18 U.S.C. § 924 (c)) that made it an offense to "use" or "carry" a firearm during a drug-trafficking crime. According to the court, to be held criminally culpable under such a statute, the "Government must show that the defendant actively employed the firearm during and relation to the predicate crime." Hence, merely having the firearm stored in the trunk or glove compartment of a vehicle during the commission of a drug-trafficking offense would be insufficient, as the firearm was not being actively utilized during the commission of the crime. After *Bailey*, it became much harder for prosecutors to win sentences under these criminal statutes, as the prosecutor needed to show actual use of the weapon. More specifically, before the *Bailey* decision, several federal circuit courts of appeals had upheld criminal convictions under the "use" prong of Section 924(c), even though the weapon was not actively utilized in the crime at question. The decision by the Supreme Court in *Bailey* overruled these lower court decisions and required lower courts to find proof that the defendant actually used or employed the firearm during the crime to uphold a conviction under Section 924(c). Additionally, as a result of the Supreme Court's decision in *Bailey*, Congress amended 18 U.S.C. Section 924(c) in 1998 to expressly provide that "possession" of a firearm during the commission of a drug-trafficking offense was also a crime. Congress amended 18 U.S.C. Section 924(c) precisely because of the Supreme Court's restrictive ruling in the *Bailey* case.

In *Bailey v. United States*, the petitioners Bailey and Robinson were both convicted of federal drug offenses and of violating section 924(c)(1) of the Gun Control Act of 1968, which imposes a prison term upon a person who "during and in relation to any . . . drug trafficking crime . . . uses or carries a firearm." Bailey's conviction was based on a loaded pistol that the police found inside a bag in his locked car trunk after they arrested him for possession of cocaine found in the car's passenger compartment. Robinson's conviction was based on an unloaded, holstered firearm that was found in a trunk in her bedroom closet after she was arrested for a number of drug-related offenses. There was no evidence that either Bailey or Robinson actually employed or utilized the weapons in committing drug-related offenses.

The government had argued successfully on appeal to a lower court that the defendants should be held criminally responsible under the above statute if the guns were sufficiently accessible and proximate to the drugs so that the jury could potentially infer that the defendant had placed the gun to further the drug offenses or protect the possession of drugs. The Supreme Court, applying standard norms of statutory construction, rejected the government's arguments and held that the term "use" correctly connotes more than mere possession of a firearm. There must be an active employment of the weapon in the underlying crime. According to the court, "use" would include such things as brandishing, displaying, bartering, striking with, and firing or attempting to fire a firearm, as well as making reference to a firearm in a defendant's possession. However, it does not include the mere placement or storage of the firearm at or near the site of crime, or at or near the proceeds, fruits, or paraphernalia, of that crime.

Congress reacted swiftly to the *Bailey* ruling. Within six months following the

ruling, both the U.S. Senate and House of Representatives set forth draft bills providing that mere possession of a firearm within the context of Section 924(c) was also a violation. While neither of the original drafts were passed, in 1997, the next Congress (the 105th Congress) amended Section 924(c) (again in response to *Bailey*) making it a separate offense to possess a firearm "in furtherance of" a crime. Thus, after *Bailey*, Congress amended Section 924(c) to expressly criminalize the "possession" of a firearm during a drug-trafficking offense. However, the qualifying language of "in furtherance of" a crime sets forth a higher standard than mere possession alone. That is, Congress required a higher standard of involvement to connect "possession" with the underlying crime ("in furtherance of" a crime). This language was inserted to placate gun advocates. Thus, according to then senator DeWine, "the purpose of adding the 'in furtherance' language is to assure that someone who possesses a gun that has nothing to do with the crime does not fall under 924(c)" (14 *Cong. Rec.*, daily ed., October 16, 1998, S12671). Likewise, according to then representative Bill McCollum, "it is also important to note that this bill will not affect any person who merely possesses a firearm in the general vicinity of a crime, nor will it impact someone who uses a gun in self-defense" (140 *Cong. Rec.*, October 9, 1998, H10330).

James A. Beckman

See also: Gun Control Act of 1968

Further Reading

Bettenhausen, Julie. "The Implications of *Bailey v. United States* on the Rise of the Convicted Criminal Claims and the Fall of 18 U.S.C. § 924(c)(1)." *Drake Law Review* 46 (1998): 677–715.

Ballistic Fingerprinting. *See* Ballistic Identification System

Ballistic Identification System

In 1999, the Bureau of Alcohol, Tobacco, Firearms and Explosives (ATF) established the National Integrated Ballistic Information Network (NIBIN) to administer and provide Integrated Ballistic Identification System (IBIS) equipment to federal, state, and local law enforcement agencies. This equipment acquires digital images of markings on spent ammunition taken from crime scenes or from test-fired crime guns. The IBIS equipment then automatically compares the markings to a database of digital images taken from earlier crime scenes or guns. If the equipment scores a match or "hit," the firearms examiner compares the two to confirm. This system allows NIBIN partners to discover links between crimes much more quickly, in a matter of hours, and in some cases making connections that would have been undiscovered without the technology (Bureau of Alcohol, Tobacco, Firearms and Explosives 2011).

The ATF's annual appropriations by Congress prohibit the agency from collecting information related to the capture or storage of ballistic information relating to the manufacture, importation, or sale of guns. Therefore, the equipment is limited to collecting ballistic information related to criminal investigations. However, the technology has allowed 156 NIBIN partner agencies to record over 1.6 million acquisitions, resulting in over 34,000 hits, linking two or more crime scene investigations to the same weapon. Importantly, the system does not match the bullets or casings fired from the same weapon, which is the duty of the firearms examiner. However, the system does provide a list of probabilities for a match according to a numerical scoring

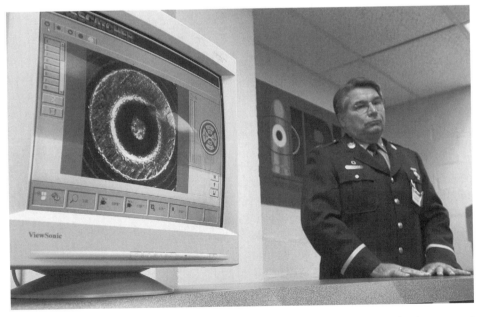

A computer monitor displays the markings of a cartridge case using the Integrated Ballistics Identification System. (AP Photo/Gail Burton)

system, which greatly speeds up the process for matching and aids the examiner by eliminating unlikely candidates (Ballistic Information Network 2011).

Robert H. Wood

See also: Association of Firearm and Tool Mark Examiners (AFTE); Bureau of Alcohol, Tobacco, Firearms and Explosives (ATF)

Further Reading

Ballistic Information Network. *Program Overview.* 2011. http://www.nibin.gov/ (accessed June 26, 2011).

Bureau of Alcohol, Tobacco, Firearms and Explosives. *ATF Fact Sheet—National Integrated Ballistic Information Network (NIBIN).* March 2011. http://www.atf.gov/publications/factsheets/factsheet-nibin.html (accessed June 26, 2011).

Barrett v. United States (1976)

Barrett v. United States (423 U.S. 212 (1976)) is the U.S. Supreme Court case that held that a convicted felon's intrastate purchase from a retail dealer of a firearm that previously, but independently of the felon's receipt, had been transported in interstate commerce, is an unlawful criminal act under the Gun Control Act of 1968 (GCA). The Supreme Court interpreted the commerce clause nexus of the GCA to apply to a purchaser's intrastate acquisition of a firearm, even if the purchaser was not directly involved in the transportation in interstate commerce. Thus, according to the Supreme Court, the GCA's interstate commerce requirement is satisfied if the firearm at any point in its past had traveled in interstate commerce.

The petitioner was convicted of violating 18 U.S.C. Section 922(h), which makes it unlawful for a convicted felon "to receive any firearm or ammunition which has been shipped or transported in interstate or foreign commerce." No evidence was presented at the petitioner's trial to show that the defendant personally participated in the interstate movement of the firearm prior to its purchase. Evidence was presented to show that the firearm, independent of the petitioner's receipt, had been transported in interstate commerce from the manufacturer to the distributor and then from the distributor to the dealer. The petitioner appealed his conviction—claiming that the GCA was not meant to reach an isolated intrastate receipt where the handgun was sold within the state by a local merchant to a local resident with whom the merchant was acquainted, and where the purchaser's transaction had no apparent connection with interstate commerce absent the handgun's attenuated out-of-state origin.

In rejecting the petitioner's claim, the court opined that the GCA clause specifying that felons were prohibited "to receive any firearm or ammunition which has been shipped or transported in interstate or foreign commerce" was without ambiguity. The court stated that this provision was directed unrestrictedly at the felon's receipt of any firearm that "has been" previously shipped in interstate commerce. Additionally, the court ruled that had Congress intended to confine the GCA to direct interstate receipt, it would have so provided as it did in other sections of the GCA.

James A. Beckman

See also: Gun Control Act of 1968

Further Reading

Streit, Kevin T. "Note: Can Congress Regulate Firearms? Printz v. United States and the Intersection of the Commerce Clause, the Tenth Amendment, and the Second Amendment." *William and Mary Bill of Rights Journal* 7 (1999): 645–70.

Barron v. Baltimore (1833)

The U.S. Supreme Court case *Barron v. Baltimore* (32 U.S. 243 (1833)) set the precedent that the Bill of Rights applied only to the national government, not to state and local governments. This left the individual states free to develop gun legislation without oversight from the federal government. *Barron v. Baltimore* was overturned through the incorporation doctrine that was a combination of congressional amendments and court action, including ratification of the Fourteenth Amendment and the Supreme Court case *Gitlow v. New York* (1925).

When the Bill of Rights to the Constitution was adopted in 1791, each state had its own bill of rights. Most people believed that the national Bill of Rights applied only to the federal government. Hence, a literal interpretation of the Constitution and the Bill of Rights would not prohibit state and local governments from passing legislation that infringed upon freedom of speech, religion, or the right to keep and bear arms. In 1813, Kentucky became the first state to pass a ban on concealed weapons.

In 1833, the Supreme Court affirmed the limitations on the Bill of Rights. The city of Baltimore was engaged in a series of infrastructure projects that diverted several streams from their natural courses. This caused a buildup of sand around John Barron's wharf that prevented ships from being able to approach the dock. Barron brought suit against the city claiming that since the Fifth Amendment forbade taking property without compensation, he ought to be reimbursed for the loss of business. Central to Barron's case was the notion that the Fifth Amendment should also apply to state and city governments.

Barron won his case and was awarded $4,500 in damages. However, the state court of appeals reversed the verdict and Barron appealed to the Supreme Court, which sided with the city. Led by Chief Justice John Marshall, the court found that the Bill of Rights applied only to the national government.

In spite of *Barron v. Baltimore*, most states accepted the premise that the right to keep and bear arms was a fundamental right of citizenship. States such as Kentucky, Georgia, Louisiana, Tennessee, Texas, and Virginia all had legal or constitutional protections for gun ownership. Many states did, however, place limitations on the types of weapons, usually making a distinction between weapons "suitable" for use by the militia and those not fit for civilized warfare. For instance, in 1840, the Tennessee Supreme Court in *Aymette v. State* distinguished between civilized weapons, such as pistols and rifles, and uncivilized ones, such as bowie knives.

Prior to the Civil War, *Barron v. Baltimore* would be used as justification for unequal treatment of state citizens, mainly in the slave states. For instance, while most states allowed private ownership of firearms, there were restrictions against slaves or former slaves owning guns or other weapons. These measures were driven by efforts to prevent a slave insurrection, and especially forestall free blacks from selling or providing weapons to slaves. Following the Civil War and the ratification of the Fourteenth Amendment, such overtly racial restrictions could not be maintained. However, many southern states used outwardly nonracial laws to restrict gun ownership. For example, in 1881, Arkansas adopted legislation that limited the type of guns that could be owned to weapons that had military use. The practical impact of such laws was that former Confederate soldiers were able to keep their firearms from the war, but poorer citizens, including African Americans, were unable to purchase new weapons. Concerns over the ability of African Americans to arm themselves were responsible for the passage of concealed-weapons legislation throughout the South. Concurrently, such sentiments also led many states to expand the legal doctrine of self-defense as a means to better protect specific classes.

Tom Lansford

See also: Black Codes; Civil War and Small Arms; Fourteenth Amendment; *McDonald v. City of Chicago*; *United States v. Tot*

Further Reading

Currie, David. *The Constitution in the Supreme Court: The First Hundred Years, 1789–1888*. Chicago: University of Chicago Press, 1985.

George, Robert P., ed. *Great Cases in Constitutional Law*. Princeton, NJ: Princeton University Press, 2001.

Harrison, Maureen, and Steve Gilbert, eds. *Landmark Decisions of the United States Supreme Court*. Beverly Hills, CA: Excellent Books, 1991.

Bartley-Fox Carrying Law

The 1974 Bartley-Fox law in Massachusetts imposed a mandatory one-year prison sentence for carrying a gun without a permit. This was the first law of its kind in the nation. The law is considered a model by gun control advocates and a horror story by gun rights advocates.

The Bartley-Fox law became effective on April 1, 1975 (Mass. Statutes 1975, chapter 113, section 2). Although widely described as a carrying law, it actually applies to any unlicensed possession of any gun (whether loaded or unloaded), or even a single round of ammunition, outside one's "residence or place of business" (Mass. Gen. Laws Ann.

chapter 269, section 10, 2001 ed.). While one year is the mandatory minimum, the sentence can be up to two and a half years in city or county jail or from two and a half to five years in state prison.

In 1994, a White House working group convened by the Clinton administration issued a secret (but leaked) report setting forth objectives for future national gun control laws. Among the objectives was a national law modeled on Bartley-Fox, providing a mandatory sentence for carrying a gun without a permit. In Massachusetts, local police chiefs and sheriffs have complete discretion about the issuance of handgun-carrying permits (Mass. Gen. Laws Ann. ch. 140, section 131; *Chief of Police of Shelburne v. Moyer*, 16 Mass. App. 543, 453 N.E.2d 461 (1983); *MacNutt v. Police Com'r of Boston*, 30 Mass. App. 632, 572 N.E.2d 577 (1991)). In practice, this means that in most jurisdictions, no one can obtain a carry permit, while some jurisdictions issue to friends of the chief or people with other political connections.

The Massachusetts Civil Liberties Union (CLU) opposed Bartley-Fox because of the risk that nondangerous people might be sent to prison. The Massachusetts legislature's Black Caucus also opposed the bill, because of concern about discriminatory licensing and arrests.

The enactment of Bartley-Fox did generate some of the kinds of cases that the Massachusetts CLU had warned about. The first prosecution under Bartley-Fox was of an old woman who was passing out religious literature in a rough part of Boston.

An early test case of the law was the successful prosecution of a young man who had inadvertently allowed his gun license to expire. To raise money to buy his high school class ring, he was driving to a pawn shop to sell his gun. Stopping the man for a traffic violation, a policeman noticed the gun. The teenager spent the mandatory year in prison (*Commonwealth v. McQuoid*, 369 Mass. 925, 344 N.E. 2d 179 (1976)).

The most famous Bartley-Fox case, however, involved a man who started carrying a gun after a coworker assaulted him and repeatedly threatened to kill him. The coworker did attack later, and the victim successfully defended himself. The crime victim was then sentenced to the mandatory one year in prison for carrying a gun without a permit. The Massachusetts high court summarized as follows:

> The threat of physical harm was founded on an earlier assault by Michel with a knife and became a real and direct matter once again when Michel attacked the defendant with a knife at the MBTA [subway] station. . . . [D]efendant is a hard-working, family man, without a criminal record, who was respected by his fellow employees (Michel excepted).
>
> Michel, on the other hand, appears to have lacked the same redeeming qualities. He was a convicted felon with serious charges pending against him. . . . It is possible that defendant is alive today only because he carried the gun that day for protection. Before the days of a one-year mandatory sentence, the special circumstances involving the accused could be reflected reasonably in the sentencing or dispositional aspects of the proceeding. That option is no longer available in the judicial branch of government in a case of this sort. (*Commonwealth v. Lindsey*, 396 Mass. 840, 489 N.E. 2d 666 (1986))

The *Lindsey* case generated such an outcry that the defendant Lindsey was eventually pardoned by Massachusetts governor Michael Dukakis, even though Dukakis was a staunch gun-prohibition advocate.

The Bartley-Fox law is vigorously enforced, regardless of the circumstances of possession. Even new residents have received the mandatory year sentence, including a college student from Louisiana (*Commonwealth v. Wood*, 398 Mass. 135, 495 N.E. 2d 835 (1986)). Although the law is, on its face, nondiscretionary, the effect has been to remove judicial discretion in sentencing, leaving prosecutors with discretion about whether to bring charges. Police, who lack the discretion about whether to make an arrest when they find a gun, will sometimes avoid conducting frisks on some persons who they do not believe deserve to be arrested.

Scholarly evaluations of Bartley-Fox have generated mixed results. Part of the problem is that studies assume that the only thing Bartley-Fox did was impose the mandatory sentence for unlicensed carrying. But in fact, Bartley-Fox also imposed mandatory sentences for use of a gun in a crime. Accordingly, it has been difficult to disentangle the effects of the two different parts of the Bartley-Fox law—one aimed at violent criminals, the other aimed at citizens who merely lack a permit.

One study was conducted by the U.S. Department of Justice, which concluded that "the effect may be to penalize some less serious offenders, while the punishment for more serious offenses is postponed, reduced, or avoided altogether" (Carlson 1982, 15). The Wright, Rossi, and Daly study *Under the Gun*—conducted under the auspices of the National Institute of Justice—found that the law reduced the casual carrying of firearms but did not significantly affect the gun-use patterns of determined criminals.

David B. Kopel

See also: Gun Control; Massachusetts Gun Law; Wright, James D.

Further Reading

Beha, James A., II. "And *Nobody* Can Get You Out": The Impact of a Mandatory Prison Sentence for the Illegal Carrying of a Firearm on the Use of Firearms and on the Administration of Criminal Justice in Boston—Part I and Part II." *Boston University Law Review* 57 (1977): 96–146, 289.

Carlson, Kenneth. "Mandatory Sentencing: The Experience of Two States." Department of Justice, National Institute of Justice Policy Brief. Washington, DC: Abt Associates, 1982.

Pierce, Glenn L., and William J. Bowers. "The Bartley-Fox Gun Law's Short-Term Impact on Crime in Boston." *Annals American Academy of Political and Social Science* 455 (1981): 120–37.

Wright, James, Peter Rossi, and Kathleen Daly. *Under the Gun: Weapons, Crime and Violence in America.* Hawthorne, NY: Aldine de Gruyter, 1983.

Bates, Madeleine "Lyn" (1946–)

Madeleine "Lyn" Bates is a founder and the vice president of Arming Women Against Rape and Endangerment (AWARE), a nonprofit organization dedicated to educating women on self-defense. She is a competitive shooter and teacher of self-defense techniques. AWARE focuses on helping women to protect themselves from a variety of crimes, including stalking. AWARE's mission is to "educate the public, organizations, and individuals about issues related to personal safety" (2011). Founded in 1990, AWARE provides training, education, and support for those learning to deal with violence, with a focus on women. Bates writes regularly for *Women & Guns* magazine (2011).

Bates received her BS from Carnegie Mellon University and her PhD from Harvard University. As a skilled shooter and a leading educator in self-defense and firearms for women, she won the Tactical Advocate Award for teaching and writing from the American Tactical Shooting Association in 1997. Bates has lectured for the American Society of Law Enforcement Training, Women in Federal Law Enforcement, the International Women Police Association, the American Society of Criminology, and the American Women's Self-Defense Association. In addition to writing for *Women & Guns*, she wrote the self-published *Safety for Stalking Victims: How to Save Your Privacy, Your Sanity, and Your Life* (2001).

Gregg Lee Carter and Walter F. Carroll

See also: Arming Women Against Rape and Endangerment (AWARE); Women and Guns; *Women & Guns* Magazine

Further Reading

Arming Women Against Rape and Endangerment (AWARE). http://www.aware.org/aboutaware.shtml (accessed March 14, 2011).

Bates, Lyn. *Safety for Stalking Victims: How to Save Your Privacy, Your Sanity, and Your Life.* Bloomington, IN: IUniverse, 2001.

Carter, Gregg Lee. *Gun Control in the United States: A Reference Handbook.* Santa Barbara, CA: ABC-CLIO, 2006.

Women & Guns. http://www.womenshooters.com/ (accessed March 14, 2011).

Beard, Michael K. (1941–)

Michael K. Beard, president of the Coalition to Stop Gun Violence (CSGV), has headed the organization since founding it in 1974. The organization, originally named the National Coalition to Ban Handguns, is composed of many groups with interests in social justice, public health, religion, civic, and child welfare—all of which strive for the reduction of firearms-related death and injury. An important branch of CSGV is the Educational Fund to Stop Gun Violence (EFSGV). CSGV and EFSGV have focused their efforts on trying to close illegal gun markets, creating a greater grassroots gun control movement, strengthening laws regulating firearms, and filing litigation against the gun industry. Their latest campaign focuses on guns, democracy, and freedom.

Beard graduated from the School of Government and Public Administration and the School of International Service at American University. He appears frequently on television and radio talk shows, where he promotes stronger gun control, and his writing on the topic regularly appears in newspapers across the country. In addition, he has testified before the U.S. House of Representatives and the U.S. Senate, during which he spoke against the McClure-Volkmer (Firearm Owners Protection) Act of 1986. Before founding CSGV, he was executive director of the Communication for Congressional Reform, Self-Determination for D.C. and the World Federalist Youth. He was a staff member for Representative Walter E. Fauntroy (D-DC), Representative Walter Moeller (D-OH), and Senator John F. Kennedy (D-MA). Beard belongs to the Screen Actors Guild and the American Federation of Radio and Television Artists.

Gregg Lee Carter and Walter F. Carroll

See also: Coalition to Stop Gun Violence (CSGV)

Further Reading

Carter, Gregg Lee. *Gun Control in the United States: A Reference Handbook*. Santa Barbara, CA: ABC-CLIO, 2006.

Coalition to Stop Gun Violence (CSGV). http://www.csgv.org/index.php (accessed March 14, 2011).

Beecham v. United States (1994)

In *Beecham v. United States* (511 U.S. 368 (1994)), the U.S. Supreme Court held that a state restoration of civil rights does not invalidate a federal conviction under the Gun Control Act of 1968 (GCA), which requires that civil rights be restored under the law of the jurisdiction where the earlier proceedings were held. The Supreme Court unanimously indicated that the determination as to the restoration of civil rights is an issue of federal, not state, law when the federal firearm disability was imposed as a result of a federal conviction.

The petitioners in *Beecham* were each convicted of violating 18 U.S.C. Section 922(g), which makes it unlawful for a convicted felon to possess a firearm. While each petitioner was previously convicted of a federal felony offense, both of the petitioners had also obtained a restoration of their civil rights by their respective states. Under the definitional section of the GCA contained at 18 U.S.C. Section 921(a)(20), a conviction is determined in accordance with the law of the jurisdiction in which the proceedings were held (choice-of-law clause), and any conviction that has been expunged or set aside or for which a person has been pardoned or has had civil rights restored shall not be considered a conviction for purposes of the GCA (exemption clause). The petitioners construed these clauses as supporting the proposition that the restoration of civil rights related to state restoration procedures alone.

In rejecting the petitioners' claim, the court utilized standard norms of statutory construction and held that the choice-of-law and exemption clauses should be read and construed in conjunction with each other, and not separately as claimed by the petitioners. The result of such statutory interpretation is that if "the law of the jurisdiction in which the proceedings were held" was a federal prosecution, any restoration of civil rights must be determined pursuant to that same jurisdiction, namely the federal government. Conversely, if the underlying proceedings were held in a state court, any restoration of civil rights must be determined by that state jurisdiction. In so ruling, the Supreme Court also rejected the notion that the arguable dearth of federal law procedure for restoring civil rights meant that Congress intended all felons to have access to all the procedures specified in the exemption clause at the state level.

While the court expressed no opinion on whether or not a federal felon can have his civil rights restored under federal law, the law in this area is unsettled. However, two sets of federal procedure processes for the restoration of civil rights should be noted. First, under Article II of the Constitution, the president may pardon any offense, which would act as a restoration of civil rights under the GCA. Second, section 925(c) of the GCA allows the secretary of the treasury to accept applications and grant relief from the disability imposed by section 922(g). The secretary of the treasury has delegated this authority to the Bureau of Alcohol, Tobacco, Firearms and Explosives (ATF). However, this is largely an illusory right at present because the ATF has been prohibited by Congress in each of its annual appropriations since 1992 from taking any action on these applications.

James A. Beckman

See also: *Caron v. United States*; Enforcement of Gun Control Laws; Gun Control Act of 1968

Further Reading

Pals, Gregory. "Notes: Judicial Review under 18 U.S.C. § 925(c): Abrogation through Appropriations?" *Washington University Law Quarterly* 76 (1998): 1095–119. http://lawreview.wustl.edu/inprint/76-3/763-1095.pdf (accessed June 8, 2011).

Beecher's Bibles

"Beecher's Bibles" was a nickname for rifles that were sent to Kansas by New England abolitionists to help antislavery settlers who were being persecuted and disarmed by the proslavery territorial government.

Pursuant to the 1854 Kansas-Nebraska Act, the question of slavery in the future states of Kansas and Nebraska was to be decided by a vote of the settlers. Both pro- and antislavery forces encouraged their allies to move into Kansas. The proslavery forces, with heavy support from "Border Ruffians" in Missouri, stuffed ballot boxes, violently drove Free Soilers away from the polls in 1855, disarmed the Free Soilers, and expelled all slavery opponents from the territorial legislature. (Free Soilers were immigrants from northern states who wanted to prevent slavery in Kansas.)

The Free Soil settlers let their New England supporters know of their need for firearms. Among the strongest supporters of arming the settlers was the Reverend Henry Ward Beecher, one of eight children of the eminent preacher Lyman Beecher and brother of Harriet Beecher Stowe, whose sensational best-seller *Uncle Tom's Cabin* helped inflame the North against slavery.

In his *Ordeal of the Union*, historian Allan Nevins (1947, 431) wrote that Beecher sent a letter to a Yale congregation of abolitionists, stating "there are times when self-defense is a religious duty. If that duty was ever imperative, it is now, and in Kansas." Nevins explained: "Beecher's remark that such weapons were a greater moral urgency among Border Ruffians than the Scriptures gave currency to the phrase 'Beecher's Bibles.' " According to one version of the story, Beecher and his church shipped 25 Sharps carbines (short rifles) in a crate concealed underneath 25 Bibles. When the settlers opened the crate, they were disappointed to find Bibles, then delighted at what lay underneath. In any case, various groups in New England—such as the Massachusetts Emigrant Aid Company—began smuggling firearms to Kansas.

The Sharps were high-tech rifles invented in 1848, incorporating the new breech-loading design—as opposed to loading from the muzzle. They could fire five rounds a minute; they rapidly displaced muzzle-loading guns and were especially popular in the West. John Brown's raiders carried the Sharps carbine.

Not far from Lawrence, Kansas (the territorial capital), is the Beecher's Bible Church. During the territorial-era wars in Kansas, the church contributed a "Beecher's Bible Regiment" to the antislavery forces. The Kansas state capitol in Topeka features a mural with a large picture of John Brown, and Henry Beecher in the background.

David B. Kopel

See also: Civil War and Small Arms; *Dred Scott v. Sandford*; Frontier Violence

Further Reading

Beecher Bible and Rifle Church. http://www.visitwamego.com/Things-To-Do/History/Beecher-Bible-and-Rifle-Church/default.aspx (accessed January 16, 2011).

Coates, Jerry, and John McAulay. *Civil War Sharps, Carbines, and Rifles*. Gettysburg, PA: Thomas Publications, 1996.

Kopel, David B. "The Second Amendment in the 19th Century." *Brigham Young University Law Review* 4 (1998): 1359–1545.

Nevins, Allan. *Ordeal of the Union: A House Dividing 1852–1857*. Vol. 2. New York: Collier, 1947.

Bellesiles, Michael A. *See* Arming America Controversy

Beretta U.S.A. Corporation. *See Dix v. Beretta U.S.A. Corp.*

Berkowitz, Leonard (1926–)

Leonard Berkowitz is a social psychologist whose research has focused on the causes of aggression and violence. Berkowitz has proposed a "weapons effect," in which exposure to a weapon leads to aggressive feelings and behavior. Berkowitz argues that weapons can serve as conditioned stimuli, eliciting both the thoughts and motor responses associated with their use.

Berkowitz received his PhD in social psychology from the University of Michigan in 1951 and began his academic career at the University of Wisconsin in 1955, where he taught until his retirement in 1993. Though retired, Berkowitz, in his own words, is "still trying to develop [his] analysis of the formation, operation, and regulation of emotional states, particularly anger" and continues to publish scholarly research (personal website). During his career, he wrote three major books on aggression. *Aggression: A Social Psychological Analysis* was published in 1962, *Aggression: Its Causes, Consequences, and Control* in 1993, and *Causes and Consequences of Feelings* in 2000. His research explored many sources of aggression: anger, frustration, exposure to violence in television and movies, and the presence of weapons.

Berkowitz argued that feelings, ideas, memories, and "expressive motor reactions" were linked associatively through an emotion-state network. If any of these elements were activated, the result would be some activation of the entire network.

According to Berkowitz, aggressive feelings and behavior could be caused by exposure to cues that were associated with violence. In this way, the presence of a gun could arouse an emotional state that made the use of that gun more likely, because of associations between guns and violence from television, movies, and life.

Berkowitz contended that "the finger pulls the trigger," but the trigger may also pull the finger. It is not just that having a gun is a convenient way of settling an argument. The weapon itself is a stimulant to violence (Kramer 1995). Because guns are associated with violence and aggression, they stimulate violent thoughts and impulses.

Berkowitz's research was primarily experimental. A frequent protocol would involve a college student who might be exposed to some kind of frustration and then in some cases provided with additional stimuli that might be associated with aggressive responses. The student was then given the opportunity to exhibit a violent response, usually by administering electrical shocks to subjects. The shocks were not real, but students were told that they were. Students might observe a short film in which a movie actor was involved in a violent altercation and then be offered the opportunity to shock a student whose name was similar to that of the movie actor. In some cases, weapons were present in the experimental laboratory or in the office in which students were initially briefed for the experiment.

In another experiment, students were permitted to throw wet sponges at clowns. The experimenters varied several conditions, including whether the clown insulted the subject. In one condition, a gun was visible in the booth; in another, it was absent. A clown who hurled insults did not incite more sponge throwing, but the presence of a gun did lead to a statistically significant increase.

Critics of Berkowitz's work have argued that the experiments evoked strong demand characteristics. Students could easily guess when they were expected to administer severe shocks and would be eager to please a professor by complying. Few would believe that a gun lying on a university desk or in a circus booth was accidental. Yet Berkowitz has varied his experimental protocols, always with the same result, and his experiments have been duplicated in other countries. Studies by other scholars have also shown that children who play with toy guns are more aggressive than those who do not.

Some of Berkowitz's more recent research involves the media's influence on aggression and violence. His work on the rise in violent crime after President Kennedy's assassination and after the mass killings committed by Charles Whitman and Richard Speck has been referenced in the linkage between media reportage and the subsequent "copycat" effect. In 2003, Berkowitz served on a panel of media scholars who reported that the "[r]esearch on violent television and films, video games, and music reveals unequivocal evidence that media violence increases the likelihood of aggressive and violent behavior in both immediate and long-term contexts" (Anderson et al. 2003). The panel further noted that while the media effects are larger for milder than for more severe forms of aggression, the latter is still substantial. Assessing a large and diverse range of existing research on the subject, the panel found its overall conclusion to be consistent, particularly in the most well-analyzed domain of television and film violence; moreover, the emerging evidence on video games is effectively the same.

Clyde Wilcox and Christine Kim

See also: Demonization of Guns; Legal Implications of Firearms Characteristics; Media

Violence; Violent Video Games and Gun Violence

Further Reading

Anderson, Craig, Leonard Berkowitz, et al. "The Influence of Media Violence on Youth." *Psychological Science in the Public Interest* 4 (2003): 81–110.

Berkowitz, Leonard. "Affect, Aggression, and Antisocial Behavior." In *Handbook of Affective Science*, edited by R. Davidson, K. Scherer, and H. Goldsmith. New York: Oxford University Press, 2003.

Berkowitz, Leonard. *Aggression: Its Causes, Consequences, and Control.* Philadelphia: Temple University Press, 1993.

Berkowitz, Leonard. "Appraisals and Anger: How Complete Are the Usual Appraisal Accounts of Anger?" In *International Handbook of Anger: Constituent and Concomitant Biological, Psychological and Social Processes*, edited by Michael Potegal, Gerhard Stemmler, and Charles Spielberger. New York: Springer, 2010.

Berkowitz, Leonard. *Causes and Consequences of Feelings.* New York: Cambridge University Press, 2000.

Berkowitz, Leonard. "The Frustration-Aggression Hypothesis: Examination and Reformulation." *Psychological Bulletin* 106 (1989): 59–73.

Berkowitz, Leonard. "Len Berkowitz." Social Psychology Network, http://berkowitz.socialpsychology.org/ (accessed May 16, 2011).

Berkowitz, Leonard. "Mood, Self-Awareness, and the Willingness to Help." *Journal of Personality and Social Psychology* 52 (1987): 721–29.

Berkowitz, Leonard. "On the Consideration of Automatic as Well as Controlled Psychological Processes in Aggression." *Aggressive Behavior* 34 (2008):117–29.

Berkowitz, Leonard. "On the Formation and Regulation of Anger and Aggression: A Cognitive-Neoassociationistic Analysis." *American Psychologist* 45 (1990): 494–503.

Berkowitz, Leonard. "Some Effects of Thoughts on the Anti- and Prosocial Influences of Media Events: A Cognitive Neoassociationistic Analysis." *Psychological Bulletin* 95 (1984): 410–27.

Berkowitz, Leonard, and Eddie Harmon-Jones. "Toward an Understanding of the Determinants of Anger." *Emotion* 4 (2004):151–55.

Kramer, Michael. "Why Guns Share the Blame." *Time* 145 (1995): 48. http://www.time.com/time/magazine/article/0,9171,982920,00.html (accessed May 16, 2011).

University of Wisconsin, Department of Psychology. "Faculty and Staff." http://glial.psych.wisc.edu/index.php/psychsplashfacstaff/93 (accessed May 16, 2011).

Biden, Joseph, Jr. (1942–)

As the long-time Democratic U.S. senator from Delaware, Joseph Biden Jr. made significant contributions to gun control policy, including cosponsoring the Crime Control Act of 1990 and writing the Violent Crime Control and Law Enforcement Act of 1994. However, his contributions as Barack Obama's vice president have been more limited. Although a gun owner himself, Biden's voting record over the course of his political career displays a strong commitment to gun control. As a result, the National Rifle Association (NRA) assigned him the lowest grade, an "F," for failing to protect gun rights.

Biden was born in Scranton, Pennsylvania, on November 20, 1942. At the age of 10, he moved to Delaware, which he served as senator from 1973 to 2009. During his tenure in the Senate, Biden was a member of the Judiciary Committee and the Foreign Relations Committee, both of which he served for a time as chair. On the Judiciary Committee, Biden focused on issues of crime, illegal drugs, and civil liberties, which placed him at the center of debates concerning guns.

The Crime Control Act, cosponsored by Biden and signed into law by President George H. W. Bush on November 29, 1990, increased penalties for those found guilty of gun-related crimes. A key provision allowed the federal government to crack down on the transfer of firearms across state lines, the trafficking of stolen guns, and the importation of parts for banned semiautomatic weapons, by extending Congress's power to regulate interstate commerce. An additional section of the law, the Gun-Free School Zones Act, also drew upon this expanded interpretation of the Commerce Clause, but was later declared unconstitutional by the Supreme Court in *United States v. Lopez* (1995)—though, after revision, it passed judicial review in its 1994 form.

Biden was also the primary author of the Violent Crime Control and Law Enforcement Act, signed into law by President Bill Clinton on September 13, 1994, which further increased penalties for all gun-related crime. However, its most well-known and controversial provision was the Public Safety and Recreational Firearms Use Protection Act, commonly referred to as the federal Assault Weapons Ban, which prohibited the manufacture of 19 types of semiautomatic weapons and their possession or transfer unless legally owned prior to the act's passage. The assault-weapons ban was not reauthorized by Congress and allowed to expire in 2004.

As Obama's running mate in 2008, Biden campaigned for repealing the Tiahrt Amendment, which limits law enforcement access to gun trace information, reinstating the expired Federal Assault Weapon Ban, closing the gun show loophole, and making guns childproof. He also provided rhetorical cover for Obama, accused of planning to take away Americans' guns, by speaking proudly as a gun owner and reassuring voters. However, since taking office, the Obama administration has notably avoided the gun issue. The one significant exception occurred in the immediate wake of the shooting of Representative Gabrielle Giffords (D-AZ) and 18 others in Tucson, Arizona, on January 8, 2011. The vice president's office was involved in meetings with gun control advocates during early efforts to reform federal gun policy, though no legislation has resulted.

Richard Holtzman and Drew Green

See also: Assault Weapons Ban of 1994; Clinton, William J.; Gun-Free School Laws; Gun Shows; National Rifle Association (NRA); Obama, Barack; Smart Guns; Trigger Locks; Tucson, Arizona, Massacre; *United States v. Lopez*

Further Reading

Spitzer, Robert J. *The Politics of Gun Control.* 5th ed. Boulder, CO: Paradigm Publishers, 2012.

Black Codes

After the Civil War, southern legislatures, determined to maintain their control over former slaves, passed comprehensive sets of repressive regulations known as "Black Codes." These codes deprived the freedmen of a variety of rights, including the right to travel, the right to serve on a jury, the right to engage in certain businesses, the right to testify against whites, and the right to possess firearms. As U.S. Supreme Court justice Clarence Thomas put it in his 2010 meticulous concurring with the *McDonald v. City of Chicago* opinion, southern legislatures took "particularly vicious aim at the rights of free blacks and slaves to . . . keep and bear arms for their defense."

Drafted during this time that represents the dusk of slavery and the dawn of freedom, the codes were passed by the legislatures of Mississippi, South Carolina, Alabama, and Louisiana in 1865, and Arkansas, Florida, Virginia, Georgia, North Carolina, Texas, and Tennessee in 1866. Antislavery Pennsylvania congressman Thaddeus Stevens vividly described the motivating sentiment of the day: "When it was first proposed to free the slaves, and arm the blacks, did not half the nation tremble? The prim conservatives, the snobs, and the male waiting-maids in Congress, were in hysterics."

Mississippi planter E. G. Baker's letter to members of the state legislature on October 22, 1865, provides additional unvarnished insight into the discriminatory mindset motivating the drafting of these codes: "It is well known here that our negroes through the country are well equipped with fire arms, muskets, double barrel shot guns, and pistols—and furthermore, it would be well if they are free to prohibit the use of fire arms until they had proved themselves to be good citizens in their altered state."

Mississippi was in fact the first state to adopt these means of social and economic control over the newly freed black population. Its code, tellingly titled an "Act to Regulate the Relation of Master and Apprentice Relative to Freedmen, Free Negroes, and Mulattoes," provided in part that "no freedman, free negro or mulatto, not in the military . . . and not licensed to do by the board of police of his or her county, shall keep or carry fire-arms of any kind, or any ammunition, . . . and all such arms or ammunition shall be forfeited to the former." Though varied in approach, at their heart, the Black Codes sought to ensure continued economic and social domination of white over black in the South.

It is important to remember that the U.S. Constitution, as well as the various state constitutions, all guaranteed citizens the right to bear arms (and were during this time popularly viewed as guaranteeing such). Attempts by southern legislators to use the Black Codes to disarm the South's black population were consequently a direct affront to those northern and southern abolitionists who sought equality. Furthermore, these codes represented a willful blindness to the fact that the former slaves were now full citizens entitled to all of the rights held by their white countrymen.

Aside from the symbolic and theoretical effect of the racially discriminatory Black Codes, they also had a very direct impact on those black citizens who were prevented from lawfully arming themselves for purposes of self-defense. An 1867 Special Report of the Anti-Slavery Conference recognized that blacks were "forbidden to own or bear firearms, and thus were rendered defenseless against assaults." In fact, two weeks after the Mississippi code was enacted, Calvin Holly, a black private assigned to the Freedmen's Bureau in Mississippi, wrote a letter relating an article in the *Vicksburg Journal* to bureau commissioner Howard. In the letter, Holly said that "the Rebels are going about in many places through the State and robbing the colored people of arms, money and all they have and in many places killing."

The southern legislators who proposed, drafted, and enacted the Black Codes knew well that an armed black populace was far less likely to be preyed upon by white mobs, and would be in an improved position to prevent re-enslavement by those white southerners who were willing to use any means necessary to preserve antebellum social order. What is more, an armed black populace in the South could potentially play a part in maintaining the Union. While former Confederate soldiers could keep their firearms, Black Codes sought to disarm the one group with unionist sympathies, namely freedmen.

Northern Republicans, able to see clearly the discriminatory motivations reflected in the Black Codes, grew increasingly concerned and irritated. They considered these codes blatant attempts to de facto relegalize and relegitimize slavery in the South. Their concern over the South's perceived attempts to circumvent the freeing of slaves provided the backdrop to the 39th Congress's drafting of the Fourteenth Amendment to the U.S. Constitution. Sen. Jacob Howard introduced the Fourteenth Amendment in the Senate. He stated that the amendment would protect the personal rights in the Bill of Rights from state deprivation, specifically mentioning the right of the people to keep and bear arms. This period of congressional Reconstruction, fueled by northern anger over southern intransigence, ultimately resulted in the repeal of the onerous and unjust Black Codes.

T. Markus Funk

See also: African Americans and Gun Violence; Fourteenth Amendment; Ku Klux Klan; *McDonald v. City of Chicago*; NAACP and Gun Control; Racism and Gun Control; *United States v. Cruikshank*

Further Reading

Cottrol, Robert J., and Raymond T. Diamond. "The Second Amendment: Toward an Afro-Americanist Reconsideration." *Georgetown Law Journal* 80 (1991): 309–61. http://www.constitution.org/2ll/2ndschol/12cd-r.pdf (accessed April 12, 2011).

Funk, T. Markus. "Gun Control and Economic Discrimination: The Melting-Point Case-in-Point." *Journal of Criminal Law and Criminology* 85 (1995): 764–806. http://www.constitution.org/2ll/2ndschol/30econ.pdf (accessed April 12, 2011).

Funk, T. Markus. "Is the True Meaning of the Second Amendment Really Such a Riddle? Tracing the Origins of an Anglo-American Right." *Howard Law Journal* 39 (1995): 411–36.

Halbrook, Stephen P. "Personal Security, Personal Liberty, and the Constitutional Right to Bear Arms: Visions of the Framers of the Fourteenth Amendment." *Seton Hall Constitutional Law Journal* 5 (1995): 341–434.

McDonald v. City of Chicago (Justice Thomas's concurring opinion). http://scholar.google.com/scholar_case?case=5141154246897960488&q=McDonald+v.+Chicago&hl=en&as_sdt=2,40 (accessed April 12, 2011).

Black Market for Firearms

The black market for firearms in the United States consists of transactions in which stolen and/or purchased firearms (including both new and secondhand guns) are illegally transferred between buyers and sellers. Individuals who divert firearms from the legal to the illegal marketplace are engaged in firearms trafficking. While not all guns bought and sold on the black market are involved in the commission of crimes, trafficking (or firearms diversion) is the primary source of guns used in criminal activity, with approximately five out of six firearms used in crime having been obtained illegally. As many as one-quarter of individuals identified as gun traffickers are convicted felons, and almost half of all firearms-trafficking investigations involve convicted felons as either the buyer or seller.

The Bureau of Alcohol, Tobacco, Firearms and Explosive (ATF), an arm of the U.S. Department of Justice, is the agency with primary responsibility for combating gun trafficking and curtailing the black market for firearms. There are four basic means by which firearms make their way onto the black market: licensed sellers (including pawn brokers) selling to prohibited purchasers (e.g., convicted felons), unlicensed individuals (e.g., private collectors) selling to prohibited purchasers, individuals purchasing guns on behalf of prohibited purchasers (i.e., straw purchases), and firearms theft.

Federal law requires firearms dealers to obtain a federal firearms license from the Federal Firearms Licensing Center. In addition to meeting federal regulations, gun dealers are required to abide by all local and state laws regarding the sale and possession of firearms. Firearms dealers are prohibited from selling firearms to certain classes of individuals, including juveniles, convicted felons, those who have been adjudicated to be mentally defective, illegal aliens, and dishonorably discharged members of the armed services. Firearms dealers are also prohibited from selling guns (except for rifles and shotguns) to unlicensed individuals from outside their state.

Licensed dealers serve as a source of firearms for the black market when they choose to sell to purchasers without conducting the federally required background check (through the National Instant Check System operated by the Federal Bureau of Investigation) or knowingly sell to prohibited purchasers who have provided falsified information. While licensed firearms dealers are involved in only a minority of ATF firearms investigations, they account for almost half of all firearms recovered in those investigations.

Not all individuals are required to obtain a federal dealer's license to sell firearms. Collectors and hobbyists who make only occasional sales and trades to enhance personal collections or who sell their collections in part or in whole are not required to do so. While such individuals are prohibited from

knowingly selling guns to prohibited purchasers, they are not required to conduct background checks, as licensed dealers are required to do. Firearms make their way into the black market when unlicensed sellers knowingly sell guns from their private collections to prohibited buyers, or when they legally purchase guns with the intention of reselling them illegally. Common venues for such illegal sales include gun shows (for both licensed and unlicensed individuals), flea markets, and want ads (both print and electronic). Unlicensed sellers account for almost a third of all firearms involved in ATF investigations.

Individuals who purchase guns on behalf of prohibited purchasers are called straw buyers and also contribute to the black market for guns. The straw buyer is legally eligible to purchase a gun but does so illegally by providing false information to the federally licensed seller regarding who the actual purchaser is. Friends (especially fellow gang members), relatives, and spouses are commonly used as straw buyers. As many as one-quarter of straw buyers are juveniles. Individual straw buyers tend to be involved with the purchase of only one or a few firearms rather than the bulk purchase of firearms. However, the number of individuals who act as straw buyers can be quite substantial, leading to a heavy influx of firearms into the black market. Working with the National Shooting Sports Association, the ATF instituted a special program christened "Don't Lie for the Other Guy," directed specifically at reducing straw purchases. The program is educational in nature and involves educating dealers about the detection of straw buyers as well as to prospective buyers regarding what constitutes a straw buy.

Not all stolen firearms make their way to the black market, but firearms stolen from individual owners as well as federally licensed dealers are an important source of guns for the black market. Less frequently, firearms are also stolen during shipping. However, though such transport thefts are relatively few in number compared to thefts from residences and licensed dealers, they typically involve large numbers of guns per incident. In addition, guns stolen during shipment are more likely to be newer guns, including semiautomatic pistols, which are preferred over older revolvers.

The ATF combats firearm trafficking and the black market for guns through a variety of programs administered by the agency's criminal enforcement division. Enforcement activities include inspection of federal licensees, background checks for gun purchasers, and criminal investigations of suspected firearm traffickers. Project Gunrunner is a recent initiative of the ATF directed at gun trafficking, specifically targeting the trafficking of guns to Mexico from the United States. Under the auspices of Project Gunrunner, and working in conjunction with state, local, tribal, and Mexican law enforcement, the ATF has undertaken about 4,500 investigations, resulting in the seizure of over 10,000 firearms destined for Mexico. Recently, however, Project Gunrunner (Bureau of Alcohol, Tobacco and Firearms 2011) has come under fire after guns involved in a sting operation were associated with the scenes where two law enforcement officers were killed.

Wendy L. Martinek

See also: Background Checks; Bureau of Alcohol, Tobacco, Firearms and Explosives (ATF); Felons and Gun Control; Firearm Dealers; Gun Shows; Licensing; National Instant Criminal Background Check System; National Tracing Center (NTC)

Further Reading

Bradford, Kevin D., Gregory T. Gundlach, and William L. Wilkie. "Countermarketing in the Courts: The Case of Marketing Channels and Firearms Diversion." *Journal of Public Policy & Marketing* 24 (2005): 284–98.

Bureau of Alcohol, Tobacco and Firearms. *Commerce in Firearms in the United States.* Washington, DC: U.S. Department of the Treasury, 2000.

Bureau of Alcohol, Tobacco and Firearms. *Following the Gun: Enforcing Federal Laws against Firearms Traffickers.* Washington, DC: U.S. Department of the Treasury, 2000.

Bureau of Alcohol, Tobacco, Firearms and Explosives. "Project Gunrunner." Washington, DC: Bureau of Alcohol, Tobacco, Firearms and Explosives, 2011. http://www.atf.gov/firearms/programs/project-gunrunner/ (accessed July 21, 2011).

Bureau of Justice Assistance. *Reducing Illegal Firearms Trafficking: Promising Practices and Lessons Learned.* Washington, DC: U.S. Department of Justice, 2000.

Pierce, Glenn L., et al. "Characteristics and Dynamics of Illegal Firearms Markets: Implications for a Supply-Side Enforcement Strategy." *Justice Quarterly* 21 (2004): 391–422.

Black Panthers

The Black Panther Party for Self Defense was founded in October 1966 in Oakland, California, by Huey P. Newton and Bobby Seale, based on the belief that only violent revolution would secure liberation for American blacks. To that end, all blacks were urged to arm themselves. The name was shortened to the Black Panthers, and the ideology spread across the country to urban minority communities. The Black Panthers terrified mainstream America, which enacted gun control laws aimed directly at the Black Panthers.

In California in the mid-1960s, the Panthers began carrying rifles and shotguns

Poster showing Black Panther leaders Bobby Seale and Huey P. Newton. (Library of Congress)

openly—as California law allowed—to protect victims of police brutality. The California legislature promptly enacted legislation restricting the carrying of long guns in public places. Governor Ronald Reagan, a strong opponent of the Black Panthers, signed the bill into law. More generally, the 1960s black militancy of which the Panthers were an especially visible element helped set the stage for the federal Gun Control Act of 1968, in which restrictions on inexpensive imported firearms were intended, in part, to prevent the urban unrest that was associated with the Black Panthers.

During the heyday of the Panthers, leaders were involved in a number of violent confrontations with police, resulting in deaths on both sides. Panther members believed that the Federal Bureau of Investigation's Counter Intelligence program was employed in an attempt to break the Black Panthers. Charges brought against Panthers failed to be substantiated in several high-profile cases. Newton was tried three times for killing a police officer in 1967. Each one resulted in a mistrial, the last in 1971. Seale was convicted as a codefendant in the "Chicago Eight" case of conspiracy to disrupt the Democratic Party convention in Chicago in 1968. The conviction was later overturned. In 1971, Seale was acquitted on charges of murdering an alleged police informant. Finally, in 1971, 13 Panthers were acquitted on charges of conspiracy to bomb public locations in New York City.

Sam Anderson claims to have been a founding member of the Harlem Panthers, whose founding in May 1966 predated the Oakland party. The Harlem party lasted only 18 months, which Anderson claims was a result of media preference for the more militant Oakland branch.

In 1972, the Panthers experienced an ideological schism when Newton and Seale announced their intent to abandon violence as a Panther tenet. Former chief publicist Eldridge Cleaver resisted the change. The conflict was resolved in 1974 when Seale resigned as leader of the Panthers and Newton fled to Cuba to avoid drug charges. During the remainder of the 1970s, the Panthers refocused and provided services to the black community such as free breakfasts for children, free medical clinics, and free food and clothing to the homeless. The Black Panther Party continued to decline in influence and notoriety and essentially disappeared in the late 1970s.

Carol Oyster

See also: Black Codes; Gun Control Act of 1968; NAACP and Gun Control; Racism and Gun Control

Further Reading

Leonardatos, Cynthia Deitle. "California's Attempt to Disarm the Black Panthers." *San Diego Law Review* 36 (1999): 947–96.

Pearson, H. *The Shadow of the Panthers: Huey Newton and the Price of Black Power in America*. Boston: Addison-Wesley, 1994.

Black Talon

The Black Talon (since renamed the Ranger Talon) is a jacketed hollow-point handgun bullet produced by the Winchester gun company. Like all such bullets, it is designed to expand upon impact, the lead core bulging at right angles to the bullet's axis to produce more shock and a larger wound channel, while the copper jacket splits and rolls back. A typical expanded bullet of this type assumes a mushroom shape, with the copper jacket rolled back behind the expanded, or mushroomed, lead core.

A unique feature of the Talon's design was that the copper jacket was thickened toward the point. Winchester advertised the Talon as possessing increased wounding power, since the thickened copper jacket would not roll back under the expanded lead core, but rather protrude at near-right angles to the bullet axis, making for a larger-diameter wound channel. Whether this actually made for increased lethality, or was merely an advertiser's puffing, was disputed by ballistics experts, but Winchester's ad copy showed the Talon's jacket assuming the form of sharp points extending outward from the expanding bullet to inflict additional damage.

In July 1993, gunman Gian Luigi Ferri killed six persons in an office shooting in San Francisco. Ferri used Black Talons for at least part of his murderous assault, and Winchester's publicity promptly rebounded upon the company. The design drew heavy media and political criticism, based both on its claimed lethality and the potential for points of the split jacket to penetrate surgical gloves during emergency surgery. In response,

Winchester limited sales to law enforcement and renamed the projectile the Ranger Talon.

David T. Hardy

See also: Ammunition, Types of; Dum-Dum Bullet

Further Reading

Peterson, Julie. "This Bullet Kills You Better." *Mother Jones* 18, no. 5 (September–October 1993): 15. http://motherjones.com/politics/1993/09/motherjones-so93-bullet-kills-you-better (accessed January 11, 2011).

Body Armor

The concept of body armor dates well into antiquity; however, until the development of synthetic fabrics capable of resisting high-velocity projectiles in the latter half of the twentieth century, only steel provided significant protection from modern firearms. Prior to the development of Kevlar, so-called bulletproof vests were essentially updates on medieval armor. However, Kevlar made possible lighter, more flexible vests that could be worn under clothing for extended periods. Beginning in the early 1970s, police agencies began to require uniformed officers to wear these vests when working. Officers in other assignments began wearing them for specific purposes, such as raids or arrests. As use increased, the number of police officer deaths reversed a rising trend and began a sustained decline (National Law Enforcement Memorial Fund 2010). The National Institute of Justice credits body armor with saving over 3,000 law enforcement lives over the past four decades (National Institute of Justice 2010).

Like all defensive armor, from medieval castles to modern tanks, soft body armor is not "bulletproof," but bullet resistant. As the velocity, mass, and density of the projectile increases, the difficulty of stopping it also increases. In addition to velocity, mass, and composition, bullet shape influences penetration. In heavier-caliber weapons, designed specifically to defeat armor plate, explosives are incorporated into the projectile and focus energy on the target and literally melt through the armor.

Vests are rated by level of protection (National Institute of Justice 2008). Types IIA, II, and III are composed of bullet-resistant fabric and capable of stopping pistol and revolver bullets ranging from 9 mm to .40 caliber; Type IIA, to .357 SIG, and Type III, up to a .44 Magnum. The additional resistance of the Type II and IIIA vests is attained by adding layers of fabric, which results in more weight and less flexibility. Thus Type II and IIA vests are most commonly used for daily wear. Resistance to all types of high-velocity military and civilian rifle bullets requires the addition of metal or ceramic inserts. These vests, rated as Type III and IV, are heavy, bulky, and conspicuous. They are primarily utilized by the military and SWAT teams.

Federal law places prohibits possession of body armor by persons convicted of violent felonies (18 U.S.C. § 931), and several states have laws restricting felons from possessing body armor.

William J. Vizzard

See also: Ammunition, Types of; Armor-Piercing Ammunition

Further Reading

National Institute of Justice. *Ballistic Resistance of Body Armor NIJ Standard–0101.06*. Washington, DC: National Institute of Justice, 2008.

National Institute of Justice. "Body Armor." http://www.nij.gov/topics/technology/body-armor/welcome.htm (accessed May 27, 2011).

National Law Enforcement Memorial Fund. "Following a 50-Year Low, Law Enforcement Fatalities Surge 43 Percent during the First Half of 2010." http://www.nleomf.org/newsroom/news-releases/2010-midyear-fatality-report.html (accessed May 27, 2011).

Boomtowns, Cowtowns, and Gun Violence

Boomtowns and cowtowns possess similar characteristics. Cowtowns of the Old West (e.g., Fort Worth, Abilene, Wichita) were boomtowns in their beginnings. Some boomtowns that were mining-oriented, such as Tombstone, Arizona, are popularly and erroneously assumed to be primarily cowtowns. Some other celebrated boomtowns with a mining backdrop included San Francisco, Sacramento, and Virginia City. The economic bases of some cowtowns were also somewhat more diverse, as a number were typified by such activities as gold mining and oil-well drilling. But there are many economic bases for boomtowns, and they continue to exist on a number of "frontiers," including Brazil, the former Soviet Union, and the inner cities of today's United States.

Both boomtowns and cowtowns traditionally feature male-intensive industries (e.g., mining, the cattle industry, the sale of crack cocaine). Both involve the systematic exploitation of the male workforce through vice-related industries and costly provisioning and resupply. Boomtowns and cowtowns are both typified by extremely high ratios of young men to women and an absence of "respectable" women; both are environments where the use of alcohol and other intoxicants is common, encouraged, expected, and even demanded. Historically, in both sorts of towns, knives and firearms are frequently carried and used as weapons of first resort, at

Scene still from *Gunfight at the O.K. Corral* (1957). (Photofest)

least in the early days of the boom. Accordingly, both are known as environments where violence flourishes, at least until tamed by "respectable" women. Indeed, the role of late-coming women "from back East" as "town tamers" is profound.

Although it may seem counterintuitive, by this set of criteria, certain American inner cities from the 1980s to the present might be thought of as boomtowns of a sort—places where young men and women of ill repute sell drugs (a boom crop), other vice flourishes, respectable women are in short supply (as successful individuals of both sexes leave with the mass exodus of the middle class), the use of alcohol and other drugs is widespread, and advanced weaponry and their possession is not uncommon (Courtwright 1996). In the early stages of the

boom, violence is especially prevalent, as different factions jockey for territorial dominance or exclusivity. Little legitimate activity occurs in some of these unhappy communities abandoned by the middle class and respectable poor, and they become free-fire or combat zones, to use local and/or police parlance.

The role of law enforcement in boomtowns and cowtowns has traditionally been portrayed as heroic (e.g., the "Gunfight at the O.K. Corral"), but more recent, revisionist interpretations show lawmen as opportunistic careerists—political animals, pimps, and gamblers protecting their own selfish interests (for example, in the Hollywood hit *Tombstone*). Far from being disinterested upholders of law and order or avatars of civilization, many lawmen in the

Old West were, at best, little more than tools of the local mercantile and vice interests. While a few were primarily concerned with establishing order, justice was often incidental in that endeavor.

It was to this end that Dodge City, Kansas, established a "deadline" (in this case, the railroad tracks), north of which firearms could not be carried. In this and other cowtowns where this form of gun control operated, cowboys and drovers checked their weapons in at the sheriff's or town marshal's office, or at various kiosks built for that purpose, and received a numbered metal token. Upon leaving town, the weapons would be restored to them. This had the effect of allowing local law enforcement to both monitor and temporarily disarm vice-bound potential troublemakers. Thus, they could be told to have a good time and also be warned "not to let the sun set" on them in that specific jurisdiction. The idea of town marshals or deputies facing down equally well-armed outlaws in fast-draw shootouts is the fiction of dime novels, the movies, and the television western of the 1950s and 1960s. Preemptive gun-possession ordinances in Dodge City, for example, render the opening sequence of the popular television series *Gunsmoke* a gross inaccuracy.

Prostitutes and gamblers made life more tolerable for the male workforce but complicated law enforcement considerably. As both were seen as necessary, they were often protected industries. Even some lawmen, such as Wyatt Earp, were reputed to have interests in prostitution and other vice industries. Earp, along with his brothers, ran a gambling house during his off-and-on career in law enforcement. Brothels were common, sometimes in such numbers as to constitute a district. Several western cities claim the distinction of coining the term "red-light district" to refer to the practice of railroad

brakemen leaving their lanterns outside prostitutes' "cribs" to prevent interruption, an act that apparently bathed entire streets in red light.

Prostitutes were often quite young and not particularly good-looking by the standards of that day or any other. However, reformed "soiled doves" and single women "visiting from back East" found plenty of eager suitors among the male population, and not a few married and vanished into respectable domesticity. Oftentimes in a boomtown, gamblers, prostitutes, and other residents would fall out, and feuding and violence might follow. In the river boomtown of Natchez, Mississippi, in 1835, a short-lived conflict developed and escalated rapidly, in which a hastily constituted "anti-gambling" society lynched five gamblers who had been involved in the killing of a local doctor. Sanity and gamblers returned soon after. Natchez-Under-the-Hill, as a vice district, remained a boomtown hot spot until river traffic lost its viability and cachet later in the century. Most violence involving prostitutes and cowboys/miners was considerably more prosaic and the circumstances not nearly as dramatic—resembling nothing more than a "Saturday Night" shooting on the "mean streets" of any major contemporary city. It should be added that boomtowns and cowtowns were not infrequently at ground zero in range "wars" that broke out in the West following the Civil War.

Another feature of incipient boomtowns, particularly those based on mining, was their reliance on vigilance committees, kangaroo courts, and swift private justice. The case of California, though illustrative, is not necessarily typical. After California came under U.S. jurisdiction, but before it achieved statehood, it was legally under the aegis of the U.S. Army. As might be expected, it was stretched very thin and was not equipped to handle law enforcement duties, a characteristic that still holds true. Accordingly, law enforcement in the gold fields and cities was chaotic. Vigilance committees, almost all politically based, sprang up. At many "trials," "jurors" were drunk and were biased toward harsh punishment. Almost all of these private justice efforts had explicitly racist subtexts. In many communities, all non-European miners—i.e., Hispanics and Asians—were driven from the gold fields. In yet others, even French, German, and Irish miners fared poorly. The vigilante fervor reached a crescendo in San Francisco, certainly a boomtown in 1851 and 1856, when vigilance committees, using crime as a pretext, seized guns from armories, lynched a few offenders, and harassed and expelled Democratic Party stalwarts from the city. Frankly, this was little more than an excuse for launching a violent and retributive political coup. Leading vigilantes in later years transferred their allegiance from their own "Peoples Party" to the Republican Party. Those who romanticize the good old days of vigilante justice in "Old San Francisco," one hopes, are ignorant of the ugly racist and class-oriented agenda of this movement.

Boomtowns are an economic phenomenon that is not limited to the Old West or early American history. Rather, one can expect to find boomtowns wherever men work (in male-dominated industries) in predominately pastoral extractive industries, where paydays may be few but generally lucrative, and where vice industries exist primarily to service and exploit those workers. Violence flourishes in boomtowns and cowtowns due to the widespread presence of weaponry, a subculture endorsing violent solutions to personal problems, and ambivalent law enforcement responses. The arrival of respectable women in force usually puts

an end to boomtown vice and violence, be it in Arizona, Mississippi, or Uganda—or in the contemporary inner-city United States.

Francis Frederick Hawley

See also: Dime Novels and the Sensationalization of Frontier Violence; Frontier Violence

Further Reading

Brown, Richard M. *Strain of Violence: Historical Studies of American Violence and Vigilantism.* New York: Oxford University Press, 1975.

Courtwright, David T. *Violent Land: Single Men and Social Disorder from the Frontier to the Inner City.* Cambridge, MA: Harvard University Press, 1996.

Roth, Randolph. *American Homicide.* Cambridge, MA: Belknap Press, 2009.

Boone, Daniel (1734–1820)

Daniel Boone—arguably America's greatest cultural hero of the Jacksonian and antebellum era—gained fame as a trailblazer, hunter, and Indian fighter. Boone's reputation rested, in part, on his contests with Indians in Kentucky and his participation in the Indian campaign known as Lord Dunmore's War of 1774 and then in the American Revolution. Indeed, on separate occasions, Indians had killed one of Boone's sons, Israel, and had taken captive Boone's daughter, Jemima, who was rescued by her father and his friends. Yet in later life, Boone said that he bore no ill will toward Indians. Some of the Shawnee who had once held Boone captive and who had adopted him into their tribe even came to visit Boone after both he and they had removed to Missouri.

At various times in his life, Boone also surveyed frontier lands, operated a country store, and tried his hand at planting tobacco. Never, however, did Boone prosper. After being sued by men who had lost their land because of his faulty surveying (and because of Kentucky's notoriously complicated land titles), Boone escaped his creditors by immigrating to Spanish-held Missouri in 1799. There, the Spanish granted Boone about 8,500 acres of land and declared him a "syndic," an office comparable to justice of the peace. After Spain transferred the Louisiana Territory to the United States in 1803, Boone lost his Missouri lands because he had failed to cultivate them. In 1814, Congress finally stepped in to grant Boone, now in his 70s, a small plot of land as a reward for having played a critical role in the settlement of the West.

No doubt the dispossession of Indians and the settlement of the West by whites would have proceeded apace without Daniel Boone. Congress awarded Boone a small parcel of land, however, because he—through the efforts of John Filson, a schoolteacher and land speculator whose promotional tract, *The Discovery, Settlement, and Present State of Kentucke*, was published in 1784—had become the United States' great hero of expansion. Filson attached to his promotional tract a so-called autobiography of Boone (the tale was based on Boone's reminiscences but written by Filson). Though the publication of Filson's Boone tale caused little stir in the United States, it caught the imagination of Europeans, leading Lord Byron to write stanzas about Boone in his poem *Don Juan*.

Americans became familiar with Boone's exploits through a condensed version of Filson's tale that was published by a Connecticut printer in 1786. Boone's popularity grew with each subsequent decade and peaked—judging by the output of art and literature on Boone—in the antebellum years. No less than seven Boone biographies appeared before the Civil War, one of which, Timothy Flint's *Biographical Memoir of Daniel Boone, the First Settler of Kentucky*, was reprinted 14 times between 1833 and 1868. Flint and others portrayed Boone as a "self-possessed" hero who rose to greatness solely through his own efforts. The wilderness that Boone inhabited—a place where men succeeded or failed through their individual initiative and energy—came to symbolize the libertarian values of the market revolution that transformed the United States during the Jacksonian and antebellum decades.

Whereas in the colonial era, frontier hunters were frequently equated with savagery, the market revolution gave rise to a celebration of frontier individualists who epitomized desirable traits like "self-possession, self-control, and promptness in execution" (Peck 1847, 15). The "most striking instance" of Boone's "peculiar self-possession," according to Flint, occurred when Boone, as a schoolboy, had coolly shot a panther while other boys had fled (Flint 1847, 21). That event seemed to presage Boone's

Daniel Boone. (Library of Congress)

independence, wanderlust, skill with a gun, and love of hunting. Boone's "peculiar habits of character," waxed Flint, "were fortified by his long cherished habit of wandering for days together with no other companionship than his rifle and his own thoughts" (Flint 1833, 51). To Francis Lister Hawks (1844), another Boone hagiographer, Boone was simply "the Kentucky Rifleman."

The particular gun with which Boone wandered was a Kentucky (or long) rifle, a small-bore (generally under .45 caliber), lightweight, long-barreled gun that was first produced by German gunsmiths who resided in western Pennsylvania. Though handmade by artisans and hence potentially expensive (gun prices varied greatly prior to the era of mass production), such guns became standard weapons among American farmers and frontiersmen. Fancier versions of the Kentucky rifle with gold and silver inlay—though still more expensive—appealed to a growing cadre of elite sport hunters in the early national era who identified themselves with both English aristocrats and with American frontiersmen like Boone.

If Boone's love for guns and hunting helped popularize sport hunting, it also helped popularize Manifest Destiny. Though earlier generations of Americans had claimed land through farming (backwoods hunters could make no claim to lands that they failed to improve), Boone transformed expansion into a sort of jousting match. Through his battles with bear, buffalo, and Indian, Boone—like his fellow Americans—became the noble claimant of a vast domain.

In the Jacksonian and antebellum decades, Daniel Boone became a new hero for a new era. Like Andrew Jackson, Boone became an icon of the self-made man. Just as important, Boone—or at least the Boone of literature—taught Americans that the use of guns had made them great, a lesson that

would be remembered by writers, painters, and politicians. "Out of the long and brilliant list of patriots—whether orators, or warriors, or statesmen, or divines," wrote George Canning Hill in 1859, "no name shines with a purer lustre than that of Daniel Boone" (Hill 1859, 59).

Daniel Justin Herman

See also: Long Rifle (Pennsylvania/Kentucky)

Further Reading

Aron, Stephen Anthony. *How the West Was Lost: The Transformation of Kentucky from Daniel Boone to Henry Clay.* Baltimore: Johns Hopkins University Press, 1996.

Bakeless, John. *Daniel Boone: Master of the Wilderness.* Lincoln: University of Nebraska Press, 1939.

Faragher, John Mack. *Daniel Boone: The Life and Legend of an American Pioneer.* New York: Holt, 1992.

Flint, Timothy. *The First White Man of the West, or the Exploits of Col. Daniel Boone, the First Settler of Kentucky.* Cincinnati: G. Conclin, 1847. Originally published under the title *Biographical Memoir of Daniel Boone: The First Settler of Kentucky.* Cincinnati: N. & G. Guilford & Co., 1833.

Flint, Timothy. *Indian Wars of the West.* Cincinnati: E. H. Flint, 1833.

Hawks, Francis Lister [Uncle Philip, pseud.]. *The Adventures of Daniel Boone, the Kentucky Rifleman.* New York: D. Appleton & Co., 1844.

Herman, Daniel Justin. *Hunting and the American Imagination.* Washington, DC: Smithsonian Institution Press, 2001.

Hill, George Canning. *Daniel Boone, the Pioneer of Kentucky.* Chicago: Donohue, 1859.

Lofaro, Michael A. *The Life and Adventures of Daniel Boone.* Lexington: University Press of Kentucky, 1978.

Peck, John Mason. *Life of Daniel Boone, the Pioneer of Kentucky.* Library of American Biography, edited by Jared Sparks, 2nd ser., vol. 13. Boston: C. C. Little and J. Brown, 1847.

Slotkin, Richard. *Regeneration through Violence: The Mythology of the American Frontier, 1600–1860.* Middletown, CT: Wesleyan University Press, 1973.

Borinsky, Mark (1945–)

Dr. Mark Borinsky—a victim of gun violence—started the modern gun control movement when he founded the National Council to Control Handguns (NCCH) in Washington, D.C., in 1974 (Carter 1997, 72). NCCH became Handgun Control, Inc. (HCI), the leading gun control advocacy organization in the country. In 2001, HCI changed its name to the Brady Campaign to Prevent Gun Violence.

While a psychology graduate student at the University of Chicago in 1973, Borinsky had a traumatic experience that led directly to his founding of NCCH. Borinsky and a friend were walking back to campus one evening when three young men robbed them at gunpoint. One of the young men kept urging the others to shoot their victims. Understandably shaken by this experience, Borinsky decided that after finishing his degree, he would work to fight the problem of gun violence.

After finishing his PhD, Borinsky moved to Washington, D.C., to start a new job. Assuming that the assassinations of John F. Kennedy, Robert Kennedy, and Dr. Martin Luther King would have spawned numerous gun control groups, Borinsky searched for a gun-lobbying group to join, but found none that he thought were effective. Using his own money, Borinsky rented a tiny office at 1710 H Street NW, hired a secretary, and launched NCCH. Because he had a full-time job, he could not run the organization on a day-to-day basis. He placed an ad for

someone to work with him in the *Northwest Current*, a small neighborhood newspaper.

Edward O. Welles, a retired Central Intelligence Agency officer, responded to the ad. Welles and Borinsky really were the organization until N. T. "Pete" Shields joined them in 1975. Shields, whose son had been killed by an assailant with a handgun, contributed greatly to the success of the organization. Most commentators acknowledge Shields's importance, but some minimize Borinsky's contribution, sometimes referring to Welles as the founder of NCCH. Welles and Shields were crucial to the success of NCCH and HCI, but Borinsky did initiate the organization. The three men all contributed greatly to HCI's success. That success was also due to the social and political environment within which they were working.

Carter (1997, 73) suggests that the mid-1970s was a propitious time for the "formation of HCI and the beginnings of the gun control movement." First, the social movements of the 1960s encouraged people to see personal troubles—such as being mugged at gunpoint—as public issues that would be amenable to solutions through social policy. Second, a huge lobbying industry had developed in Washington, D.C., and that industry provided numerous opportunities for social issues-oriented organizations. Third, there was no effective interest group focused solely on gun control. Finally, the federal government provided opportunities for HCI—congressional representatives, the Department of Justice's Bureau of Justice Statistics, and the Centers for Disease Control all worked with HCI in the 1970s.

Having founded the organization, Borinsky moved away from it in the 1970s to work in the private sector. Since 2001, he has volunteered at Johns Hopkins Bloomberg School of Public Health. In 2007, he founded the Johns Hopkins Sustainability Store, which has shelf space in the Johns Hopkins Hospital Gift Shop. Borinsky is working on creating an organization to establish an environmental rating for individuals similar to a credit rating and has started a tutoring practice for children in grades 1–12, according to his LinkedIn (2011) profile.

Walter F. Carroll

See also: Brady, James S.; Brady, Sarah Kemp; Brady Campaign to Prevent Gun Violence; Brady Center to Prevent Gun Violence; Gun Control; Shields, Nelson T. "Pete"; Welles, Edward O.; Zebra Killings

Further Reading

Borinsky, Mark. LinkedIn profile. http://www .linkedin.com/pub/mark-borinsky/6/82a/ 770 (accessed February 28, 2011).

Carter, Gregg Lee. *The Gun Control Movement*. New York: Twayne, 1997.

DeConde, Alexander. *Gun Violence in America: The Struggle for Control*. Boston: Northeastern University Press, 2001.

Shields, Pete. *Guns Don't Die—People Do*. New York: Arbor House, 1981.

Boston Gun Project (BGP)

The Boston Gun Project (BGP) was part of a set of linked programs aimed at reducing gun violence among young people in Boston in the 1990s. Levels of violent crime, usually involving firearms, had reached epidemic proportions in the late 1980s to the early 1990s. For example, homicides of those under 24 years of age increased 230 percent from 1987 (22) to 1990 (73). After this jump, the rates remained high, averaging 44 youth homicides a year from 1991 to 1995. Some criminologists predicted that crime rates would climb even higher in the coming years, due largely to a group of young men they

referred to as "super predators." The subsequent crime drop in the 1990s occurred all over the country in cities that had adopted differing crime reduction strategies. Under the rubric of the Boston Strategy to Prevent Youth Violence, funded by the National Institute of Justice (NIJ), the BGP was a gun suppression and interdiction strategy linked to Operation Ceasefire, an enforcement strategy initiated in 1996 to lessen gang gun violence. The connected programs succeeded in reducing youth homicide in Boston and provided model programs for reducing gun violence nationally.

The Boston Strategy to Prevent Gun Violence involved a wide spectrum of federal, state, and local agencies; nonprofit community service organizations; businesses; religious leaders; parents; and others. The BGP itself involved Alcohol, Tobacco and Firearms (ATF), the Boston Police Department (BPD), the Suffolk County District Attorney's Office, and the U.S. Attorney's Office. These individuals and organizations had long been concerned about youth violence, and the epidemic of violence heightened their desire to take effective action. Researchers at the Harvard University's John F. Kennedy School of Government joined with these constituencies to develop the BGP. David M. Kennedy, of the Kennedy School, and his colleagues Anthony Braga and Anne M. Piehl directed the project. They wanted to find out whether gun violence could be reduced by limiting access to guns.

The BGP, a supply-side initiative, attempted to interdict gun trafficking. Based on close cooperation between ATF and BPD, the project received resources that enabled it to investigate gun-trafficking cases, trace recovered handguns, and inspect federally licensed firearms dealers to monitor their compliance with regulations. The inspections led 80 percent of the licensed dealers in

Boston to give up their licenses. ATF agents worked with BPD ballistics and crime laboratories, attempting to trace recovered handguns through ATF's National Tracing Center. The working group developed guidelines to help it disrupt illegal gun markets and also developed a local tracing data set. They gave priority to tracing guns that had been used in a crime in less than 30 months and focused on semiautomatic pistols, because research had revealed that those were the most popular guns used by youth; guns with obliterated serial numbers that had been restored; those found in high-risk neighborhoods; and those associated with gangs and gang areas. The group also emphasized federal prosecution for gun crimes, which typically had longer sentences and took those convicted far from home (Office of Justice Programs 1999; Kennedy et al. 2001).

The local trace database was also helpful for Operation Ceasefire, a demand-side initiative. The Boston Police Department's Youth Violence Strike Force developed this part of the Boston Strategy to Prevent Youth Violence and implemented it in May 1996. It was based, in part, on findings from the Kansas City Gun Experiment (KCGE). The KCGE was based on the premise that additional patrols in a given area could result in increased gun seizures and a reduction in gun crime. Rogan, Shaw, and Sherman (1995) matched two beats that had exceptionally high crime rates—including many homicides and drive-by shootings. Over a 29-week period in 1992, one beat (the "target area") received extra patrols focused on gun crime. The other beat (the "control area") received the usual amount of patrol and police presence. There were several promising, although not statistically significant, findings. Gun seizures in the target area increased, gun crimes decreased in the target area, and fear of crime declined significantly in the target area. The latter constituted the only statistically significant findings; however, the researchers concluded that focusing on particular areas showed great promise.

The upbeat conclusions of the KCGE led to creation of Operation Ceasefire, an enhanced version of the KCGE. The program focused on reducing gang violence by going to gang leaders and telling them there would be a crackdown on any violations, regardless of how minor they were. Response to violence would take the form of swift prosecutions. Gang violence dropped as a result of this approach, together with the other aspects of the Boston Strategy. Another part of the overall program was Operation Night Light, which had begun in 1992 as a police and probation collaboration to deter juvenile violence.

The success of the Boston Gun Project, and its linked programs, was evident in major reductions in homicides in Boston. In 1995, there were 45 homicides, and that that dropped to 26 in 1996 and 15 in 1997. The programs were recommended as promising strategies to reduce gun violence (Office of Justice Programs 1999) and were used as models in other cities. For example, a successful gun violence strategy based on the Boston model but modified for local conditions was successful in East Los Angeles in the late 1990s (Tita et al. 2003).

More generally, as a result of the Kansas City and Boston programs, "directed patrol" strategies are now seen as critical in combating gun crime (Ludwig 2005; Walker 2006). They are viewed as most successful when combined with interagency cooperation—such as the aggressive sentencing of the Boston-area U.S. attorney general combined with the aggressive and directed street patrols of the Boston police. In 1995, Chicago created the Chicago Project for Violence

Prevention, which includes a Ceasefire component. The project takes a public health approach to reducing violence. The Ceasefire program, adapted from successful programs in other cities, notably Boston, was initiated in 2000. The success of these programs gave birth to the broader and more comprehensive U.S. Department of Justice's Project Safe Neighborhoods initiative in 2001.

Walter F. Carroll and Sean Maddan

See also: Black Market for Firearms; Firearm Dealers; National Tracing Center (NTC); Project Exile; Project Safe Neighborhoods; Project Triggerlock

Further Reading

Braga, Anthony. "Serious Youth Gun Offenders and the Epidemic of Youth Violence in Boston." *Journal of Quantitative Criminology* 19 (2003): 33–54.

Kennedy, David M., et al. *Reducing Gun Violence: The Boston Gun Project's Operation Ceasefire.* Research Report NCJ 188741. Washington, DC: National Institute of Justice, 2001. http://www.ncjrs.gov/pdffiles1/nij/188741.pdf (accessed May 31, 2011).

Ludwig, Jens. "Better Gun Enforcement, Less Crime." *Criminology and Public Policy* 4 (2005): 677–716.

Office of Justice Programs. *Promising Strategies to Reduce Gun Violence.* Report NCJ 173950. Washington, DC: U.S. Department of Justice, Office of Justice Programs, February 1999. http://www.ojjdp.gov/pubs/gun_violence/contents.html (accessed May 31, 2011).

Rogan, Dennis, James W. Shaw, and Lawrence W. Sherman. "The Kansas City Gun Experiment." *National Institute of Justice Research in Brief.* Washington, DC: U.S. Department of Justice, National Institute of Justice, January 1995. https://www.ncjrs.gov/pdffiles/kang.pdf (accessed July 25, 2011).

Sheppard, David. *Strategies to Reduce Gun Violence.* Washington, DC: U.S. Department of Justice, Office of Justice Programs, OJJDP, 1999. http://www.ojjdp.gov/pubs/gun_violence/173950.pdf (accessed May 31, 2011).

Tita, George, K., et al. *Reducing Gun Violence: Results from an Intervention in East Los Angeles.* Santa Monica, CA: RAND, 2003. http://www.rand.org/content/dam/rand/pubs/monograph_reports/2010/RAND_MR1764-1.pdf (accessed May 31, 2011).

Walker, Samuel. *Sense and Nonsense about Crime and Drugs.* Belmont, CA: Thompson-Wadsworth, 2006.

Boxer, Barbara (1940–)

Sen. Barbara Boxer (D-CA) has been a forceful advocate for gun control in the U.S. House of Representatives and now in the U.S. Senate. Boxer has used her position as a senator from the most populous state to garner media attention to her gun control policies, but has also worked quietly in the Senate to introduce bills and amendments, to alter language in bills, and to direct appropriations to gun control projects. When the Democrats regained the majority in the Senate in 2001, Boxer became an even more influential player in the gun control debate.

Working as a stockbroker and newspaper editor before entering politics, Boxer first served as a congressional aide during 1974–1976. She was elected to the Marin Board of Supervisors in 1976 and served for six years. She was elected to the House in 1983, where she served four terms. In 1992, she was elected to the Senate in the "Year of the Woman" (Cook, Thomas, and Wilcox 1993). She has been called "the iconoclastic feminist, environmentalist, anti-war and anti-corporate crusader that has made her a hero to liberals in home state and around the country" (Koszczuk and

Angle 2007, 71). Boxer currently serves as the chair of the Environment and Public Works Committee and of the Select Committee on Ethics, the first woman to hold this position. She also sits on the Committees on Foreign Relations and Commerce, Science, and Transportation.

Boxer supported the Brady Bill and the assault-weapons ban. She introduced the American Handguns Standards Act, which sought to ban Saturday night specials and other cheap handguns, in 1996. She introduced the Firearms Rights, Responsibilities, and Remedies Act in an effort to protect the ability of cities and groups to sue gun manufacturers, dealers, and importers for civil damages resulting from gun violence. In the wake of the 9/11 terrorist attacks, Boxer wrote the legislation that required air marshals be on board high-risk flights and supported laws that would allow passenger and cargo pilots to carry firearms in the cockpit. Later, she was among a small handful of Democrats who spoke out against legislation that would exempt gun makers from civil liability lawsuits (the Protection of Lawful Commerce in Arms Act of 2005). She has been an outspoken advocate of renewing the assault-weapons ban, which was enacted in 1994 but expired in 2004.

More recently, she criticized proposed legislation that would permit visitors to national parks to carry loaded and concealed weapons and another that would allow individuals with permits in their home states to carry concealed weapons into another state. She also voted "no" on legislation that would allow firearms in checked baggage on Amtrak trains. In the wake of the attempted assassination of Rep. Gabrielle Giffords (D-AZ) in Tucson, Arizona, in January 2011, which killed six individuals and wounded 13, Boxer became a cosponsor of a trio of legislation introduced by Sen.

Frank Lautenberg (D-NJ)—the Large Capacity Ammunition Feeding Device Act, which would prohibit the make and sale of ammunition magazines with a more-than-10-round capacity; the Denying Firearms and Explosives to Dangerous Criminal Act, which closes the "Terror Gap" loophole; and the Gun Show Background Check Act. During the opening days of the 112th Congress, she also singly introduced the Common-Sense Concealed Firearms Act, which would require minimum standards for granting permits in states that allowed concealed weapons. Aside from the legislation front, Boxer also argued for the importance of images and rhetoric in the discussion on gun issues.

Much of Boxer's legislative activity has centered on protecting children from gun violence. In 1997 and again in 1999, she introduced with Sen. Herb Kohl (D-WI) the Child Safety Lock Act, which would require child-safety locks on all handguns sold in the United States. A version of this bill was adopted as an amendment to a Juvenile Justice Bill, but the legislation did not pass the House. In 2005, the amendment passed successful by a 70–27 vote in a broader legislation that prohibited civil liability lawsuit against gun makers. She proposed another amendment to the Juvenile Justice Bill that directed the Federal Trade Commission to study manufacturers' efforts to market guns to children; this amendment was also adopted. In the floor debate, Boxer argued that gun manufacturers are targeting children as young as four years of age. She also introduced the Youth Access to Firearms Act, which would ban the sale or transfer of guns to people under 18, with exceptions for parents, grandparents, and guardians.

These efforts to control guns are part of a larger legislative agenda to reduce violence among youth. Boxer introduced the School

Safety Fund Act, which would direct funds to local school districts for a variety of programs aimed at identifying and counseling potentially violent students, and for establishing violence prevention programs. She has also worked on funding for after-school programs, more police on campus, and more funding for hiring police.

Boxer is one of the most liberal members of the Senate. Although she has worked on military procurement issues (especially those dealing with California contractors), her greatest focus has been on women's issues. She sponsored the Violence against Women Act while serving in the House and helped to pass it in the Senate. She is also a strong supporter of abortion rights and the environment. Boxer is the author of *Strangers in the Senate: Politics and the New Revolution of Women in America*, and is a coauthor of *Nine and Counting: The Women of the Senate*.

Clyde Wilcox and Christine Kim

See also: Assault Weapons Ban of 1994; Brady Handgun Violence Prevention Act (Brady Bill); Democratic Party and Gun Control; Lawsuits against Gun Manufacturers; Protection of Lawful Commerce in Arms Act of 2005; Tucson, Arizona, Massacre

Further Reading

Barone, Michael, and Grant Ujifusa. *The Almanac of American Politics 2000*. Washington, DC: National Journal Group, 1999.

Boxer, Barbara. *Strangers in the Senate: Politics and the New Revolution of Women in America*. Washington, DC: National Press Books, 1994

Boxer, Barbara, Catherine Whitney, and Dianne Feinstein. *Nine and Counting: The Women of the Senate*. New York: HarperCollins, 2001.

"Boxer, Barbara, D-California." In *CQ's Politics in America 2008: The 110th Congress*, by Jackie Koszczuk and Martha Angle. Washington, DC: CQ Press, 2007.

Cook, Elizabeth Adell, Sue Thomas, and Clyde Wilcox. *Women of the Year*. Boulder, CO: Westview Press, 1993.

"The U.S. Congress Votes Database." *Washington Post*. http://projects.washingtonpost.com/congress/members/b000711/ (accessed May 16, 2011).

"U.S. Senator Barbara Boxer." http://boxer.senate.gov/ (accessed May 16, 2011).

Brady, James S. (1940–)

James S. Brady was a lifelong member of the Republican Party and career public servant when he was wounded in the 1981 assassination attempt on President Ronald Reagan. He subsequently became a staunch advocate for gun control. After he left public service in 1989, Brady and his wife Sarah led the effort to enact the Brady Bill, which mandated background checks and a waiting period before the purchase of a handgun. In 2001, the gun control advocacy organization Handgun Control, Inc., was renamed the Brady Campaign to Prevent Gun Violence, and the Center to Prevent Handgun Violence was renamed the Brady Center to Prevent Gun Violence, in honor of the efforts of James and Sarah Brady.

James Scott Brady was born on August 29, 1940, in Centralia, Illinois. He attended the University of Illinois, where he majored in political science and communications. He graduated in 1962. Brady became interested in politics at an early age and was a staunch Republican. While in college, he served as a staff member for Sen. Everett M. Dirksen, who was the Republican minority leader in the U.S. Senate. During the summer of 1962, Brady worked for the Justice Department's Antitrust Division as an honor intern.

James and Sarah Brady, 2004. (Luke Frazza/AFP/Getty Images)

After college, Brady worked for a number of private firms before reentering public service. In 1973, he married Sarah Kemp, and the couple went on to have a son, James S. Brady Jr. The same year that he married, Brady became a communications consultant for the U.S. House of Representatives. He soon joined the Nixon and Ford administrations, accepting the post of special assistant to the secretary of housing and urban development. This post was followed by a stint from 1975 to 1976 as special assistant to the director of the Office of Management and Budget. Brady finished out the Ford administration as an assistant to the secretary of defense. He then joined the staff of Sen. William V. Roth Jr. (R-DE). Brady left Roth's staff in 1979 to serve as the press secretary of presidential candidate John

Connally of Texas. He then joined the team of presidential candidate Ronald Reagan as the director of public affairs and research. Following Reagan's election, Brady was appointed spokesman for the office of the president-elect. In January 1981, Brady became the assistant to the president and White House press secretary.

On March 30, 1981, John Hinckley Jr. tried to assassinate President Reagan. During the attempt, Reagan, Brady, and two others were wounded. Brady was seriously injured by a gunshot to the head, which struck him just above his left eye. The injury left Brady partially paralyzed and permanently disabled. Although Brady was unable to continue to carry out all of the functions of his demanding position, Reagan retained Brady as the official press secretary for the remainder of both of his terms in office. Brady left office on January 20, 1989.

Since the assassination attempt in 1981, Brady has worked with a number of groups that advocate for the disabled. He traveled the nation as a spokesperson for the National Head Injury Foundation. Brady eventually became vice chair of the organization as well as vice chairman of the National Organization on Disability. In 2000, President Bill Clinton named the White House Press Briefing Room the James S. Brady Press Briefing Room. This honor was in recognition of Brady's work on behalf of the disabled and his contributions to gun control efforts.

It was Brady's work on behalf of gun control legislation that led to his greatest impact on American politics. While he remained Reagan's press secretary, Brady supported the president's staunch anti–gun control stance. However, once out of office, Brady joined his wife in championing gun control legislation. The centerpiece of Brady's efforts was the bill that soon came to bear his name—the Brady Bill. Brady undertook a seven-year effort to gain passage of the bill. The Brady Bill was signed into law by Clinton on November 30, 1993. The law required a mandatory five-day waiting period and a background check before a handgun could be purchased. Brady later worked to secure passage of the federal Assault Weapons Ban of 1994, which forbade the manufacture and sale of such weapons. In recognition of his efforts on gun control, Clinton awarded Brady the Presidential Medal of Freedom in 1996. Brady continued to lobby at both the state and national level, advocating on behalf of his twin causes—gun control and the rights of the disabled. However, he also became estranged from the Republican Party. He did not support George W. Bush's presidential campaigns in 2000 and 2004, or Sen. John McCain (R-AZ) in the 2008 election. Instead, Brady increasingly backed pro-control Democrats for state and national office.

Tom Lansford

See also: Assault Weapons Ban of 1994; Brady, Sarah Kemp; Brady Campaign to Prevent Gun Violence; Brady Center to Prevent Gun Violence; Brady Handgun Violence Prevention Act (Brady Bill); Hinckley, John Warnock, Jr.; Reagan, Ronald Wilson; Republican Party and Gun Control

Further Reading

Brady, Sarah, with Merrill McLoughlin. *A Good Fight*. New York: Public Affairs, 2002.

Brady Campaign to Prevent Gun Violence. "Biographies: Jim Brady." 2011. http://www.bradycampaign.org/about/bio/jim (accessed July 10, 2011).

Cook, Philip J., and Jens Ludwig. *Gun Violence: The Real Costs*. New York: Oxford University Press, 2000.

Dickinson, Mollie. *Thumbs Up: The Life and Courageous Comeback of White House Press Secretary Jim Brady*. New York: William Morrow, 1987.

Brady, Sarah Kemp (1942–)

Sarah Brady is the wife of former White House press secretary James S. Brady. After her husband was seriously wounded in an assassination attempt against President Ronald Reagan in 1981, Sarah became active in the gun control movement. She became the chair of Handgun Control, Inc. (HCI), and later chair of the Center to Prevent Handgun Violence. Sarah Brady is best known for her efforts to enact the Brady Bill, which mandated a waiting period and background check before the purchase of a handgun.

Sarah Kemp was born on February 6, 1942, in Missouri, although she grew up in Alexandria, Virginia. She attended the College of William and Mary. After graduation in 1964, she became a teacher in the Virginia public school system. However, in 1968, she began a career in politics, serving in a variety of positions within the Republican Party. From 1968 to 1970, she was an assistant to the campaign director of the National Republican Congressional Committee. She then accepted a position as an administrative aide for Rep. Mike McKevitt (R-CO). In 1972, she accepted the same position in the office of Rep. Joseph J. Maraziti (R-NJ) and held that post for the next two years. In 1973, she married James Brady. The couple has one son, James Scott Brady Jr. From 1974 through 1978, Sarah held the posts of coordinator of field services and director of administration for the national Republican Party. She also served as a delegate to five Virginia Republican Party conventions.

On March 30, 1981, Sarah's husband James was seriously wounded in an assassination attempt on President Reagan. He became partially paralyzed and remained disabled. The episode prompted Sarah to become active in the gun control movement. She advocated for what she termed "sensible" gun laws that did not infringe extensively upon the ability of responsible citizens to own or acquire weapons, but which limited access by criminals. As such, she initially sought to forge a compromise between the extremes of both sides of gun control issues.

In 1989, Sarah became the chair of HCI, an advocacy group that worked to promote gun control laws. While still in this capacity, Sarah became chair of HCI's sister organization, the Center to Prevent Handgun Violence (CPHV). Both organizations were private, nonprofit groups that lobbied on behalf of gun control legislation and supported educational programs. They also helped coordinate legal work in challenges against the gun industry and specific state and/or national laws through the CPHV's Legal Action Project.

Under Sarah's leadership, HCI worked to ensure passage of a 1993 measure in Virginia that limited handgun purchases to one per month. Both HCI and the CPHV also lobbied on behalf of the Assault Weapons Ban that was passed by Congress and signed into law by President Bill Clinton in 1994. However, the main effort of Sarah and both organizations was the passage of the Brady Bill, named in honor of her husband. The Brady Bill mandated background checks and required a five-day waiting or cooling-off period for those attempting to purchase handguns. After an intensive multiyear lobbying effort, the Brady Bill was passed in 1993.

In the wake of the Assault Weapons Ban of 1994 and the Brady Law, Sarah led the CPHV in an intensive campaign to develop a series of educational programs. For instance, the CPHV launched Steps to Prevent Firearm Injury (STOP) in coordination with the American Academy of Pediatrics in 1995 to train physicians to counsel families with small children on the potential risks of gun ownership. She also directed the CPHV to support legal action against the gun industry, including the 1998 lawsuit brought by New Orleans against firearm manufacturers. However, her increased efforts on behalf of gun control led many of her former supporters in the Republican Party to perceive that Sarah had abandoned her moderate position. When she spoke at the 1996 Democratic National Convention on gun control, her credibility as a moderate within the Republican Party was further eroded. In the 2000 election, HCI and the CPHV actively worked to defeat Republican presidential candidate George W. Bush.

In 2001, HCI and the CPHV were renamed in honor of Sarah and Jim Brady. Handgun Control, Inc., became the Brady Campaign to Prevent Gun Violence. The Center to Prevent Handgun Violence became the Brady Center to Prevent Gun Violence. Sarah and her husband emerged as fierce critics of the NRA and typically opposed candidates endorsed by the pro-gun group. The Bradys opposed Bush in the 2004 presidential election and backed Sen. Barack Obama (D-IL) in the 2008 balloting.

Tom Lansford

See also: Brady, James S.; Brady Campaign to Prevent Gun Violence; Brady Center to Prevent Gun Violence; Brady Handgun Violence Prevention Act (Brady Bill); Hinckley, John Warnock, Jr.; Legal Action Project (LAP); One-Gun-per-Month Laws; Reagan, Ronald Wilson; Republican Party and Gun Control

Further Reading

Brady, Sarah, with Merrill McLoughlin. *A Good Fight*. New York: Public Affairs, 2002.

Brady Campaign to Prevent Gun Violence. "Biographies: Sarah Brady." 2011. http://www.bradycampaign.org/about/bio/sarah (accessed July 10, 2011).

Cook, Philip J., and Jens Ludwig. *Gun Violence: The Real Costs*. New York: Oxford University Press, 2000.

DeConde, Alexander. *Gun Violence in America: The Struggle for Control*. Boston: Northeastern University Press, 2001.

Dickinson, Mollie. *Thumbs Up: The Life and Courageous Comeback of White House Press Secretary Jim Brady*. New York: William Morrow, 1987.

Brady Campaign to Prevent Gun Violence

The Brady Campaign to Prevent Gun Violence is the nation's largest citizen organization working for stronger gun laws. The Brady Campaign works to prevent gun violence by advocating and defending sensible gun laws, regulations, and public policies; mobilizing grassroots activists; electing pro–gun control public officials; and increasing public awareness of the realities of gun violence.

Headquartered in Washington, D.C., and with regional staff in other parts of the country, the Brady Campaign works with allied organizations; victims of gun violence; law enforcement; the medical community; civic, educational, and religious groups; lawmakers; and citizens across the country who support stronger gun laws. It is a nonpartisan, not-for-profit organization funded almost entirely through membership and individual donations.

Victims have always been at the heart of the organization. In the early 1970s,

Chicago graduate student Mark Borinsky was held up at gunpoint and almost killed. Determined to do something about gun crime after finishing his degree, Borinsky expected to find several gun control organizations in Washington, D.C., to which he could lend his support. Finding that there were none, he used his own resources to start the National Council to Control Handguns (NCCH) in 1974.

That same year, 23-year-old Nick Shields was shot and killed in San Francisco as he prepared for lacrosse practice, a victim of the "Zebra" killers. Nick's father, N. T. "Pete" Shields, an executive at the DuPont Company, wanted to do something to give meaning to his son's senseless murder. Shields became involved with NCCH in 1975 and soon took a year's leave of absence from his job to devote more time to NCCH. By the end of 1976, Shields went to work full time for NCCH as executive director.

By 1981, NCCH had been renamed Handgun Control, Inc. (HCI), and Shields was now chair of the organization. On March 30, 1981, a mentally disturbed man, John Hinckley Jr., tried to assassinate President Ronald Reagan, wounding the president, two law enforcement officers, and, most seriously, Press Secretary James Brady.

In 1983, realizing that legislation alone would not stem the nation's gun-violence epidemic, Shields founded HCI's sister organization, the Center to Prevent Handgun Violence, to change public attitudes and behavior surrounding guns. While the focus of HCI was on legislation and elections, the center's focus was on education, research, litigation, and outreach.

In 1985, another encounter with guns spurred Sarah Brady to join HCI. The Bradys' six-year-old son Scott found a loaded gun in the backseat of a friend's car and started playing with it. She was outraged that firearms had become so common and accessible in our society that even a child could easily get hold of one. After reading that the gun lobby, led by the National Rifle Association, was pushing a bill in Congress to roll back the nation's already weak gun laws, Sarah Brady called HCI and asked what she could do to help.

She quickly became the organization's primary spokesperson. HCI helped with the passage of legislation to ban armor-piercing ammunition and to ban guns that are not detectable by X-ray machines. When Shields retired in 1989, Sarah Brady became chair of HCI. She and James stepped up their advocacy for HCI's number-one priority: legislation to require background checks on gun purchasers—legislation that became known as the Brady Bill.

The Brady Bill was passed in 1993 after a seven-year battle and signed into law by President Bill Clinton as the Brady Handgun Violence Prevention Act. It closed a gaping loophole in the nation's gun laws. In most states, a gun buyer could simply sign a form, attesting that he or she was not a prohibited purchaser, and walk out with a gun. The form would simply get filed away with no follow-up or verification conducted to determine the accuracy of the information. The man who almost killed James Brady purchased his $29 gun at a gun store in Texas, where he was not a resident and not a legal gun purchaser. He was able to buy the gun because no background check was conducted. The Brady Law requires a background check on gun sales by licensed gun dealers. Through the end of 2010, the law had blocked 2.2 million attempts to purchase a gun by people legally prohibited from doing so, such as felons, the dangerously mentally ill, and drug criminals.

In 1994, the Brady Campaign worked to pass the law banning military-style assault weapons and assault clips holding more than 10 bullets. The law sunsetted in 2004, despite George W. Bush having campaigned in favor of the ban.

In the wake of multiple school shootings in the late 1990s, Colorado and Oregon overwhelmingly passed statewide referenda in 2000 to close the "gun show loophole," requiring a background check for all gun sales at gun shows.

On June 14, 2001, the boards of trustees of Handgun Control, Inc., and the Center to Prevent Handgun Violence officially changed the names of the organizations to the Brady Campaign to Prevent Gun Violence and the Brady Center to Prevent Gun Violence, respectively, in honor of James and Sarah Brady. In October 2001, the Brady Campaign and the Brady Center entered into a partnership with the Million Mom March, a grassroots movement that started in 1999 in the wake of the Columbine High School massacre and other mass shootings.

In 2003, the California Assembly approved far-reaching gun control legislation, sponsored by the Brady Campaign, that would require handgun manufacturers to redesign new handguns to prevent accidental shootings. This effectively established a new national safety standard for handgun production.

In 2007, after the mass shooting at Virginia Tech, the Brady Campaign worked to pass legislation, signed by President George W. Bush on January 8, 2008, to provide incentives to states to submit records of prohibited gun purchasers to the National Instant Criminal Background Check System (NICS). The NICS Act will help block hundreds of thousands of prohibited buyers who are not presently stopped by the Brady Law because their names are not in NICS.

On June 26, 2008, the U.S. Supreme Court's landmark Second Amendment case,

District of Columbia v. Heller, held that the Second Amendment protects an individual right to possess handguns specifically for use in self-defense in a person's home. Justice Antonin Scalia, writing for the 5–4 majority, stressed, however, that this individual right "is not unlimited."

All nine justices agreed that a wide variety of gun laws are "presumptively lawful," including bans on gun possession by dangerous persons such as felons and the mentally ill; laws forbidding the carrying of firearms in "sensitive places," such as schools and government buildings; laws imposing conditions and qualifications on gun sales, which could include background checks, licensing, and limits on bulk sales of handguns; prohibitions on carrying concealed weapons; prohibitions on dangerous and unusual weapons, such as machine guns and military-style semiautomatic assault weapons; and safe storage laws to prevent gun accidents.

The Brady Campaign continues the fight to close these and other loopholes in U.S. gun laws and to pass measures that make it easier to enforce those laws. In the wake of the shooting in Tucson, Arizona, involving Arizona congresswoman Gabrielle Giffords, Brady's efforts focused on strengthening the Brady background check system by extending it to nearly all gun sales, banning "assault clips" holding more than 10 rounds of ammunition; and strengthening law enforcement's authority and resources to enforce federal gun laws effectively.

Nancy M. Hwa and Rebecca Knox

See also: Assault Weapons Ban of 1994; Background Checks; Borinsky, Mark; Brady, James S.; Brady, Sarah Kemp; Brady Center to Prevent Gun Violence; Brady Handgun Violence Prevention Act (Brady Bill); *District of Columbia v. Heller*; Gun Control; Gun Lobby; Gun Shows; Helmke, Paul; Legal Action Project (LAP); NICS Improvement Act;

Shields, Nelson T. "Pete"; Tucson, Arizona, Massacre; Virginia Tech Massacre; Zebra Killings

Further Reading

Brady, Sarah, with Merrill McLoughlin. *A Good Fight*. New York: Public Affairs, 2002.

Brady Campaign to Prevent Gun Violence. http://www.bradycampaign.org (accessed January 16, 2011).

Carter, Gregg Lee. *The Gun Control Movement*. New York: Twayne, 1997.

Dickenson, Mollie. *Thumbs Up: The Life and Courageous Comeback of White House Press Secretary Jim Brady*. New York: William Morrow, 1987.

Shields, Pete. *Guns Don't Die—People Do*. New York: Arbor House, 1981.

Brady Center to Prevent Gun Violence

The Brady Center to Prevent Gun Violence, founded in 1983 as the Center to Prevent Handgun Violence, is a nonpartisan, nonprofit organization dedicated to reducing gun violence through litigation, policy research, and public education. The Brady Center is an affiliate of the Brady Campaign to Prevent Gun Violence (formerly known as Handgun Control, Inc.), which works for the passage of local, state, and federal gun control laws.

The guiding principle of the Brady Center is that gun control legislation, although necessary, is not a comprehensive solution to the gun violence problem. Thus, the activities of the Brady Center include such non-legislative initiatives as providing pro bono legal representation to gun violence victims, performing comprehensive policy research, and engaging in broad public education efforts to dramatize the problem of gun violence and analyze potential solutions.

The Legal Action Project (LAP) of the Brady Center seeks to use the courts to establish legal principles that will reduce gun violence. The LAP provides pro bono representation to individual gun violence victims, as well as to cities and counties in lawsuits against the gun industry. LAP lawyers brought the first lawsuit against the industry by a city seeking to recover the public costs of gun violence, as well as the first suit seeking to hold a gun manufacturer liable for failing to personalize guns to prevent misuse by children and other unauthorized persons. Through the filing of "friend of the court" briefs and other assistance, the LAP also plays a key role in defending gun control laws under attack in the courts.

The Brady Center has frequently issued reports on key policy issues involving gun violence and gun laws. Examples include *The NRA: A Criminal's Best Friend: How the National Rifle Association Has Handcuffed Gun Law Enforcement* (2006); *Brady Background Checks: 15 Years of Saving Lives* (2008); *Exporting Gun Violence: How Our Weak Gun Laws Arm Criminals in Mexico and America* (2009); *No Check. No Gun. Why Brady Background Checks Should Be Required for All Gun Sales* (2009); and *Guns and Hate: A Lethal Combination* (2009).

In 2005, the Brady Center launched its Gun Industry Watch program to monitor and publicly expose gun industry practices that contribute to gun violence, with the goal of bringing about lifesaving reforms. Reports issued by Gun Industry Watch include *Without a Trace: How the Gun Lobby and the Government Suppress the Truth About Guns and Crime* (2006) and *Shady Dealings: Illegal Gun Trafficking from Licensed Gun Dealers* (2007). Gun Industry Watch also has published a series of reports profiling the activities of specific gun dealers whose irresponsibility contributed substantially to the flow of guns into the illegal market.

Dennis A. Henigan

See also: Gun Control; Lawsuits against Gun Manufacturers; Legal Action Project (LAP)

Further Reading

Brady Center to Prevent Gun Violence. http://www.bradycenter.org/ (accessed January 22, 2010).

Carter, Gregg Lee. *The Gun Control Movement*. New York: Twayne, 1997.

Dorélien, Astrid, Michael Miller, and Peter Brody. *Guns and Hate: A Lethal Combination*. Brady Center to Prevent Gun Violence, July 2009. http://www.bradycenter.org/xshare/pdf/reports/guns-hate.pdf (accessed January 22, 2010).

Haile, Elizabeth S. *Without a Trace: How the Gun Lobby and the Government Suppress the Truth About Guns and Crime*. Brady Center to Prevent Gun Violence, April 2006. http://www.bradycenter.org/xshare/pdf/reports/giw.pdf (accessed January 22, 2011).

Henigan, Dennis A. *Lethal Logic: Exploding the Myths that Paralyze American Gun Policy*. Dulles, VA: Potomac Books, 2009.

Knox, Rebecca. *Brady Background Checks: 15 Years of Saving Lives*. Brady Center to Prevent Gun Violence, November 30, 2008. http://www.bradycenter.org/xshare/pdf/reports/brady-law-15years.pdf (accessed January 22, 2011).

Lowry, Jonathan, et al. *Exporting Gun Violence: How Our Weak Gun Laws Arm Criminals in Mexico and America* (2009). http://www.bradycenter.org/xshare/pdf/reports/exporting-gun-violence.pdf (accessed January 22, 2011).

Siebel, Brian J. *No Check. No Gun. Why Brady Background Checks Should be Required for All Gun Sales*. Brady Center to Prevent Gun Violence, March 2009. http://www.bradycenter.org/xshare/pdf/reports/no-check-no

-gun-report.pdf (accessed January 22, 2011).

Siebel, Brian J., and Elizabeth S. Haile. *Shady Dealings: Illegal Gun Trafficking from Licensed Gun Dealers*. Brady Center to Prevent Gun Violence, January 2007. http://www.bradycenter.org/xshare/pdf/reports/shady-dealings.pdf (accessed January 22, 2011).

Vice, Daniel R. *The NRA: A Criminal's Best Friend: How the National Rifle Association Has Handcuffed Gun Law Enforcement*. Brady Center to Prevent Gun Violence, October 2006. http://www.bradycenter.org/xshare/pdf/reports/criminals-best-friend.pdf (accessed January 22, 2011).

Brady Handgun Violence Prevention Act (Brady Bill)

The Brady Handgun Violence Prevention Act, or Brady Bill, is a 1993 law passed by Congress (PL 103-159; 107 Stat. 1536) that required a five-business-day waiting period for the purchase of a handgun, for the purpose of conducting a background check on the prospective buyer and to provide a cooling-off period to minimize impulse purchases that might lead to violence. Five years after enactment of the law, the five-day waiting period was eliminated and replaced by an instant background-check system, as per the terms of the law.

From 1987 to 1993, gun control proponents, led by Handgun Control, Inc. (HCI; later renamed the Brady Campaign), placed their primary political emphasis on the enactment of a national waiting period for handgun purchases. The purpose of such a rule was twofold: first, to provide authorities with the opportunity to conduct a background check on the prospective purchaser to void handgun purchases by felons, the mentally incompetent, or others who should not have handguns; and second, to provide a cooling-off period for those who seek to buy and perhaps use a handgun in a fit of temper or rage. On its face, the proposal represented a modest degree of government regulation, since it merely postpones a handgun purchase by a few days and denies handguns only to those whom everyone agrees should not have them. Yet the struggle over enactment of a waiting period took on epic proportions in the form of a bitter power struggle between regulation opponents and proponents.

The Brady Bill was named after James Brady, the former White House press secretary and subsequent gun control advocate who was seriously injured in the assassination attempt against President Ronald Reagan in 1981. It was first introduced in Congress in 1987—in the Senate by Howard Metzenbaum (D-OH) and in the House of Representatives by Edward F. Feighan (D-OH). It quickly became the top priority of HCI and Sarah Brady, James Brady's wife and HCI leader. The National Rifle Association (NRA) opposed the measure, saying that it would merely be a prelude to stronger regulation, that it would not stop criminals from getting guns, and that it merely inconvenienced those entitled to guns. As late as the mid-1970s, however, the NRA had supported the idea of waiting periods.

The Brady Bill was put up to a chamber-wide vote in the House for the first time in 1988, when opponents led by the NRA succeeded in defeating the bill by substituting an NRA-backed amendment for the waiting period, despite a concerted effort by HCI and a coalition of police organizations called the Law Enforcement Steering Committee. By its own account, the NRA spent from $1.5 million to $3 million in the successful effort to kill the bill, mostly on a media campaign and grassroots efforts. Assessing the failed effort, Representative Feighan noted that at least two dozen House members had privately spoken of their support for the bill, but had refused to vote for it not because they feared losing their seats, but because of "the aggravation" that accompanied opposing the NRA.

Two years later, both chambers voted to approve the Brady Bill. Initial House approval for a seven-day waiting period came in May 1991 (by a 239–186 vote), with Senate approval (by a 71–26 vote) following a month later. Before passing the Brady Bill, the House defeated an NRA-backed substitute, sponsored by Rep. Harley O. Staggers (D-WV), which called instead for an instant computerized background check of prospective handgun purchasers, a measure that would eventually become a part of the final bill.

The problem with the proposal at the time it was first offered was that for such a system to work, it would require the full automation of pertinent records from all the states. Yet in 1991, only 10 states had such automation; eight states still handled files manually, and nine states did not even maintain the necessary felony records. These data problems were mostly resolved in the late 1990s.

President George H. W. Bush publicly opposed the Brady Bill throughout 1991 and 1992, but linked it with the larger crime bill to which it was attached, saying that he would sign the measure even if Brady was included—but only if the larger crime bill was to his liking. Bush's veto threat hung over the bill, yet it also opened the door to presidential approval, since it provided a means whereby he could sign the measure into law without seeming to entirely abandon his inclination to oppose most gun control measures.

The Brady Bill struggle climaxed in 1993, when supporters promoted a five-business-day waiting period bill. House Judiciary

Committee approval was won on November 4, despite the objections of committee chair and gun control opponent Jack Brooks (D-TX), who also boosted the bill's chances by reluctantly consenting to separate the measure from a new crime bill. Six days later, the full House approved the Brady Bill after fending off several amendments (sponsored by Republicans and Brooks) designed to weaken the bill. One such amendment, to phase out the waiting period after five years, was adopted. The final vote to pass the bill, H.R. 1025, was 238–189.

Following the lead of the House, the Senate separated the Brady Bill (S.R. 414) from the larger crime package. The bill faced a Republican filibuster almost immediately, but this move was forestalled by an agreement between the political party leaders to allow floor consideration of a substitute version that included two NRA-backed provisions. The first called for all state waiting periods to be superseded by the federal five-day waiting period (24 states had waiting periods of varying lengths in 1993; 23 also had background checks). This was objectionable to Brady supporters because many states had waiting periods longer than five days, and the move was seen as a violation of states' rights. This amendment was stricken from the bill by a Senate floor vote. The second measure called for ending the five-day waiting period after five years. It survived a vote to kill it. The Senate then faced a filibuster, which looked as though it would be fatal to the bill. Brady supporters and congressional allies all conceded that the bill was dead for the year. The postmortems proved to be premature, however, because within a couple of days, the Republicans decided to end their opposition on November 20, sensing a rising tide of impatience and no sense that they could win further concessions from

Democratic leaders. The bill was passed that day by a 63–36 vote.

The bill then went to a contentious House-Senate conference on November 22. Opposing factions finally reached an accommodation, and the bill was approved in the Senate by voice vote on November 24, with a promise to consider several modifications in early 1994. President Bill Clinton signed the bill into law on November 30.

As enacted, the Brady Law codified a five-business-day waiting period for handgun purchases for the succeeding five years. According to the law, handgun purchases are to be rejected if the applicant has been convicted of a crime that carries a sentence of at least a year (not including misdemeanors); if there is a violence-based restraining order against the applicant; if the person has been convicted of domestic abuse, arrested for using or selling drugs, is a fugitive from justice, is certified as mentally unstable or is in a mental institution, or is an illegal alien or has renounced U.S. citizenship. The law also authorized $200 million per year to help states improve and upgrade their computerization of criminal records; increased federal firearm license fees from $30 to $200 for the first three years, and $90 for renewals; made it a federal crime to steal firearms from licensed dealers; barred package labeling for guns being shipped to deter theft; required state and local police to be told of multiple handgun sales; and said that police must make a "reasonable effort" to check the backgrounds of gun buyers. In addition, it provided for ending the five-day wait after five years and replacing it with an instant background check, which began in December 1998. Such checks are conducted through information provided by the Federal Bureau of Investigation's National Instant Criminal Background Check System (NICS). The check must be completed within three days,

but 95 percent of the background checks are completed within two hours, according to a U.S. Justice Department report. Even though waiting periods are no longer required by the national government, 11 states have their own, ranging from a few days to several months.

Opponents of the law, including the NRA, challenged its constitutionality—not as a violation of the Second Amendment's right to bear arms, but as a violation of states' rights under the Tenth Amendment. In 1997, the U.S. Supreme Court struck down the law's provision requiring local police to conduct background checks in the case of *Printz v. United States* (521 U.S. 898). The ruling did not challenge the propriety of restricting handgun sales. Despite the ruling, handgun background checks generally continued. From the time of the law's enactment through 2008, about 1.8 million handgun sales were blocked as the result of the law (about 2 percent of all handgun purchases). In 2009, the government passed its 100 millionth background check. In addition, the increase in federal firearm license fees helped reduce the number of license holders from nearly 300,000 to about 50,000 by 2007, as most license holders were not storefront dealers but private individuals who were willing to pay the low fee to save money on their own gun purchases. The Clinton administration issued regulations to monitor dealers more closely as well. Critics argued that the federal government failed to prosecute most Brady Law violators. In response, the Clinton administration proposed hiring several hundred additional Bureau of Alcohol, Tobacco and Firearms agents and federal prosecutors to focus on gun-law violators. Congress approved the proposal in 2000.

Brady Law supporters also continued to note that the background-check provision only applied to licensed dealers. At gun shows and flea markets in most states, guns can be bought and sold by unlicensed individuals. An estimated 40 percent of gun sales occur at gun shows, flea markets, and other unregulated "secondary market" venues (over 4,000 gun shows are held every year). National legislative efforts to close this so-called "gun-show loophole" have failed. As of 2008, 17 states required background checks for all handgun purchases, even those from unlicensed sellers. Since 2004, federal law has required the destruction of background check data within 24 hours (known as the Tiahrt Amendment, named after Rep. Todd Tiahrt [R-KS], who sponsored the measure), making it unavailable for law enforcement examination.

Robert J. Spitzer

See also: Background Checks; Brady, James S.; Brady, Sarah Kemp; Brady Campaign to Prevent Gun Violence; Enforcement of Gun Control Laws; Gun Shows; National Instant Criminal Background Check System; National Rifle Association (NRA); NICS Improvement Act; *Printz v. United States*; Reagan, Ronald Wilson; Waiting Periods

Further Reading

Bureau of Alcohol, Tobacco and Firearms. *Gun Dealer Licensing and Illegal Gun Trafficking*. Washington, DC: U.S. Department of the Treasury, 1997.

Bureau of Alcohol, Tobacco and Firearms. *Gun Shows: Brady Checks and Crime Gun Traces*. Washington, DC: U.S. Department of the Treasury, 1999.

Spitzer, Robert J. *The Politics of Gun Control*. 5th ed. Boulder, CO: Paradigm Publishers, 2012.

Branch Davidians

The Branch Davidians are an obscure offshoot of the Seventh-Day Adventist Church who achieved sudden worldwide notoriety on February 28, 1993, when a bungled attempt by the Bureau of Alcohol, Tobacco and Firearms (ATF) to serve a search-and-arrest warrant concerning illegal weapons went horribly wrong. The mismanaged raid and the intense firefight that it provoked resulted in the deaths of four agents and six residents of the Branch Davidians' Mount Carmel Center outside Waco, Texas.

The ATF justified the raid with the claim that the residents of Mount Carmel were illegally converting semiautomatic weapons into machine guns, among other things. During the ensuing 51-day siege, however, those inside Mount Carmel countered that many of them knew nothing at all about any illegal guns and that only a few of them were involved in the purchase and resale of firearms at local gun shows. In negotiations, first with the ATF and then with the Federal Bureau of Investigation (FBI), the Branch Davidians portrayed themselves as a peaceful group of Bible students who had gathered at Mount Carmel to study with David Koresh, whom they believed to be the only man ever to unravel the mysteries of the biblical book of Revelation and its message about the imminent end of the world. Government agents, in turn, portrayed Koresh as a deranged con man who had duped gullible people into following him, exploited them for his own purposes, and would willingly lead them to their deaths.

The tense standoff ended on April 19, 1993, when, after a prolonged attempt by armored vehicles to punch holes in the rickety wood-framed building, the Mount Carmel Center was consumed in flames, taking the lives of 74 residents and leaving only nine survivors. Despite reports from the U.S. departments of Treasury and Justice, hearings by Senate and House committees, a July 2000 report from Special Counsel John

Danforth, and extensive reviews of the evidence by journalists and scholars, many aspects of the "Waco" incident remain in contention. Not the least of these is the role of firearms, and violence, in the beliefs and practices of the Branch Davidians and in the teaching of David Koresh.

History

The Branch Davidians and their predecessors, the Davidians, had been a presence in the Waco area for nearly 60 years at the time of the raid. For virtually all of that time, they had lived in peaceful coexistence with their neighbors. They could trace their spiritual lineage to Victor Houteff, a dissident Seventh-Day Adventist who preached about the imminent, literal establishment of a millennial "Davidian" kingdom in Palestine. In 1935, Houteff bought a 189-acre tract of land outside of Waco to serve as the headquarters for his tiny movement. He intended to gather together a group of 144,000 "servants of God," as mentioned in Revelation chapter 7, and lead them to the land of ancient Israel where they would soon meet Christ at his messianic return. Although their move to Israel did not occur as soon as expected, throughout the 1940s Houteff's group conducted a vigorous international missionary enterprise from its Texas headquarters. That largely unsuccessful effort was funded in part by selling off sections of the original parcel of land. Houteff died in 1955 and was succeeded by his wife Florence. In 1957, she sold the original parcel of land and relocated the group to 941 acres of land in Elk, nine miles east of Waco. That was the same land on which David Koresh would take up residence and eventually assume leadership of the group.

Florence became convinced that the end of the world and the dawning of the kingdom of God would begin during the Passover season in 1959. When her expectations went unfilled, the community was shattered, and it dwindled to fewer than 50 people during the mid-1960s. The group was revivified under the leadership of first Ben and then Lois Roden during the 1970s and 1980s. David Koresh, then known as Vernon Howell, came to Mount Carmel in 1981, an aimless high school dropout with twin passions for the electric guitar and the Bible. Like Houteff and the Rodens before him, Koresh believed that the Seventh-Day Adventist Church had become corrupted and could not claim to represent those who would be saved at God's imminent judgment. Lois Roden quickly recognized Koresh's facility with the Bible and, to the dismay of her son George, recognized him as her successor. Lois Roden died in 1986, and by the summer of 1988, after several conflicts with George, Koresh assumed leadership of the community.

David Koresh, the "Lamb of God"

Soon after joining the group of bible students led by Lois Roden, the young man then known as Vernon Howell began to fashion a unique identity for himself. The turning point came during a 1985 visit to Israel, where Howell claimed to have had an extraordinary religious experience. Although his comments to those outside the group were very cryptic, it appears that he understood his experience as an ascent into the heavens, similar to the one recounted by the apostle Paul in 2 Corinthians 12 and to the "night journey" attributed to Muhammad in the Islamic tradition. On March 5, for example, he told one of the FBI negotiators that he had been taken up into the heavens, shown everything concerning the seven seals, and commissioned by God to spread the truth to all humanity. The 1985 experience thus lay behind Koresh's most provocative assertion, that he was a

"Christ," an anointed one. That assertion, however, did not involve a claim of identity with Jesus Christ, but rather a similarity of function. Like Jesus and others who are called "Christs" or "messiahs" in the Bible, Koresh saw himself as having been chosen to execute God's will on earth. One of those "Christs," the sixth-century-BCE Persian king Cyrus who liberated the people of Israel from their captivity in Babylon, gave Howell the surname that he legally adopted in 1990, Koresh.

Koresh's specific task was to reveal, for the first time in human history, the message of the scroll sealed with seven seals that is mentioned in the book of Revelation, chapters 4 and 5. Koresh's message concerned not only the imminent last judgment and the cataclysmic end of the world as we know it, but also the roles that he and his devoted followers would play in that apocalyptic scenario. Koresh identified himself as the Lamb of Revelation, and his students fervently hoped that they would be among the 144,000 who would be saved. Revelation was the fixed point around which all Branch Davidian discourse revolved. All of Koresh's interpretive forays into the rest of the Christian scriptures, which ranged widely through the prophets and Psalms in his "Bible Studies," were explicitly designed to clarify and extend the message of the seven seals.

Koresh's message included references to all of the violent natural, social, and cosmic upheavals that are typical of biblical apocalypticism. He embraced Revelation's image of a climactic battle between the forces of good and evil at Armageddon and anticipated that he and his small band of followers might be called upon to fight on behalf of God. There is, however, no evidence that Koresh urged his followers to take matters into their own hands to hasten the apocalypse; nor is there evidence that the cache of weapons at the Mount Carmel Center was intended to be used to provoke the battle that would signal the end of the world. Koresh did not doubt that the day of judgment would hold terrible violence for those who have shunned the truth, but that violence would be enacted by God alone.

After Koresh

Only nine Branch Davidians survived the April 19 fire. Many of those who were outside Mount Carmel at the time of the siege have not kept the faith, and few new believers have been added since 1993. Nonetheless, two prominent representatives have emerged to continue, and even expand upon, David Koresh's teaching. Livingstone Fagan, who had been sent out of Mount Carmel on March 23 to serve as a theological spokesperson for the community, has written several small tracts and a larger manuscript, *Mt. Carmel: The Unseen Reality*, during his incarceration on charges of conspiracy to commit murder. Fagan's writings constitute a faithful representation of Koresh's teaching and he has continued to write tracts since his release from prison and deportation from the United States in 2007. Another figure, known only as "The Chosen Vessel" but identified as the Mount Carmel survivor Renos Avraam, has attempted to supplement Koresh's teachings with his own innovations, most recently focusing on August 2012 as the time of the end. In neither body of writings, however, is there any indication of an endorsement of violence on the part of the faithful. The responsibility of the students of the seven seals is still to study the apocalyptic message of Revelation and prepare themselves for the imminent judgment of the Lord.

Eugene V. Gallagher

See also: Bureau of Alcohol, Tobacco, Firearms and Explosives (ATF); Waco, Texas, Raid

Further Reading

Fagan, Livingstone. *A Discussion of Branch Davidian Theology.* http://david.koresh-lf-2009.angelfire.com/page_4.html (accessed January 23, 2011).

Gallagher, Eugene V. "The Persistence of the Millennium: Branch Davidian Expectations of the End after "Waco." *Nova Religio* 3 (2000): 303–19.

Moore, Carol. *The Davidian Massacre: Disturbing Questions about Waco Which Must Be Answered.* Franklin, TN, and Springfield, VA: Legacy Communications and Gun Owners Foundation, 1995.

Reavis, Dick. *The Ashes of Waco: An Investigation.* New York: Simon and Schuster, 1995.

Tabor, James D., and Eugene V. Gallagher. *Why Waco? Cults and the Battle for Religious Freedom in America.* Berkeley: University of California Press, 1995.

Thibodeau, David, and Leon Whiteson. *A Place Called Waco: A Survivor's Story.* New York: Public Affairs, 1999.

Wessinger, Catherine. *How the Millennium Comes Violently: From Jonestown to Heaven's Gate.* New York: Seven Bridges Press, 2000.

Wright, Stuart A. *Armageddon at Waco: Critical Perspectives on the Branch Davidian Conflict.* Chicago: University of Chicago Press, 1995

British American Security Information Council (BASIC)

The British American Security Information Council, commonly known as BASIC, is a nongovernmental research body that explores security and military issues and works to promote the nonproliferation of weapons. The organization produces a variety of publications on security and weapons issues and sponsors international forums to address these matters.

Founded in 1987, BASIC has twin offices in London and Washington, D.C. When it was originally established, the Cold War was just beginning to wind down, and arms control and nuclear nonproliferation dominated BASIC's activities. However, after the end of the superpower conflict in the early 1990s, BASIC shifted its focus to more on efforts to control the international arms trade and the traffic in light weapons. The organization brings together a variety of academics and policymakers who produce studies and analyze trends in weapons proliferation. BASIC also sponsors workshops and conferences on security and proliferation matters for government officials, scholars, and the general public. In addition, BASIC collaborates with other nongovernmental bodies to facilitate research and nonproliferation programs.

BASIC undertook a variety of specific programs that target areas of concern. For instance, the organization's Project on European Security worked to coordinate arms-control cooperation between such international bodies as the North Atlantic Treaty Organization, the European Union, and the Organization for Security and Co-operation in Europe. One of BASIC's major programs was its Project on Light Weapons. This project sought to evaluate the role and importance of light weapons in regional and substate conflicts. It further endeavored to counter the spread of small arms in all countries, including the United States. Specifically, BASIC worked to decrease the number of weapons worldwide. Among the steps that BASIC took was support for the destruction of weapons and strengthening gun control measures throughout the world. BASIC also lobbied individual governments and international organizations such as the United Nations for more restrictive controls on the export of light weapons and bans on specific types of arms.

In the United States, BASIC worked to limit the import of inexpensive handguns from such nations as Brazil and China. Furthermore, the organization supported legislation that would limit the export of light weapons to nations with high rates of gun violence as the result of the illicit drug trade, such as Colombia, or political instability, such as Liberia. Finally, BASIC research and reports were utilized as effective monitors of the domestic gun trade and both state and national endeavors to limit access to illegal weapons.

In the 2000s, BASIC returned to its earlier concentration on nuclear nonproliferation and disarmament. The organization worked to limit tactical nuclear weapons within the North Atlantic Treaty Organization and to establish a nuclear weapons–free zone in the Middle East, including efforts to end Iran's nuclear weapons program. One of BASIC's goals is now the complete elimination of all nuclear weapons.

Tom Lansford

See also: United Nations (UN)

Further Reading

British American Security Information Council. http://www.basicint.org/ (accessed June 20, 2011).

Brown Bess

"Brown Bess" is the familiar name for any one of several pattern muskets put into service by the British military between the 1720s and the 1840s. The "Bess" was the first of the eighteenth-century pattern muskets to gain adoption as a standard military weapon, and as such, it was widely copied and imitated.

The Brown Besses were fabricated under the direction of the Board of Ordinance for the Land Service at the Tower of London. This close direction of arms production was a novelty in the early eighteenth century, and the British Board of Ordinance led the way in centralizing arms procurement (removing responsibility from the colonel commanding each local unit). In the process, the board developed a system to produce "pattern" arms. Private contractors fabricated components of the muskets (locks, stocks, and barrels) from patterns. The board inspected each lock and proved (test-fired) each barrel. Separate contractors then took components from the board's inventory to assemble muskets of standardized specifications of bore, weight, furniture, lock design, and length. Although the parts in each individual weapon were fit by hand (not interchangeable), use of this pattern system made the completed weapons interchangeable in the hands of the soldiers who carried them. Individual differences in weight, balance, and handling were minimal. Every unit in the army could be equipped with weapons of standard bore, reliability, and handling characteristics. Moreover, the Board of Ordinance could control the supply of arms to ensure consistent quality and supply.

The development of pattern arms and centralized ordinance meant that soldiers could be trained to operate in very closely coordinated units firing virtually identical weapons. Technologically, the pattern musket and its associated socket bayonet provided the basis for the tactical revolution that finally banished the pike completely from European battlefields. As pattern muskets improved and their use in the hands of trained troops became the standard, the deadliness of coordinated fire from flintlock muskets put an end to the use of cavalry as shock troops on the battlefield. Thus, these flintlock muskets of the eighteenth century put an end to a tactical constant that dated to the eighth century.

Fitted with the socket bayonet, the Brown Bess was the first in a new class of weapons that provided the technological basis for establishing heavy infantry as the dominant force in tactical planning. Planning based on dominance of heavy infantry—massed formations of troops armed with a bayonet-equipped musket (or rifle)—lasted until World War I. At that point, the heavy machine gun and the artillery barrage changed tactical realities once again.

Strictly applied, the name Brown Bess refers only to the Long Land Pattern Musket produced for the British army from the 1720s to the 1790s. More commonly, however, the name appropriately describes the several variants based on the Long Land Musket that were in regular use until the 1840s. Less appropriately, the name Brown Bess is often applied as a more general term to describe eighteenth-century muzzle-loading flintlocks, especially the weapons carried by troops of the Continental army during the American Revolution. In fact, the Bess was not standard issue among the Continentals, nor were the British Besses particularly popular with the Americans. They were among the heaviest, most cumbersome, and most difficult to use of the pattern muskets. The Bess called for real strength and highly trained skills.

The most important of the Brown Bess variants include the Short Land Pattern Musket and another model produced originally for the East India Company. The original Long Land Pattern Musket had a barrel length of 46 inches. The Short Land Pattern Musket, introduced in the 1760s, simply cut the barrel to 42 inches. That change may seem minor, but it had a real effect on the handling of the weapon in the close-packed ranks of troops who carried the Bess. This Short Land Musket, which is also called the New Land Pattern Musket, became the standard weapon for British troops in both the American Revolution and the Napoleonic Wars. Modified to accept percussion caps, the British army carried on with the Bess until the 1840s. The East India Company's variant was a lighter, cheaper version of the rugged and reliable military weapons provided by the Board of Ordinance at the Tower. These less-rugged Besses, which had an even shorter barrel, are particularly known for their use as trade guns, especially in the North American fur trade.

The origins of the name Brown Bess are unclear, and the term was never more than a nickname of familiar use, which accounts for its frequent misapplication as a generalized term applied to eighteenth-century flintlock muskets. The first appearances of the term Brown Bess in print occurred relatively late (1780s), but almost certainly the name was in common use among the troops who carried the weapon much earlier than the 1780s. The most widely accepted explanation for the name makes it a corruption of one of any number of Dutch or German terms related to guns and gun barrels: *bus*, *büsse*, *byssa*, or *busche*. The original name, then, would have meant nothing more than "brown barrel."

As a class, the weight and ruggedness of Brown Besses set them apart from other eighteenth-century military flintlocks. These were .75-caliber weapons weighing in excess of 10 pounds. Most other standard-issue pattern muskets from the period were of lesser caliber and somewhat lighter. French pattern muskets such as the Charlevilles, for example, were .69 caliber, and that was still widely considered a heavy infantry weapon. It was the 1763 Charleville that the French supplied in large quantities (over 80,000) to their American allies during the American Revolution. Thus, while the popular imagination has the Continentals of the American Revolution equipped with the Brown Bess, most American troops were actually issued the somewhat smaller-bore Charleville. The British had never allowed widespread distribution of the Besses in the colonies, even for militia use. The Brown Besses (about 17,000) actually used by Americans during the Revolutionary War were captured arms. The Charlevilles received from France beginning in 1777 supplied the American military needs for long arms well into the 1790s, and the first of the long arms produced at the Springfield Armory was a copy of the Charleville, not the Brown Bess. Indeed, the muskets on which Eli Whitney set out to perfect manufacturing by interchangeable parts was an American pattern based on the Charleville.

The Bess was considered heavy and difficult to master. It was designed to fire a very heavy ball, to stand up to violent use in bayonet charges, or to be turned end-for-end and used as a club. It fired with considerably more "kick" than such weapons as the Charleville, and it was thought that effective use required more highly trained and disciplined troops. The efficient use of the Bess, in fact, put the British regulars among the most effective and feared troops of the period. British regulars of the late eighteenth and early nineteenth centuries were particularly noted for their discipline and their coolness under fire. Equipped with the Brown Bess, their discipline and training gave them truly formidable military capability that is often underappreciated in light of

the subsequent development of effective breech-loading and rifled weapons.

Looking back, especially in light of the mythology surrounding sharpshooters and the use of irregular troops armed with rifles, it is tempting to marvel at the foolishness of battlefield tactics that had red-coated regulars marching forward in their closely packed ranks. In fact, the red-coated regular marching forward in the serried ranks of the American Revolution had a better statistical chance of survival than did the combat infantryman crouching in the trenches of World War I or the GIs huddled in the foxholes of World War II. The British infantry square of the Napoleonic era was a truly formidable fighting formation, and its effectiveness was built on training and discipline designed to make the best use of the technical capabilities inherent in the Brown Bess. The Bess's ball was very large and heavy (16 balls to the pound) and it produced smashing and shattering effects in the wounds it created. Given the relatively low muzzle velocities possible with black powder, the inertia of this very large ball (three-fourths of an inch in diameter) gave it considerably greater stopping power than what was possible with any weapon of lesser caliber.

The discipline and training of close-order drill for the redcoats was intended to pack the troops together to provide a formation with the maximum possible rate of fire. Three lines of troops firing in a coordinated fashion could effectively deploy one musket for each 14 inches of firing line. At least for short periods, coordinated fire from closely packed troops trained to use the Bess could produce a screen of projectiles that will bear comparison with the effects of modern automatic weapons. Even the use of the smooth-bore musket (as opposed to rifles) was calculated to increase the rate of fire. An effectively trained soldier equipped with smooth-bore muskets could fire at least three rounds per minute on command. In contrast, the muzzle-loaded rifles of the eighteenth century required several minutes of loading time for each round fired. Firing by platoons grouped into three lines, a well-trained battalion of soldiers equipped with the Brown Bess could keep a screen of musket balls in the air in front of their formation at all times. No contemporary formation of riflemen could produce anything comparable. Even when riflemen were used effectively during the American Revolution, as they were at the Battle of Saratoga, they were screened and protected from counterattack by troops armed with muskets and bayonets.

With a musket, even a good marksman could not expect to hit a man-sized target at any more than 40 to 50 yards. Individual aiming, however, was not called for. The Brown Bess, in fact, was not fitted with any sights at all; infantrymen were trained to point and shoot—not to aim at any individual target. A compact infantry formation could establish an effective screen of musket fire out to at least 150 yards—even on a battlefield swathed in black-powder smoke—simply by loading and firing on command. Such a screen of fire made it very dangerous for either cavalry or enemy infantry to approach a trained infantry formation, and it usually made it possible for a formation to move across a battlefield at will unless opposed by a comparably equipped and trained force or by massed artillery fire. It was the effectiveness of closely coordinated musket fire that finally ended any expectation that heavy cavalry could deliver a shock force capable of breaking massed infantry formations on the battlefield. The combination of the flintlock musket and the bayonet gave the battlefield advantage to the heavy infantry.

Despite several notorious incidents in the French and Indian War—and several others during the American Revolution—in which skirmishers, irregulars, or sharpshooters managed to break the discipline of British troops (or kill their officers), well-trained regulars equipped with muzzle-loading muskets dominated the wars of the late eighteenth and the early nineteenth centuries. The muzzle-loading pattern musket and its associated bayonet were key parts in a technology system that maximized the rate of fire and emphasized the need for highly skilled and trained infantrymen. As one of the heaviest and most rugged of the eighteenth-century pattern muskets, the Brown Bess was also among the most effective. It was also the first of the pattern muskets to be adopted as a standard weapon for a national army. Its weight, kick, and cumbersomeness made it more difficult to use than many other muskets, but in the hands of properly trained troops, these same characteristics also made it just that much more deadly. The British army's reputation for reliance on a small number of long-service, highly trained professionals with particular expertise in the use of small arms was first established in the wars of the eighteenth and early nineteenth centuries. In that respect, the reputation of the modern British army was first built around the use of the Brown Bess.

David S. Lux

See also: American Revolution; Long Rifle (Pennsylvania/Kentucky)

Further Reading

Jones, Archer. *The Art of War in the Western World*. New York: Oxford University Press, 1987.

Neumann, George C. "The Redcoat's Brown Bess." *American Rifleman Magazine* 149 (April 2001): 49.

Wilkinson, Frederick. *The World's Great Guns*. London: Hamlyn Publishing Group, 1977.

Browning, John Moses (1855–1926)

John Browning revolutionized the gun industry. He was a prodigious inventor and one of the most successful gun manufacturers in modern history. Although he died in 1926, many of his weapons remain in use in the twenty-first century. Browning became noted for his innovations and the reliability of his designs. Among Browning's most celebrated designs were the Colt .45-caliber pistol, the Browning automatic rifle, and the Browning automatic shotgun.

John Moses Browning was born on January 23, 1855, in Ogden, Utah, to Mormon parents. His father was a gunsmith, and the younger Browning learned his trade working in his father's shop. At age 14, John Browning built his first gun—a single-shot rifle that he gave to his brother Matt. After the death of their father in 1879, the two brothers opened their own gunsmith shop, which they named the Browning Arms Company. That same year, Browning married Rachel Teresa Child. The couple went on to have eight children.

Soon after starting the company, Browning patented his first weapon, a single-shot rifle. While Browning created a variety of designs, the family arms business remained small and limited, since the brothers could not expand their sales beyond their small town. However, in 1883 a representative of the Winchester Arms Company became interested in one of Browning's designs. Winchester paid Browning $8,000 for the rights to produce his rifle. This marked the start of a lengthy relationship between Browning and the Winchester Company.

Ultimately, Browning gained 44 patents for Winchester.

Browning utilized his genius to design a variety of weapons and different styles of firearms. Besides working for Winchester, Browning also designed guns for such firearm companies as Remington, Colt, and the Belgian company Fabrique Nationale (FN). Browning far preferred to work on his inventions rather than manage the family's company.

Browning's business relationship with Winchester proved fruitful for both parties. In 1887, Browning invented one of the most popular and widely used weapons in the American West, the Winchester Model 1887 lever-action repeating rifle. This gun used a lever to reload and cock the weapon prior to firing. This gave the gun a high rate of fire compared with the single-action rifles commonly in use at the time. Browning produced this design in a shotgun for Winchester as well. Browning followed these innovations with a pump-action mechanism for shotguns—the basic model for all pump-action shotguns manufactured through contemporary times.

One of Browning's most important innovations involved the use of compressed gas to operate weapons. Browning's inspiration for this new design came when he observed the tremendous amount of gas and air produced by the explosion that occurred when a bullet was fired. The gunsmith sought to utilize this power in such a way that would allow the gun to reload automatically. His design did just that. The gases produced when a shell was fired created a recoil that moved the weapon's firing pin back. This allowed the spent bullet to be ejected and a new round to enter the chamber.

This automatic system was an integral component in the development of the modern machine gun. Browning personally designed two highly effective and popular machine guns. The first was the 1895 Colt Peacemaker, which became the standard heavy machine gun for the U.S. Army. His second design was the Browning automatic rifle (BAR), a lighter machine gun that could be fired by an individual. The BAR would be used in both world wars and the conflicts in Korea and Vietnam.

One of Browning's greatest contributions to gunsmithing came with his development of automatic pistols. His first automatic handgun was a .32-caliber pistol that automatically reloaded using a slide mechanism. This model was followed by a variety of weapons, including the famous Colt .45-caliber M1911 government model. This heavy pistol became the standard sidearm for both the military and law enforcement. Browning also developed a lighter 9 mm pistol known as the P-35, which was widely used by military and police forces around the world.

Browning also developed an automatic shotgun. However, Winchester decided not to produce the weapon because it was deemed too expensive to manufacture, and the market was thought to be too small. Browning found a new partner in Belgium's FN. Not only did FN reap significant financial rewards by producing Browning's shotgun, but other companies, including Remington and Savage, contracted to use Browning's design in the production of their automatic shotguns. The Browning automatic (A5) shotgun, which was first produced in 1902, is still produced and sold today. The association between the Browning Arms Company and FN survived long after Browning's death; in 1977 the Belgian corporation actually purchased the Browning Company. Browning has continued to operate under its own name, and through the 1990s, it recorded average annual sales of $100 million.

All of Browning's firearms were noted for both their reliability and their durability. The weapons were popular with the military and law enforcement because of their effectiveness and their consistency. The weapons were also marked by their simplicity of design and utility of function. The automatic weapons also provided far more firepower than contemporary firearms when Browning first introduced the weapons. Eventually, Browning would patent over 100 different weapons. These ranged from pistols to artillery pieces for the army. A testament to Browning's design genius has been the continued manufacture of his weapons, decades after his death on June 21, 1926. In fact, at the time of his death, there were still a number of new designs left that kept arms companies busy for a decade. It was not until 1935 that his final handgun design went into production.

Tom Lansford

See also: Colt, Samuel; Firearm Dealers; Ruger, William Batterman; Smith & Wesson (S&W); Winchester, Oliver Fisher

Further Reading

Miller, David. *The History of Browning Firearms: Fortifications around the World*. Guilford, CT: Lyons Press, 2006.

Winders, Gertrude Hecker. *Browning: The World's Greatest Gunmaker*. New York: John Day Co., 1961.

Buffalo Bill Cody. *See* Cody, William "Buffalo Bill"

Bullet Serial Numbers. *See* Micro-Stamping (Bullet Serial Numbers)

Bureau of Alcohol, Tobacco, Firearms and Explosives (ATF)

The Bureau of Alcohol, Tobacco, Firearms and Explosives (ATF) is a federal law enforcement organization located within the Department of Justice. It is responsible for enforcing laws related to the illegal diversion of alcohol and tobacco products as well as the illegal use and trafficking of firearms. The ATF is also responsible for administering and enforcing both criminal and regulatory laws regarding bombs, explosives, and arson. Previously, the ATF possessed regulatory functions related to the permitting, labeling, and marketing of tobacco and alcohol. However, the Homeland Security Act of 2002 vested those responsibilities in the newly created Alcohol and Tobacco Tax and Trade Bureau (TTB). While the TTB is located within the Department of Treasury, the former home of the ATF, the Homeland Security Act moved the ATF to the Department of Justice.

The ATF is headquartered in Washington, D.C., with field divisions located in over two dozen states and additional field offices located in several foreign countries, including Canada, Colombia, Iraq, and Mexico. The director of the ATF reports to the deputy attorney general in the Department of Justice. A chief of staff, chief counsel, and deputy director assist the director. The deputy director serves as the chief operating officer for the bureau and oversees eight separate offices that constitute the ATF. Those offices include Enforcement Programs and Services, Field Operations, Management, Professional Responsibility and Security Operations, Public and Governmental Affairs, Science and Technology, Strategic Intelligence and Information, and Training and Professional Development.

The earliest predecessors of contemporary ATF agents were the individuals charged by Secretary of the Treasury Alexander Hamilton with collecting a federal spirits tax imposed in 1791, a levy that later gave rise to the Whiskey Rebellion of 1794. The first

twentieth-century precursor to the ATF was the Prohibition Unit, an organization within the Bureau of Internal Revenue of the Treasury Department devoted to the enforcement of the Eighteenth Amendment and the Volstead Prohibition Enforcement Act. Perhaps the most colorful character in the bureau's history was Eliot Ness, whose story spawned both a television series and movies. Ness and his agents, nicknamed the Untouchables, became famous during the Prohibition period for pursuing gangster Al Capone and helping to build a successful case against him on tax-evasion charges. Tobacco came within the purview of the ATF during the 1950s, when the bureau was given the responsibility to collect a federal tobacco tax.

Even before the tobacco- and alcohol-related regulatory functions of the ATF were moved to the TTB, firearms regulation and enforcement dominated the bureau's agenda, both in terms of expenditures and regulatory activity. The regulation of firearms possession (including licensing firearm dealers) and criminal investigations (including tracing guns used in criminal activity) are the bureau's major firearms-related activities. The National Firearms Act of 1934 (aimed at curtailing the easy availability of firearms for criminal activities) and the Federal Firearms Act of 1938 (prohibiting certain classes of people from owning firearms) gave the bureau its original entry into firearms regulation. Its current responsibilities with regard to firearms derive mostly from the Gun Control Act of 1968 and its subsequent amendments, including the Firearms Owners' Protection Act of 1986 and the Brady Handgun Violence Prevention Act of 1998.

As part of its responsibilities with regard to firearms, the ATF is tasked with issuing federal licenses for gun manufacturers and dealers. The ATF's National Licensing

Center is based in Atlanta and handles these licensing responsibilities. Dealers are required to maintain a permanent place of business from which to conduct their firearms business and are barred from selling to prohibited classes of individuals, including felons, juveniles, and those adjudicated to be mentally incompetent. Individuals who collect guns for personal collections and make sales only occasionally as part of their hobby are also required to obtain a federal collector's license.

To ensure compliance with licensing requirements, the ATF conducts occasional inspections of existing licensees but has historically been plagued with insufficient personnel for effective monitoring. The Brady Handgun Violence Prevention Act requires dealers to obtain a criminal background check on a prospective buyer prior to making a sale. They do so through the National Instant Criminal Background Check System (NICS), which is operated by the Federal Bureau of Investigation (FBI). Though the ATF does not operate the NICS, it is responsible for ensuring dealer compliance with this provision of the Brady Bill, including the background check requirement.

In addition, the ATF operates the National Tracing Center (NTC) located in Martinsburg, West Virginia. The NTC is responsible for tracing the ownership of guns recovered from criminal investigations. The NTC collects information on firearms sales, stolen guns, and chains of possession (from manufacturer to purchaser) to aid local, state, and national law enforcement agencies. Such information is part of a computerized database used to identify firearms-trafficking corridors and black markets for guns. In fiscal year 2009, the NTC processed more than 340,000 requests from domestic and international law enforcement agencies to trace guns related to crimes. The NTC also

serves as the repository for firearms transaction records from federal firearm licensees that discontinue business, maintains records of multiple sales (i.e., the sale of two or more handguns to the same person within five consecutive business days), and provides assistance in identifying firearms with altered or destroyed serial numbers.

The ATF's current responsibilities with regard to arson and explosives derive from the Gun Control Act of 1968, which gave the ATF federal jurisdiction for destructive devices, and the Organized Crime Control Act of 1970, which established regulations regarding the manufacture, storage, and sale of explosives. As part of its role in the enforcement of laws regarding explosives and arson, the ATF administers the Federal Explosives License (FEL) Program. There are approximately 11,000 licensees working with commercial explosives, including fireworks and those used in the mining industry. The ATF also maintains a cadre of explosives specialists, fire investigators, and criminal profilers who engage in explosives investigations, assist with bomb disposal, and provide technical assistance to the commercial explosives industry. In conjunction with the U.S. Bomb Data Center, the ATF maintains the Bomb Arson Tracking System, which provides arson and explosives information to aid police officers, bomb technicians, and fire investigators at the state and local level.

No longer playing a role in the regulation of the alcohol or tobacco industries, the ATF's focus in this area is now strictly on the reduction of alcohol smuggling and contraband tobacco trafficking. The objective is to reduce or remove sources of revenue for criminal and terrorist organizations. The ATF directs more of its efforts at tobacco trafficking than at alcohol smuggling because tobacco trafficking is more common. Tobacco has become increasingly more attractive to trafficking organizations that previously focused only on weapons and drugs, as some states have dramatically increased their tobacco taxes. Tobacco diversion is estimated to cost federal, state, and local governments upward of $5 billion in unpaid excise taxes each year.

The relationship between the firearms industry and the ATF is volatile and exacerbated by the intense opposition of anti–gun control groups, such as the National Rifle Association (NRA). The ATF has been the target of a number of intense attacks and efforts to dismantle it. For example, when the bureau proposed to computerize records to facilitate meeting its regulatory obligations in the 1980s, Congress prohibited the ATF from spending any of its funds to do so and went so far as to cut the funds the ATF had estimated computerization would have cost from the bureau's budget. During his 1980 presidential campaign, Ronald Reagan included promises to dissolve the bureau, spurred in part by NRA lobbying and analyses conducted by conservative groups suggesting that major budget savings would accrue from folding the ATF into other agencies.

Most recently, the ATF has attracted intense scrutiny and the ire of lawmakers and gun rights groups over its Operation Fast and Furious—a sting operation intended to trace weapons moving illegally across the border between the United States and Mexico and result in the prosecution of illegal drug sellers. Guns sold to suspects in the sting operation were later traced to the scenes of death for two U.S. border agents. When U.S. attorney general Eric Holder was asked about details of the operation, he claimed not to know many of them; almost immediately, the NRA began a petition to have him fired (National Rifle Association

2011). Other fallout included the call for ATF acting director Kenneth Melson's resignation, as well as calls for the dissolving of the bureau itself (Gerstein 2011; Stolberg 2011)—which has been the aim of many in the gun rights camp for more than two decades.

Wendy L. Martinek

See also: Background Checks; Black Market for Firearms; Brady Handgun Violence Prevention Act (Brady Bill); Branch Davidians; Federal Firearms Act of 1938 (Public Law No. 75-785); Firearm Dealers; Gun Control Act of 1968; Gun Registration; Gun Shows; National Firearms Act of 1934; National Instant Criminal Background Check System; National Rifle Association (NRA); National Tracing Center (NTC); Ruby Ridge; Youth Crime Gun Interdiction Initiative

Further Reading

Bureau of Alcohol, Tobacco and Firearms. *An Introduction to the Bureau of Alcohol, Tobacco, and Firearms and the Regulated Industries*. Washington, DC: U.S. Department of the Treasury, 1998.

Gerstein, Josh. "Could Controversy Kill the ATF?" *Politico.com*, July 8, 2011. http://www.politico.com/news/stories/0711/58532.html (accessed July 20, 2011).

Martinek, Wendy L., Kenneth J. Meier, and Lael R. Keiser. "Jackboots or Lace Panties? The Bureau of Alcohol, Tobacco, and Firearms." In *The Changing Politics of Gun Control*, edited by John M. Bruce and Clyde Wilcox, 17–44. Lanham, MD: Rowman & Littlefield, 1998.

Moore, James. *Very Special Agents: The Inside Story of America's Most Controversial Law Enforcement Agency—the Bureau of Alcohol, Tobacco, and Firearms*. New York: Pocket Books, 1997.

National Rifle Association. "National Campaign to Fire Attorney General Eric Holder." July 2011. https://www.nra.org/fireholder/ (accessed July 20, 2011).

Spitzer, Robert J. *The Politics of Gun Control.* 5th ed. Boulder, CO: Paradigm Publishers, 2012.

Stolberg, Sheryl Gay. "Firearms Bureau Finds Itself in a Rough Patch." *New York Times,* July 4, 2011. http://www.nytimes.com/2011/07/05/us/politics/05guns.html (accessed July 6, 2011).

Vizzard, William J. *In the Cross Fire: A Political History of the Bureau of Alcohol, Tobacco and Firearms.* Boulder, CO: Lynne Rienner, 1997.

Bureau of Justice Statistics (BJS)

The Bureau of Justice Statistics (BJS), a component of the Office of the Justice Program in the U.S. Department of Justice, is the primary source for criminal justice statistics in the United States. The BJS collects, analyzes, publishes, and disseminates information to the criminal justice community on crime, crime rates, criminal offenders, victims, and the operation of the justice system at all levels of government. These data are critical to policymakers at all levels in promulgating legislation that ensures the administration of justice is efficient and fair while effectively combating crime.

The BJS annually publishes statistical findings on federal criminal offenders and case processing, correctional populations, and criminal victimization. The BJS periodically publishes statistical findings on a series of other topics, including felony convictions, practices and policies of state and federal prosecutors, the administration of law enforcement agencies and correctional facilities, and the characteristics of correctional populations. The BJS will also undertake special data collections and analyses to respond to the policy and legislative needs of the Department of Justice, the administration, Congress, and the criminal justice community. The BJS has made its data accessible in both print and digital format, with many of the BJS databases being accessible via the Internet. The BJS maintains more than two dozen major data collection series, which it publishes and distributes nationwide. The BJS website also contains links to several helpful reports on firearms usage, such as "Firearm Injury and Death from Crime: 1993–1997" and "Guns and Crime: Handgun Victimization, Firearm Self-Defense, and Firearm Theft."

James A. Beckman

See also: Department of Justice, U.S.; National Crime Victimization Survey (NCVS)

Further Reading

Bureau of Justice Statistics. http://bjs.ojp.usdoj.gov/ (accessed June 8, 2011).

Office of the Federal Register, National Archives and Records Administration. *The United States Government Manual.* Washington, DC: Government Printing Office, 1997.

Bush, George H. W. (1924–)

George Herbert Walker Bush was elected president of the United States in 1988. During the campaign, he emphasized his opposition to gun control and his lifetime membership in the National Rifle Association (NRA). As president, Bush provided rhetorical support for the NRA, but he also implemented a ban on imported assault rifles, along with other modest gun control measures. In 1994, Bush publicly resigned from the NRA and issued a letter denouncing fund-raising efforts by the organization that described federal agents as "jackbooted government thugs." In 2000, his son, George W. Bush, was elected president of the United States. Like his father, Bush campaigned in opposition to gun control.

George H. W. Bush. (George Bush Presidential Library)

George H. W. Bush was born on June 12, 1924, in Milton, Massachusetts, to Dorothy Walker Bush and Prescott Bush (who later served as a Republican senator for Connecticut in 1952–1962). Bush ran unsuccessfully for the Senate in 1964, then won a seat in the House of Representatives in 1966 representing Texas's Seventh District. Bush served on the Ways and Means Committee, and was reelected to the House in 1968 with no opposition. In 1970, he again lost a bid for the Senate.

During the 1970s, Bush held a number of appointed positions. In 1971, he was named U.S. ambassador to the United Nations. In 1973, he was appointed chair of the Republican National Committee. In 1974, he became chief of the U.S. Liaison Office in Peking during a period of normalizing relations between the United States and the People's Republic of China. In 1976, Bush became director of the Central Intelligence Agency.

Bush ran for the Republican presidential nomination in 1980. He won the Iowa caucuses but lost in New Hampshire to Ronald Reagan, who eventually won the nomination. Reagan picked Bush to be his running mate. Bush went on to serve two full terms as vice president. As vice president, Bush was in charge of the administration's antiterrorism policy and coordinated the war on drugs. He also headed a task force on regulatory relief.

In 1988, Bush won the GOP nomination for president and came from far behind to defeat Democrat Michael Dukakis in the general election. As president, he assembled an international coalition to drive Iraq from Kuwait in 1991, and for a time he enjoyed the highest popularity ratings of any incumbent president. But the economy slipped into recession, and Bush was defeated in his bid for reelection by Bill Clinton in 1992.

As a candidate, Bush emphasized his opposition to gun control. He repeatedly claimed that states with the strictest gun controls had the highest crime rates and called for stricter sentencing for criminals. In 1988, Bush won the endorsement of the NRA.

While in office, Bush introduced Operation Triggerlock, a program that directed U.S. attorneys to vigorously prosecute violations of gun laws committed by convicted felons and drug traffickers. This program provided increased support to the Bureau of Alcohol, Tobacco and Firearms (ATF), an agency that had already benefited from Bush's backing as part of his strategy for the war on drugs as vice president. This operation reinvigorated the ATF and changed their mission.

Bush's opposition to gun control was tested in 1989, when a gunman armed with a semiautomatic assault rifle massacred 17 schoolchildren in Stockton, California. Two years later, a man killed 23 people (including himself) and wounded more than 20 others in a cafeteria in Killeen, Texas. Political pressure built during this period for controls on semiautomatic weapons and large weapon clips.

Bush's advisers were divided, with drug czar William Bennett and many police groups urging that limits be placed on the weapons, but others pushing Bush to focus instead on an anticrime policy. Bush waffled and vacillated on the subject before finally issuing an executive order in early 1989 temporarily banning the import of certain assault weapons. He later made the ban permanent and expanded the number of guns covered by the policy. The NRA reacted angrily and refused to endorse Bush in 1992. Yet Bush's ban did not cover domestically produced weapons, thereby avoiding a clash with gun manufacturers.

In May 1995, after the bombing in Oklahoma City, Bush made public a letter to the NRA in which he resigned his lifetime membership. Bush angrily denounced statements by NRA president Wayne LaPierre defending the group's characterization of federal law enforcement agents as "wearing Nazi bucket helmets and black storm trooper uniforms" and "attack[ing] law abiding citizens." The strongly worded letter served as a coda on Bush's complicated relationship with the NRA. Bush's break with the NRA has been continually referenced, particularly in regard to the NRA's endorsement of presidential candidates. Among Bush's Republican successors, Bob Dole failed to garner a NRA endorsement in 1996, but Bush's son, George W. Bush, did receive the official nod in 2000 and 2004, as did John McCain in 2008.

On January 8, 2011, 19 individuals, including Rep. Gabrielle Giffords (D-AZ), fell victim to a mass shooting at a public meeting held by the congresswoman for her constituents. Six, including a nine-year-old girl and the chief federal judge in Arizona, did not survive. The tragedy, like other recent mass shootings, such as the Virginia Tech massacre in 2007, reawakened the gun control debate. In the wake of the Tucson event, the National Institute for Civil Discourse, a new nonpartisan center for debate, research, education, and policy about civility in public discourse, was established at the University of Arizona. George H. W. Bush and Bill Clinton serve as inaugural honorary chairs.

Clyde Wilcox and Christine Kim

See also: Killeen, Texas, Massacre; LaPierre, Wayne R., Jr.; McVeigh, Timothy; Republican Party and Gun Control; Stockton, California, Massacre; Tucson, Arizona, Massacre; Virginia Tech Massacre

Further Reading

Carter, Gregg Lee. *The Gun Control Movement.* New York: Twayne, 1997.

Davidson, Osha Gray. *Under Fire: The NRA and the Battle for Gun Control.* Iowa City: University of Iowa Press, 1998.

Duffy, Michael. *Marching in Place: The Status Quo Presidency of George Bush.* New York: Simon and Schuster, 1992.

George Bush Presidential Library and Museum. http://bushlibrary.tamu.edu/ (accessed May 16, 2011).

National Institute for Civil Discourse. http://nicd.arizona.edu/ (accessed May 16, 2011).

Spitzer, Robert J. *The Politics of Gun Control.* 5th ed. Boulder, CO: Paradigm Publishers, 2012.

Vizzard, William J. *Shots in the Dark: The Policy, Politics, and Symbolism of Gun Control.* New York: Rowman & Littlefield, 2000.

The White House. "George H. W. Bush." http://www.whitehouse.gov/about/presidents/georgehwbush (accessed May 16, 2011).

Bush, George W. (1946–)

George W. Bush was elected president in 2000 and reelected in 2004, with strong support from the National Rifle Association (NRA). Although never a NRA member himself, Bush's position in favor of an individual's right to bear arms led the vice president of the association to declare to supporters: "If we win [in the 2000 election], we'll have a president . . . where we'll work out of their office" (Connolly and Neal 2000, A01). The major gun-related issues that marked Bush's tenure in the White House were the D.C. sniper case in 2002, the expiration of the federal Assault Weapons Ban in 2004, the passage of federal legislation shielding gun manufacturers and sellers from lawsuits in 2005, the Virginia Tech shootings in 2007, and the Supreme Court decision in *District of Columbia v. Heller* (2008).

Bush was born in New Haven, Connecticut, on July 6, 1946. The eldest son of Barbara and George H. W. Bush, who served as vice president from 1981 to 1989 and president from 1989 to 1993, he grew up in Midland, Texas. After an unsuccessful run for Congress in 1978, Bush worked in business until elected governor of Texas in 1994. During his six years as governor of one of the most gun-friendly states in the country (he was reelected in 1998), Bush was a strong advocate for gun rights policy, signing bills allowing concealed handguns and barring cities from suing gun manufacturers.

In his first campaign for the White House, Bush defeated former vice president Al Gore, whose strong gun control stance likely cost him rural votes. Running for national office only a year after the shootings at Columbine High School in Colorado, Bush used campaign rhetoric that appealed to more moderate voters, while signaling support to gun rights advocates. As a candidate, he voiced support for stronger enforcement of already existing guns laws, more resources to prosecute those who commit crimes with guns, instant background checks at gun shows, voluntary trigger locks, moving the purchase age for firearms from 18 to 21 years old, and extending the federal Assault Weapons Ban. As president, however, Bush never pushed for these policies, apart from designating a minimal increase in funding for the prosecution of those charged with gun crimes. Instead, upon taking office, he frustrated gun control advocates by nominating John Ashcroft, an outspoken supporter of individual gun rights, to lead the Department of Justice.

During the search for the D.C. sniper in 2002, Bush pleased the NRA by deflecting calls to implement a nationwide ballistic fingerprinting system, which would allow law enforcement to track the origins of bullets using a centralized database. Beginning in 2003, Bush focused on passing a federal law that would indemnify gun manufacturers and sellers from lawsuits, just as he had done in Texas as governor. As the expiration of the 10-year-old Federal Assault Weapons Ban approached prior to the 2004 election, broad bipartisan support emerged in the Senate for a comprehensive gun policy that would extend the ban, establish background checks for purchases at gun shows, and shield manufactures and sellers from lawsuits. However, despite public opinion polls indicating that a majority of Americans supported the renewal of the ban, House Republicans balked at the gun control restrictions, and Bush ignored his campaign promises by failing to pressuring members of his party to take action. Although many members of the NRA felt betrayed that the president had offered rhetorical support for extending the ban, after he let it lapse on

September 13, gun rights groups organized large-scale efforts to assure his reelection.

In 2005, the long-sought indemnity bill for gun manufacturers and sellers was overwhelmingly passed, without previously proposed gun control amendments, by a new Republican-majority Congress. Bush signed the Protection of Lawful Commerce in Arms Act into law on October 26. Despite this early success, Bush's second term in office was marked by a spate of school shootings, which increased public pressure from gun control advocates. In 2006, there were four school shootings during a two-week period, including the killing of 10 girls in a one-room Amish schoolhouse in Pennsylvania. In response, the Bush administration organized an invitation-only White House Conference on School Safety, which included neither Democrats nor gun control advocates. During the one-hour discussion moderated by the president, he never once used the word "guns." On April 16, 2007, a student gunman killed 33 people (including himself) at Virginia Polytechnic Institute and State University. The deadliest shooting in U.S. history, this event reignited calls by gun control advocates for additional restrictions on the acquisition of firearms. Unable to ignore the issue, Bush supported the subsequent bipartisan legislation aimed at preventing the mentally ill from purchasing guns by improving the record-keeping of the National Instant Criminal Background Check System (NICS)—and he signed the NICS Improvement Act on January 8, 2008.

The most significant change to gun policy that occurred during Bush's tenure was the Supreme Court's decision in *District of Columbia v. Heller*, announced on June 26, 2008, which significantly reinterpreted the Second Amendment of the Bill of Rights. Specifically, this decision declared that the possession of a gun was an individual right, rather than a collective right, as in the case of a militia. This interpretation supported the position that had been administration policy since then attorney general Ashcroft declared it in a letter to the NRA in 2001. In his official public statement regarding this decision, Bush stated: "As a longstanding advocate of the rights of gun owners in the America, I applaud the Supreme Court's historic decision today confirming what has always been clear in the Constitution: The second amendment protects an individual right to keep and bear firearms" (Bush 2008, 921).

Richard Holtzman

See also: Assault Weapons Ban of 1994; Ballistic Identification System; *District of Columbia v. Heller*; National Rifle Association (NRA); Protection of Lawful Commerce in Arms Act of 2005; Virginia Tech Massacre; Washington, D.C., Sniper Attacks

Further Reading

Ashcroft, John. "Letter to the National Rifle Association Regarding Bush Administration's Interpretation of the Second Amendment, May 17, 2001." http://www.nraila.org/images/ashcroft.pdf (accessed July 14, 2011).

Baum, Dan. "Bush and Guns." *Rolling Stone*, July 6, 2000: 64–66.

Bush, George W. "Statement on the United States Supreme Court Ruling on Individual Gun Rights, June 26, 2008." *Weekly Compilation of Presidential Documents* 44 (2008): 921. http://www.gpo.gov/fdsys/pkg/WCPD-2008-06-30/pdf/WCPD-2008-06-30-Pg921-2.pdf (accessed December 29, 2011).

Connolly, Ceci, and Terry M. Neal. "Bush Denies He'd Toe the NRA Line; Gore Seizes on Video for Gun Control Attack." *Washington Post*, May 4, 2000, A01. http://www.highbeam.com/doc/1P2-524281.html (accessed July 14, 2011).

Dao, James. "N.R.A. Open an All-Out Drive for Bush and Its Views." *Washington Post*, April 16, 2004, A14. http://www.democratic underground.com/discuss/duboard.php?az =view_all&address=102x489788 (accessed July 14, 2011).

Milbank, Dana. "Guns Are in Schools but Not in the President's Vocabulary." *Washington Post*, October 11, 2006, A02. http://www .washingtonpost.com/wp-dyn/content/ article/2006/10/10/AR2006101001390 .html (accessed July 14, 2011).

Buyback Programs. *See* Gun Buyback Programs

C

Calguns Foundation

The Calguns Foundation is a 501(c)3 nonprofit organization that promotes gun rights for California residents. Placing much emphasis on concealed carry (CCW), the foundation aims to educate governments and protect the rights of individuals to acquire, own, and lawfully use firearms in California. Defining itself as a "grassroots civil rights" organization, Calguns Foundation provides Second Amendment–related education, pursues strategic litigation, and defends California gun owners from what it sees as improper prosecution. These activities further the foundation's goals of supporting the California firearms community through education, defense, and protection of the civil rights of California gun owners. In addition to supporting a public discussion forum at Calguns.net (Calguns Foundation 2011), the foundation also maintains a Facebook page, a profile on LinkedIn, a Twitter account, and a wiki with a wide range of information.

Gene Hoffman Jr. is the chairman and, apparently, the founder of the foundation. He is chairman and CEO of Vindicia, a firm that provides integrated payment and fraud management services. Brett Thomas, the treasurer and a director of the foundation, is also associated with Vindicia. All of the Calguns Foundation's directors have had extensive business careers, many in areas related to software and technology. They also have long-term interests in guns and gun ownership, with several being NRA life members.

Illustrative of the foundation's efforts is a suit filed against the Santa Clara County sheriff, Laura Smith. The suit, filed with Tom Scocca and the Madison Society, is in response to the sheriff's refusal to grant a carry permit to Scocca, director of security for a Silicon Valley semiconductor business. The suit argued that Scocca has "good cause" for a concealed carry permit and that the sheriff should grant it. The Madison Society focuses on education and litigation to remove restrictions on the right to "keep and bear arms" (Madison Society Foundation).

The foundation has also been successful with its Carry License and Sunshine Initiative. This program gathers and analyzes information about license issuance statistics, policies, and processing in various counties. The initiative then shares the information with counties that are not in compliance with California law in these areas. For example, Solano County has agreed to change their concealed carry fee to comply with the state law (Calguns Foundation 2011).

Walter F. Carroll

See also: Concealed Weapons Laws

Further Reading

Calguns Foundation. http://www.calgunsfoundation.org/ (accessed May 22, 2011).

Madison Society Foundation. http://www.madison-society.org/ (accessed May 16, 2011).

California Street (101) Massacre

On July 1, 1993, Gian Luigi Ferri entered the law offices of Pettit and Martin at 101 California Street in San Francisco, armed with three handguns and several hundred rounds of ammunition. Ferri was a former client who believed that the law firm had cheated him and contributed to his recent financial failures. He opened fire, killing eight people and wounding six more in the law firm and other offices before the police cornered him in a stairwell and he committed suicide. Public attention soon focused on a similarity between this mass killing and the Stockton schoolyard massacre of four years before: both gunmen had used assault weapons. Ferri used two TEC-DC9s, semiautomatic assault pistols manufactured by Navegar, Inc., of Miami, Florida, and equipped with military-style features that allow the user to fire many rounds of ammunition in a short period of time. Although California had banned the sale of assault weapons after the Stockton shooting, Ferri easily obtained his at a gun show and pawnshop in Nevada.

The 101 California Street massacre galvanized public opinion toward increased firearm regulation and contributed to the passage of the federal Assault Weapons Ban the following year. (The federal law had a 10-year "sunset" provision and expired in 2004.) Another important outgrowth of the massacre was *Merrill v. Navegar*, a historic lawsuit that produced the first appeals court decision to hold that a gun manufacturer may be held responsible for negligent conduct that increases the risk of criminal violence.

Navegar, doing business under the name Intratec, throughout the 1980s manufactured high-capacity assault pistols under the names KG-9 and TEC-9. The weapons quickly gained popularity among criminals. One study showed that the TEC-9 was the leading assault weapon seized by law enforcement agencies in large cities in 1990 and 1991, accounting for 24 percent of all such weapons seized. When the District of Columbia and other jurisdictions enacted laws restricting the TEC-9 and other assault weapons by model name, Navegar made a minor alteration to the weapon and renamed it the "TEC-DC9" to evade the laws. The features that criminals found so appealing, however, remained the same: the ability to accept high-capacity magazines, which can hold 50 rounds or more; a barrel shroud, which allows the shooter to grasp the gun with both hands and spray-fire, while protecting the hand from the heat generated by rapid fire; and a threaded barrel to accommodate silencers. The company advertised in survivalist publications like *Soldier of Fortune* and *Combat Handguns*, touting the TEC-DC9's "firepower," "excellent resistance to fingerprints," and other features of little value to law-abiding gun purchasers.

In the lawsuit, filed in May 1994, massacre victims and their families argued that Navegar should be liable for negligence in selling assault weapons to the general public (rather than restricting sales to the military, police, and shooting ranges) and using advertising that increased the appeal of the guns to criminals and other high-risk gun buyers. Navegar executives testified that they were well aware of their product's stature as the preeminent assault weapon used in crime and that they welcomed the publicity stemming from its use in notorious acts of violence because of the resulting spike in sales.

A California Superior Court judge dismissed the suit before trial, concluding that Navegar owed no duty to the victims because the weapons were legally manufactured and sold. In a landmark ruling in September 1999, the California Court of Appeals disagreed. The court held that although the manufacture and sale of a lawful firearm is not negligent in itself, Navegar owed the plaintiffs a duty to exercise reasonable care not to create risks above and beyond those inherent in the presence of firearms in society. It was the first appellate court decision imposing such a duty on a gun manufacturer.

On August 6, 2001, the California Supreme Court voted 5–1 to reverse the court of appeals ruling on other grounds, finding that a California statute, passed in 1983, barred the application of general common law principles to impose liability on Navegar. The court held that the statute, Civil Code Section 1714.4, precluded any claim for negligence or strict liability against a gun manufacturer involving an assessment of the risks versus the benefits of a firearm. In dissent, Justice Kathryn Mickle Werdegar argued that the statute did not apply to the plaintiffs' claim because "[t]hough plaintiffs' claim does require a weighing of risks and benefits, the risk and benefits involved are not those *of the product as such*, but those created by defendant's choice of distribution channels" (emphasis original). She further found that Navegar, under general legal principles, owed a duty of care in its "design, distribution, and marketing activities."

Largely as a result of the *Merrill* decision, in 2002, the California legislature repealed Section 1714.4, ending special immunity for the gun industry in California. However, in 2005, President George W. Bush signed into law the Protection of Lawful Commerce in Arms Act, imposing new federal limits on the liability of gun manufacturers and sellers.

Dennis A. Henigan

See also: Assault Weapons Ban of 1994; Lawsuits against Gun Manufacturers; Protection of Lawful Commerce in Arms Act of 2005; Stockton, California, Massacre; TEC-DC9 Pistol

Further Reading

Fried, Rinat. "California Lets Massacre Suit against Gunmaker Proceed: Ruling Is First to Green-Light Crime-Based Cause of Action." *National Law Journal* 7 (1999): A9.

Henigan, Dennis A. *Lethal Logic: Exploding the Myths that Paralyze American Gun Policy.* Dulles, VA: Potomac Books, 2009.

Sward, Susan. "Legacy of Horror: Highrise Massacre Left Behind Change, Challenges." *San Francisco Chronicle*, June 30, 1998, A1.

Calling Forth Act of 1792

The Calling Forth Act of 1792 (1 U.S. Stat. 264) represented the culmination of three years of political wrangling over how to implement congressional authority over militias. The compromise was for Congress to delegate this power to the president, leaving him a relatively free hand in the case of invasion, but circumscribing this power to some extent in the case of domestic insurrection, when the president needed to seek approval from a federal judge. It also invited the states to request militia help from the federal government in times of need, yet also made clear that the federal government could act against one or more states "whenever the laws of the United States shall be opposed, or the execution thereof obstructed." The larger objective was to balance federal and state power by making sure that the national government could act decisively, yet also to address antifederalist fears of an overly strong national government. The Second Amendment's assurance to the states that they would be able to form and maintain their own militias would not, this act said, absolve them of national connections, needs, or obligations. Any state that refused to call forth or commit its militias in appropriate circumstances could expect to find other state militias sent to its soil.

The language of the law was sweeping, saying:

> [W]henever the United States shall be invaded, or be in imminent danger of invasion from any foreign nation or Indian tribe, it shall be lawful for the President of the United States, to call forth such number of the militia of the state or states most convenient to the place of danger or scene of action, as he may judge necessary to repel such invasion, and to issue his orders for that purpose, to such officer or officers of the militia as he shall think proper; and in case of an insurrection in any state, against the government thereof, it shall be lawful for the President of the United States, on application of the legislature of such state, or of the executive . . . to call forth such number of the militia of any other state or states, as may be applied for, or as he may judge sufficient to suppress such insurrection.

Six days after the enactment of this law, Congress enacted the companion Uniform Militia Act of 1792, which stipulated in detail the manner in which the state militias were to be organized, even requiring militia-eligible men to keep firearms ammunition, and related materials. Lacking any enforcement mechanism, however, this law was generally ignored.

Although the Calling Forth Act included a time limit of two years, subsequent legislation was enacted to confirm and extend federal power over the militias, notably in 1795 and 1807.

Robert J. Spitzer

See also: Militia Act of 1792; Militias

Further Reading

Spitzer, Robert J. *Gun Control: A Documentary and Reference Guide*. Westport, CT: Greenwood Press, 2009.

Campaign to Protect Sane Gun Laws

The Campaign to Protect Sane Gun Laws was mounted by a coalition of national organizations that joined Handgun Control, Inc. (HCI), in 1995 to mobilize public opposition against attempts to weaken federal gun control laws, especially the Brady Bill and the Assault Weapons Ban.

HCI (now the Brady Campaign to Prevent Gun Violence) viewed alliances with other organizations as keys to achieving its goals through influencing government. On March 30, 1995, the 14th anniversary of the shooting of President Reagan and James Brady, HCI joined with 108 national organizations to oppose efforts by the gun lobby to repeal the Brady Handgun Violence Prevention Act and the Assault Weapons Ban of 1994. The organizations joining the campaign represented some 140 million Americans and included such well-known organizations as the American Medical Association, the American Academy of Pediatrics, the NAACP, the United States Catholic Conference, and the United States Conference of Mayors.

Each of the organizations in the campaign pledged to oppose the repeal of sensible gun laws such as the Brady Bill and the Assault Weapons Ban. At that time, gun rights groups

Canada, Gun Laws | 133

were pressuring Congress to repeal and weaken both laws. In April 1995, Congress began hearings on a bill to repeal the Assault Weapons Ban. The Campaign to Protect Sane Gun Laws successfully mobilized public opinion and generated intense lobbying pressure that helped prevent repeals.

Walter F. Carroll

See also: American Academy of Pediatrics (AAP); American Medical Association (AMA); Assault Weapons; Assault Weapons Ban of 1994; Brady Campaign to Prevent Gun Violence; Brady Handgun Violence Prevention Act (Brady Bill); Coalition to Stop Gun Violence (CSGV); Interest Groups and Gun Legislation; National Rifle Association (NRA); United States Congress and Gun Legislation

Further Reading

Carter, Gregg Lee. *The Gun Control Movement.* New York: Twayne Publishers, 1997.

Spitzer, Robert J. *The Politics of Gun Control.* 5th ed. Boulder, CO: Paradigm Publishers, 2012.

Canada, Gun Laws

Historically, Canada has had stricter gun control legislation than the United States, as well as lower rates of criminal violence and a higher suicide rate. As in the United States, Canada's urban areas have lower rates of legal gun ownership but higher rates of criminal violence than rural areas. Canada's low rates of criminal violence antedate recent gun legislation. Responsibility for making criminal law lies with the federal government in Canada, unlike the United States, where the states have that power. Canada is much more centralized than the United States. For example, the prime minister unilaterally appoints all senators and all Supreme Court justices. Moreover, individual rights have less

protection under the Canadian Charter of Rights and Freedoms than under the American Bill of Rights.

In 1995, the Canadian government passed the Firearms Act (Bill C-68), which mandated universal firearm registration and owner licensing. This legislation surprised some observers, as Canada already had a strict firearm regime. The safe handling of long guns (rifles and shotguns) was regulated through provincial hunting regulations, and handguns had been registered since 1934. In 1977, police scrutiny had been required for all purchasers of firearms, and a wide range of weapons were prohibited. In 1991, large-capacity magazines and a large number of semiautomatic rifles were prohibited or restricted. Opponents argue that the 1995 legislation was unconstitutional, unworkable, and ineffective, and would just create a costly bureaucracy.

The Liberal Party pushed the Firearms Act though Parliament in 1995. Three of the four opposition parties (Reform, Progressive Conservatives, and New Democrats) were united against Bill C-68. The only opposition party to support this legislation was the Quebec Party, possibly because Quebec was allowed to run a separate firearm registry. The Supreme Court of Canada rejected a constitutional challenge by six provincial governments (including Ontario) in 2000.

When firearm registration was introduced, it was claimed that it would cost taxpayers C$85 million (US$55 million). By early 2007, the known governmental costs had climbed to over C$2 billion. Unfortunately, no solid evidence can be found linking Canadian gun laws to a decline in either violent crime rates or suicide rates (Dandurand 1998; Mauser 2007). Since the early 1990s, homicide rates have fallen faster in the United States than in Canada.

To gun rights observers, the history of gun control in Canada demonstrates the slippery slope of gun control. Gun laws are passed during periods of fear and political instability. Despite no convincing empirical support of being effective, politicians periodically call for more gun laws, and the bureaucracy surrounding them continues to grow.

During the 1930s, the Canadian government feared labor unrest as well as American rumrunners. As a result, in 1934 it passed firearm legislation that mandated handgun registration. There were separate permits for British subjects and for aliens. Before 1947, few Asians or blacks qualified as British subjects even if born in Canada. World War II introduced additional gun control laws. In 1941, Asians were forbidden to own firearms and their firearms were confiscated. This is difficult to understand because China was a wartime ally of the British Commonwealth.

Terrorism in Quebec dominated the late 1960s and the early 1970s. In 1969, another firearm law was introduced that created the categories of "restricted weapons" and "prohibited weapons" for the first time. The Royal Canadian Mounted Police (RCMP) was given the authority to attach any "reasonable conditions" to the "use, carriage or possession of the [restricted] weapon . . . or ammunition, as [deemed] desirable in the interests of the safety of other persons."

Restrictions were increased for "restricted weapons" (mostly handguns), including requiring a "specific purpose" for use, and at this point they were subjected to stricter conditions, including the requirement that separate permits must be obtained each time handguns were taken to gunsmiths, gun shows or target ranges. Permits for "protection" were limited to a handful of people, such as retired police, judges, geologists, and prospectors. Citizens were allowed to purchase a restricted weapon only if the police judged them to be suitable owners.

"Prohibited weapons" (including fully automatic firearms, silencers, switchblades, nunchakus, and rifles and shotguns shorter than 66 cm) were made subject to more stringent conditions than restricted weapons. (A fully automatic firearm continues to shoot as long as the trigger is held down, or until the magazine is empty.) It became illegal to purchase or sell a prohibited weapon, though individuals who happened to own them before the introduction of the legislation could keep them and sell them amongst themselves but not take them to a shooting range. The government also gave itself the authority to restrict or prohibit, through Order-in-Council, any firearm "not commonly used in Canada for hunting or sporting purposes." (Orders-in-Council are decisions made at the cabinet level and therefore undergo no parliamentary review.)

In 1977, firearm legislation was amended again. A new permit was required to obtain ordinary rifles and shotguns (the Firearms Acquisition Certificate, or FAC). A new crime was declared regarding "unsafe storage of firearms," although no definition of safe storage was provided. The protection of property was eliminated as a suitable reason for acquiring a restricted firearm, and owners could no longer register handguns at their business address. The police began to refuse an FAC to anyone who indicated she or he desired to acquire a firearm for self-protection (even though in a typical year, tens of thousands of Canadians claim to use firearms to protect themselves or their families from violence; see Mauser 1996).

In 1991, notable changes were made to firearm law in response to a horrific shooting in Montreal that had shocked the country in 1989. After a lengthy investigation of the shooting, the Quebec coroner concluded that poor police response time rather than the particular weapon used was primarily responsible for the high number of deaths. The Progressive Conservative government decided there should be new firearm legislation. The 1991 legislation (Bill C-17) expanded the list of prohibited weapons to include converted full-automatics and a large number of semiautomatic military-style rifles and shotguns. A semiautomatic firearm requires a separate press of the trigger for each shot, although it automatically readies itself for the next. No empirical studies had been conducted to determine which, if any, types of firearms posed a threat to public security. Military-style firearms were restricted primarily because of their cosmetic differences from other firearms. This legislation changed the FAC system so that it now required applicants to provide a photograph and two references and imposed a mandatory 28-day waiting period and safety training before obtaining an FAC. At the same time, the application form was expanded to include 35 questions. If the applicant was married or divorced, one of their references was required to be a spouse or former spouse.

Applicants were now more thoroughly screened by police. The screening often involved telephone checks with neighbors and spouses or ex-spouses. Other major changes included new Criminal Code offenses, new definitions of prohibited and restricted weapons, new regulations for firearm dealers, and explicit regulations for the safe storage, handling, and transportation of firearms.

A major focus of the new legislation was semiautomatic military-style guns. The class of prohibited weapons was expanded to include semiautomatic firearms that had been converted from fully automatic ones. Owners of the newly prohibited firearms

were faced with eventual confiscation without compensation. The legislation also prohibited high-capacity cartridge magazines for automatic and semiautomatic firearms. A series of Orders-in-Council prohibited or restricted many semiautomatic rifles and some types of nonsporting ammunition.

Bill C-17's requirement for FAC applicants to show knowledge of the safe handling of firearms came into effect in 1994. To demonstrate such knowledge, applicants had to pass a test or a firearm safety course approved by a provincial attorney general, or a firearm officer had to certify that the applicant was competent in handling firearms safely. The mandated safety courses had to cover firearm laws as well as firearm safety.

Upon being elected in 1993, the Liberals brought in new gun legislation (Bill C-68). The government prohibited over half of all registered handguns in Canada (smaller handguns that could be carried concealed) and initiated plans to confiscate them. There was no evidence provided that these handguns had been misused. The auditor general of Canada found that no evaluation of the effectiveness of the 1991 firearm legislation had ever been undertaken (Auditor General 1993: 647–55). Bill C-68 became law on December 5, 1995; the main provisions began to be phased in when owner licensing and long-gun registration began in 1998; licensing became mandatory in 2001, and all long guns were required to be registered by 2003. Any person who allows his or her license to expire is subject to arrest and their firearms confiscated.

In addition to requiring licensing owners and registering firearms, Bill C-68, formally known as the Firearms Act of 1995, broadened police powers of search and seizure and expanded the types of officials who could make use of such powers; it weakened constitutionally protected rights against self-incrimination, and it imposed stricter requirements for obtaining a firearm license (the application retained the personal questions required by the previous legislation and now required two personal references plus endorsements from current or former "conjugal partners").

Gary A. Mauser

See also: Canadian Firearms Program (CFP); Erfurt, Germany, Massacre; Finland, Gun Laws; Gun Control; Gun Registration; Italy, Gun Laws; Japan, Gun Laws; Russia, Gun Laws; Switzerland, Gun Laws; United Kingdom—History of Gun Laws since 1900; United Kingdom—History of Gun Laws through 1900; Victimization from Gun Violence

Further Reading

Auditor General of Canada. *May Status Report of the Auditor General*. Chap. 4. Ottawa: Queen's Printer, 2006. http://www.oag-bvg.gc.ca/internet/English/parl_oag_2006_05_04_e_14961.html (accessed June 14, 2011).

Auditor General of Canada. *Report of the Auditor General*. Ottawa: Queen's Printer, 1993. http://www.oag-bvg.gc.ca/internet/English/parl_oag_199312_27_e_5966.html (accessed June 14, 2011).

Breitkreuz, Garry. "Firearms Quick Facts." http://www.garrybreitkreuz.com/firearmsquickfacts.htm (accessed June 14, 2011).

Dandurand, Yvon. *Firearms, Accidental Deaths, Suicides and Violent Crime: An Updated Review of the Literature with Special Reference to the Canadian Situation*. Canadian Firearms Centre, Policy Sector, WD1998–4e, 1998. http://www.rcmp-grc.gc.ca/cfp-pcaf/res-rec/summaries/dandurand-eng.htm (accessed June 14, 2011).

Kopel, David B. *The Samurai, the Mountie, and the Cowboy: Should America Adopt the Gun Controls of Other Democracies?* Buffalo, NY: Prometheus Books, 1992.

Mauser, Gary A. "Armed Self-Defense: The Canadian Case." *Journal of Criminal Justice* 24 (1996): 393–406.

Mauser, Gary A. *Hubris in the North: The Canadian Firearms Registry*. Vancouver, BC: Fraser Institute, 2007.

Royal Canadian Mounted Police. "Canadian Firearms Program." http://www.rcmp-grc.gc.ca/cfp-pcaf/index-eng.htm (accessed June 14, 2011).

Royal Canadian Mounted Police. "Commissioner of Firearms—2009 Report." http://www.rcmp-grc.gc.ca/cfp-pcaf/rep-rap/2009-comm-rpt/index-eng.htm (accessed June 14, 2011).

Canadian Firearms Centre. *See* Canadian Firearms Program (CFP)

Canadian Firearms Program (CFP)

The Canadian Firearms Centre was created in 1996 within the Department of Justice to oversee the administration of the 1995 Firearms Act and the Canadian Firearms Program (CFP). In 2003, as a result of monumental administrative problems, the Centre was established as a freestanding agency in the Ministry of Public Safety. In 2006, responsibility for the CFP was transferred to the Royal Canadian Mounted Police (RCMP).

The CFP is tasked with licensing firearm owners, registering all firearms, and coordinating with a sprawling network of federal agencies including the provincial police forces, Public Safety Canada, Canada Border Services Agency, Department of Justice, Department of Indian and Northern Affairs, and the Department of Foreign Affairs and International Trade. The Firearms Act does not generally apply to military or police personnel, but police agencies have been required since 2008 to report agency and protected firearms to the registry.

The main provisions of the 1995 Firearms Act came into effect in 1998 when owner licensing and long-gun registration began. In 2001, it became mandatory to have a license to own a firearm, and all long guns (rifles and shotguns) were required to be registered by 2003. Any person who allows a license to expire is subject to arrest and having firearms confiscated. Handguns have been registered since 1934. Between 1977 and 1998, a police-issued Firearms Acquisition Certificate (FAC) was required to acquire a firearm. Obtaining an FAC required passing a firearm safety course and a police background check.

The complexity of the 1995 law stimulated the Justice Department to create an extensive bureaucracy. In addition to the head office in Ottawa, there are 10 offices for the Canadian Provincial Firearms Officers (CPFO); two processing centers, one in Montreal, Quebec, and another in Miramichi, New Brunswick; and three call centers. The CFP quickly grew to 1,744 paid, full-time positions by July 2000. This does not include an unreported number of people employed by the CFP or its partners part time who also work in the area. The provinces of British Columbia, Alberta, Saskatchewan, Manitoba, and Newfoundland and Labrador refused to cooperate with the CFP, forcing the program to be directly administered for those provinces.

Since its inception, the CFP has been plagued by serious problems. It was originally budgeted at C$85 million, but by early 2007, the known governmental costs had climbed to over C$2 billion. A 1999 review by PriceWaterhouse found the CFP to have exceeded its budget and to have a high error rate and unusually slow processing times. Average waits for licenses were found to be over six months. In 2001, despite the huge backlog of applications, the CFP began to cut staff. The CFP is the subject of a management case that identified numerous problems in how the way the government of Canada managed the project (Duval 2004).

The Auditor General (December 2002, 2006) identified serious problems with the CFP, including mismanagement, corruption and misleading Parliament. Her reports led to RCMP investigations, arrests and convictions, and they ultimately contributed to the fall of the Liberal government in 2006. The RCMP has stated that it cannot rely upon the quality of the information in the registry.

In recent years, the CFP has become much more efficient. The CFP budget for 2010–2011 is C$97 million. This budget does not include all costs incurred by the provincial and federal partners in managing or enforcing the CFP; nor does it include compliance costs.

To reduce the likelihood that a person shown to be a risk to public safety will be permitted to retain possession of firearms, all current holders of firearms licenses are automatically checked with Canadian Police Information Centre (CPIC) every night to determine if they have been the subject of an incident report. All matches are automatically forwarded to the CPFO, who can decide to confiscate the flagged person's firearms.

The vast majority of Canadian gun owners are hunters who own rifles or shotguns; smaller numbers of Canadians own handguns. In 1998, the Department of Justice estimated there were over 3.5 million firearm owners and between 8 million and 20 million firearms. In January 2001, the CFP announced that 1.9 million owners had obtained a license or had applied for a license out of an estimated 2.4 million gun owners. In 2003, the CFP announced that 6.8 million firearms had been registered. In

2010, the RCMP reported there were 1.8 million licensed owners and 7.5 million firearms registered.

No solid evidence can be found linking Canadian gun laws to declines in either violent crime rates or suicide rates. Firearms have been persistently involved in about one-third of homicides since 1975. Canadian homicide rates fell 22 percent between 1990 and 1998, before the beginning of firearm licensing and registration, but slid just 2 percent between 1998 and 2009. In contrast, homicide rates in the United States fell 33 percent between 1990 and 1998, and 20 percent between 1998 and 2009. Suicides involving firearms started declining before the 1995 law came into effect, falling from 1,110 in 1991 to 818 in 1998. After licensing and long-gun registration became mandatory in 1998, suicides continued to fall, dropping to 534 in 2007 (the most recent data available). Unfortunately, total suicides have remained relatively constant (3,593 in 1991; 3,613 in 2007), as alternative suicide methods remain readily accessible.

Some observers from the gun rights camp believe the safety culture in Canada has gone too far—the society is becoming increasingly frightened by what was formerly normal firearms usage. Hunters are charged with "unsafe storage" when carrying unloaded firearms on hunting trips, high school students have been charged for merely carrying a BB gun, and widows are harassed by police attempting to confiscate their deceased's husband's firearm. Even though defending oneself against criminal attack is legal, legitimate defensive uses of firearms routinely result in charges of "possessing a weapon for a purpose dangerous to public peace," assault with a weapon, or even murder. The Conservative Party maintains that the long-gun registry is ineffective and a waste of taxpayers' money, and

promises that they will abolish it when they win a majority government. The opposition parties remain supportive.

Gary A. Mauser

See also: Canada, Gun Laws; National Firearms Association of Canada

Further Reading

Breitkreuz, Garry, MP. "The Canadian Firearms Act Means You Can't Take Your Fundamental Rights for Granted." http://www.garrybreitkreuz.com/breitkreuzgpress/guns29.htm (accessed June 15, 2011).

Duvall, Mel. "Canada Firearms: Armed Robbery." *Baseline*, July 1, 2004. http://www.baselinemag.com/c/a/Projects-Management/Canada-Firearms-Armed-Robbery/ (accessed June 15, 2011).

Kopel, David B. *The Samurai, the Mountie, and the Cowboy: Should America Adopt the Gun Controls of Other Democracies?* Buffalo, NY: Prometheus Books, 1992.

Mauser, Gary A. *Bill C-391—Countering Ten Misleading Claims. Presentation to the Standing Committee on Public Safety and National Security*, House of Commons. Ottawa: Canada, 2010.

Mauser, Gary A. *Hubris in the North: The Canadian Firearms Registry*. Vancouver, BC: Fraser Institute, 2007.

Office of the Auditor General of Canada. "2002 April Status Report of the Auditor General of Canada: Chapter 4—The Criminal Justice System: Significant Challenges." http://www.oag-bvg.gc.ca/internet/English/parl_oag_200204_04_e_12377.html (accessed June 15, 2011).

Office of the Auditor General of Canada. "2002 December Status Report of the Auditor General of Canada: Chapter 11—Other Audit Observations." http://www.oag-bvg.gc.ca/internet/English/parl_oag_200212_11_e_12405.html (accessed June 15, 2011).

Office of the Auditor General of Canada. "2006 May Status Report of the Auditor

General of Canada: Chapter 4—Canadian Firearms Program." http://www.oag-bvg .gc.ca/internet/English/parl_oag_200605_04 _e_14961.html (accessed June 15, 2011).

Royal Canadian Mounted Police. "Canadian Firearms Program." http://www.rcmp -grc.gc.ca/cfp-pcaf/index-eng.htm (accessed June 15, 2011).

Caron v. United States (1998)

This U.S. Supreme Court case (524 U.S. 308) held that the federal law forbidding felons from possessing firearms and enhancing criminal sentences for violations of this prohibition can be applied to someone who is allowed under state law to possess rifles and shotguns but not handguns. The Supreme Court interpreted the felon-in-possession prohibition and the sentence enhancement provision of the Gun Control Act (GCA) of 1968 to apply to a felon who under state law was forbidden to have some guns after his original conviction but was permitted to possess other guns. Thus, if the state placed any restrictions on the types of guns the felon could possess when his civil rights were restored, such restrictions had the effect of making the felon fully accountable to the firearm possession prohibition and the enhanced punishment provisions of the GCA.

A petitioner was convicted of violating 18 U.S.C. Section 922(g)(1), which forbids a person convicted of a serious offense to possess any firearm and requires that a three-time violent felon who violates this provision receive an enhanced sentence. The GCA further specifies that a person cannot be held to the above standard if the offender's civil rights have been restored, "unless such . . . restoration . . . expressly provides that the person may not . . . possess . . . firearms." The petitioner claimed that he should not be accountable under this law, as he had his civil rights restored with respect to his ownership of rifles and shotguns. The state at issue permitted a convicted felon to possess rifles but restricted possession of handguns to inside one's home or business.

In rejecting the petitioner's claim, the Court opined that the petitioner's restoration of civil rights was a defense to the GCA, as the state in question placed some restrictions on what sort of firearms he could possess. The Court stated that the restoration of civil rights has no effect on the GCA even if the state allows the possession of certain types of guns, some long, as possession of at least some categories of guns is not permissible. The Court further held that it was the likely congressional intent of the GCA to prohibit felons from possessing any guns if the state restoring the felon's civil rights forbade the possession of any type of gun.

James A. Beckman

See also: *Beecham v. United States*; Gun Control Act of 1968

Further Reading

Caron v. United States (97-6270). Legal Information Institute. http://www.law.cornell .edu/supct/html/97-6270.ZO.html (accessed June 11, 2011).

Carter, Harlon (1913–1991)

A lifelong gun activist and National Rifle Association (NRA) leader who spearheaded the organization's extremist and more political turn in the 1970s, Carter was born in a small Texas town in 1913, where guns were a part of his early life. He became a skilled marksman and joined the NRA at the age of 16. A year later, Carter was charged with murder for shooting and killing a 15-year-old with a shotgun. Carter claimed self-defense, as the murdered boy had a knife.

A jury found Carter guilty of murder without malice and sentenced him to a maximum of three years in prison. Carter appealed the conviction, which was reversed on procedural grounds. The appeals court cited incorrect instructions by the judge to the jury regarding self-defense as the justification for reversal. The charges were eventually dropped.

In 1951, Carter won election to the NRA's national board of directors. He served as the organization's vice president from 1963 to 1965 and as president from 1965 to 1967; he then became a member of the NRA's executive council. Carter's professional career fell outside of the NRA. He worked for the U.S. Border Patrol for many years and became its head in 1950. Eleven years later, he became a regional commissioner for the Immigration and Naturalization Service (of which the Border Patrol was a part), a position from which he retired in 1970.

In 1975, Carter was named head of the newly created NRA Institute for Legislative Action (ILA). From that position, he, along with other hard-liners, argued for a tougher, less compromising, and more political role for the NRA. For example, Carter voiced his opposition to any restriction on the availability of cheap handguns, called Saturday night specials. In response, in 1976, the ruling NRA old guard leaders fired 75 hard-liners, who were also critical of old guard plans to build a World Sports Center in Colorado Springs, move the NRA there, and place greater organizational emphasis on hunting and sporting activities. Carter resigned in protest in 1976. He and his allies, including gun activist Neal Knox, plotted to win control of the NRA at its 1977 annual convention in Cincinnati. In what was later dubbed the Cincinnati Revolt, the hard-line (also called "new guard") faction won some key procedural changes, which they then used to their advantage. By the end of the convention, the hard-liners had prevailed, and Carter was elected NRA executive vice president. Carter appointed Neal Knox to head the ILA after the short tenure of Robert Kukla.

From this point forward, the NRA adopted a no-compromise approach to any and all gun control proposals. It also adopted a more strident and heated rhetorical style, and focused ever more organizational resources on its anti–gun control political efforts. Its immediate priority was to repeal the Gun Control Act of 1968, an effort that partially succeeded with enactment of the Firearms Owners' Protection Act of 1986, also known as the McClure-Volkmer bill. Under Carter, the NRA also pressed to increase its membership and began extensive merchandising efforts. It also decided that its new, harsher image needed softening, which led to the launching of its "I'm the NRA" advertising campaign in 1982. These ads featured women, actors, politicians, and others to portray gun ownership and gun sports as a less threatening, and more mainstream activity. In 1982, Carter fired Knox, who had become too radical even for Carter. In failing health, Carter left the NRA presidency in 1985, and passed away in 1991.

Robert J. Spitzer

See also: Firearms Owners' Protection Act of 1986; Institute for Legislative Action (ILA); National Rifle Association (NRA)

Further Reading

Brown, Peter Harry, and Daniel G. Abel. *Outgunned: Up Against the NRA*. New York: Free Press, 2003.

LaPierre, Wayne, and James Jay Baker. *Shooting Straight: Telling the Truth about Guns in America*. Washington, DC: Regnery Publishing, 2002.

Spitzer, Robert J. *The Politics of Gun Control.* 5th ed. Boulder, CO: Paradigm Publishers, 2012.

Cartridges

Cartridge names follow one of two broad customs. Nonmetric cartridges are commonly referred to by their caliber (in theory, in hundredths or thousandths of an inch). Metric cartridges are commonly referred to by their caliber in millimeters followed by the case length in millimeters: thus a 7 × 57 mm refers to a cartridge with a 7 mm diameter bullet and an empty cartridge case 57 mm long. Some American metric cartridges are used with an additional designation (e.g., the 6 mm Remington).

The nonmetric designation has a problem in that there may be a multitude of cartridges firing bullets of the same diameter, so an additional designation is needed. This takes a near-universe of forms. In cartridges of the black powder era, it was customary to hyphenate the weight of black powder that the cartridge would hold. Thus a .30-30 and a .45-70 held 30 and 70 grains of black powder, respectively. More modern cartridges were often named for the company that first introduced them (e.g., the .280 Remington, .308 Winchester, and .45 ACP, or Automatic Colt Pistol), the nation or group that adopted them (the .303 British, 7.62 mm Russian, and .223 NATO), or sometimes for its individual inventor (the .257 Roberts). The venerable .30-06, on the other hand, takes its descriptor from the date of its introduction (1906). Sometimes the designation is simply a trade label suggesting velocity: the .22 Hornet, the .220 Swift, the .219 Zipper, or the .250-3000 (the first factory cartridge to exceed 3,000 feet per second in velocity). Particularly high-power cartridges may be designated "magnum"; when that

A handful of rifle cartridges. (Stocksnapper)

description is already used in a given caliber, "maximum" is sometimes used to designate an even more powerful round.

From time to time, individual gunsmiths or enthusiasts have created "wildcat" cartridges, a type not made by any factory, usually by taking a factory cartridge and "necking it down" to fire a smaller-caliber bullet, "necking it up" to take a larger one, or "blowing it out" to reduce its taper and increase its powder capacity. These may be designated in a variety of ways, such as by hyphenating its original caliber (e.g., .22-250 refers to a .25 caliber cartridge necked down to .22), using its inventor's name (e.g., .35 Whelen), or in other ways (e.g., a .30-06 necked down to .25 becomes the .25-06, and if "blown out" becomes the .25-06 Improved).

As if the above were not sufficiently complicated, it must be noted that a given cartridge may have multiple names. For example, the .308 Winchester, .308 NATO, and 7.62 × 51 all refer to the same cartridge, and the .22-250 began its life as the .22 Varminter.

A further complication is that the cartridge name may not reflect the actual bullet diameter! Most .38 and .44 handguns fire bullets of .357 and .429 diameter. The .38-40 is actually .40 caliber. The .219 Zipper, .222 Remington, .223 Remington, and .224 Weatherby all fire bullets of the same diameter, but the .45-70, .45 ACP, and .45 Long Colt use three slightly different bullet diameters.

Prior to invention of the modern metallic cartridge, military firearms used paper cartridges. These were tubes of waxed or greased paper, with the bullet at one end and powder at the other. The shooter bit the end off the powder side, poured the gunpowder down the barrel, and then rammed the bullet home.

David T. Hardy

See also: Ammunition, Types of; Black Talon; Dum-Dum Bullet; Gunpowder

Further Reading

Hogg, Ian. *Jane's Directory of Military Small Arms Ammunition*. New York: Jane's Publishing, 1985.

Logan, Herschel C. *Cartridges: A Pictorial Digest of Small Arms Ammunition*. Harrisburg, PA: Stackpole, 1959.

Cases v. United States. *See* United States Constitution and Gun Rights

Castle Doctrine

The castle doctrine deals with the rights and responsibilities of persons to defend themselves or others, in their home. In some cases, the law also deals with a person outside the home. The major question is when a person has the right to use deadly force against a potential attacker and when the person has the responsibility to retreat.

In 2010, 25 states had some form of a castle doctrine or "stand-your-ground" statute (Alabama, Alaska, Arizona, California, Colorado, Connecticut, Florida, Hawaii, Kansas, Louisiana, Maine, Maryland, Massachusetts, Michigan, Missouri, Ohio, Oregon, New Jersey, North Carolina, Rhode Island, Texas, Utah, West Virginia, and Wyoming). Generally, the intruder must be making or have made an attempt to illegally enter the home or place occupied by the potential victim(s). The occupant must believe that the intruder plans to inflict bodily harm and/or commit another felony by entering the home. If those conditions are met, then the occupant may use deadly force against the intruder. Some statutes also provide civil liability immunity to the occupant.

Castle doctrine statutes usually replace a "duty to retreat" law that requires the occupant to retreat as much as possible in the house and verbally warn the intruder that they intend to shoot prior to discharging any firearm.

Both the duty to retreat and the castle doctrine trace their roots to English law. William Blackstone wrote of the duty to retreat, and English law recognized that only the state had the right to sanction homicide. English common law, though, did recognize the right of an individual in their home to defend themselves against intruders. Early American jurisprudence recognized the castle doctrine, and in the nineteenth century, the courts and state legislatures began to expand the sphere of protection beyond the home itself.

A flurry of legislative activity in the late twentieth century was ignited by the 2005 passage of a castle doctrine law in Florida. Some critics of the law predicted a bloodbath of vigilantism, while supporters argued that law-abiding citizens would now be able to protect themselves without fear of prosecution.

The Florida stature is more of a stand-your-ground law in that it expanded the area that could be legally defended to any space that was legally occupied. It clearly eliminated the duty to retreat as a legal requirement. It also created a media frenzy, and it was followed by increased legislative activity in the area in many other states that continues today.

Castle doctrine laws may be framed in a cultural and/or politically ideological framework. Some see the laws as recognition of individual rights, while others see them as an attempt to reintroduce the Wild West and individual justice. Some cast the laws as the result of ascendance of a conservative political philosophy. Others see the laws as part of a movement toward enhanced rights for victims of crime. Still others see them as preempting the police power of the state.

The impact of castle doctrine statutes is difficult to assess. While anecdotal evidence on both sides may be found, at present there are no systematic, sound studies of the impact of castle doctrine laws.

Harry L. Wilson

See also: Right to Self-Defense, Philosophical Bases; Self-Defense, Legal Issues

Further Reading

Barros, D. Benjamin. "The Evolution of Home as Castle." http://lawprofessors.typepad.com/property/2005/11/the_evolution_o.html (accessed May 25, 2011).

Boots, Denise Paquette, Jayshree Biharn, and Euel Elliott. "The State of the Castle: An Overview of Recent Trends in State Castle Doctrine Legislation and Public Policy." *Criminal Justice Review* 34 (2009): 515–35.

Levin, Benjamin. "A Defensible Defense?—Reexamining Castle Doctrine Statutes." *Harvard Journal of Law* 47 (2010): 523–54. http://www.harvardjol.com/wp-content/uploads/2010/07/523-554.pdf (accessed May 25, 2011).

National Rifle Association, Institute for Legislative Action. "Fortifying the Right to Self Defense." http://www.nraila.org/Issues/factsheets/read.aspx?ID=188 (accessed May 25, 2011).

Total Criminal Defense. "What Is the Castle Doctrine?" http://www.totalcriminaldefense.com/overview/castle-doctrine.aspx (accessed May 25, 2011).

Castle Law. *See* Castle Doctrine

Cease Fire, Inc.

Cease Fire, Inc., a national, not-for-profit organization, aimed to save lives by reducing the number of handgun-related deaths and injuries in the United States, especially among children. The organization focused on the public health implications of handgun violence and endeavored to educate people about the dangers of keeping firearms in the home. Jann Wenner—founder, editor-in-chief, and publisher of *Rolling Stone* magazine—founded Cease Fire, Inc., in 1996. Funding was provided in part by singer Courtney Love, widow of rock start Kurt Cobain who killed himself with a handgun. Its advisory board consisted of a broad array of public figures including former President Jimmy Carter, Senators Bill Bradley and Dianne Feinstein, corporate leaders, and entertainment celebrities.

Wenner had been a good friend of John Lennon. Lennon's murder in 1980 impelled Wenner to become active in the gun control movement and to eventually found Cease Fire. Its stated mission was to "reshape the gun violence debate in America" with a specific goal to promote "handgun-free homes and families" through public education, using a public health model to disseminate public messages and research on death rates of children due to guns, especially guns in the home.

In 1997, Cease Fire launched a national awareness campaign that included TV public service announcements (PSAs) and print ads in major newspapers and magazines. The PSAs and print ads noted that 10 children were killed by a gun every day. Each ad or PSA presented the true story of a child who had been killed by a handgun in his or her home. The focus on the tragic death of one child made these ads and PSAs very powerful. The print ads showed a picture of a small child or children with captions such as "John Higgins hid his handgun so well, it took his son three years to find it." The ad then explained the circumstances in which the child found the gun and the ensuing tragedy. In the case of the John Higgins

ad, Billy Higgins accidentally shot and killed his two-year-old sister.

Cease Fire, Inc., advisory board member and actor Michael Douglas narrated the television PSAs. One ad showed a young boy who was perhaps five or six years old standing on a stack of boxes on a chair to reach a box that contained a gun. The child plays with the gun, the scene fades to black, and a shot is heard. Other PSAs were similar; some featured a group of children playing and then gaining access to a gun in the home. In all of the ads, the message is "Think your kids don't know where your gun is? Think again."

Cooperating with Cease Fire on the campaign were the American College of Emergency Physicians, the National Association of Children's Hospitals and Related Institutions, the National Association of County and City Health Officials, the National Association of Secondary School Principals, and the National Education Association. Cease Fire also worked with leaders from a variety of other organizations and industries, including those in law, law enforcement, entertainment and media, and academia.

Cease Fire launched the campaign in Boston, in conjunction with the unveiling of Stop Handgun Violence's huge highway billboard drawing attention to handgun-related deaths of children. The campaign then moved to Albuquerque, Austin, Cleveland, Miami, Portland, and Salt Lake City. Cease Fire also worked with parent-teacher associations to promote the campaign.

After three years of national operations, the financial drain of the organization led Wenner to shut it down. When Cease Fire stopped operating in 1999, Wenner gave Physicians for Social Responsibility (PSR) the rights to use the powerful Cease Fire ads and PSAs. PSR added its name to the materials and continued to distribute them as part of its "Risk: Gun in the Home" public awareness campaign. The print ads could be downloaded from the PSR website and the PSAs still appeared on television.

Although it had a short-lived existence, Cease Fire developed an influential model that continued after its demise to shape public efforts at gun control. Projects were developed in many communities across the nation modeled on Cease Fire, crediting it as influential in their development and success. A notable example is the Chicago Project for Violence Prevention, which reported that its Cease Fire Project in West Garfield Park reduced shootings by as much as 67 percent in one year (Skogan et al. 2008). Similar community projects in other areas, such as the U.S. Department of Justice's Project Safe Neighborhoods, developed community-based programs using Cease Fire's model of integrating law enforcement agents and community leaders in successful gun and violence reduction programs.

Robin L. Roth

See also: Child Access Prevention (CAP) Laws; Lennon, John; Project Safe Neighborhoods; Safe Kids USA; Trigger Locks

Further Reading

Cease Fire Chicago. "CeaseFire: The Campaign to STOP the Shooting." http://www.ceasefirechicago.org (accessed May 31, 2011).

Skogan, Wesley G., et al. "Executive Summary Evaluation of CeaseFire-Chicago." http://www.northwestern.edu/ipr/publications/ceasefire_papers/executivesummary.pdf (accessed May 31, 2011).

U.S. Department of Justice. "Project Safe Neighborhoods: America's Network against Gun Violence." http://www.ncjrs.gov/pdffiles1/bja/205263.pdf (accessed May 31, 2011).

Center for Gun Policy and Research

The Center for Gun Policy and Research (CGPR) aims to prevent gun-related injuries and deaths through applying a public health perspective to the issue of gun violence prevention. In pursuit of these goals, the CGPR carries out a broad range of activities, including "original scholarly research, policy analysis, and agenda-setting public discourse" (Center for Gun Policy and Research 2011). The CGPR carries out research on topics such as gun trafficking, domestic violence and guns, keeping guns from young people, and legal issues related to guns and gun violence. Its faculty and affiliated experts pursue strategies for reducing gun violence. The center is based at the Johns Hopkins Bloomberg School of Public Health in Baltimore, Maryland. In addition to being the oldest and largest school of public health in the country, the Bloomberg School is internationally acclaimed, with over 500 full-time faculty and more than 2,000 students from 86 countries. Investigation into the cause and prevention of gun injuries and fatalities began at the Bloomberg School more than 20 years ago as part of an overall injury prevention research effort. Center codirectors Jon Vernick and Daniel Webster have worked on gun violence prevention research for the past decade. In 1995, the center was formally established with funding from the Joyce Foundation.

The center examines the public health effects of guns in society and serves as an objective resource for the media, policy makers, advocacy groups, and attorneys. For the past two decades, it has helped shape the public agenda in the search for solutions to gun violence. Graduates of the school's academic programs hold leadership positions in the field of gun violence prevention worldwide. The center carries out a broad range of activities including scholarly research, policy analysis, and agenda-setting public discourse. It strives to bring public health expertise and perspectives to the complex policy issues related to gun violence prevention. The center's priority areas of activity and research include the following:

- *Gun Trafficking*: The center studies gun dealer regulation and oversight with the goal of reducing the transfer of firearms from legal to illegal markets. The center focuses on this area because the illegal transfer of guns by corrupt dealers is the single largest channel for guns into the illegal market.
- *Domestic Violence and Guns*: Because guns are the most common weapons used in domestic violence, the center studies policies and behaviors related to gun violence by domestic violence offenders.
- *Keeping Guns from Youth*: The center studies policies and behaviors related to gun access and carrying among youth. The center also designs and evaluates interventions and other policies designed to keep guns from criminals and other high-risk groups. Center researchers study the risk factors for youth violence and help to develop policies and programs to lessen that violence.
- *Legal Issues*: The center monitors and evaluates the effectiveness of major gun laws, including laws banning Saturday night specials, concealed weapons laws, handgun registration laws, handgun licensing laws, and child firearm access prevention laws. The center holds to the position that litigation is

an important tool for protecting the public's health. Center faculty assist with litigation designed to change the way guns are designed, marketed, distributed, and sold.

In addition to these major foci, the center has made numerous contributions in other areas related to gun violence, including the following:

- *Guns as Consumer Products*: The center redefined the debate on gun violence prevention by proposing that the safe design of guns could be regulated in much the same way as the safety of cars, toys, and other consumer products. This new approach opened the way for legislation and litigation to protect consumers. The center's research interests also include the marketing of guns and the regulation of gun sales.
- *Technology for "Safer" Guns*: The center pioneered the concept of "personalized" guns that can be fired only by their intended owner. Such guns could potentially prevent childhood gun deaths, youth suicides, and homicides committed with stolen guns. The center promotes incorporating "safer gun" technology into the design and manufacture of all guns through litigation, legislation, regulation, and public education.
- *Model Legislation*: In 1996, the center developed a model law that would require all new handguns to be personalized. This model law, revised in 1998, has been used by Pennsylvania, New Jersey, New York, and other states in their efforts to draft effective legislation.
- *Tracking Public Opinion on Gun Use and Prevention Strategies*: Since 1996, the center has annually conducted a

national poll in conjunction with the National Opinion Research Center to assess public attitudes toward guns and prevention strategies. The findings provide an important basis for the development of new public policies.

- *Testimony and Expertise:* Center faculty and affiliated experts are frequently invited to advise federal, state, and city legislators on gun laws and regulations, and to regularly testify at congressional and state hearings.
- *Public Education:* A key center function is providing the public with accurate information about gun injuries and prevention strategies. Fact sheets as well as center publications, bibliographies, published articles, and information for the media and general public are available by contacting the center.

Nancy Lord Lewin and Walter F. Carroll

See also: Child Access Prevention (CAP) Laws; Gun Violence as a Public Health Problem; Lawsuits against Gun Manufacturers; Medicine and Gun Violence; Motor Vehicle Laws as a Model for Gun Laws; Product Liability Lawsuits; Smart Guns; Trigger Locks; Violence Prevention Research Program (VPRP)

Further Reading

Center for Gun Policy and Research. http://www.jhsph.edu/gunpolicy/ (accessed May 18, 2011).

Center for the Study and Prevention of Violence (CSPV)

The Center for the Study and Prevention of Violence (CSPV) assists individuals and groups seeking to understand and prevent violence, especially adolescent violence. Acting as a bridge between researchers on one hand and practitioners and policy makers on the other, CSPV acts as an information clearinghouse, provides technical assistance, and carries out research on the causes and prevention of violence. Although the center does provide information on firearms and their role in violence, it does not emphasize gun and gun control–related issues.

Founded in 1992 with a grant from the Carnegie Corporation, CSPV is a research center within the Institute of Behavioral Science at the University of Colorado at Boulder. University of Colorado Distinguished Professor of Sociology Emeritus Delbert S. Elliot directs the center, which has a threefold mission. First, and most basic, its Information House is a central location for collecting, evaluating, storing, and disseminating violence-related information. Focusing primarily on youth violence, Information House acts as a clearinghouse providing bibliographic information to the public. It also provides fact sheets and position papers. For example, the "Fact Sheet on Youth Handgun Violence" (CSPV 2011a) provides basic information on youth handgun violence in Colorado and the United States. The fact sheet notes that handgun homicides by males aged 15–18 increased by over 150 percent from 1980 to 1995. The CSPV "Position Summary on Gun Control Prevention Efforts" suggests that research on the effectiveness of gun control laws is inconclusive. The CPSV also publishes Center Papers, which include CSPV-014, "Preventing Youth Handgun Violence." This paper was published in 1999, and most other Center Papers predate it.

The second part of the CSPV mission is providing technical assistance in evaluating and developing violence prevention programs. For example, in 1996 CSPV received funding from the Colorado Division of

Criminal Justice, the Centers for Disease Control and Prevention, and the Pennsylvania Commission on Crime and Delinquency to develop "Blueprints for Violence Prevention," a national project to identify and replicate effective violence prevention programs. The project has reviewed over 500 programs, identifying 11 effective violence prevention programs, called Blueprints, and 19 promising programs. CSPV provides technical assistance and training to these programs. CSPV also provides technical assistance to 16 Colorado schools and school districts as part of the Safe Communities–Safe Schools Initiative.

Third, CSPV carries out research and data analysis. For example, in 1997, the Colorado Trust, a private foundation dedicated to the health and well-being of the people of Colorado, funded CSPV to conduct research on youth and guns. The CSPV (2011b) was to document the nature and extent of youth handgun violence in Colorado and nationally, find out what people in Colorado think about the handgun problem and possible solutions, and identify effective programs to prevent youth handgun violence. As a result of this project, the Colorado Trust funded a further project to evaluate the effectiveness of three programs aimed at reducing youth gun violence. Three organizations that partnered with CSPV in this initiative set up gun violence prevention curricula based on the results of this assessment. The CSPV website allows online database searches. It also provides extensive links to other violence resources on the Internet.

Walter F. Carroll

See also: Centers for Disease Control (CDC); Children's Defense Fund (CDF); Columbine High School Tragedy; Gun Violence as a Public Health Problem; Media Violence; National School Safety Center (NSSC); Schoolyard Shootings; Student Pledge against Gun Violence; Youth and Guns; Youth Gun Control Legislation: The Juvenile Justice Bill of 1999

Further Reading

Arredondo, Sabrina, et al. *Preventing Youth Handgun Violence: A National Study with Trends and Patterns for the State of Colorado*. Boulder, CO: Center for the Study and Prevention of Violence, 1999. http://www.colorado.edu/cspv/publications/papers/CSPV-014.pdf (accessed March 8, 2011).

Center for the Study and Prevention of Violence (CSPV). "CSPV Fact Sheet: Youth Handgun Violence" (2011a). http://colorado.edu/cspv/publications/factsheets/cspv/FS-006.pdf (accessed February 28, 2011).

Center for the Study and Prevention of Violence (CSPV). "The Colorado Trust: Youth and Guns" (2011b). http://www.colorado.edu/cspv/research/past.html#youthguns (accessed February 28, 2011).

Center for the Study and Prevention of Violence (CSPV). http://www.colorado.edu/cspv/ (accessed February 28, 2011).

Center to Prevent Handgun Violence. *See* Brady Center to Prevent Gun Violence

Centers for Disease Control and Prevention (CDC)

The Centers for Disease Control and Prevention (CDC) is a federal agency located in the cabinet-level Department of Health and Human Services. Formed in 1946 as the Communicable Disease Center and located in Atlanta, Georgia, its mission is to monitor health problems; detect and investigate health problems; conduct research on the prevention of health problems; develop and advocate sound public health policies; implement prevention strategies; promote healthy behaviors; foster safe and healthful environments; and provide leadership and training. In 1992, the CDC's gun violence program was charged to its National Center for Injury Prevention and Control (NCIPC) division. The reports to Congress, newsletters, and published articles based on CDC-supported research identified firearms ownership and use as a public health problem, a position disputed by gun rights writers, who have argued that this research is biased and flawed.

The CDC's connection to firearms research dated to 1983, when the CDC declared firearms violence to be a significant public health threat and, in effect, a preventable disease. That year the CDC created a unit to gather and encourage research on gun-related violence within its Violence Epidemiology Branch, which in turn spawned considerable public health and medical research underscoring the public health threat posed by guns. President Ronald Reagan's surgeon general, C. Everett Koop, and President Bill Clinton's first surgeon general, Joycelyn Elders, both weighed in strongly to push the public health definition of the problem. By tagging guns with the "public health threat" label and comparing them to such public health risks as smoking and automobile accidents, members of the medical community sought to redefine the gun issue to improve gun-related research and knowledge, reduce gun-related injuries and deaths, and influence public policy outcomes. In 1993, the American Medical Association and the American Academy of Pediatrics formally entered the national debate by publishing numerous articles on the subject. Also that year, former surgeon general Koop and *Journal of the American Medical Association* editor George Lundberg called for

increased gun control measures to stem what they termed a public health emergency related to gun violence.

Opposition to this research mobilized among the gun rights community spearheaded by the National Rifle Association. It launched an effort in 1995 to get Congress to stop funding for CDC research on gun issues, which that year amounted to $2.6 million (about 0.1 percent of the CDC's total budget). It also organized a group of pro-gun rights doctors, called Doctors for Integrity in Policy Research, to press the gun rights view. The following year and in each succeeding year, Congress barred the CDC from engaging in any research that "may be used to advocate or promote gun control." This eliminated most gun-related research (in 2001, the CDC spent about $400,000 on gun-related research). By 2009, however, the National Institutes of Health had regularized some funding for public health studies of gun violence, amounting to under $5 million for the previous seven years. Still, the gun research funding bar has, according to one researcher, "largely succeeded in choking off the development of evidence upon which that [gun] policy could be based" (Luo 2011).

Carol Oyster and Robert J. Spitzer

See also: Gun Violence as a Public Health Problem; Victimization from Gun Violence

Further Reading

Centers for Disease Control and Prevention. http://www.cdc.gov/ (accessed June 4, 2011).

Centers for Disease Control and Prevention. "National Center for Injury Prevention and Control." http://www.cdc.gov/injury/index .html (accessed June 4, 2011).

Goss, Kristin. *Disarmed: The Missing Movement for Gun Control in America*. Princeton, NJ: Princeton University Press, 2006.

Kates, Don B., Jr., et al. "Guns and Public Health: Epidemic of Violence or Pandemic of Propaganda?" *Tennessee Law Review* 62 (1994): 513–96.

Kellermann, Arthur L., et al. "Validating Survey Responses to Questions about Gun Ownership among Owners of Registered Handguns." *American Journal of Epidemiology* 131 (1990): 1080–84.

Luo, Michael. "Sway of N.R.A. Blocks Studies, Scientists Say." *New York Times*, January 26, 2011. http://www.nytimes.com/2011/01/26/us/26guns.html (accessed June 4, 2011).

Spitzer, Robert J. *The Politics of Gun Control.* 5th ed. Boulder, CO: Paradigm Publishers, 2012.

Child Access Prevention (CAP) Laws

Child Access Prevention (CAP) laws, also known as safe storage laws, attempt to minimize harm to young people by keeping firearms out of their hands. CAP laws do this by establishing criminal penalties for gun owners who do not store their firearms safely. By 2008, 27 states and the District of Columbia had established CAP laws (Legal Community against Violence 2008). In some states, violation of the CAP law is a felony. The potential importance of these laws is evident in data on shooting deaths among the young. In 2007, homicide was the leading cause of death for those 10–24 years of age, and 84 percent of them were killed with a firearm (Centers for Disease Control 2010).

Recognition of the threats to young people from firearms led to the passage of CAP laws. In 1989, Florida became the first U.S. state to pass a child access prevention gun law. CAP laws, which require gun owners to store their firearms in a manner that would prevent children and teens from gaining unauthorized access, vary in how "safe storage" is defined, but generally require firearms to be securely locked in a cabinet or gun safe, or, in some states, with a trigger lock. Some CAP laws hold gun owners criminally liable only if unsafe storage leads to an injury, while others are not dependent upon injurious outcomes. Another way in which state CAP laws vary is in the maximum penalty allowed for law violations, with a minority of states allowing for felony prosecutions in cases of CAP law violations.

The first study of such laws used data through 1994 to estimate the effects of the first 12 state CAP laws that went into effect (see Cummings et al. 1997). The authors estimated that these laws were associated with a significant reduction (41 percent) in the rate of unintentional firearm deaths among youths up to age 14, but only in states with felony prosecution. Data from this study also indicated that there was a negative association between the adoption of these laws and teen firearm suicide rates that approached statistical significance.

Webster and Starnes (2000) conducted a subsequent study with data through 1997 that assessed the effects of CAP laws on unintentional firearm deaths among youth under age 15 in the first 15 states to adopt these laws. They found that CAP-law effects were not uniform across states. Florida's CAP law was associated with a 51 percent drop in the rate of unintentional firearm deaths to youths, but there was no effect of the law in the other 14 CAP-law states.

Lott and Whitley (2001) examined the effects of CAP laws on crime as well as on unintentional firearm deaths and suicides among youth. They hypothesized that CAP laws could increase criminal victimization within the home by making guns less accessible for home occupants to defend themselves against home intruders. Despite the relative rarity of unintentional firearm deaths to youths under age 15 in most states in a given year, the authors estimated CAP laws' effects within five-year age groups. They report no statistically significant CAP-law effects on unintentional firearm deaths or suicides across all CAP-law states, among those that allow felony prosecutions for CAP-law violations, or in any single state that adopted a CAP law. The study also found that the introduction of CAP laws were associated with statistically significant increases in police-reported rapes (9 percent), robberies (8–10 percent), and burglaries (4–6 percent). Under various assumptions about prelaw trends, the authors report even greater law-associated increases in crime, including increases in aggravated assaults.

It is difficult to discern exactly why Lott and Whitley do not find significant CAP-law effects on unintentional firearm deaths when such effects were so striking in Webster and Starnes's research. Breaking up the 0–14 age group into three five-year subsets weakens statistical power to detect statistically significant effects. Lott and Whitley also use a statistical model (Tobit) not typically used to study data with many zero values for specific states and years, because the model can be highly sensitive to model specification. Model specification is also at issue in the derivation of the laws' effects on crime, as no specification tests are offered and some of the findings are difficult to reconcile. For example, their models also reveal that laws prohibiting individuals from bulk handgun purchases increase crime both in the state that adopts the measure and in adjacent states. The findings on CAP laws' effects on crime are also not consistent with other relevant research findings. Kellermann et al. (1995) found that citizens attempted to use a gun in defense in less than 2 percent of

home invasion crimes. The 8–10 percent increase in total robberies associated with the adoption of CAP laws does not seem plausible given that only 11 percent of *all* robberies occur in residences (Federal Bureau of Investigation 1998), most of which will not have either children or guns. If such effects were true, CAP laws would have to double the number of robberies in residences. The reduction in burglaries also seems implausible. By definition, such crimes do not involve criminal contact with victims, and most criminals are unlikely to be aware of laws concerning firearm storage.

A more recent study by Grossman and his colleagues (2005) indicated that the practices associated with CAP laws do reduce youth suicide and unintentional injury in homes with children and teenagers. The latest assessment of the effectiveness of CAP laws was carried out by the Public Health Law Research project, funded by the Robert Wood Johnson Foundation and housed at the Temple University Bradley School of Law. Surveying the available evidence on the effectiveness of the laws, the project finds that CAP laws "may represent a promising intervention for reducing gun-related morbidity and mortality among children," but that currently the research is insufficient to "validate their effectiveness" (Public Health Law Research 2009).

Daniel W. Webster and Walter F. Carroll

See also: Defensive Gun Use (DGU); Gun Control; Gun Violence as a Public Health Problem; Kellermann, Arthur L.; Lott, John R., Jr.; Motor Vehicle Laws as a Model for Gun Laws; Victimization from Gun Violence; Youth and Guns

Further Reading

Centers for Disease Control. "Facts at a Glance: Youth Violence: 2010." http://www.cdc.gov/ViolencePrevention/pdf/YV-DataSheet-a.pdf (accessed May 14, 2011).

Cummings, Peter, et al. "State Gun Safe Storage Laws and Child Mortality Due to Firearms." *Journal of the American Medical Association* 278 (1997):1084–86.

Federal Bureau of Investigation. *Crime in the United States, 1997: Uniform Crime Reports.* Washington, DC: U.S. Department of Justice, 1998.

Grossman, David, et al. "Gun Storage Practices and Risk of Youth Suicide and Unintentional Firearm Injuries." *Journal of the American Medical Association* 293 (2005): 707–14.

Kellermann, Arthur L., et al. "Weapon Involvement in Home Invasion Crimes." *Journal of the American Medical Association* 273 (1995): 1759–62.

Legal Community Against Violence. "Child Access Prevention Brief." 2008. http://www.lcav.org/content/child_access_prevention.pdf (accessed May 15, 2011).

Lott, John R., Jr., and John E. Whitley. "Safe Storage Gun Laws: Accidental Deaths, Suicides, and Crime." *Journal of Law and Economics* 44 (2002): 659–89.

Public Health Law Research. "Child Access Prevention (CAP) Laws for Guns: Evidence Brief." 2009. http://publichealthlawresearch.org/public-health-topics/injury-prevention/gun-safety/evidence-brief/child-access-prevention-cap-laws-gu (accessed May 15, 2011).

Webster, Daniel W., and Marc M. Starnes. "Reexamining the Association between Child Access Prevention Gun Laws and Unintentional Firearm Deaths among Children." *Pediatrics* 106 (2000): 1466–69.

Childproof Guns. *See* Smart Guns

Children's Defense Fund (CDF)

A private, nonprofit child advocacy group, the Children's Defense Fund has regularly advocated strict gun control measures in the United States. The organization was founded in 1973 by Marian Wright Edelman, an African American lawyer deeply involved in civil rights activism in the South during the 1960s. Under Edelman's leadership, the Washington, D.C.–based CDF has sought to inform the U.S. public on the state of children's health, welfare, and education, and to lobby government at all levels in favor of policy initiatives aimed, for example, at expanding access to early childhood education and health insurance. Its primary focus is on issues affecting poor children, minority children, and children with disabilities, with improvement in the health indices of these groups being a central goal of the organization. Evidence indicating that Americans under the age of 19—especially male African Americans—are far more likely than children and youth in other industrialized nations to suffer firearm-related injury or death has led the CDF to argue that the prevention of gun violence is a vital issue of children's health in the United States.

For many years, the CDF campaigned vigorously for tighter restrictions on the ownership and availability of firearms, attributing high numbers of gun-related homicides, suicides, and accidental deaths among young people in the United States to a lack of such restrictions. The measures supported by the organization have included the registration of all firearms to facilitate police tracking of guns that end up in the hands of children as well as licensing requirements for potential gun owners to ensure firearms competency and knowledge of safe storage. As of 2010, however, legislative action addressing the issue of gun violence occupies a less prominent position among the CDF's list of priorities, a development owing in part to recent U.S. Supreme Court rulings challenging the constitutionality of the sort of legal controls on firearms ownership and proliferation advocated by the organization (the landmark rulings were made in *District of Columbia v. Heller* and *McDonald v. City of Chicago*). The dramatic overall decline in gun deaths among U.S. children and youths since the mid-1990s, a trend evident in statistics published by the CDF, also appears to have diminished the urgency of the issue. Nonetheless, the frequency of such deaths remains sufficiently elevated, especially among African Americans, to keep the level of gun violence affecting U.S. children on the list of "unwanted distinctions" cited by the organization in its comparative assessments of U.S. conditions with those elsewhere.

In addition to its national headquarters, the CDF maintains 14 offices in 11 states and encourages a wide range of activism in support of its legislative and policy agenda. The organization's "Protect Children, Not Guns" publication recommends a variety of approaches to reducing gun violence, ranging from public pressure in favor of "common-sense gun safety measures" such as childproof features for firearms, to the active cultivation in homes, schools, and community institutions of nonviolent conflict resolution skills. Its best-known contribution to policy debates is an annual report on the status of children and youth in the United States. This report provides a wide array of statistical and other information to policy makers and the public on a number of issues of concern to the organization, gun violence among them.

Paul Lokken

See also: *District of Columbia v. Heller*; *McDonald v. City of Chicago*; Youth and Guns

Further Reading

Children's Defense Fund. "About Us." http://www.childrensdefense.org/about-us/ (accessed June 20, 2011).

Children's Defense Fund. "Protect Children Not Guns 2010." http://www.childrensdefense.org/child-research-data-publications/data/protect-children-not-guns-2010-report.pdf (accessed June 20, 2011).

Children's Defense Fund. "The State of America's Children." http://www.childrensdefense.org/child-research-data-publications/data/state-of-americas-children.pdf (accessed June 20, 2011).

Cho, Seung-hui (1984–2007)

On April 17, 2007, Seung-hui Cho, a senior at Virginia Polytechnic Institute and State University, went on a shooting spree killing 32 people and wounding 25 others in what became known as the Virginia Tech massacre. It is recorded as "the deadliest shooting incident by a single gunman in U.S. history" (Council of State Government 2009).

Cho, whose suicide followed just minutes after his murderous rampage, had a long history of social anxiety disorder and mental illness. Such impediment did not stop Cho from acquiring two deadly arsenals, more specifically, a Glock-19 pistol and a Walther P22, well-known semiautomatic pistols with which he accomplished his bloody massacre (Luo 2007).

In frustration, Virginia governor Tim Kaine told gun politicos to take the debate somewhere else (Associated Press 2007)— but this soon proved to be a foot-in-the-mouth comment. Within hours after the incident, pro- and antigun lobbyists ignited their debates with politicians who were (1) hounded by journalists, and (2) forced to take a stand on the gun control issues (Helmke 2007; Perino 2007).

Within days of relentless coverage by the press of the massacre, foreign criticisms of U.S. gun control law poured in (Wier 2007). Further, a loophole in the Virginia law failed to flag Cho—despite his court-ordered psychiatric treatment (Luo 2007). This mishap was amplified by MSNBC's rehashing of the deranged gunman's ramblings (MSNBC.com 2007), and it prompted Governor Kaine to hastily issue an executive order prohibiting sales of firearms to mentally ill patients who a Court had ordered to undergo psychiatric treatment (Commonwealth of Virginia, Office of Attorney General, 2007).

Governor Kaine's order is significant because it makes no distinction between voluntary and involuntary commitment to undergo a psychiatric treatment as long as the court found the person "dangerous." Moreover, there is no distinction between persons found to be "dangerous" only to him- or herself versus those persons who pose a danger to the community. The executive order also does not differentiate between inpatient and outpatient treatment. The point of the order is that once there is a court order declaring a person dangerous and in need of psychiatric treatment, it must be reported to the data bank. As a result, when a licensed gun dealer conducts a background check on a potential customer in the data bank, the dealer will find that the customer is barred from buying any firearms or ammunition.

Gun control advocates strive to eliminate any appearance of insensitivity to people with mental disability since they have no desire to negate mental illness as a medical condition. Many are aware that there are privacy issues and stigma attached to mental illness and understand the reasons behind many mental health advocates' objections—as mandatory federal database disclosures could appear unscrupulous by categorizing a person with mental illness in the same category as a criminal offender.

Certainly, being part of a central criminal record database, for anyone, is not an attractive position to be in—especially when one is, for example, seeking employment or trying to travel in and out of the United States. Problems can also arise when a court order has been fully complied with—i.e., the person has been treated and released, but no papers were filed to indicate such. These are some areas where the law is still murky and opens the possibility of mentally ill being subjected to discrimination, and it is here where discretion and judgment of the person reviewing the data is critical. For people who are in this position of responsibility, there must be thorough training to identify such issues and a specific set of protocols to follow in these cases.

In today's world, where terrorists have—and do—come into the United States to kill and maim the population, defense readiness, proper procedures, and the security of its citizens must be weighed carefully against privacy concerns and political correctness. There is no doubt that a person's medical records are confidential. However, when one's mental illness becomes so magnified and uncontrollable and poses possible danger to others, a court intervention may be necessary to protect the public. In these instances, one may reasonably argue that registering these court-ordered cases into the federal criminal data bank may be justified to prevent these individuals from obtaining firearms, which can be implements of terrible destruction. Thus, it seems reasonable to err on the side of public safety and protection than on the side of privacy when it is specifically related to purchase of firearms. Most educators, however, like in Cho's case where laws safeguarding privacy are confusing and administrators can be exposed to liability for breach of confidence, often err on the side of caution not to disclose even when public safety is at risk (Davies 2008, 11).

In Cho's case, cumbersome and confusing sets of privacy laws regarding patient health care and state gun control laws that are open to interpretation got in the way of protecting public safety. Throughout his early childhood to high school years, he was a child with special needs who was diagnosed with both selective mutism (the inability to speak in certain social situations) and social anxiety disorder. He did not talk, became withdrawn, and showed symptoms of depression. For nearly a year, he was on the antidepressant Paroxetine—a drug that seemed to significantly improve his mental state (Virginia Tech Review Panel 2007, 35). Cho's medical history reveals that prior to his college years, there were interventions and support from his family—with coordinated efforts by therapists, a psychiatrist, and school staff to help him cope with emotional problems. His sister, who is fluent in both English and Korean, seemed to be an effective facilitator between the Cho family and the outside specialists and support systems.

In college, the "multifaceted support system" disappeared (Virginia Tech Review Panel 2007, 40), and Cho was basically left on his own to handle his problems. Nothing remarkable unfolded until his junior year, at which time he became withdrawn—wearing reflector glasses with his hat pulled down to cover his face and writing papers with violent and anger-filled themes. His strange behavior included taking unauthorized pictures of his classmates with his cell phone, calling his suitemates from outside identifying himself as his twin brother "question mark" and asking to speak to Cho, and posting disturbing (but not threatening) messages on a female student's Facebook page (Virginia Tech Review Panel 2007, 46). At least one incident report was filed with the campus police, an a few days before this filing, the Virginia Tech Judicial

Affairs office received an e-mail regarding Cho's "odd behavior" and "stalking" (Virginia Tech Review Panel 2007, 44).

In his English courses, Cho's aberrant behavior earned him not only low grades but reports by the professors to the department head. An instant message to a suitemate that he may kill himself prompted the campus police to take Cho in for a mental health assessment. Upon completion of the assessment, a clinical social worker found him to be "mentally ill and was an imminent danger to self or others." Since Cho was not willing to be treated voluntarily, she recommended an involuntary psychiatric hospitalization and contacted the magistrate for a temporary detention order, or TDO (Virginia Tech Review Panel 2007, 47). The TDO was issued, and Cho was admitted to St. Albans; diagnosis was "Mood Disorder, NOS" (nonspecific), and he was prescribed Ativan for anxiety. An independent evaluator, a licensed clinical psychologist, certified to the court that although Cho was mentally ill, he did not present an imminent danger to himself or others, and he did not require involuntary hospitalization. A psychiatrist also affirmed the independent evaluator's findings and suggested outpatient treatment and counseling (but gave no primary diagnosis or prescription). The special justice who presided over the commitment hearing concluded that Cho was dangerous to himself and ordered outpatient treatments (Virginia Tech Review Panel 2007, 48).

During this time, Cho's parents were never notified of police incidents, reports to judicial affairs, and commitment hearings. In his senior year, he became more withdrawn and his lack of speech—as observed by his professors and others—is speculated to be one of the first signs of schizophrenia (Welner 2007). The college intervention staff ("The Care Team"), established to identify and work with students with problems, was also unfamiliar with the details of these occurrences. Inept communication among the various school departments contributed to the further demise of any support and follow-up system that may have helped Cho. This administrative inefficiency, together with "overly strict interpretations of federal and state privacy laws," hampered the school administration to adequately investigate and properly evaluate Cho regarding the risks he posed to public safety (Virginia Tech Review Panel 2007, 5).

While notifying his parents may have been an intuitively correct decision, it may not have been allowed give federal privacy laws encompassing education (the Family Educational Records Privacy Act, or FERPA) and health (the Health Insurance Portability and Accountability Act, or HIPPA). These laws can be confusing and inconsistent (Davies 2008, 11). Under FERPA, although medical records remain within the realm of privacy, personal observations and conversations with a student are exempt; thus, teachers and administrators who observe erratic behavior can share the information with law enforcement officers, other administrators, and parents. In Cho's case, the sharing of information, especially with his parents, would have perhaps launched the support system that had been so successful during his high school years.

Balancing an individual's privacy against public safety continues to be a formidable task. This delicate balance is especially difficult to maintain when there appear to be so many loopholes and inconsistencies in state and federal laws regarding privacy, public safety, and gun control. These are compounded when competing administrative policies of schools and health care facilities are added into the equation. What is clear, however, is that because of the Virginia Tech incident, the public became mobilized in making changes to gun control laws regarding mental health record-keeping. On March 24, 2008, President Bush signed a measure requiring mandatory reporting by the states to the National Instant Criminal Background Check System (NICS) of those disqualified to purchase guns (Cochran 2008). It included felons, domestic violence offenders, and those declared dangerous and mentally ill by the courts. It represented a rare occasion when gun control advocates (the Brady Campaign) and gun rights advocates (the National Rifle Association) joined in support of the same legislation involving firearms.

Jongsung Kim

See also: Brady Campaign to Prevent Gun Violence; Colleges and Gun Violence; National Rifle Association (NRA); NICS Improvement Act; Students for Concealed Carry on Campus; Virginia Tech Massacre

Further Reading

Associated Press. "Candidates on Spot over Gun-Control." Politics on MSNBC, April 18, 2007. http://www.msnbc.msn.com/id/18170829/ns/politics (accessed June 27, 2011).

Cochran, John. "New Gun Control Law is Killer's Legacy." ABC News/Politics, January 12, 2008. http://abcnews.go.com/Politics/story?id=4126152&page= (accessed June 27, 2011).

Commonwealth of Virginia, Office of Attorney General. "Governor Kaine Issues Executive Order Expanding background Checks for Gun Purchases." http://www.vachiefs.org/index.php/news/item/governor_issues_eo_expanding_background_checks_for_gun_purchases (accessed December 29, 2011).

Council of State Governments. "Protecting Students and Students' Rights a Delicate Issue." *Campus Violence and Mental Health.* 2009. http://www.csg.org/knowledgecenter/docs/

MentalHealth-CampusSafety.pdf (accessed June 27, 2011).

Davies, Gordon K. "Connecting the Dots: Lessons from the Virginia Tech Shootings." *Change*, January–February 2008. http://www .changemag.org/Archives/Back%20Issues/ January-February%202008/full-connecting -the-dots.html (accessed July 9, 2011).

Helmke, Paul. "Nation Again Grieves a Tragedy of 'Monumental Proportions.' " Brady Campaign to Prevent Gun Violence, April 16, 2007. http://www.bradycampaign .org/media/press/view/884 (accessed June 27, 2011).

Luo, Michael. "U.S. Rules Made Killer Ineligible to Purchase Gun." *New York Times*, April 21, 2007. http://www.nytimes.com/ 2007/04/21/us/21guns.html (accessed June 27, 2011).

MSNBC.com. "High School Classmates Say Gunman Was Bullied." MSNBC, April 19, 2007. http://www.msnbc.msn.com/id/ 18169776/ns/us_news-crime_and_courts (accessed June 27, 2011).

Perino, Dana. "Press Briefing by Dana Perino." White House, April 17, 2007. http://georgewbush-whitehouse.archives .gov/news/releases/2007/04/20070416-1 .html (accessed June 27, 2011).

Virginia Tech Review Panel. *Mass Shootings at Virginia Tech: Report of the Review Panel*. August 2007. http://www.governor .virginia.gov/TempContent/techPanelReport -docs/FullReport.pdf (accessed June 27, 2011).

Welner, Michael. "Cho Likely Schizophrenic, Evidence Suggests." ABC News/Health, April 17, 2007. http://abcnews.go.com/ Health/VATech/story?id=3050483&page=2 (accessed June 27, 2011).

Wier, Keith. "Massacre Sparks Foreign Criticism of U.S. Gun Culture." *The Star Online*, April 27, 2007. http://thestar.com.my/ news/story.asp?file=/2007/4/18/worldupdates/ 2007-04-17T212204Z_01_NOOTR_RTRJO NC_0_-294575-1&sec=Worldupdates (accessed June 27, 2011).

Citizens Committee for the Right to Keep and Bear Arms (CCRKBA)

The Citizens Committee for the Right to Keep and Bear Arms is a nonprofit organization that describes itself as "the common sense gun lobby." With an estimated membership of 650,000, an advisory board that includes members of Congress, and an affiliated political action committee, the CCRKBA aggressively promotes gun rights. The CCRKBA serves mainly to promote political activities in support of gun rights, while its companion organization, the Second Amendment Foundation, focuses more on education, legal action, and publications.

The CCRKBA is part of a network of gun rights organizations overseen by Alan Gottlieb. Its stated mission is "to educate grass root activists, the public, legislators, and the media. Our programs are designed to help all Americans understand the importance of the Second Amendment and its role in keeping Americans free." Gottlieb has served as chair of the CCRKBA, and Joe Waldron, a retired Marine Corps officer, has served as executive director. According to the *Encyclopedia of Associations*, the organization has a staff of 40, although it appears that some staff may be shared with other organizations. The CCRKBA offers a $15 annual membership, which comes with a subscription to its monthly newsletter, *Point Blank*.

CCRKBA and the Second Amendment Foundation share offices in Bellevue, Washington. The two organizations cosponsor an annual Gun Rights Policy Conference. They also share ownership of several talk radio stations, and the CCRKBA purchased part of Oregon station KBNP in 2009. Marketing services are contracted with Merril Associates as well.

The CCRKBA has a lobbyist, John Snyder, based in Washington, D.C. It has averaged over $600,000 per year in lobbying expenses since at least the 1990s, according to data compiled by the Center for Responsive Politics. The $723,532 spent in 2009 ranked third among gun rights organizations, well below the National Rifle Association and Gun Owners of America. It has had an affiliated political action committee, the Right to Keep and Bear Arms Political Victory Fund, but a 2011 search of the Federal Elections Commission website did not indicate any recent activity.

In 2011, the CCRKBA added to its advocacy efforts though a billboard truck that is used at events across the country to promote its "Guns Save Lives" campaign. The CCRKBA is a direct response to a billboard truck campaign sponsored by Mayors Against Illegal Guns that includes a counter of the number of gun violence victims since the Representative Gabrielle Giffords shooting in Tucson, Arizona, in early 2011.

While the CCRKBA supports a gun rights agenda, it has been criticized by some activists for its willingness to compromise with gun control supporters. Gottlieb and the CCRKBA supported a 1999 proposal in Washington State related to storage of unlocked guns. However, recent activities appear to reflect a willingness to engage in both dialogue and political posturing. For example, the CCRKBA offered in 2011, via a press release, to meet with President Obama's staff on gun control issues. At the same time, it reiterated support for gun rights and included criticism of a federal investigation that allowed drug dealers to purchase guns and transport them to Mexico in an attempt to follow the weapons to cartel leaders.

Marcia L. Godwin

See also: Gottlieb, Alan Merril; Gun Owners of America (GOA); Gun Rights Policy Conference (GRPC); Gun Shows; *Gun Week*; National Rifle Association (NRA); Second Amendment Foundation (SAF); *Women & Guns* Magazine

Further Reading

Atterberry, Tara. *Encyclopedia of Associations*. 49th ed. Vol. 1, *National Organizations of the United States*. Farmington Hills, MI: Gale Group/Cengage Learning, 2010.

Center for Responsive Politics. "OpenSecrets .org: Center for Responsive Politics." http://www.opensecrets.org/ (accessed May 18, 2011).

Citizens Committee for the Right to Keep and Bear Arms. http://www.ccrkba.org/ (accessed May 18, 2011).

GuideStar. http://www2.guidestar.org/ (accessed May 18, 2011).

Utter, Glenn H. *Encyclopedia of Gun Control and Gun Rights*. Westport, CT: Greenwood, 2000.

City of Chicago v. Beretta U.S.A. Corp. *See* Lawsuits against Gun Manufacturers

City of Cincinnati v. Beretta U.S.A. Corp. *See* Lawsuits against Gun Manufacturers

City of Gary v. Smith & Wesson Corp. *See* Lawsuits against Gun Manufacturers

City of Las Vegas v. Moberg (1971)

City of Las Vegas v. Moberg (82 N.M. 626 (1971)) was the first of several 1970s decisions that reversed a several-decade decline in the use of state constitution right-to-keep-and-bear-arms provisions. Perhaps unsurprisingly because of the increasing disorder of the

1960s, by the time the *Moberg* case was decided, the guarantees of a right to keep and bear arms had been disregarded by most state courts. The *Moberg* decision, while agreeing that *concealed* carrying of arms could be regulated or completely prohibited, also found that a law that prohibited the *open* carrying of arms was unconstitutional, since it violated Article II, Section 6, of the New Mexico Constitution.

Leland James Moberg had entered a police station in Las Vegas, New Mexico, wearing a holstered pistol, to report a theft from his automobile. A city ordinance prohibited carrying of any deadly weapon, openly or concealed, including "guns, pistols, knives with blades longer than two and half inches, slingshots, sandbags, metallic metal knuckles, concealed rocks, and all other weapons, by whatever name known, with which dangerous wounds can be inflicted."

Moberg appealed his conviction based on Article II, Section 6, of the New Mexico Constitution: "The people have the right to bear arms for their security and defense, but nothing herein shall be held to permit the carrying of concealed weapons." The New Mexico Court of Appeals agreed that "ordinances prohibiting the carrying of concealed weapons have generally been held to be a proper exercise of police power," but also asserted that "as applied to arms, other than those concealed, the ordinance under consideration purports to completely prohibit the 'right to bear arms.' It is our opinion that an ordinance may not deny the people the constitutionally guaranteed right to bear arms, and to that extent the ordinance under consideration is void."

The court of appeals cited *State v. Rosenthal* (Vt. 1903), *In re Brickey* (Idaho 1902), *State v. Woodward* (1937), and *State v. Kerner* (1921) as precedents for its position. With the exception of the *Woodward* case, this list of decisions was perfectly appropriate for the facts in *Moberg*. Each decision involved a state constitution's guarantee of a right to keep and bear arms; each involved a person charged with violating a local ordinance (not a state law) that prohibited the carrying of a pistol; and each involved a peaceful person carrying a gun openly.

The *Woodward* decision was the oddball case on the list, however, because Woodward was on trial for assault with a deadly weapon, and the dispute was not whether he was lawfully carrying a weapon at the time of the incident, but whether the judge's instructions had prejudiced the jury against Woodward by implying that carrying a gun was unlawful. While the Idaho Court of Appeals ordered Woodward to be retried with different jury instructions, there was no statute or ordinance struck down by the decision—unlike *Rosenthal*, *Brickey*, and *Kerner*, each of which had found a local ordinance unconstitutional.

The *Moberg* decision was short and contained little in the way of analysis, historical evidence, discussions of original intent, or appeals to pragmatic arguments for or against gun control.

Clayton E. Cramer

See also: Concealed Weapons Laws; Open Carry Laws; *State v. Kerner*; *State v. Rosenthal*

Further Reading

City of Las Vegas v. Moberg, 82 N.M. 626, 627, 628, 485 P. 2d 737 (App. 1971).

Commonwealth v. Ray, 218 Pa. Super. 72, 272 A. 2d 275 (1970).

Davis v. State, 146 So. 2d 892, 893, 894 (Fla. 1962).

Grimm v. City of New York, 56 Misc. 2d 525, 289 N.Y.S. 2d 358 (1968).

In Re Brickey, 8 Ida. 597, 70 Pac. 609, 101 Am. St. Rep. 215 (1902).

Photos v. City of Toledo, 19 Ohio Misc. 147, 250 N.E. 2d 916, 918, 919, 920, 921 (Ct. Comm. Pleas 1969).

State v. Bolin, 200 Kan. 369, 436 P. 2d 978, 979 (1968).

State v. Dawson, 272 N.C. 535, 545, 546 (1967).

State v. Kerner, 181 N.C. 574, 107 S.E. 222 (1921).

State v. Rosenthal, 75 Vt. 295, 55 Atl. 610 (1903).

State v. Schutzler, 249 N.E. 2d 549 (Ohio Ct. Comm. Pleas 1969).

State v. Woodward, 58 Ida. 385, 74 P. 2d 92 (1937).

City of New York v. A-1 Jewelry & Pawn, Inc. *See* Protection of Lawful Commerce in Arms Act of 2005

City of New York v. Beretta U.S.A. Corp., et al. *See* Protection of Lawful Commerce in Arms Act of 2005

City of St. Louis v. Cernicek. *See* Lawsuits against Gun Manufacturers

City of Salina v. Blaksley (1905)

The 1905 Kansas Supreme Court decision *City of Salina v. Blaksley* (83 P.619, 72 Kan. 230 (1905)) is the foundation of the theory that the Second Amendment does not guarantee an individual right. As such, *Salina* is perhaps the most important state court decision involving the Second Amendment, although *Salina* was overruled by implication in a 1979 Kansas Supreme Court decision.

In 1842, a concurring opinion by an Arkansas Supreme Court judge said that the Second Amendment right was merely "an assertion of that general right of sovereignty belonging to independent nations, to regulate their military force" (*State v. Buzzard*, 4 Ark. 18, 32 (1842); Dickinson, concurring). This is the only known document from the nineteenth century asserting that the Second Amendment does not guarantee a right of individuals to possess firearms. The concurring opinion was not cited by any other nineteenth-century courts. Even in Arkansas, subsequent case law in the nineteenth century regarded the Second Amendment as an individual right (e.g., *Fife v. State*, 31 Ark. 455, 456 (1876)).

In the town of Salina, Kansas, James Blaksley was convicted of carrying a pistol while intoxicated. When he appealed his conviction, neither Blaksley nor the prosecutor argued that the right to arms did not pertain to individuals, and the matter was therefore never briefed. The government attorney had simply argued that the local law was a reasonable gun control. Nevertheless, the Kansas Supreme Court chose to issue a decision announcing that the Second Amendment, and the right to arms in the Kansas state constitution, did not belong to individual citizens.

According to the *Salina* court, the "right to arms" meant only that the state militia, in its official capacity and while in actual service, could not be disarmed. The *Salina* court rejected or misdescribed every nineteenth-century source of authority that it used. (No eighteenth-century or prior sources were cited.)

The Kansas court rejected the Kentucky case of *Bliss v. Commonwealth* (12 Ky. 90 (1822)) and the long line of cases holding that to secure a well-regulated militia, individual citizens needed to be able to own and practice with guns. The court quoted a sentence from Bishop's *Statutory Crimes* that "the keeping and bearing of arms has reference only to war, and possibly also to insurrections." The quote was accurate, but the Kansas court neglected the language surrounding the quote and other writings by Bishop, which made it clear that Bishop thought the right to arms was "declaratory of personal rights" and therefore belonged to individuals, not the state.

Lastly, the court quoted *Commonwealth v. Murphy*, an 1896 decision that had upheld, against a state constitutional claim, a Massachusetts law (similar to the Illinois law upheld by the U.S. Supreme Court in *Presser v. Illinois*) that banned mass parades with weapons. The Massachusetts court had written: "The right to keep and bear arms for the common defense does not include the right to associate together as a military organization, or to drill and parade with arms in cities or towns, unless authorized so to do by law" (44 N.E. 138 (Mass. 1896)). But holding that the right to arms does not authorize individuals to behave in a certain manner is not the same as the Kansas ruling that there is no individual right at all.

The *Salina* court did not discuss the pre–Civil War history of Kansas, when the pro-slavery territorial government's disarmament of individual citizens was denounced nationally as a violation of the Second Amendment. The main basis of the *Salina* holding is the Kansas court's textual analysis of the implications of the Kansas arms right provision and of the Second Amendment. The Second Amendment was not at issue in the case and was simply discussed as a guide to textual analysis of the Kansas provision. The court did not explain why the framers of the Kansas Constitution, in the middle of an article titled "Bill of Rights," suddenly inserted a provision that had nothing to do with rights but instead tautologically affirmed a power of the state government: in essence, that the militia is under the complete power of the state government.

Decades later, the Kansas Supreme Court moved away from *Salina* by declaring a local gun control ordinance unconstitutional (*Junction City v. Mevis*, 601 P.2d 1145 (Kan. 1979)). By then, however, *Salina*'s no-right theory had spread far beyond the Kansas state line. The next case to adopt a nonright theory was *United States v. Adams* (11 F. Supp. 216, S.D. (Fla. 1935)), which stated that the Second Amendment "refers to the militia, a protective force of government; to the collective body and not individual rights." The *Salina* nonrights position was widely adopted by federal district and appellate courts in the last three decades of the twentieth century, although the *Salina* case itself was not always acknowledged.

David B. Kopel

See also: *Presser v. Illinois*; Second Amendment

Further Reading

Kopel, David B. "The Second Amendment in the Nineteenth Century." *Brigham Young University Law Review* 4 (1998): 1359–1554.

Kruschke, Earl R. *The Right to Keep and Bear Arms*. Springfield, IL: Charles C. Thomas, 1985.

Civil War and Small Arms

The American Civil War has been characterized as the first "modern" war. One of the most important changes was the shift from Napoleonic tactics in the field. The practice of massing infantry for frontal assaults (which often involved firing a volley at point-blank range and then resorting to the bayonet and/or using the musket as a club) proved disastrous in the face of new firearm technology and munitions that were brought

Row of stacked Union rifles at Petersburg, Virginia, April 3, 1865. (Library of Congress)

to bear in this conflict. Specifically, the use of the "minie ball," the replacement of the musket with the rifle, and the supplanting of the single-shot rifle with the breech-action, rapidly firing carbine all led to the demise of the tactic of frontal assault.

It took commanders on both sides a while to learn this lesson, however. Confederate general Robert E. Lee, looking for a decisive victory on northern soil and buoyed by the fighting spirit and mettle of his troops, made the same fundamental error at Gettysburg that Union general Ambrose Burnside had made against the Army of Northern Virginia in 1862, at Fredericksburg. Union general Ulysses S. Grant made the same mistake in 1864 at Cold Harbor, a catastrophe that cost the North 13,000 casualties to the South's 2,500.

The arms and munitions that spelled the end of the "age of frontal assault" were mass-produced in the North but hard to come by in the South. At the beginning of the war, both sides were using single-shot, muzzle-loading rifles that were very similar. Early in the war, the North used the Springfield .58-caliber musket, while the South relied on the .577-caliber British Enfield— among other arms secured in Europe. The efforts of Confederate agents such as Caleb Huse, a Massachusetts native, were crucial in this regard. Increasingly, a wide variety of weapons salvaged from the battlefield proved critical to southern armies as the northern blockade became more effective.

The North, also initially short of arms, used numerous European suppliers as well. By the time production at northern armories reached capacity late in the war, Union forces were well armed. Northern armories produced 3 million firearms during the war, and Union agents purchased another million in Europe. Of the total of 500,000 guns in

Confederate hands, well over two-thirds had been purchased in Europe. The greater part of the remainder was provided by the battlefield or seized from Union facilities occupied by the Confederate government immediately following secession.

Union forces also benefited from innovative rapid-fire firearms such as the .52-caliber Sharps and the .52 rimfire Spencer carbines, as well as the .44-caliber Henry rifle. Only the innate conservatism of their army ordnance office bound the Union troops to the less efficient Springfield until relatively late in the war.

Colt's revolvers found favor with both sides; the .36-caliber Navy model was especially popular in the South. Union forces favored the .44-caliber version, and it was later almost supplanted by the sturdier and less expensive Remington .44 Army. Revolvers quickly displaced sabers in the cavalry; increased firepower was far more effective and less hazardous than slashing about with a sword in close quarters. Many infantrymen carried a variety of pocket pistols and other handguns foraged from the battlefield or brought from home—also useful in hand-to-hand fighting after exhausting the single shot from the rifle (bayonet charges were thankfully rare). Numerous revolvers made by other manufacturers, domestic and European, were obtained by both government and individuals throughout the war. Rudimentary but very functional machine guns, Gatling guns, and other precursors made their appearance in the war but played no major part.

The importance of the Civil War for the history of firearms and the development of the gun culture in the United States is that after the Union's huge advantage in industrial weapons production crushed the agrarian South, huge numbers of used and surplus weapons went home with both victor and vanquished. A generation of combat-hardened young men had learned the relatively new lesson that firepower prevails. Disastrous and abortive Reconstruction-era violence followed, and much of the "wildness" in the West can be attributed to these young men and their arsenal. Furthermore, the gun manufacturers of the Connecticut Valley, who had profited mightily from federal contracts, sold the surplus inexpensively and began to advertise and dump their wares to those in the cities and on the frontiers. The government itself engaged in sales of large lots of this surplus in the postwar period. Some of the sales were at government facilities in the United States, and many of these arms and gun parts found their way to private owners and gunsmiths. (A surprising amount of U.S. surplus firearms was offered on the international market, being sold to the French and ending up as Prussian war booty following the Franco-Prussian War. The Prussians sold much of it to Turkey.) Immigrants and those on the way west made heavy emotional investment in the incipient gun mythos. With highly accurate rifles like those developed during the war, professional hunters exterminated the buffalo, and the forces of the victorious Union, with massive firepower including the Gatling gun, firmly put the remaining Native Americans in what the white man considered their place—the reservation. The aftermath of the war allowed the innovations in weaponry of the first modern war to be carried by all and sundry, and may have been the critical period in the formation of an American gun culture.

Francis Frederick Hawley

See also: Civil War Reenactments; Colt, Samuel; Gun Culture; Remington, Eliphalet, II; Surplus Arms

Further Reading

Coggins, Jack. *Arms and Equipment of the Civil War*. Wilmington, NC: Broadfoot, 1990.

Edwards, William B. *Civil War Guns*. Harrisburg, PA: Stackpole Press, 1962.

Nosworthy, Brent. *The Bloody Crucible of Courage: Fighting Methods and the Combat Experience of the Civil War*. New York: Carroll and Graf, 2003.

Civil War Reenactments

Civil War reenactment units are largely composed of civilian hobbyists and historians whose aim is to recreate landmark Civil War battles with replica and authentic black-powder weapons once used by the infantry, artillery, and cavalry during the four-year American conflict of 1861–1865. Civil War reenactors are a loosely confederated group of volunteers comprised of regiments geographically and culturally similar to Civil War regiments. Unlike the actual conflict that had a well-defined command structure, reenactor regiments are not governed by any one private or government organization and typically muster at reenactment events according to army. At site- and calendar-specific events, such as the annual Gettysburg reenactment, army positions and movements retrace the historical events, but verisimilitude is guided by a regiment's enactment of "Hardee's tactics" based on military handbooks used by northern and southern armies during the Civil War. Reenactors also offer "Living Histories," which offer the public a more intimate view of military camp life including "first-person" reenactor presentations on military drills, skirmishing tactics, period music, and field hospital operations, for example. Standard-issue small arms play a vital yet fairly uniform role in many of today's Civil War reenactments.

The actual conflict between the northern and southern states served as a technological catalyst for modern weaponry, introducing a range of small-arm developments from smaller yet more accurate ballistics to the prototype of today's machine gun. However, reenactors personally finance their pastime and generally stick with a greatly modified arsenal of reproduction weaponry, placing more emphasis on safety and recreating battlefield tactics than on a wide range of firepower.

Enlisted men in the infantry are required to purchase a .58-caliber, percussion-cap, muzzle-loading long arm. The most commonly used weapons during the war and those found in today's reenactments are the 1861 or 1863 models of the Springfield-rifled musket and an Americanized version of the British 1853 Enfield-rifled musket. All of these weapons must be "three-band," or have three metal bands securing the metal barrel to the wooden stock. "Three-band" denotes a weapon of greater length and prevents ear damage to a comrade when shooting over his shoulder in a firing line. Another safety feature is the prohibition of bullets and ramrods lest they are accidentally left in a barrel charged with black powder. Infantry officers carry a percussion cap sidearm modeled on early 1860s issuances such as the .36-caliber Colt and the Remington .44-caliber pistols, both single action, six-shot revolvers.

For safety reasons, of course, reenactments do not feature "bayonet charges" into opposing trenches. The initial designs of Civil War–rifled muskets, such as the .58-caliber Springfield and Enfield, required weapons to be almost five feet in length, thus greatly improving shooting accuracy

Civil War reenactors portray Union soldiers, bayonetted muskets in hand. (William Sherman)

and bayonet-thrusting distance. The artillery, however, typically did not share these concerns. Operating from a relatively immobile position and ideally at great distance from the enemy, artillerists placed less value on large infantry weapons. Today's artillery reenactors are lightly armed with the Remington or Colt revolvers or the short, two-band, .58-caliber artillery carbine. Some "Living Histories" may include artillery demonstrations, but large-scale reenactments often incorporate an artillery battery.

Conversely, the general thrust of the cavalry was mobility and its purpose to outpace the enemy. Many cavalry reenactors are terrific horsemen and quite adept at staged swordplay. Most are also armed with the Colt or Remington revolvers or the much larger and heavier .44-caliber Dragoon pistols that serve as "clubs" when out of ammunition. The cavalry also totes the .54-caliber Sharps carbine, a short, breech-loading rifle

that is much easier to load and fire on horseback.

Much like the tack taken by Civil War reenactors who recreate four years of varied warfare that took place in many locales, this essay necessarily generalizes their small-arms use. Though there are some basic requirements based on the company's role in the regiment (e.g., rifle for infantryman, horse if cavalry), the reenactor is welcome to accrue as much authentic or replicated weaponry as he or she can afford—again provided it meets safety and regiment standards.

The rise of the Internet has proven to be a great resource for Civil War reenactors. In addition to regimental websites, there are several notable organizations that post online information on national and international reenactment events, sell replica and authentic Civil War weapons, and provide a forum for both the public and reenactor. Reenactors draw inspiration from and contribute to a variety of online and hard-copy periodicals devoted to Civil War history such as *The Civil War Times*, and the *Blue and Gray Magazine*. Publications devoted to Civil War reenactments such as the *Camp Chase Gazette* provide reviews on weapon usage, and most authentic and reproduced weapons are purchased through Dixie Gun Works in Union City, Tennessee, a company dedicated to black powder and Civil War weapons.

James Manning

See also: Civil War and Small Arms; North-South Skirmish Association, Inc.

Further Reading

American Civil War Reenactor Images: A Photographic Gallery. http://www.wild-westweb.net/cw.html (accessed January 19, 2011).

Blue and Gray Magazine. http://www.blue-graymagazine.com (accessed January 19, 2011).

Camp Chase Gazette. http://www.campchase.com (accessed January 19, 2011).

The Civil War Reenactor's Home Page. http://www.cwreenactors.com/index.php (accessed January 19, 2011).

Civil War Times. http://www.historynet.com/civil-war-times (accessed January 19, 2011).

Hadden, Robert Lee. *Reliving the Civil War: A Reenactor's Handbook.* Mechanicsburg, PA: Stackpole Books, 1999.

Horwitz, Tony. *Confederates in the Attic.* New York: Vintage Books, 1999.

Lee, James K. *The Volunteer's Hand Book: Containing an Abridgement of Hardee's Infantry Tactics Adapted to the Use of the Percussion Musket in Squad and Company Exercises, Manual of Arms for Riflemen, and United States Army Regulations as to Parades, Reviews, Inspections, Guard Mounting, Etc.* Richmond, VA: West & Johnson, 1860. http://books.google.com/books?id=U0FFAAAAYAAJ&printsec=frontcover&source=gbs_ge_summary_r&cad=0#v=onepage&q&f=false (accessed January 23, 2011).

Reenactor.net's American Civil War. http://www.reenactor.net/forums/index.php?page=20 (accessed January 23, 2011).

Civilian Marksmanship Program.

See National Board for the Promotion of Rifle Practice (NBPRP)

Clinton, William J. (1946–)

In 1992, William Clinton became the first president of the United States to be elected with a public stance that was antithetical to the National Rifle Association (NRA). During his first term (1993–1997), significant gun control legislation was enacted, and after his party lost control of Congress in 1994, the president continued to propose additional legislation while also pursuing nonlegislative means.

With Clinton's support, the "Brady Bill" (named for James Brady, President Reagan's press secretary, who was shot and seriously wounded along with Reagan and two law enforcement officers in 1981) was enacted by Congress after seven years of debate under previous administrations (including a veto by President George H. W. Bush) and signed into law by Clinton in November 1993 (PL 103-159). The law established a five-business-day waiting period for handgun sales through licensed dealers. The statute also required local law enforcement authorities to conduct background checks on handgun purchasers (this provision was declared unconstitutional by the Supreme Court in *Printz v. United States* (95-1478), 521 U.S. 98 (1997)). In 1994, Congress enacted the administration's crime bill (PL 103-322). The statute's key gun control provision was a ban on the manufacture, sale,

William J. Clinton. (The White House)

and importation of 19 assault weapons (this provision of the statute had a "sunset clause," and lapsed on September 13, 2004). Congress also passed the Gun-Free Schools Act of 1994 (PL 103-382), which required schools receiving federal funds to expel for at least one year any student who brought a weapon to the school.

After the Democratic Party lost control of Congress in the 1994 election (in his 2004 autobiography, Clinton acknowledges that his support of gun control measures hurt his party in the midterm elections), Clinton resorted to nonlegislative means to pursue his gun control policies. In 1997, Clinton and the nation's eight largest gun manufacturers agreed that they would include child safety locks with all new handguns. Clinton had previously issued an executive memorandum ordering federal law enforcement authorities to provide child safety locks for their officers' firearms. In 1998, he issued an executive order banning the importation of 50 assault weapons.

In March 2000, the Clinton administration announced that Smith & Wesson, the nation's largest gun manufacturer, had agreed to reform the way it designed, distributed, and marketed the company's products. The agreement settled a number of lawsuits brought by the U.S. Department of Housing and Urban Development (HUD) and a number of local jurisdictions against major U.S. gun manufacturers. The suits sought compensation for the damages that the guns produced by the manufacturers had inflicted upon the aggrieved communities. Smith & Wesson became the first defendant to settle.

In April 2000, in the aftermath of a shooting at the National Zoo, where seven children were wounded, Clinton announced that HUD and the District of Columbia government would spend $350,000 to buy 7,000 guns as part of a local gun buyback program. The Washington program was the largest of HUD's BuyBack America program, a $15 million initiative that more than 80 local jurisdictions had already joined.

Clinton's efforts to convince a Republican-controlled Congress to enact additional gun control legislation were unsuccessful. After the Columbine High School massacre in April 1999, the president proposed raising the legal age for owning a gun from 18 to 21 and extending the Brady Law waiting-period requirement to weapons sold at gun shows. These measures were rejected by Congress, many of the opponents arguing that additional gun control legislation would not prevent incidents like that at Columbine and that more effective enforcement of existing gun laws could have a more significant impact.

Jeffrey Kraus

See also: Antiterrorist Legislation; Assault Weapons Ban of 1994; Background Checks; Brady Handgun Violence Prevention Act (Brady Bill); Columbine High School Tragedy; Democratic Party and Gun Control; Elections and Gun Control; Gun-Free School Laws; Gun Shows; McVeigh, Timothy; *Printz v. United States*; Smith & Wesson Settlement Agreement

Further Reading

Clinton, William Jefferson. *My Life*. New York: Knopf, 2004.

Clinton, William Jefferson. *Proposed Legislation: "Saving Law Enforcement Officers' Lives Act of 1995": A Message from the President of the United States Transmitting a Draft of Proposed Legislation to Save the Lives of America's Law Enforcement Officers*. Washington, DC: U.S. Government Printing Office, 1995.

U.S. Congress. House of Representatives. Committee on the Judiciary. *Brady Handgun Violence Prevention Act: Report Together with Additional and Dissenting Views to Accompany H.R. 1025*. Washington, DC: U.S. Government Printing Office, 1993.

U.S. Congress. House of Representatives. *Federal Firearms Licensing: Hearing before the Subcommittee on Crime and Criminal Justice of the Committee on the Judiciary, House of Representatives*. 103rd Cong., 1st sess., June 17, 1993. Washington, DC: U.S. Government Printing Office, 1993.

U.S. Congress. House of Representatives. *Pending Firearms Legislation and the Administration's Enforcement of Current Gun Laws: Hearing before the Subcommittee on Crime of the Committee on the Judiciary, House of Representatives*. 106th Cong., 1st sess., May 27, 1999. Washington, DC: United States Government Printing Office, 2000.

U.S. Congress. House of Representatives. Subcommittee on Crime. *Implementation of the National Instant-Check System for Background Checks of Firearm Purchasers: Hearing before the Subcommittee on Crime of the Committee on the Judiciary, House of Representatives*. 105th Cong., 2d sess., June 11, 1998. Washington, DC: U.S. Government Printing Office, 2000.

U.S. Congress. House of Representatives. Subcommittee on Crime and Criminal Justice. *Brady Handgun Violence Protection Act: Hearing before the Subcommittee on Crime and Criminal Justice of the Committee on the Judiciary, House of Representatives, 103rd Congress, 1st Session on H.R. 1025, September 30, 1993*. Washington, DC: U.S. Government Printing Office, 1994.

U.S. Department of Justice, Office of Justice Programs, Office of Juvenile Justice and Delinquency Prevention. "Reducing Youth Gun Violence: An Overview of Programs and Initiatives: Program Report." Washington, DC: U.S. Department of Justice, Office of Justice Programs, Office of Juvenile Justice and Delinquency Prevention, 1996.

U.S. General Accounting Office. *Gun Control: Implementation of the Brady Handgun Violence Prevention Act: Report to the Committee on the Judiciary, U. S. Senate, and the Committee on the Judiciary, House of Representatives*. Gaithersburg, MD: U.S. General Accounting Office, 1996.

Coalition to Stop Gun Violence (CSGV)

The Coalition to Stop Gun Violence (CSGV) is a national, 501(c)(4) nonprofit gun control advocacy organization. CSGV's sister organization, the Educational Fund to Stop Gun Violence, is a 501(c)(3) organization that focuses on public education. The coalition's leadership includes Josh Horwitz, executive director, and Michael Beard, president emeritus.

In 1974, the United Methodist General Board of Church and Society formed the

National Coalition to Ban Handguns, a group of 30 religious, labor, and nonprofit organizations with the goal of addressing "the high rates of gun-related crime and death in American society" by licensing gun owners, registering firearms, and banning private ownership of handguns with "reasonable limited exceptions" for "police, military, licensed security guards, antique dealers who have guns in unfireable condition, and licensed pistol clubs where firearms are kept on the premises." In 1989, the organization ceased advocating for a national ban on handguns and changed its name to the Coalition to Stop Gun Violence.

CSGV currently has 48 national organizations as members, including faith-based groups, child welfare advocates, public health professionals, and social justice organizations. Its stated mission is "to secure freedom from gun violence through research, strategic engagement and effective policy advocacy."

In 2001, CSGV launched a campaign to close "illegal gun markets," a paradigm that has now become the operating principle of the modern gun control movement. Current CSGV projects include the following efforts:

- *Close the "Gun Show Loophole"*: The "Gun Show Loophole" allows for private individuals to sell firearms at gun shows without conducting background checks on purchasers or maintaining records of sale. CSGV has been working to close the loophole in the U.S. Congress and at the state level in the Commonwealth of Virginia.
- *Redefine the Debate on Guns, Democracy, and Freedom*: CSGV executive director Josh Horwitz coauthored a book entitled *Guns, Democracy, and*

the Insurrectionist Idea in 2009. The book, and Horwitz's blogs at the *Huffington Post*, contest the gun lobby's claim that the Second Amendment provides an *individual* right to confront "tyranny" in government with force of arms.

- *Defend the District of Columbia's New Gun Laws*: In the wake of the Supreme Court's *District of Columbia v. Heller* decision in 2008, the District of Columbia revised its gun laws to comply with the ruling. CSGV has worked to defend the city's new gun laws from repeated legislative challenges by the National Rifle Association.
- *Implement "Micro-stamping" Laws in States across the Country*: Micro-stamping technology uses lasers to make microscopic engravings on the breech face and firing pin of a gun. As the gun is fired, a code identifying the weapon's serial number is stamped onto the cartridge. CSGV implemented a multiyear public education campaign to promote micro-stamping technology in California. This effort bore fruit when Governor Arnold Schwarzenegger signed legislation in October 2007 mandating the micro-stamping of all new models of semiautomatic handguns in the state. In 2009, the District of Columbia enacted a micro-stamping law while revising its laws following the *Heller* decision. As of this writing, CSGV was advocating for micro-stamping technology in New York, Wisconsin, and Connecticut.

Ladd Everitt

See also: Beard, Michael K.; Black Market for Firearms; *District of Columbia v. Heller*; Gun Shows; Micro-Stamping (Bullet Serial Numbers); Washington, D.C.

Further Reading

Coaltion to Stop Gun Violence. http://www
.csgv.org/ (accessed June 16, 2011).

Cocaine and Gun Violence. *See*
Drugs, Crime, and Guns, United States

Code of Responsible Conduct. *See*
Gun Industry Responsibility Act (GIRA)

**Code of Responsible Conduct for
Gun Dealers and Manufacturers.**
See Gun Industry Responsibility Act

Cody, William "Buffalo Bill" (1846–1917)

William "Buffalo Bill" Cody was one of the
most famous Americans of his era. He
served as a member of the Pony Express,
an army scout, and a buffalo hunter. His
exploits were dramatized and immortalized
in a series of novels. Cody also managed
the traveling Wild West Show, which
brought the frontier to Americans in the
eastern areas of the nation. For many contemporary Americans, Cody remains the
symbol of the West and the embodiment of
the role of guns in the settlement of the
nation.

William Frederick Cody was born on February 26, 1846, near Le Claire, Iowa. His
father died in 1857, and the family subsequently moved from Iowa to Kansas. At
age 11, Cody began working as a mounted
messenger for the Majors and Russell Company. When gold was discovered two years
later in Colorado, Cody moved west to pros-
pect. The following year, at age 14, Cody
joined the Pony Express as a rider. In 1860,
he made the third-longest trip in the organization's history (some 322 miles).

In 1863, during the Civil War, Cody volunteered for the Seventh Kansas Cavalry

and fought in Missouri and Tennessee. After
the war, he continued to work for the army
as a scout and dispatch rider. In 1866, Cody
married Louisa Frederici in St. Louis. From
1867 to 1868, Cody was contracted to provide buffalo meat for the Kansas Pacific
Railroad. By his own account, Cody shot
4,280 buffaloes in 17 months and earned
the nickname "Buffalo Bill."

After his hunting expedition, Cody
returned to service with the army for the
next four years as chief of scouts with the
Fifth Cavalry. During this period, Cody took
part in 16 battles against Native Americans,
culminating in the defeat of the Cheyenne
at Summit Springs, Colorado. In 1872, Cody
was awarded the Medal of Honor for his
service.

Meanwhile, author Ned Buntline began to
write a series of dime novels based on the
exploits of Cody. Buntline created "Buffalo
Bill" as the alter ego to the real-life Cody.
Buntline eventually wrote 550 of these novels, which were packed with violence and
gunplay. They were enormously popular
and made Buffalo Bill a household name.
Although he was only 26 years old, Cody
was already a national folk hero.

In 1872, Buntline convinced Cody to portray his character in a stage play, *Scouts of
the Prairie*. In between occasional periods
of service with the army, Cody continued
acting in the show for the next 11 years.
The success of this venture led Cody to
establish his own show, "Buffalo Bill's Wild
West Show," in 1883. The Wild West Show
combined theater and historical drama.
Cody used live animals, including buffalo.
He employed a number of the Old West's
most famous people, including Annie
Oakley and Chief Sitting Bull (who had led
the attack against Custer). Cody employed
Native Americans from government reserva-
tions and often used his show to speak out

Lithograph of Buffalo Bill on horseback, holding a smoking rifle. (Library of Congress)

about the treatment of the various tribes. In fact, after the massacre at Wounded Knee in 1890, Cody and a number of the Native American performers in his show traveled to the reservation to help restore order and prevent further violence.

Meanwhile, both of the great herds of buffalo, the southern and northern groups, had been hunted to extinction by the year that Cody launched his extravaganza. In addition, the frontier had begun to close and open spaces were quickly being fenced in and settled. Cody bemoaned the loss of the frontier in his shows, which were becoming increasingly popular. In 1887, the Wild West Show was part of the American Exposition at Queen Victoria's Silver Jubilee in London. For 10 years, the show made regular appearances in Europe. Cody used the financial bonanza produced by his show to fund a variety of projects. His concern with the loss of wildlife and habitat led him to establish game preserves in Colorado and Wyoming. He also worked to limit the length of hunting seasons in a number of states. Cody served as a model of the later hunter-conservationist and would inspire figures such as Theodore Roosevelt.

Cody also sought to develop his own town. Along with a group of investors, he established a town that bore his name in Wyoming in 1896. Cody had grand visions for his town, but they never matured. Still, three major canals and two dams were built, and 16,200 acres were placed under irrigation. While Cody was a master showman, he was a poor businessman. By the end of his life, he had lost most of his fortune. Cody died on January 10, 1917.

Tom Lansford

See also: Boomtowns, Cowtowns, and Gun Violence; Dime Novels and the Sensationalization of Frontier Violence; Frontier Violence; Hickok, James Butler "Wild Bill"; Oakley, Annie

Further Reading

Blackstone, Sarah J. *Buckskins, Bullets, and Business: A History of Buffalo Bill's Wild West*. Westport, CT: Greenwood Press, 1986.

Buffalo Bill Museum and Grave. http://www.buffalobill.org/ (accessed June 29, 2011).

Cody, William F. *Buffalo Bill's Life Story: An Autobiography*. Reprint ed. Mineola, NY: Dover Publications, 1998.

Wetmore, Helen Cody. *Last of the Great Scouts: The Life Story of Col. William F. Cody*. Charlottesville: University of Virginia Library, 1998.

Collectors

Collecting firearms appears to be one of the more popular hobbies in the United States. While it is difficult to produce a precise estimate of the number of gun collectors in the United States, the activity is sufficiently widespread to support a very large number of publications, websites, and chat rooms. These communications outlets are organized in almost every conceivable fashion. While some publications, such as the National Rifle Association's quarterly journal *Men at Arms*, are intended for general audiences, other magazines and websites cater to much narrower clienteles. Some publications target readers interested in particular time periods, such as those of the Old West, the American Civil War, or World War II; while others focus attention on collectors of specific brands of firearms, such as Browning, Winchester, Colt, or Smith & Wesson. Still others are organized around a geographical unit, such as the Dallas Arms Collectors' Association or the New Mexico Gun Collectors' Association.

While it is difficult to generalize about such a diverse group of communications outlets, these magazines and websites tend to emphasize four different types of messages. First, these media constitute an important means of exchange. Information about gun sales, shows, and innovations are spread to interested readers through both substantive articles and paid advertisements. In addition to providing information about the purchases of guns and ammunition, these publications also provide access to further information. Some of these, such as *Men at Arms* or the more specialized *Guns of the Old West*, contain reviews of books on topics of interest to gun collectors.

Second, many of the articles in publications for gun collectors consist of descriptions of historical events in which firearms played important roles. These might include accounts of battles, military and scientific expeditions, or the depiction of firearms in the general media culture. The emphasis on history appears to fulfill an important rhetorical purpose, which involves pointing out the constructive use of guns in significant events in U.S. and world history.

Third, many of the articles in gun-oriented publications focus on the technical, performance-related characteristics of various weapons. Often, several different firearms of the same general type (such as revolvers, rifles, or shotguns of a particular caliber) are tested and compared to one another along different technical criteria. These might include accuracy, durability, aesthetics, and reliability. The theme of safety is often emphasized in articles of this type, since associations of gun owners and collectors are often eager to live down a perceived reputation for recklessness.

Finally, some of these publications and sites carry explicit political messages. These are generally labeled clearly and set off from the rest of the publication in question. Explicitly political communications seem generally to fall into one of two distinct types. One set of messages emphasizes the legitimacy of gun ownership and the folly of gun control. These will often contain messages about the Constitution generally (or, more specifically, the Second Amendment) or about American history. The American Revolution is a popular theme in these communications, as the notion of a "citizen militia" is a very powerful rhetorical symbol to members of these groups. The connection between this type of political socialization and the historical articles described above is quite obvious, and there is considerable overlap between the two categories. Somewhat more rarely, other political messages will emphasize short-term tactics and will contain descriptions of candidate positions on firearm-related issues, information about pending legislation in Congress or in state legislatures, or analyses of recent court decisions.

The popularity of gun collecting in the United States has contributed to the phenomenon of the "gun show," in which gun enthusiasts can gather to exchange information and perspectives on aspects of gun ownership. Gun shows are often settings in which guns, ammunition, and accessories can be purchased with legal or practical exemptions from government regulations.

The general point is that gun collecting is far from a private activity. Although individual collections may appear isolated from one another, gun collectors have created elaborate communications networks, which in turn promote shared cultural values and ideological perspectives.

Ted G. Jelen

See also: Gun Culture; Gun Ownership; Gun Shows; *Gun Week*; Recreational Uses of Guns; Target Shooting

Further Reading

Horwitz, Joshua, and Casey Anderson. *Guns, Democracy, and the Insurrectionist Idea*. Ann Arbor: University of Michigan Press, 2009.

Shideler, Dan. *2012 Standard Catalog of Firearms: The Collector's Price and Reference Guide*. Iola, WI: Krause, updated annually.

Colleges and Gun Violence

The issue of guns on campus is of concern to educators and the broader community. In general, the carrying and possession of firearms on college campuses is forbidden by state law or institutional rules. Even colleges that support the shooting sports typically store the guns away from students.

Some people view colleges as safe havens from violence, but events over the past several decades have proven otherwise. During the 1990s, the *Chronicle of Higher Education* ("A Look at Campus Crime," 2000), reported increasing weapons arrests on college campuses, and the first decade of the twenty-first century saw the bloodiest mass shooting in U.S. history at Virginia Tech, as well as other small incidents at other campuses—including a much publicized and bloody shooting at Northern Illinois University.

There are three sources of violence and thus concern. Colleges, like the rest of society, may suffer acts of workplace violence. Violent behavior by terrorists, disgruntled employees, family members, significant others, and stalkers could occur on college campuses. In this way, colleges seem no different from other work environments.

The second concern is the possibility of drug-related gun violence spreading to college campuses, especially to schools that are close to urban centers with many gun-related crimes. Neighborhood residents may wander onto campus or engage in drug dealing. There is a risk associated with outreach programs: students involved in gangs may carry weapons on campus for personal protection. Many high school students cite personal protection as a reason for carrying a weapon to school, and there is no reason to think the urban college campus may be different. There is also concern that drug and alcohol usage on campus may lead to violent behavior. The *Chronicle of Higher Education* has discussed this issue in some depth. Some critics, however, have criticized such reports as focusing on minority institutions and students to a much greater extent than necessary and for being unduly alarmist.

A third major risk is that of rampage shootings, which not surprisingly receive the most prominent coverage in the media. One of the most infamous incidents was the Texas Tower Massacre committed by Charles Whitman at the University of Texas, Austin, in 1966, when he killed 14 out of the 45 people he shot. Among the most notable of these kinds of incidents was the 1989 slaying of 14 women at the University of Montreal's Ecole Polytechnique.

However, the current generation was most stunned by the horrific events at Virginia Polytechnic Institute and State University in Blacksburg, Virginia, on April 16, 2007. Referred to as the Virginia Tech massacre, it saw 32 people killed and wounded by student Seung-hui Cho. Several important points came out the tragedy. First, there were clear warning signs that the individual had behavioral problems, which should have caused the institution to take action and perhaps his being prevented from buying firearms. These have led to lawsuits against the institution and members of its administration. Key points were their failure to deal with Cho early on and, most importantly, not locking down the university after the first shooting that occurred before the main massacre. As in many of these cases, the shooter killed himself as the police closed in. It was also clear that attempts to protect oneself were futile in many cases. Unarmed students were shot down attempting to tackle Cho. Cho broke through barricades and shot those attempting such. Playing dead was successful for some (Giduck and Chi 2008).

A similar incident occurred at Northern Illinois University on February 14, 2008, where a past student, Steven Kazmierczak, killed 6 and injured 18. Kazmierczak had a psychiatric history and also killed himself.

Incidents are not confined to students as aggressors. On February 12, 2010, Dr. Amy Bishop, a biology professor who had been denied tenure, killed three faculty members and wounded three others. Once again, the shooter had a past history of violence and problems that might have been predictive.

The Virginia Tech incident, in part, led to the passing of the NICS Improvement Act in 2008. The act encourages, through a system of incentives and financial punishments, the individual states to improve their data collection and reporting of individuals who are denied gun possession by the Gun Control Act of 1968, including convicted felons and those with adjudicated mental disabilities. Current focus has been on the nature of the killers (their ages, environmental contexts, mental illnesses, and previous warnings to their peers) and whether gun control laws would have had any effect in preventing their crimes.

Predicting who will become violent is extremely difficult and may be counterproductive if it leads to scapegoating. Some success has been achieved in secondary schools, with other students reporting threats. This has increased given the new sensitivity to such threats. However, the consensus seems to be that prediction is still far off, if even possible (Borum et al. 2010; U.S. Secret Service 2000). College counselors have little knowledge of firearms issues or how to discuss them with students (Price et al. 2009).

Gary Kleck (2009), a noted criminologist, has argued that gun control laws would not be effective in preventing rampages. Schools have now formed crisis management teams to evaluate risks and develop critical incident plans. They range from actual emergency trials to plans for handling the operational and legal aftermath, as well as public relations. Alert systems based on phone systems or sirens have been installed. The actual utility of such methods are doubted by experts (Fox 2008), but the plans' existence might serve as an after-the-fact liability defense in court. Alert systems cannot save the victims of the initial attack in a large lecture hall. Time to institute and alert or lock down may take from 15 minutes to several hours. The actual killing may be over by then.

Some gun rights proponents contend that current laws deprive educators and staff of any option for armed self-defense. This has led to a movement to allow concealed carry on college campus by legislative action, as most college administrations oppose such. Utah has mandated that concealed carry be allowed on public campuses. Several schools in Colorado now allow concealed carry. Legislation to allow carry (against the wishes of the school) has been introduced in many states. Interestingly, it is opposed by college administrations and business interests. Antigun views and liability concerns seem the major reasons for the opposition such as in Texas (Texas State Rifle Association 2011). Colleges are worried that recent Supreme Court decisions favorable to gun rights (*District of Columbia v. Heller*; *McDonald v. City of Chicago*) may impact them (Kelderman 2010).

One interesting report is that schools respond to rampages with memorials, celebrations of life, and services right after the incident and anniversaries. Experts argue that these might be counterproductive, as social cognitive learning theory suggests that they are just priming the next shooter, who is vicariously rewarded by seeing the pain produced in the past massacre and how his or her actions might do the same—justifying their own suicidal ideation in some cases (American Psychiatric Association 2007; Fox 2008).

Other issues relevant to guns on campus are college student opinions about firearms and the rate of possession of firearms. A study by Miller, Hemenway, and Wechsler (1999) found that 3.5 percent of college students nationally reported having a handgun with them at college. This is probably an underestimate of ownership given college possession restrictions. Meyer (2001) found that 12 percent of men and 3.5 percent of women in a Texas and Oregon sample reported owning handguns. Surveys about gun laws themselves are always suspect, as it is easy to manipulate answers through the forms of questions asked (Vizzard 2000). Nevertheless, it is clear that the college-educated population does not dramatically differ from other segments of the public on these issues. Kleck (1997) summarizes data indicating that most people in the United States favor weak to moderate controls on gun purchases (e.g., waiting periods and background checks) but not outright bans. Meyer (2001) found a similar pattern, with some support for licensing requirements but not for outright bans. Interestingly, about 48 percent of that sample (whose members did not own a handgun) indicated that they might buy one in the future. In comparison, the Meyer sample of faculty found that about 20 percent owned a handgun, with about 15 percent not owning one but contemplating a future purchase.

The last issue is the status of firearms research on college campuses. To the gun world, academics are seen as mostly wild-eyed liberals who strongly oppose the Second Amendment. Redding (2001) documents such tendencies in psychology. Certainly, most academic writings tend to focus on the problems of firearms in society. However, some of the most serious support for the Second Amendment has come from liberal scholars such as Lawrence Tribe of Harvard Law School. The work of John Lott Jr. (2010) and Gary Kleck (1997) on the utilitarian value of guns in society has bolstered the case for a strong defense of the Second Amendment. Such works have even led to calls for liberal scholars to censor themselves because their analyses hurt the gun control cause (Etzioni 2001).

Glenn E. Meyer

See also: Cho, Seung-hui; *District of Columbia v. Heller*; *McDonald v. City of Chicago*; NICS Improvement Act; Students for Concealed Carry on Campus; Texas Tower Shooting; Virginia Tech Massacre; Workplace Shootings

Further Reading

American Psychiatric Association. "APA Urges Media to Stop Airing Graphic Cho Materials." http://www.psych.org/Main Menu/Newsroom/NewsReleases/2007News Releases/07-25openletteronchomaterials .aspx?FT=.pdf (accessed May 31, 2011).

Borum, Randy, et al. "What Can Be Done about School Shootings? A Review of the Evidence." *Educational Researcher* 39 (2010): 27–37. http://youthviolence.eds chool.virginia.edu/pdf/school-shootings -article-by-borum-cornell-2010.pdf (accessed May 31, 2011).

Cullen, Dave. *Columbine*. New York: Twelve, 2009.

Etzioni, Amitai. "Are Liberal Scholars Acting Irresponsibly on Gun Control?" *Chronicle of Higher Education* 47 (2001): B14–B15. http://www.gwu.edu/~ccps/etzioni/B350 .html (accessed May 31, 2011).

Fox, James A. "Topics in University Security: Lockdown 101." *New York Times*, April 16, 2008. http://www.nytimes.com/2008/04/ 16/opinion/16fox.html?ref=choseunghui (accessed May 31, 2011).

Giduck, John P., and Walter D. Chi. "After Action Review: An Evaluation and Assessment of the Law Enforcement Tactical Response to the Virginia Tech University Shootings of Monday, 16 April 2007." Archangel Group, Ltd., September 5, 2008. http://www.roanoke.com/news/092508 _archangel.pdf (accessed May 31, 2011).

Kelderman, Eric. "Campus Gun Bans Are Still on Solid Legal Grounds, Experts Say." *Chronicle of Higher Education*, June 29, 2010. http://chronicle.com/article/Campus -Gun-Bans-Are-Still-on/66089/ (accessed May 31, 2011).

Kleck, Gary. "Mass Shootings in Schools: The Worst Possible Case for Gun Control" *American Behavioral Scientist* 52 (2009): 1447–64.

Kleck, Gary. *Targeting Guns: Firearms and Their Control.* Hawthorne, NY: Aldine de Gruyter, 1997.

"A Look at Campus Crime." *Chronicle of Higher Education*, June 9, 2000. http:// chronicle.com/article/A-Look-at-Campus -Crime/7333 (accessed May 31, 2011).

Lott, John R., Jr. *More Guns, Less Crime: Understanding Crime and Gun Control Laws.* 3rd ed. Chicago: University of Chicago Press, 2010.

Meyer, Glenn E. "Campus Weaponry: Student and Faculty Attitudes, Fears, and Behavior." *Prevention Researcher* 6 (1999): 12–23.

Miller, Matthew, David Hemenway, and Henry Wechsler. "Guns and Gun Threats at College." *Journal of American College Health* 48 (1999): 7–12. http://www.hsph .harvard.edu/cas/Documents/Gunthreats2/ gunspdf.pdf (accessed May 31, 2011).

Price, James, et al. "College Counselors' Perceptions and Practices Regarding Anticipatory Guidance on Firearms." *Journal of American College Health* 58 (2009): 133–39.

Redding, Richard E. "Sociopolitical Diversity in Psychology: The Case for Pluralism." *American Psychologist* 56 (2001): 205–15.

Students for Concealed Carry on Campus. http://www.concealedcampus.org/ (accessed May 31, 2011).

Texas State Rifle Association. "Concealed Carry on Campus Prefiled." https://www .tsra.com/index.php?option=com_content &view=article&id=274:concealed-carry -on-campus-prefiled&catid=55:tripp-talk &Itemid=113 (accessed May 31, 2011).

U.S. Secret Service. "Preventing School Shootings: A Summary of a U.S. Secret Service Safe School Initiative Report." http://www.ncjrs.gov/pdffiles1/jr000248c .pdf (accessed May 31, 2011).

Vizzard, William J. *Shots in the Dark: The Policy, Politics, and Symbolism of Gun Control.* Lanham, MD: Rowman & Littlefield, 2000.

Colt, Samuel (1814–1862)

For more than a century, beginning in 1855, Colt revolvers were manufactured in the brownstone armory that Samuel Colt built near the Connecticut River in Hartford. At the time, it was the largest private armory in the world, crowned with a blue, onion-shaped dome, still a Hartford landmark.

Inventor, entrepreneur, and promoter Samuel Colt was born in Hartford in 1814. His passion for firearms and explosive devices as a youngster made him an indifferent student, to the chagrin of his father. Christopher Colt had difficulties with his son from the beginning. The senior Colt apprenticed Samuel to a farmer when the boy was 11. He was an indifferent hand and spent more time reading up on gunpowder, galvanic experiments, and inventors than seemed proper. His reading program ultimately inspired an obsession for inventing what contemporaries called an "impossible gun"—one that would shoot five or maybe six times without reloading. Brought back

Samuel Colt. (Hayward Cirker, ed., *Dictionary of American Portraits*, 1967)

to work in his father's factory in 1829, Samuel quickly created a ruckus by using a galvanic cell (a battery) to explode an underwater charge of gunpowder. In 1832, Christopher Colt apprenticed his wayward son as a sailor on the brig *Corvo*, bound from Boston to Calcutta. While aboard, the 16-year-old youth conceived of the revolutionary idea of the revolver by watching the action of the ship's wheel. This inspiration led him to carve a wooden model of would become a six-shooter. After Samuel returned from the sea, Christopher Colt, a successful entrepreneur, proved willing to finance the fabrication of two prototypes of Colt's six-shooter. Both failed to give satisfactory performance.

Undeterred, but penniless, Colt set out to earn the money needed to carry on his experiments by becoming an itinerant performer of spectacles. He billed himself as "the celebrated Dr. Coult of New York, London, and Calcutta." With knowledge of the properties of the newly discovered nitrous oxide gas, he toured Canada and the East Coast for three years giving demonstrations of "laughing gas." With his earnings, he engaged a competent mechanic, John Pearson, to fabricate improved models or his six-shooter. Then, borrowing $1,000 from his father, Colt set out in 1835 to secure patent protection for his idea in Europe. Still only 21, he received patents in London (December 8, 1835) and France— and, the following February, U.S. Patent No. 138. On the strength of these, he raised $200,000 in capital from New York and New Jersey investors.

Colt's first attempt at manufacturing took place in Paterson, New Jersey, in a leased section of a silk mill. The company failed in 1842, despite the fact that 100 of his revolvers had met with success against the Seminole Indians in Florida and in Texas, where the newly formed Texas Rangers used them in their fights against the fierce Comanche. Even with these successes, Colt faced a familiar problem among nineteenth-century manufacturers of novel and complex mechanical devices. Their inventions stretched the limits of contemporary technological capabilities for volume production. The capital and labor costs required for a precision product simply rendered volume sales impossible. Without the volume, the potential revenue could not repay the investment. In this period of the 1840s, even the national armories at Springfield and Harpers Ferry were just beginning to achieve their first truly effective interchangeability of parts for long arms—a much less demanding set of machining tasks than Colt faced with his handgun. The "filing and fitting" necessary for Colt's guns made volume sales an elusive dream—even if he could find willing buyers.

Five years later, at the outset of the Mexican War, the U.S. Army gave Colt an order for 1,000 revolvers. Even this relatively small run was beyond his capacity. Still "poor as a churchmouse," as he said, and clearly lacking production facilities, Colt turned to Eli Whitney Jr. in Whitneyville, Connecticut, to partner in the manufacture of the Colt-Whitney-Walker model.

Everyone had known the guns were effective since the days of their use against the Seminoles and the Comanche. It was the Mexican War and the development of manufacturing capacity, however, that really launched Colt on his way to fame and fortune. Colt returned to Hartford to set himself up in a rented facility and set out to produce the Colt Dragoon model. By 1852, he was able to purchase 250 acres of flood-prone land in the South Meadows and began work building a great armory and a self-sufficient community called Coltsville. Ignoring the skepticism and hostility of the city fathers, he built a dike along his property for flood protection, laid out streets, erected houses for his employees, and even built a hall for their entertainment.

Always on the lookout for more business, Colt saw an opportunity to furnish weapons to both sides in the Crimean War. The first American to manufacture abroad, he opened a factory in London in 1853 to make the Model 1849 Pocket and the Model 1851 Navy. Unfortunately, the plant was mismanaged and closed in 1857.

The operating genius of the Colt Armory was Elisha K. Root, the most brilliant machinist of his era in New England. Adapting the system of interchangeable parts pioneered by Eli Whitney and the Springfield Armory, Root developed equipment and processes that made possible the mass production of firearms on machines, except for the finishing and final assembly. By 1857,

the armory turned out 250 guns a day. It also became a training center for a succession of gifted mechanics, like Pratt and Whitney, who went on to apply Root's methods in companies of their own. It is said that Root was the inspiration for the hero in Mark Twain's novel *A Connecticut Yankee in King Arthur's Court.*

Colt himself functioned as president and salesman extraordinaire through aggressive marketing and close relations with military officials, legislators, and foreign heads of state. Thousands of his revolvers were shipped to California during the Gold Rush. He traveled abroad, wangling introductions to government officials and making them gifts of beautifully engraved weapons. In less than a decade, Colt had become the United States' first tycoon, a bibulous millionaire and cigar-puffing bachelor who had everything except a wife and home.

Colt set out to acquire the wife and a mansion with his usual dispatch, showmanship, and pomp. For his bride, he chose the gracious and gentle Elizabeth Jarvis, daughter of a Middletown minister. At age 30, Elizabeth Jarvis was 12 years junior to Colt. For Colt, it was the perfect match. The extravagance of their wedding in June 1856 shocked Hartford's staid society. Likewise, Colt's extravagant and palatial Armsmear on the western end of his domain caused a great deal of society chatter.

As North and South raced toward the cataclysm of the Civil War, Colt busily harvested profits from both the U.S. Army and the southern states. A Democrat, he opposed the election of Lincoln out of fear the Union would be destroyed—and a lucrative market thereby lost. In his view, slavery was not a moral wrong, just an inefficient economic system. Anticipating the onset of conflict, he shrewdly prepared the armory for a five-year struggle and the arming of a million men. To that end, he erected a duplicate facility that mirrored his existing H-shaped factory.

The demands of wartime production seemed to sap strength and wear down his seemingly inexhaustible energies. Plagued by frequent attacks of inflammatory rheumatism, he continued to drive himself as if he knew his days were numbered. At the age of 47, he died on January 14, 1862, leaving his widow and son Caldwell an estate that was adjudged enormous at the time.

Samuel Colt had adopted as his motto "*Vincit qui patitur*" (he conquers who suffers). But a more apt key to his character is the remark he once wrote to his half brother William: "It is better to be at the head of a louse than at the tail of a lion ... If I can't be first I won't be second in anything."

A catastrophe almost put an end to the armory two years after his death, as 1,500 men worked two 10-hour shifts to keep Ulysses S. Grant's Union troops supplied with muskets and revolvers. Fire destroyed the original factory and most of the machines. Undaunted, Elizabeth Colt ordered the building of a new armory. At the height of the Civil War, production had reached 100,000 revolvers and nearly 50,000 muskets annually.

The coming of peace, however, brought an end to the military's demand for arms. The company tried to keep its workforce busy making machine tools, steam engines, sewing machines, printing presses, and both the Gatling and Browning machine guns. In 1872, the company brought out the six-shot Colt .45, or "Peacemaker," the gun that became a legend among cowboys and frontiersmen. It was said that while Lincoln made all men free, Colt made all men equal.

In 1901, four years before her death, Mrs. Colt, the grande dame of Hartford society, sold the Colt Armory to Boston and New York financiers. The company earned huge profits until the end of World War I, paying its investors annual dividends averaging 22 percent. Making and selling arms and munitions was a business like any other, and the moral aspects of being "dealers in death" did not disturb the conscience of management. Certainly, Hartford did not regard gun making as a sin. Connecticut had been the arsenal of the nation since colonial times.

During World War I, the Colt Armory achieved the highest production levels in its history. Before U.S. entry into the war, because of demand from Canada and Great Britain, the company's order backlog extended to three years, employment rose to nearly 4,000, and its stock quintupled in value. By the end of the war in 1918, it had delivered 425,500 automatic pistols, 151,700 revolvers, 13,000 Maxim-Vickers machine guns, and 10,000 new Browning machine guns, while handling smoothly the subcontracting of nearly 100,000 more. Employment peaked at 10,000. The three most responsible for this spectacular achievement were Colt president William C. Skinner; Fred Moore, head of production; and the inventor John Browning, whose .45 pistol was the army's standard sidearm. Besides his .30-caliber machine gun, he also invented a lightweight automatic rifle. His son, Lt. Val A. Browning, was the first to fire both weapons in France.

Peacetime called for a different strategy. Anticipating a severe drought in military sales, Skinner and his successor, Samuel Stone, set in motion a diversification program, as was done after the Civil War. They obtained contracts for adding machines and commercial dishwashers to be marketed under the name of someone other than Colt. Stone acquired a company engaged in molding hard plastics, which he renamed "Colt rock," and another company that made electrical products.

Colt weathered the Great Depression better than most other Hartford manufacturers, reducing the work week, cutting salaries, keeping more men on the payroll than were needed, and eating up surplus. On Pearl Harbor Day in 1941, the company was still the largest private armory in the United States and the only one turning out machine guns. As it had in two previous conflicts, Colt Armory stretched itself to the limit, winning the army-navy "E" for outstanding production in 1942. But a few months later, it was evident that the armory was in the incipient stage of its eventual downfall. It began losing money every month. The root of the trouble was partially its fatigued and strife-torn labor force, but more important was the obsolescence of both management and manufacturing techniques.

In September 1955, the directors voted to merge Colt Armory with an upstart conglomerate called Penn-Texas, which had acquired Pratt & Whitney Machine Tool the same year. Under the new ownership, the most significant achievement was the introduction of the M16 automatic rifle, which became the standard army and air force weapon. In recent years, Colt Armory suffered one blow after another: more mismanagement, heavy deficits, obsolete products, loss of markets and contracts, defense cutbacks, a four-year strike, another buyout, and bankruptcy. Yet it recovered from all of these reversals and now operates not in the old downtown armory, but in a modern plant in West Hartford. The departure in 1994 marked the end of 147 years of gun making in Hartford, during which not only Colt Armory, but also Sharps, Pope Manufacturing, and Pratt & Whitney Machine Tool had led the state to an unprecedented era of power and prosperity. The armory is being renovated for small businesses, artists' studios, and possibly a museum of industrial technology.

Ellsworth S. Grant, with updates by
David S. Lux

See also: Browning, John Moses; Remington, Eliphalet, II; Ruger, William Batterman; Whitney, Eli; Winchester, Oliver Fisher

Further Reading

Barnard, Henry. *Armsmear: The Home, the Arm, and the Armory of Samuel Colt: A Memorial*. New York: Alvord, 1866.

Edwards, William B. *The Story of Colt's Revolver*. Harrisburg, PA: Stackpole, 1953.

Flayderman, Norm. *Flayderman's Guide to Antique American Firearms*. Iola, WI: F+W Media, Inc., 2007.

Grant, Ellsworth S. *The Colt Armory*. Lincoln, RI: Andrew Mowbray, 1995.

Haven, Charles T., and Frank A. Belden. *A History of the Colt Revolver*. Special edition. Fairfax, VA: National Rifle Association (Odysseus Editions), 1997.

Hosley, William. *Colt: The Making of an American Legend*. Amherst: University of Massachusetts Press, 1996.

Lindsay, David. *Madness in the Making: The Triumphant Rise and Untimely Fall of America's Show Inventors*. Lincoln, NE: iUniverse, Inc., 1997, 2005.

Rohan, Jack. *Yankee Arms Maker: The Story of Sam Colt and His Six-Shot Peacemaker*. Rev. ed. New York: Harper, 1948.

Serven, James Edsall, and Carl Metzger. Paterson Pistols, First of the Famous Repeating Firearms Patented and Promoted by Sam'l Colt. n.p.: Foundation Press, 1946.

Wilson, R. L. *The Colt Heritage: The Official History of Colt Firearms, from 1836 to the Present*. New York: Simon and Schuster, 1979.

Columbine High School Tragedy (1999)

On April 20, 1999, Eric Harris and Dylan Klebold, both seniors at Columbine High School near Littleton, Colorado, entered the school and killed 12 fellow students and one teacher before taking their own lives. An additional 23 students were injured in the shooting spree. Arguably, the Columbine murders shook the American psyche more than any shooting since the 1968 assassination of Sen. Robert F. Kennedy. While Columbine deeply unsettled the United States initially, the crime's long-term impact on gun policy was much smaller than had originally been expected. The Columbine events did, however, have a variety of positive and negative long-term impacts on some parts of American society, and the debate that followed revealed one of the fundamental fault lines within the country.

Well over a year's planning came to culmination when Harris and Klebold entered Columbine High School on the morning of April 20 and deposited duffel bags containing 20-pound propane tanks in the cafeteria, with a timer set to detonate the tanks at 11:17 a.m. According to the report released by the Jefferson County Sheriff's Office, the tanks contained sufficient explosive power to "kill the majority of students" who would be in the cafeteria for lunch. The killers then positioned themselves in the parking lot outside the school, to be ready to shoot fleeing students. They also set timers on bombs in their parked cars, to kill the first responders.

None of the bombs worked as planned. So at 11:19, Harris and Klebold began shooting outside the school. The first five students shot (two of whom were killed) were sitting on the steps outside the school cafeteria. Seventeen-year-old Rachel Scott was murdered specifically because she had revealed her Christian faith to one of the killers several weeks before. When one of the killers put a gun to her head and tauntingly asked if she still believed in God, she replied, "You know I do." "Go be with Him, then," he answered, and pulled the trigger.

At 11:24, the school resource officer, Deputy Sheriff Neil Gardner, returned from lunch and exchanged fire in a long-distance gun battle with Harris and Klebold before they entered the building. A nearby officer on motorcycle patrol arrived and also exchanged shots. Neither officer entered the building to pursue the killers, nor did any of the many other officers who arrived within minutes. A SWAT team quickly assembled outside the school, but the team did not enter the building until approximately 12:06 p.m.

In the meantime, Klebold and Harris were shooting people inside the school. Among their victims was teacher Dave Sanders (age 47), who was holding a door open so that students could flee. Harris and Klebold entered the school library where students were hiding under desks and tables. Inside the library, a teacher had called 911 on a portable phone, and the 911 operator had told the teacher to keep the students in the library because help was on the way. Because Columbine High School sits on a sloping hill, students could have fled the library through an exit door on an outside wall.

Another 911 call revealed that Harris and Klebold had entered the library. Inside, they taunted students as they shot them one by one. The police remained outside. The last victim in the library was killed at about 11:35 a.m. Klebold and Harris returned to the cafeteria, shooting randomly and hurling pipe bombs, most of which failed to detonate. While Harris and Klebold had used a variety of explosives with which a skilled bomb-maker could have killed hundreds, the two murderers failed to kill anyone with their homemade devices—although shrapnel from the explosives did cause a number of injuries. Columbine demonstrated it is easy to kill people with firearms, but while a trained person (such as Timothy McVeigh) can kill hundreds of people with explosives, it is difficult for an untrained person to do so.

Harris and Klebold returned to the library (the surviving students had fled), where they put guns to their heads, and killed themselves at 12:08 p.m. The first SWAT personnel entered the east side of the school (far from where the killers were known to be) at 12:06 p.m. For the next several hours, the police continued to "contain the perimeter"—searching and securing one room at a time, starting with the rooms farthest from where the killers had last been spotted.

Every injured person who received prompt medical care survived. But police did not reach the room where teacher Dave Sanders was bleeding for nearly three hours, despite pleas from cellular phone callers in the room with him. He eventually bled to death; he was the only teacher killed that day. SWAT team personnel entered the library for the first time at 3:22 p.m. Authorities repeatedly refused opportunities to rescue Sanders, and falsely and repeatedly claimed that medical care was on the way.

The murderers' weapons consisted of an Intratec TEC-DC9 semiautomatic pistol, obtained from Mark Manes, a petty criminal and the son of a gun control activist. He was later sentenced to prison for knowingly providing a handgun to minors in violation of Colorado law and for using an unlicensed sawed-off shotgun (during a filmed target practice with the killers) in violation of federal law. The other three weapons were a Hi-Point 9 mm carbine, a Savage 67H pump-action shotgun, and a Stevens 311-D side-by-side, double-barreled 12-gauge shotgun. These were obtained by Robyn Anderson, who on the Saturday before the Tuesday murders would be Klebold's prom date. She bought the guns for the youths at the Tanner Gun Show on November 22, 1998, from private individuals.

After the murders, Anderson told various stories about her role. At first, when interrogated by law enforcement, she admitted being at the gun show, but denied purchasing the weapons. In January 2000 testimony before the Colorado legislature, she asserted that she would not have bought the guns if there had been background checks on gun buyers. She had previously said the opposite, when appearing on *Good Morning America* on June 4, 1999.

Eric Harris was a classic psychopath—a person who feels little or no empathy, but who is a skilled liar, able to manipulate others. Dylan Klebold was shy, depressed, and willingly led by Harris. Harris fantasized about a world in which all humans were dead. Both Harris and Klebold loved the 1994 Oliver Stone film *Natural Born Killers*, about a pair of mass murderers, and they referred to their murder plot as "NBK."

Narcissists and sadists, both Harris and Klebold imagined themselves to be greatly superior to everyone else, and supposedly more self-aware. During their high school career together, they were bullies, vandals, arsonists, and thieves. Their diaries and videos of themselves exulted in murderous rage against humanity in general. On the day of the murders, Harris wore a T-shirt with the words "Natural Selection," reflecting his oft-stated belief in his own superiority and his right to kill inferiors.

Harris and Klebold had been arrested on January 30, 1998, and pled guilty to first-degree criminal trespass, theft, and criminal mischief for breaking into a parked van and stealing $1,719 of electronic equipment and other goods. They spent one year in a juvenile diversion program consisting of community service, counseling, and anger management classes, from which they were released on February 3, 1999.

On March 18, 1998, Harris was reported to the Jefferson County Sheriff's Department by Randy Brown, the father of a classmate. The Browns provided the department with pages of hateful, homicidal material from Harris's website, including a specific death threat against classmate Brooks Brown, and the intention to murder many people soon. The department prepared an affidavit for an application to obtain a search warrant for Harris's home, supported by evidence that Harris might be manufacturing bombs. But the department failed to ask a court for a warrant, perhaps because the detective in charge was assigned to another matter and never finished the Harris case. For years, the Sheriff's Department covered up the existence of the affidavit and its extensive prior knowledge of the danger Harris posed. Sheriff John Stone's statements to the media on April 20 and thereafter were frequently inaccurate and lacking an appropriate factual basis.

The cover-up began in a meeting held (to evade the media) at the Jefferson County Open Space Department on the afternoon of April 20. Media requests for files, pursuant to the Colorado Open Records Act, helped partially undo the cover-up, but much of the important work in discovering hidden documents was performed by attorneys Barry Arrington and Jim Rouse, on behalf of Brian Rohrbough, whose son Danny was murdered.

If the Jefferson County Sheriff's Department had obtained and carried out a search warrant, or even informed the diversion program or the district attorney's office, Harris and Klebold would probably have been sent to prison for their felony theft. If the Sheriff's Department had informed Columbine High School or the parents, action might

have been taken when the incipient killers obliquely revealed their plans—as when Harris's father picked up a phone call from a gun store saying that the ammunition magazines had arrived, when Harris's father found a pipe bomb in Harris's room, or when a teacher informed Klebold's parents and a school counselor about Klebold's creative writing essay detailing a mass murder moment by moment from the killer's exultant perspective.

Overall, there had been at least 15 Sheriff's Department contacts involving Harris and Klebold before April 20, but (as in the period before the September 11, 2001, terrorist attacks), there was a failure to connect the dots. Many other warnings were known to various people, such as Harris's accumulation of a large quantity of propane tanks.

The societal reaction to Columbine fit the pattern of "moral panics," which sociologists have described as hysterical community reactions designed to reestablish norms of control by cracking down on outcasts—regardless of whether the outcasts are really the cause of the problem.

Although preliminary media reports identified the killers as members of the "Trench Coat Mafia," a group of about a dozen students who regularly wore black trench coats to school, Harris and Klebold were not members. The false reports led some school districts to ban the wearing of trench coats, and many schools began to crack down on "Goth" culture. ("Goth" is a youth subculture with an interest in Dark Ages imagery and other forms of darkness, including dark clothing.)

Corrupting music was also blamed, particularly the singer Marilyn Manson and KMFDM, the latter of which was a Harris favorite. Columbine spurred many movie theaters to begin strict enforcement of the rule against unaccompanied minors viewing R-rated movies.

Video games also came in for scrutiny, since the killers spent a great deal of time playing "first-person-shooter" games such as *Postal* and *Doom*. But no substantial changes in marketing or sales resulted, and video game defenders pointed out that the vast majority of people who play such games do not commit violent crimes, just as the vast majority of children in earlier generations who played "cowboys and Indians" did not later shoot real people with bows or guns.

Over the following years, Columbine copycat crimes were attempted at schools around the nation. Several such crimes were prevented because, post-Columbine, students were ready to speak up about rumors and suspicious behavior. Some media critics charged that excessive, sensational coverage of Columbine was an important cause of additional school shootings. Columbine received far more publicity than any other mass murder at a school, either before or since, and the media fully cooperated in Harris's plan to create a made-for-TV event. Newspapers and magazines put the killers' pictures on their covers.

While media practices remained largely unchanged after Columbine, many schools— especially high schools—became notably more authoritarian and began in some cases to share characteristics with minimum-security prisons. Many schools added guards and security cameras. Most schools already had "zero-tolerance" policies forbidding students from carrying firearms on school grounds, but these policies were now enforced in ways that would have seemed absurd a decade before. Children were suspended or expelled for playing "cops and robbers" on the playground, for playing with "finger guns," for drawing pictures of soldiers, for making cutout guns from paper, for expressing support for the Second Amendment, and

for other activities not involving real weapons. The draconian application of zero tolerance was, in part, a reflection of the determination of the American school establishment to "do something." Various invasions of student privacy also became more common.

Some people, including conservative radio commentator Paul Harvey, House of Representatives majority whip Tom Delay (R-TX), and Darrell Scott (the father of slain student Rachel Scott), blamed the absence of school prayer and, more broadly, the decline of religious values. Whether organized school prayer would have made any difference for Harris and Klebold is doubtful, and it is plain that they were nihilistic. In their diaries, videotapes, and the Harris website, they claimed to be accountable to no one and entitled to enforce their will against everyone else.

Columbine spurred a surge of activism among Christian youth groups. Many young Christians were inspired by Rachel Scott and Cassie Bernall, evangelical Christians who were murdered at Columbine, and by Valeen Schnurr, a Catholic who was severely wounded but who made a quick recovery that defied medical explanation. Many Christians agreed that Satan had been at work at Columbine.

In a videotape made a month before the killings, Eric Harris expressed his desire to "get a chain reaction going," and indeed copycat crimes followed Columbine. Rachel Scott, a devout Christian who had made a point of showing kindness to outcasts, the handicapped, and others at Columbine High School, hoped for a different kind of chain reaction: "I have a theory that if one person can go out of their way to show compassion, then it will start a chain reaction of the same," she had written in her diary. Scott's diary had been in her backpack and was held elder Mauser joined the staff of a new Colorado gun control organization, SAFE (Sane Alternatives to the Firearms Epidemic), as its top professional lobbyist.

At the NRA convention, NRA president Charlton Heston rebuked Mayor Webb: "Don't come? We're already here," Heston said, pointing to the large number of NRA members in Colorado and in the Columbine community. The speech was in keeping with Heston's long-standing efforts to portray the NRA as a pervasive part of mainstream America. Heston's speech, though well received by its audience, was instantly overshadowed by the surprise appearance of the next speaker, Colorado secretary of state Vikki Buckley (a black Republican). Buckley spoke about her own past as a victim of gun violence, and described Columbine as "a New Age hate crime." (The killers greatly admired the Nazis, called Isaiah Shoels a "nigger" before murdering him, and apparently targeted Rachel Scott for being a Christian.) Buckley excoriated Webb for attacking constitutional amendments, and demanded that the gun prohibition advocates spend less time obsessing about guns and more time preventing children from being born out of wedlock. The crowd gave her a standing ovation, and a few days later the *Wall Street Journal* suggested that Republicans consider Buckley for national office. Buckley died in July 1999, however.

When Sen. Orrin Hatch (R-UT) brought his juvenile crime bill (S. 254, the Violent and Repeat Juvenile Accountability and Rehabilitation Act of 1999) to the floor of the U.S. Senate in mid-May, the NRA was forced to refrain from opposing several antigun amendments so as to conserve its political capital. Even after acquiescing to an amendment to impose background checks on sales by private individuals at gun shows, the NRA was defeated 51–50 (with Vice President Gore casting the tie-breaking vote) on a much harsher amendment that gave the Bureau of Alcohol, Tobacco and Firearms the regulatory authority to abolish or severely curtail gun shows.

After the juvenile crime bill, which was laden with antigun amendments, passed the Senate, gun control advocates in the House wanted a quick vote on their own juvenile crime bill. But the House Republican leadership decided to wait until after the Memorial Day recess. Rep. Anthony Weiner (D-NY) objected, warning, "It doesn't take the NRA long to reload."

When the full House voted on the juvenile justice bill in mid-June, the gun measures had been split off into a separate bill. The final version of the bill included a gun show background check measure that the NRA could live with (no extra regulatory power granted to the ATF), some additional gun restrictions (including on imports of certain magazines and on long-gun possession by people under 18), as well as repeal of the 1976 Washington, D.C., municipal handgun ban. A surprise coalition of mostly Republican gun rights supporters (who thought the bill went too far) and mostly Democratic gun control advocates (who thought the House bill did not go nearly far enough) ended up defeating the House gun bill. The result was fine with the Clinton White House, which planned to use gun control as a major issue in the 2000 elections. In January 2000, Tom Mauser attended President Clinton's State of the Union speech in Washington, D.C., where Clinton praised him for his advocacy of gun control.

Back in Colorado, the aftermath of Columbine blocked the NRA's efforts to pass legislation for a concealed handgun carry licensing law, and for a state law prohibiting most local gun control laws, although both proposals would be enacted in 2003. In the summer of 1999, Governor Bill Owens endorsed a variety of gun controls. The focus of the Colorado 2000 legislative session was on guns more than any other issue. By the time the session was over, all gun control proposals had been defeated, except for some "tough-on-crime" measures that the NRA had supported, such as the "Robyn Anderson bill" prohibiting the transfer of long guns to minors without parental consent. The legislature passed and the governor signed the broadest law in the nation prohibiting lawsuits against gun manufacturers.

That fall, SAFE brought a "gun show" initiative on the statewide ballot and passed it with 70 percent of the vote. A similar measure was passed by Oregon voters with 60 percent of the vote. At Columbine High School itself, beloved principal Frank DeAngelis helped lead the 2,000 students to take back their school, to not allow themselves or their school to be defined by the crimes, and to protect students from aggressive and intrusive media who used anniversaries to revisit the place that had brought them such a ratings bonanza in April 1999. In coming years, DeAngelis would often by consulted by principals at other schools that had been victimized by shooters.

Columbine changed, probably permanently, the dynamics of the debate on gun shows, turning them from an obscure topic of interest only to gun control activists into a well-known national issue. A second effect was to energize, at least temporarily, antigun activists. The most famous of these was talk show host Rosie O'Donnell, who declared the day after Columbine that there should be a mandatory jail sentence for gun ownership. In the long run, her shrill rhetoric probably harmed her cause.

In an October 11, 2000, presidential debate, the Columbine issue was raised.

Vice President Al Gore pointed to guns, and Texas governor George W. Bush pointed to values. The two answers exemplified the cultural divide revealed by the gun debate in general and so sharply intensified by the horror of Columbine. Is human evil a product of a wicked character, or of a bad environment in which dangerous objects like guns are available? Were Harris and Klebold "good kids," as Tom Mauser had said, whose lives showed that guns should be banned?

Thus, even as Columbine was a uniquely traumatizing mass shooting, it ultimately revealed the same philosophical fault lines that have characterized the gun debate from the very beginning. Indeed, the "material versus spiritual" debate is as old as philosophy itself. Michael Moore's gun control advocacy film *Bowling for Columbine* won the 2003 Academy Award for Best Documentary, although it was criticized for numerous errors and fabrications. Jefferson County district attorney Dave Thomas received the Democratic nomination for U.S. House of Representatives in 2004, but he lost the election by a wide margin after a new round of information about the cover-up was revealed.

Perhaps the ultimate illustration of how Columbine had finally faded as a factor in gun policy discussion was provided by Tom Mauser, in an April 7, 2010, gun control debate at Colorado State University in Fort Collins. The debate was put on by Students for Concealed Carry on Campus, a group that had formed the night of the Virginia Tech mass murders. Rejecting the argument that people who are licensed to carry guns in all other public places should be allowed to carry on college campuses, Mauser said that mass shootings are so rare that they should not lead to changes in gun control policy.

David B. Kopel and Carol Oyster

Community Oriented Policing Services (COPS)

Community policing suggests that police officers do better in keeping the peace when they work with community partners. Such partnerships include law enforcement agencies collaborating with other government agencies, selected individual community members, community groups, nonprofit organizations, service providers, private businesses, and the media.

In an effort to better realize the ideals of community policing, Congress created the Office of Community Oriented Policing Services (COPS) as part of the broader Violent Crime Control and Law Enforcement Act of 1994. COPS creates linkages among local groups and individuals by providing information on crime control to all levels of law enforcement (including county sheriffs and municipal police officers), government leaders, first responders, scholars, students, and the general public. Some of this information includes how to build partnerships and how to better use technology to combat crime. Over the years, COPS has variously focused on terrorism, child abuse, bullying, violent crime, campus crime, gangs, and illegal drugs.

Some of its key programs—including Accelerated Hiring, Education, and Deployment (AHEAD), Funding Accelerated for Smaller Towns (FAST), Making Officer Redeployment Effective (MORE), and the Universal Hiring Program (UHF)—have provided funding for the hiring of hundreds of thousands of officers throughout the country, as well as new technology and equipment for these officers. COPS also has funded training on immigration law enforcement, DNA, ethics, federal law enforcement, regional community policing, and tribal law enforcement.

Community-oriented policing programs have been shown to be the effective in reducing gun crime. Building relationships with gangs—while sending the strong and repeated message that "if you use a gun, you'll go to prison"—and cooperating with local nonprofit agencies and businesses to help get young people get off the streets and back into school (or gainful employment) represent two of the most important strategies that community-oriented policing programs use to reduce gun violence. Among the better known of these "carrot-and-stick" programs are Project Safe Neighborhoods, Project Triggerlock, Project Exile, Operation Ceasefire, and the Boston Gun Project.

Sean Maddan

See also: Boston Gun Project (BGP); Project Exile; Project Safe Neighborhoods

Further Reading

Alpert, Geoffrey P., and Alex R. Piquero. *Community Policing: Contemporary Readings*. Long Grove, IL: Waveland Press, 2000.

COPS. http://www.cops.usdoj.gov (accessed January 22, 2010).

Concealed Carry Magazine. *See* United States Concealed Carry Association (USCCA)

Concealed Weapons Laws

Concealed weapons laws are one of the most common forms of gun control regulation throughout the states. Adopted by most states in the early twentieth century as alternatives to a total ban of weapons, these laws prohibited citizens from carrying concealed firearms. These laws were generally restrictive, though some states gave discretion to local police or judges to issue permits to those they felt were "trustworthy." These laws were often backed by opponents of gun control such as the National Rifle Association (NRA).

They reemerged as an important part of the gun control debate in the 1980s and 1990s as gun control opponents organized to modify most of the laws to end the discretion of local police chiefs and sheriffs to require mandatory issuance of permits to those who meet certain requirements. Before 1987, only Georgia, Indiana, Maine, New Hampshire, North Dakota, South Dakota, Vermont, and Washington had "shall-issue" laws requiring law enforcement officials or courts to issue firearm-carrying permits to the average citizen. In 1987, Florida enacted a "shall-issue" right-to-carry law that eventually served as the framework for other states. In 2011, 38 states have such laws. Only Illinois does not issue permits and prohibits all concealed carry.

In general, there is a brief spike in the number of individuals applying for a permit to carry a concealed weapon as soon as the more lenient laws are implemented, but this increase levels off after about a year. The number of permit holders in a state typically levels off after several years.

The most common requirements are demonstration of a minimum level of proficiency with a firearm (usually through completion of a training course or passing a test) and a criminal background check that reveals no felony convictions. Some states also include any convictions for domestic abuse or sex offense in the category of disqualifying events.

It is interesting that the opponents of gun control sparked the movement to change the laws they helped craft decades earlier. In some states, such as Virginia, they responded to sentiment that some of the judges were improperly exercising their discretion in denying permits to qualified citizens. In many cases, it was simply a preference to fight the legislative battles at the state level. State laws generally prohibit local jurisdictions from passing their own gun control measures (so-called preemption laws). This means that the interest groups involved in trying to influence policy can focus their attention on the state legislatures rather than concerning themselves with a much larger number of city councils.

The debate in "shall-issue" states tends to take place over the issue of restrictions on where concealed firearms may be carried. Typically, permit holders are not allowed to carry into schools, government buildings, churches, or restaurants that serve alcohol. The NRA and other strong gun rights groups have lobbied diligently, with mixed success, in reducing the number of areas in which firearms may not be carried.

The debate over these laws hinges largely on whether one believes that they increase the safety of the carrier by giving her or him the opportunity to fend off would-be assailants and deter potential criminals because they know their intended victim might be armed, or whether one believes that they lead to an increase in the crime rate because more people own and carry guns.

This field has become one of the most hotly disputed in gun control research. Researchers such as Lott (2010) and Moody and Marvell (2009) claim that more lenient restrictions on carrying concealed firearms result in lower violent crime rates due to deterrence. Others, such as Ayres and Donohue (2009), argue that, at best, concealed carry has no impact on the violent crime rate, and, at worst, lenient laws might actually increase violent crime. While this debate may seem esoteric to those not enamored of disputes regarding the correct usage of quantitative studies and statistics beyond the understanding of most citizens who are not trained economists or statisticians, the debate has significant impact on those who make public policy.

In 2004, the National Academy of Sciences issued a report stating that the evidence in the field was ambiguous and that further research was necessary (see Wellford, Pepper, and Petrie). If the academy reconvened its panel today, it is unlikely they would reach a different conclusion.

Harry L. Wilson

See also: Cook, Philip J.; Defensive Gun Use (DGU); Gun Control; Hemenway, David; Kleck, Gary; Lott, John R., Jr.; More Guns, Less Crime Thesis; Preemption Laws; Right to Self-Defense, Philosophical Bases; Self-Defense, Legal Issues; Self-Defense, Reasons for Gun Use; Substitution Effects

Further Reading

Ayres, Ian, and John J. Donohue III. "More Guns, Less Crime Fails Again: The Latest Evidence from 1977–2006." *Econ Journal Watch* 6 (2009): 218–38.

Lott, John R., Jr. *More Guns, Less Crime: Understanding Crime and Gun Control Laws*. 3rd ed. Chicago: University of Chicago Press, 2010.

Moody, Carlisle, and Thomas Marvell. "The Debate on Shall-Issue Laws." *Econ Journal Watch* 5 (2008): 269–93.

Wellford, Charles E., John V. Pepper, and Carol V. Petrie. *Firearms and Violence: A Critical Review*. Washington, DC: National Research Council of the National Academies and National Academies Press, 2004. http://www.nap.edu/openbook.php?isbn=0309091241 (accessed July 18, 2011).

Congressional Voting Patterns on Gun Control

Members of the U.S. Congress demonstrate three predictable patterns of voting on gun control issues. First, regional voting differences are evident. Southern members of Congress are notably inclined to vote against gun regulation, whereas eastern members of Congress largely favor firearms regulation. Second, urban-rural differences are striking. Members of Congress representing rural constituents are much more likely to oppose gun control measures than are their colleagues who represent urban populations. Third, party cleavage is prominent. Gun control proposals traditionally find Democrats in support of firearms regulation and Republicans against it. Starting in the decade of the 2000s, however, more Democrats, especially at the national level, have embraced gun rights.

Regional Differences

Congressional decision making on gun control bills aligns closely with regional origins. This regional cleavage is most notable between the South and West and the rest of the country. Southern members of Congress are notably inclined to oppose firearms regulation. This is not surprising, since, relative to the East, private ownership of guns is highest in the South. And although midwesterners and westerners have similar levels of gun ownership, the proportion of multiple gun owners is substantially higher in the West (except for the Pacific coast states) and in the South than in the Midwest and East.

Reviewing the voting patterns for the Brady Act of 1993 and the Assault Weapons Ban of 1994 illustrates these regional differences. The Brady Act of 1993 required a background check and waiting period for gun purchasers, and the Assault Weapons Ban of 1994 prohibited the manufacture and importation of certain semiautomatic weapons. Southern members of Congress were relatively unreceptive to these gun control measures. About 42 percent of the southern representatives and 46 percent of the southern members of the Senate voted in favor of the Brady Bill. Southern congressional support of the Assault Weapons Ban of 1994 was even more anemic—with 34 percent of the southern representatives favoring the bill, and 31 percent of southern senators voting for its passage.

In sharp contrast to their southern colleagues, eastern members of Congress overwhelmingly supported these measures. A sizable 79 percent of eastern senators voted in favor of the Brady Bill, as did approximately 75 percent of eastern representatives. Support for the Assault Weapons Ban was similarly robust. Seventy-five percent of eastern senators approved the bill, and 70 percent of eastern representatives gave it the nod.

Among western and midwestern legislators, patterns of support for the Brady and assault weapons bills fell mostly between the solid backing from eastern members of Congress and the relatively weak support from southern congresspersons. Midwestern and western representatives were strikingly close in their voting preferences. Fifty-six percent of both groups assented to the Brady Bill. Fifty-two percent of the western House members voted for the assault weapons bill, and a nearly identical 51 percent of the midwestern House members approved the measure. But midwestern and western senators were not so homogeneous in their voting—largely because of party differences. Midwestern senators staked their positions closer to their eastern comrades, whereas western senators aligned more closely to their southern colleagues. A hefty 87 percent of midwestern senators favored the Brady Bill, while only 46 percent from the West did so. And, in contrast to the 42 percent of western senators' votes, 78 percent of

midwestern senators approved of the Assault Weapons Ban.

Urban-Rural Differences

Regional voting differences partly reflect urban-rural cleavages. Irrespective of regional and party differences, urban legislators are much more likely to favor gun control measures than are their rural counterparts. This urban-rural difference reflects distinct patterns of gun ownership. Studies consistently report that the incidence of gun ownership is highest in rural areas and lowest in cities. Many more guns are used for hunting and sporting purposes in rural areas than in cities, so rural citizens, not surprisingly, are much less amenable to gun regulation than are urbanites. Moreover, because cities tend to have high rates of violent crime compared to the rural United States, urban legislators strongly support gun control bills to try to keep guns out of the hands of criminals.

Examining the congressional votes on the Brady and Assault Weapons Ban bills reveals the urban-rural split over positions on gun control. Urban House members overwhelmingly supported both measures; rural representatives strongly opposed them. Nearly all urban House Democrats voted for the Brady and Assault Weapons Ban bills. And although urban House Republican support of the Brady and Assault Weapons Ban bills was far weaker (hovering just below 50 percent) than that of urban House Democrats, it was nearly double that of the rural House Republicans. The urban-rural voting differences on these bills also existed when controlling for regions of the country, although it was strongest in the South and West.

Party Differences

Political party differences in gun control politics increased markedly from the 1960s to the 1990s. In 1968, both the Republican and Democratic parties had platforms expressing some support for federal gun regulation. When the Gun Control Act of 1968 went to the floors of Congress for vote, overwhelming majorities of both parties in the House and Senate expressed their support for the bill. The little opposition to the bill that existed was similarly bipartisan, coming mainly from the South. By the 1990s, gun control had become a beacon to illuminate the difference between the Republican and Democratic parties. Gun control had become a polarizing issue in Congress, with Republicans predominantly opposing controls and Democrats favoring them. Congressional voting patterns on the Brady and Assault Weapons Ban bills reflected this divide. House Democratic support for the bills exceeded House Republican support by margins of 42 and 48 percentage points, respectively. These sizable party differences remained across all regions. Although support for gun control in the South was lower than in other regions, the difference between the party's yes-vote percentages on these measures was still greater than 30 percentage points in both the House and Senate.

The last major gun control measure to come to a vote in Congress was a package of gun regulations considered in 1999 in the aftermath of the Columbine High School shooting earlier that year. Voting in both chambers mostly followed party lines, with most Democrats in support and most Republicans opposed. In the 2000s, however, Democrats in Congress and around the country began to retreat from support for stronger gun laws, feeling that the issue had hurt them in the 2000 elections, and while Democrats as a whole were still seen as more pro-control, party differences on the issue shrunk.

Keith Rollin Eakins, with updates by
Robert J. Spitzer

See also: Assault Weapons Ban of 1994; Brady Handgun Violence Prevention Act (Brady Bill); Democratic Party and Gun Control; Firearms Owners' Protection Act of 1986; Gun Control; Gun Control Act of 1968; Gun Ownership; Republican Party and Gun Control; United States Congress and Gun Legislation

Further Reading

Davidson, Osha Gray. *Under Fire: The NRA and the Battle for Gun Control.* New York: Henry Holt, 1993.

Jelen, Ted G. "The Electoral Politics of Gun Ownership." In *The Changing Politics of Gun Control,* edited by John M. Bruce and Clyde Wilcox, 224–46. Lanham, MD: Rowman & Littlefield, 1998.

Lambert, Diana. "Trying to Stop the Craziness of This Business: Gun Control Groups." In *The Changing Politics of Gun Control,* edited by John M. Bruce and Clyde Wilcox, 172–95. Lanham, MD: Rowman & Littlefield, 1998.

Langbein, Laura I. "PACs, Lobbies, and Political Conflict: The Case of Gun Control." *Public Choice* 77 (1993): 551–72.

Patterson, Samuel C., and Keith R. Eakins. "Congress and Gun Control." In *The Changing Politics of Gun Control,* edited by John M. Bruce and Clyde Wilcox, 45–73. Lanham, MD: Rowman & Littlefield, 1998.

Spitzer, Robert J. *The Politics of Gun Control.* 5th ed. Boulder, CO: Paradigm Publishers, 2012.

Conservatism and Gun Control.

See Ideologies—Conservative and Liberal

Consumer Product Safety Laws

Consumer product safety policy aims to protect consumers from certain types of hazards. For firearms, product safety has been pursued by firearms industry standard setting; by tort lawsuit; by focused legislative statutes; and by administrative implementation of broad, general statutes.

Two controversies predominate: whether particular requirements that claim to promote safety actually do so, and whether administrators should have the power to ban guns without legislative consent. At the federal level, the Consumer Product Safety Commission is forbidden to regulate guns, precisely because of fears of indirect gun prohibition. In Massachusetts, the attorney general, claiming authority from a consumer fraud statute, imposed a wide variety of gun restrictions.

The original consumer safety regulations for American firearms were the standards set for the firearms industry by the Sporting Arms and Ammunition Manufacturers Institute (SAAMI), an industry trade association. SAAMI was created in 1926, pursuant to a request from the federal government. SAAMI has created over 700 standards, which are updated every five years. SAAMI standards are examined and reviewed by the American National Standards Institute (ANSI) and by the National Institute of Standards and Technology.

Although SAAMI standards are not legally binding, manufacturers who wish to obtain government contracts must meet the standards, since the FBI, the U.S. military, and many state or local government agencies often require that procured firearms meet SAAMI specifications.

In American law, the most traditional form of consumer safety protection is the right of a consumer to bring a tort lawsuit against the manufacturer of a defective product. Consumer lawsuits against manufacturers of defective guns (e.g., the gun's barrel explodes, or the gun discharges when accidentally dropped) have helped improve the quality of firearms sold and driven many

substandard guns off the market. In contrast to lawsuits brought against makers of properly functioning guns (e.g., lawsuits filed in 1998–1999 by big-city mayors), consumer lawsuits against genuinely defective guns are uncontroversial.

Legislatures may also choose to enact firearms laws designed to protect consumers (as opposed to firearm laws intended to prevent gun crime, the more common objective). For example, in 2000, Maryland enacted legislation requiring that all guns sold in the state beginning on January 1, 2003, be equipped with internal locking devices (Md. Ann. Code § 442c(d)). The Maryland law is an example of consumer legislation that is premised on the idea that many consumers are incapable of judging their own best interests. Currently, some guns have internal locks and some do not. The Maryland law assumes that consumers who choose guns without locks are making a mistake.

Some states have enacted bans on so-called junk guns or Saturday night specials. The bans are often touted as protecting consumers from unreliable guns, although this claim is not entirely consistent with the fact that all the gun bans contain an exemption allowing police possession of the banned guns. If the banned guns really were unreliable and dangerous to the user, then it is difficult to see why anyone would want the police to have such guns.

Another proposal, not currently enacted in any state, would require that all guns (or all handguns, or all self-loading handguns) have a "loaded indicator." Lawsuits have been brought against manufacturers of guns without a loaded indicator, although none of the lawsuits as of 2011 have succeeded.

As the name suggests, a "loaded indicator" shows that a firearm is loaded. Advocates of mandatory loaded indicators, such handguns that (1) did not have tamper-resistant serial numbers, (2) did not meet standards that the attorney general created for durability and for being dropped on hard surfaces, (3) did not have the types of locks that the attorney general thought best, (4) did not have heavy trigger pulls that would make the guns impossible for an average five-year-old child to fire, and (5) had a barrel less than three inches long. For the last requirement, the manufacturer could sell short-barreled guns as long as certain disclosures about accuracy were made (see 940 Code Mass. Regs. §§ 16.00 et seq.).

The American Shooting Sports Council (a trade association, which later merged with the National Shooting Sports Foundation) filed suit, claiming that the Massachusetts law against "unfair and deceptive trade practice" did not give the attorney general the authority to invent a detailed code of gun manufacture. The lawsuit also argued that particular details of the attorney general's regulations were illogical, nearly impossible to meet, or counterproductive. The attorney general lost in the trial court but won in the Massachusetts Supreme Court (*American Shooting Sports Council, Inc. v. Attorney General*, 711 N.E.2d 899 (Mass. 1999)). The Massachusetts legislature mooted the issue by enacting a law granting the attorney general the power to create the regulations he had created. When the regulations initially went into effect in Massachusetts, the result was to bar the sale of all handguns except those made by Smith & Wesson, which is based in Springfield, Massachusetts.

After the 2000 election of George W. Bush reduced the prospects for broad new federal gun controls, the Center to Prevent Handgun Violence (CPHV)—which later changed its name to the Brady Campaign to Prevent Gun Violence—urged state attorneys general to follow the lead of the Massachusetts attorney general. The CPHV suggested that 20 states had consumer protection laws that could be used to impose gun controls.

Another consumer-related issue bears not only on firearms themselves but on their advertising. In 1996, the CPHV filed a petition (consisting of a request letter and supporting documentation) with the Federal Trade Commission (FTC) asking the FTC to ban gun advertising that encourages defensive gun ownership. A similar petition was filed by Professors Teret and Vernick in conjunction with Dr. Garen Wintemute of the University of California. The CPHV petition asked that defensive gun ads be banned as "deceptive" because gun ownership does not increase safety in the home but in fact is very dangerous.

Under current FTC policy, an advertisement is "unfair" if it causes "substantial injury to consumers which is not reasonably avoidable by consumers themselves and not outweighed by countervailing benefits to consumers or to competition." The CPHV argued that the defensive gun advertisements are unfair because they encourage people to own guns for protection. Gun ownership leads to injuries and deaths, the CPHV pointed out. There are no countervailing benefits, the organization argued, since defensive gun use is very rare.

Opponents of the advertising ban argued that defensive gun ownership does increase safety among lawful gun owners; that harm from guns is "reasonably avoidable by consumers themselves" because consumers can obey gun safety rules and laws against committing gun crimes; and that the FTC should not censor speech on a controversial policy topic. The FTC rejected the request to restrict firearms advertising.

David B. Kopel

See also: Bureau of Alcohol, Tobacco, Firearms and Explosives (ATF); Lawsuits against Gun Manufacturers; Loaded-Chamber Indicator; Massachusetts Gun Law; National Instant Criminal Background Check System; Saturday Night Specials; Smart Guns; Sporting Arms and Ammunition Manufacturers' Institute (SAAMI)

Further Reading

Bejar, Benjamin. "Wielding the Consumer Protection Shield: Sensible Handgun Regulation in Massachusetts: A Paradigm for a National Model." *Boston University Public Interest Law Journal* 7 (1998): 59–91.

Brady Campaign to Prevent Gun Violence. "How State Attorneys General Can Act Now to Save Lives." January 2001. http://www.bradycenter.org/xshare/pdf/reports/targetingsafety.pdf (accessed January 14, 2011).

Consumer Product Safety Commission. "PSC, Master Lock Co. Announce Recall to Replace Gun Locks." Revised April 28, 2004. http://www.cpsc.gov/cpscpub/prerel/prhtml00/00149.html (accessed January 14, 2011).

Dobray, Debra, and Arthur J. Waldrop. "Regulating Handgun Advertising Aimed at Women." *Whittier Law Review* 12 (1991): 113–29.

Kopel, David B. "Treating Guns like Consumer Products." *University of Pennsylvania Law Review* 148 (2000): 1213–46.

Sporting Arms and Ammunition Manufacturers Institute. http://www.saami.org/ (accessed January 14, 2011).

Vernick, Jon S., and Stephen P. Teret. "Public Health Approach to Regulating Firearms as Consumer Products." *University of Pennsylvania Law Review* 148 (2000): 1193–1212.

Violence Policy Center. "The Firearms Safety and Consumer Protection Act: To Regulate the Manufacture and Safety of Firearms." http://www.vpc.org/fact_sht/torkenfs.htm (accessed January 14, 2011).

Consumer Protection Regulations on Handgun Safety. *See* Massachusetts Gun Law

Conyers, John (1929–)

John Conyers (D-MI) has served in the House of Representatives since 1965. He is the second-most senior member of the House. From 1989 to 1994, he chaired the House Committee on Government Operations (now the Committee on Oversight and Reform). For the 110th and 111th Congresses, he also chaired the Committee on the Judiciary. Conyers has emerged as one of the leading advocates of gun control in the House. He helped found the Congressional Black Caucus and is generally considered to be dean of the group.

After a four-year stint in the army in Korea in the early 1950s, Conyers received a law degree in 1958. He served for three years as legislative assistant to John Dingell and was active in civil rights and labor groups before he won a seat in the House as part of the Democratic landslide of 1964, representing northern Detroit. Conyers was one of only a handful of African Americans in Congress in the 1960s, and was a vocal opponent of the Vietnam War and a supporter of a guaranteed income and racial reparations. He has one of the most liberal voting records in Congress—often receiving ratings of 100 from the liberal political organization Americans for Democratic Action and 0 from the American Conservative Union. His greatest visibility came during the Judiciary Committee hearings on the impeachment of President Bill Clinton. As ranking minority member of the committee, Conyers presented the Democratic arguments clearly and with a subtle sense of humor.

Conyers has been active in the area of criminal justice. He introduced the Hate

Harry Frank Guggenheim Foundation supported his study of stolen-gun markets. In 1994, the National Institute of Justice provided a grant to the Police Foundation for a study of guns in the United States. Cook and Jens Ludwig (1997) carried out the National Survey of Private Ownership of Firearms (NSPOF), the most comprehensive overview of gun inventory and gun ownership in the country. The survey generated numerous important findings related to the size, composition, and ownership of the nation's gun inventory; the methods of and reasons for firearm acquisition; the storage and carrying of guns; and DGUs.

In 1995, Cook chaired a symposium sponsored by the Guggenheim Foundation on youth violence. The symposium focused on the role of guns in homicides, especially among young inner-city men. The Duke University School of Law journal *Law and Contemporary Problems* published the conference papers in 1996 under the title *Kids, Guns, and Public Policy*. Cook edited the issue and emphasized that, although homicide rates in general had been falling, those for youths had greatly increased, and all of that increase had been due to guns.

Cook's research on the effects of gun availability on robberies and murders committed during robberies shed light on the "instrumentality effect," the idea that the instrument used in a crime influences whether the crime is lethal. Cook's research on robbery showed that robbers who chose to use firearms in committing their crime did so to ensure control and compliance on the part of their victims. When robbers used guns, there was less likely to be a physical attack; but if there was a physical attack, the victims were more likely to be killed. In fact, "the case-fatality rate for gun robbery is three times as high as for robberies with knives and ten times as high for robberies with other weapons" (Cook and Ludwig 2001, 35).

Cook (1979) also studied the 50 largest cities in the United States to find out whether gun availability influences crime. He found that in cities with low gun ownership rates, the percentage of homicides and suicides involving guns is low. In cities with many guns, robbers are more likely to use guns in their crimes, and the robberies are more likely to be lethal than in cities with fewer guns.

Cook has also made important contributions to the discussion of DGUs, taking issue with Kleck and Gertz's estimate of 2.5 million DGUs annually (Kleck 1997; Kleck and Gertz 1995). Kleck and Gertz argue that there are more DGUs than crimes committed with handguns. If true, this might weaken arguments for gun control, although Cook points out that, aside from the dispute over the numbers, it is not clear that all these DGUs add to public safety. Cook and his colleagues refer to the estimate of 2.5 million DGUs as "the gun debate's new mythical number" (Cook, Ludwig, and Hemenway 1997). The National Crime Victimization Survey (NCVS) generates an estimate of about 100,000 DGUs a year. Cook and his colleagues suggest that the higher estimate is at least partly due to the likelihood of having many more "false positives"—those who did not use a gun for self-defense during the period studied but say that they did—than "false negatives"—those who did use a gun for self-defense but did not report it (Cook and Ludwig 2001; Cook, Ludwig, and Hemenway 1997; Hemenway 1997).

Cook and Ludwig's own National Survey of Private Ownership of Firearms (NSPOF) generates an estimate of about 1.5 million DGUs. Cook and Ludwig suggest that this figure is an overestimate and that accurate estimates of DGUs are unlikely to emerge from such large sample surveys because of the likelihood of false positives outweighing false negatives. Pro-gun groups have gleefully seized on Cook and Ludwig's suggestion that their own survey overestimated DGUs and argued that the results prove Kleck and Gertz's estimate. In fact, Cook and Ludwig exercise sound methodological judgment in reaching their cautious conclusions.

Sociologist Tom Smith (1997) has urged a "truce in the DGU war," arguing that the Kleck and Gertz estimate of 2.5 million DGUs annually is too high and that the NCVS estimate of about 100,000 DGUs is too low. He suggests a possible figure of 1,210,000 DGUs per year. Smith argues that the debate would benefit from more data and less speculation.

In a major, controversial contribution to thinking about gun policy, Cook and Ludwig have estimated the net costs of gun violence in the United States (Cook and Ludwig 2001). Rather than focusing only on the costs of handgun violence in terms of the medical costs and lost productivity associated with gun injuries and deaths, Cook and Ludwig develop an economic-cost framework to calculate the *full* or *real* costs of handgun violence. Their goal is "to document how gun violence reduces the quality of life for everyone in America" (Cook and Ludwig 2001, viii), and they estimate that gun violence costs about $100 billion. They derive most of this estimate, which is much higher than most such figures, from a "contingent-valuation" survey. The National Opinion Research Center (NORC) of the University of Chicago asked the questions in its 1998 General Social Survey (GSS). The survey asked respondents what they would pay to reduce gun crime in their communities. Extrapolating from those figures, Cook and Ludwig reached an estimated cost of $80 billion a year, to which they added

additional costs to arrive at the $100 billion figure. This research broadens the debate over gun violence and gun control by emphasizing that all Americans are potential victims of gun violence.

Subsequently, Ludwig and Cook edited *Evaluating Gun Policy: Effects on Crime and Violence* (2003). This collection examines gun policy and research from a variety of perspectives and is useful for anyone who wishes to better understand gun policy.

Walter F. Carroll

See also: Acquisition of Guns; Availability of Guns, Effects on Crime; Black Market for Firearms; Crime and Gun Use; Defensive Gun Use (DGU); General Social Survey (GSS); Guggenheim Foundation, Harry Frank; Gun Ownership; Gun Violence as a Public Health Problem; Kleck, Gary; Lethality Effect of Guns; Ludwig, Jens Otto; National Crime Victimization Survey (NCVS); National Institute of Justice (NIJ); Weapons Instrumentality Effect; Zimring, Franklin

Further Reading

Bijlefeld, Marjolijn. "Philip J. Cook." In *People for and against Gun Control: A Biographical Reference*, edited by Marjolijn Bijlefeld, 64–68. Westport, CT: Greenwood Press, 1999.

Cook, Philip J. "The Effect of Gun Availability on Robbery and Robbery Murder: A Cross-Section Study of Fifty Cities." *Policy Studies Review Annual* 3 (1979): 743–81.

Cook, Philip J. "Kids, Guns, and Public Policy." *Law and Contemporary Problems* 59 (1996): 1–4.

Cook, Philip J., and Jens Ludwig. "Guns in America: National Survey on Private Ownership and Use of Firearms." *National Institute of Justice Research in Brief*. Washington, DC: U.S. Department of Justice, National Institute of Justice, May 1997. http://www.ncjrs.gov/pdffiles/165476.pdf (accessed March 7, 2011).

Cook, Philip J., and Jens Ludwig. *Gun Violence: The Real Costs*. New York: Oxford University Press, 2000.

Cook, Philip J., Jens Ludwig, and David Hemenway. "The Gun Debate's New Mythical Number: How Many Defensive Gun Uses per Year?" *Journal of Policy Analysis and Management* 16 (1997): 463–69. http://home.uchicago.edu/~ludwigj/papers/JPAM_Cook_Ludwig_Hemenway_2007.pdf (accessed March 7, 2011).

Cook, Philip J., Mark H. Moore, and Anthony A. Braga. "Gun Control." In *Crime: Public Policies for Crime Control*, edited by James Q. Wilson and Joan Petersilia, 2nd ed., 291–330. San Francisco: ICS Press, 2002.

Kleck, Gary. *Targeting Guns: Firearms and Their Control*. Hawthorne, NY: Aldine de Gruyter, 1997.

Kleck, Gary, and Marc Gertz. "Armed Resistance to Crime: The Prevalence and Nature of Self-Defense with a Gun." *Journal of Criminal Law and Criminology* 86 (1995): 150–87.

Ludwig, Jens, and Philip J. Cook, eds. *Evaluating Gun Policy: Effects on Crime and Violence*. Washington, DC: Brookings Institution, 2003.

Smith, Tom. "A Call for a Truce in the DGU War." *Journal of Criminal Law and Criminology* 87 (1997): 1462–69.

Cooling-Off Periods. *See* Waiting Periods

Cop Killer Bullets. *See* Armor-Piercing Ammunition

Cornell, Saul (1960–)

Saul Cornell is the Paul and Diane Guenther Chair in American History at Fordham University and author of *A Well-Regulated Militia: The Founding Fathers and the Origins of Gun Control in America* (2006), which won the 2006 Langum Prize for Legal History.

He holds a PhD (1989) in history from the University of Pennsylvania, and his dissertation on antifederalist thought was the basis for his first book, *The Other Founders: Anti-Federalism and the Dissenting Tradition in America, 1788–1828* (1999) which won the 2001 Cox Book Prize from the Society of the Cincinnati. His work on the antifederalists drew him into the debate over the original meaning of the Second Amendment, finding it odd that scholars would "lavish so much attention on the losing side's thoughts in the original struggle over the Constitution" (Cornell 2006, x).

Professor Cornell's contribution to the originalist debate over the Second Amendment is his assertion that the Founders understood the "right to bear arms" to be civic in nature. Finding fault with both the individual and collective-right models that have dominated scholarship since the 1980s, Cornell argues that individuals needed the right to keep and bear arms to fulfill their legal obligation to provide for the common defense by serving in a well-regulated militia. Cornell has advocated for the civic rights model in numerous articles, essays, lectures, and conference papers. He has used his expertise to coauthor *amicus* briefs for *District of Columbia v. Heller* and *McDonald v. City of Chicago*, and to consult for many other briefs. He has authored several articles on the *Heller* decision, criticizing the Court's historical methodology and reliance on plain-meaning originalism. Cornell's civic rights model has generally been well received in the academic community but has drawn sharp criticism from legal scholars. While political scientist Robert J. Spitzer believes that Cornell "argues persuasively and brilliantly that civic obligation was the essence of the Second Amendment" (2006, 455), senior NRA attorney David T. Hardy asserts that Cornell offers "a partial, selective, and often unreliable account of the development of the American right to arms" (2007, 1242).

In 2002, with a $400 000 grant from the Joyce Foundation, Cornell founded and served as director of the Second Amendment Research Center (SARC), housed at the John Glenn Institute for Public Policy at the Ohio State University. SARC maintained a comprehensive digital archive of Second Amendment articles written by scholars with full-time academic affiliations, compiled militia laws from the early republic, and developed materials for classroom use. The Center cosponsored several symposia including one with the Fordham University School of Law in the fall of 2004 titled, "The Second Amendment and the Future of Gun Regulation: Historical, Legal, Policy and Cultural Perspectives." SARC abandoned its website after falling victim to repeated attacks by hackers, and ceased operation after its funding expired. Cornell eventually left Ohio State for Fordham University and has continued to publish on early American constitutional topics.

Nathan Kozuskanich

See also: *District of Columbia v. Heller*; *McDonald v. City of Chicago*; Second Amendment

Further Reading

Cornell, Saul. "Originalism on Trial: The Use and Abuse of History in *District of Columbia v. Heller*." *Ohio State Law Journal* 69 (2008): 625–40

Cornell, Saul. *A Well-Regulated Militia: The Founding Fathers and the Origins of Gun Control in America*. Oxford: Oxford University Press, 2006.

Cornell, Saul, and Nathan DeDino. "Well Regulated: The Early American Origins of Gun Control." *Fordham Law Review* 73 (2004): 487–528.

Hardy, David T. "Review of *A Well-Regulated Militia*." *William and Mary Bill of Rights Journal* 15 (2007): 1237–84.

Spitzer, Robert J. "Review of *A Well-Regulated Militia*." *American Journal of Legal History* 48 (2006): 454–55.

Corporation for the Promotion of Rifle Practice and Firearms Safety. *See* National Board for the Promotion of Rifle Practice

Cottrol, Robert J. (1949–)

Robert J. Cottrol is the Harold Paul Green Research Professor of Law at George Washington University (GWU). He is also professor of law, of history, and of sociology. Cottrol earned his BA and PhD from Yale University, and his JD from Georgetown Law School. He joined the law faculty at GWU in 1995. Cottrol's research focuses on race relations in the contexts of U.S. legal history and criminal law. He edited the much-cited *Gun Control and the Constitution: Sources and Explorations on the Second Amendment* (1993). Cottrol's studies have led him to endorse background checks for firearms purchases to screen out those who should not own a gun—most importantly, convicted felons. However he also argues that guns are a tool for self-defense and that the ordinary citizen should have ready access to them. In particular, Cottrol contends that African Americans and other minorities need to possess guns as a countervailing power to a racist society—a society that has produced the likes of the Ku Klux Klan and police forces that have been known to treat minorities with extreme and undue harshness.

Currently, gun rights and gun control advocacy groups do not work together on any aspect of the pressing social problem of gun violence in the United States. Cottrol believes this situation needs rectification and that there are several areas in which the two types of advocacy groups could profitably work together, especially in developing more creative means of preventing guns from ending up in the hands of dangerous individuals. Cottrol's reasonableness is evident in one of his more recent writings on guns and the right to bear arms. In this coauthored piece, "Public Safety and the Right to Bear Arms" (Cottrol and Diamond 2008), although clearly favoring an individual-rights interpretation of the Second Amendment, the authors present a relatively even-handed overview of the topic.

Cottrol has published in the *Yale Law Journal*, *Georgetown Law Review*, *American Journal of Legal History*, and the *Law and Society Review*. His books include *The Afro-Yankees: Providence's Black Community in the Antebellum Era* (1983) and his edited volume *From African to Yankee: Narratives of Slavery and Freedom in Antebellum New England* (1998).

Gregg Lee Carter and Walter F. Carroll

See also: Black Codes; Racism and Gun Control; Second Amendment

Further Reading

Carter, Gregg Lee. *Gun Control in the United States: A Reference Handbook*. Santa Barbara, CA: ABC-CLIO, 2006.

Cottroll, Robert J. *Gun Control and the Constitution: Sources and Explorations on the Second Amendment*. New York: Garland, 1993.

Cottroll, Robert J. "The Second Amendment: Toward an Afro-Americanist Reconsideration." *Georgetown Law Journal* 80 (1991): 309–61. http://www.constitution.org/2ll/2ndschol/12cd-r.pdf (accessed October 14, 2011).

Cottroll, Robert J., and Raymond T. Diamond. "Never Intended to Be Applied to the White Population: Firearms Regulation and Racial Disparity—the Redeemed South's Legacy to a National Jurisprudence?" *Chicago-Kent Law Review* 70 (1995): 1307–35. http://www.constitution.org/2ll/2ndschol/11cd-reg.pdf (accessed October 14, 2011).

Council for Responsible Firearms Policy. *See* National Council for Responsible Firearms Policy

Cowboy Action Shooting (CAS)

Participants in Cowboy Action Shooting (CAS) wear costumes inspired by the Old West and shoot replica or vintage firearms in events organized according to a specific set of rules established by the Single Action Shooting Society (SASS). Similar to tactical shooting exercises on the one hand and historical reenactments on the other, CAS imitates real-life shooting situations and aims for historical accuracy. However, unlike most other simulations, Cowboy Action shooters use live ammunition—heavy loads and lots of them—in their shooting events. CAS is a combination of both competitive and recreational shooting. By the close of the twentieth century, it had become the fastest-growing outdoor shooting sport in the United States, popular among both men and women.

Participants in CAS span all walks of life and income levels. What brings them together is a common interest in the history and traditions of the American West: what SASS refers to as "The Spirit of the Game." They wear accurate reproductions of Old West attire in fabrics available in the nineteenth century (no synthetics or vinyl) and authentic styles (most women eschew pants for skirts and bustles). Some wear vintage clothes and shoot antique guns. Most of the

Sam Elliott (as Virgil Earp) and Kurt Russell (as Wyatt Earp) in an archetypal cowboy shootout scene from the 1993 film *Tombstone*. (Photofest)

guns used, however, are replicas of firearms produced before 1900: single-action revolvers, black-powder or lever-action rifles, and pump- or lever-action shotguns. The only concession to modernity is that all shooters must wear eye and ear protection.

Shooters are required to adopt aliases, some of which recall heroic western figures or types (Judge Roy Bean, Wyatt Earp, Bounty Hunter), while others are clever plays on frontier themes (Aimless Annie, Buck Roo, Chili King), and still others on participants' real-life identities (a biochemist named "Lady Doc," an attorney named "Lilly Lawless"). They get together for shooting matches in which the various tests of skill pitting shooters against wooden or steel targets conform to scenarios based on famous incidents of western history or in classic western films (stagecoach robberies, saloon shootouts, and shooting from horseback). Originally, the "horses" were strictly

mechanical, but now there are also Cowboy Mounted Shooting competitions using the real thing. Prizes are awarded in different shooting classes, as well as for the best costumes; to qualify for the costume competition, one must be an active shooter.

SASS, the largest association of CAS shooters, celebrated its 30th anniversary in 2011. Its global membership is expected to reach 100,000 in 2012. As of 2011, there were 674 affiliated clubs in all 50 states as well as Canada, Australia, New Zealand, South Africa, and several European nations. Club presidents are called territorial governors, and clubs bear names like the Alamo Moderators, the Hole in the Wall Gang, and Doc Holliday's Immortals. At shooting matches, groups of contestants are organized into posses. Major CAS shooting events have evocative names like Helldorado, Range War, and Mule Camp. The world championship CAS event is End of Trail, held annually in June at SASS's national headquarters in Edgewood, New Mexico.

Mary Zeiss Stange

See also: Civil War Reenactments; Recreational Uses of Guns; Tactical Training

Further Reading

Anderson, Hunter Scott. *The Top Shooter's Guide to Cowboy Action Shooting*. Iola, WI: Krause Publications, 2000.

Laws, Susan. *Cowgirl Action Shooting*. Wimberly, TX: Aimless Annie Enterprises, 2000.

Taffin, John. *Action Shooting: Cowboy Style*. Iola, WI: Krause Publications, 1999.

Cowtowns and Gun Violence. *See* Boomtowns, Cowtowns, and Gun Violence

Cox v. Wood (1918)

In *Cox v. Wood* (247 U.S. 3 (1918)), the Supreme Court affirmed that the federal government may conscript military-eligible men to serve in the American military when sent to fight outside of the borders of the United States under its constitutional powers of war, including the calling up of the militia. The appellant Cox, drafted to serve in the military during World War I, argued that, while the government had the right to conscript him for military service, it did not have the right to send him abroad for military service, asserting that militia service as stipulated in Article I, Section 8, of the U.S. Constitution is limited to the three purposes for militias set out in the section: "To execute the laws of the Union, suppress insurrections, and repel invasions." Since military service in a foreign country is not among the listed purposes of militias, the appellant argued, he was entitled to a

discharge from service. This case was one of several that challenged the constitutionality of aspects of the military draft system instituted when the United States entered World War I in 1917.

Citing its own recent ruling in the *Selective Draft Law Cases* (1918), the court sided with the government, saying that Congress's powers to declare war and raise and support a military were not constrained by the conditions for militias described in Article I, Section 8. As the court concluded, "the power to call for military duty under the authority to declare war and raise armies and the duty of the citizen to serve when called were coterminous with the constitutional grant from which the authority was derived, and knew no limit deduced from a separate and, for the purpose of the war power, wholly incidental, if not irrelevant and subordinate, provision concerning the militia found in the Constitution." Thus, the federal government's control over militia service coincided with its control over other aspects of power over the military and war-related matters.

Robert J. Spitzer

See also: Militias; National Guard

Further Reading

Spitzer, Robert J. *Gun Control: A Documentary and Reference Guide*. Westport, CT: Greenwood Press, 2009.

Crime and Gun Availability. *See* Availability of Guns, Effects on Crime

Crime and Gun Use

Throughout its history, the United States has had a relatively high rate of violent crime compared with other developed nations. Initially, the inexpensiveness and widespread availability of guns were major contributing factors to crime. In addition, disadvantaged groups in society traditionally had limited access to firearms and were therefore more often the victims of violent crime and intimidation. Gun use as a factor in committing crimes peaked in the 1980s and has steadily declined.

During the early era of colonization in North America, effective law enforcement was rare. Law enforcement was the responsibility of local sheriffs recruited from the community. If there were large bands of bandits, the militia would be called out. The result of all this was that law enforcement was reactive, though if criminals were caught, justice was often severe.

This pattern of crime and gun use continued as the frontier moved west. The massive influx of people into California in the wake of the discovery of gold in 1849 led to a dramatic rise in crime as people fought over claims to land. Strikingly, the homicide rate in the region tripled between 1849 and 1850. In the aftermath of the Civil War, there was a corresponding rise in crime and gun use in the West as renewed waves of settlers moved westward, many carrying the firearms that they had used during the war. The influx of well-armed people and little effective law enforcement in the West led to increases in a variety of crimes and ushered in the era of the gunfight. Bands of well-organized and armed bandits robbed trains and banks. Many of these groups, including the James Gang, were comprised of veterans of the Civil War who had served in irregular guerilla units such as Quantrill's Raiders. Meanwhile, the gunfight became a relatively common means for men to settle disputes, though the practice was not as widespread as they were portrayed in popular fiction.

The closing of the frontier in the 1890s and the subsequent increase in both the scale and scope of law enforcement brought a decline in gun-related crimes in the West. However, large-scale immigration in the East and the extreme poverty faced by many immigrants drove crime rates higher in the East, although gun use was not as widespread as it was in the West. In addition, the municipal police forces of the urban areas of the East were more efficient than their counterparts in the South and West.

The onset of Prohibition in 1920 led to the outbreak of another era of serious gun crime. Organized crime gangs dominated the illegal procurement and sale of alcohol. The spread of speakeasies (illegal bars that served alcohol) brought enormous profits to organized crime. Mobsters such as Al Capone built immense empires (Capone's organization brought in an estimated $60 million per year). The rise of the Mafia led to bitter and often bloody turf wars over control of territory and markets. During the 1920s, in Chicago alone, there were 500 Mafia-related murders. Crimes such as racketeering and extortion also rose. In the aftermath of World War I, many former servicemen had experience with automatic weapons. The introduction of such firearms as the Thompson submachine gun and automatic handguns, including the .45-caliber Colt Model 1911A, exacerbated the violence.

Other factors also influenced crime and gun use during the 1920s and 1930s. The proliferation of automobiles increased the mobility of criminals. The onset of the Great Depression in 1929 added vast numbers of Americans to the unemployment rolls, with 3 million Americans out of work by 1930. With bank and business failures, the number of homeless people increased dramatically. Petty theft, mainly of food and other sundries, grew more common, as did more serious crime, especially bank robberies. The widespread poverty and despair provoked a backlash against disadvantaged groups in the United States, including recent immigrants and African Americans. Throughout the nation, hate groups such as the Ku Klux Klan grew dramatically during the late 1920s and the 1930s. In addition, the number of hate crimes, including lynchings, tripled. During the 1920s and 1930s, the nation's homicide rate rose to a level that would not be seen again until the 1980s.

The advent of World War II led to a drop in violent crime, and the prosperity of the 1950s continued this trend. However, racial violence continued throughout the South as the civil rights movement gained momentum and white supremacists sought to intimidate the pro-integrationists. Crime rates in the United States increased in the early 1960s, for despite the affluence of the period, a significant proportion of the population lived below the poverty line. The 1960 census showed that 25 percent of the nation, or about 40 million Americans, were poor.

As the nation's social fabric began to come apart in the 1960s, drug use increased, the counterculture grew, and crime rose dramatically. This last trend was exacerbated by the influx of relatively inexpensive handguns known as Saturday night specials. Violent race riots in major cities such as Detroit, Los Angeles, and Newark left scores dead and hundreds injured from gunshots. In the South, political violence related to the civil rights movement continued, while the assassinations of John F. Kennedy in 1963, Martin Luther King Jr. in 1968, and Robert F. Kennedy in 1968 brought gun violence to the forefront of the public's attention. Meanwhile, groups from both the political left and right began to engage in antigovernment activities, including bombings of public buildings and bank robberies. The rise in gun crime led Congress to enact the nation's

first federal firearm control law in over three decades, the Gun Control Act of 1968.

Throughout the 1970s, crime continued to increase as drug use expanded, especially in urban areas. Furthermore, there were turf wars between organized crime organizations and a rise in gang-related violence. The introduction of a powerful new form of cocaine, known as crack, accelerated the violence as gangs fought each other for control of the market. Many police forces were unprepared to deal with the violence and increased gun use that was engendered by the spread of crack. Between 1985 and 1991, homicides among African American males under the age of 20 doubled, while overall homicide rates involving the use of a gun climbed by 71 percent. Between 1960 and 2000, 1 million Americans died from firearms (including in homicides, suicides, and accidental shootings). The rise in gun violence corresponded with the dramatic increase in guns. By 2000, Americans owned an estimated 200 million guns. This figure included an estimated 40 million handguns that had been produced since 1973. The guns used in crimes came from a variety of sources, but the majority were purchased legally. According to a 1991 survey by the Justice Department, 10 percent of guns used in crimes were stolen, while 28 percent were bought or acquired illegally (the remainder were purchased through legitimate sources).

The rates of gun use in nonfatal crimes, such as theft, sexual assault, and aggravated assault, also increased dramatically during the late 1980s. About one-third of these crimes were committed by perpetrators using firearms. In comparison, approximately 70 percent of homicides were committed with firearms. Handguns were the weapons of choice because they were easy to conceal and relatively inexpensive. Handguns accounted for

86 percent of all gun-related crimes (3 percent were perpetrated with rifles, 5 percent with shotguns, and 5 percent with undetermined types of firearms). In 1992, a record 931,000 crimes were committed with handguns.

After the surge in gun violence during the late 1980s, gun crime began to decline significantly in the 1990s. Between 1993 and 2000, crimes perpetrated with firearms declined by almost 40 percent. This drop was the result of a variety of factors. First, tougher sentencing laws were enacted by a number of states and the federal government. These new measures expanded the length of prison time for those convicted of violent crime. By 2000, the nation's prison population had expanded to 1.3 million people, four times the number of inmates in 1980. Second, new legislation made it more difficult to obtain guns. The Brady Handgun Violence Prevention Act, which went into effect in 1994, placed limitations on people's access to guns. The law required background checks and waiting periods before handguns could be purchased. In addition, the 1994 Violent Crime Enforcement Act made the possession of semiautomatic assault weapons manufactured after the act illegal. Third, the maturation of the crack cocaine market and the growing popularity of other illicit drugs caused a decrease in the gun violence related to the sale and importation of illicit drugs. Fourth, new methods of policing have improved the efficiency of law enforcement. Programs such as community policing have improved relations between law enforcement and the communities it serves, while buyback programs have had minor success in reducing the number of weapons available. Fifth, the economic expansion of the 1990s brought more people into the workforce and, like other periods of economic expansion, led to a general decrease in the crime rate. While the 1990s witnessed a general decline in gun crime, this decline was not uniform. Specific segments of the nation continued to experience high rates of gun violence. This was especially true of African American and Hispanic males under the age of 20.

In the 2000s, gun crimes initially declined in overall terms, before stabilizing in 2004–2005. By 2009, the firearm crime rate had fallen to 1.4 victims per 1,000 people, down from 5.9 per 1,000 in 1993 and 2.4 per 1,000 in 2000. Meanwhile, that year, gun crimes fell to 8 percent of all violent crimes, down from 11 percent in 1993, but up from 7 percent in 2000. Guns were most often used in robberies. In 2004, the ban on assault weapons was allowed to expire. The number of guns held by private citizens increased during the 2000s, with a significant rise following the election of Barack Obama as president in 2008 (this rise was attributable to concerns that gun ownership would be restricted). By 2010, 39 percent of all U.S. homes had a firearm on the premises (and only 2 percent of respondents said they had a gun, but not kept at home), and there were more than 250 million privately owned guns (*Sourcebook of Criminal Justice Statistics* 2011). A number of spectacular gun crimes, including the 2007 Virginia Tech massacre, which left 32 dead, refocused attention on gun use during violent crimes.

Tom Lansford

See also: African Americans and Gun Violence; Assault Weapons Ban of 1994; Availability of Guns, Effects on Crime; Black Market for Firearms; Brady Handgun Violence Prevention Act (Brady Bill); Concealed Weapons Laws; Drive-by Shootings; Drugs, Crime, and Guns: United States; Federal Firearms Act of 1938 (Public Law No. 75-785); Felons and Gun Control; Frontier Violence; Gun Buyback Programs; Gun Violence as a

Public Health Problem; Ku Klux Klan; National Firearms Act of 1934; Vigilantism; Virginia Tech Massacre

Further Reading

Carter, Gregg Lee. *The Gun Control Movement*. New York: Twayne Publishers, 1997.

Cook, Philip J., and Jens Ludwig. *Gun Violence: The Real Costs*. New York: Oxford University Press, 2000.

DeConde, Alexander. *Gun Violence in America: The Struggle for Control*. Boston: Northeastern University Press, 2001.

Kleck, Gary, and Don B. Kates. *Armed: New Perspectives on Gun Control*. Amherst, NY: Prometheus Books, 2001.

Miller, Maryann. *Drugs and Gun Violence*. New York: Rosen Publishing Group, 1995.

"Table 2.59.2010: Respondents Reporting Having a Gun in their Home or on Property (United States, Selected Years 1959–2010)." *Sourcebook of Criminal Justice Statistics.* 2011. http://www.albany.edu/sourcebook/tost_2.html#2_ak (accessed June 25, 2011).

U.S. Department of Justice. *National Crime Victimization Survey, 2008*. Washington, DC: Government Printing Office, 2009. http://www.bjs.gov/content/pub/pdf/cv08.pdf (accessed December 28, 2011).

Cross-National Comparisons of Gun Violence. *See* Victimization from Gun Violence

D

Defense of Habitation Law. *See* Castle Doctrine

Defensive Gun Use (DGU)

Defensive gun use is the use of a firearm for defensive purposes against an immediate threat. The "use" may involve firing the gun, but more commonly it amounts to simply brandishing a gun. Scholarly research suggests that the overwhelming majority of DGUs are "successful"—although whether such successes are morally legitimate is a subject of controversy. There is a heated dispute about how many DGUs take place in the United States annually; Kleck's (1997) National Self-Defense Survey suggests 2.5 million or more, whereas the National Opinion Research Center (Smith 1997) estimates that a figure of several hundred thousand is more plausible.

Defensive gun use should be distinguished from the deterrent effects of firearm ownership. DGUs involve crimes in progress, whereas deterrence involves crimes that are never attempted because the criminal fears that the victim might be armed. Thus, Lott's *More Guns, Less Crime* (2000), which finds that violent crime drops 5–8 percent and that mass murders in public places drop about 90 percent after the enactment of "shall-issue" handgun carry licensing laws, is not really part of the DGU debate, since Lott's research involves deterrence much more than the thwarting of attempted crimes.

The National Crime Victimization Survey (NCVS) is conducted annually by the U.S. government to estimate the prevalence of crime and to study related matters. Examining survey results from 1979 to 1985, Kleck (1997) found that respondents who reported using a firearm to resist a violent crime were injured less often than were people who resisted by other means or who did not resist at all.

The lowest crime completion rates were found when the victim used a firearm. For example, when robbery victims did not resist, the robbery succeeded 88 percent of the time, and the victim was injured 25 percent of the time. If the victim resisted with a gun, the robbery success rate fell to 30 percent and the victim injury rate to 17 percent. In less than 1 percent of DGUs did the criminal take the gun away from the victim. Other forms of resistance (e.g., shouting for help or using a weapon other than a firearm) had crime success rates somewhere in between the extremes of nonresistance and resistance using a firearm. All other forms of resistance had higher victim injury rates than did nonresistance or firearm resistance.

Many gun control advocates argue that DGUs are harmful to society. For example, the United Methodist Church, which founded the National Coalition to Ban Handguns (now named the Coalition to Stop Gun Violence), declares that people should submit to rape and robbery rather than endanger the criminal's life by shooting him (Polsby and Kates 1997). Opposing gun ownership by battered women, Betty Friedan argues that "lethal violence even in self-defense only engenders more violence" (Japenga 1994, 54). Under this view, violence is per se evil, and it is irrelevant whether that violence is used to perpetrate a crime or to prevent one.

The only national study of how frequently firearms are used against burglars was conducted by Ikeda (1997) and four other researchers for the Centers for Disease Control and Prevention (CDC). In 1994, random-digit-dialing phone calls were made throughout the United States, resulting in 5,238 interviews. The interviewees were asked about use of a firearm in a burglary situation during the last 12 months. The CDC researchers found that 6 percent of the sample population had used a firearm in a burglary situation during that 12-month period. Extrapolating the polling sample to the national population, the researchers estimated that in the last 12 months, there were 1,896,842 incidents in which a householder retrieved a firearm but did not see an intruder. There were an estimated 503,481 incidents in which the armed householder *did* see the burglar, and 497,646 incidents in which the burglar was scared away by the firearm. As detailed by Kleck (1997), other research suggests that there are about two dozen cases annually in which an innocent person is fatally shot after having been mistaken for a burglar.

While the CDC burglary data have attracted little controversy, estimates of the total number of DGUs are the subject of great debate. The accompanying table, adapted from Kleck (1997), summarizes all American studies aimed specifically at estimating DGU numbers. The later studies tend to be considerably more sophisticated methodologically than the earlier surveys and include various safeguards to weed out respondents who might invent a DGU story.

Gun control advocates argue that all of the above surveys are wrong and that the only correct figure for DGUs comes from the NCVS. The NCVS data for 1992–2005

suggest an average of about 97,000 DGUs annually. Kleck and other critics respond that the NCVS never directly asks about DGUs (but instead asks an open-ended question about how the victim responded), and that because the NCVS is nonanonymous and is conducted by U.S. Department of Justice officials, respondents may be reluctant to disclose DGUs.

Hemenway (1997) and Kleck have engaged in an extended debate about the validity of Kleck's figures (and the other surveys) versus those of the NCVS. Smith (1997) of the National Opinion Research Center concludes that the NCVS's figures probably are too low (partly because it only asks about some crimes, and not the full scope of crimes from which a DGU might ensue), and that the Kleck figure is too high. Smith estimates that the true number of DGUs annually is somewhere between 256,500 and 1,210,000.

David B. Kopel

See also: Coalition to Stop Gun Violence (CSGV); Cook, Philip J.; Kleck, Gary; Lott, John R., Jr.; More Guns, Less Crime Thesis; National Crime Victimization Survey (NCVS); Right to Self-Defense, Philosophical Bases; Self-Defense, Legal Issues; Self-Defense, Reasons for Gun Use

Further Reading

Hemenway, David. "Survey Research and Self-Defense Gun Use: An Explanation of Extreme Overestimates." *Journal of Criminal Law and Criminology* 87 (1997): 1430–45.

Ikeda, Robert M., et al. "Estimating Intruder-Related Firearms Retrievals in U.S. Households, 1994." *Violence and Victims* 12 (1997): 363–72.

Japenga, Ann. "Would I Be Safer with a Gun?" *Health*, March–April 1994, 54–65.

Kleck, Gary. "Degrading Scientific Standards to Get the Defensive Gun Use Estimate

Table 1 Defensive Gun Use

Survey	Field	Bordua	DMI one	DMI two	Hart	Ohio
Area	California	Illinois	U.S.	U.S.	U.S.	Ohio
Year of interviews	1976	1977	1978	1978	1981	1982
Gun type covered	Handguns	All guns	All guns	All guns	Handguns	Handguns
Recall period	Ever/1, 2 years	Ever	Ever	Ever	5 years	Ever
Excluded uses against animals?	No	No	No	Yes	Yes	No
Excluded military, police uses?	Yes	No	Yes	Yes	Yes	No
DGU question refers to	Respondent	Respondent	Household	Household	Household	Respondent
% who used gun	8.6/1.4/3[a]	5.0	15	7	4	6.5
% who fired gun	2.9	n.a.	6	n.a.	n.a.	2.6
Implied number of defensive gun uses	3,052,717	1,414,544	2,141,512	1,098,409	1,797,461	771,043

Survey	Mauser	Gallup	Gallup	Kleck & Gertz	L.A. Times	Tarrance	Police Foundation
Area	U.S.	U.S.	U.S.	U.S.	U.S.	U.S.	U.S.
Year of interviews	1990	1991	1993	1993	1994	1994	1994
Gun type covered	All guns	All guns	All guns	All guns	All guns	All guns	All guns
Recall period	5 years	Ever	Ever	1 year	Ever	5 years	1 year
Excluded uses against animals?	Yes	No	No	Yes	No	Yes	Yes
Excluded military, police uses?	Yes	No	Yes	Yes	Yes	Yes	Yes
DGU question refers to	Household	Respondent only	Resp.	Resp.	Resp.	Resp./Household	Resp.
% who used gun	3.79	8	11	1.326	8[c]	1/2[d]	1.44
% who fired gun	n.a.	n.a.	n.a.	0.63	n.a.	n.a.	0.70
Implied number of defensive gun uses[b]	1,487,342	777,153	1,621,373	2,549,862	3,609,682	764,036	1,460,000

[a]1,4% in past year, 3% in past two years, 8.6% ever.

[b]Estimated annual number of DGUs of guns of all types against humans, excluding uses connected with military or police duties, after any necessary adjustments were made, for United States, 1993.

[c]Covered only uses outside the home.

[d]1% of respondents, 2% of households.

Source: Adapted from Kleck, Gary. *Targeting Guns: Firearms and Their Control* (Hawthorne, NY: Aldine de Gruyter), pp. 187–188.

Republican administrations. Signed by Clinton in November 1993, Public Law 103-159 mandated a five-business-day waiting period for handgun sales through licensed dealers and required local law enforcement authorities to conduct background checks on handgun buyers (this provision was declared unconstitutional by the U.S. Supreme Court in *Printz v. United States* (95-1478), 521 U.S. 98 (1997)). In 1994, the Democratic-majority Congress enacted the Clinton administration's crime bill (PL 103-322). The law's major gun control provision was a ban on the manufacture, sale, or importation of 19 assault weapons (the ban was allowed to "sunset" by President George W. Bush and a Republican-controlled Congress in 2004). Also that year, Congress approved the Gun-Free Schools Act of 1994 (PL 103-382), which required schools receiving federal funds to expel for one year any student caught with a weapon in the school or on school grounds.

In 1994, the Republicans gained control of both houses of Congress, picking up nine Senate seats and 53 seats in the House of Representatives. This overwhelming defeat represented a repudiation of Clinton and the Democratic Congress's policies in the first two years of the administration, including the Democrats' position on gun control. A 1992 Clinton voter, interviewed by *Time* magazine, offered some insight into the 1994 midterm defeat: "I voted for him, but he's just got it all wrong about where we all stand on gays and guns and taxes" (Stacks 1994, 46).

Clinton would also acknowledge the role that the party's gun control position played in 1994. In an April 1995 press conference, the president stated: "There are some who would be on this platform today who lost their seats in 1994 because they voted for the Brady Bill and they voted for the assault weapons ban" (White House Press Office 1995).

Clinton was reelected in 1996. However, his party would remain the congressional minority. While Clinton pursued nonlegislative avenues to continue his gun control agenda, congressional Democrats found that they could push neither Clinton's nor their own legislative proposals through a Republican-controlled Congress.

In the 2000 presidential election, the party's platform (2000) stated: "Democrats passed the Brady Law and the Assault Weapons Ban. We increased federal, state, and local gun crime prosecution by 22 percent since 1992. Now gun crime is down by 35 percent. Now we must do even more. We need mandatory child safety locks. We should require a photo license identification, a background check, and a gun safety test to buy a new handgun. We support more federal gun prosecutors and giving states and communities another ten thousand prosecutors to fight gun crime." In contrast, the only reference to gun control in the Republican platform was that the party asserted that "any juvenile who commits any crime while carrying a gun should automatically be detained."

Bush's narrow election win was attributed by many to the Democratic Party's support of gun control. President Clinton, in an election postmortem, stated that the NRA "probably had more to do with anyone else with the fact that we didn't win the House this time, and they hurt Al Gore" (Dao 2001, 1). Max Sardin, a Democratic congressman from Texas, offered a similar assessment: "If the Democrats and the Gore campaign had not been so strident in opposition to gun rights . . . there's absolutely no doubt that Vice President Gore would be president . . . It cost him a tremendous amount of support across the South. It cost him support in his home state of Tennessee. It was a big issue in West Virginia, Arkansas . . . and hurt him in voter turnout throughout the country with the labor vote" (Moscoso 2001). Steve Cobble, director of the Campaign for a Progressive Future, a liberal political action committee, said that gun control has become the shorthand for why Democrats don't do well" (Dao 2001, 1).

Since Gore's defeat, the Democrats have been less strident in their support of gun control. Ross Baker observed that, "On the national level, the issue is considered toxic by Democrats. I think part of it has to do with [the Democrats'] remarkable success in capturing seats previously held by Republicans. Many of these new Democrats ran on platforms of not tampering with Second Amendment rights, and they don't want to pull the rug out from under them" (O'Toole 2009).

President Barack Obama, when he accepted his party's nomination in 2008, said "The reality of gun ownership may be different for hunters in rural Ohio than for those plagued by gang violence in Cleveland, but don't tell me we can't uphold the Second Amendment while keeping AK-47s out of the hands of criminals" (O'Toole 2009). However, as president, Obama has signed into law a number of gun rights pieces of legislation enacted by a Democratic-controlled Congress. He signed legislation that included a provision permitting guns to be taken into national parks (Public Law 111-24) and signed an appropriations bill that contained an amendment allowing guns as checked baggage on Amtrak. When Attorney General Eric Holder announced that the Justice Department would seek reinstatement of the Assault Weapons Ban, the White House instructed Holder to end public discussion of the proposal.

In the post-Clinton era, the Democrats distanced themselves from gun control. The party's inability to attract votes from white male voters in the rural South and Midwest caused the party to step away. Electoral success in the pro-gun South, Midwest, and West by moderate Democrats opposed to gun control has impacted the party's position. Unlike 1993–1994, when a Democratic president and Congress enacted major gun control laws, a Democratic president and Congress in 2008 has not taken up the cause of the Clinton-era party.

Jeffrey Kraus

See also: Assault Weapons Ban of 1994; Biden, Joseph, Jr.; Boxer, Barbara; Brady, James S.; Brady Handgun Violence Prevention Act (Brady Bill); Clinton, William J.; Congressional Voting Patterns on Gun Control.; Elections and Gun Control; Gun Lobby; Kennedy, Edward M.; McCarthy, Carolyn; Obama, Barack; Republican Party and Gun Control; Schumer, Charles E.

Further Reading

Attlesey, Sam. "Both National Parties Focusing on Texas." *Dallas Morning News*, June 30, 1985, A52.

Baer, Kenneth S. *Reinventing Democrats: The Politics of Liberalism from Reagan to Clinton.* Lawrence: University Press of Kansas, 2000.

Congressional Quarterly. *Guide to U.S. Elections.* Washington, DC: Congressional Quarterly, 1994.

Dao, James. "New Gun Control Politics: A Whimper, Not a Bang." *New York Times*, March 11, 2001, sec. 4, 1. http://www.nytimes.com/learning/teachers/featured_articles/20010312monday.html (accessed June 16, 2011).

Democratic Leadership Council. *The New American Choice: Opportunity, Responsibility, Community.* Washington, DC: Democratic Leadership Council, 1991.

Democratic National Committee. *Party Platform.* Washington, DC: Democratic National Committee, 2000.

Disorders. The word's root is "hoplon"—from an ancient Greek shield that could be used offensively or defensively.

Of course, having a strong dislike or hatred of something is not in itself an indication of mental illness. Something becomes a Specific Phobia, clinically speaking, only when it significantly interferes with ordinary life activities. For example, few people enjoy being laughed at, but this normal fear would be a mental illness, "gelotophobia," if a person avoided all social interactions for fear that someone might laugh at him.

Imagining guns or gun owners to all have evil moral characteristics could readily lead to hoplophobia; indeed, the phobia would seem eminently rational from the phobic's point of view. Demonization is most successful, politically speaking, when it induces in the general public a "moral panic"—defining of a group of people or a certain behavior as a threat to social values. In a moral panic, the media presents persons, objects, or activities in a stereotyped and hysterical fashion, urging that immediate action be taken, without time for reflection. A moral panic is often set off by an "atrocity tale," which is an event (real or imaginary) that evokes moral outrage, implicitly justifies punitive actions against those considered responsible for the event, and mobilizes society to control the perpetrators (see Goode and Ben-Yehuda 2009).

Since the late 1960s, some scholars have been searching for scientific proof for demonization, which they call "the weapons effect." That a gun can change behavior is not seriously disputed; for example, if a scrawny 15-year-old is contemplating the robbery of a liquor store where two strong men stand behind the counter, the 15-year-old might attempt the robbery only if he had a handgun, since the firearm would enable him to genuinely threaten the clerks in a manner that would be impossible if he had to rely only on his bodily strength. The "weapons effect" theory, however, goes much further than pointing out that guns are tools that can be used to carry out a person's objectives, for good or ill. Rather, the weapons effect asserts that the mere presence of a firearm makes a person more aggressive and antisocial.

A few studies have claimed to have found a weapons effect, but other research has found the opposite—that firearms inhibit aggression. To the extent that any pro-aggression effect has been found, it appears confined to people who have no prior familiarity with guns. Most importantly, the few studies claiming to find harmful effects have little relation to the actual presence of guns. For example, one study found that people became angrier at dangerously aggressive drivers if the aggressive driver's car had a "pro-gun" bumper sticker. At most, the study demonstrated greater social disapproval of an obviously dangerous person if the person were thought to own a gun. Another study tested how quickly university students reacted to particular words, depending on whether they had first been shown a drawing of a gun (Anderson, Benjamin, and Bartholow 1998).

Kleck's review of 21 weapons-effect studies found that "the more closely the experiments simulated real-world situations . . . the less likely they were to support the weapons hypothesis" (1991, 158–62). Another literature survey, by Gallant and Eisen (2002) examined the Anderson study and others, and found the weapons-effect hypothesis to be poorly supported, but to have been used as a justification for many policies that caused real-world harms by depriving violent crime victims of defensive firearms.

David B. Kopel

See also: Berkowitz, Leonard; Coaltion to Stop Gun Violence (CSGV)

Further Reading

Anderson, Craig A., Arlin J. Benjamin Jr., and Bruce D. Bartholow. "Does the Gun Pull the Trigger? Automatic Priming Effects of Weapon Pictures and Weapon Names." *Psychological Science* 9 (1998): 308–14. http://www.psychology.iastate.edu/faculty/caa/abstracts/1995-1999/98ABB.pdf (accessed July 3, 2011).

Dunlop, Boadie W., and Philip T. Ninan. *Handbooks in Health Care*. Newtown, PA: Handbooks in Health Care, 2006.

Gallant, Paul, and Joanne D. Eisen. "Trigger Happy: Rethinking the 'Weapons Effect.'" *Journal on Firearms and Public Policy* 14 (2002): 89–124.

Goode, Erich, and Nachman Ben-Yehuda. *Moral Panics: The Social Construction of Deviance*. 2nd ed. Cambridge, MA: Wiley-Blackwell, 2009.

Gusfield, Joseph. *Symbolic Crusade: Status Politics in the Temperance Movement*. 2nd ed. Urbana: University of Illinois Press, 1986.

Hyde, W. W. "The Prosecution of Animals and Lifeless Things in the Middle Ages and Modern Times." *University of Pennsylvania Law Review* 64 (1916): 696–730.

Kleck, Gary. *Point Blank: Guns and Violence in America*. Hawthorne, NY: Aldine de Gruyter, 1991.

Kopel, David B. *The Samurai, the Mountie, and the Cowboy: Should America Adopt the Gun Controls of Other Democracies?* Amherst, NY: Prometheus Books, 1992.

McGrory, Mary. "Plastic Guns: The NRA Gets the Drop." *Washington Post*, October 25, 1987.

Wills, Garry. "Gun Rules . . . or Worldwide Gun Control?" *Philadelphia Inquirer*, May 17, 1981.

Wills, Garry. "John Lennon's War." *Chicago Sun-Times*, December 12, 1980.

Department of Justice, U.S.

Often described as the largest law firm in the nation, the Department of Justice (DOJ) serves as counsel for the citizenry and the public at large by representing them in enforcing the federal civil and criminal laws of the land. The DOJ is specifically responsible for enforcing all federal criminal prosecutions regarding guns, weapons, and explosive violations in the federal courts. The DOJ also conducts all cases in the Supreme Court in which a federal issue is at stake and represents the government in legal matters generally. The DOJ is charged with enforcing the laws and defending the interests of the United States according to the law, providing federal leadership in deterring and controlling crime, punishing those guilty of illegal behavior, and administering and enforcing the nation's immigration laws.

In September 1789, the office of the attorney general was created and the occupant accorded membership in the president's cabinet. It was not until June 1870, however, that the attorney general became the head of the Department of Justice, as the department was first established by an act of Congress on June 22, 1870. Since 1870, the attorney general has presided over the Department of Justice and served as the chief law enforcement officer of the federal government. The mission of the office of the attorney general is to supervise and direct the administration and operation of the Department of Justice, including the Federal Bureau of Investigation, Drug Enforcement Administration, Bureau of Prisons, Bureau of Alcohol, Tobacco, Firearms and Explosives, Office of Justice Programs, and the U.S. marshals, which are all within the DOJ. The attorney general also supervises and directs the various activities of the DOJ as represented by the U.S. attorneys and U.S. marshals in the various judicial districts around the country. Since 1870, the DOJ has been a cabinet-level department of the federal government.

James A. Beckman

See also: Bureau of Alcohol, Tobacco, Firearms and Explosives (ATF); Bureau of Justice Statistics (BJS); Federal Bureau of Investigation (FBI)

Further Reading

Bureau of Justice Statistics. http://bjs.ojp .usdoj.gov/ (accessed June 8, 2011).

Connor, Roger, Michael Dettmer, and Redding Pitt. "The National Symposium on the Changing Role of U.S. Attorneys' Offices in Public Safety: A Brief History Prepared for the Changing Role of U.S. Attorneys' Offices in Public Safety Symposium." *Capital University Law Review* 28 (2000): 753–73.

Office of the Federal Register, National Archives and Records Administration. *The United States Government Manual*, 328–65. Washington, DC: U.S. Government Printing Office, 1997.

Department of the Treasury v. Galioto (1986). *See* Mental Disabilities and Gun Use and Acquisition

Derringers

Derringers are very small one- or two-shot pistols designed to be carried in the pocket and used for defense at very close quarters. The derringer originated from a one-shot, muzzle-loading pistol designed by Henry Deringer of Philadelphia in the 1850s. The design quickly became popular, and Deringer faced many competitors. Deringer's gun was high in both quality and price, and many of his competitors put out cheaper models stamped with his name. He responded with

Derringer used by John Wilkes Booth to assassinate President Abraham Lincoln on April 14, 1865. (Library of Congress)

trademark infringement suits; in an attempt to evade them, the competitors began to stamp their firearms "Derringer" (with two "r's"), and this spelling became generally accepted as the name of the firearm type. Deringer's original guns were of relatively large caliber, .33 to .52, whereas the modern derringer is most commonly chambered for .22 rimfire. An authentic Henry Deringer pistol is today a collector's item commanding a high price.

David T. Hardy

See also: Handguns; Miniguns

Further Reading

Eberhardt, L. D., and Robert L. Wilson. *The Deringer in America*. New York: Andrew Mowbray, 1985.

Parsons, John E. *Henry Deringer's Pocket Pistol*. New York: William Morrow, 1952.

Dick Act (Militia Act of 1903)

The Militia Act of 1903, often referred to as the Dick Act in honor of Rep. Charles Dick (OH) a longtime Ohio National Guard officer, was a major reorganization of the American militia system to develop new federal recognition, control, and funding of state National Guards. The act gave the president new powers to command the militias in times of crisis and required National Guards to meet requirements of regular drills and training. In return, the federal government provided major new funding for the militias, new equipment, and new training, so that they would have the same capabilities and recognition as the regular army. This expansion of federal control angered some "states' rights" supporters, and the legislation raised new questions about what constituted the "well-regulated militia" described in the Second Amendment.

Historically, the United States had maintained a small regular army and relied on the mobilization of militias in times of crisis. The militias were organized under the Militia Act of 1792, which stated that all white, male citizens between the ages of 18 and 45 should purchase their own weapon and join a local militia. The state-organized militias were often poorly funded and organized, plus the federal government could not require their service even during times of war. The problems of this system were highlighted in the Spanish-American War of 1898. Secretary of War Elihu Root concluded that if the United States was to become a world power, it needed a new military system. He carefully cultivated support among National Guard leaders and in Congress, so that new legislation was easily adopted in 1903.

Under the Dick Act, the president could mobilize Guard units for nine months, although in times of peace, the Guard remained under state control. All state-organized militias were required to conform to regular army organization, to attend 24 drills and five days of annual training each year, and to face inspection by regular army officers. In return, the federal government supplied the states with new rifles, ammunition, and training. Between 1903 and 1916, the federal government spent over $53 million on state Guard units, more than had been spent over the previous century. The law affected over 120,000 soldiers and officers in over 2,300 companies across the country. It did not fully solve U.S. preparedness issues or clashes between members of the regular army and the Guards, but it is generally regarded as an important step in building U.S. military power.

At the time of its passage and still today, some have objected to federal control over state militias. Supporters of the legislation noted that the states retained control over their Guard in most circumstances and would now be benefitting from a more professional, well-equipped force. However, some with a strong gun rights/pro-militia, antigovernment ideology contend that the Founding Fathers intentionally wanted state militias as a check on a possibly tyrannical central government.

Furthermore, the opening section of the Dick Act reaffirmed that all male citizens were part of the country's militia. Now, though, there would be formally organized militias "to be known as the National Guard of the State . . . and the remainder would be known as the Reserve Militia." Over time, many analysts have argued that it is now the National Guard that qualifies as a well-regulated militia. Other observers have argued that all citizens remain part of the militia and therefore have the right, and even duty, to arm and practice their marksmanship. For example, in court, some lawyers have suggested that Chicago's prohibition on firing guns in the city for any reason other than self-defense is a violation of personal rights to target practice and preparedness.

G. Edward Richards, with updates by
John W. Dietrich

See also: Militia Act of 1792; National Guard; Second Amendment

Further Reading

Donnelly, William M. "The Root Reforms and the National Guard." http://www.history .army.mil/documents/1901/Root-NG.htm (accessed March 18, 2011).

Parker, James. "The Militia Act of 1903." *North American Review* 177 (1903): 278–87.

Spitzer, Robert J. *The Politics of Gun Control.* 5th ed. Boulder, CO: Paradigm Publishers, 2012.

Dime Novels and the Sensationalization of Frontier Violence

By the eve of the Civil War, American publishers discovered the "dime novel" (or "half dime novel," which sold for a nickel), a form of fiction that excited the reading public with its rambunctiously violent plots. Advancements in printing and papermaking allowed for drastic drops in price for cheaply printed, portable books for a booming (and increasingly literate) urban population hungry for rousing stories about the trans-Mississippi West. Over the next few decades, the dime novel flourished and became one of the most important influences on American perceptions of the "Wild West."

The publisher Erastus Beadle led the way in 1860 by reprinting an 1839 magazine serialization entitled *Malaeska: The Indian Wife of the White Hunter* by Ann S. Stephens. The book sold at least half a million copies. Later that year, Edward A. Ellis established the typical dime novel plot with *Seth Jones; Or, the Captives of the Frontier.* Overnight, the dime novel western became male-centered and Eurocentric, adding dash and thrilling exploits to the old captivity narrative motif. Now a white hunter rescued the captives in the name of white westward progress.

The dime novel format hit the peak of its popularity with the arrival of "Buffalo Bill" Cody novels in 1869. E. Z. C. Judson, better known by his pen name Ned Buntline, discovered Cody, who was a scout and bison hunter for the railroads, and fashioned him as the legendary hero. Ten years later, Prentiss Ingraham picked him as the author of the series, which cemented "Buffalo Bill" in the national imagination as the embodiment of the spirit of the West. This blended with Cody's own commercialization of the

Cover art for *Gentleman Joe, the Bonanza King*—a classic example of the dime novel. (Library of Congress)

western imagery in his enormously popular Wild West Shows that toured the United States and Europe into the 1910s. "Buffalo Bill" relied constantly on his rifle to produce food or for protection, or on his Colt pistols to establish law and order or to rescue white captives. Other dime novel heroes, such as Edward Wheeler's "Deadwood Dick," added some slight variations on the theme; but basically by the 1880s, the formula of the genre was set. Later dime novel western series in the twentieth century repeated the familiar themes almost to the point of exhaustion. In their pages, far many more instances of gun-related violence, murder, and retribution occurred than could have ever happened in the actual West.

In the movie *Unforgiven*, Clint Eastwood's 1992 antiwestern masterpiece, Richard Harris played a gunslinger whose reputation was the product of dime novels, but who, according to his own answers to an eager young journalist, had not performed even one of those fantastic literary exploits. The movie's irony is obvious, but in the nineteenth century, many Americans believed fervently in the violent imagery of the dime novels. Central to that violence were the ever-present six-shooters and repeater rifles. Many a cover featured "Buffalo Bill" or "Deadwood Dick" locked in combat with a fearsome Indian or rapscallious rustler, the hero having just fired his trusty Colt or Spencer at close range into the villain's body. Even before reading a single word, the reader knew that Anglo-American civilization was safe for another day, that Manifest Destiny was becoming more of a reality each month in the American West. The prose, full of shootouts, hairbreadth escapes, and revenge killings, simply confirmed for late-nineteenth-century Americans the righteousness of the American conquest westward.

Thomas Altherr

See also: Boomtowns, Cowtowns, and Gun Violence; Cody, William "Buffalo Bill"; Frontier Violence; Hickok, James Butler "Wild Bill"

Further Reading

Bold, Christine. "Malaeska's Revenge; or, The Dime Novel Tradition in Popular Fiction." In *Wanted Dead or Alive: The American West in Popular Culture*, edited by Richard Aquila, 21–42. Urbana: University of Illinois Press, 1996.

Bold, Christine. *Selling the Wild West: Popular Western Fiction, 1860 to 1960*. Bloomington: Indiana University Press, 1987.

Carter, Gregg Lee. *The Gun Control Movement*. New York: Twayne Publishers, 1997.

Jones, Daryl. *The Dime Novel*. Bowling Green, OH: Bowling Green State University Press, 1978.

Slotkin, Richard. *Gunfighter Nation: The Myth of the Frontier in Twentieth-Century America*. New York: HarperCollins, 1992.

Tompkins, Jane. *West of Everything: The Inner Life of Westerns*. New York: Oxford University Press, 1992.

Dingell, John D. (1926–)

John Dingell (D-MI) is one of the staunchest opponents of gun control in the U.S. House of Representatives. A master tactician, Dingell has frequently used procedural maneuvers and amendments to defeat or weaken gun control legislation. In June 1999, after the Senate had approved a gun control measure, Dingell managed to block legislation by use of a killer amendment. Dingell served for many years on the NRA Board of Directors, and once referred to Bureau of Alcohol, Tobacco and Firearms (ATF) agents as "fascists." Rep. Carolyn McCarthy (D-NY), a strong gun control advocate in the Congress, once called Dingell "Mr. NRA."

John D. Dingell. (U.S. House of Representatives)

The son of a congressman, Dingell received his law degree from Georgetown Law School in 1952. He served as assistant prosecuting attorney for Wayne County, Michigan, from 1954 to 1955, and then won a special election to succeed his father, who died in office in 1955. Dingell won reelection in each succeeding election since 1956. In 2002, the redistricting of Michigan to reflect population changes created a new 15th District that comprised parts of Dearborn and southwestern Wayne County, eastern Washtenaw County, and all of Monroe. As a result, Dingell was thrown into a scrutinized and cutthroat Democratic primary with another Democratic incumbent, Lynn Rivers. The latter had represented Ann Arbor, a university town, and another brand of the Democratic Party. The congresswoman was backed by pro-choice groups, in particular EMILY's List, environmentalists, and gun control advocates such as the Brady Campaign. Dingell, on the other hand, was supported by the NRA and the United Auto Workers. Rivers attempted to galvanize electoral support around the issue of gun control, and the Brady Center to Prevent Gun Violence sent volunteers to the new district for six weeks and taped get-out-the-vote messages by actor Martin Sheen. Even founder Sarah Brady campaigned personally for Rivers in the district. Despite Rivers's and her endorsers' efforts, Dingell won the primary by a margin of 59 percent to 41 percent.

Dingell served as chair of the powerful House Committee on Energy and Commerce from the 97th through the 103rd Congresses, when Republicans gained control of the House. Political analysts consider Dingell to have built one of the most "expansive congressional power centers of the post–World War II era" (CQ's Politics in America 2008). A picture of the earth once hung in the committee office, representing the committee's jurisdiction, which included energy, health care, and telecommunication. However, health care has been the most important to Dingell, who helped to write the legislation that created Medicare in 1965. For decades, he has been a staunch supporter of nationalized health care. Dingell lost his chairmanship of the committee to Henry Waxman (D-CA) in 2008.

Dingell represents Detroit and thus has been a staunch supporter of the auto industry. He has consistently fought against stricter air pollution controls for cars and trucks, often clashing with members of his own committee. Dingell has never shied away from political conflict, however, and he has earned a reputation as a master strategist. In one highly publicized incident, Dingell was told by a colleague on the Energy and Commerce Committee that he lacked the votes to win on an issue. Dingell retorted, "Yeah, but I've got the gavel," and banged it down to adjourn the meeting.

For many years, Dingell used his powerful position as chair of Energy and Commerce to bottle up gun control legislation in the House. In 1981, he was part of an effort to shut down the ATF, and was quoted in an NRA-produced film as referring to ATF agents as "a jack-booted group of fascists who are . . . a shame and a disgrace to our country." Dingell used his power in the House to effectively block gun control legislation during the 1980s and 1990s. When the Republicans took control of the chamber in 1995, Dingell took a low profile on gun control. But in 1999, he managed to insert an amendment in a House bill that would have weakened regulations on background checks of those who sought to buy guns at gun shows. The Dingell amendment would have given officials just 24 hours to conduct a background check and permitted the sale to be completed if officials had failed to finish their investigation. The amendment was a "killer amendment" because it sufficiently weakened the provisions of the overall bill that gun control advocates voted against final passage, and it permitted gun control opponents a "free vote" in favor of gun control.

Despite Dingell's earlier strong language about ATF agents, he resigned his seat on the NRA board after the organization mailed fund-raising letters accusing the ATF of using "storm trooper" tactics and being "jack-booted thugs." Dingell's resignation came at a time when former president George Bush resigned his membership and General H. Norman Schwarzkopf criticized the NRA publicly. But Dingell has never backed away from his strong support for NRA policies, often leading him to conflict publicly with John Conyers, who once served as his aide.

In the wake of the 2007 Virginia Tech massacre, in which a student gunman killed 32 individuals and wounded many more, Dingell played an instrumental role in securing the successful House passage of the first major gun legislation in more than a decade. Sponsored by Rep. Carolyn McCarthy and cosponsored by Dingell, among others, earlier iterations of the National Instant Criminal Background Check System (NICS) Improvement Act of 2007 mostly languished in the Congress. The Virginia Tech shooting, however, renewed congressional and public urgency on the issue. McCarthy enlisted the help of Dingell, who worked with the NRA to broker legislative language that would protect Second Amendment rights but would still be acceptable to gun control advocates. The eventual bill did receive the support of both the NRA and the Brady Campaign. The act authorized funding to states to transmit background check data to the federal government and keep the NICS database updated; it also created a mechanism for individuals wrongfully included in the database to petition for removal. The bill was signed into law in January 2008, and three years after its enactment, Dingell, among other authors of the original bill, requested that the Government Accountability Office conduct an audit of the NICS.

Clyde Wilcox and Christine Kim

See also: Bureau of Alcohol, Tobacco, Firearms and Explosives (ATF); Conyers, John; McCarthy, Carolyn; NICS Improvement Act; Virginia Tech Massacre

Further Reading

Anderson, Jack. *Inside the NRA: Armed and Dangerous, an Exposé.* Beverly Hills, CA: Dove Books, 1996.

"Dingell, John, D-Mich." In *CQ's Politics in America 2008: The 110th Congress,* by Jackie Koszczuk and Martha Angle. Washington, DC: CQ Press, 2007.

John D. Dingell. http://dingell.house.gov/ (accessed May 16, 2011).

Martinek, Wendy, Kenneth J. Meier, and Lael Keiser. "Jackboots or Lace Panties? The Bureau of Alcohol, Tobacco, and Firearms." In *The Changing Politics of Gun Control*, edited by John M. Bruce and Clyde Wilcox, 17–44. Lanham, MD: Rowman & Littlefield, 1998.

Spitzer, Robert J. *The Politics of Gun Control*. 5th ed. Boulder, CO: Paradigm Publishers, 2012.

Washington Post. "The U.S. Congress Votes Database." http://projects.washingtonpost.com/congress/members/d000355/ (accessed May 16, 2011).

District of Columbia v. Beretta U.S.A. Corp. *See* Lawsuits against Gun Manufacturers

District of Columbia v. Heller (2008)

Summary

The watershed *District of Columbia v. Heller* decision of June 26, 2008, marked the first time the U.S. Supreme Court enforced a claim of any description under the Second Amendment, and the first time the Court clearly acknowledged a Second Amendment right independent of service in the lawfully established militia and delinked from possession of weapons held for militia service. As proposed by Congress in 1789, and ratified by the requisite ninth state in 1791, the Second Amendment proclaims "A well regulated Militia, being necessary to the security of a free State, the right of the people to keep and bear Arms, shall not be infringed." Writing for a sharply divided 5–4 Court in *Heller*, Justice Antonin Scalia relied heavily on his signature jurisprudential theories of plain-meaning textualism and original public understanding to hold unconstitutional both the District of Columbia's ban on handgun possession in the home and the requirement that permissible weapons kept in the home be disassembled or fitted with trigger locks. For Justice Scalia and the majority, the District's strict gun control regime vitiated a right of personal self-defense, and particularly a right to defend the home, that rests at the core of the Second Amendment. In separate dissents authored by Justices Breyer and Stevens, the court's four dissenters maintained the amendment could not be fairly construed to say anything about weapons possession unrelated to militia service. For the dissenters, regulation of weapons possession unconnected to militia service is consistent with founding-era practice and should remain a matter of discretion for the politically accountable branches of local, state, and national government.

Precedent

Prior to deciding *Heller*, the Supreme Court had addressed Second Amendment claims on only four prior occasions. The decisions, *United States v. Cruikshank* (1876), *Presser v. Illinois* (1886), *Miller v. Texas* (1894), and *United States v. Miller* (1939), were old, in three cases arguably obsolete, and in the fourth allegedly ambiguous. The first three of these cases involved claims raised against state and local governmental actors and individuals alleged to be acting under color of state law in an era when Bill of Rights guarantees were not yet enforced against the states by the federal judiciary. The particular issue of enforcing the Second Amendment against the states was not implicated by Heller's claim since it arose in the District of Columbia. Moreover, since the Supreme Court did not enforce noneconomic liberties guaranteed in the Bill of Rights against state actors through the Due

Process Clause of the Fourteenth Amendment until well into the twentieth century, the continuing precedential value of nineteenth-century decisions holding that the Second Amendment did not speak to state infringement of the right to arms was subject to question by the time *Heller* was argued. (Indeed, two years after *Heller*, in *McDonald v. City of Chicago*, the Supreme Court held that the Second Amendment right to arms was incorporated against the states through the Due Process Clause of the Fourteenth Amendment, even though the Court had held in *Cruikshank*, *Presser*, and *Miller v. Texas* that the Privileges or Immunities Clause of the Fourteenth Amendment did not require application of the right to arms against the states). The fourth pre-*Heller* case, *United States v. Miller*, was the most significant respecting the substantive scope of the constitutional right to arms. The case reversed a decision of the federal district court for the Western District of Arkansas quashing an indictment of two Depression-era gangsters for transporting a sawed-off shotgun across state lines in violation of the National Firearms Act of 1934. The federal district court had sustained a demurrer on the grounds that the conduct for which the defendants were indicted was protected by the Second Amendment. Writing for the court, Justice McReynolds stressed "[c]ertainly it is not within judicial notice that this weapon is any part of the ordinary military equipment or that its use could contribute to the common defense." Thus, the weapon at issue was not protected by the Second Amendment, and application of the National Firearms Act to punish its possession was not constitutionally infirm.

Perhaps Justice McReynolds's opinion did not set out with crystalline clarity a test for distinguishing weapons protected by the Second Amendment from those subject to governmental regulation and prohibition. In any case, the opinion has been subject to radically different readings by subsequent commentators, with one group wishing to exempt from Second Amendment protection all weapons not actually carried in service in the lawfully established militia, and another wanting to subject to Second Amendment protection any weapon that might be of a class that conceivably has some utility for military or paramilitary purposes. Federal courts of appeals uniformly read *Miller* as a severe limitation on the scope of the constitutional right to arms for many decades, but the Fifth Circuit's decision in *United States v. Emerson* (2001) and the D.C. Circuit's decision in *Parker v. District of Columbia* (2007; the case that became *Heller* upon appeal to the Supreme Court) recognized a Second Amendment right unrelated to militia service and created a split in the circuits, suggesting that the Second Amendment was ripe for reconsideration in the Supreme Court.

Lower-Court Litigation

Dick Heller was one of six District of Columbia residents to challenge various aspects of the city's strict gun control regime in *Parker v. District of Columbia* (decided 2004 in the federal district court, and in 2007 in the U.S. Court of Appeals for the District of Columbia). In his capacity as a special police officer, Heller was authorized under the D.C. law to carry a handgun while on duty at the Federal Judicial Center, but he was not permitted to register or obtain a license to keep a handgun at home. The Parker plaintiffs argued unsuccessfully in federal district court that the city's bar on registration and licensure of handguns for home protection violated the Second Amendment. Heller was the only one of the

Parker litigants who had actually applied for a registration certificate to keep a handgun; and since his claim focused on the concrete harm allegedly flowing from denial of that application, he alone could claim to have suffered adverse governmental action as a consequence of the District's laws. According to Judge Silberman writing for a split three-judge panel of the D.C. Circuit in 2007, Heller was therefore the only *Parker* plaintiff to satisfy standing requirements, and the only one allowed to challenge the unfavorable federal trial court decision in the court of appeals. Judge Silberman embraced an individualistic reading of the Second Amendment and held for Heller on the merits, ruling that the District's prohibition on registering handguns for home protection was unconstitutional. In justifying his decision, Judge Silberman relied principally on the Fifth Circuit's *Emerson* opinion, which in turn drew heavily on the self-proclaimed "standard model" of the Second Amendment, a revisionist interpretation of the constitutional right to arms that won favor among gun rights advocates and law professors committed to libertarian principles in the last decades of the twentieth century. The "standard model," which Justice Scalia went on to endorse in *Heller*, depends on textual exegesis and the weight of often isolated historical quotations to buttress a private-rights reading of the Second Amendment even as it rejects more contextualized accounts favored by academic historians. Thus, while most historians writing on the original meaning of the Second Amendment focus on the role of the militia in late-eighteenth-century Anglo-American political discourse, standard modelers, Judge Silberman, and eventually Justice Scalia have zeroed in on the image of the individual rights bearer defending home and hearth against all enemies (including potentially governmental ones) as the arch-

etypal embodiment of Second Amendment freedoms.

Justice Scalia's Analysis

The District of Columbia appealed the D.C. Circuit's adverse decision to the Supreme Court in hopes of preserving what was effectively a total handgun ban. The District maintained that the Second Amendment did not concern weapons possession unrelated to service in the lawfully established militia, and, in the alternative, that even if the court chose to recognize a private right to self-defense disconnected from militia service, that right would not be violated by the District's gun control laws. Justice Scalia rejected both arguments and endorsed a broader reading of the Second Amendment that embraces at its core a purely private right to self-defense, particularly of the home. That right, the majority reasoned, could not tolerate restrictions as severe as those imposed by the District. For the majority, the time required to assemble, unlock, and aim a more cumbersome weapon than a handgun imposed unacceptable burdens on Heller's right to defend himself against intruders into his own home.

Justice Scalia began his analysis by dividing the text of the amendment into a "prefatory clause" concerning the militia and an "operative clause" concerning the right to arms. This division of the text implies a hierarchical ordering that proved outcome-determinative in the court's analysis. For the majority, the purpose of preserving the militia announced in the so-called prefatory clause did not limit the meaning of the text labeled operational. Indeed, the court went so far as to assert that preservation of the militia was but one of many purposes behind the amendment, and likely not the most important. Both during oral argument and in the opinion of the court, the majority celebrated a private right to self-defense assumed to rest at the core of the amendment. The court played down evidence respecting original intent such as the fact that none of the reported commentary during the House of Representatives debates on the proposed amendment in 1789 touched on a private right to arms, while 12 members went on record to discuss a right related to militia service. (Since the Senate debated behind closed doors until 1794, only House of Representatives debates were reported—and even these were only partially reported – during the First Congress). Rather, the court focused on original public understanding; that is, the alleged meaning attached to the text by the general public participating in the ratification process that gave life to the new constitutional text. The court stressed the amendment's reference to a "right of the people," which for the court implied individualist liberties analogous in application to rights belonging to "the people" described in the Fourth Amendment. Perhaps more controversially, the court proceeded to endorse a nonmilitary sense of "keep and bear Arms," which it supported by citations to various dictionaries of the times, in the face of countervailing evidence respecting standard usage cited by the dissenters. The court acknowledged that bearing arms at least sometimes means rendering military service, but this usage according to the majority was "idiomatic" rather than "natural." According to the court, the orthodox construction of the amendment's operational language, and the one enshrined in the Constitution, guarantees not a narrow right to carry weapons in military or militia service, but "the individual right to possess and carry weapons in case of confrontation."

While five justices signed off on this meaning, oral argument also suggested differences among the majority respecting the scope of the constitutional right to arms, and these differences led to Justice Scalia crafting a narrower opinion than his own comments and questions indicated he might have wished to pursue. Alan Gura, counsel for Heller, urged an extremely potent version of the right to arms for purposes of self-defense, and Justice Scalia made clear during oral argument that he felt government action impacting an individual's ability to engage in armed self-defense should be permitted only if it could withstand strict scrutiny; that is, only if the government measures served a compelling interest and employed means necessary to achieving that interest. Chief Justice Roberts, in contrast, expressed reticence about subjecting gun control legislation to a heightened form of judicial scrutiny, and in the end, the court left open the question of what standard lower courts should apply in reviewing gun laws in the future. Justice Kennedy, for his part, expressed great skepticism about *United States v. Miller* during argument in *Heller*, and made clear that he did not think gun possession unrelated to militia service was protected under the *Miller* interpretation of the Second Amendment. Kennedy was willing to overturn *Miller*, but the greater reluctance of other justices including Chief Justice Roberts to lay aside precedent pushed the majority toward a strained reading of *Miller* rather than forthright confrontation with that decision's severely skeptical approach to private-rights claims under the Second Amendment. Meanwhile, the law-and-order sensibilities of the justices comprising the *Heller* majority militated against the potentially boundless version of the right to self-defense urged by Gura and in some libertarian-leaning *amici curiae* briefs. Thus, Justice Scalia readily conceded that some gun control measures might not run afoul of the amendment, writing that "nothing in our opinion should be taken to cast doubt on longstanding prohibitions on the possession of firearms by felons and the mentally ill, or laws forbidding the carrying of firearms in sensitive places such as schools or government buildings, or laws imposing conditions and qualifications on the commercial sale of arms." In addition, Justice Scalia limited the right to "weapons in common use" thereby excluding "dangerous and unusual weapons." The opinion strongly suggests, and oral argument made entirely clear, that Justice Scalia conceded the constitutionality of federal prohibitions on machine guns precisely because they are "dangerous and unusual" and not "in common use" among the population. This allowance gives rise to a paradox, namely that in the court's reading of the Second Amendment, arms particularly suitable for militia service such as M16 rifles are not constitutionally protected, while weapons of very little military utility, such as target shooting pistols, are constitutionally secured against government confiscation.

Dissents

Justices Stevens and Breyer developed different lines of objection to the court's opinion in their separate dissents, each of which was joined by all four dissenting justices. Both Stevens and Breyer took issue with Justice Scalia's focus on original public understanding, in each instance both because they disagreed that Justice Scalia had accurately and faithfully rendered the original public understanding of the amendment, and also because they disagreed as a jurisprudential matter whether original public understanding should be the dominant consideration in constitutional questions. For Justice Stevens, the majority's claim that the amendment was originally understood to

focus on private self-defense unrelated to militia service was simply wrong as a matter of text and history. Stevens highlighted studies raised by *amici* demonstrating that contrary to the majority's assertions, bearing arms had an overwhelmingly military meaning in the late eighteenth century. Stevens also considered broader questions of original intention, and these allowed him to focus on debates in Congress and scholarship on late-eighteenth-century American political ideology that undermined the majority's reasoning. For his part, Justice Breyer expressed agreement that Justice Stevens had demonstrated the absence of a private-rights dimension to the Second Amendment, but accepted for the sake of argument the court's determination that the amendment does include the right to self-defense. Even if the constitutional text did encompass the right to defend the home against intruders, Breyer then argued, the District's measures were consistent with founding-era practice, including many municipal laws severely restricting the ability to use guns in urban settings in the late colonial and early national periods. Justice Breyer also strongly objected to the court's decision on grounds of localism and democratic legitimacy. Since in his view, the text of the Constitution provided no solid basis for judicial intervention, the people of the District of Columbia should be free to choose strict gun control even if their preferences do not harmonize with those in other regions of the country or of a bare Supreme Court majority.

Reaction

Heller was hailed by gun rights enthusiasts as a major landmark in the Supreme Court's checkered history of rights enforcement and as vindication of popular support for a robust, individualistic Second Amendment. Popular constitutionalists favoring traditional values associated with the founding era were not alone in singing *Heller*'s praises. Prominent constitutional scholars Randy Barnett and Eugene Volokh, who champion the theory that judicial reliance on original public meaning of constitutional text can minimize the dangers of judges' personal political preferences infecting judicial review, celebrated Justice Scalia's opinion as the high-water mark of originalist constitutional interpretation. But noted constitutional historians including Jack Rakove and Saul Cornell responded that Justice Scalia's version of the historical understanding of the amendment was objectively untenable, and their suspicions of *Heller*'s jurisprudential *bona fides* were echoed by jurists with otherwise unimpeachable conservative credentials such as Richard Posner and Harvey Wilkinson, who labeled the decision activist and insufficiently supported by the Constitutional text.

Significance

Heller left open for future consideration at least four broad questions about the right to armed self-defense. One of these questions—whether the constitutional right to arms would be applied against the states and municipalities—was answered affirmatively two years later in *McDonald v. City of Chicago*. A second question, whether there is a constitutional right to weapons possession for purposes other than self-defense or militia service, has not been addressed at all by the Supreme Court. Two other broad classes of questions adumbrated in *Heller* and *McDonald* remain, and burgeoning litigation in the lower courts will likely bring them before the Supreme Court in the coming years. These concern the standard of judicial review, and permissible classes of gun regulation. In *Heller*, the court deliberately shied away from announcing that a particular level of scrutiny would

automatically be triggered by Second Amendment claims, and given the chief justice's skepticism respecting tiered scrutiny and the skepticism of four justices regarding a personal right to arms, it is likely that the current court will address Second Amendment claims on a case-by-case basis, carving out doctrinal niceties incrementally as the justices did in the Fourth, Fifth, and Sixth Amendment arenas during the Warren, Burger, and Rehnquist years. The permissible reasonable limitations on the right to arms endorsed by the court in *Heller* were recited once more in *McDonald*, but since issues such as carrying guns in schools or prohibiting the mentally ill from acquiring arms were not litigated in either *Heller* or *McDonald*, it might be tempting for gun rights enthusiasts to argue that the court's endorsement of restrictions amount to mere *obiter dicta* and are not part of the holdings of the cases that form binding precedent. For their part, government attorneys defending gun control regulations and statutes will almost certainly argue that the exceptions listed in *Heller* do not form a complete class, and that other analogous or conceptually related limitations on the right to arms should also be tolerated under the Second Amendment. The future, of course, remains unwritten, but gun rights litigation, for the first time in the nation's history, has solid (if not impregnable) constitutional underpinnings.

Civil litigation challenging licensing regimes has increased apace since *Heller*, although the *Heller* court took for granted that licensing was not in itself unreasonable. Perhaps more dramatically, Second Amendment claims are rapidly becoming part of the criminal defense attorney's arsenal to be deployed alongside Fourth, Fifth, Sixth, and Eighth Amendment claims in gun cases. In the longer term, it is possible that *Heller* may be confined to its facts, standing for the important but limited principle that the government may not render impossible armed defense against home invaders. As of this writing, however, the scope of the right to armed self-defense of the home and the applicability of the right to armed defense to spaces outside the home remain very much in play, and criminal defense counsel, private litigants, lobbyists and action groups, and the judicial and legislative branches of local, state, and national government are all poised to participate in determining the metes and bounds of these rights.

William G. Merkel

See also: *Barron v. Baltimore*; Cornell, Saul; Fourteenth Amendment; Gura, Alan; *McDonald v. City of Chicago*; *Miller v. Texas*; *Presser v. Illinois*; Second Amendment; *United States v. Cruikshank*; *United States v. Emerson*; *United States v. Miller*

Further Reading

Doherty, Brian. *Gun Control on Trial: Inside the Supreme Court Battle over the Second Amendment.* Washington, DC: Cato Institute, 2009.

Korwin, Allan, and David B. Kopel. *The Heller Case: Gun Rights Affirmed.* Scottsdale, AZ: Bloomfield Press, 2008.

Lund, Nelson. "The Second Amendment, *Heller*, and Originalist Jurisprudence." *UCLA Law Review* 56 (2009): 1343–76. http://uclalawreview.org/?p=104 (accessed June 27, 2011).

"Symposium: District of Columbia v. Heller." *Syracuse Law Review* 59 (2008).

Dix v. Beretta U.S.A. Corp.

Dix v. Beretta U.S.A. Corp. is the first lawsuit ever filed seeking to establish the liability of a gun manufacturer for failing to "personalize" guns to prevent their use by children, teenagers, and other unauthorized persons.

Brought in April 1995 in Alameda County Superior Court in northern California, the *Dix* case arose from the tragic shooting a year earlier of 15-year-old Kenzo Dix by his friend Michael S. Michael had taken a 9 mm Beretta 92 Compact L pistol from a bag beside his father's bed, replaced the gun's full magazine with an empty one, and brought the gun to his room to show to his friend Kenzo. Michael did not know that a bullet remained hidden in the pistol's firing chamber. Thinking the gun was unloaded, Michael pointed the gun at Kenzo and pulled the trigger, inflicting a fatal wound.

Kenzo's parents, Griffin and Lynn Dix, filed suit against Michael's father and stepmother for leaving the pistol accessible to Michael. The claims were settled for $100,000. The suit also included a groundbreaking product liability claim against Beretta that asserted that the Beretta pistol was defective because it was designed without personalized safety features, such as internal locking devices, that would prevent its unauthorized use. Other product liability claims asserted that the gun lacked an effective chamber-loaded indicator and that the warnings accompanying the gun were insufficient. The filing of the lawsuit commenced a protracted legal battle in the California courts.

Following discovery proceedings, in May 1998, a California trial judge denied Beretta's motion for summary judgment, ruling that a gun maker can be strictly liable for failing to personalize guns. Beretta's petition for review of this decision to the California Court of Appeals failed, clearing the way for a jury trial.

In November 1998, a deeply divided jury returned a 9–3 verdict in favor of Beretta. However, in June 2000, the California Court of Appeals reversed the judgment against the Dixes, finding that the trial judge had improperly failed to consider evidence of juror bias. Following remand to the lower court, the trial judge ordered a new trial, concluding that at least one juror had pre-judged the case in favor of Beretta. The new trial order was upheld by the court of appeals in February 2002. A second trial was held in December 2003, resulting in a deadlock. A third trial commenced in July, 2004 and resulted in a verdict for Beretta.

The *Dix* case became prominent in the national debate over the feasibility and wisdom of requiring guns to have safety mechanisms to prevent misuse by children and teenagers. For example, most of the lawsuits filed by over 30 municipalities against the gun industry during the period 1998–2002 made claims, modeled after *Dix*, that the manufacturers should be liable for failing to incorporate feasible personali-zation systems and sought to recover the public costs of gun violence that could have been prevented by such systems. These law-suits asserted that personalization of guns would not only prevent unintentional shoot-ings by juveniles, but would also reduce the number of teenage suicides committed with guns stored in the home and deter theft of guns by making stolen guns unusable by thieves or by purchasers of stolen guns.

Even though the *Dix* case did not result in a victory for the plaintiffs, the threat of liability from it and similar cases has had a profound impact on gun design. After the *Dix* case was filed, several major gun makers began to market guns with personalization systems, such as combination locks or key-operated locks integral to the firearm. In addition, the case helped to galvanize sup-port for legislation to mandate consumer safety standards for handguns in California. As of January 1, 2007, all new models of handguns sold in California were required to have a chamber-loaded indicator, among other safety devices.

Future design defect cases like *Dix* may be affected by the Protection of Lawful Com-merce in Arms Act, enacted in 2005, which shields gun manufacturers and dealers from certain civil liability actions. Although the act includes an exception for actions involv-ing injuries or other damages "from a defect in design or manufacture of the product, when used as intended or in a reasonably foresee-able manner," the scope of the exception is unclear. The "defect" exception is limited by language providing that "where the discharge of the product was caused by a volitional act that constituted a criminal offense, then such act shall be considered the sole proximate cause of any resulting death, personal injuries or property damage."

In *Adames v. Sheahan*, 909 N.E.2d 742 (2009), the Illinois Supreme Court ruled that the act barred a product liability lawsuit stemming from an accidental shooting by a 13-year-old boy who found his father's semiautomatic pistol in a closet and thought he had unloaded the gun by removing the ammunition magazine. Because the shooter had been adjudicated delinquent based on a finding that he had committed involuntary manslaughter and reckless discharge of a firearm, the court held that the "defect" exception did not apply because the shoot-er's discharge of the gun "was caused by a volitional act that constituted a criminal offense." It is possible that the statute will diminish, over time, the effect of the threat of civil liability on gun manufacturer incen-tives to make guns safer.

Dennis A. Henigan

See also: Lawsuits against Gun Manufac-turers; Loaded-Chamber Indicator; Product Liability Lawsuits; Protection of Lawful Com-merce in Arms Act of 2005; Smart Guns;

Smith & Wesson Settlement Agreement; Suicide, Guns and

Further Reading

Brady Center to Prevent Gun Violence. http://www.bradycenter.org (accessed January 22, 2010).

Henigan, Dennis A. *Lethal Logic: Exploding the Myths that Paralyze American Gun Policy.* Dulles, VA: Potomac Books, 2009.

Doctors for Responsible Gun Ownership (DRGO)

Doctors for Responsible Gun Ownership (DRGO) is an organization that promotes the "safe and legitimate" use of firearms and opposes attempts by public health professionals and organizations to classify gun violence as a medical epidemic. The organization is a project of the Claremont Institute for Statesmanship and Political Philosophy, a nonprofit, politically conservative, research institution. Although based in California, it has a national and international membership.

By the early 1990s, medical journals were increasingly publishing research on the causes of gun violence. In 1992 the Centers for Disease Control and Prevention (CDC) established the National Center for Injury Prevention and Control, which has funded research on firearms use. Organizations such as the American Medical Association and the American Academy of Pediatrics (AAP) also began advocating more directly for the adoption of gun control measures. For example, the AAP adopted a policy statement in 1992, which was revised in 2000 and reaffirmed in 2004, that recommends that doctors ask parents questions about gun storage and advise parents to remove weapons from residences. In California these efforts became especially visible when the California Wellness

Foundation sponsored a multimillion-dollar violence prevention initiative.

DRGO was formed in late 1993 by Dr. Timothy Wheeler and other doctors concerned about these activities. Wheeler is a full-time surgeon and serves as director and spokesperson for the organization. The organization became a project of the Claremont Institute in 1994, although it maintains a separate mailing address. According to DRGO, the membership is about 1,300. About 60 percent are physicians; most other members are scientists and medical professionals. Most of the membership is from the United States, but there are a few members from other countries.

DRGO focuses on educational activities and policy advising. With the Claremont Institute, it has sponsored *amicus* briefs for legal cases, including a brief to the U.S. Supreme Court in 2008 *District of Columbia v. Heller* (128 S. Ct. 2783) that was written by Don Kates and Marc Ayers. Dr. Wheeler himself has testified before Congress, written opinion articles for major newspapers across the United States, and made numerous media appearances, including interviews on *60 Minutes* and for the *Cam & Co.* webcast on the National Rifle Association's Internet network.

Marcia L. Godwin

See also: American Academy of Pediatrics (AAP); American Medical Association (AMA); *District of Columbia v. Heller*; Health Care Professionals and Gun Violence; Hemenway, David; Kates, Don B., Jr.; Medicine and Gun Violence

Further Reading

American Academy of Pediatrics, Committee on Injury and Poison Prevention. "Firearm-Related Injuries Affecting the Pediatric Population." *Pediatrics* 105 (2000): 888–95. http://aappolicy.aappublications.org/cgi/

content/full/pediatrics;105/4/888 (accessed April 12, 2011).

Christoffel, Katherine Kaufer. "Firearm Injuries: Epidemic Then, Endemic Now." *American Journal of Public Health* 97 (2007): 626–29. http://ajph.aphapublications.org/cgi/content/full/97/4/626 (accessed April 12, 2011).

Doctors for Responsible Gun Ownership. http://www.claremont.org/ (accessed April 12, 2011).

Finch, Stacia, et al. "Impact of Pediatricians' Perceived Self-Efficacy and Confidence on Violence Prevention Counseling: A National Study." *Maternal and Child Health Journal* 12 (2008): 75–82.

Godwin, Marcia L., and Jean Reith Schroedel. "Policy Diffusion and Strategies for Promoting Policy Change: Evidence from California Local Gun Control Ordinances." *Policy Studies Journal* 28 (2000): 760–76.

Kates, Don B., Jr., with John K. Lattimer and James Boen. "Sagecraft: Bias and Mendacity in the Public Health Literature on Gun Usage." In *The Great American Gun Debate: Essays on Firearms and Violence*, edited by Don B. Kates Jr. and Gary Kleck, 123–47. San Francisco: Pacific Research Institute for Public Policy, 1997.

Nathanson, Constance A. "Social Movements as Catalysts for Policy Change: The Case of Smoking and Guns." *Journal of Health Politics, Policy and Law* 24 (1999): 421–88.

Okoro, Catherine, et al. "Prevalence of Household Firearms and Firearm-Storage Practices in the 50 States and the District of Columbia: Findings from the Behavioral Risk Factor Surveillance System, 2002" *Pediatrics* 116 (2005): e370–e376. http://pediatrics.aappublications.org/cgi/content/abstract/116/3/e370 (accessed April 12, 2011).

Paola, Frederick A. "Firearm Counseling by Physicians: Coverage under Medical Liability Insurance Policies." *Southern Medical Journal* 96 (2003): 647–51.

Wheeler, Timothy, and E. John Wipfler III. *Keeping Your Family Safe: The Responsibilities of Firearm Ownership.* Bellevue, WA: Merril Press, 2009.

Domestic Violence and Guns. *See* Lautenberg, Frank R.

Domestic Violence Offender Gun Ban. *See* Lautenberg, Frank R.

Dred Scott v. Sandford (1857)

Dred Scott was an intensely controversial 1857 Supreme Court case involving slavery, the citizenship of free blacks, and the Missouri Compromise. Chief Justice Roger Taney's opinion addressed the Second Amendment in two ways: First, the court said that if free blacks were American citizens, state laws would not be able to prevent them from carrying guns. Second, the court said that Congress could not violate the Bill of Rights by disarming American citizens who lived in territories that were not yet states.

Dred Scott was the slave of a federal army officer who had taken Scott to live with him in an army post in the state of Illinois and later to an army post in part of a territory comprising the future state of Wisconsin. Slavery had been outlawed there by Congress when it passed the Northwest Ordinance; Congress extended the slavery ban to some other new territories with the 1820 Missouri Compromise. Ownership of Scott eventually passed to someone in Missouri (Sanford, but misspelled in the case name as "Sandford"). Scott sued in federal court to be declared free, since he had resided on free soil, having been brought there by his master.

A divided Supreme Court ruled that Scott could not sue in a federal court, because he

Dred Scott. (Library of Congress)

was not a U.S. citizen. The majority opinion was written by Chief Justice Roger Taney, a Maryland Democrat who personally despised slavery, but was intensely concerned with preservation of the Union.

Among Taney's proofs that free blacks were not citizens was the fact that blacks were often excluded from militia service. The Taney opinion explained that the parties to the original American social compact were only those "who, at that time [of American independence], were recognized as the people or citizens of a State, whose rights and liberties had been outraged by the English Government; and who declared their independence, and assumed the powers of Government to defend their rights by force of arms." The new nation's federal militia law of 1792 had enrolled only free white males in the militia of the United States, and blacks had been excluded from the New Hampshire militia. These facts

suggested to Chief Justice Taney that free blacks were not recognized as citizens, since they were not in the militia.

In dissent, Justice Benjamin Curtis retorted by pointing to the language of the 1792 Militia Act, which enrolled "every free, able-bodied, white male citizen." Justice Curtis noted the implication of the language that "citizens" included people who were not able-bodied, male, or white; otherwise, there would have been no need to limit militia membership to able-bodied white males.

The *Dred Scott* majority offered a list of the allegedly unacceptable consequences of black citizenship: Black citizens would have the right to enter any state, to stay there as long as they pleased, and within that state they could go where they wanted at any hour of the day or night, unless they committed some act for which a white person could be punished. Further, black citizens would have "the right to . . . full liberty of speech in public and private upon all subjects which [a state's] own citizens might meet; to hold public meetings upon political affairs; and to keep and carry arms wherever they went." Thus, Chief Justice Taney claimed that the "right to . . . keep and carry arms" (like "the right to . . . full liberty of speech" and "the right to . . . hold public meetings on political affairs") was a right of American citizenship.

Most of the rights mentioned by Chief Justice Taney appear to be rephrasings of explicit rights contained in the Bill of Rights. Instead of "freedom of speech," Justice Taney discussed "liberty of speech"; instead of the right "peaceably to assemble," he discussed the right "to hold meetings"; and instead of the right to "keep and bear arms," he discussed the right to "keep and carry arms."

All the justices in *Dred Scott* were apparently unaware of an early case that appears to be nearly conclusive on the citizenship question. Justices of the Supreme Court used to be required to "ride circuit" part of the year, and preside over cases in the federal district courts. In 1793, Supreme Court justice Samuel Chase was riding circuit in Connecticut, and he presided over a case in which a free black man, who was a resident of Connecticut, successfully sued a Massachusetts man for illegally enslaving the Connecticut resident's daughter. Chief Justice Chase was a notorious stickler on jurisdiction, and he allowed the black man's lawsuit to be heard in federal court. The plaintiff won, and the case was reported in many newspapers throughout the United States. The case provides strong evidence that, at least in terms of original public meaning of the Constitution, free blacks were indeed citizens with a right to sue in federal courts.

Although resolution of the citizenship issue was sufficient to end the *Dred Scott* case, the Taney majority decided to address what it considered to be an error in the opinion of the circuit court. The Supreme Court ruled that Congress had no power to outlaw slavery in a territory, as Congress had done in the 1820 Missouri Compromise for the future territory of Nebraska.

Chief Justice Taney's treatment of the territories question began with the universal assumption that the Bill of Rights constrained congressional legislation in the territories: "No one, we presume, will contend that Congress can make any law in a territory respecting the establishment of religion, or the free exercise thereof, or abridging the freedom of speech or of the press, or the right of the people of the territory peaceably to assemble and to petition the government for redress of grievances. Nor can Congress deny to the people the right to keep and bear arms, nor the right to trial by jury, nor compel anyone to be a witness against himself in a criminal proceeding." From the universal assumption that Congress could not infringe the Bill of Rights in the territories, Taney concluded that Congress could not infringe the property rights of slave owners by abolishing slavery in the territories.

It is sometimes argued that the Second Amendment right does not belong to individual citizens but instead protects a "state's right" to have a militia. This argument is not consistent with *Dred Scott*, because *Dred Scott* viewed the amendment as enforceable in the territories—which, of course, are not states and therefore cannot exercise state's rights. Chief Justice Taney's list of the rights of territorial citizens that could not be infringed by Congress included only individual rights.

Chief Justice Taney's opinion in *Dred Scott* (which was shared by six members of the seven-member court on the citizenship issue, and by five on the territories issue) was not casual. The court knew that *Dred Scott* would be one of the most momentous cases ever decided, as the court deliberately thrust itself into the raging national controversy over slavery. The case was argued in two different terms, and the chief justice's opinion began by noting that "the questions in controversy are of the highest importance." Unlike most Supreme Court cases, *Dred Scott* became widely known and was hotly debated among the general population. The court majority's statement listing the right to arms as one of several individual constitutional rights that Congress could not infringe was widely quoted during antebellum debates about congressional power over slavery (see, for example, Douglas 1859). *Dred Scott*'s holding about black citizenship was implicitly overruled by the first sentence of the Fourteenth Amendment, which declares that all persons born in the

United States are citizens of the United States and of the state in which they reside.

David B. Kopel

See also: Second Amendment; *United States v. Emerson*

Further Reading

Douglas, Stephen. "The Dividing Line between Federal and Local Authority: Popular Sovereignty in the Territories." *Harper's*, September 1859.

Dred Scott v. Sandford, 60 U.S. (19 How.) 393 (1857).

Fehrenbacher, Don E. *The* Dred Scott *Case: Its Significance in American Law and Politics*. New York: Oxford University Press, 2001.

Finkelman, Paul, ed. Dred Scott v. Sandford: *A Brief History with Documents*. Boston: Bedford Books, 1997.

Kopel, David B. "The Supreme Court's Thirty-five *Other* Gun Cases: What the Supreme Court Has Said about the Second Amendment." *St. Louis University Public Law Review* 18 (1999): 99.

Krauss, Stanton D. "New Evidence that Dred Scott was Wrong about Whether Free Blacks Could Count for the Purposes of Federal Diversity Jurisdiction." *Connecticut Law Review* 37 (2004): 25.

Drive-by Shootings

Drive-by shootings, or "drive-bys," are defined to be when a firearm is discharged from a vehicle at a person, another vehicle, a building, or other target. They can allow a shooter to approach a victim quickly and without being noticed, to get some protection from possible return fire, and to leave the area before either retaliation or police action. They are often associated with gang violence, but also stem from road rage, regular disputes between individuals, and random actions.

There are no fully reliable national statistics on drive-bys, but studies have been conducted at local levels and using samples of national news. A 1994 article in the *New England Journal of Medicine* reviewed 1991 Los Angeles police files. In that year alone, over 2,000 people were victims; 670 adolescents and children were shot at, resulting in 393 wounded and 36 killed. The majority of the victims were gang-related individuals, but other criminals and innocent bystanders were also shot. The Violence Policy Center (2010) has conducted two national surveys of drive-bys using data collected from news reports. They acknowledge that this method is not fully scientific or comprehensive. Their data shows that from July 1, 2008, to December 31, 2008, there were 733 drive-by incidents reported in the media. All but four states had an incident in this period, but California, Texas, and Florida led the nation. They found most of the incidents happen between 7:00 p.m. and 7:00 a.m. In nearly half, the incidents the victims were at a residence, and in about one-sixth, they were in another car.

Drive-by shootings have helped focus national attention on gun-related violence and have fueled the desires of gun control advocates for stricter gun control measures. Several famous people such as former Northwestern University coach Ricky Byrdsong and rap artist Tupac Shakur have been killed in drive-bys. Drive-by shootings have, however, been celebrated in certain music and popular video games despite their violence.

G. Edward Richards, with updates by John W. Dietrich

See also: Crime and Gun Use; Drugs, Crime, and Guns: United States

Further Reading

Dedel, Kelly. "Drive-By Shootings." *Problem-Oriented Guides for Police, Problem-Specific Guides Series (No. 47)*. Washington, DC: U.S. Department of Justice, Office of Community Oriented Policing Services, 2007. http://www.cops.usdoj.gov/files/ric/Publications/e02072864.pdf (accessed February 7, 2011).

Hutson, H. Range, Deirdre Anglin, and Michael J. Pratts Jr. "Adolescents and Children Injured or Killed in Drive-by Shootings in Los Angeles." *New England Journal of Medicine* 330 (1994): 324–27.

The Violence Policy Center. *Drive-by America*. 2nd ed. 2010. http://www.vpc.org/studies/driveby2010.pdf (accessed February 7, 2011).

Drugs, Crime, and Guns: Cross-National Comparisons

Drug crimes are often associated with violence and the use of lethal weapons. Without question, the number of people killed in Mexico has spiked considerably as a result of the development and upsurge of drug cartels in the region. According to the U.S. Department of Justice (2010, 15), between 6,500 and 8,000 individuals were killed in Mexico in 2009 as a result of drug trafficking organizations battling one another for control of narcotics supply and sales. Despite these alarming numbers, very little of this violence has spread across the border into the United States. While the city of Juarez in Mexico is one of the hardest-hit areas with regard to drug-related homicides, El Paso, Texas, the American city that borders Juarez, has one of the lowest homicide rates in the country. The overlap of drugs, violent crimes, and use of weapons is indeed not unexpected; however, their correlations and outcome are more complex than policies or media portrayals and reports would lead the average observer to believe.

Prohibitions and the Demand for Violence

The hypothesis that prohibitions can increase violence is based on the following reasoning: Prohibitions of goods for which there is substantial demand and imperfect substitutes generally give rise to black markets; and in such markets, participants cannot resolve disputes via standard nonviolent mechanisms. For example, black-market producers cannot use the legal system to adjudicate commercial disputes such as nonpayment of debts. Black-market employers risk legal penalties if they report their employees for misuse of "company" property. Purchasers of black-market goods cannot sue for product liability, nor can sellers use the courts to enforce payment. And rival firms cannot compete via advertising and thus might wage violent turf battles instead. In black markets, disagreements are thus much more likely to be resolved with violence than in conventional markets.

The hypothesis that prohibitions increase violence is consistent with a number of facts. Numerous sources, anecdotal and otherwise, report the use of violence in the alcohol trade during Prohibition (1920–1933) but not before or after. Violence committed by pimps or johns against prostitutes is widely regarded as a feature of prostitution markets, in which prostitutes cannot easily report violence without risking legal sanctions themselves. Similarly, violence was an important feature of the gambling industry during its early years in the United States, when entry was prohibited in most places; the incidence has decreased as legal gambling has mushroomed.

Yet many prohibitions are associated with minimal levels of violence. For example, compulsory schooling laws are prohibitions against not attending school, but there is little violence associated with them. Minimum wage laws are prohibitions against hiring employees at subminimum wages; yet, at least in the United States, there is little violence associated with them, too. More generally, a broad range of regulatory policies (e.g., environmental, occupational health and safety, labor market) can be characterized as prohibitions but do not appear to generate violence. And the pre-1920 state prohibitions of alcohol and the federal prohibitions of drugs in the 1940s and 1950s were not associated with nearly the levels of homicide experienced in the last several decades. Most relevant to this analysis, Western European countries have drug prohibition laws similar to those in the United States, yet substantially lower rates of violence.

There are several reasons why some prohibitions might not generate violence. The most important of them is that prohibitions are unlikely to create violence unless there is substantial enforcement. And the amount of violence will increase with the degree of enforcement (Miron 1999). There are two parts to this argument. Prohibitions are unlikely to create substantial black markets unless there is a substantial degree of enforcement, and the size of the black market will increase with the degree of enforcement. The reason is that prohibitions generally contain exceptions that permit legal or quasi-legal production and consumption of the good, thus allowing use of nonviolent mechanisms to resolve many disagreements. But increased enforcement in the form of new laws that decrease the scope of the exceptions, or increased monitoring of existing exceptions, places some add-itional transactions outside the mechanisms for resolving legal disputes.

Enforcement is also critical to the degree of violence under prohibition because participants in black markets are likely to develop mechanisms for avoiding violence, but enforcement makes this more difficult. For example, rival suppliers might agree to cartelize a market, thus reducing the need for advertising; but the arrest of one supplier generates violence among the remaining suppliers, who attempt to capture new market shares. Alternatively, black-market suppliers can create private, nonviolent mechanisms for resolving disputes, but enforcement that creates turnover among suppliers makes such arrangements difficult to maintain. Still another mechanism is that, given higher dispute resolution costs, black-market participants can choose production and distribution methods that minimize transactions (e.g., home production), but heightened enforcement makes this difficult. Likewise, consumers of the prohibited commodity can purchase repeatedly from a reliable supplier, but enforcement that generates turnover among suppliers makes this harder, increasing the scope for disagreements.

This reasoning suggests the following hypotheses for empirical examination. First, differences in the degree of drug prohibition enforcement across countries might explain differences in violence. Second, greater gun control might itself increase violence by driving gun markets underground; thus, differences in gun control across countries might also explain differences in violence.

Evidence

In recent years, the United States has averaged about 5.5 homicides per 100,000 people (see *Sourcebook of Criminal Justice Statistics* 2011). According to World Health

Organization and the European Institute for Crime Prevention and Control (Harrendof, Heiskanen, and Malby 2010), the comparable figure for Canada is 2 homicides per 100,000 people, while for Mexico, it is 10 homicides per 100,000. Similarly, the United Kingdom, Ireland, Hungary, and Slovenia reported 3 homicides per 100,000 people. For the past two decades, the Russian Federation has experienced some of the world's highest homicide rates, averaging 30 homicides per 100,000 people—despite having a low gun ownership percentage. Collated crime data from all reporting nations indicate that Central America, the Caribbean region, South America, and North America have gun use in more than 50 percent of their total homicides. All European nations, including the Russian Federation, Asian nations, and Oceania have gun use in less than 15 percent of their homicides. While the level of homicide in the United States stands out in comparison to other wealthy, democratic countries, it does not in comparison to the world as a whole. Similarly, the rate of gun ownership is not consistently associated with homicides throughout the world.

On the one hand, violence rates are high in the countries of the Caribbean and Latin America, most of which are key producers of, or transit points for, illegal drugs. Colombia's homicide rate, in particular, is at least seven times the U.S. rate. The fact that these countries produce and ship illegal drugs does not necessarily mean they will be violent; the hypothesis is that the degree of enforcement plays the crucial role. But the existence of a substantial amount of black-market activity is a necessary condition for enforcement to encourage violence.

On the other hand, violence rates are also high in the countries of the former Soviet bloc, which are less substantial producers or shippers of illegal drugs. This does not mean that enforcement of drug prohibition is not playing a role in these elevated violence rates; these countries have illegal drug markets that are potentially violent. But much of their violence likely reflects ethnic conflict, corruption or the lack of an effective criminal justice system; these possibilities imply that the high violence rates are unrelated to drug prohibition or gun control. If the violence is due to either of these two mechanisms, however, it is still consistent with the broader perspective described, which is that violence is high when alternative dispute resolution mechanisms are not readily available.

Discussion

General assumptions about guns, drugs, and crimes cannot easily be drawn from data collected worldwide. While it may be convenient to assume that gun restrictions reduce violent crimes, and drug trafficking always generates more violent crimes, we learn from data collected worldwide that this is not the case. The Russian Federation has one of the developed world's highest homicide rates that occur via stabbings, strangling, or beating. The United States has a higher than average (when compared to developed countries) homicide rate that is closely related to gun use. It appears the greatest impact on murder and suicide rates comes from social, economic, and cultural elements within a society. Prohibitions on weapons and narcotics influence crime in general and violent crime in particular, but do not have an absolute direct relationship with violent deaths. The belief that more guns equates with more crimes, and fewer guns lead to less crime, is not borne out by statistics either within or outside of the United States. Drug distribution, sales, production, and consumption are closely associated with some of the most common crimes: burglary, robbery, assault, and theft. In Europe, there is more drug-related crime than in the United States; but the United States has more guns and violent crime. For those who suggest that drug legalization will reduce violent crime or that lax gun laws will stimulate more crime, there is no evidence to suggest that either of those commonly referenced ideas will reduce violence or enhance crime.

Jeffrey A. Miron and Karen K. Clark

See also: Drugs, Crime, and Guns: United States; Gun Control; Victimization from Gun Violence

Further Reading

Harrendof, S., M. Heiskanen, and S. Malby. *International Statistics on Crime and Justice*. New York: United Nations Office of Drugs and Crime, 2010. http://www.unodc.org/documents/data-and-analysis/Crime-statistics/International_Statistics_on_Crime_and_Justice.pdf (accessed July 26, 2011).

Kates, Don B., and Gary Mauser. "Would Banning Firearms Reduce Murder and Suicide? A Review of International and Some Domestic Evidence." *Harvard Journal of Law and Public Policy* 30 (2007): 649–94.

Killias, Martin. "International Correlation between Gun Ownership and Rates of Homicide and Suicide." *Canadian Medical Association Journal* 148 (1993): 1721–25.

Kleck, Gary. *Targeting Guns: Firearms and Their Control*. Hawthorne, NY: Aldine de Gruyter, 1997.

Kopel, David B. *The Samurai, the Mountie, and the Cowboy*. Buffalo, NY: Prometheus, 1992.

Miron, Jeffrey A. "Violence, Guns, and Drugs: A Cross-Country Analysis." *Industry Studies* Working Paper no. 107, Boston University, 2001.

Sourcebook of Criminal Justice Statistics Online. "Table 3.106.2009: Estimated Number and Rate (per 100,000 Inhabitants) of Offenses Known to Police, by Offense, United States, 1960–2009." http://www.albany.edu/sourcebook/pdf/t31062009.pdf (accessed July 26, 2011).

U.S. Department of Justice. *National Drug Threat Assessment 2010*. Washington, DC: National Drug Intelligence Center, U.S. Department of Justice, ID: 2010-Q0317-001, February, 2010. http://www.justice.gov/ndic/pubs38/38661/38661p.pdf (accessed July 26, 2011).

Drugs, Crime, and Guns: United States

Presumed links among drugs, crime, and guns are staples of public perceptions and governmental and media analyses of urban social problems. Yet studies show that popular understanding is much in need of qualification and specification. Not all criminals use or sell drugs, not all drug users and sellers are criminal predators, and neither violent offenders nor drug users and sellers necessarily employ firearms in the conduct of their activities. And while many people would argue that gun possession fosters social problems, especially among the young, few would accord gun possession the status of the single cause of either drug-related activity or predatory criminal behavior.

Much about drug use and firearms is inferred from positive associations between hard-drug abuse (primarily of heroin and cocaine, but in some places also methamphetamine) and predatory crime. Fourteen percent of juveniles incarcerated for robbery in long-term, state-operated facilities in 1987, for example, had committed their crimes under the influence of drugs, excluding alcohol (Beck, Kline, and Greenfeld become involved with peer structures and values whereby "hanging out," using (and perhaps selling) drugs, and carrying and using guns become part and parcel of the daily routine of existence (Fagan 1990). Thus, no one element is causally prior to the other.

Notable as well, neither drug-related nor criminal activity is the primary motivator of gun possession and carrying among youths. The average youth who possesses and carries firearms (even the average youth involved in crime or drugs) does so because he views himself as in need of protection in a hostile social environment (Decker, Pennell, and Caldwell 1997; Sheley and Wright 1995, 1998). By most accounts, serious and frequent involvement as a seller or buyer in drug exchanges places one in dangerous situations. Areas where such exchanges occur appear to be more dangerous than those where they do not occur. Heavy drug use also places one in the company of others whose substance abuse level is sufficient to promote armed exploitation of peers. Finally, firearms that are carried for protection in the conduct of life in the drug world translate to weapons at hand in what otherwise would be social conflicts played out with less violence. They also lead to chance encounters where people are relieved of property. In this sense and those noted above, the association between drug-related and firearm-related activities is considerably more complicated than commonly expressed in the public debate.

Joseph F. Sheley

See also: Availability of Guns, Effects on Crime; Crime and Gun Use; Drugs, Crime, and Guns: Cross-National Comparisons; Felons and Gun Control; Youth and Guns

Further Reading

Altschuler, David M., and Paul J. Brounstein. "Patterns of Drug Use, Drug Trafficking, and Other Delinquency among Inner City Adolescent Males in Washington, DC." *Criminology* 29 (1991): 589–621.

Anglin, M. Douglas, and George Speckart. "Narcotics Use, Property Crime, and Dealing: Structural Dynamics across the Addiction Career." *Journal of Quantitative Criminology* 2 (1986): 355–75.

Beck, Allen, Susan Kline, and Lawrence Greenfeld. *Survey of Youth in Custody, 1987.* Washington, DC: Bureau of Justice Statistics, 1988.

Callahan, Charles M., and Frederick P. Rivara. "Urban High School Youth and Handguns." *Journal of the American Medical Association* 267 (1992): 3038–42.

Decker, Scott H., Susan Pennell, and Ami Caldwell. *Illegal Firearms: Access and Use by Arrestees.* Washington, DC: National Institute of Justice, 1997. http://www.nij.gov/pubs-sum/163496.htm (accessed May 31, 2011).

Fagan, Jeffrey. "Drug Selling and Illicit Incidents in Distressed Neighborhoods." In *Drugs, Crime, and Social Isolation*, edited by A. Harrell and G. Peterson, 99–146. Washington, DC: Urban Institute Press, 1992.

Fagan, Jeffrey. "Social Processes of Delinquency and Drug Use among Urban Gangs." In *Gangs in America*, edited by C. Ronald Huff, 183–219. Newbury Park, CA: Sage, 1990.

Goldstein, Paul J. "The Drugs/Violence Issue: A Tripartite Conceptual Framework." *Journal of Drug Issues* 15 (1985): 493–506.

Johnson, Bruce D., et al. "Drug Abuse in the Inner City: Impact on Hard-Drug Users and the Community." In *Drugs and Crime*, edited by Michael Tonry and James Q. Wilson, 9–47. Chicago: University of Chicago Press, 1990.

Lizotte, Alan J., et al. "Patterns of Adolescent Firearms Ownership and Use." *Justice Quarterly* 11 (1994): 51–73.

National Institute of Justice. *Annual Report on Drug Use among Adult and Juvenile*

Arrestees. Washington, DC: National Institute of Justice, 2001.

Nurco, David N., et al. "Differential Criminal Patterns of Narcotic Addiction over an Addiction Career." *Criminology* 26 (1988): 407–23.

Sheley, Joseph F., and James D. Wright. "High School Youths, Weapons, and Violence: A National Survey." *National Institute of Justice Research in Brief*. Washington, DC: U.S. Department of Justice, National Institute of Justice, October 1998. https://www .ncjrs.gov/pdffiles/172857.pdf (accessed July 25, 2011).

Sheley, Joseph F., and James D. Wright. *In the Line of Fire: Youth, Guns, and Violence in Urban America*. Hawthorne, NY: Aldine de Gruyter, 1995.

Staley, Samuel R. "Same Old, Same Old: American Drug Policy in the 1990s." In *Criminology: A Contemporary Handbook*, edited by Joseph F. Sheley, 3rd ed., 543–59. Belmont, CA: Wadsworth, 2000.

U.S. Department of Justice. *Profile of Jail Inmates, 1996*. Washington, DC: U.S. Department of Justice, 1998 http://www .bjs.gov/content/pub/pdf/pji96.pdf (accessed December 29, 2011).

U.S. Department of Justice. *Substance Abuse and Treatment, State and Federal Prisoners, 1997*. Washington, DC: U.S. Department of Justice, 1999.

Wright, James D., and Peter H. Rossi. *Armed and Considered Dangerous: A Survey of Felons and Their Firearms*. Hawthorne, NY: Aldine de Gruyter, 1994.

Dueling

During the early period of American history, dueling was relatively common in the country. Both swords and guns were used, but pistols emerged as the weapon of choice. By the 1800s, the rules and customs surrounding dueling had become codified and the practice was deemed an acceptable means for gentlemen to settle their differences. Following the deaths of several prominent Americans, however, including Alexander Hamilton, public pressure began to mount to abolish the practice. But it was not until the Civil War that dueling came into disfavor in the South.

Dueling had its roots in medieval European practices whereby noblemen would fight to avenge their honor or to prove their innocence. The concept behind such judicial combat centered around the belief that God would only allow the person who was in the right to win. This legitimized the violence and even gave it state sanction. Later attempts to ban dueling during the 1600s and 1700s met with little success, despite efforts by the church to suppress the practice.

The first recorded duel in American history occurred in 1621 in Massachusetts. The combatants fought with swords, but pistols quickly became the favorite weapons in the British North American colonies. By the time of the American Revolution (1775–1783), dueling had become widespread, but it was particularly popular among the landed gentry of the South. In 1777, the "Code Duello" was published by a group of Irish dueling enthusiasts. The code contained specific rules of conduct for duels, including stipulating the number or severity of wounds or the number of shots that were necessary to satisfy the honor of the grieved party. In 1838, John Lyde Wilson, the governor of South Carolina, published an American version of the code.

Dueling customs and the "Code Duello" mandated that once a grievance had been registered, all action was coordinated through seconds. The second was usually a close friend or relative. Ideally, the seconds were supposed to try to mediate the dispute before violence ensued. If reconciliation

The dum-dum and all similar designs were forbidden for wartime use by the Hague Declaration of 1899, which prohibited use of bullets designed to flatten or expand in the human body.

David T. Hardy

See also: Ammunition, Types of; Black Talon; Hollow Point Bullet

Further Reading

Hogg, Ian. *Jane's Directory of Military Small Arms Ammunition*, 13–14. New York: Jane's Publishing, 1985.

Dunne v. People (1879)

Dunne v. People (94 Ill. 120 (1879)) was an Illinois state court case in which the Illinois court addressed the extent and nature of state and federal power over militias, including the relevance of the U.S. Constitution's Second Amendment's right to bear arms. A man named Peter J. Dunne refused to serve on a jury because, according to state law, as a member of the Illinois National Guard, he was exempted from jury duty. His refusal to serve nevertheless resulted in a fine, which he appealed to the state court. It ruled that his service under state law was a proper exercise of state power to regulate militias within the rubric of federal laws and the U.S. Constitution concerning militias. The fine levied against the man was overturned. At the request of both parties, the court examined at great length the powers of Illinois regarding the regulation of militias.

In the court's detailed examination of state and federal control over militias, the court referenced the Second Amendment several times, noting that the Second Amendment's wording was designed to reserve to the states their ability to organize and maintain a militia to carry out the purposes of militias listed in Article I, Section 8, of the U.S. Constitution:

"to execute the laws . . . suppress insurrections and repel invasions." The federal government and the states had "concurrent power" over militias, said the court, meaning that each level of government possessed the power, just as both the federal government and the states have the power to tax.

The court asked whether the militia law, to be valid, must enroll and arm every single militia-eligible male, or whether it could just enroll and arm a "select corps" consisting only of volunteers. Such an arrangement was entirely acceptable, said the court, as "The citizen is not entitled under any law, State or Federal, to demand as a matter of right that arms shall be placed in his hands. . . . It is with the legislative judgment of what number the active militia of the State shall consist." To drive home the militia-based nature of the Second Amendment and its irrelevance to personal ownership and use of weapons, the court stated flatly that "The right of the citizen to 'bear arms' for the defence of their person and property is not involved, even remotely, in this discussion." In the twentieth century, state control over the militias would be reduced by a succession of federal laws that increased federal control. This rebalancing of power in favor of the national government would be upheld by the Supreme Court in several cases including *Perpich v. Department of Defense* (1990).

Robert J. Spitzer

See also: Militias; National Guard; *Perpich v. Department of Defense*; Second Amendment

Further Reading

Spitzer, Robert J. *Gun Control: A Documentary and Reference Guide*. Westport, CT: Greenwood Press, 2009.

Duty-to-Retreat Doctrine and Gun Control Laws. *See* Castle Doctrine

E

Eddie Eagle

The Eddie Eagle program was created by the National Rifle Association (NRA) in 1988 to teach children to avoid gun accidents. The core of the program, symbolized by the costumed cartoon character Eddie Eagle, consists of a four-line slogan designed to tell children from prekindergarten to sixth grade how to react if they encounter a gun: "Stop! Don't touch. Leave the area. Tell an adult." The NRA makes available various instructional materials, including workbooks, posters, and an animated video. According to the NRA, the program has been used in all 50 states and has reached more than 21 million children. The NRA says that Eddie Eagle offers no value judgments about whether guns are good or bad, but is designed to promote protection and safety.

Critics of the program argue that it has less honorable purposes. In its report "Joe Camel with Feathers," the Violence Policy Center (VPC), a pro–gun control research organization, argues that the program was developed as a lobbying tool to defeat gun child-safety legislation then being considered in Florida by offering the program as a voluntary, NRA-controlled substitute for government regulation. The VPC further criticizes the

National Rifle Association gun safety mascot Eddie Eagle stands beside Wayne LaPierre, NRA executive vice-president, during a news conference in Washington on February 28, 1997. (AP Photo/Dennis Cook)

and membership contacts. While the exact amount of money groups spend on these activities is difficult to determine, we have begun to see that these efforts are very extensive. The NRA is one of the groups heavily involved in this type of campaign activity.

Harry L. Wilson

See also: Brady Campaign to Prevent Gun Violence; Bush, George W.; Democratic Party and Gun Control; Obama, Barack; National Rifle Association (NRA); Political Victory Fund (PVF); Republican Party and Gun Control

Further Reading

Magleby, David B. *The Change Election: Money, Mobilization, and Persuasion in the 2008 Federal Elections*. Philadelphia: Temple University Press, 2010.

National Rifle Association, Political Victory Fund. http://www.nrapvf.org/default.aspx (accessed May 25, 2011).

OpenSecrets.org. "National Rifle Assn." http://www.opensecrets.org/orgs/summary.php?id=D000000082 (accessed May 25, 2011).

Spitzer, Robert J. *The Politics of Gun Control*. 5th ed. Boulder, CO: Paradigm Publishers, 2012.

Vizzard, William J. *Shots in the Dark: The Policy, Politics, and Symbolism of Gun Control*. Lanham, MD: Rowman & Littlefield, 2000.

Wilson, Harry L. *Guns, Gun Control, and Elections: The Politics and Policy of Firearms*. Lanham, MD: Rowman & Littlefield, 2007.

Emergency Committee for Gun Control

In 1968, the National Council for a Responsible Firearms Policy (NCRFP) founded the Emergency Committee for Gun Control to lobby on behalf of the Gun Control Act of 1968 (GCA). The Emergency Committee supported national gun registration, national gun licensing, a ban on interstate gun sales, and a ban on mail-order sales of long guns. The bipartisan committee—headed by former astronaut and future senator John Glenn—played an important role in getting the GCA passed.

In the late 1960s, the NCRFP was the only lobbying or advocacy group focusing specifically on gun control. However, the organization was underfunded and not very effective. President John F. Kennedy's assassination in 1963 had engendered some support for gun control, but that support did not generate any gun control legislation. The climate for gun control changed dramatically in 1968, however, with the murders of the Reverend Martin Luther King Jr. and Robert Kennedy. Those assassinations opened up the possibility of gun control legislation (Vizzard 2000, 102). On June 6, 1968, the day after Robert Kennedy died, President Lyndon Johnson went on national television to call for Congress "to enact a strong and effective gun law governing the full range of lethal weapons" (DeConde 2001, 183). Several days later, he created the National Commission on the Causes and Prevention of Violence.

On May 24, 1968, the Senate had passed and sent to the House of Representatives Title IV of the Omnibus Crime Control and Safe Streets Act. Title IV was the gun control section of the act. Although Title IV banned felons and a few other categories of people from receiving, possessing, or transporting firearms, Johnson was not satisfied with it. He signed the bill into law but continued to work on getting Congress to pass his own, more comprehensive gun control bill—the Gun Control Act of 1968 (DeConde 2001; Vizzard 2000).

The Emergency Committee for Gun Control played a crucial role in getting the GCA passed. Attorney General Ramsey Clark had gone to the NCRFP to request that it set up a broader, more effective group. The NCRFP then met with representatives of 38 groups that favored comprehensive gun control. The groups included the AFL-CIO, the American Bar Association, the National Council of Churches, and the American Civil Liberties Union. Individual members included New York mayor John Lindsay, Johnny Carson, Joe DiMaggio, Ann Landers, Vince Lombardi, and Frank Sinatra. These groups and individuals established the Emergency Committee. To head the committee, the group chose John Glenn, a close friend of the Kennedy family and a staunch supporter of gun control.

The Emergency Committee effectively lobbied Congress and publicized the need for more comprehensive gun control. In October, Congress passed the Gun Control Act of 1968. The more comprehensive GCA replaced Title IV of the Omnibus Crime Control and Safe Streets Act. Having been formed to lobby on behalf of the GCA, the Emergency Committee did not operate long after the bill passed. Despite its brief existence, the committee played a key role at an important point in the development of gun control legislation and policy in the United States.

Although the GCA was the first important gun control legislation passed since the Federal Firearms Act of 1938, gun control supporters felt that to gain passage, the bill had been substantially weakened. Indeed, in a standard pattern, gun control opponents succeeded in weakening the bill and then later argued that the weakened law was ineffective.

Walter F. Carroll

See also: Brady Campaign to Prevent Gun Violence; Coalition to Stop Gun Violence (CSGV); Gun Control Act of 1968; National Council for a Responsible Firearms Policy (NCRFP); Omnibus Crime Control and Safe Streets Act

Further Reading

DeConde, Alexander. *Gun Violence in America: The Struggle for Control*. Boston: Northeastern University Press, 2001.

Patterson, Samuel C., and Keith R. Eakins. "Congress and Gun Control." In *The Changing Politics of Gun Control*, edited by John M. Bruce and Clyde Wilcox, 45–73. Lanham, MD: Rowman & Littlefield, 1998.

Vizzard, William J. *Shots in the Dark: The Policy, Politics, and Symbolism of Gun Control*. Lanham, MD: Rowman & Littlefield, 2000.

Enforcement of Gun Control Laws

The issue of enforcement of gun laws is really a cover for opposing new gun laws. Those on one side of the issue argue that "we need to make a law restricting guns," while those on the other side say "we don't need new laws—we need enforcement of existing gun laws." Though there is always, of course, some enforcement of existing laws, it is a relevant issue whether the amount of enforcement is optimal. The rate of arrests by both state and federal agencies for weapons offenses is shown in Figure 1.

The rate of arrests per 1,000 people increased substantially from 1.0 in 1983 to about 1.3 in 1994 and decreased thereafter until 1998, when it was 1.1. It has remained in a small range since then. The number of arrests reported by the FBI ranged from about 150,000 to 200,000 per year.

There are at least two competing explanations for the later decline in the number of arrests. First, enforcement may have been

Table 1   Result of Gun Arrests (2004)

	State	Federal	Overall
Arrests	117,610	9,936	127,546
Convictions	93,010	8,082	101,092
Percent	79.1%	81.3%	79.3%
Sentence			
Prison	44.0%	93.0%	47.9%
Jail	29.0%		26.7%
Probation	27.0%	6.7%	25.4%
Mean Length			
Months			
Prison	42	84	49
Jail	7		7
Probation	34	40	34
Percent of time served (1999)	48.7%	50.7%	49.0%
Average time served per conviction	8.72	32.31	10.52
Est. Gun Crimes			651,665
Time served per crime			2.06

Source: *Sourcebook of Criminal Justice Statistics*

Once a person is convicted, the next step is sentencing. As shown in Table 1, about 25 percent of convicted firearm felons are given probation. This is even more pronounced at the state level. Also, a substantial fraction of those convicted at the state level are sentenced to jail rather than prison, and the sentences are considerably shorter there, averaging seven months in state courts; probably, in many cases, equal to the time served before the trial; state courts averaged 217 days between arrest and sentencing in weapons offenses in one year (see *Sourcebook of Criminal Justice Statistics 1999*, 2000, table 5.55).

Of those sentenced to prison, the average sentence is 42 months at the state level and 84 months at the federal level. The fraction of the sentence actually served is also shorter at the state level. The result is that a person convicted of a felony gun crime (when that crime is the most serious part of the conviction) can expect to serve an average of less than 9 months in prison if in a state court or 33 months if in a federal court. The average across all such convictions is 11 months in prison. Since only about 79 percent of those arrested are actually convicted and, of course, only a small percentage of those who violate the gun laws are unlucky enough to be arrested and charged, the expected cost of violating the gun laws in terms of prison time is very small. Based on these data, we can estimate about 2 months per violent crime; it is lower if we were to also consider weapons crimes that were not committed in conjunction with a violent crime.

While inspecting people to ensure that they do not have illegal firearms is infeasible, increasing the sentences for illegal use of those firearms is not. It should be possible, if desired by society, to substantially increase the penalties, especially at the state level. Further, enhancement of the sentences for other crimes when they are done with illegal guns should help reduce the incentive to use guns in committing such crimes.

For violent crimes in which the weapons offense is not the most serious charge, the sentence for the more serious crime may be enhanced by a penalty for using or possessing a firearm in the offense, such as a robbery. That is not counted in the weapons arrests noted above. There are regular enhancements currently used. The average enhancement seems to be about six years, and about 40 percent of state courts and 56 percent of federal courts include sentence enhancements on criminals using firearms in their crime (see *Almanac of Policy Issues 2003*).

When considering the violation of gun laws, note that the "little old lady" who lives in a crime-prone area and who has a handgun as an equalizer is unlikely to be arrested even if her gun is illegal. Her purpose is self-defense, and few juries would convict her even if she uses the gun to shoot an intruder. It might be legal for her to have a long gun, such as a shotgun, but that would not serve as well for self-defense inasmuch as the intruder might take it away, a task that is more difficult with a handgun. Also, keeping a handgun handy and using it is easier than it is for a longer gun. Of course, the handgun is less deadly, but the intruder is more likely to be frightened off rather than shot in any such confrontation.

The real concern is keeping the guns out of the hands of criminals and the dangerously mentally ill or other persons who should not be trusted with guns because of the danger they pose. To that end, numerous laws have been passed to keep guns out of such hands. The Bureau of Justice Statistics lists a number of different categories under which felony charges on the federal level may be made (see *Sourcebook of Criminal Justice Statistics*). These are divided into three major categories: transfer, regulatory, and possession.

In 2008, some 8,320 defendants were charged with firearm-related crimes. Most of these crimes are of the two types of possession by a prohibited person (4,992 arrests), Section 922G; and possession or use of a firearm during a violent or drug trafficking crime (2,037 arrests), Section 924C. Another 29 arrests were for causing death with a firearm while committing other violent or drug trafficking crimes, Section 924J. The remaining 1,262 arrests were for other violations. In 2008, there were approximately 170,000 weapons arrests by the states and their subdivisions. It is likely that most of these are of the possession type.

In deciding how many resources to devote to pursuing firearm offenders, it should be kept in mind that there are limited resources available to the criminal justice system. Resources have to be allocated to countering other crimes, too. The optimal allocation will result in the marginal benefit of each criminal justice activity, relative to its cost, being equal across activities. Important questions to be asked include how much people fear other crimes relative to firearm crimes (which are usually possession), how effective additional enforcement will be in reducing the actual number of such crimes and the attendant fear of those crimes, and how effective firearm enforcement will be in actually reducing other crimes. Until these questions are answered, the question of whether additional enforcement is warranted cannot be answered. However, we can certainly conclude that prosecution of illegal gun possession does occur in fairly substantial numbers. On the other hand, if we look at data from 1990–2005, we see that the numbers of murders using guns has a correlation of +0.95 with the weapons arrests, suggesting that the arrests are after the crime and are simply added charges once the perpetrator has been charged with the major crime.

Lawrence Southwick Jr.

See also: Gun Control; Gun Courts

Further Reading

Almanac of Policy Issues. "Firearms and Crime Statistics." August 2003. http://www.policyalmanac.org/crime/archive/firearms_and_crime.shtml (accessed December 29, 2011).

Bureau of Justice Statistics. http://bjs.ojp.usdoj.gov/ (accessed May 31, 2011).

Carroll, Joseph. "Gun Ownership and Use in America." Gallup Poll, November 22, 2005. http://www.gallup.com/poll/20098/gun-ownership-use-america.aspx (accessed May 31, 2011).

Loftin, Colin, Milton Heumann, and David McDowall. "Mandatory Sentencing and Firearms Violence: Evaluating an Alternative to Gun Control." *Law and Society Review* 17 (1983): 287–318.

Sourcebook of Criminal Justice Statistics. Washington, DC: U.S. Department of Justice, Office of Justice Programs, Bureau of Justice Statistics, various years.

Statistical Abstract of the United States Annual. Washington, DC: U.S. Bureau of the Census.

Wright, James D., Peter H. Rossi, and Kathleen Daly. *Under the Gun: Weapons, Crime and Violence in America.* New York: Aldine, 1983.

Erfurt, Germany, Massacre

The first school shooting in German history occurred on the morning of April 26, 2002, at the Gutenberg Gymnasium in Erfurt (Thuringia). The shooter was Robert Steinhäuser, a former student at the gymnasium. Steinhäuser had been expelled in October 2001 after forging a doctor's excuse to cover several days of absence the previous month. Unlike most secondary schools in other German states, Thuringia neither conferred a high school diploma on its students after the 10th class, nor allowed them to take an exam certifying their academic competence—meaning that expellees like Steinhäuser faced grim employment prospects. The ignominy of expulsion along with the vocational hopelessness he faced might have been the triggers to his rampage.

Steinhäuser chose the last day of student written examinations (*Abiturprüfungen*) to launch his massacre. He entered the gymnasium building in the late morning, carrying two weapons along with ammunition in his backpack: a Glock 17 pistol and a pump-action shotgun. (Of the two, he would use only the pistol.) Entering the men's bathroom on the ground floor, he donned a ski mask and discarded his wallet, jacket, ammunition, and backpack before departing the bathroom with the pistol and shotgun, as well as cartridges for both weapons.

Steinhäuser's first stop was the administrative offices of the gymnasium, in which he shot his first victims, the deputy school director and secretary. He had already left the administrative offices when the director discovered the bodies. She locked herself in her office and called the authorities. In the meantime, Steinhäuser mounted the stairs to the second floor. While still on the stairway, he shot a teacher repeatedly in the back before entering a classroom and shooting a teacher as he stood before his horrified students. Moving on to the third floor, Steinhäuser fired five shots at a teacher in the hallway, then entered another occupied classroom, where he shot the teacher five times.

On the third floor, the killer shot another teacher in her classroom. At this point, he reloaded his pistol for the first time and shot three more victims—two teachers and a student instructor. During his rampage on the third floor, Steinhäuser was recognized by a student. Unfazed, he chased after terrified students and teachers, who now were in full flight from the building. One of the victims, absorbing a bullet from the killer, fell through a half-open doorway to the ground. Steinhäuser stepped over her and shot her again. Reloading the Glock 17 a second time, he tried to force his way into a locked classroom; unable to break down the door, he fired eight bullets through the closed door, mortally wounding two of the students. Returning to the second floor, the shooter fired through the door of the men's room, narrowly missing a student standing beside the lavatory sink.

At this point, Steinhäuser entered the schoolyard, where he shot a teacher who was trying to evacuate students from the gymnasium premises. For the last time, he reloaded his pistol in time to exchange shots with an arriving police officer. He ran back into the gymnasium and shot a police officer from a second-floor window. The end came for Steinhäuser when he met a teacher named Rainer Heise in front of Room 111. The killer had earlier removed his ski mask, allowing Heise to recognize him. He reportedly told Steinhäuser, "You can shoot me now," to which the killer replied, "Herr Heise, that's enough for today." Heise then invited Steinhäuser to join him in Room 111 for a private conversation. When the killer walked in front of Heise through the doorway, Heise shoved him from behind, locking him in the room. A short time later, police heard a gunshot from Room 111—the sound of Steinhäuser committing suicide. In addition to the killer himself, the rampage took the lives of 12 teachers, the gymnasium secretary, two students, and a police officer.

Aftermath of the Erfurt Massacre

The events at Erfurt in April 2002 were the impetus to intense national soul searching in Germany, as well as substantive changes to federal weapons laws and the juvenile protection law (*Jugendschutzgesetz*). Debate in the Bundestag concerning the latter advanced briskly after the massacre, leading to its passage in the weeks following the tragedy. The new juvenile protection law enhanced regulation of violent computer games (an inquiry into the massacre found that Steinhäuser owned several of these). The federal weapons law—ironically, passed in its original form on the same day as the Erfurt shootings—was amended on October 11, 2002, in response to Erfurt. The October changes included raising the minimum age for legal acquisition of a high-caliber weapon for sport shooting (other than shotguns) from 18 to 21; requiring applicants under 25 years of age to submit to a psychological examination before issuance of a gun license; the blanket prohibition of pump-action shotguns with pistol grips, throwing stars, switchblades, push daggers, and butterfly knives; and setting a minimum age for sport shooting of 12 years. In addition, the amended weapons law enjoined storage of firearms and ammunition in certified repositories.

At the state level, the shootings prompted a delayed reform of Thuringia's school law. Before 2003, Thuringia's gymnasium students received no diploma after completing the 10th class. As noted above, students who failed to satisfy the requirements for the comprehensive examination (*Abitur*) had few chances for gainful employment—a factor cited by critics as a possible condition precedent to Steinhäuser's rampage. In

2003, state authorities altered their policy to allow students at their own election to sit for a test at the end of their 10th class. Students who passed the examination received a certificate vouching for their academic "capability." (The designation reads "Special Certificate of Capability," or *Besondere Leistungsfeststellung*.) In 2004, the state required all of Thuringia's gymnasium students to take this exam.

Together with a memorial plaque erected in the Erfurt town square, and haunting questions of why and how the massacre could have happened, the legal responses described above are among the long-term effects of the Erfurt shootings visible in Germany today.

Michael S. Bryant

See also: Child Access Prevention (CAP) Laws; Germany, Gun Laws; Violent Video Games and Gun Violence

Further Reading

Becker, Jens. *Kurzschluß – Der Amoklauf von Erfurt*. Reinbek: Schwartzkopff Buchwerke, 2005.

Beyer, Christopf. *Der Erfurter Amoklauf in der Presse—Unerklärlichkeit und die Macht der Aufklärung: Eine Diskursanalyse anhand zweier ausgewählter Beispiele*. Verlag Dr. Kovač, 2004.

Bundesminsterium des Innern. "Verschärfungen des Waffenrechts aufgrund der Novelle des Waffengesetzes 2002." 2002.

Dicke, Wolfgang. "Waffen im Visier—doch das Problem ist viel komplexer." *Deutsche Polizei* 5 (2009): 6–8.

"18 Dead in German School Shooting." BBC News, April 26, 2002. http://news.bbc.co .uk/2/hi/europe/1952869.stm (accessed January 6, 2012).

Geipel, Ines. *Für heute reicht's*. Berlin: Rowohlt, 2004.

"How Teacher Stopped the School Slaughter." *The Observer/The Guardian*, April 28, 2002. http://www.guardian.co.uk/world/ 2002/apr/28/schools.education (accessed January 6, 2012).

Spiegel On-Line. "Tod in der Schule: das Massaker von Erfurt." 2010. http://www.spiegel .de/sptv/special/0,1518,245253,00.html (accessed December 30, 2011).

Ergonomics and Firearms Design

Ergonomic considerations in firearms design are aimed toward making guns more efficient, lighter, and easier to use, as well as toward reducing the likelihood of accidental discharges.

Rifles manufactured before World War II tended to be heavy and have limited capacity—examples include Mauser 98s, Enfields, Springfields, and Mosin-Nagants. Military guns were optimized for long-range encounters with powerful ammunition and sized for the average Western European or American male. Operation was manual and relatively slow, though intensive training could achieve fast rates of fire.

Desire for lightweight guns with greater rates of fire in World War II led to the production of lower-powered guns using less powerful rounds (including pistol rounds)—such as the American M1 carbine and M3 "Grease Gun" in 45 ACP; the British Sten and Sterling submachine guns in 9 mm; the German MP-38 and MP-40; and Russian PPSh-41. Even greater firing rates were quickly developed, including the German Sturmgewher 44, the USSR AK-47, and the U.S. M16 family. More recent developments have emphasized less recoil and adjustable stock lengths, which are especially valuable to the smaller shooter.

Similar trends can be seen in handgun development. While the revolver was revolutionary when it was introduced in the middle of the nineteenth century with its offering of multiple rounds, in the modern era, the semiautomatic handgun dominates the military, police, and self-defense markets. Soon after its introduction in the early 1980s, the Glock 17 set what would become the dominant paradigm: a light-polymer frame, with a high-capacity magazine. One advantage of polymers is that grip size can be made alterable to accommodate different hand sizes.

Gun sights have seen many improvements over the past several decades. The most obvious are the increasingly powerful and more sophisticated telescopic sights. Other important developments include colored, fiber-optic sights and night sights that make targets glow. More passive sights using Gestalt perceptual principles to align front and rear have also been developed, including the triangular sites found on modern Steyr handguns, Suresights (SureSight 2006), and Hex sights (Goshen Enterprises 2011)—though none of these have become popular.

On the other hand, laser sights, as those developed by Crimson Trace and Lasermax, have become increasingly popular. A bright red dot is projected on the target and aligned with the gun's point of impact at a chosen distance. The advantages are that one can see the point of impact, the gun does not have to be brought to eye level, and they can be intimidating. Developed in the late 1970s, they were popularized in the movie *The Terminator*. Problems include the shooter losing the dot in bright light and "chasing" it rather than focusing on the target. To improve daylight usage, green lasers have been developed to take advantage of the human's greater sensitivity to that wavelength band and thus are more visible.

Dominating the rifle market are Red dot or Reflex sights, such as the Aimpoint or Eotech offerings. Patented by John Arne Ingemund in 1973, they use reflexive optics to project a dot on a target seen through the sight without parallax error. They offer much faster target acquisition and much better performance in low light compared to old-fashioned iron sights. The armed forces are major users of this type of sights. The sights are relatively large for handgun usage and thus far are usually seen only at competitions. However, smaller ones are being developed.

Visual performance is also enhanced by adding illumination devices to firearms. Most modern military rifles and other long arms can have a flashlight attached to them. The same is true of modern semiautomatic handguns. Numerous companies manufacture such devices. They serve to identify targets and also have an intimidation effect. The downside of such devices is that they necessitate pointing the gun at a target with the risk of an accidental or negligent discharge.

One crucial aspect of firearms design is to avoid accidental or negligent discharges. A key problem is that even when a firearm is pointed at a wrong target (e.g., an innocent bystander in a police or military setting), there is a natural impulse to put one's finger on the trigger. Modern training stresses keeping the finger off the trigger and to the side of the firearm unless you are to shoot. A "startle response" can generate a 14-pound trigger pull. A squeezing reaction of the hand not holding the gun can cause a sympathetic squeeze in the gun hand, causing it to fire. And even simply swinging one's hand with the finger on the trigger can set off the gun. Attempting to activate a gun-mounted flashlight in too close a proximity to the trigger has also been seen to lead to an accidental pulling of the trigger. In more extreme cases, officers have reached for a pistol-shaped taser, pulled their handgun instead, and have shot someone that they were trying to restrain.

The firearms world sometimes attempts to deal with such problems with training mantras, the most famous of which is "all guns are always loaded." Unfortunately, training may not overcome errors unless it is long and intense—much longer and much more intense than most gun users have experienced. For example, several studies show that even trained police officers put their fingers on the trigger in simulations when they swore they did not. To prevent the accidental trigger pulling that can ensue, one solution has been to increase the trigger pull pressure. However, intensive training seems the best solution.

Other designs to prevent accidental discharges include (1) adjustable handgrip and stock sizes so that weapons can be personalized for users of different heights, arm lengths, and grip strengths; (2) magazine release designs that discourage the incorrect loading of guns; (3) loaded-chamber indicators to prevent accidents in which someone thinks a firearm is unloaded but a round is still in the chamber (with magazine-fed weapons, it is common to assume that removing the magazine removes all ammunition—but this is not true and leads to tragic accidents); and (4) safeties that have designs guaranteeing that a firearm does not discharge if it is dropped.

Glenn E. Meyer

See also: AK-47; Loaded-Chamber Indicator; Magna-Trigger; Smart Guns

Further Reading

Christopher, John Chivers. *The Gun*. New York: Simon and Schuster, 2010.

Goshen Enterprises, Inc. "HexSite Sighting Systems." http://www.goshen-hexsite.com/index2.php (accessed May 31, 2011).

Green, Marc. "Human Error vs. Design Error." Human Factors Blog, July 16, 2010. http://humanfactorsblog.org/2010/07/16/the-human-factors-of-weapons/ (accessed May 31, 2011).

Hendrick, Hal, Paul Paradis, and Richard J. Hornick. *Human Factors Issues in Handgun Safety and Forensics*. Boca Raton, FL: CRC Press, 2007.

Ingemund, John Arne. "Optical Sighting Instrument with Means for Producing a Sighting Mark" U.S. Patent 3,942,901, 1973. http://www.google.com/patents?id=RLc7AAAAEBAJ&printsec=abstract&zoom=4#v=onepage&q&f=false (accessed May 31, 2011).

L-3 Communications EOTech. "Origins of the Holographic Weapon Sight." 2011. http://www.eotech-inc.com/page.php?id=11 (accessed May 31, 2011).

Norman, Donald A. *The Psychology of Everyday Things*. New York: Basic Books, 1988.

SureSight. 2006. http://www.suresight.com (accessed May 31, 2011).

F

Faiths United to Prevent Gun Violence. *See* National Council of Churches (NCC) and Gun Control

Fatalities. *See* Victimization from Gun Violence

Federal Bureau of Investigation (FBI)

The Federal Bureau of Investigation, as the federal law enforcement agency in charge of the National Instant Criminal Background Check System (NICS), plays an important enforcement role in the regulation of guns in the United States. Federal law requires that any gun buyer be subjected to this instant background check prior to purchasing a firearm. The purpose of the NICS is to determine whether a potential gun buyer is complying with the laws that limit which persons may or may not purchase firearms (e.g., persons with a felony record may not purchase firearms). In most states, however, transactions between private parties are not required to go through the NICS system. Eighteen states do require gun sales between private parties to be made with the assistance of a federally licensed firearms dealer—who can ensure that the backgrounds of the buyer and seller are run through NICS and thus meet federal requirements for the possession and purchase of a firearm. (Those states are Alabama, California, Connecticut, Hawaii, Illinois, Indiana, Iowa, Maryland, Massachusetts, Michigan, Minnesota, Missouri, Nebraska, New Jersey,

New York, North Carolina, Rhode Island, and South Carolina.)

While the FBI is the primary federal law enforcement agency responsible for implementation and operation of the NICS, it plays a secondary role in the investigation and enforcement of federal gun laws. That is, the Bureau of Alcohol, Tobacco, Firearms and Explosives (ATF) has primary jurisdiction in the investigation, prevention, and enforcement of federal laws involving firearms, ammunition and explosives relating to interstate commerce. The jurisdictional primacy of ATF in this area has led to what has been often described as a "turf war" between ATF and FBI. According to a *Washington Post* article dated May 10, 2008, entitled "FBI, ATF Battle for Control of Cases: Cooperation Lags Despite Merger Five Years Ago," the agencies have "fought each other for control, wasting time and money and causing duplication of effort." Furthermore, according to the above article, "at crime scenes, FBI and ATF agents have threatened to arrest one another and battled over jurisdiction and evidence." As part of the Homeland Security legislation in 2002, the law enforcement aspects of ATF were transferred from the Department of the Treasury to the Department of Justice (DOJ). While ATF remained as a separate agency, the law enforcement aspects of its mission are now housed under the same parent department as the FBI, namely DOJ (the tax collection functions of ATF were left under the auspices of the Department of the Treasury). Part of the impetus for this transfer was to minimize jurisdictional conflicts between the ATF and FBI. Yet, since the FBI is the primary federal law enforcement agency in the investigation of terrorism related offenses, and ATF retains primary jurisdiction over incidents involving explosives, conflicts continue to arise between the agencies.

The FBI also publishes the annual *Crime in the United States*, which is based on its Uniform Crime Reports (UCRs)—information provided voluntarily by police departments throughout the United States. The FBI provides standardized forms for recording the data. The UCRs are the only source of information for deducing trends in crime in the United States as a whole and in localities within the country. They are the primary source of crime statistics for elected officials, criminal justice agencies, administrators, and other policy makers as well as the news media and the general public. The reports also analyze and inform policy makers on issues pertaining to crime and gun offenses, and they inform agents and officers in the field. For instance, a 2006 FBI report entitled "Violent Encounters: Felonious Assaults on America's Law Enforcement Officers," found (among other things) that handguns were predominantly utilized in assaulting police officers, and that the offenders often showed outward signs of possessing a weapon that the assaulted officer misses.

Although the FBI has traditionally played an important role in the enforcement of existing firearm laws, the appointment of John Ashcroft as attorney general of the United States in 2001 altered the enthusiasm with which the bureau has pursued those who are in possession of firearms illegally or who attempt to possess them illegally. Ashcroft (2001), in a May 17, 2001, letter to the executive director of the National Rifle Association, made it clear that he interpreted the Second Amendment's guarantee to a right to bear arms as one that applies to individual citizens rather than organized militias. In response to this letter, others pointed out that the federal courts had, in fact, consistently ruled that the Second Amendment applies to the right of individual states to have militias and not to the rights of individual citizens to keep and bear firearms for any other purpose. However, in the landmark cases of *District of Columbia v. Heller* (2008) and *McDonald v. City of Chicago* (2010), the individual-rights interpretation was upheld by the U.S. Supreme Court. It is notable that Ashcroft's beliefs on gun policy have affected the FBI's activities in the area of gun checks. For example, the *New York Times* reported on December 6, 2001, that Ashcroft barred the FBI from checking records to determine whether any of the people detained after the terrorist attacks on September 11 of that year had bought guns.

Elizabeth K. Englander and Patricia Snell

See also: Bureau of Alcohol, Tobacco, Firearms and Explosives (ATF); *District of Columbia v. Heller*; *McDonald v. City of Chicago*; National Instant Criminal Background Check System; NICS Improvement Act; Second Amendment; Uniform Crime Reports (UCR)

Further Reading

Ashcroft, John. "Letter to Mr. James Jay Baker, Executive Director of the National Rifle Association." Sent May 17, 2001. http://www.nraila.org/images/Ashcroft.pdf (accessed April 12, 2011).

Cole, George F., and Christopher E. Smith. *The American System of Criminal Justice.* 8th ed. Belmont, CA: Wadsworth, 2000.

Federal Bureau of Investigation. http://www.fbi.gov (accessed April 12, 2011).

Federal Bureau of Investigation. "Violent Encounters: Felonious Assaults on America's Law Enforcement Officers." http://www

.fbi.gov/stats-services/publications/law-enforcement-bulletin/2007-pdfs/jan07leb.pdf (accessed July 11, 2011).

Markon, Jerry. "FBI, ATF Battle for Control of Cases: Cooperation Lags Despite Merger Five Years Ago," *Washington Post*, May 10, 2008. http://www.washingtonpost.com/wp-dyn/content/story/2008/05/09/ST2008050903113.html (accessed July 11, 2011).

Federal Firearms Act of 1938 (Public Law No. 75-785)

The Federal Firearms Act of 1938 imposed the first federal limitations on the sale of ordinary firearms. It was aimed at those selling and shipping firearms through interstate or foreign commerce. The law required manufacturers, dealers, and importers of guns and handgun ammunition to obtain a federal firearms license (at an annual cost of one dollar) from the Internal Revenue Service. Dealers had to maintain records of the names and addresses of persons to whom firearms were sold. Gun sales to persons convicted of violent felonies were prohibited.

The legislation was substantially weakened by the National Rifle Association, as it was able to convince Congress to strike a provision that would have empowered the Justice Department to prosecute gun shippers and manufacturers who put guns into the hands of criminals (Carter 1997, 68). They could only be prosecuted if they "knowingly" sold guns to criminals (Spitzer 2012).

Jeffrey Kraus

See also: Firearm Dealers; Gun Control; National Firearms Act of 1934

Further Reading

Ascione, Alfred M. "The Federal Firearms Act." *St. John's Law Review* 13 (1939): 437–49.

Barnes Company. *Handgun Laws of the United States.* Fairfield, CT: Barnes Company, 1974.

Carter, Gregg Lee. *The Gun Control Movement.* New York: Twayne Publishers, 1997.

Leff, Carol Skalnik, and Mark H. Leff. "The Politics of Ineffectiveness: Federal Firearms Legislation, 1919–1938." *Annals of the American Academy of Political and Social Sciences* 455 (1981): 48–62.

Spitzer, Robert J. *The Politics of Gun Control.* 5th ed. Boulder, CO: Paradigm Publishers, 2012.

Federal Firearms Licensee (FFL).
See Firearm Dealers

Federal Gun Control Act of 1968.
See Gun Control Act of 1968

Federalism and Gun Control

The U.S. Constitution established a system of governance, federalism, whereby governing powers are divided between the national or federal government on the one hand, and state governments on the other. In the realm of gun control, laws regulating guns, gun use, and gun possession were the exclusive province of state and local governments from colonial times until the twentieth century. State and local laws regulating gun carrying, gun ownership, gun use, hunting practices, and laws requiring militia-eligible men to own guns were common among the colonies and, later, states. Even today, the vast majority of gun laws and regulations exist at the state and local level.

The first federal gun law imposed a federal excise tax on guns enacted as part of the War Revenue Act of 1919. In 1927, responding to rising gun use by criminals, Congress enacted a bill to bar the sale of handguns to private individuals through the mail. The first major national gun law, the National Firearms Act of 1934, imposed restrictions on so-called "gangster weapons," including machine guns and sawed-off shotguns. Subsequently, periodic national gun laws were enacted as the result of societal violence and high-profile assassinations.

The federal government's involvement in gun regulations paralleled the dramatic expansion of federal power that occurred during the New Deal era in the 1930s. As with the national government's greatly expanded influence in many areas, Congress's power to regulate interstate commerce became a key means by which it sought to shape national gun policy.

From the end of the 1930s until the 1990s, the federal courts consistently upheld the national government's more expansive definition of the commerce power. In 1995, however, in the case of *United States v. Lopez*, the Supreme Court overturned a federal law that barred guns from public schools, the Gun Free School Zones Act of 1990, concluding that the government's chief basis for the law—that the presence of guns in schools impeded the educational process, and that education was vital to the commerce of the nation—was an inadequate basis for use of the commerce power. Less noticed in the fracas over this court decision was the fact that all of the states already had legal proscriptions to gun carrying in schools. In 1996, Congress enacted a new version of the Gun Free School Zones Act, this time including wording stating that any firearm-based prosecution must be accompanied by evidence that the firearm in question must have "moved in or otherwise affects interstate commerce."

The *Lopez* decision was followed by others that imposed limits on Congress's application of the commerce power. The Supreme Court's decision in *United States v. Morrison* (2000), for example, struck down the civil remedy portions of the Violence against Women Act of 1994 as beyond Congress's powers to regulate interstate commerce. In 2005, however, the high court upheld Congress's use of the commerce power to regulate the local cultivation and use of marijuana in California in the case of *Gonzales v. Raich*, even though state law did not criminalize these activities.

The Supreme Court also ruled that Congress may not require state officials to participate in federal gun control efforts. In *Printz v. United States* (1997), the court struck down a provision of the federal Brady gun control law that required local law enforcement officials to conduct background checks on gun purchasers. The court held that Tenth Amendment principles of state sovereignty protected the states from having their officials told what to do by the federal government.

State gun laws came under uniform scrutiny because of a landmark ruling by the Supreme Court in 2010. In the case of *McDonald v. City of Chicago*, strict local handgun bans in Chicago and Oak Park, Illinois, were challenged as a violation of the Second Amendment's right to bear arms. While numerous such Second Amendment–based challenges of state and local gun laws had been rejected in federal courts in the past, the door to this challenge was opened by the Supreme Court's 2008 ruling in *District of Columbia v. Heller*, when a closely divided court ruled, for the first time in history, that the Second Amendment provided an individual right of citizens to possess handguns for the purpose of personal self-protection in the home (setting aside the militia-based interpretation that had been accepted by past courts). That ruling had applied to the District of Columbia's handgun ban because D.C. is a federal enclave. In *McDonald*, however, the court extended its ruling to the states, thus applying or "incorporating" this amendment to the states. While this ruling opened the door to hundreds of challenges to state and local gun laws around the nation, the court majority opinion, authored by Justice Samuel Alito, went to great pains to note that it considered most existing gun regulations to be legal within this newfound gun right.

Glenn Harlan Reynolds and
Robert J. Spitzer

See also: Brady Handgun Violence Protection Act (Brady Bill); *District of Columbia v. Heller*; Gun Control; Gun-Free School Laws; Gun Registration; Licensing; National Firearms Act of 1934; *McDonald v. City of Chicago*; *Printz v. United States*; Second Amendment; Tenth Amendment; United States Congress and Gun Legislation; *United States v. Lopez*

Further Reading

Cornell, Saul. *A Well-Regulated Militia.* New York: Oxford University Press, 2006.

Ducoff, John A. "Yesterday: Constitutional Interpretation, the Brady Act, and *Printz v. United States*." *Rutgers Law Journal* 30 (1998): 209–45.

"Gun Free School Zones Act—As Reenacted." http://www.gunlaws.com/Gun_Free_School _Zones_Act.pdf (accessed January 27, 2011).

Jones, Melissa Ann. "Legislating Gun Control in Light of *Printz v. United States*." *University of California–Davis Law Review* 32 (1999): 455–83. http://lawreview.law.ucda vis.edu/issues/Vol32/Issue2/DavisVol32No2 _Jones.pdf (accessed January 18, 2011).

"Reflections on *United States v. Lopez*: Symposium." *Michigan Law Review* 94 (1995): 533–831.

Federation for NRA

Federation for NRA is an ad hoc organization formed independently of the National

Rifle Association (NRA) in 1977 by disgruntled NRA hard-line members who felt that the NRA's old-guard leadership was insufficiently tough on gun and related political issues. Formed and headed by gun activist Neal Knox and including NRA dissidents Harlon Carter, Robert Kukla, David Caplan, and Joseph Tartaro, the federation became the umbrella group that laid plans to wrest control of the NRA from the old-guard leaders at the NRA's 1977 annual convention in Cincinnati. In what was later dubbed the Cincinnati Revolt, federation members, identifiable by their orange caps, coordinated their activities at the convention using bullhorns and walkie-talkies. They used parliamentary procedures to alter the NRA's bylaws to give the members attending the convention greater influence over organizational decisions. They then used these revised procedures to vote out of office the old-guard leaders and to vote in Carter to head the NRA. Federation members were elected or appointed to other NRA leadership posts.

The federation was revived by Knox in 1982 after he was forced to resign as head of the Institute for Legislative Action (ILA) by Carter. By this time, a rift had developed between the two men. Knox believed that Carter had become soft and complacent, corrupted by the authority of his office; Carter believed Knox had become too extremist. Knox objected to Carter's five-year term as president (NRA presidents before and since serve one-year terms) and charged that Carter had interfered with ILA activities. Knox and the federation proposed a return to one-year terms and other procedural changes. At the NRA's 1983 convention, these efforts were easily defeated by Carter and his allies, who had led the NRA to a broader membership and financial base. In 1984, Knox became the first NRA Board of Directors member ever voted off that body. In 1991, Knox returned to the board and again gained power in the NRA, only to be thwarted in 1997 by Wayne LaPierre and his candidate for vice president (who became NRA president in 1998), actor Charlton Heston.

Robert J. Spitzer

See also: Carter, Harlon; Heston, Charlton; Knox, Neal; National Rifle Association (NRA)

Further Reading

Brown, Peter Harry, and Daniel G. Abel. *Outgunned: Up against the NRA*. New York: Free Press, 2003.

Leddy, Edward F. *Magnum Force Lobby*. Lanham, MD: University Press of America, 1987.

Tartaro, Joseph. *Revolt at Cincinnati*. Buffalo, NY: Hawkeye, 1981.

Feinstein, Dianne (1933–)

A forceful advocate of gun control, Dianne Feinstein has been a Democratic senator from California since winning a special election to that post in 1992. Using her membership on the Senate's Judiciary Committee as a platform, Feinstein frequently has focused on efforts to strengthen the federal role in combating crime and on gun control as one approach to reducing the nation's violent crime rate. Early in her Senate career, Feinstein played a leadership role in the passage of two important federal gun control measures: the Gun-Free Schools Act and the Assault Weapons Ban of 1994. Subsequently, she has been less successful: she was unable to win an extension of the Assault Weapons Ban past 2004, unable to prevent passage of the gun liability bill (Protection of Lawful Commerce in Arms Act of 2005), and could not close the gun show loophole. She is a frequent prominent

commentator and major congressional force on gun control measures and judicial appointments.

Feinstein's strong support of gun control was rooted in her experiences in San Francisco city government. In 1978, as president of the city's Board of Supervisors, she was called upon to announce the gunshot murders of Mayor George Moscone and board member Harvey Milk. She made the announcement soon after discovering the two bodies in City Hall. Her experiences in the tragedy were recalled during a noteworthy exchange she had with a fellow senator during a gun control debate. Larry Craig (R-ID), a member of the National Rifle Association's board, questioned her knowledge of guns. Feinstein replied that she certainly knew of the effects of guns after trying to find Milk's pulse after he was fatally shot. She later became mayor of San Francisco, where she won approval of a municipal ordinance banning handgun ownership within the city. Then, in a public ceremony, Feinstein surrendered the .38-caliber pistol she had carried in response to death threats, the shooting-out of her windows, and an attempted bombing of her home. Passage of the ordinance greatly angered gun control opponents, some of whom initiated an effort to recall the mayor. Feinstein won the subsequent election by an overwhelming margin, a victory that seemed to solidify her political base in preparation for subsequent statewide contests. In comments on gun issues, Feinstein very often refers to her time as mayor as giving her insight into urban violence.

In the Senate, Feinstein continued her antiviolent crime and gun control efforts. The Gun-Free Schools Act of 1994, which she cosponsored with Byron Dorgan (D-ND), established uniform nationwide guidelines to make elementary and secondary schools

Dianne Feinstein. (U.S. Senate)

gun-free "safe havens" to protect children and youth from gun-related violence. Feinstein noted that school gun prohibition standards varied enormously among the states; her goal was to ensure that all children would be assured legal protection from gun-related violence.

In 1994, Feinstein also succeeded in winning passage of a 10-year ban on 19 forms of combat-type assault weapons. Her proposal, inserted as an amendment to the 1994 crime bill, listed specific types of rapid-fire weapons, partly to separate them from arms commonly used for hunting or target shooting. The law only applied to guns manufactured after the law went into effect. Another key provision of this bill banned the manufacture and sale of ammunition clips carrying 11 or more rounds. Feinstein argues the limits reduced the level of weapons used in crime, but critics contended it was impossible to prove the ban had lowered crime and that gun manufacturers easily circumvented the ban by making minor design modifications.

In 2004, the Assault Weapons Ban was due to sunset unless it was renewed. President Bush indicated he would sign a renewal law if it reached his desk, but he would not push Congress on the issue. Feinstein introduced an amendment that would have extended the ban for another 10 years to a bill that would have shielded the firearms industry from lawsuits. The amendment passed on a 52–47 vote, with most support coming from Democrats and northeastern Republicans. Lead sponsors of the liability bill opposed the renewal amendment and also a successful amendment to close the gun show loophole, so they called for defeat of their own bill. The bill died in a 90–8 vote. In subsequent years, Feinstein and others submitted bills to renew the ban, but they made little progress in Congress. She has stated that she remains committed to renewing and even expanding the Assault Weapons Ban, but is waiting for the right political moment.

In 2005, the liability bill was raised again. Feinstein sharply opposed the measure, calling it "highly offensive," and "a give-away" to the gun industry. The bill passed and became law (the Protection of Lawful Commerce in Arms Act). Feinstein also has been unsuccessful with legislation on gun shows. In 2008, she, Sen. Frank R. Lautenberg (D-NJ) and Sen. Jack Reed (D-RI) led nine other cosponsors in introducing legislation to require background checks at gun shows. The group unveiled the effort at a press conference featuring victims and family members of the Virginia Tech shooting. The legislation never made it out of committee.

Feinstein was more successful in playing a role in expansion of the National Instant Criminal Background Check System (the NICS Improvement Act). The Judiciary Committee approved her amendment to require that anyone found to be not guilty by reason of insanity or incompetent to stand trial be reported to the database.

Robert Dewhirst, with updates by
John W. Dietrich

See also: Assault Weapons Ban of 1994; Gun-Free School Laws; Gun Shows; NICS Improvement Act; Protection of Lawful Commerce in Arms Act of 2005

Further Reading

Koszczuk, Jackie. "Sen. Dianne Feinstein." *Congressional Quarterly Weekly Report* 57 (2002): 21–22.

Roberts, Jerry. *Dianne Feinstein: Never Let Them See You Cry.* New York: Harper Collins, 1994.

Whitney, Catherine. *Nine and Counting: The Women of the Senate.* New York: Harper-Collins, 2000.

Felons and Gun Control

Where, how, and why felons obtain, carry, and use guns have been central issues in the gun control debate for decades. One goal of many gun control advocates is to find some mechanism that disrupts the flow of firearms into criminal hands but does not infringe upon the legitimate gun ownership rights of law-abiding citizens. Many recent gun control measures have been enacted with this specific end in mind. Unfortunately, the criminal population has always found it relatively easy to circumvent gun control measures.

The most comprehensive survey of felons and their firearms was undertaken by Wright and Rossi (2008) in the early 1980s and is still cited in the scholarly literature with regularity. As recently as 2005, *Armed and Considered Dangerous* was described as "the only available survey of attitudes of (imprisoned) felons" concerning guns (Hahn et al. 2005). The study showed that relatively few felons (about one in six) attempted to obtain guns through customary retail channels; the illicit firearm market was dominated by informal purchases, swaps and trades with family members, friends, street sources, drug dealers, and other hard-to-regulate sources. The study also showed that most crime guns (somewhere between one-half and three-quarters of them) entered the stream of illicit commerce through theft from legitimate gun owners. The *Armed and Considered Dangerous* survey findings have also been substantiated by surveys conducted by the U.S. Department of Justice in 1991 and 1997 (Bureau of Justice Statistics [BJS] 2002). In the 1997 survey of state inmates, among those who possessed a gun at the time of their arrest, 80 percent bought their firearm from family, friends, a street buy, or an illegal source (BJS 2002, 1).

These results give reason to doubt the efficacy of gun controls imposed at the point of retail sale (e.g., the prohibition in the Gun Control Act of 1968 against retail sale of firearms to persons with felony records, the five-day waiting period for new firearm purchases enacted as part of the Brady Handgun Violence Prevention Act of 1993, or the instant criminal records check now required of new gun purchasers). The national five-day waiting period was implemented to give police departments ample time to undertake background checks on prospective gun buyers; the instant record check obviated the need for a waiting period. Whether or not a significant number of gun purchases by felons have been thwarted by these measures has been a matter of dispute. Proponents cite the number of purchases disallowed because of the background checks; opponents argue that the principal effects have been to divert an even higher proportion of felonious gun acquisitions into the secondary or informal market. Regardless, the most comprehensive evaluation of the effects of the five-day waiting period found no significant effects on rates of homicide and suicide (Ludwig and Cook 2000).

The five-day waiting period expired in 1998 and was replaced by the National Instant Criminal Background Check System (NICBCS) managed by the Federal Bureau of Investigation. The heart of the NICBCS is a national database containing information on all felony convictions; in theory, it allows for instantaneous presale background checks of all prospective gun purchasers. A report by the General Accounting Office (2002) on implementation of the NICBCS showed that most applicants (88%) were successfully checked within one hour. Further, about 95 percent of background checks were completed within three calendar days. If the background check is not completed within three business days, the transfer is allowed to proceed by default.

Restrictions at the point of retail sale, even the NICBCS background checking restriction, are readily circumvented by criminals. Another General Accounting Office (GAO) report released in March 2001 revealed that GAO investigators using fake identification successfully purchased guns from licensed gun dealers in every state they tried. Another easy circumvention is the use of proxy purchasers, associates with "clean" records who purchase guns from retailers in quantity for distribution to their felonious friends. Despite these obvious strategies that allow felons to evade retail-sales controls, the preponderance of evidence continues to show that most felons acquire guns through one-at-a-time and off-the-record transactions with friends, family, and other informal sources (Pierce et al. 2004). Consistent with this conclusion, the Bureau of Alcohol, Tobacco and Firearms' (ATF) *Gun Crime Trace Reports* (2000b) concludes that few possessors of crime guns

(about 11 percent) purchased their firearms directly from federally licensed gun dealers.

Given the above findings, it is anomalous that most guns used in crimes, confiscated by the police, and traced through the ATF paperwork system prove to be relatively new guns. The elapsed time between a gun's first retail sale and its use in a crime is called "time-to-crime," and numerous ATF reports and other studies have concluded that, on average, time-to-crime is relatively short. This implies a criminal preference for new guns and, perhaps, a larger role for organized gun trafficking in supplying the illicit firearm market than is suggested by the studies reviewed above, a conclusion endorsed by the ATF (Bureau of Alcohol, Tobacco and Firearms 2000a). Kleck (1997) resolves the anomaly by noting that criminals are, on average, relatively young and would therefore be expected to own relatively newer firearms. Consistent with this conclusion, one study (Kennedy, Piehl, and Braga 1996) found that the younger the criminal, the younger his gun.

Among gun owners in general, the secondary or informal market (private purchases or swaps and trades that do not involve licensed gun retailers) accounts for about 40 percent of annual firearm sales (Cook and Ludwig 1996). The preponderance of evidence is that among felons, that fraction is substantially higher. And while it is illegal under federal law to knowingly transfer a firearm to a felon even in a private transaction, this restriction is for all practical purposes unenforceable; as a result, the immense secondary market in firearms is essentially unregulated—a free-market free-for-all that felons can and do exploit to obtain guns of every description, in any desired quantity. A serious effort to prevent firearms from falling into felons' hands will require some regulation of this secondary market, and so far, no one has come up with a workable strategy to accomplish this end.

James D. Wright and Rachel L. Rayburn

See also: Assault Weapons Ban of 1994; Background Checks; Black Market for Firearms; Brady Handgun Violence Prevention Act (Brady Bill); Crime and Gun Use; Enforcement of Gun Control Laws; Gun Control Act of 1968; Gun Shows; National Instant Criminal Background Check System; Youth Crime Gun Interdiction Initiative

Further Reading

Bureau of Alcohol, Tobacco and Firearms. *Following the Gun: Enforcing Federal Laws against Firearms Traffickers.* Washington, DC: Bureau of Alcohol, Tobacco and Firearms, 2000a. http://www.mayorsagainstillegalguns.org/downloads/pdf/Following_the_Gun%202000.pdf (accessed May 31, 2011).

Bureau of Alcohol, Tobacco and Firearms. *Gun Crime Trace Reports (1999).* Washington, DC: Bureau of Alcohol, Tobacco and Firearms 2000b. http://www.atf.gov/publications/download/ycgii/1999/ycgii-report-1999-highlights.pdf (accessed May 31, 2011).

Bureau of Justice Statistics (BJS). *Firearm Use by Offenders.* Washington, DC: Department of Justice, 2002. http://bjs.ojp.usdoj.gov/content/pub/pdf/fuo.pdf (accessed May 31, 2011).

Cook, Philip J., and Jens Ludwig. *Guns in America: Results of a Comprehensive Survey of Gun Ownership and Use.* Washington, DC: Police Foundation, 1996. http://www.policefoundation.org/pdf/GunsinAmerica.pdf (accessed May 31, 2011).

General Accounting Office. *Firearms: Purchased from Federal Firearm Licensees Using Bogus Identification.* Washington, DC: General Accounting Office, 2001.

General Accounting Office. *Opportunities to Close Loopholes in the National Instant Criminal Background Check System.* Washington, DC: General Accounting Office, 2002. http://www.gao.gov/products/GAO-02-720 (accessed May 31, 2011).

Hahn, Robert A., et al. "Firearms Laws and the Reduction of Violence: A Systematic Review." *American Journal of Preventative Medicine* 28 (2005): 40–71.

Kennedy, David M., Anne M. Piehl, and Anthony A. Braga. "Youth Violence in Boston: Gun Markets, Serious Youth Offenders, and a Use Reduction Strategy." *Law and Contemporary Problems* 59 (1996): 147–96.

Kleck, Gary. *Targeting Guns: Firearms and Their Control.* Hawthorne, NY: Aldine de Gruyer, 1997.

Ludwig, Jens, and Philip J. Cook. "Homicide and Suicide Rates Associated with Implementation of the Brady Handgun Violence Prevention Act." *Journal of the American Medical Association* 284 (2000): 585–91.

Pierce, Gary L., et al. "Characteristics and Dynamics of Illegal Firearms Markets: Implications for a Supply-Side Enforcement Strategy." *Justice Quarterly* 21 (2004): 391–422.

Wright, James D., and Peter H. Rossi. *Armed and Considered Dangerous.* 2nd ed. Piscataway, NJ: Aldine Transaction, 2008.

Ferguson, Colin. *See* Long Island Railroad Massacre

Fifty Caliber Shooters Association, Inc. (FCSA)

The Fifty Caliber Shooters Association (FCSA) was founded in 1985 by a small group dedicated to advancing the sporting uses of the .50-caliber Browning Machine Gun (BMG) cartridge. FCSA, a nonprofit organization registered in Tennessee and Utah, publishes a quarterly magazine, *Very High Power*; maintains a website providing comprehensive information on .50-caliber shooting; and sanctions shooting competitions. The primary focus of the shooting competitions is on 1,000-yard competitions; the organization sponsors 10 to 15 of these each year in different locations in the United States (FCSA n.d.). Although most of its 4,000 members are in the United States, FCSA now has members in 22 countries. FCSA is a pro–Second Amendment, strongly gun rights organization.

FCSA also includes the Fifty Caliber Institute. The institute focuses on education, represents the organization to the media, and advocates politically on behalf of .50-caliber owners and manufacturers. Political advocacy is especially important to FCSA because of its belief that the .50-caliber shooting community has been under continual attack by gun control advocates. For example, the association was greatly concerned about Senator Dianne Feinstein's (D-CA) "Military Sniper Weapon Regulation Act," which aimed to put .50-caliber rifles under the control of the National Firearms Act (Burtt n.d.). The legislation did not pass.

Walter F. Carroll

See also: Feinstein, Dianne; Second Amendment

Further Reading

Burtt, John. "Position Statement." Fifty Caliber Shooters Association, n.d. http://www.fcsa.org/wwwroot/visitors/position_statement.php (accessed April 12, 2011).

Fifty Caliber Shooters Association (FCSA). "Fact Sheet." n.d. http://www.fcsa.org/wwwroot/visitors/about.php (accessed April 12, 2011).

Finland, Gun Laws

Finland is a small Nordic country of 5.3 million inhabitants and approximately 1.6 million firearms. Traditionally, Finland has a strong, hunting-related, shooting-sports culture. It has more firearms per person than most European countries, and the government promotes the idea that maintaining and nurturing the country's strong firearm culture is in the best interests of its citizens.

Legislation on firearms has been collected into a single statute covering all aspects of firearm ownership, commerce in firearms, and punishments for violating the law. This statute has been modified several times in an effort to promote security and prevention of violence with firearms. Firearms are highly regulated, and the gun statute is very detailed. The more important aspects of the statute follow.

A person must be 18 years old to purchase a firearm. He or she must first submit an application to the police, part of which requires that the reasons for wanting to own the gun must be stated. Accepted reasons include hunting, sport shooting, gun collecting, museum display, security work, and filming. Applicants must back up the reason for wanting to own the gun with some kind of specific evidence—for example, a membership card from a shooting or hunting club or proof of being in the security field. If the application is accepted, the potential gun owner must then apply for a permit for possession.

Out of the approximately 1.7 million gun permits that have been granted, 50 percent have been given for hunting. Hunting is a popular pastime in Finland, and there are 300,000 hunters there (5.4 percent of the population). These figures are the highest in Europe. A small number of these hunters—about 3 percent—are women. The quantity of hunters has remained steady for decades, with approximately 5,000 new hunters taking hunting license tests annually.

The number of applications for gun permits declined slightly during the 1990s. In the early 1990s, 125,000 permits were handled annually, but the number dropped to 55,000 after the stricter firearm law amendments went into effect in 1998. The number of permits per year has leveled to around 70,000 per year. It has been argued that the relatively high number of permits in the early 1990s was due to the government push to control World War II weapons and the belief that gun laws would become stricter.

There are approximately 15,000 new firearms sold annually. Police departments across the country are required to keep records of guns and permits within their area. All such records are classified.

One of the peculiarities of Finnish gun control is the attention paid to vintage World War II weapons. In the aftermath of the war with Russia, many, if not most, males chose to keep both their sidearms and long weapons as war mementos. The trend was replicated by larger unofficial hidings of weapons by private groups and individuals for fear of a Russian invasion. Most of these private firearms were not reported to the police at the time or in the following decades; they were sold illegally or handed over as family heirlooms. In the early 1990s, the government wanted to include such firearms in official records and offered amnesty for those who turned in such firearms. Those wishing to keep these historical firearms were offered permits. The police estimate that between 100,000 and 150,000 illegal firearms are still in Finland; many of these may be old guns, but they also include newer illegal firearms obtained for criminal purposes.

Finnish firearm owners are obligated by law to prevent their firearms from falling into the wrong hands. Thus, for example, if a gun owner has more than five weapons, they must be kept in a locked gun safe or stored with the gun parts separated. In addition, all firearms carried outside the home must be unloaded and—in most cases—disassembled.

Firearm collectors are required to apply for a collector's license. Approximately 1,000 such licenses have been issued. Collectors submit a timetable and collection content outline along with the application. The applicant is furthermore expected to give detailed information about his or her expertise in firearm history and technology. Collectors are required to keep detailed records of their collections.

The European Firearms Pass is used in Finland. This is the identification card for gun owners in which the owner's name, address, identification number, place of birth, and citizenship are displayed along with information about firearm permits and owned firearms both in Finland and in other European Union countries. The European Firearms Pass enables gun owners to transport firearms used for hunting and sport shooting within Europe.

Commerce in firearms is regulated to a high degree by the Ministry of Interior. Gun stores are required to keep detailed records of all firearms held by the store and to provide the police with such records in situations specified by law. All persons working at a gun store need to have a permit to handle firearms.

Finland has its fair share of violent crime, murder, and manslaughter, the rates of which have risen slightly from the beginning of the 1980s through 2000 only to decrease again during the 2000s. For example, in 1990, there were 7.8 homicides and attempts per 100,000 people, and this rose to 9.2 by 2000 (though virtually all of the increase was due to attempts, as the actual number of murders was nearly identical—145 in 1990 and 146 in 2000; by 2006, this had fallen to 138 homicides). The rate of actual murders (2.6 per 100,000 people) is about half that of the United States (5.5)—despite the fact that both nations are awash in firearms. Moreover, unlike in the United States, the majority of homicides in Finland are *not* related to firearms. For example, of the homicides committed between 2002 and 2006, only 15.4 percent were related to firearms; in comparison, 39.7 percent were committed with a sharp instrument (Savolainen, Messner, and Kivivuori 2001, 53; Kivivuori, Lehti, and Aaltonen 2007).

Analyses of the socioeconomic, cultural, and personal attributes of the killers and the types of weapons used reveal that proposed legislative changes that would restrict firearms would not deter homicide or solve many of the other problems surrounding firearms; rather, such analyses find the root causes in broader social problems (such as alcohol abuse and inequality, as research found that 80 percent of the offenders were intoxicated at the time of the homicide).

Firearms have been noticeably uncontroversial in Finland over the years. Some of the problematic issues in the U.S. gun control debate do not apply to Finland and other countries. For example, "self-protection" is strikingly missing as a right of Finnish citizens. Also, instances where private property has been protected with firearms (against animal rights activists, for example) have been condemned by the authorities. Even Finland's first-ever two school shooting incidents (Jokela, November 2007, and Kauhajoki, September 2008) resulted in only mild calls for stricter firearms regulation. Instead, the discussion in both cases focused on better treatment of mental health problems. Moreover, unlike in the United States, the majority of Finnish males (due to conscription) and a significant minority of women (due to voluntary military

service) have a good deal of familiarity with firearms. Military training not only focuses on the defensive and combat usage of firearms, but also highlights safety training.

Tiia Rajala

See also: Availability of Guns, Effects on Crime; Canada, Gun Laws; Germany, Gun Laws; Italy, Gun Laws; Japan, Gun Laws; Mexico, Gun Laws; Russia, Gun Laws; Self-Defense, Reasons for Gun Use; Switzerland, Gun Laws; United Kingdom—History of Gun Laws since 1900; Victimization from Gun Violence

Further Reading

Kivivuori, Janne, Martti Lehti, and Mikko Aaltonen. "Homicide in Finland, 2002–2006. A Description Based on the Finnish Homicide Monitoring System (FHMS)." Research Brief. Helsinki, Finland: National Research Institute of Legal Policy, March 2007. http://www.optula.om.fi/Satellite?blobtable =MungoBlobs&blobcol=urldata&SSURIapp type=BlobServer&SSURIcontainer=Default &SSURIsession=false&blobkey=id&blob headervalue1=inline;%20filename=homin fin2007.pdf&SSURIsscontext=Satellite %20Server&blobwhere=1284991870697&blob headername1=Content-Disposition&ssbinary =true&blobheader=application/pdf (accessed March 2, 2011).

Savolainen, Jukka, Steven F. Messner, and Janne Kivivuori. "Contexts of Lethal Violence in Finland and the United States." In *Homicide in Finland*, edited by Tapio Lappi-Setälä, 41–60. Helsinki, Finland: National Research Institute of Legal Policy, 2001.

Firearm and Injury Center at Penn (FICAP)

Founded in 1997, the Firearm and Injury Center (FICAP) was established in the Division of Traumatology and Surgical Critical Care of the University of Pennsylvania, in response to an increase and change in lethality of gunshot wound patients. A collaboration between the schools of nursing and medicine, FICAP produced a variety of research studies on firearms, including a comparison of rural versus urban firearm death and injury, the injury risks associated with guns in the home, the injury risks associated with gun carrying, and suicide among African American males.

Over time, FICAP broadened its base, scope, and mission. It now includes researchers from the schools of education, engineering, communication, social policy, business, and arts and sciences. From a focus on firearms, it now has a goal to help create safer communities by helping to reduce all types of injuries and violence.

The FICAP website (http://www.uphs .upenn.edu/ficap) includes a resource book that provides an overview of firearm injury in the United States and a series of Issue Briefs describing research findings.

David Hemenway

See also: Gun Violence as a Public Health Problem

Further Reading

Firearm and Injury Center at Penn. *Firearm Injury in the U.S.* (2009). http://www.uphs .upenn.edu/ficap/resourcebook/pdf/mono graph.pdf (accessed July 8, 2011).

Firearm and Injury Center at Penn. http:// www.uphs.upenn.edu/ficap/ (accessed July 8, 2011).

Firearm Dealers

Virtually all civilian sales of new firearms in the United States are made through federally licensed firearm dealers (FFLs), regulated under a scheme established by the federal Gun Control Act of 1968 (GCA). Retail dealers range from tiny enterprises, such as mom-and-pop sidelines in rural general stores, to vast specialized emporia with racks of guns and affiliated shooting ranges. Retailers get most of their guns from wholesale distributors, who are also federally licensed. Even so, about 40 percent of all gun sales each year are of used guns bought and sold through unregulated transactions in the secondary market.

Enacted in the wake of the assassinations of President John F. Kennedy, Sen. Robert F. Kennedy, and Dr. Martin Luther King Jr., the GCA replaced the Federal Firearms Act of 1938 as the primary federal law regulating commerce in firearms. The 1968 law created a licensing system aimed primarily at regulating the interstate movement of firearms. By restricting interstate movement of firearms to transactions between FFLs, the law was intended to enhance the ability of the individual states to effectively enforce their own gun laws by barring "gun runners" from buying guns in states with lax laws and transporting them to states with more restrictive laws. The GCA also barred certain prohibited classes of persons, such as convicted felons, illegal aliens, and drug addicts from receiving or possessing firearms.

Central to the federal regulatory scheme is the requirement that any person "engaged in the business" of manufacturing, importing, or dealing in firearms obtain a license from the Bureau of Alcohol, Tobacco, Firearms and Explosives (ATF). The ATF issues 11 types of licenses, depending on the nature of the licensee's activity. The most common license, Type 01, is issued to retail dealers (70 percent), but some other common licenses include Type 02 for pawnbrokers (10 percent), Type 06 for ammunition manufacturers (2 percent), Type 07 for firearm manufacturers (2 percent), and Type 08 for importers (less than 1 percent).

A dealer's license grants the holder the privilege of purchasing and shipping guns in

Mark Diaz, manager of Schrank's Smoke 'n Gun Shop, displays six handguns for sale at the store in Waukegan, Illinois. (AP Photo/M. Spencer Green)

any quantity across state lines to and from other licensees, including retailers, wholesale distributors, and manufacturers. Licensees are required to maintain detailed records of firearm transactions and are subject to periodic inspection by the ATF. Although some states impose their own licensing requirements, most do not, limiting their regulation to collateral matters such as zoning restrictions and generic business licensing and tax collection.

The GCA's original wording limited the ATF's discretion in denying licenses. The law required ATF to issue a license within 45 days of an application to anyone who was 21 years old, had business premises,

and was not prohibited from possessing firearms. Although the law required anyone "engaged in the business of dealing in firearms" to have a license, it failed to define the term "engaged in the business."

As a consequence of these regulatory features, two issues quickly developed. First, the number of FFLs quickly ballooned. Persons who had no intention of engaging in a full-fledged retail business easily got licenses at an annual fee of only $10. With license in hand, these so called "kitchen-table" dealers could buy guns out of state, sometimes at wholesale prices, for themselves, their friends, and others, often evading local zoning and tax laws in the process and without undergoing background checks or waiting periods imposed on individual retail customers. By 1992, there were 245,000 licensed gun dealers in the United States—more than the 210,000 gas stations in the country. The sheer number of dealers made meaningful regulation by the ATF virtually impossible. As a result, some licensees who appeared on the surface to be operating only as a convenience to friends were in fact selling firearms in volume without records. . By 1993, when the number of FFLs reached its peak of 286,000, the ATF estimated that 74 percent of FFLs were kitchen-table dealers, and 46 percent conducted no business at all. By 2010, the ATF reported that the number of licensed dealers and pawnbrokers had declined to 54,600—primarily due to federal gun legislation in 1993 and 1994 (see below).

The second issue problem associated with the law resulted directly from the failure to clearly define "engaging in the business." Unlicensed dealers sold from flea markets, gun shows, their homes, and their cars while claiming to be simply collectors. Efforts to police dealers and to prosecute unlicensed dealers generated substantial resistance within the firearms enthusiasts and advocacy groups who advanced legislation designed to restrict the authority of ATF to inspect dealers, narrow the definition of engaging in the business, and reduce record-keeping violations by dealers to misdemeanors (Vizzard 2000). This legislation passed Congress in 1986 as the Firearms Owners Protection Act (FOPA). As a result, the capacity of ATF to control unlicensed dealing and diversion of firearms by licensed dealers into the unlicensed market was greatly reduced (Vizzard 2000).

Although the 1993 Brady Handgun Violence Prevention Act (the "Brady Bill") primarily was aimed at requiring uniform criminal record checks of all persons purchasing guns from federally licensed dealers, it also increased the dealer licensing fee to $200 for the first three years and $90 for each additional three-year period. It also requires applicants to certify that they have notified the chief law enforcement officer in their area of their intent to apply for a license. The 1994 Violent Crime Control and Law Enforcement Act (the "Assault Weapons Ban") further required applicants to submit photographs and fingerprints, and to certify that their business complies with all state and local laws, including zoning regulations. Finally, ATF field offices initiated cooperative efforts with state and local authorities to ensure that applicants met all relevant state and local laws.

As a result of these changes, the number of Type 01 FFLs dropped from 245,628 in January 1994 to 66,500 in February 2001, a decrease of 73 percent. Gun rights advocates complained that the reforms infringed on their rights, and the industry complained that the dramatic decrease in dealers hurt sales. But regulators welcomed the drop, arguing that it was easier to supervise fewer dealers and that the drop in casual dealers discouraged criminal gun trafficking. Even so, the ATF reported that in 1998, about 31 percent of FFLs had sold no guns during the preceding year.

Federal law does not require all gun sellers to obtain a license. On the contrary, the FOPA exempts a person who makes occasional sales, exchanges, or purchases of firearms for the enhancement of a personal collection or for a hobby, or who sells all or part of a personal firearms collection, and requires a showing that they are in business for livelihood and profit. Although such hobbyists and personal sellers do not enjoy the privilege of interstate sales, they have inspired commercial complaint and regulatory concern, principally in the context of gun shows, venues at which firearms are often sold informally. Forty percent of all gun sales each year are made through such informal secondary market outlets.

Because federal gun control laws have focused primarily on screening gun buyers in an attempt to "keep guns out of the wrong hands," licensed dealers are required to keep specific records on all guns they buy or sell and to initiate background checks on all potential purchasers. Hobbyists and personal sellers are free from these requirements. Licensed dealers complain that this disparity puts them at a competitive disadvantage, especially at gun shows, where the only difference between a licensed dealer and an unlicensed private seller is that a person buying from the latter is free of bothersome paperwork and background checks. Gun regulators argue that unlicensed sellers have become a major source of firearms for felons, juveniles, and others who have been effectively barred from getting guns by the background checks imposed by the Brady Bill. Closing this "gun show loophole" has become a contentious goal of the gun control movement.

Thomas Diaz, with updates by
William J. Vizzard

See also: Assault Weapons Ban of 1994; Brady Handgun Violence Prevention Act (Brady Bill); Bureau of Alcohol, Tobacco, Firearms and Explosives (ATF); Federal Firearms Act of 1938 (Public Law No. 75-785); Firearms Owners' Protection Act of 1986; Gun Control Act of 1968; Gun Shows

Further Reading

Bureau of Alcohol, Tobacco and Firearms. *Commerce in Firearms in the United States.* Washington, DC: U.S. Government Printing Office, 2000. http://www.mayorsagainstillegalguns.org/downloads/pdf/Commerce_in_Firearms_2000.pdf (accessed May 27, 2011).

Diaz, Tom. *Making a Killing: The Business of Guns in America.* New York: New Press, 1999.

Violence Policy Center. *Firearms Production in America: 2000 Edition.* Washington, DC: Violence Policy Center, 2000. http://www.vpc.org/graphics/prodcov.pdf (accessed May 27, 2011).

Vizzard, William J. *Shots in the Dark: The Policy, Politics, and Symbolism of Gun Control.* Lanham, MD: Rowman & Littlefield, 2000.

Firearm Sentence Enhancement (FSE) Laws

Firearm sentence enhancement laws are those criminal laws that impose upon criminal offenders increased penalties if the use of a firearm was involved in the offender's criminal offense. FSE laws, often also called "gun-use laws," typically result in significantly longer terms of imprisonment for perpetrators of crimes committed with guns. By increasing the term of imprisonment, FSE laws were envisioned as a way to decrease violent crimes, including gun assaults and homicides, through deterrence. FSE laws have been assumed by legislators to have a derivative deterrent effect on violent gun assaults and homicides, because the potential criminal offender would presumably leave the guns at home to avoid the imposition of greater punishments if apprehended. The arguable assumption behind FSE laws is that the existence of such laws might influence the decision-making process of the criminal offender on whether or not to carry a firearm or whether or not to use the firearm during the commission of a felony.

In the gun control and firearm policy areas, few measures have received as much attention at both the state and federal levels as FSE laws. Multiple state statutes and the federal Gun Control Act of 1968 impose increased punishments in criminal cases through the use of FSE provisions. FSE laws have been viewed by state and federal legislators as an attractive means of gun control, as one of their most important expectations is that they will reduce gun-related crime without imposing further constraints on the behavior of "law-abiding" citizens who wish to possess firearms. It is for this reason that interest groups such as the National Rifle Association frequently lend their support to the advancement of FSE laws.

The federal FSE law is contained in section 924(c) of the Gun Control Act (GCA) of 1968. In its original form, the FSE law in the GCA provided a mandatory minimum sentence of between 1 and 10 years for criminals who used or carried a firearm unlawfully during the commission of any federal felony. Since the federal FSE law's original enactment, Congress has amended it many times, including by expanding the coverage to drug crimes, distinguishing among the types of firearms, and raising the penalty to up to 30 additional years if the firearm is a machine gun, an assault rifle, or equipped with a silencer. Congress has also clarified the meaning of "use" and "possession" of a firearm in the FSE provision in response to several Supreme Court cases restricting the interpretation of the FSE provision. To date, no systematic studies have been published that reveal the effectiveness of FSE laws.

James A. Beckman

See also: *Bailey v. United States*; Gun Control Act of 1968; *Muscarello v. United States*

Further Reading

Hofer, Paul. "Federal Sentencing for Violent and Drug Trafficking Crimes Involving Firearms: Recent Changes and Prospects for Improvement." *American Criminal Law Review* 37 (2000): 41–73.

Firearms Coalition

The Firearms Coalition was founded in 1984 by Neal Knox and is an umbrella organization of sorts for gun rights organizations and individuals. Membership is available on two levels: one that is at no cost and offers basic services; the other, Executive Membership Status, is available through financial contributions and offers access to the coalition's resources.

The Internet is a powerful tool for any advocacy group, and many gun organizations have focused on building elaborate websites to gain support and publicize their messages. The Firearms Coalition at first used phone messages and fax alerts, but it moved quickly to the online format. The Internet not only helps the coalition increase its fund-raising efforts, but, more importantly, places the information in the public domain. Members and nonmembers alike are able to view Knox's columns, alerts, and general gun-related news articles via the site. The Firearms Coalition website has also collected gun-related Internet links whose content and quality are briefly described.

Tiia Rajala

See also: Knox, Neal

Further Reading

Firearms Coalition. http://www.firearmscoalition.org/ (accessed February 28, 2011).

Firearms Industry

The U.S. firearms industry is unique in several aspects. Unlike most manufacturing industries, it has limited potential for export sales, as most nations more strictly control civilian firearms sales than does the United States. Even for classifications of small arms that are less restricted, such as traditional hunting rifles and shotguns, demand does not match that in the United States. In addition, firearms technology has changed very slowly, and firearms are very durable (Vizzard 2000, 23–24). Thus the two forces that drive demand for other products, consumption and obsolescence, provide very little impetus for firearms sales.

Over the past half century, the gun market in the United States has evolved from one dominated by sporting rifles and shotguns ("long guns") to one dominated by firearms designed primarily for combat. Beginning in the early 1960s, gun sales increased rapidly as baby boomers came of age and consumer product sales generally increased. At the same time, the composition of the market began to change (Vizzard 2000, 24). Between 1960 and 2009, handgun sales increased far more rapidly than long gun sales; expanding from about a quarter of the market to over half of all new gun sales (ATF 2000; ATF 2010; USITC 2010). In addition, military (nonsporting style) firearms became a progressively larger portion of the rifle and shotgun market (Vizzard 2000, 24–26), and the handgun market shifted from domination by revolvers to domination by semiautomatic pistols (ATF 2000; ATF 2010; USITC 2010). Actual volume of sales for new guns has fluctuated over the past 50 years, climbing from just over 2 million in 1960, to a high of 6.4 million in 1980 and then declining (ATF 2000). The election of 1992 and subsequent push by the Clinton administration for a ban on certain semiautomatic, military-style rifles, commonly called "assault rifles," ignited a fear of new gun control and spurred sales to over seven million by 1994, which was followed by another decline (ATF 2000). The 2008 election generated another significant increase in buying (Gregory 2009), which peaked in 2009, with sales approaching nine million new firearms (ATF 2010; USITC 2010). (Note: to calculate the number of firearms sold in the United States, the total firearm imports, from USITC import data, were added to total firearms manufactured, from ATF data; then total firearms exported, from ATF data, were subtracted.) This latest increase in sales seems particularly ironic, as purchasers responding to fear of new firearms restrictions apparently ignored the Supreme Court's landmark opinion in *District of Columbia v. Heller* (2008), which interpreted the Second Amendment as guaranteeing an individual's right to own firearms—as well as the absence of firearms regulation in either the congressional or presidential legislative agenda. The shift from a market dominated by sporting-style long guns to one dominated by handguns and combat-style long guns—combined with a pattern of sales that appears to respond primarily to perceived changes in the political climates—implies that the gun market has moved from one dominated by sport shooters to one more dominated by persons who perceive a need for personal defense. The number of hunting licenses issued in the United States has declined over the past four decades, as has access to wildlife habitat and rural populations (U.S. Fish and Wildlife Service 2011). The percentage of households reporting gun ownership in the General Social Survey (National Opinion Research Center 2011), 32.3 percent in 2010, has been in a concurrent decline. Although legitimate scholars have questions regarding the calculation of the true rate of gun ownership by individual citizens (Ludwig, Cook, and Smith 1998), some decline seems irrefutable.

Yet, the number of firearms in private hands in the United States, conservatively estimated at 220 million in 2000 (Vizzard 2000), has likely grown to around 300 million today. The exact rate of growth cannot be calculated, as the total number of guns confiscated by police and illegally exported is not precisely known. Given this increase in the gun population, concurrent with a declining number of gun owners, one can only conclude that a limited number of gun owners continue to acquire firearms beyond the number needed to engage in sport or accomplish personal protection. Given the pattern of behavior by purchasers of other products in the United States, impulse buying would seem to offer the most reasonable explanation for much of the buying. In addition, the sudden spike in buying around elections implies an influence from hoarding due to fear of future restrictions.

Based on data from federal excise taxes, firearms and ammunition accounted for about $2 billion in retail sales in 2009. This represented about 0.05 percent of the U.S. retail economy. The Small Arms and Ammunition Manufacturers Institute (SAAMI) estimated the total economic impact of hunting and shooting on the U.S. economy at $36.4 billion in 2004 (SAAMI 2004). This figure includes sales of clothing, equipment, and accessories as well as travel and other spending by shooters and hunters. The figure is difficult to verify, but would represent about 0.25 percent of the national economy if correct.

According to ATF, there were fewer than 54,000 licensed firearms dealers in the United States as of September 1, 2010. Although this represents a significant decline from the peak of 286,000 in 1993, many of these are not conducting regular, full-time retail or wholesale sales.

William J. Vizzard

See also: *District of Columbia v. Heller*; Ergonomics and Firearm Design; Firearm Dealers; Hunting; National Association of Firearms Retailers (NAFR); National Shooting Sports Foundation (NSSF); Protection of Lawful Commerce in Arms Act of 2005; Second Amendment; Surplus Arms

Further Reading

Bureau of Alcohol, Tobacco, Firearms and Explosives (ATF). *Annual Firearms Manufacturers and Export Report.* http://www.atf.gov/statistics/afmer/ (accessed June 26, 2011).

Bureau of Alcohol, Tobacco, Firearms and Explosives (ATF). *Commerce in Firearms in the United States.* Washington, DC: U.S. Government Printing Office, 2000.

Gregory, Sean. "Boom in Gun Sales Fueled by Politics and the Economy." *Time*, April 8, 2009. http://www.time.com/time/printout/0,8816,1889886,00.html (accessed June 26, 2011).

Ludwig, Jens, Philip J. Cook, and Tom W. Smith. "The Gender Gap in Reporting Household Gun Ownership." *American Journal of Public Health* 88 (1998): 1715–18.

National Opinion Research Center. General Social Survey, 2011. ("Do you happen to have in your home (or garage) any guns or revolvers?" If yes, "Is it a pistol, shotgun, rifle, or what?") http://www.norc.uchicago.edu/GSS+Website/ (accessed July 6, 2011).

Small Arms and Ammunition Manufacturers Institute (SAAMI). "Market Size and Economic Impact of the Sporting Firearms and Ammunition Industry in America." 2004. http://www.saami.org/specifications_and_information/publications/download/SAAMI_ITEM_222-Market_Size_and_Economic_Impact_of_the_Sporting_Firearms_and_Ammunition_Industry_in_America.pdf (accessed June 27, 2011).

United States International Trade Commission (USITC). http://dataweb.usitc.gov/ (accessed May 27, 2011).

U.S. Fish and Wildlife Service. "Wildlife and Sport Fish Restoration Program: National

Survey—15 Year Trend Information." Last updated May 18, 2011. http://wsfrprograms.fws.gov/subpages/NationalSurvey/15_year_trend.htm (accessed May 27, 2011).

U.S. Government Accountability Office. *Firearms Trafficking: U.S. Efforts to Combat Arms Trafficking to Mexico Face Planning and Coordination Challenges*. Washington, DC: United States Government Accountability Office, GAO-09-709, June 2009. http://www.gao.gov/new.items/d09709.pdf (accessed May 27, 2011).

Vizzard, William J. *Shots in the Dark: The Policy, Politics, and Symbolism of Gun Control*. Lanham, MD: Rowman & Littlefield, 2000.

Firearms Owners Against Crime (FOAC)

This organization is a nonpartisan political action committee, based in Pennsylvania and chaired by Kim Stolfer. Its purpose is to promote the election of legislators and politicians who support unregulated gun ownership. The organization is supported by individual donations. FOAC is involved at both the state and federal levels in promoting legal gun ownership. The group supports the prosecution of illegitimate use of firearms but does not support the regulation or restriction of gun ownership for legitimate use, "including personal and property protection." In support of its position, FOAC cites the Second Amendment and the First Article of the Constitution of the Commonwealth of Pennsylvania.

The organization keeps its membership aware of those legislative initiatives and voting records that are relevant to its mission. It publishes voter guides for those wanting to support unregulated gun ownership. FOAC

also organizes meetings and speaker events, and it provides a website with informational links.

Elizabeth K. Englander and Patricia Snell

See also: Citizens Committee for the Right to Keep and Bear Arms (CCRKBA); Gun Owners of America (GOA); National Rifle Association (NRA); Second Amendment

Further Reading

Firearms Owners Against Crime (FOAC). http://www.foac-pac.org/ (accessed March 25, 2011).

Firearms Owners' Protection Act of 1986

This federal law relaxed several gun restrictions that were first enacted in 1968. The move to relax federal gun regulations was a top agenda item of a new and more politically aggressive leadership faction that took control of the National Rifle Association in 1977. Congressional sponsors of the bill were Sen. James McClure (R-ID) and Rep. Harold Volkmer (D-MO). The bill that passed in 1986 (Public Law 99-308, 100 Stat. 449) came to be known as the McClure-Volkmer bill.

As early as 1978, Rep. Volkmer proposed legislation at the behest of the NRA to repeal much of the Gun Control Act of 1968. Sen. McClure joined this effort in the early 1980s. This political drive picked up important momentum from the presidential election of gun control foe Ronald Reagan in 1980 and the more conservative mood of the country, and from the fact that the Republicans won control of the Senate after the 1980 elections.

Earlier versions of the McClure-Volkmer bill had been approved by the Senate Judiciary Committee in 1982 and 1984, but full floor consideration was not obtained until

1985, when at the urging of the bill's sponsors, Senate Majority Leader Robert Dole (R-KS) authorized the unusual move of bypassing the Judiciary Committee and placing the bill directly on the Senate calendar. Once on the floor, the bill was subjected to a barrage of amendments designed to strengthen gun controls; none of these amendments was accepted, however, except for a restriction adopted by the Senate to ban the importation of gun parts for cheap handguns called Saturday night specials.

Opponents of the bill, led by Sen. Edward Kennedy (D-MA) and Sen. Howard Metzenbaum (D-OH), threatened a filibuster in June if some of the bill's provisions were not softened. Supporters yielded, and after intense negotiations the bill, S. 49, was passed on July 9, 1985. The final vote for passage of the bill was 79–15. The relatively speedy passage was attributed to the pressure of the NRA and its allies, and to the fact that the Republican-controlled Senate had a sympathetic Judiciary Committee chair, Strom Thurmond (R-SC), and majority leader.

Deliberations in the Democratic-controlled House posed a far greater problem for McClure-Volkmer supporters. House Judiciary Committee chair Peter Rodino (D-NJ), a staunch gun control proponent, had announced early in 1985 that the bill arrived " D.O.A.—Dead on Arrival." Bill opponents were still confident that Rodino would succeed as he had in the past in keeping the bill bottled up in committee. Yet Rodino was unable to fulfill his prediction. By the fall of 1985, bill supporters had begun a discharge petition that, if signed by a majority of the House membership (218 representatives), would force the bill out of committee and onto the floor. The drastic and unusual nature of the House discharge petition is revealed by the fact that from 1937 to 1986, discharge petitions had succeeded in only 20 instances.

Of those, only two such bills were actually enacted into law.

Despite the initial opposition of Rodino and Rep. William J. Hughes (D-NJ), the chair of the Judiciary Subcommittee on Crime, they both realized that unless they formulated a substitute compromise bill, the full committee would be forced to report McClure-Volkmer. The committee thus held a markup session on a compromise bill and reported it to the floor by unanimous vote. This remarkable turn of events occurred in March 1986 as the result of a successful discharge petition. By reporting the Rodino-Hughes bill to the floor first (on March 11) before the actual filing of the discharge petition on behalf of McClure-Volkmer (on March 13), gun control supporters hoped to salvage some parliamentary flexibility that would allow priority consideration of the Rodino-Hughes bill. This maneuver failed, however, because Volkmer was able to offer his version of the bill as a substitute for that of the Judiciary Committee in a vote on the floor.

On April 9, Representative Hughes offered a package of law enforcement amendments to McClure-Volkmer, including a ban on interstate sale and transport of handguns and stricter record-keeping regulations. The package was rejected by a wide margin (248–176). During the vote, police officers stood in full uniform at "parade rest" at the entrance to the House floor as a sign of their opposition to McClure-Volkmer. After several other votes on motions to strengthen certain gun control provisions (all were defeated), the House adjourned and then reconvened the next day. On the third try, the House approved (by 233–184) a ban on interstate handgun sales after proponents stressed the difference between sale and transport. A final amendment to bar all future possession and sale of machine guns by private citizens also passed. The bill was approved by a 292–130 vote on April 10. President Reagan signed the measure into law on May 19, 1986.

As passed into law, McClure-Volkmer amended the 1968 act by allowing for the legal interstate sale of rifles and shotguns as long as the sale was legal in the states of the buyer and seller. The act also eliminated record-keeping requirements for ammunition dealers, made it easier for individuals selling guns to do so without a license unless they did so "regularly," allowed gun dealers to do business at gun shows, and prohibited the Bureau of Alcohol, Tobacco and Firearms (ATF) from issuing regulations requiring centralized records of gun dealers. The law also reduced the penalty for falsifying firearm records from a felony to a misdemeanor. In addition, the act limited to one per year the number of unannounced inspections of gun dealers by the ATF and prohibited the establishment of any system of comprehensive firearm registration. Finally, the act barred future possession or transfer of machine guns and retained existing restrictions (except for transport) on handguns.

In a final move to tighten up elements of the bill, which was also a concession to law enforcement groups that had opposed McClure-Volkmer, the Senate passed a separate bill on May 6 that tightened licensing, record-keeping, and interstate transport requirements. That bill easily passed the House on June 24 and was signed into law on July 8, 1986. The passage of McClure-Volkmer represented a high point in the NRA's influence in Washington. In all, the NRA spent about $1.6 million in lobbying and advertising costs to win passage of the bill. At the same time, however, gun control supporters, led by Handgun Control, Inc. (now called the Brady Campaign), also won some concessions in the bill, prompting them to claim victory as well. In addition, this bill marked a public and permanent split between police organizations and the NRA. Formerly, links between the two had been strong. After this, however, most police organizations would side with efforts to strengthen gun control, including the Brady Bill and the Assault Weapons Ban. Despite the NRA's victory, leaders within the organization considered it inadequate, and several dozen NRA employees were fired after the bill's enactment as a consequence.

Robert J. Spitzer

See also: Assault Weapons Ban of 1994; Brady Campaign to Prevent Gun Violence; Brady Handgun Violence Prevention Act (Brady Bill); Bureau of Alcohol, Tobacco, Firearms and Explosives (ATF); Gun Control Act of 1968; National Rifle Association (NRA)

Further Reading

Spitzer, Robert J. *The Politics of Gun Control.* 5th ed. Boulder, CO: Paradigm Publishers, 2012.

Vizzard, William J. *Shots in the Dark: The Policy, Politics, and Symbolism of Gun Control.* Lanham, MD: Rowman & Littlefield, 2000.

Firearms Research Digest

The *Firearms Research Digest* (http://www.firearmsresearch.org) is an online database that provides succinct summaries of academic firearms articles that appear in social science, criminology, medical, and public health journals. Launched by the Harvard Injury Control Research Center at the Harvard School of Public Health in 2010, the digest makes scholarly articles more accessible to reporters, law enforcement, public health officials, policymakers, and the general public. Each article is summarized in simple, clear, and accessible language.

Initially, the website covered six years of research published between 2003 and 2008. The digest is being expanded to include articles from 1988 to the present. Funding to create this online library was provided by the Chicago-based Joyce Foundation.

Despite the increased ease of accessing articles through search engines such as Google Scholar or PubMed, the sheer volume of returned information in technical jargon can be daunting. The principal objective of the *Firearms Research Digest* is to highlight the key research findings in lay language so anyone can readily understand the study results.

The digest includes research published in academic journals that were identified through a search of academic indexes: the social science indexes Academic Search Premier and EconLit; the educational literature database ERIC; the psychiatry/psychology index PsychInfo; the public health and medical index MEDLINE; and the legal and public records LexisNexis database. Not included are books, or articles from nonacademic sources (including government, law enforcement, and advocacy groups); studies of a purely medical nature (e.g., treatment of gunshot wounds); or studies of a purely historical or antiquarian nature (e.g., Civil War firearms).

An advanced search engine allows for searching by keyword, title, author, topic (subject taxonomy), publication, or year. Search results provide full bibliographic citation as well as the brief summary of findings. The site had over 6,000 unique visits in its first six months of operation.

David Hemenway

See also: Center for Gun Policy and Research; Violence Prevention Research Program (VPRP)

Further Reading

Firearms Research: Prevalence, Patterns, and Prevention of Firearms Violence. http://www.firearmsresearch.org (accessed January 24, 2011).

First Monday: Unite to End Gun Violence, 2000–2001

First Monday was an annual, campus-based organizing campaign that focused on a different social justice issue each year. The campaign began each year on the first Monday in October to coincide with the opening of the Supreme Court term. First Monday focused on a different social justice issue each year starting in 1994. In 2000 and 2001, it focused on gun violence. That decision reflected the organization's view of how critical gun violence is. First Monday 2000 emphasized the victims of gun violence and the importance of gun control laws. The 2001 campaign focused on the gun industry, the gun lobby (especially the National Rifle Association), and how their practices exacerbate gun violence in the United States.

First Monday was a project of the Alliance for Justice in conjunction with Physicians for Social Responsibility. The campaign pointed out that the United States tolerates levels of gun violence that are much higher than those in most other industrialized societies, with more than 80 people a day dying from gun violence, at that time. Of those 80 people, about 23 were between 20 and 30 years of age. The organization suggested that this epidemic of gun violence was a public health issue and developed Unite to End Gun Violence as a broad-based, multifaceted campaign.

First Monday aimed to involve students in high schools, colleges and universities, and schools of law, medicine, nursing, social work, and public health in its national education and advocacy campaigns. The campaigns suggest activities and roles appropriate to different groups of students. For example, high school students could start groups on gun violence prevention in their schools. College students might raise awareness on campuses by distributing information on gun violence or hosting speakers. First Monday suggested that medical, public health, and nursing students should get involved because gun violence is a national public health crisis. Law students could do research on the legal aspects of guns, gun control legislation, and gun violence. Social work departments and students played an active role in the campaign, which stressed the importance of education on gun violence for social work practitioners.

First Monday organized its events around several documentary films. In 2000, the campaign produced *America: Up in Arms*, featuring Martin Sheen. That film examined the public health costs of gun violence. First Monday 2001 produced *Deadly Business*, directed by Glen Pearcy. This film focused on the gun industry, including its marketing practices and product design issues. The film drew close parallels between the gun and tobacco industries. The First Monday website provides extensive information on these films and many other resources for those wishing to participate in the campaign. Over 100 organizations cosponsored First Monday 2001, including the American Academy of Pediatrics, the American Bar Association, the Child Welfare League of America, the National Association of School Nurses, the National Education Association, and the Police Foundation.

Although First Monday moved on to a different social justice issue on the first Monday of 2002, the work on gun violence continued through Gun Industry Watch, a new student network that monitored the gun industry and the National Rifle Association. Gun Industry Watch members engaged in grassroots activities to expose deceptive advertising by firearm manufacturers, expose and boycott corporate partners and sponsors of the gun lobby, and work toward achieving higher safety standards for firearms. Gun Industry Watch is now part of the Brady Campaign to Prevent Gun Violence.

Walter F. Carroll

See also: Accidents, Gun; American Academy of Pediatrics (AAP); American Medical Association (AMA); Background Checks; Brady Campaign to Prevent Gun Violence; Centers for Disease Control (CDC); Consumer Product Safety Laws; Crime and Gun Use; Gun Shows; Gun Violence as a Public Health Problem; Gunshot Wounds; Medicine and Gun Violence; National Rifle Association (NRA); National Violent Death Reporting System; Suicide, Guns and

Further Reading

Alliance for Justice. "The First Monday Campaign." http://www.afj.org/for-students-expired/past-programs/the-first-monday-campaign.html (accessed February 28, 2011).

Brady Campaign to Prevent Gun Violence. Legal Action Project: Gun Industry Watch Reports. http://www.bradycenter.org/legal action/giwreports (accessed February 28, 2011).

Cook, Philip, and Jens Ludwig. *Gun Violence: The Real Costs*. New York: Oxford University Press, 2000.

Force-on-Force Training. *See* Tactical Training

Fourteenth Amendment

The Fourteenth Amendment granted full citizenship to African Americans and was designed to guarantee the "equal protection" of the law to all citizens. It was one of three amendments passed in the wake of the Civil War that were designed to integrate African Americans into the broader spectrum of American politics and to provide full rights of citizenship. Since the 1897 Supreme Court case *Chicago, Burlington, and Quincy Railroad v. Chicago*, the Fourteenth Amendment has been used to incorporate the protections of the Bill of Rights at the state and local levels. Passed in 1868, the Fourteenth Amendment is the only component of the U.S. Constitution that specifically addresses the issue of equality by mandating "equal protection of the laws." The due process clause of the amendment declares that states could not "deprive any person of life, liberty, or property, without due process of law." It was used in successive court cases to extend basic civil rights and liberties to disadvantaged groups such as African Americans after the Supreme Court in the 1873 *Slaughter-House Cases* ruled that the privileges and immunities clause of the amendment applied only to the federal government and not the states.

Following the Civil War, southern states passed a variety of restrictive gun laws that were designed to prevent African Americans from obtaining guns. Southern elites feared that if African Americans were armed, they would be less compliant, and laws such as the "Black Codes" were passed to deny rights to the community. A number of states, including Alabama, Louisiana, and Mississippi, enacted laws that expressly forbade African Americans from acquiring guns. The passage of the Fourteenth Amendment led to the repeal of race-based restrictions on gun ownership. However, these gun laws were often replaced with more restrictive legislation that was race-neutral in language, but its impact was to limit access to weapons. For instance, restrictions on gun ownership were often unequally enforced. While law enforcement vigorously enforced bans on certain weapons in the African American community, the white-dominated police forces ignored possession of guns in the white community.

The disparity of gun ownership and the advent of racially motivated attacks in the South led Congress to debate legislation that would have outlawed southern militias and placed restrictions on the ability of all southerners to possess firearms. However, the majority of members of Congress from both parties ultimately agreed that efforts to ban or prohibit militias would be overturned by the Supreme Court. Since Congress could not limit the ability of whites to acquire weapons, the national legislature concentrated on measures to ensure equal access to firearms. Support for arming African Americans also had an ideological component. Just as Americans had to resort to force to gain independence from Great Britain and now had to use force to free the slaves, many Radical Republicans envisioned a well-armed African American citizenry as the optimum means to ensure the equality granted under the Fourteenth Amendment and subsequent legislation.

Through the Fourteenth Amendment, the Republican-controlled Congress endeavored to provide African Americans with the means to defend themselves from racist organizations such as the Ku Klux Klan (KKK). In response to racial violence, Congress passed the Anti-KKK Act in 1871. Weapons were also seen as a necessary tool to protect African American families from corrupt local law enforcement, and during Reconstruction, the federal government provided weapons to arm black militias for purposes of self-defense.

In spite of the intentions of the measure, the Fourteenth Amendment initially failed to provide the protections contained within it. A succession of Jim Crow laws were passed in the South that institutionalized segregation. Legal segregation was approved by Supreme Court cases in the 1880s and in the infamous *Plessy v. Ferguson* (which endorsed the concept of "separate but equal") in 1896. Nonetheless, the amendment would also serve as the basis for later efforts to repeal segregation and ensure political equality.

The Fourteenth Amendment continues to be a core element of the gun control debate in the United States. Contemporary gun rights advocates base their arguments against gun regulation on the equal protection clause of the amendment. According to this line of reasoning, all citizens have the right to self-defense since the Fourteenth Amendment guarantees equal protection for all Americans. In 2008, in *District of Columbia v. Heller*, the Supreme Court ruled that the Second Amendment allowed individuals to own firearms for personal protection or self-defense. Two years later, the court used the due process clause of the Fourteenth Amendment to apply the Second Amendment to states and localities in *McDonald v. City of Chicago*. The decision overturned broad prohibitions against firearms ownership by the states or local governments. It did permit the continuation of some restrictions, including laws against carrying weapons in public areas such as schools or prohibitions against felons owning firearms.

Tom Lansford

See also: Black Codes; *District of Columbia v. Heller*; Ku Klux Klan; *McDonald v. City of Chicago*; *Miller v. Texas*; National Rifle Association (NRA); *Presser v. Illinois*; Right to Self-Defense, Philosophical Bases; Second Amendment; *United States v. Cruikshank*

Further Reading

Bland, Randall, and Joseph V. Brogan. *Constitutional Law in the United States: A Systematic Inquiry into the Change and Relevance of Supreme Court Decisions*. San Francisco: Austin & Winfield, 1999.

Curtis, Michael Kent. *No State Shall Abridge: The Fourteenth Amendment and the Bill of Rights*. Durham, NC: Duke University Press, 1987.

Epps, Garret. *Democracy Reborn: The Fourteenth Amendment and the Fight for Equal Rights in Post–Civil War America*. New York: Holt, 2007.

George, Robert P., ed. *Great Cases in Constitutional Law*. Princeton, NJ: Princeton University Press, 2001.

Halbrook, Stephen P. *Securing Civil Rights: Freedman, the Fourteenth Amendment, and the Right to Bear Arms*. Washington, DC: Independent Institute, 2010.

Harrison, Maureen, and Steve Gilbert, eds. *Landmark Decisions of the United States Supreme Court*. Beverly Hills, CA: Excellent Books, 1991.

Fourth Amendment

The Fourth Amendment forbids unreasonable searches and seizures. The amendment was one of the 10 original amendments to the Constitution (the Bill of Rights). The Fourth Amendment was designed to protect Americans from general or arbitrary searches by the police or government by requiring a specific warrant to be issued by a judge or magistrate before a search is undertaken. The rise in handgun violence during the 1960s and 1970s led to a gradual erosion of Fourth Amendment rights as the courts granted the police greater latitude in searches for weapons and firearms.

The amendment has its roots in English common law. By the time of the American Revolution, it had become a legal precedent in Great Britain that the police or other forces of the Crown needed an official writ before entering a personal home. In fact, one of the factors that created tension between the colonies and Great Britain was the suspension of such protections. Throughout the colonies, royal magistrates and judges issued writs of assistance and general warrants that allowed British soldiers to search houses and seize property without cause or provocation. The lingering resentment against such actions prompted the adoption of the Fourth Amendment.

The amendment forbade the government from conducting "unreasonable searches and seizures" and guaranteed the "right of the people to be secure in their persons, houses, papers, and effects." The amendment requires that the police obtain a warrant that specifically describes what place will be searched and what, if any, items are to be seized or people arrested. For the police to gain a search warrant, they have to swear under oath that there is "probable cause" for such a warrant.

Since the ratification of the Bill of Rights in 1791, courts have allowed exemptions to the Fourth Amendment. For instance, police are permitted to arrest people who are in the midst of committing a crime or when they have probable cause to suspect someone is about to break the law. In 1912, the Supreme Court began using the exclusionary rule whereby evidence that was seized without a warrant or legally valid probable cause cannot be introduced in a criminal trial. The rule initially applied only to federal cases. It was not until 1961 and the Supreme Court case *Mapp v. Ohio* that the exclusionary rule was applied to state and local court cases.

The Supreme Court has allowed some exceptions to the exclusionary rule. In *Nix v. Williams* in 1984, the court decided that the police and prosecutors could use evidence, even if it was seized illegally, if the discovery of that evidence led police to a discovery that they would have reached without the illegal evidence. That same year, the court in *United States v. Leon* further expanded the exemptions to the exclusionary rule by finding that evidence could be used for prosecution if it was obtained when the police were acting in "good faith" even if they were mistaken about the scope or breadth of a search warrant. In *Herring v. United States* (2009), the court found that evidence could also be used even if there was unintentional police negligence in preparing a search warrant. Meanwhile, in *Illinois v. Webster* (2004), the high court ruled that police could use roadblocks in response to specific crimes or searches (but not general roadblocks). Roadblocks had become an increasingly common tactic of police.

Critics of some specific gun control efforts claim that these programs violate the Fourth Amendment. For instance, the courts have granted the police wide latitude to search for and seize guns even without probable cause. One result of such latitude has been the police tactic of "profiling," whereby police units stop motorists on the highways or people in certain neighborhoods if they fit a specific set of guidelines, which usually mirror the profiles of those engaged in criminal activity. The police defend these warrantless stops by claiming that they fall under the doctrine of probable cause. Furthermore, many localities have adopted programs that are designed to reduce violence and crime in certain neighborhoods. Central to these programs is the ability of the police to run "sweeps" or warrantless searches of public housing areas to confiscate

Police officers arrest suspected gang members during a sweep in Los Angeles, California. (Jean-Marc Giboux/Getty Images)

guns or illicit drugs. For example, in 1988, Chicago began Operation Clean Sweep in which the police randomly "swept" through public housing buildings and seized illegal materials. After the American Civil Liberties Union filed a lawsuit against the tactic, the scope of the sweeps was limited, but they have continued. Concern over crime and gun violence in certain urban areas has increased the popularity of these programs that erode an individual's Fourth Amendment protections against unreasonable search and seizure.

Tom Lansford

See also: American Civil Liberties Union (ACLU)

Further Reading

Bland, Randall, and Joseph V. Brogan. *Constitutional Law in the United States: A Systematic Inquiry into the Change and*

Relevance of Supreme Court Decisions. San Francisco: Austin & Winfield, 1999.

George, Robert P., ed. *Great Cases in Constitutional Law.* Princeton, NJ: Princeton University Press, 2001.

Harrison, Maureen, and Steve Gilbert, eds. *Landmark Decisions of the United States Supreme Court.* Beverly Hills, CA: Excellent Books, 1991.

Hoffman, Ronald, and Peter J. Albert, eds. *The Bill of Rights: Government Proscribed.* Charlottesville: University Press of Virginia, 1997.

Fraternal Order of Police (FOP)

The Fraternal Order of Police (FOP) is the world's largest organization of rank-and-file police officers. Founded in 1915 by police officers in Pittsburgh as the Fort Pitt Lodge No. 1, the FOP soon spread to other states, and in 1955, it became a national organization. The FOP now has over 2,100 local and state chapters, or lodges, with over 325,000 members. The national organization, known as the Grand Lodge, has three offices: the Labor Services Division in Columbus, Ohio; the Steve Young Law Enforcement Legislative Advocacy Center in Washington, D.C., and the Atnip-Orms Center National Headquarters in Nashville, Tennessee.

State and local lodges independently determine the services they provide to their members. Through its national offices, the FOP maintains an active legislative agenda, lobbying and testifying before Congress and regulatory agencies on legislation it favors or opposes. Local lodges provide members with legal defense and counsel, and sponsor and provide practical and financial support to injured officers and their families. FOP offices provide labor representation to members, although its founders were reluctant to call the organization a union due to the virulent antiunion sentiment of their founding period. Through its history, however, the FOP has functioned much like a labor union in advocating for a broad range of labor benefits and protecting members from perceived unsatisfactory work conditions.

The FOP has been an active legislative lobbying force on firearms-related issues. The FOP does not have an overall position on gun control; rather, it takes varying positions on gun control legislation based on its assessment of their implications for law enforcement officers and the law enforcement community.

For many years, the FOP as well as other law enforcement associations maintained close ties to the National Rifle Association (NRA) because of the NRA's role in sponsoring firearm safety classes and promoting the responsible use of firearms. However, the NRA's increasing resistance to any kind of gun control gradually alienated the FOP and other police organizations. In 1994, the FOP broke from the NRA when it supported the Brady Bill's establishment of federal background checks on firearms purchasers.

The NRA opposed regulation of armor-piercing (so-called "cop killer") bullets. Spitzer (2012) suggests the split became final when the NRA began to run advertisements attacking police chiefs who had opposed NRA policies. Carter notes that the passage of the McClure-Volkmer Act in 1986 also contributed to the disaffection of law enforcement organizations—including the FOP—from the NRA. The NRA strongly supported the McClure-Volkmer Act, which "removed record-keeping requirements for ammunitions dealers and allowed mail-order sales of rifles, shotguns, and ammunition to resume" (Carter 1997, 103).

Its estrangement from the NRA led the FOP and other police organizations to ally themselves with Handgun Control, Inc. (HCI, now called the Brady Campaign to Prevent Gun Violence). In reaction to the split with the established law enforcement organizations, the NRA supported and subsidized the creation of the Law Enforcement Alliance of America (LEAA) as an alternative to the mainstream law enforcement organizations. LEAA is small, not very influential, and generally takes NRA positions on gun control issues and legislation.

The FOP—and a coalition of other police organizations—supported the Brady Act, allying itself with HCI. The FOP strongly opposes the 1996 Domestic Violence Offender Gun Ban, also known as the Lautenberg Amendment. This amendment—to a federal spending bill—prohibits anyone with a misdemeanor conviction for domestic violence against a spouse or child from purchasing or owning a handgun. According to the FOP, the amendment has cost some police officers their jobs for having committed one domestic violence infraction in the past. The FOP argues that it is unfair to apply the ban retroactively and supports amending the Lautenberg Amendment so that it would not apply retroactively.

The FOP also supported passage of the Law Enforcement Safety Act, passed by Congress in 2004, that allows active-duty and off-duty law enforcement officers as well as retired officers to carry concealed weapons, even outside of their jurisdictions. The FOP and the bill's sponsors argued that it would allow those trained in law enforcement to intervene in criminal situations and protect communities. FOP president Chuck Canterbury argued in the legislative hearings that this is not a firearms issue, but "an officer safety issue, a public safety issue, and a homeland security issue" (Canterbury 2004). Furthermore, he said the FOP supported a federal law to supplant the ineffective patchwork of states' conceal-and-carry laws.

The National Legislative Office of the FOP also opposes a wide variety of other handgun control legislation, including legislation to require the licensing and registration of all handguns with the federal government, legislation to require anyone owning a handgun or ammunition to have a license from their state, legislation to prohibit individuals from purchasing more than one handgun in a 30-day period, and legislation to ban the manufacture of guns that cannot be personalized.

The FOP also supports legislative actions that are not directly related to violence, gun control and other police-related legislation. Most notably in recent years, these have included several bills and acts regulating Social Security, such as the Social Security Fairness Act, and President Bush's Commission to Strengthen Social Security's recommendation to privatize Social Security.

Robin L. Roth

See also: Ammunition, Regulations of; Armor-Piercing Ammunition; Brady Campaign to Prevent Gun Violence; Brady Handgun Violence Prevention Act (Brady Bill); Concealed Weapons Laws; Firearms Owners' Protection Act of 1986; Lautenberg, Frank R.; National Rifle Association (NRA)

Further Reading

Canterbury, Chuck. *Testimony of Chuck Canterbury, National President, Grand Lodge, Fraternal Order of Police, on H.R. 218, the Law Enforcement Officers Safety Act of 2003, before the House Subcommittee on Crime, Terrorism, and Homeland Security Committee on the Judiciary*, June 15, 2004. http://www.fop.net/legislative/testimony/20040615_HR218.pdf (accessed July 30, 2011).

Carter, Gregg Lee. *The Gun Control Movement*. New York: Twayne, 1997.

Fraternal Order of Police. http://www.grandlodgefop.org/ (accessed May 31, 2011).

Spitzer, Robert J. *The Politics of Gun Control*. 5th ed. Boulder, CO: Paradigm Publishers, 2012.

Fresno Rifle and Pistol Club, Inc. v. Van de Kamp. See Halbrook, Stephen P.

Frontier Violence

Many different forms of violence took place on the American frontier. The violence played an important role in creating and shaping the American gun culture. Even today, the effects of the frontier are powerful.

The most common form of frontier violence was hunting. In the British Isles, France, and other parts of Western Europe—the sources of almost all of the white population of the British colonies and then the United States before the late nineteenth century—hunting was strictly controlled for the benefit of the aristocracy. A farmer might even be forbidden to kill deer or rabbits that were eating his crops. In theory, all game belonged to the king.

But in the wilds of the United States, hunting was wide open. Anyone could hunt, and for people living on the frontier— whether in western Massachusetts in the 1670s or Idaho in the 1870s—hunting often made a difference in whether the family would go hungry or not. Even today, there are many poor people in rural parts of the United States for whom the results of the fall hunting season determine how much meat the family will be eating over the winter. The ready availability of hunting gave ordinary people an important reason for owning firearms, and the practical requirements of hunting—such as shooting a squirrel out of a tree dozens of yards away—promoted the development of shooting skills.

Most of the American Revolution and the Civil War did not take place on the frontier, but some important engagements occurred there. The Indian wars took place almost exclusively on the frontier. But perhaps the most important military violence involving the American frontier was the Battle of New Orleans on January 8, 1815. (New Orleans itself was not on the frontier, but the port was the key to the economy of much of the frontier, and frontiersmen played a major role in the battle.) The Treaty of Ghent, signed on December 24, 1814, had officially ended the War of 1812, but news of the treaty had not reached North America. Had the British captured New Orleans—the port through which almost all trade from the United States' recently acquired Louisiana Territory flowed—it is doubtful that the British would have relinquished it, despite what the Treaty of Ghent required. Indeed, the British had violated the Treaty of Paris, which ended the American Revolution, by

refusing to evacuate their forts east of the Mississippi.

The British army was fresh from its triumph over Napoleon, and the forces invading New Orleans were the best in the world—the victors of the Peninsular Campaign in Spain. Against the best-trained, best-equipped army in the world, the Americans did not have enough weapons for their forces. Historian Robert Remini's *The Battle of New Orleans* quotes a contemporary observer: "From all the parishes the inhabitants could be seen coming with their hunting guns" because "there were not enough guns in the magazines of the United States to arm the citizens" (Remini 1999, 45).

The Tennessee militia hardly looked like a professional army, with their rough clothes, unshaven faces, and raccoon caps. The Kentucky militia was even worse, arriving in rags and disappointed to find out that there were no blankets in the city for them. The redcoats called them "dirty shirts." Yet, as Remini explains, "most of these men could bring down a squirrel from the highest tree with a single rifle shot. Their many years living in the Tennessee wilderness had made them expert marksmen" (1999, 71).

The Americans who fought at New Orleans were a diverse combination of professional soldiers, militiamen, irregulars, lawyers, privateers, farmers, and shopkeepers. They included free blacks, Creoles, Cajuns, Spaniards, Frenchmen, Portuguese, Germans, Italians, Indians, and Anglos. When objections were raised to arming the free blacks of Louisiana, General Andrew Jackson replied, "Place confidence in them, and . . . engage them by every dear and honorable tie to the interest of the country who extends to them equal rights and privileges with white men."

The Battle of New Orleans, fought on January 8, 1815, was the final battle of the War of 1812. (Library of Congress)

As the British maneuvered outside the city, nightly raids by the dirty shirts killed British sentries, took their equipment, and kept the whole army off balance. During an engagement by the Cypress Swamp on December 28 (11 days before the main battle), the Tennesseans waded through the muck and leapt from log to log like cats, driving off the British beefeaters.

In one encounter on the day of the main battle, a dirty shirt took aim at a wounded British officer who was walking back to his camp. "Halt Mr. Red Coat," yelled the American. "One more step and I'll drill a hole through your leather." The officer complied, sighing, "What a disgrace for a British officer to have to surrender to a chimney-sweep."

Although the British greatly outnumbered the Americans, the day of January 8, 1815, turned into one of the worst days in British military history. Over 2,000 British soldiers were killed, captured, or wounded. The Americans lost only 7 killed and 6 wounded, although their total casualties from skirmishes on other days amounted to 333.

As news of the victory spread throughout the United States, the Americans' sense of inferiority to the British began to recede. The Americans had smashed the best that Britain could throw at them. Newspapers quoted Shakespeare's *Henry VI*: "Advance our waving colors to the wall, rescued is Orleans from the English wolves." Jackson's upset victory was as important for the United States' future as Joan of Arc's was for France.

Until the Civil War, the Battle of New Orleans was celebrated nearly on a par with the Fourth of July. It became a tremendous source of American pride, helping to shape the national identity. The victory also helped propel Jackson to election as president in 1828. The popular song "The Hunters of Kentucky" celebrated the accomplishments of American frontiersmen and their rifles. One version of the song concluded:

> But Jackson he was wide awake,
> And was not scared of trifles,
> For well he knew Kentucky's boys,
> With their death-dealing rifles.
> He led them down to Cypress Swamp,
> The ground was low and mucky,
> There stood John Bull in martial pomp,
> And here stood old Kentucky.
> But steady stood our little force,
> None wished it to be greater,
> For every man was half a horse,
> And half an alligator.
> (chorus) Oh, Kentucky, hunters of
>   Kentucky!
> Oh, Kentucky, hunters of Kentucky!
> And when so near we saw them wink,
> We thought it good to stop them,
> It would have done you good, I think,
> To see Kentuckians drop them.
> And so if danger e'er annoys,
> Remember what our trade is,
> Just send for us Kentucky boys,
> And we'll protect you ladies.

Many of the American rifles at New Orleans were of a superbly crafted and effective type originally made by the Pennsylvania Dutch. Thanks in part to the song, though, the Pennsylvania rifles became known as "Kentucky rifles."

The Kentucky rifles were well suited for both hunting and self-defense. In contrast, British guns were more specialized, reflecting who would be using them. Muskets were mass-produced for infantry soldiers, who were not even trained to aim at an individual enemy; but in tightly controlled linear formations, the redcoats could produce massive, devastating firepower. In contrast, British aristocrats hunted on their estates with exquisite shotguns and other firearms tailored for them personally. The way guns were made in the United States—mass-produced for a mass market and intended for multiple uses—reflected frontier conditions, as "civil and military uses of firearms dovetailed as they had not generally done in Europe" (Kennett and Anderson 1975, 41).

The second great frontier-related military experience that shaped American attitudes toward firearms was the Texas Revolution. As the military dictatorship of General Santa Anna began systematically denying Texans their right to self-government (which the Mexican government had guaranteed to Texan settlers) and other rights guaranteed to all Mexicans by the 1824 Mexican Constitution, Texans began to contemplate a war for independence. At Gonzales, the Mexicans tried to seize a small cannon that the settlers had used to scare away Indians. The Texans were armed only with bowie knives, a few pistols, and flintlock rifles, many of which dated back to the American Revolution. The Texans raised a flag, which dared, "Come and Take It." The Mexicans tried unsuccessfully and then retreated.

At the Alamo, a fort in San Antonio, 136 Texans withstood a siege by the main Mexican standing army from February 23 to March 6, 1836, before finally being destroyed, having refused all demands to surrender. The defenders of the Alamo had bought Sam Houston crucial time to rally the Texan people.

On April 21, 1836, the Texans met the Mexican army at San Jacinto. Although outnumbered two to one, the Texans launched a surprise attack. "Remember the Alamo," they yelled, rushing into battle with their rifles and bowie knives, as a single fife and a single drum played the love song "Will You Come to the Bower?"

In the first hour of battle, the Texans killed 600 Mexicans and captured 200 more. Within a day, the rest of the Mexican army, including Santa Anna himself, had been captured. Texan casualties were 6 dead and 30 wounded. The Mexican standing army was crushed, and although Mexico refused formally to recognize Texan independence, the dictatorship gave up trying to conquer Texas.

The "Texan War Cry"—sung to the same tune as the "Star Spangled Banner"—celebrated the victory of a self-armed people over the professional army of a tyrant:

Oh Texans rouse hill and dale with your cry,
No longer delay, for the bold foe advances.
The banners of Mexico tauntingly fly,
And the valleys are lit with the gleam of their lances.
With justice our shield, rush forth to the field,
And stand with your posts, till our foes fly or yield.
For the bright star of Texas shall never grow dim,
While her soil boasts a son to raise rifle or limb.
Rush forth to the lines, these hirelings to meet,
Our lives and our homes, we will yield unto no man.
But death on our free soil we'll willingly meet,

Ere our free temple soiled by the feet of the foe man.
Grasp rifle and blade with hearts undismayed,
And swear by the temple brave Houston has made.
That the bright star of Texas shall never be dim,
While her soil boasts a son to raise rifle or limb.

The frontier attitudes expressed in the "Texan War Cry" and "The Hunters of Kentucky" deeply shaped American culture. Even in the early twenty-first century, these ideas are at the core of the American gun culture: A true man will use a firearm to protect women from predators (the British soldiers had been promised a rape-and-pillage spree—"beauty and booty"—if they captured New Orleans); the free people of a nation must defend it personally with their own arms; professional soldiers ("hirelings") in the pay of unfree governments are—despite the soldiers' intimidating "martial pomp"—morally and militarily inferior to American soldiers; dying in defense of freedom is better than living under tyranny; and the quintessence of freedom—the precise reason why the stars of liberty shine—is the patriot's rifle.

These attitudes did not start with the frontier, of course. The American Revolution is the most important part of their foundation. And the attitudes were reinforced, with modification, by American participation in World War II. Yet it would be a serious mistake to underestimate the influence of Alamo imagery on almost every generation of American youth until almost the end of the twentieth century. The Battle of New Orleans and the Texan War of Independence helped ensure that the firearms-related "moral lessons" of the American Revolution were not seen as one-time events but recurring facts of the eternal struggle between freedom and tyranny.

In September 2000, Michael Bellesiles's book *Arming America: The Origins of a National Gun Culture* was published with great critical acclaim. Bellesiles, with an obvious eye on the contemporary gun control debate, argued that before the Civil War, few Americans owned guns, even on the frontier; that hunting was mostly confined to professionals; and that guns were unimportant in the United States until the federal government promoted mass armament as a result of the Civil War.

But historians who investigated Bellesiles's claims have found them to be contrary to the facts, and indeed contrary to the very sources that Bellesiles cited (e.g., Cramer 2001; Lindgren and Heather 2001). The Bellesiles book was exposed as a fraud, and withdrawn by the publisher. Bellesiles was forced to resign his professorship at the History Department at Emory University.

If some Americans today wish to imagine a "gun-free" America in colonial days and during the early republic, Americans of the late nineteenth century had different wishes. For many people in the United States and around the world, knowledge of the American "Wild West" reflects that of the city audiences who attended the enormously popular "Buffalo Bill Wild West Show." The show opened in 1883 and featured a stagecoach robbery, shooting contests, numerous gunfights, and terrifying Indians. In his book *The Mythic West*, Robert Athearn explains how the Wild West, exemplified (or invented) by the Buffalo Bill show, became a symbol of the purest, most rugged form of Americanism. The western frontier,

a reasonably calm place in real life, was revered as bloody and heroic.

While the Buffalo Bill show and movie "westerns" are responsible for popular understanding of the western frontier in the late nineteenth century, the reality was not so violent. The most thorough investigation of gun ownership and gun violence in the American western frontier is Roger McGrath's *Gunfighters, Highwaymen, and Vigilantes*, an examination of the nineteenth-century Sierra Nevada mining towns of Aurora and Bodie. Aurora and Bodie certainly had as much potential for violence as any place in the West. Their populations were mainly young, transient males subject to few social controls. There was one saloon for every 25 men; brothels and gambling houses were also common. Governmental law enforcement was ineffectual, and sometimes the sheriff was himself the head of a criminal gang. Nearly everyone carried a gun. Aurorans usually toted a Colt Navy .36 six-shot revolver, while Bodieites sported the Colt double-action model known as the "Lightning," a double-action version of the famous "Peacemaker," or "Frontier," revolver.

The homicide rate in those towns was extremely high, as the "bad men" who hung out in saloons shot each other at a fearsome rate: 64 per 100,000 annually in Aurora, and 116 in Bodie. These rates are comparable to the highest homicide rates in the worst parts of American cities during the late twentieth century. The presence of guns turned many petty drunken quarrels into fatal encounters—as they sometimes do today.

But in Aurora and Bodie, other crime was virtually nonexistent. McGrath, writing in 1984, compared the Aurora and Bodie crime rates to the 1980 crime rates in the United States. The per capita annual robbery rate in Aurora and Bodie was only 7 percent of modern New York City's rate. The burglary rate was a mere 1 percent of New York's. Rape was unknown in Aurora and Bodie. Bodie had a robbery rate of 84 per 100,000 persons per year. The rate in 1980 New York City was 1,140; in San Francisco–Oakland, it was 521; and in the United States as a whole, it was 243. The Bodie burglary rate was 6.4 per 100,000 people per year. The 1980 New York City rate was 2,661; the San Francisco–Oakland rate was 2,267; and the overall rate for the United States was 1,668.

"The old, the weak, the female, the innocent, and those unwilling to fight were rarely the targets of attacks," McGrath found. One resident of Bodie did "not recall ever hearing of a respectable woman or girl in any manner insulted or even accosted by the hundreds of dissolute characters that were everywhere. In part this was due to the respect depravity pays to decency; in part to the knowledge that sudden death would follow any other course." Everyone carried a gun, and except for young men who liked to drink and fight with each other, everyone was secure from crime.

The experiences of Aurora and Bodie were repeated throughout the West. One study of five major cattle towns with a reputation for violence—Abilene, Ellsworth, Wichita, Dodge City, and Caldwell—found that all together, the towns had fewer than two criminal homicides per year (Dykstra 1983).

During the 1870s, Lincoln County, New Mexico, was in a state of anarchy and civil war. The homicide rate was astronomical, but (as in Bodie and Aurora) it was confined almost exclusively to drunken males upholding their "honor." Modern big-city crimes such as rape, burglary, and mugging were virtually unknown (Utley 1990).

A study of the Texas frontier from 1875 to 1890 found that burglaries and robberies (except for bank, train, and stagecoach robberies) were essentially nonexistent. People did not bother with locking doors, and murder was rare, except for young men shooting each other in "fair fights" they engaged in voluntarily (Holden 1940).

John Umbeck's (1981) investigation of the High Sierra goldfields in the mid-nineteenth century yielded similar results. After the Gold Rush brought on by Sutter's Mill in 1848, thousands of prospectors rushed to goldfields in the California mountains. There was no police force. Indeed, there was no law at all regarding property rights, since the military governor of California had just proclaimed the Mexican land law invalid (without offering a replacement). There was intense competitive pressure and greed for gold, and nearly everyone carried firearms. Yet there was hardly any violence. Similarly, when much of the Indian territory of Oklahoma was opened all at once for white settlement, heavily armed settlers rushed in immediately to stake their claims, and the settlers with their guns arrived long before effective law enforcement did. Yet there was almost no violence (Day 1989).

In sum, historian W. Eugene Hollon (1974) observes that "the Western frontier was a far more civilized, more peaceful, and safer place than American society is today." Americans living in the "Wild West," with its many guns, were far safer than Americans living in many modern cities.

In the modern era, some people argue that the inner cities of the United States constitute a frontier. Sen. Frank Church (D-ID) contended that most people "would not go into ghetto areas at all except in broad daylight under the most optimum conditions—surely not at night, alone or on foot. But some people have no choice. To live or work or have some need to be on this 'frontier' imposes a fear which is tempered by possession of a gun" (Church 1979).

In contrast, historian Joe B. Frantz (1969) advanced the case for the irrelevance of the gun culture to modern problems. He acknowledged that the frontier experience promoted important American values: individualism, mobility (both physical and social), and nationalism. These frontier values, including the attachment to firearms, Frantz continued, are no longer appropriate, for "direct action does not befit a nation whose problems are corporate, community, and complex" (1969, 152–53).

The statements of Church and Frantz encapsulate the competing views about the legitimacy of "direct action" against crime. Is it reasonable for a person who must walk alone in an inner city to carry a handgun for protection, or should she instead rely entirely on community protection and lobby for such things as better streetlights? Whatever the answers to the questions about the modern frontier, it is clear that on the American frontier throughout the seventeenth, eighteenth, and nineteenth centuries, firearms were not only a very important survival tool, but also a preeminent symbol of personal and national independence and self-sufficiency.

David B. Kopel

See also: American Revolution; *Arming America* Controversy; Boomtowns, Cowtowns, and Gun Violence; Civil War and Small Arms; Long Rifle (Pennsylvania/Kentucky); Native Americans and Gun Violence; Urbanism and Gun Violence; Vigilantism

Further Reading

Athearn, Robert G. *The Mythic West*. Lawrence: University Press of Kansas, 1986.

Bellesiles, Michael. *Arming America: The Origins of a National Gun Culture*. New York: Knopf, 2000.

Church, Frank. "Foreword." In *Restricting Handguns: The Liberal Skeptics Speak Out*, edited by Don B. Kates Jr. Croton-on-Hudson, NY: North River Press, 1979.

Cramer, Clayton. *Armed America: The Remarkable Story of How and Why Guns Became as American as Apple Pie*. Nashville, TN: Thomas Nelson, 2007.

Day, Robert. " 'Sooners' or 'Goners,' They Were Hell Bent on Grabbing Free Land." *Smithsonian* 20 (1989): 192–203.

Dykstra, Robert R. *The Cattle Towns: A Social History of the Kansas Cattle Trading Centers*. Lincoln: University of Nebraska Press, 1983.

Frantz, Joe B. "The Frontier Tradition." In *Violence in America: Historical and Comparative Perspectives*, edited by Hugh Davis Graham and Ted Robert Gurr, 127–53. New York: Bantam Books, 1969.

Holden, William C. "Law and Lawlessness on the Texas Frontier, 1875–1890." *Southwestern History Quarterly* 44 (1940): 188–203.

Hollon, W. Eugene. *Frontier Violence: Another Look*. New York: Oxford University Press, 1974.

Kennett, Lee, and James LaVerne Anderson. *The Gun in America: The Origins of a National Dilemma*. Westport, CT: Greenwood Press, 1975.

Lindgren, James, and Justin Lee Heather. "Counting Guns in Early America." *William and Mary Law Review* 43 (2001): 1777–842.

McGrath, Roger D. *Gunfighters, Highwaymen, and Vigilantes: Violence on the Frontier.* Berkeley: University of California Press, 1984.

Remini, Robert. *The Battle of New Orleans.* New York: Viking Press, 1999.

Umbeck, John. *A Theory of Property Rights: With Application to the California Gold Rush.* Ames: Iowa State University Press, 1981.

Utley, Robert M. *High Noon in Lincoln: Violence on the Western Frontier.* Albuquerque: University of New Mexico Press, 1990.